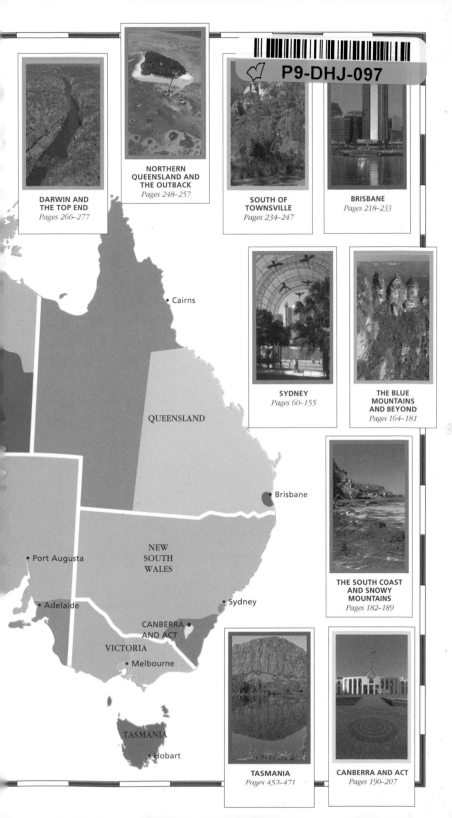

P9-DHJ-097

Cairns

QUEENSLAND

Brisbane

NEW SOUTH WALES

Port Augusta

Adelaide

Sydney

CANBERRA AND ACT

VICTORIA

Melbourne

TASMANIA

Hobart

EYEWITNESS TRAVEL
AUSTRALIA

EYEWITNESS TRAVEL

AUSTRALIA

DK

LONDON, NEW YORK,
MELBOURNE, MUNICH AND DELHI
www.dk.com

Produced by Duncan Baird Publishers
London, England

MANAGING EDITOR Zoë Ross
MANAGING ART EDITORS Vanessa Marsh
(with Clare Sullivan and Virginia Walters)
EDITOR Rebecca Miles
COMMISSIONING DESIGNER Jill Mumford
DESIGNERS DAWN DAVIS-COOK, Lucy Parissi

CONSULTANT Helen Duffy
MAIN CONTRIBUTORS Jan Bowen, Helen Duffy, Paul Kloeden, Jacinta
le Plaistrier, Sue Neales, Ingrid Ohlssen, Tamara Thiessen.

PHOTOGRAPHERS
Max Alexander, Alan Keohane, Dave King,
Rob Reichenfeld, Peter Wilson.

ILLUSTRATORS
Richard Bonson, Jo Cameron, Stephen Conlin, Eugene Fleury,
Chris Forsey, Steve Gyapay, Toni Hargreaves, Chris Orr, Robbie Polley,
Kevin Robinson, Peter Ross, John Woodcock.

Reproduced by Colourscan (Singapore)
Printed and bound by South China Printing Co. Ltd., China

First American Edition 1998

12 13 14 15 10 9 8 7 6 5 4 3 2

Published in the United States by DK Publishing
375 Hudson Street, New York, New York 10014

Reprinted with revisions
1999, 2000, 2001, 2002, 2003, 2005, 2006, 2008, 2010, 2012

Copyright 1998, 2012 © Dorling Kindersley Limited, London
A Penguin Company

A CATALOG RECORD FOR THIS BOOK IS AVAILABLE FROM THE LIBRARY OF CONGRESS.
ISSN 1542-1554
ISBN 978 0 75668 414 3

*Front cover main image: Uluṟu (Ayers Rock),
Uluṟu-Kata Tjuṯa National Park*

MIX
Paper from
responsible sources
FSC
www.fsc.org   FSC™ C018179

**The information in this
DK Eyewitness Travel Guide is checked regularly.**
Every effort has been made to ensure that this book is as up-to-date
as possible at the time of going to press. Some details, however,
such as telephone numbers, opening hours, prices, gallery hanging
arrangements and travel information are liable to change. The
publishers cannot accept responsibility for any consequences arising
from the use of this book, nor for any material on third party
websites, and cannot guarantee that any website address in this book
will be a suitable source of travel information. We value the views and
suggestions of our readers very highly. Please write to: Publisher,
DK Eyewitness Travel Guides, Dorling Kindersley, 80 Strand,
London WC2R 0RL, Great Britain, or email: travelguides@dk.com.

◁ **A flock of budgerigars, western New South Wales**

CONTENTS

Giraffe in Sydney's Taronga Zoo

Ben Boyd National Park on the south coast of New South Wales

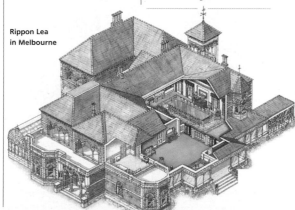

Rippon Lea in Melbourne

HOW TO USE THIS GUIDE

This guide helps you to get the most from your visit to Australia. *Introducing Australia* maps the whole country and sets it in its historical and cultural context. The 17 regional chapters, including *Sydney*, describe important sights with maps, pictures and illustrations, as well as introductory features on subjects of regional interest. Suggestions on restaurants, accommodation, shopping and entertainment are in *Travellers' Needs*. The *Survival Guide* has tips on getting around the country. The cities of Sydney, Melbourne and Brisbane also have their own *Practical Information* sections.

SYDNEY

The centre of Sydney has been divided into four sightseeing areas. Each area has its own chapter which opens with a list of the sights described. All the sights are numbered and plotted on an *Area Map*. Information on each sight is easy to locate within the chapter as it follows the numerical order on the map.

Sights at a Glance lists the chapter's sights by category: Historic Streets and Buildings, Museums and Galleries, Parks and Gardens etc.

All pages relating to Sydney have orange thumb tabs.

1 Area Map
Sights are numbered on a map. Sights in the city centre are also shown on the Sydney Street Finder *(see pp148–55).* Melbourne *also has its own* Street Finder *(see pp414–21).*

A locator map shows where you are in relation to other areas of the city centre.

2 Street-by-Street Map
This gives a bird's-eye view of the heart of each sightseeing area.

A suggested route for a walk covers the more interesting streets in the area.

Stars indicate sights that no visitor should miss.

3 Detailed Information on Each Sight
All the sights in Sydney are described individually. Useful addresses, telephone numbers, opening hours and other practical information are provided for each entry. The key to all the symbols used in the information block is shown on the back flap.

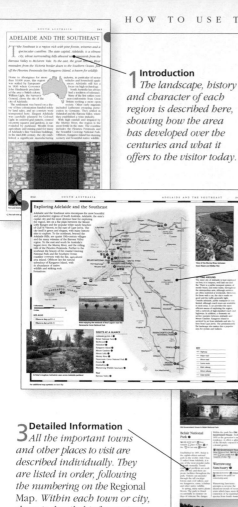

ADELAIDE AND THE SOUTHEAST

1 Introduction
The landscape, history and character of each region is described here, showing how the area has developed over the centuries and what it offers to the visitor today.

AUSTRALIA AREA BY AREA
Apart from Sydney, Australia has been divided into 16 regions, each of which has a separate chapter. The most interesting towns and places to visit are numbered on an *Regional Map* at the beginning of each chapter.

Each area of Australia can be identified quickly by its own colour coding, which is shown on the inside front cover.

2 Regional Map
This shows the main road network and gives an illustrated overview of the whole area. All interesting places to visit are numbered and there are also useful tips on getting around the region.

3 Detailed Information
All the important towns and other places to visit are described individually. They are listed in order, following the numbering on the Regional Map. Within each town or city, there is detailed information on important buildings and other sights.

Ayers House

For all the top sights, a visitors' checklist provides the practical information needed to plan your visit.

4 Australia's Top Sights
Historic buildings are dissected to reveal their interiors; museums and galleries have colour-coded floorplans; the national parks have maps showing facilities and trails. Major towns have maps, with sights picked out and described.

Story boxes explore specific subjects further.

INTRODUCING
AUSTRALIA

DISCOVERING AUSTRALIA

Australia offers unequalled experiences and a wealth of diversity. Its 18,000-km (11,180-mile) coastline boasts everything from the world's best coral reefs, to endless white sandy bays, stunning tropical islands and buzzing surf beaches. The massive interior includes vast red deserts, ancient Aboriginal sites, snow-topped

Aboriginal necklace

mountains and lush green vineyards. You will be spoilt for choice whether you want to experience thrilling outdoor adventure, enjoy the laid-back beach culture, or sample the best in international cuisine and wine. These pages detail regional highlights that will whet your appetite and help you to plan and make the most of your trip.

SYDNEY

- **Stunning Sydney Harbour**
- **Sydney Opera House**
- **The historic Rocks**
- **Relaxed beach culture**

Australia's largest city offers a magnificent array of cultural and architectural delights. The city's crowning glory is **Sydney Harbour** *(see pp70–73)* – a stunning natural asset that other cities can only dream about. **Sydney Opera House** *(see pp84–5)* is a world-class venue and an architectural icon that enjoys the most spectacular setting of any cultural institution. Nearby is the pretty historic quarter, **The Rocks** *(see pp76–7)*, where the first British fleet settled in 1788. A string of gorgeous ocean beaches line the east coast, such as famous **Bondi** *(see p127)*, where surfers gather at dawn and the beach cafés are perfect for people-watching.

Sydney Opera House, one of the world's most striking buildings

Lush vineyards in the fertile Hunter Valley, New South Wales

THE BLUE MOUNTAINS AND BEYOND

- **Outdoor activities**
- **Hunter Valley wine tasting**
- **Prehistoric Mungo World Heritage Area**

Escape from Sydney to the cool refuge of the **Blue Mountains** *(see pp170–73)*. The striking Three Sisters rocks at Echo Point frame a breathtaking panorama, and act as a backdrop for adventure activities, such as bushwalking and rock climbing. **Hunter Valley** *(see pp174–5)* is world-famous for its superb wines, which can be sampled in local cellars. North of Newcastle, secluded towns dot the coast all the way to Queensland. Some are sleepy hideaways, but for those seeking a party, Byron Bay *(see pp178–9)* is the place to go. Out west, the **Mungo World Heritage**

Area *(see p181)* reminds visitors of the Aborigines' 40,000-year occupation of this ancient land.

THE SOUTH COAST AND SNOWY MOUNTAINS

- **Glorious hiking and cycling**
- **Browsing in antique shops**
- **World-class skiing**

Perfect for those who love the great outdoors, this region boasts the **Royal National Park** *(see p186)* on Sydney's southeastern fringe – a fantastic playground for cyclists, bushwalkers and hang-gliders. Further south are the lush, idyllic villages of the **Southern Highlands** *(see pp186–7)*. Known as a retreat for Sydneysiders in summer, they are ideal in winter for browsing antique shops. The **South Coast**'s *(see pp188–9)* fishing villages are a hit with anglers and families, while the **Snowy Mountains** *(see p187)* offer world-class ski resorts, trout fishing and horse-riding in summer.

◁ *Kangaroo Dreaming with Rainbow Serpent, 1992 by Michael Nelson Tjakamarra*

CANBERRA AND ACT

- **Impressive city architecture**
- **World-class art and artifacts**
- **A breathtaking wilderness**

Australia's capital sprang to life under the harmonious designs of its architect, Walter Burley Griffin. Impressive colonial and indigenous art and artifacts are displayed at the world-class **National Museum of Australia** *(see p205)* and the **National Gallery of Australia** *(see pp202–3)*. To the south, the wild **Namadgi National Park** *(see p207)* offers great hiking amid snowy mountains, glistening river valleys and ancient Aboriginal rock art.

Cuddly koala at the Lone Pine Koala Sanctuary, Brisbane

BRISBANE

- **Arts and culture**
- **Exotic botanic gardens**
- **Bustling South Bank**

Cosmopolitan Brisbane has as its creative hub the **Queensland Cultural Centre** *(see pp228–9)*. This thriving institution houses the state's Art Gallery, Gallery of Modern Art, Museum and Performing Arts Centre. The **Botanic Gardens** *(see p230)* feature exotic herbs, delicate mangrove and walking trails. Across the river, the **South Bank** *(see p227)* abounds with buskers, markets and cafés. Admire adorable koalas at the **Lone Pine Koala Sanctuary** *(see p230)*.

The Great Barrier Reef, one of the natural wonders of the world

SOUTH OF TOWNSVILLE

- **The magnificent Great Barrier Reef**
- **Sunshine and beaches**
- **Fraser Island's giant dunes**

With astonishing natural wonders, this region is one of Australia's highlights, and its undisputed gem is the **Great Barrier Reef** *(see pp212–17)*. The world's largest coral reef is a must-see for anyone who has ever dreamt of coming face to face with tropical fish. The **Sunshine Coast** *(see pp238–9)* lives up to its name, with a sunny climate and superb resorts. **Fraser Island** *(see p242)* is the world's biggest sand island, with rainforests, lakes and beaches.

NORTHERN QUEENSLAND AND THE OUTBACK

- **Partying in Cairns**
- **Coastal rainforest**
- **The vast Gulf Savannah**

Cairns *(see pp254–5)* is famed for its party atmosphere. The city also makes a good base for exploring the Great Barrier Reef and **Daintree National Park** *(see p253)*, where the rainforest meets the sea. The **Gulf Savannah** *(see p256)* is an empty wilderness of salt pans and flatlands, a breeding ground for birds in spring and a birdwatchers' paradise. Drive into the Outback and discover the harsh realities of life as an Aussie farmer in the town of **Longreach** *(see p257)*.

DARWIN AND THE TOP END

- **Spectacular landscapes at Kakadu National Park**
- **Ancient Aboriginal rock art**
- **Bathurst Island culture**

Darwin's *(see pp270–73)* remote location and history of migration have given it a multicultural, wild-west character. The world's best Aboriginal art collection is displayed at Darwin's **Museum and Art Gallery of the Northern Territory** *(see p273)*. Rock art is also a highlight of one of Australia's most extraordinary places, **Kakadu National Park** *(see pp276–7)*, with its dramatic escarpments and spectacular lightning storms in the build-up to the wet season. Day trips from Darwin to **Bathurst Island** *(see p274)* offer a unique glimpse of Aboriginal, Indonesian and Tiwi islanders' traditional way of life.

Aboriginal cave art, Kakadu National Park, Darwin

THE RED CENTRE

- **Awe-inspiring Uluru**
- **Desert wildflowers in spring**
- **Adventure camel treks**

At the heart of this vast red landscape is a site of enormous spiritual significance for the Aboriginal community: **Uluru** *(see pp286–9)*. The chance to admire the immense presence and ever-changing colours of this monolith is one of the highlights of a trip to Australia. Spring is a magical time to visit as, after the rains, the desert erupts into a carpet of wildflowers. Lively **Alice Springs** *(see pp282–3)* is the Red Centre's only city, and from here you can arrange outdoor adventure activities, such as **camel treks** *(see p567)* in the desert.

Uluru, the emblem of Australia and a sacred Aboriginal site

the region's prettiest coastal towns, **Margaret River** *(see pp314–15)*, which has become synonymous with gourmet food, fine wine and international surf competitions.

NORTH OF PERTH AND THE KIMBERLEY

- **The extraordinary Pinnacles**
- **Dazzling Ningaloo Reef**
- **The dramatic Kimberley**

Remote Western Australia contains hidden treasures. Strange limestone Pinnacles stand to attention amid the dunes at **Nambung National Park** *(see p324)*, while the magnificent **Ningaloo Reef** *(see p328)* is a snorkeller's dream. Swim from exquisite turquoise bays to observe its sea turtles, whale sharks and reef fish. Spring is the best time to explore the **Kimberley** *(see p330)*, with its vast deserts and deep-river canyon.

Coastal dunes on the Eyre Peninsula, South Australia

Surfing off the coast of Perth, Western Australia

PERTH AND THE SOUTHWEST

- **The isolated city of Perth**
- **Bike rides on Rottnest Island**
- **Surfing at Margaret River**

Perth *(see pp302–7)*, the world's most remote city, is a modern metropolis with superb beaches and great surf. On lovely **Rottnest Island** *(see pp308–9)* you can hire bikes to explore its idyllic coves and encounter its unique furry inhabitants: the quokkas. Within easy access of Perth, the historic port of **Fremantle** *(see pp310–11)* is the ideal spot for a laid-back café crawl. To the southwest lies one of

ADELAIDE AND THE SOUTHEAST

- **Charming Adelaide**
- **Barossa Valley vineyards**
- **Unspoilt Kangaroo Island**

Adelaide *(see pp344–7)*, the graceful "City of Churches", is a cosmopolitan city with a vibrant restaurant scene. Don't miss a tour of one of the world-class wineries set amid the rolling hills of the **Barossa Valley** *(see pp356–7)*. To the southwest of Adelaide, **Kangaroo Island** *(see p354)* is a haven for wildlife, while the beautiful lagoons of **Coorong National Park** *(see p351)* are protected from the Southern Ocean by sand dunes.

THE YORKE AND EYRE PENINSULAS AND SOUTH AUSTRALIAN OUTBACK

- **Coffin Bay Oysters**
- **Walk the Flinders Ranges**
- **Going underground at Coober Pedy**

Some of Australia's best oysters are to be had at **Coffin Bay National Park** *(see pp366–7)* on the Eyre Peninsula *(see p366)*, which is also home to wonderful spring wildflowers and birdlife. To the west, clifftops are prime vantage points for whale watching. Inland, the arid **Flinders Ranges** *(see p369)* are popular with bushwalkers, while in **Coober Pedy** *(see p368)*, residents live in subterranean dwellings to escape the extreme temperatures.

MELBOURNE

- **A botanical paradise**
- **European café culture**
- **International cuisine**
- **Great sporting venues**

Melbourne *(see pp380–421)* prides itself on its green spaces, multicultural lifestyle and strong sporting tradition. Take a stroll though the tranquil 19th-century **Royal Botanic Gardens and Kings Domain** *(see pp398–9)* and enjoy one of the finest botanic collections in the world. Melbourne is also home to several great sporting venues, notably Australia's world-famous cricketing temple, the **Melbourne Cricket Ground** *(see p397)*, and the international tennis mecca at **Melbourne Park** *(see p397)*. European, Middle-Eastern and Asian immigrants have given the city a variety of world-class restaurants and a lively, usually alfresco, café culture *(see pp552–6)*.

Outdoor café in the centre of Federation Square, Melbourne *(see p402)*

National Park *(see p427)*. Paddlesteamers cruise the lazy **Murray River** *(see p430)* passing pioneer river towns such as **Swan Hill** *(see p431)*. Down south, the highlight is a scenic drive down the **Great Ocean Road** *(see pp428–9)*, a winding coast road that hugs the rugged clifftops overlooking the mighty Twelve Apostles, giant eroded monoliths.

Penguin, Phillip Island

WESTERN VICTORIA

- **Gold fever in Ballarat**
- **Awesome climbing**
- **Drive the mighty Great Ocean Road**

The 19th-century gold-rush went wild in **Ballarat** *(see pp434–5)*, **Bendigo** and **Maldon** *(see p432)*, where the extravagant buildings are evidence of former wealth. Westwards, climbers and bushwalkers have a field day in the rugged **Grampians**

EASTERN VICTORIA

- **Majestic Yarra Valley**
- **Alpine National Park Skiing**
- **Penguins of Phillip Island**

Fertile Eastern Victoria boasts intense natural beauty. The **Yarra Valley** *(see p443)* is home to some of Australia's finest vineyards, and the **Healesville Sanctuary** *(see p443)*, is a fascinating wildlife park that features indigenous species, such as the elusive platypus. Victoria's **Alpine National Park** *(see pp448–9)* offers world-class cross-country and

downhill ski resorts. Tranquil **Phillip Island** *(see p442)* is famous for the thousands of Little penguins that waddle out of the ocean at dusk. **Wilsons Promontory** *(see p444)* is a stunning coastal park with shady gullies, secluded beaches and windswept heathlands that are made for nature-lovers. The calm waters of **90 Mile Beach** *(see p444)*, an unbroken stretch of beaches and sand dunes, and the beautiful **Gippsland Lakes** *(see p445)*, Australia's largest inland lake system, offer fantastic sailing, fishing, camping and diving.

TASMANIA

- **Historic Hobart**
- **Port Arthur gaol**
- **White-water rafting at Franklin-Gordon Wild Rivers**

Steeped in maritime history, pretty **Hobart** *(see pp460–61)*, is Australia's second oldest city. Its beautiful waterfront bustles with markets, cafés, restaurants, entertainment and nightlife. The city's dark past as a penal colony has been preserved at isolated **Port Arthur** prison *(see pp470–71)*. **Cradle Mountain Lake Saint Clair National Park** *(see p467)* is loved by bushwalkers, many of whom make the pilgrimage to its pristine alpine lake. **The Franklin-Gordon Wild Rivers National Park** *(see p468)* is a wild region of cool-climate rainforests, fern gullies and white-water rafting.

Tasmania, an island of stunning natural beauty

Putting Australia on the Map

Australia lies in the southern hemisphere and
covers 7,772,535 sq km (3,842,675 sq miles) of land.
A continent, it is bordered by the Pacific Ocean to
the east and the Indian Ocean to the west. More
than 70 per cent of its 22 million people
reside along the coastline with its more
hospitable climate. The capital, Canberra,
is in the Australian Capital Territory,
but the most populous city is
Sydney. Tasmania, an island
state, lies 240 km (150 miles)
off the southern tip of the
country, across the
Bass Strait.

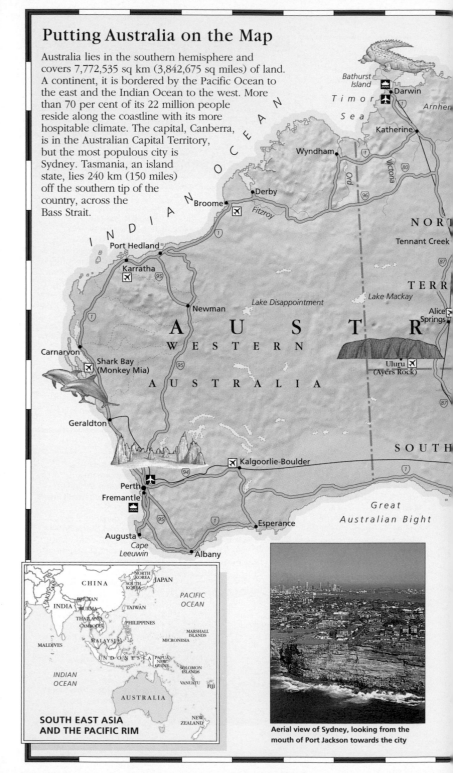

INDIAN OCEAN

Bathurst
Island

Darwin

Timor Sea

Arnhem

Katherine

Wyndham

Ord

Victoria

80

96

Derby

Broome

Fitzroy

NORT

Port Hedland

Tennant Creek

87

Karratha

95

TERR

Lake Disappointment

Lake Mackay

Newman

Alice
Springs

Carnarvon

A U S T R

W E S T E R N

Shark Bay
(Monkey Mia)

A U S T R A L I A

Uluru
(Ayers Rock)

87

Geraldton

S O U T H

Kalgoorlie-Boulder

94

1

Perth

Fremantle

Great
Australian Bight

95

1

Esperance

Augusta

Cape
Leeuwin

Albany

CHINA

NORTH
KOREA

JAPAN

SOUTH
KOREA

PACIFIC
OCEAN

BHUTAN

INDIA

BURMA

TAIWAN

THAILAND

CAMBODIA

PHILIPPINES

MALDIVES

MALAYSIA

MARSHALL
ISLANDS

MICRONESIA

INDONESIA

PAPUA
NEW
GUINEA

SOLOMON
ISLANDS

INDIAN
OCEAN

VANUATU

FIJI

AUSTRALIA

NEW
ZEALAND

**SOUTH EAST ASIA
AND THE PACIFIC RIM**

Aerial view of Sydney, looking from the
mouth of Port Jackson towards the city

Aerial view of Melbourne, along the Yarra River looking towards the casino

Arafura Sea

Torres *Strait*

Cape York

Gulf of Carpentaria

Groote
Eylandt

Mornington
Island

and

Cooktown

Cairns

HERN

Flinders

Townsville

Proserpine

Mackay

Great Barrier Reef

Mount Isa

TORY

QUEENSLAND

Longreach

Blackall

Rockhampton

Hervey Bay

Fraser
Island

ALIA

Diamantina

Charleville

Maroochydore

Brisbane

Coolangatta

Toowoomba

Moree

Bourke

Lake
Eyre

Coober
Pedy

AUSTRALIA

Lake Torrens

Lake
Gairdner

eduna

Whyalla

Darling

NEW
SOUTH
WALES

Broken Hill

Dubbo
Maitland

Newcastle

Coffs Harbour

Murray

SYDNEY

Port
Lincoln

Mildura

Wollongong

Adelaide

Wagga Wagga

CANBERRA
AUSTRALIAN
CAPITAL
TERRITORY

Kangaroo
Island

VICTORIA

Melbourne

Geelong

PACIFIC OCEAN

King
Island

Bass Strait

Flinders
Island

Tasman Sea

KEY

Devonport

Launceston

International airport

Domestic airport

Passenger ship terminal

Freeway or motorway

Railway

State boundary

TASMANIA

Hobart

0 kilometres   500

0 miles   250

A PORTRAIT OF AUSTRALIA

*A*ustralia is the world's oldest continent, inhabited for more than 60,000 years by Aborigines. It was settled by the British during their maritime heyday, in 1788, and since then has transformed from a colonial outpost into a nation with a population of about 21 million people. For visitors, its ancient, worn landscape contrasts with the vitality and youthful energy of its inhabitants.

Covering an area as large as the United States of America or the entire European continent, Australia's landscape is highly diverse, encompassing the dry Outback, the high plateaus of the Great Dividing Range, the lush woods of Tasmania, the rainforests and coral reefs of the tropical north and almost 18,000 km (11,000 miles) of coastline. The Great Dividing Range forms a spine down eastern Australia, from Queensland to Victoria, separating the fertile coastal strip from the dry and dusty interior.

Dominating the vegetation is the eucalypt, known as the "gum tree", of which there are some 500 varieties.

Aboriginal image of Namerredje

Australian trees shed their bark rather than their leaves, the native flowers have no smell and, with the exception of the wattle, bloom only briefly.

Australia has a unique collection of fauna. Most are marsupials, such as the emblematic kangaroo and koala. The platypus and echidna are among the few living representatives in the world of mammals that both lay eggs and suckle their young. The dingo, brought to Australia by the Aborigines, is considered the country's native dog.

Australia's antiquity is nowhere more evident than in the vast inland area known as the Outback.

Sydney Opera House, jutting into Sydney Harbour

◁ Typical red soil and spinifex grass of Australia's Outback

Ancient, eroded landscape of the Olgas, part of Uluṟu-Kata Tjuṯa National Park in the Northern Territory

Once a huge inland sea, its later aridity preserved the remains of the creatures that once inhabited the area. Some fossils found in Western Australia are 350 million years old – the oldest forms of life known on earth.

THE ABORIGINES

The indigenous inhabitants of Australia, the Aborigines, today constitute almost 1.6 per cent of the national population. Their rights and social status are gradually being improved.

Aboriginal Australian

The early days of European colonialism proved disastrous for the Aborigines. Thousands were killed in hostilities or by unfamiliar diseases.

During the 1850s, many Aborigines were confined to purpose-built reserves in a misguided attempt to overcome widespread poverty.

Since the 1950s there have been serious efforts to redress this lack of understanding. Conditions are improving, but even today, in almost every aspect of life, including health care, education and housing, Aborigines are worse off than other Australians. In 1992, a milestone occurred when the High Court overturned the doctrine of *terra nullius* – that Australia belonged to no one at the time of British settlement. The Native Title Act followed, which, in essence, states that where Aborigines could establish unbroken occupancy of an area, they could then claim that land as their own.

Almost all Australians support this reconciliation and are increasingly aware of the rich heritage of the Aborigines. The Aboriginal belief in the Dreamtime *(see pp30–31)* may never be completely assimilated into

The kangaroo, a famous icon of Australia

the Australian consciousness, but an understanding of ancestral beings is an invaluable guide to traditional lifestyles. Aboriginal painting is now respected as one of the world's most ancient art forms and modern Aboriginal art began to be taken seriously in the 1970s. Aboriginal writers have also come to the forefront of Australian literature. Younger Aborigines are beginning to capitalize on this new awareness to promote equal rights and, with Aboriginal cultural centres being set up throughout the country, it is unlikely that Australia will dismiss its native heritage again.

SOCIETY

Given Australia's size and the fact that early settlements were far apart, Australian society is remarkably homogeneous. Its citizens are fundamentally prosperous and the way of life in the major cities and towns is much the same however many miles divide them. It takes a keen ear to identify regional accents.

However, there is some difference in lifestyle between city dwellers and the country people. Almost 90 per cent of the population lives in the fast-paced cities along the coast and has little more than a passing familiarity with the Outback. The major cities preserve pockets of colonial heritage, but the

A fortified wine maker takes a sample from a barrel of port in the Barossa Valley, South Australia

overall impression is modern, with new buildings reflecting the country's youth. In contrast, the rural communities tend to be slow-moving and conservative. For many years, Australia was said to have "ridden on the sheep's back", a reference to wool being the country's main money-earner. However, the wool industry is no longer dominant. Much of Australia's relatively sound economy is now achieved from coal, iron ore and wheat, and as the largest diamond producer in the world. Newer industries such as tourism and wine making are also increasingly important. Australians are generally friendly and relaxed, with a self-deprecating sense of humour. On the whole, Australia has a society without hierarchies, an attitude generally held to stem from its convict beginnings.

Isolated Outback church in Silverton, New South Wales

Yet, contrary to widespread belief, very few Australians have true convict origins. Within only one generation of the arrival of the First Fleet in 1788, Australia had become a nation of immigrants. Originally hailing almost entirely from the British Isles, today one in three Australians comes from elsewhere. Australia's liberal postwar immigration policies led to an influx of survivors from war-torn Europe, most notably Greeks, Italians, Poles and Germans.

Indonesian satay stall at Parap Market in Darwin in the Northern Territory

The emphasis has shifted in recent years and today the majority of new immigrants hail from Southeast Asia. Although some racism does exist, this blend of nations has, on the whole, been a successful experiment and Australia is justifiably proud to have one of the most harmonious multicultural communities in the world.

POLITICS

Since 1901, Australia has been a federation, with its central government based in the purpose-built national capital, Canberra. Each state also has its own government. The nation inherited the central parliamentary system from England, and there is a two-party system consisting of the left (Labor) and the right (a coalition of Liberal and National Parties). The prime minister is the head of federal government, while the heads of state governments are premiers. Australia is a self-governing member of the British Commonwealth and retains the English monarch as its titular head of state. At present, the national representative of the monarch is the Governor-General, but the nation is involved in an ongoing debate about its future as a republic. There is opposition from those who argue that the system currently in place has led to one of the most stable societies in the world, while others believe that swearing allegiance to an English monarch has little meaning for the current population, many of whom are immigrants. A referendum in November 1999 saw the monarchy retained with some 55 per cent of the votes.

The nation's character has always been shaped by its sparsely populated island location, far distant from its European roots and geographically closer to Southeast Asia. Today

View of the Parliamentary area and Lake Burley Griffin in Canberra

there is a growing realization that the country must look to the Pacific region for its future. Closer ties with Asia, such as business transactions with Indonesia, China and Japan, are being developed.

ART AND CULTURE

Blessed with a sunny climate and surrounded by the sea, outdoor leisure is high on the list of priorities for Australians – going to the beach is almost a national pastime. Australians are also mad about sport: football, cricket, rugby, tennis and golf are high on the national agenda.

Yet despite this reputation, Australians actually devote more

Australian Rules football match in Melbourne

of their time and money to artistic pursuits than they do to sporting ones, and as a result the national cultural scene is very vibrant. It is no accident that the Sydney Opera House is one of the country's most recognizable symbols. The nation is probably best known for its opera singers, among whom have been two of the all-time greats, Dame Nellie Melba and Dame Joan Sutherland. Opera Australia and the Australian Ballet, both based in Sydney, are acknowledged for their high standards. Every state also has its own thriving theatre company and symphony orchestra. Major art galleries abound throughout the country, from the many excellent state galleries exhibiting international works to a multitude of

Young boogie boarder

small private galleries exhibiting local and contemporary Australian and Aboriginal art.

The Australian film industry has also come into its own since the 1970s. The best-known Australian film is possibly *Crocodile Dundee* (1985), but productions such as *Shine* (1996), *Moulin Rouge!* (2001) and *Happy Feet* (2006) compete on equal terms with films from around the world and have won international film awards.

This is not to say that Australia's cultural pursuits are entirely highbrow. Low-budget television soap operas such as *Neighbours* have become high-earning exports. Rock bands such as AC/DC also have an international following.

In almost all aspects, it seems, Australia lives up to its nickname of "the lucky country" and it is hard to meet an Australian who is not thoroughly convinced that this young and vast nation is now the best country on earth.

Film poster of the Academy-Award winning *Shine*

Australia's Landscape

Geological stability has been largely responsible for creating the landscape of the earth's oldest, flattest and driest inhabited continent. Eighty million years ago, Australia's last major bout of geological activity pushed up the Great Dividing Range, but since then the continent has slept. Mountains have been eroded down, making it difficult for rain clouds to develop. Deserts have formed in once lush areas and today more than 70 per cent of the continent is arid. However, with some of the oldest rocks on earth, its landscapes are anything but uniform, and include rainforests, tropical beaches, glacial landforms, striking coastlines and flood plains.

Australia's drift *towards the equator has brought a northern monsoon climate, as in Kakadu National Park (see pp276–7).*

Cradle Mountain (see p467) *in southwest Tasmania was created by geological upheaval, glaciation and erosion. Here jagged mountain ranges, ravines and glacial lakes have formed a landscape that is quite unique in Australia.*

KATA TJUṮA (THE OLGAS)

Geological remnants of an immense bed of sedimentary rock now almost covered by sand from erosion, Kata Tjuṯa's weathered domes may once have been a single dome many times the size of Uluṟu *(see pp286–9).*

Western Plateau

Central Lowlands

Great Dividing Range

There are three *main geological regions in Australia: the coastal plain including the Great Dividing Range; the Central Lowlands; and the Western Plateau. The Great Dividing Range is a relatively new feature in geological terms. It contains Australia's highest mountains, deep rivers, spectacular gorges and volcanic landforms. The Central Lowlands subsided when the continental margins on either side rose up – a result of rifting caused by continental drift. The Western Plateau contains many of Australia's large deserts and is composed of some of the most ancient rocks in the world.*

The area to the east *of Queensland was flooded at the end of the last Ice Age, creating ideal conditions for a coral reef. The Great Barrier Reef* (see pp212–17) *now forms one of the world's most stunning sights.*

The Nullarbor Plain (see p367) *was created by the upthrust of an ancient sea floor. Today, sheer cliffs drop away from this desert landscape dotted with sinkholes and plunge into the sea below, creating one of Australia's most startling coastlines.*

THE AUSTRALIAN CONTINENT

The Australian continent finally broke away from its last adjoining landmass, Antarctica, 40 million years ago and embarked on a long period of geographical isolation. During this time Australia's unique flora and fauna evolved and flourished *(see pp24–5)*. Aboriginal people lived undisturbed on this continent for at least 40,000 years, developing the land to their own needs, until the arrival of Europeans in 1770 *(see pp46–51)*.

Two hundred million years ago, the area of land that is now continental Australia was attached to the lower half of the earth's single landmass, Pangaea.

Between 200 and 65 million years ago, Pangaea separated to form two supercontinents, Gondwanaland in the south and Laurasia in the north.

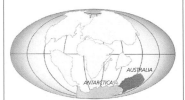

Fifty million years ago, Gondwanaland had broken up into the various southern continents with only Antarctica and Australia still attached.

Today, the drifting of the continents continues and Australia is moving northwards towards the equator at the rate of 8 cm (3 ins) a year.

Flora and Fauna

Forty million years of isolation from other major land masses have given Australia a collection of flora and fauna that is unique in the world. Low rainfall and poor soil has meant meagre food sources, and animals and plants have evolved some curious adaptations to help them cope. Surprisingly, these adverse conditions have also produced incredible biodiversity. Australia has more than 25,000 species of plants, and its rainforests are among the richest in the world in the number of species they support. Even its desert centre has 2,000 plant species and the world's greatest concentration of reptile species.

The platypus *lives in an aquatic environment like a fish, suckles its young like a mammal, lays eggs and has the bill of a duck!*

The lush rainforest is a haven for many endemic species of flora and fauna.

Epiphytes, ferns and vines abound around this rainforest creek.

At least 30 species of spinifex cover many of Australia's desert plains.

RAINFORESTS

The east coast rainforests are among the most ancient ecosystems on earth. At least 18,000 plant species exist here. Some trees are more than 2,500 years old, and many are direct descendants of species from Gondwana *(see p23)*.

ARID REGIONS

The vast reaches of Australia's arid and semi-arid regions teem with life. Desert plants and animals have developed unique and specific behavioural and physical features to maximize their survival chances in such harsh conditions.

The golden bowerbird *of the rainforest builds spectacular bowers out of sticks as a platform for its mating displays. Some bowers reach well over 2 m (6.5 ft) in height.*

The boab (baobab) tree *sheds its leaves in the dry season to survive.*

Spinifex grass, *found across the desert, stores water and needs frequent exposure to fire to thrive.*

The Wollemi pine *was discovered in 1994 and caused a sensation. It belongs to a genus thought to have become extinct between 65 and 200 million years ago.*

The thorny devil *feeds only on ants and can consume more than 3,000 in one meal.*

MAMMALS

Australian mammals are distinctive because the population is dominated by two groups that are rare or non-existent elsewhere. Monotremes, such as the platypus, are found only in Australia and New Guinea, and marsupials, represented by 180 species here, are scarce in other parts of the world. In contrast, placental mammals, highly successful on other continents, have been represented in Australia only by bats and rodents, and more recently by dingos. Mass extinctions of larger placentals occurred 20,000 years ago.

Red kangaroos *are the most common of many species of this marsupial found in Australia.*

The dingo *was introduced into Australia by migrating humans c. 5,000 years ago.*

Eucalypt trees provide food for possums and koalas.

Moist fern groundcover shelters a variety of small mammals and insects.

This coral garden is home to many molluscs, crustaceans and brightly coloured fish.

OPEN WOODLAND

The woodlands of the eastern seaboard, the southeast and southwest are known as the Australian bush. Eucalypt trees predominate in the hardy vegetation that has developed to survive fire, drought and poor-quality soil.

SEALIFE

Australia's oceans are poor in nutrients but rich in the diversity of life they support. Complex ecosystems create beautiful underwater scenery, while the shores and islands are home to nesting seabirds and giant sea mammals.

Koalas *feed only on nutrient-poor eucalypt leaves, and have evolved low-energy lives to cope, such as sleeping for 20 hours a day.*

Seagrass beds *have high-saline conditions which attract many sea creatures. Shark Bay shelters the highest number of sea mammals in the world (see pp326–7).*

Kookaburras *are very efficient breeders: one of the young birds is kept on in the nest to look after the next batch of hatchlings, leaving both parents free to gather food.*

The Australian sealion *is one of two seal species unique to Australia. Its extended breeding cycle helps it contend with a poor food supply.*

World Heritage Areas of Australia

The World Heritage Convention was adopted by UNESCO in 1972 in order to protect areas of universal cultural and natural significance. Seventeen sites in Australia are inscribed on the World Heritage List and include unusual landforms, ancient forests and areas of staggering biodiversity. Four of the locations (Kakadu National Park, Willandra Lakes, the Tasmanian wilderness and Uluṟu-Kata Tjuṯa National Park) are also listed for their Aboriginal cultural heritage.

Fossil sites *in Riversleigh (see p257) and Naracoorte chart Australia's important evolutionary stages.*

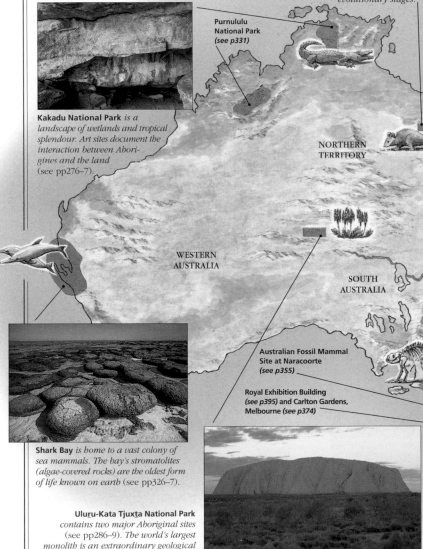

Purnululu National Park *(see p331)*

Kakadu National Park *is a landscape of wetlands and tropical splendour. Art sites document the interaction between Aborigines and the land (see pp276–7).*

NORTHERN TERRITORY

WESTERN AUSTRALIA

SOUTH AUSTRALIA

Australian Fossil Mammal Site at Naracoorte *(see p355)*

Royal Exhibition Building *(see p395)* **and Carlton Gardens, Melbourne** *(see p374)*

Shark Bay *is home to a vast colony of sea mammals. The bay's stromatolites (algae-covered rocks) are the oldest form of life known on earth (see pp326–7).*

Uluṟu-Kata Tjuṯa National Park *contains two major Aboriginal sites (see pp286–9). The world's largest monolith is an extraordinary geological phenomenon in the flat desert plains.*

KEY

World Heritage Area

World Heritage Marine Area

The Great Barrier Reef
(see pp212–13)

The Gondwana rainforests of Australia *contain a near complete record of plant evolution on the Australian continent. Some 50 per cent of all bird species and 30 per cent of marsupial species found in the country are sheltered here.*

The Willandra Lakes *are the site of archaeological finds dating back 40,000 years. The area is also remarkable for its semi-arid land-scape and ghostly lunettes (see p181).*

Fraser Island
(see p242)

QUEENSLAND

Central Eastern Rainforest Reserves
(see p175)

NEW SOUTH WALES AND ACT

The Greater Blue Mountains Area *(see pp164–81)*

VICTORIA

Sydney Opera House
(see pp84–5)

Lord Howe Island, *a crescent-shaped island, and its nearby rocky outcrops represent a chain of volcanic structures. Home to the rare woodhen, banyan trees and kentia pines, Lord Howe's isolation provides key information about the evolution of these species.*

TASMANIA

The Tasmanian wilderness, *Australia's largest conservation zone, satisfies all four natural criteria for World Heritage listing. Its rocks represent every geological period, including the Ice Age, the wide range of plants are unique to the area, and it is home to some of the oldest trees and the longest caves in the world (see pp454–5).*

0 kilometres 500

0 miles 500

The Australian Outback

Perenite goanna in the Outback

The Outback is the heart of Australia and one of the most ancient landscapes in the world. It is extremely dry – rain may not fall for several years. Dramatic red rocks, ochre plains and purple mountains are framed by brilliant blue skies. Development is sparse: "towns" are often no more than a few buildings and facilities are basic. There may be hundreds of miles between one petrol station and another. The Outback isn't easy to explore, but it can be a rewarding experience. Make sure you are well equipped *(see p590)*, or take an organized tour.

LOCATOR MAP

The Australian Outback

Camels *were brought to Australia in the 1870s from the Middle East, as a means of desert transport. The Outback is now home to the only wild camels in the world. Camel safaris for tourists are available in many places.*

Saltbush, which gets its name from its ability to withstand saline conditions, is a typical form of vegetation.

OUTBACK LIFE

The enduring image of Australia's Outback is red dust, solitary one-storey shacks and desert views as far as the eye can see. Although small areas of the Outback have seen towns spring up over the past 100 years, and many interstate roads are now suitable for most vehicles, this image remains true to life across vast stretches of the interior landscape. Most of the Outback remains pioneering country far removed from the modern nation.

Camping *in the bush is one of the highlights of any trip into Australia's Outback, whether independently or with an organized tour. You will need a camping permit, a swag (canvas-covered bed roll), a mosquito net and a good camping stove to eat and sleep in relative comfort under the stars.*

The film industry *has long been a fan of the Outback's vast open spaces and dramatic colours. Films such as the 1994 comedy* The Adventures of Priscilla, Queen of the Desert *made spectacular use of the Red Centre's sparse and dusty landscape.*

Australian "hotels" in Outback areas often operate only as public houses, re-named hotels to counteract Australia's once strict licensing laws.

A solitary building set against vast areas of open desert landscape can be an evocative landmark in the Outback.

PIONEERS AND EXPLORERS

Many European explorers, such as Edward Eyre and John Stuart, ventured into the Outback during the 19th century. The most infamous expedition was Robert O'Hara Burke's from Victoria to the Gulf of Carpentaria *(see p53).* Ironically, it was the rescue missions due to his inexperience which brought about the pioneers' most significant investigations of Australia's interior.

Robert O'Hara Burke 1820–61

The Birdsville Races *in Queensland are the biggest and best of the many horse races held in the Outback, where locals gather to bet and socialize.*

Opal mining *in towns such as Coober Pedy (see p368) is one source of the Outback's wealth. Tourists need a miner's permit, available from state tourist offices, to hunt for gems.*

Aboriginal Culture

Far from being one homogeneous race, at the time of European settlement in the 18th century, the estimated 750,000 Aborigines in Australia had at least 300 different languages and a wide variety of lifestyles, depending on where they lived. The tribes of northern coastal areas, such as the Tiwis, had most contact with outsiders, especially from Indonesia, and their culture was quite different from the more isolated Pitjantjatjaras of Central Australia's deserts or the Kooris from the southeast. However, there were features common to Aboriginal life and these have passed down the centuries to present-day traditions.

Ancient stone axe

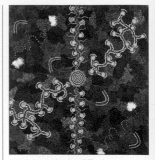

Men's Dreaming by Clifford Possum Tjapaltjarri

Aboriginal artifacts and tools, decorated in traditional ornate patterns

TRADITIONAL ABORIGINAL LIFESTYLES

For tens of thousands of years, the Aborigines were a race of hunters leading a nomadic existence. They made lightweight, versatile tools such as the boomerang, and built temporary mud dwellings. The extent of their wanderings differed from region to region – people who lived in areas with a plentiful supply of food and water were relatively more static than those in areas where such essentials were scarce.

Through living in small groups in a vast land, Aboriginal society came to be broken up into numerous clans separated by different languages and customs. Even people with a common language would live apart in extended family groups, consisting of a husband, wife, aunts, uncles and all their children to share the responsibilities of daily life. Groups would come together from time to time to conduct religious ceremonies, arrange marriages and settle inter-clan disputes. Trade was an important part of social life. Shell, ochre and wood were some of the goods exchanged along trade routes that criss-crossed the entire country.

The nomadic way of life largely ended when English settlers claimed vast tracts of land, but other aspects of traditional life have survived. In Aboriginal communities, senior members are still held in great respect, and are responsible for maintaining laws and meting out punishments to those who break them or divulge secrets of ancient rituals. Such rituals are part of the Aboriginal belief system called "Dreamtime".

THE DREAMTIME

The dreamtime (or Dreaming) is the English term for the Aboriginal system of laws and beliefs. Its basis is a rich mythology about the earth's creation. "Creation ancestors" such as giant serpents are believed to have risen up from the earth's core and roamed the world, creating valleys, rivers and mountains. Other progenitors caused the rain and sun, and created the people and wildlife. Sites where ancestral beings are thought to have emerged from the earth are sacred and are still used as the locations for ceremonies and rituals today.

The belief in the Dreamtime is, in essence, a religious ideology for all Aborigines, whatever their tribe, and forms the basis of Aboriginal life. Every Aborigine is

THE BOOMERANG

Contrary to popular belief, not all boomerangs will return to the thrower. Originally, "boomerang" simply meant "throwing stick". They were used for hunting, fighting, making fire, stoking the coals when cooking and in traditional games. A hunter did not normally require a throwing stick to return since its purpose was to injure its target sufficiently to enable capture. Over time, intricate shapes were developed that allowed sticks to swirl in a large arc and return to the thrower. The returning boomerang is limited to games, killing birds and directing animals into traps. Light and thin, with a deep curvature, its ends are twisted in opposite directions. The lower surface is flat and the upper surface convex.

Aboriginal boomerang

believed to have two souls – one mortal and one immortal, linked with their ancestral spirit (or totem). Each family clan is descended from the same ancestral being. These spirits provide protection: any misfortune is due to disgruntled forebears. As a consequence, some clan members have a responsibility for maintaining sacred sites. Anyone failing in these duties is severely punished.

Each Dreamtime story relates to a particular landscape; as one landscape connects with another, these stories form a "track". These "tracks" are called Songlines and criss-cross the Australian continent. Aborigines are able to connect with other tribes along these lines.

Aborigines being painted with white paint to ward off evil spirits

ABORIGINAL SONG AND DANCE

Aboriginal songs tell stories of Dreamtime ancestors and are intrinsically linked to the worship of spirits – the words of songs are often incomprehensible due to the secrecy of many ancestral stories. Simple instruments accompany the songs, including the didgeridoo, a 1-m (3-ft) long wind instrument with a deep sound.

Aborigines also use dance as a means of communicating with their ancestors. Aboriginal dance is experiencing a cultural renaissance, with new companies performing both traditional and new works.

ABORIGINAL ISSUES

Although few Aborigines now maintain a traditional nomadic lifestyle, the ceremonies, creation stories and art that make up their culture remain strong.

The right to own land has long been an issue for present-day Aborigines; they believe that they are responsible for caring for the land entrusted to them at birth. The Land Rights Act of 1976 has done much to improve these rights. The Act established Aboriginal Land Councils which negotiate between the government and Aborigines to claim land for its traditional owners *(see pp58–9)*. Where Aboriginal rights have been established, that land cannot be altered in any way.

Decorating bark with natural ochre stains

In areas of large Aboriginal inhabitance, the government has also agreed that white law can exist alongside black law, which allows for justice against Aboriginal offenders to be meted out according to tribal law. In many cases, this law is harsh and savage, but it allows for Aborigines to live by their own belief system.

The revival of Aboriginal art was at the forefront of seeing Aboriginal culture in a more positive light by Australians. Aboriginal artists such as Emily Kame Kngwarreye combine traditional materials such as bark and ochre with acrylics and canvas, while telling Dreaming stories in a modern idiom.

Many Aborigines have now moved away from their traditional lifestyle and live within the major cities, but they remain distinctly Aboriginal and generally choose to live within Aboriginal communities. Within designated Aboriginal lands *(see pp262–3)*, many still follow bush medical practices and perform traditional rituals.

It cannot be denied that Aborigines are still disadvantaged in comparison with the rest of Australia, particularly in terms of housing, health and education. But the growing awareness of their culture and traditions is gradually leading to a more harmonious coexistence.

Aborigines performing a traditional dance at sunset

Aboriginal Art

Aboriginal rock art sign

As a nomadic people with little interest in decorating their temporary dwellings, Aborigines have long let loose their creativity on landscape features such as rocks and caves *(see pp47–8)*. Many art sites are thousands of years old, although they have often been re-painted over time to preserve the image. Rock art reflects daily Aboriginal life as well as religious beliefs. Some ancient sites contain representations of now extinct animals; others depict human figures with blue eyes, strange weapons and horses – evidently the arrival of Europeans. Aboriginal art is also seen in everyday objects – utensils and accessories such as belts and headbands.

Bark painting, *such as this image of a fish, has disappeared from southern areas, but still flourishes in Arnhem Land and on Melville and Bathurst islands.*

Cave rock was a popular "canvas" for traditional Aboriginal art, particularly when tribes took cover during the rainy season.

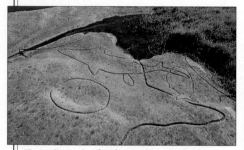

The outline style *of rock engraving was developed most fully in the Sydney-Hawkesbury area, due to vast areas of soft Hawkesbury sandstone. More than 4,000 figures have been recorded, often gigantic in size – one whale engraving is more than 20 m (65 ft) long. Groups of engravings can cover more than 1 ha (2.5 acres).*

Figures showing the human anatomy are often depicted in basic but exaggerated, stylized forms.

Darwin

Brisbane

Perth

Sydney

Adelaide

Melbourne

Hobart

MAJOR ABORIGINAL ART SITES

- Arnhem Land, Northern Territory
- Central Desert
- Uluṟu-Kata Tjuṯa National Park
- Laura, Queensland
- Melville and Bathurst islands
- Sydney-Hawkesbury area

Quinkans *are stick-like figures found in far north Queensland's Laura region. They represent spirits that are thought to emerge suddenly from rock crevices and startle people, to remind them that misbehaviour will bring swift retribution.*

Burial poles *are an example of how important decoration is to Aborigines, even to commemmorate death. These brightly coloured Tutini burial poles belong to the Tiwi people of Melville and Bathurst islands* (see p274).

The crocodile image personifies the force of nature, as well as symbolizing the relationship between humans and the natural environment. Both are common themes within Aboriginal art.

Bush Plum Dreaming *(1991) by Clifford Possum Tjapaltjarri is a modern example of ancient Aboriginal techniques used by the Papunya tribe.*

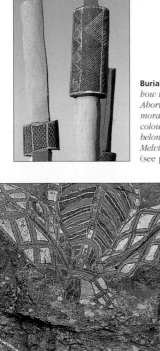

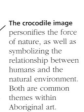

"X-ray art", *such as this figure at Nourlangie Rock in Kakadu National Park* (see pp276–7), *shows the internal and external anatomy of living subjects, including a range of animals.*

ARNHEM LAND ROCK ART

Arnhem Land is the 80,285-km (49,890-mile) Aboriginal territory which stretches from east of Darwin to the Gulf of Carpentaria *(see pp262–3)*. Magnificent rock art "galleries" in this region date from 16,000 BC *(see p47)* – some of the oldest Aboriginal art in the country.

Totemic art *at Uluru (see pp286–9) is thought to portray the beings in Aboriginal culture who are believed to have created the rock.*

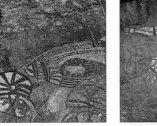

Australian Artists and Writers

The first Europeans to paint Australia were those who arrived in the *Endeavour (see pp50–51)*, but it was not until the prosperity generated by the 1850s gold rushes that art gained any public recognition. There had been colonial artists, of whom Conrad Martens (1801–78) was the best known, but in a country where survival was the most immediate problem, art was not a high priority. The first writings were also journals of early settlers; it was 100 years before Australia could claim the beginnings of a literary tradition, when Rolf Boldrewood (1826–1915) wrote *Robbery Under Arms* (1888), a heroic tale of the bush.

Frederick McCubbin

Sir Russell Drysdale

ARTISTS

The so-called "Heidelberg School", named after an area around Melbourne, was the first distinctive Australian school of painting at the end of the 19th century. Its mainstays included Tom Roberts (1856–1931), Charles Conder (1868–1909), Frederick McCubbin (1855–1917) and Arthur Streeton (1867–1943). The group drew strongly on the *plein air* methods of the French Impressionists to capture the distinctive light and openness of the Australian landscape. Then, in the early 1900s, Hans Heysen captured the national imagination with his delicately coloured gum trees and his view of the Australian landscape. Sir Sidney Nolan (1917–92),

best known for his "Ned Kelly" series of the 1940s based on the country's most notorious bushranger *(see p394)*, also produced landscape paintings which propelled Australian art on to the international scene for the first time.

The best known of the talented Boyd family, Arthur Boyd (1920–99), is another great on the Australian art scene; his "Half-Caste Bride" series catapulted him into the art world in 1960.

Probably the greatest interpreter of Australia's Outback is Sir Russell Drysdale (1912–81), whose paintings depict the harshness of this landscape. Brett Whiteley (1939–92) is a more recent talent whose sensual work reflects his view of the world.

Winner of the Archibald Prize for portraiture, William Dobell (1899–1970) is often regarded as the figurehead of the Sydney Modernist movement. He achieved some level of notoriety when, in 1944, two fellow artists mounted a legal challenge to the granting of the Archibald for his portrait of Joshua Smith, claiming it was "not a portrait but a caricature". The action was unsuccessful, but all Dobell's further work generated publicity for the wrong reasons.

Possibly the most popularly recognized Australian artist is Ken Done. Often dismissed for blatant commercialism, his brilliantly coloured work has achieved sales of which most artists only dream.

The most significant collection of Australian art can be seen at Canberra's National Gallery *(see pp202–3)*.

Toberua (1994) by Ken Done

THE ANTIPODEANS

Formed in Melbourne in 1959, the Antipodeans consisted of seven of Australia's best-known modern artists, all born in the 1920s: Charles Blackman, Arthur Boyd, David Boyd, John Brack, Robert Dickerson, John Perceval and Clifton Pugh. The aim of the group was to support figurative painting rather than abstraction. The group denied that they were creating a national style and the name Antipodeans was adopted to avoid too narrow a focus on Australia, as the group aimed for international recognition at exhibitions in London. Ironically, it later came to apply to Australian art in general.

Kelly in Spring (1956), one of Sir Sidney Nolan's "Ned Kelly" series

Portrait of Miles Franklin by Marie McNiven

WRITERS

Much of Australian fiction is concerned with the difficulties Europeans experienced in a harsh land, or the relationship between white settlers and Aborigines. The themes can be traced back to an early Australian novelist, Henry Handel Richardson, the pseudonym of Ethel Richardson (1870–1946). Her trilogy, *The Fortunes of Richard Mahoney* (1929), was published to great acclaim, including a nomination for the Nobel Prize for Literature. Contemporary novelist David Malouf (born in 1934) continues to explore these issues in *Remembering Babylon* (1993), winner of the Prix Baudelaire, and *Conversations at Curlow Creek* (1996).

Film poster of *Schindler's List*, based on *Schindler's Ark*

Australia's most celebrated novelist is Patrick White (1912–90), who won the Nobel Prize in 1973 with *The Eye of the Storm*. White had made his mark in 1957 with *Voss*, the story of the explorer Ludwig Leichhardt. Two-time Booker Prize-winner Peter Carey (born in 1943) celebrated Australia's most famous bushranger in *The True History of the Kelly Gang* (2000).

Campaigner for women's suffrage, Louisa Lawson (1848–1920), is credited with Australia's first feminist journal, *Dawn*, written between 1888 and 1905. At the same time, another feminist, Miles Franklin (1879–1954), defied traditional notions of the time by pursuing an independent life in Australia, England and the USA. Her life was documented in several autobiographies, beginning with *My Brilliant Career* (1901).

For descriptions of pre- and postwar Sydney life in the slums, the novels of Ruth Park (born in 1922), such as *Harp in the South* (1948) and *Fence around the Cuckoo* (1992), are unbeatable. Novelist Thomas Keneally (born in 1935) won the 1982 Booker Prize with *Schindler's Ark*.

Aboriginal writer Sally Morgan (born in 1951) has put indigenous Australian writing on the map with her 1988 autobiography *My Place*.

POETS

Australia's early poets were mostly bush balladeers, articulating life in the Australian bush. "The Man from Snowy River" and "Clancy of the Overflow" by AB "Banjo" Paterson (1864–1941) are classics still committed to memory by every Australian schoolchild. Writing from the late 1800s until his death in 1922, Henry Lawson similarly wrote some enduring bush verse, but his poetry also had a more political edge. His first published poem in the *Bulletin* literary magazine in 1887 was the rallying "Song of the Republic". One of Australia's leading poets, Les Murray (1938–), is known as the "bush bard" for his writing on bush life.

Poets such as Judith Wright (1915–2000) and Oodgeroo Noonuccal (1920–93), have powerfully expressed the anguish of Aboriginal people.

Henry Lawson

PLAYWRIGHTS

Australia's most prolific contemporary playwright is David Williamson, born in 1942. A satirist exploring middle-class life and values, Williamson has been an international success and several of his plays, such as *Dead White Males* (1995), have been performed both in London and New York.

Ray Lawler gained renown in 1955 with *Summer of the Seventeenth Doll*, which challenged the deep-rooted Australian concept of male friendship. The play has been adapted as an opera, with music by Australian composer Richard Meale.

Other notable contemporary playwrights are Nick Enright, Stephen Sewell and Louis Nowra.

The Wines of Australia

Grapes and wine have been produced in Australia virtually since European settlement in 1788 *(see pp50–51)*. The first vineyards were planted in Sydney in 1791 and over the next 40 years vines were planted in the Hunter Valley (1827), the Barossa Valley at Jacobs Creek (1847), the Yarra Valley (1930), and Adelaide (1937). John and Elizabeth Macarthur became Australia's first commercial wine producers with a small vintage in 1827 from their Sydney farm *(see p127)*. In the 1960s, with the introduction of international grape varieties, such as Chardonnay, small oak-barrel maturation and modern wine-making technology, the wine industry really developed. Since the 1990s Australia has earned an excellent reputation for high-quality wines and there are about 1,465 wineries operating today.

Penfold's Grange

LOCATOR MAP

Major wine-producing regions of Australia

| 0 kilometres | 500 |
| 0 miles | 500 |

Leeuwin Estate winery *in Margaret River, Western Australia* (see pp314–15) *is one of the nation's largest producers of top-quality table wines, including Chardonnay and Cabernet Sauvignon.*

PERTH

ADELAIDE

THE FATHER OF AUSTRALIAN WINE

James Busby is often regarded as the father of the Australian wine industry. Scottish-born, he arrived in Sydney in 1824. During the voyage to Australia he wrote the country's first wine book, detailing his experiences of French vineyards. He established a property at Kirkton in the Hunter Valley, New South Wales, and returned to Europe in 1831, collecting 570 vine cuttings from France and Spain. These were cultivated at Kirkton and at the Sydney and Adelaide Botanic Gardens. In 1833, having founded Australia's first wine-producing region, he emigrated to New Zealand.

James Busby

Mount Hurtle winery *produces distinctive white table wines. It is located in one of South Australia's main wine regions, McLaren Vale (see pp338–9).*

WINE REGIONS OF AUSTRALIA

Since signing a trade agreement with the European Union, Australia has had to implement a new classification system for its wine producing regions. The whole of Australia has 28 wine zones, which can be whole state (Tasmania) or parts of states (Western Victoria). Within these zones are 61 wine regions, such as Barossa Valley *(see pp356–7)*, with the main ones listed below. Some of the up-and-coming areas in Australia are Mudgee and Orange (NSW), and Geelong (VIC).

1 **South Burnett**
2 **Granite Belt**
3 **Hastings River**
4 **Hunter Valley**
5 **Mudgee**
6 **Orange**
7 **Cowra**
8 **Lachlan Valley**
9 **Canberra**
10 **Gundagai**
11 **Hilltops**
12 **Sydney**
13 **Shoalhaven**
14 **Riverina**
15 **Murray Darling**
16 **Swan Hill**
17 **Rutherglen Glenrowan King Valley**
18 **Yarra Valley**
19 **Mornington Peninsula**
20 **Geelong**
21 **Tasmania**
22 **Sunbury**
23 **Macedonl**
24 **Pyrenees**
25 **Grampians**
26 **Coonawarra**
27 **Mount Benson**
28 **Padthaway**
29 **Langhorne Creek**
30 **McLaren Vale**
31 **Adelaide Hills**
32 **Eden Valley**
33 **BarossaValley**
34 **Clare Valley**
35 **Kangaroo Island**
36 **Esperance**
37 **Great Southern**
38 **Pemberton**
39 **Manjimup**
40 **Margaret River**
41 **Swan District**
42 **Perth Hills**

Balmoral House *is part of the Rosemount Estate in the Upper Hunter Valley* (see pp162–3). *The house gives its name to the winery's excellent Balmoral Shiraz.*

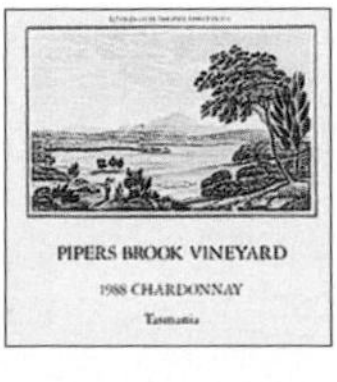

Pipers Brook *in Tasmania was established in 1973 and produces fine Chardonnays.*

VISITING A WINERY

Wine tourism is increasingly popular in Australia and information and maps are readily available at information bureaux. Most wineries are open daily (but you should ring ahead to avoid disappointment) and if they charge for tastings it will be refunded against a purchase from the "cellar door". Winery restaurants are also popular and some have barbeques and entertainment for children while others have a wine-food paired menu. With strict drink-drive laws it may be better to take a guided tour – these can be by bus or limousine.

Surfing and Beach Culture

Lifeguard and her surfboard

Australia is the quintessential home of beach culture, with the nation's beaches ranging from sweeping crescents with rolling waves to tiny, secluded coves. Almost all Australians live within a two-hour drive of the coast, and during the hot summers it is almost second nature to make for the water to cool off. The clichéd image of the sun-bronzed Australian is no longer the reality it once was, but popular beaches are still packed with tanned bodies basking on golden sands or frolicking in deep blue waves. Fines levied for inappropriate behaviour mean that the atmosphere is calm and safe at all times. Surfing has always been a national sport, with regular carnivals and competitions held on the coastline. There are also opportunities for beginners to try their hand at this daring sport.

Baked-brown bodies *and sun-bleached hair were once the epitome of beach culture.*

Surf carnivals *attract thousands of spectators, who thrill to races, "iron man" competitions, dummy rescues and spectacular lifeboat displays.*

SURFER IN ACTION

Riding the waves is a serious business. Wetsuit-clad "surfies" study the surfing reports in the media and think nothing of travelling vast distances to reach a beach where the best waves are running.

Crouching down into the wave's crest increases stability on the board.

WHERE TO SURF

The best surfing to be found in Australia is on the New South Wales coast *(see pp178–9)*, the southern Queensland coast, especially the aptly named Surfer's Paradise and the Sunshine Coast *(pp238–9)* and the southern coastline of Western Australia *(pp312–13)*. Tasmania also has some fine surfing beaches on its northwestern tip *(pp466–7)*. Despite superb north Queensland beaches, the Great Barrier Reef stops the waves well before they reach the mainland. In summer, deadly marine stingers (box jellyfish) here make surf swimming impossible in many areas, unless there is a stinger-proof enclosure.

Surf lifesaving *is an integral part of the Australian beach scene. Trained volunteer life-savers, easily recognized by their red and yellow swimming caps, ensure that swimmers stay within flag-defined safe areas and are ready to spring into action if someone is in trouble.*

BEACH ACTIVITIES

Australian beaches are not only the preserve of surfers. Winter temperatures are mild in most coastal areas, so many beach activities are enjoyed all year. Weekends see thousands of pleasure boats, from small runabouts to luxury yachts, competing in races or just out for a picnic in some sheltered cove. The sails of windsurfers create swirls of colour on gusty days. Kite-flying has become an art form, with the Festival of the Winds a September highlight at Sydney's Bondi Beach *(see p40)*. Beach volleyball, once a knockabout game, is now an Olympic sport.

Festival of the Winds

Takeaway snack food *at the beach is an Australian tradition, since many sunlovers spend entire days by the ocean. Fish and chips, kebabs and burgers are on sale at beach cafés.*

Surfboards, once made out of wood, are now built of light fibreglass, often in bright colours, improving speed and visibility.

The Australian crawl *revolutionized swimming throughout the world in the 1880s. For most Australians, swimming is an everyday sport, learned at a very early age.*

SAFETY

Beaches are safe provided you follow a few guidelines:
- *Always swim "between the flags".*
- *Don't swim alone.*
- *Note signs warning of strong currents, blue bottles or stingers.*
- *If you get into difficulty, do not wave but signal for help by raising one arm straight in the air.*
- *Use Factor 30+ sunscreen and wear a shirt and hat.*

AUSTRALIA
THROUGH THE YEAR

The seasons in Australia are the opposite of those in the northern hemisphere. In the southern half of the continent spring comes in September, summer is from December to February, autumn runs from March to May, while winter begins in June. In contrast, the tropical climate of the north coast is more clearly divided into wet and dry seasons, the former between November and April. Australia's vast interior has a virtually unchanging desert climate – baking hot days and cool nights. The weather throughout Australia is reliable enough year-round to make outdoor events popular all over the country.

Reveller enjoying the Melbourne Festival

SPRING

With the warm weather, the profusion of spring flowers brings gardens and national parks to life. Food, art and music festivals abound in cities. Footballers finish their seasons, cricketers warm up for summer matches and the horse-racing fraternity gets ready to place its bets.

Australian Football League Grand Final in September

SEPTEMBER

Open Garden Scheme *(Sep–May)*. The country's most magnificent private gardens open to the public *(see p374)*.
Mudgee Wine Festival *(date varies)*. Includes bush dances as well as wine *(see p177)*.
Festival of the Winds *(Sun, date varies)*, Bondi Beach *(see p39)*. Multicultural kite-flying festival; music, dance.

Royal Melbourne Show *(last two weeks)*. Agricultural exhibitions, rides and displays.
Australian Football League Grand Final *(last Sat in Sep)*, Melbourne *(see p397)*.
Tulip Festival *(last week Sep–first week Oct)*, Bowral. The Corbett Gardens are carpeted with flowers *(see p186)*.
Carnival of Flowers *(date varies)*, Toowoomba. Popular floral festival including spectacular garden and flower displays *(see p240)*.

OCTOBER

Melbourne Fringe Festival *(late Sep–early Oct, dates vary)*. The arts festival showcases hundreds of events, such as live performances, films, visual arts, multi-media exhibits and comedy shows.
Australian Rugby League Grand Final *(first weekend)*, Sydney. National event.

Floriade, the October spring flower festival in Canberra

Melbourne International Arts Festival *(most of Oct)*, Dance, theatre, music and visual arts events.
Henley-on-Todd Regatta *(third Sat)*, Alice Springs. Races in bottomless boats along the dry Todd River.
Melbourne Marathon *(date varies)*. Fun-run through the centre of the city.
Lygon Street Festa *(last weekend)*, Melbourne. Street carnival through the city's Italian district *(see p395)*.

Henley-on-Todd Regatta at Alice Springs

Floriade *(first three weeks),* Canberra. Magnificent flower festival in Commonwealth Park *(see p195).*
Leura Garden Festival *(second to third weekends),* Blue Mountains. Village fair and garden shows *(see p172).*
Rose and Rodeo Festival *(last weekend),* Warwick. Australia's oldest rodeo attracts riders from all over the world *(see p240).*
Jacaranda Festival *(last week),* Grafton. Australia's oldest flower festival features a Grand Float procession through the town *(see p178).*
Maldon Folk Festival *(last weekend).* Folk music concerts in this country town.

Race-goers dressed up for the Melbourne Cup in November

NOVEMBER

Sculpture by the Sea *(first week),* Sydney. Great outdoor sculptures can be seen at Bondi beach.
Great Mountain Race of Victoria *(first Sat),* Mansfield. Bush riders compete cross-country *(see p447).*
Melbourne Cup *(first Tue).* Australia's most popular horse race virtually brings the nation to a halt.

SUMMER

The beginning of the school holidays for Christmas marks the start of the summer in Australia and the festivities continue until

Santa Claus celebrating Christmas on Bondi Beach, Sydney

Australia Day on 26 January. Summer, too, brings a feast for sport lovers, with tennis, surfing events and a host of cricket matches. Arts and music lovers make the most of organized festivals.

DECEMBER

Carols by Candlelight *(24 Dec),* Melbourne. Top musicians unite with locals to celebrate Christmas.
Christmas at Bondi Beach *(25 Dec).* Holiday-makers hold parties on the famous beach *(see p126).*
Sydney to Hobart Yacht Race *(26 Dec).* Sydney Harbour teems with yachts setting off for Hobart *(see p458).*
Boxing Day Test Match *(26 Dec),* Melbourne.
New Year's Eve *(31 Dec),* Sydney Harbour. Street parties and firework displays.

JANUARY

Hanging Rock Picnic Races *(1 Jan & 26 Jan).* Premier country horse racing event *(see p437).*
Festival of Sydney *(second week-end Jan).* City throngs during this cultural festival.
Australian Open *(last two weeks),* Melbourne. Australia's popular Grand Slam tennis tournament.
Country Music Festival *(last two weeks),* Tamworth. Australia's main country music festival, culminating in the Golden Guitar Awards *(see p177).*
Midsumma Festival *(mid-Jan–first week Feb),*

Melbourne. Melbourne's annual Gay and Lesbian festival includes street parades.
Tunarama Festival *(last weekend),* Port Lincoln. Tuna tossing competitions and fireworks *(see p366).*
Australia Day Concert *(26 Jan),* Sydney. Free concert commemorating the birth of the nation *(see p56).*
Chinese New Year *(late Jan or early Feb),* Sydney.
Cricket Test Match, Sydney.

Fireworks in Sydney for the Australia Day celebrations

FEBRUARY

Festival of Perth *(Feb–Mar).* Australia's oldest arts festival.
Leeuwin Estate Winery Music Concert *(mid-Feb–Mar),* Margaret River. Concert attracting stars *(see p314).*
Adelaide Fringe *(mid-Feb–mid-Mar).* Second-largest fringe festival in the world.
Adelaide Festival of Arts *(late Feb–mid-Mar).* Multi-arts festival held biennially in even-numbered years.

Australian Grand Prix, held in Melbourne in March

AUTUMN

After the humidity of the summer, autumn brings fresh mornings and cooler days that are tailor-made for outdoor pursuits such as bushwalking, cycling and fishing, as well as outdoor festivals. There are numerous sporting and cultural events to tempt the visitor. Many of the country's wineries open their doors during the harvest season and hold gourmet food and wine events. Anzac Day (25 April) – the day in 1915 when Australian and New Zealand forces landed at Gallipoli – has been observed annually since 1916 and is a national holiday on which Australians commemorate their war dead.

Yarra Valley wine

MARCH

Australian Formula One Grand Prix *(last weekend)*, Melbourne. Top Formula One drivers compete, while the city celebrates with street parties *(see p403)*.
Gay and Lesbian Mardi Gras Festival *(varies)*, Sydney. Flamboyant street parades and events.
Yarra Valley Grape Grazing *(early Mar)*. Grape pressing, barrel races, good food and wine.
Begonia Festival *(first two weeks)*, Ballarat. Begonia displays in the Botanical Gardens *(see p435)*.
Moomba Festival *(second week)*, Melbourne. Inter-national aquatic events on the Yarra River *(see pp400–1)*.
St Patrick's Day Parade *(17 Mar or Sun before)*, Sydney. Pubs serve green beer and a flamboyant parade travels from Hyde Park.

APRIL

Melbourne International Comedy Festival *(end Mar–early Apr)*. Comedy acts from around the world perform indoors and out.
Royal Easter Show *(week preceding Good Fri)* Sydney. Agricultural shows, funfair rides, local arts and crafts displays and team games.
Rip Curl Pro Surfing Competition *(Easter weekend)*, Bells Beach. Pros and amateurs take part in this premier competition *(see p428)*.

Easter Fair *(Easter weekend)*, Maldon. An Easter parade and a colourful street carnival takes over this quaint country town *(see p432)*.
International Flower and Garden Show *(early Apr)*, Melbourne. Spectacular floral event held in the beautiful Exhibition Gardens *(see p395)*.
Bright Autumn Festival *(last week Apr–mid-May)*, Bright. Winery tours, art exhibitions and street parades *(see p447)*.
Anzac Day *(25 Apr)*. Australia's war dead and war veterans are honoured in remembrance services throughout the country.

MAY

Australian Celtic Festival *(first weekend)*, Glen Innes. Traditional Celtic events celebrate the town's British heritage *(see p176)*.
Kernewek Lowender Cornish Festival *(mid-May)*, Little Cornwall. A biennial celebration of the area's Cornish heritage which began with the copper discoveries of the 1860s *(see p363)*.
Torres Strait Cultural Festival *(even-numbered years)*, Thursday Island. Spiritual traditions of the Torres Strait Islanders celebrated through dance, song and art.

Anzac Day ceremony along Canberra's Anzac Parade

Racing in Alice Springs' Camel Cup

WINTER

Winter in the east can be cool enough to require warm jackets, and it is often icy in Victoria and Tasmania. Many festivals highlight the change of climate in celebration of freezing temperatures. Other events, such as film festivals, are arts-based and indoors. The warm rather than sweltering climate of the Outback in winter offers the opportunity for pleasurable outdoor events.

JUNE

Three-day Equestrian event *(first weekend)*, Gawler. Spectacular riding skills are displayed at Australia's oldest equestrian event.
Sydney Film Festival *(two weeks mid-Jun)*. The latest blockbusters film releases are combined with retrospectives and showcases.
Laura Dance & Cultural Festival *(odd-numbered years)*, Cape York. Celebration of Aboriginal culture.

Darling Harbour Jazz Festival *(mid-Jun)*, Sydney. Hugely popular festival featuring jazz bands.

JULY

Yulefest *(throughout Jun, Jul, Aug)*, Blue Mountains. Hotels, guesthouses and some restaurants celebrate a mid-winter "traditional Christmas" with log fires and all the usual yuletide trimmings.
Brass Monkey Festival, *(throughout Jul)*, Stanthorpe. Inland Queensland turns the freezing winter temperatures into an opportunity for celebration *(see p240)*.
Alice Springs Show *(first weekend)*. Agricultural and historical displays combined with arts, crafts and cookery demonstrations.
Cairns Show *(mid-Jul)*. A cultural celebration of historical and contemporary life in the Australian tropics *(see p254)*.
Melbourne International Film Festival *(last week Jul–mid-Aug)*. The largest and most popular film festival.

Camel Cup *(mid-Jul)*, Alice Springs. Camel racing on the dry Todd River.

Mount Isa Rodeo in August

AUGUST

Almond Blossom Festival *(first week)*, Mount Lofty. Includes almond cracking.
City to Surf Race *(second Sun)*, Sydney. A 14-km (9-mile) fun run to Bondi.
Shinju Matsuri Festival *(last weekend–first week Sep)*, Broome. Pearl festival.
Melbourne Contemporary Art Fair *(mid-Aug)*. Biennial modern art fair.
Mount Isa Rodeo *(mid-Aug)*. Largest rodeo *(see p257)*.

Dragon Boat race, part of the Shinju Matsuri in Broome

The Climate of Australia

This vast country experiences a variable climate. Three-quarters of its land is desert or scrub and has low, unreliable rainfall. The huge, dry interior is hot year-round during the day but can be very cold at night. The southern half of Australia, including Tasmania, has warm summers and mild winters. Further north, seasonal variations lessen and the Top End has just two seasons: the dry, and the wet, with its monsoon rains and occasional tropical cyclones.

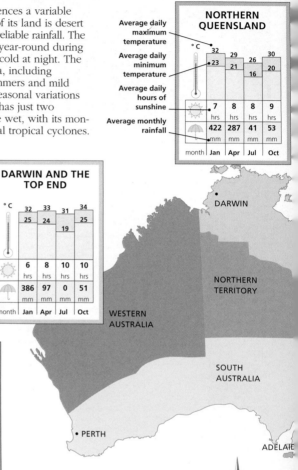

NORTHERN QUEENSLAND

Average daily maximum temperature
Average daily minimum temperature
Average daily hours of sunshine
Average monthly rainfall

°C				
max	32	29	26	30
min	23	21	16	20
☀	7 hrs	8 hrs	8 hrs	9 hrs
☂	422 mm	287 mm	41 mm	53 mm
month	Jan	Apr	Jul	Oct

NORTH OF PERTH

°C				
max	33	34	28	33
min	26	22	14	22
☀	8 hrs	9 hrs	7 hrs	9 hrs
☂	160 mm	30 mm	0 mm	1 mm
month	Jan	Apr	Jul	Oct

DARWIN AND THE TOP END

°C				
max	32	33	31	34
min	25	24	19	25
☀	6 hrs	8 hrs	10 hrs	10 hrs
☂	386 mm	97 mm	0 mm	51 mm
month	Jan	Apr	Jul	Oct

DARWIN

NORTHERN TERRITORY

WESTERN AUSTRALIA

THE RED CENTRE

°C				
max	36	27	19	31
min	21	12	4	14
☀	10 hrs	10 hrs	9 hrs	10 hrs
☂	43 mm	10 mm	8 mm	18 mm
month	Jan	Apr	Jul	Oct

SOUTH AUSTRALIA

PERTH

ADELAIDE

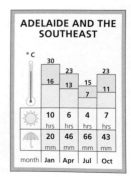

PERTH AND THE SOUTHWEST

°C				
max			17	21
min				12

THE YORKE AND EYRE PENINSULAS

°C				
max	32	26	17	26
min	19	13	7	13
☀	10 hrs	6 hrs	5 hrs	7 hrs
☂	15 mm	18 mm	18 mm	23 mm
month	Jan	Apr	Jul	Oct

ADELAIDE AND THE SOUTHEAST

°C				
max	30	23	15	23
min	16	13	7	11
☀	10 hrs	6 hrs	4 hrs	7 hrs
☂	20 mm	46 mm	66 mm	43 mm
month	Jan	Apr	Jul	Oct

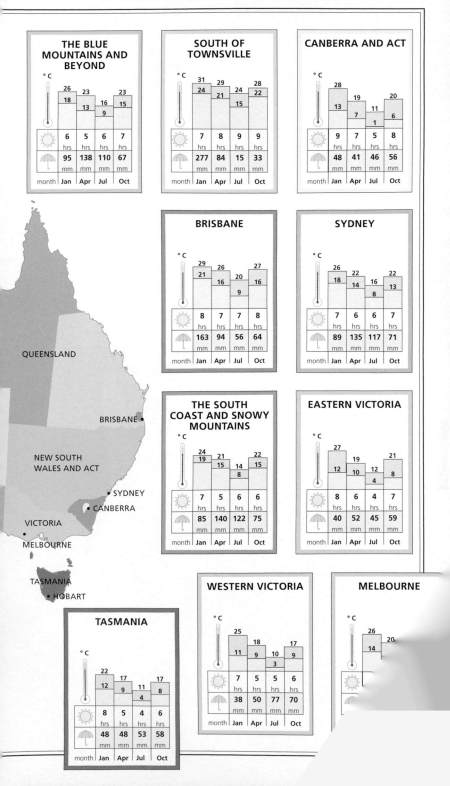

THE BLUE MOUNTAINS AND BEYOND

°C

	Jan	Apr	Jul	Oct
high	26	23	16	23
low	18	13	9	15
sun	6 hrs	5 hrs	6 hrs	7 hrs
rain	95 mm	138 mm	110 mm	67 mm

SOUTH OF TOWNSVILLE

°C

	Jan	Apr	Jul	Oct
high	31	29	24	28
low	24	21	15	22
sun	7 hrs	8 hrs	9 hrs	9 hrs
rain	277 mm	84 mm	15 mm	33 mm

CANBERRA AND ACT

°C

	Jan	Apr	Jul	Oct
high	28	19	11	20
low	13	7	1	6
sun	9 hrs	7 hrs	5 hrs	8 hrs
rain	48 mm	41 mm	46 mm	56 mm

BRISBANE

°C

	Jan	Apr	Jul	Oct
high	29	26	20	27
low	21	16	9	16
sun	8 hrs	7 hrs	7 hrs	8 hrs
rain	163 mm	94 mm	56 mm	64 mm

SYDNEY

°C

	Jan	Apr	Jul	Oct
high	26	22	16	22
low	18	14	8	13
sun	7 hrs	6 hrs	6 hrs	7 hrs
rain	89 mm	135 mm	117 mm	71 mm

THE SOUTH COAST AND SNOWY MOUNTAINS

°C

	Jan	Apr	Jul	Oct
high	24	21	14	22
low	19	15	8	15
sun	7 hrs	5 hrs	6 hrs	6 hrs
rain	85 mm	140 mm	122 mm	75 mm

EASTERN VICTORIA

°C

	Jan	Apr	Jul	Oct
high	27	19	12	21
low	12	10	4	8
sun	8 hrs	6 hrs	4 hrs	7 hrs
rain	40 mm	52 mm	45 mm	59 mm

WESTERN VICTORIA

°C

	Jan	Apr	Jul	Oct
high	25	18	10	17
low	11	9	3	9
sun	7 hrs	5 hrs	5 hrs	6 hrs
rain	38 mm	50 mm	77 mm	70 mm

MELBOURNE

°C

	26	20
	14	

TASMANIA

°C

	Jan	Apr	Jul	Oct
high	22	17	11	17
low	12	9	4	8
sun	8 hrs	5 hrs	4 hrs	6 hrs
rain	48 mm	48 mm	53 mm	58 mm

QUEENSLAND

NEW SOUTH WALES AND ACT

BRISBANE •

• SYDNEY
• CANBERRA

VICTORIA

• MELBOURNE

TASMANIA
• HOBART

THE HISTORY OF AUSTRALIA

*A*ustralia is a young nation in an ancient land. It is a nation of immigrants, past and present, forced and free. The first European settlers occupied a harsh country; they explored it, exploited its mineral wealth and farmed it. In so doing, they suffered at the hands of nature, as well as enduring depressions and wars. Out of all this, however, has emerged a modern and cosmopolitan society.

The first rocks of the Australian landscape began to form some four-and-a-half billion years ago. Over time many older rocks were covered by more recent rocks, but in places such as the Pilbara region of Western Australia erosion has exposed a landscape 3,500 million years old *(see pp330–31)*. About 500 million years ago Australia, together with South America, South Africa, India and the Antarctic, formed a supercontinent known as Gondwanaland. This landmass moved through a series of different climatic zones; today's desert interior was once a shallow sea *(see pp22–3)*.

Australian coat of arms

THE FIRST IMMIGRANTS
Australia was first settled by Aboriginal people who arrived by sea from Asia more than 60,000 years ago. On landing, they quickly adapted to the climatic and geographical conditions. Nomadic hunters and gatherers, the Aborigines moved with the seasons and spread across the continent, reaching Tasmania 35,000 years ago. They had few material possessions beyond the tools and weapons required for hunting and obtaining food. The early tools, known today as core tools, were very simple chopping implements, roughly formed by grinding stone. By 8,000 BC Aborigines had developed the sophisticated returning boomerang *(see p30)* and possibly the world's first barbed spear. So-called flaked tools of varying styles were in use 5,000 years later, finely made out of grained stones such as flint to create sharp cutting edges.

Beneath the apparently simple way of life, Aboriginal society was complex. It was based on a network of mainly nomadic bands, comprising between 50 and 100 people, bound by kin relationships, who lived according to strictly applied laws and customs. These laws and beliefs, including the spiritual significance of the land, were upheld through a tradition of song, dance and art *(see pp30–33)*. With no centralized or formal system of government, individual groups were led by prominent, generally older men, who were held in great respect. Across the continent there were mor

TIMELINE

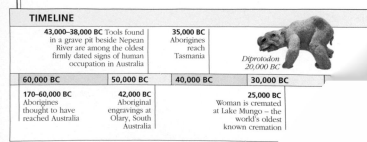

Diprotodon 20,000 BC

60,000 BC	50,000 BC	40,000 BC	30,000 BC	
43,000–38,000 BC Tools found in a grave pit beside Nepean River are among the oldest firmly dated signs of human occupation in Australia	**35,000 BC** Aborigines reach Tasmania			
170–60,000 BC Aborigines thought to have reached Australia	**42,000 BC** Aboriginal engravings at Olary, South Australia	**25,000 BC** Woman is cremated at Lake Mungo – the world's oldest known cremation		

◁ *Desmond, A New South Wales Chief (about 1825) by Augustus Earle*

Woodcut of an "antipodean man" (1493)

than 200 languages spoken and approximately 800 dialects. In many respects, Aboriginal life was also very advanced: excavations at Lake Mungo provide fascinating evidence of ancient burial rituals, including what is believed to be the world's oldest cremation 25,000 years ago *(see p181).*

THEORIES OF A SOUTHERN LAND

In Europe, the existence of a southern land was the subject of debate for centuries. As early as the 5th century BC, with the European discovery of Australia some 2,000 years away, the mathematician Pythagoras speculated on the presence of southern lands necessary to counterbalance those in the northern hemisphere. In about AD 150, the ancient geographer Ptolemy of Alexandria continued this speculation by drawing a map showing a landmass enclosing the Atlantic and Indian oceans. Some scholars went so far as to suggest that it was inhabited by "antipodes", a race of men whose feet faced backwards. Religious scholar St Augustine (AD 354– 430) declared categorically that the southern hemisphere contained no land; the contrary view was heretical. But not all men of religion agreed: the 1086 *Osma Beatus,* a series of maps illustrating the works of the monk Beatus, showed the hypothetical land as a populated region.

It was not until the 15th century, when Europe entered a golden age of exploration, that these theories were tested. Under the patronage of Prince Henry of Portugal (1394–1460), known as Henry the Navigator, Portuguese sailors crossed the equator for the first time in 1470. In 1488 they sailed around the southern tip of Africa, and by 1502 they claimed to have located a southern land while on a voyage to explore South America. The Italian navigator, Amerigo Vespucci, described it as Paradise, full of trees and colourful birds. The location of this land is not clear but it was definitely not Australia.

In 1519 another Portuguese expedition set off, under the command of Ferdinand Magellan, and was the first to circumnavigate the world. No drawings of the lands explored survive, but subsequent maps show Tierra del Fuego as the tip of a landmass south of the Americas. Between 1577 and 1580 the Englishman Sir Francis Drake also circumnavigated the world, but his maps indicate no such land. Meanwhile, maps prepared in Dieppe in France between 1540 and 1566 show a southern continent, Java la Grande, lying southeast of Indonesia.

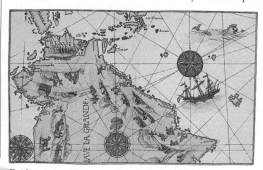
First known map of Australia known as the *Dauphin Chart,* 1530–36

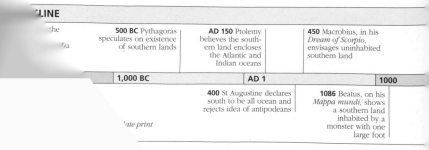

LINE

	500 BC Pythagoras speculates on existence of southern lands	AD 150 Ptolemy believes the southern land encloses the Atlantic and Indian oceans	450 Macrobius, in his *Dream of Scorpio,* envisages uninhabited southern land
1,000 BC		**AD 1**	**1000**
		400 St Augustine declares south to be all ocean and rejects idea of antipodeans	1086 Beatus, on his *Mappa mundi,* shows a southern land inhabited by a monster with one large foot

'ate print

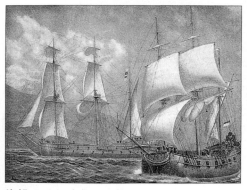

Abel Tasman's Dutch discovery ships

THE DUTCH DISCOVERY

By the 17th century Portugal's power in Southeast Asia was beginning to wane, and Holland, with its control of the Dutch East Indies (Indonesia), was the new power and responsible for the European discovery of Australia.

Willem Jansz, captain of the ship *Duyfken*, was in search of New Guinea, a land thought to be rich in gold, when he sailed along the Cape York Peninsula in 1606. He found the coast inhospitable. In 1616 Dirk Hartog, commanding the *Eendracht*, was blown off course on his way to the East Indies. He landed on an island off Western Australia and nailed a pewter plate to a pole (*see p326*).

Dutch navigator Abel Tasman charted large parts of Australia and New Zealand between 1642 and 1644, including Tasmania which he originally named Van Diemen's Land in honour of the Governor-General of the East Indies. It became Tasmania in 1855.

The Dutch continued to explore the country for 150 years, but although their discoveries were of geographic interest they did not result in any economic benefit.

THE FORGOTTEN SPANIARD

In 1606, the same year that Willem Jansz first set foot on Australian soil, Luis Vaez de Torres, a Spanish Admiral, led an expedition in search of "Terra Australis". He sailed through the strait which now bears his name between Australia and New Guinea (*see p252*). His discovery, however, was inexplicably ignored for 150 years. He sent news of his exploration to King Felipe III of Spain from the Philippines but died shortly after. Perhaps his early death meant that the news was not disseminated and the significance of his maps not realized.

Bronze relief of Luis Vaez de Torres

THE FIRST ENGLISHMAN

The first Englishman to land on Australian soil was the privateer William Dampier in 1688. He published a book of his journey, *New Voyage Round the World*, in 1697. Britain gave him command of the *Roebuck*, in which he explored the northwest Australian coast in great detail. His ship sank on the return voyage. The crew survived but Dampier was court martialled for the mistreatment of his subordinates.

Portrait of Willia[m] Dampier

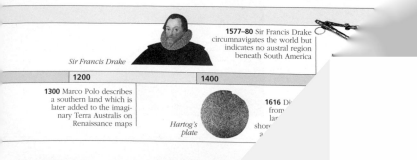

Sir Francis Drake

1577–80 Sir Francis Drake circumnavigates the world but indicates no austral region beneath South America

1200	1400

1300 Marco Polo describes a southern land which is later added to the imaginary Terra Australis on Renaissance maps

Hartog's plate

1616 Di[rk] from lan[d] shor[e]

The Colonization of Australia

By the mid-18th century England had taken over as the world's main maritime power. In 1768 Captain James Cook set off to find Australia in the *Endeavour* and in 1770 King George III formally claimed possession of the east coast, named New South Wales. Overcrowding of jails and the loss of American colonies in the War of Independence led the English to establish a penal colony in the new land. The First Fleet, consisting of two men-of-war and nine transport ships, arrived in Sydney Cove in 1788. The initial settlement consisted of 750 convicts, approximately 210 marines and 40 women and children. Faced with great hardship, they survived in tents, eating local wildlife and rations from England.

Hat made from cabbage palm

Captain James Cook *(c.1800)*
The English navigator charted eastern Australia for the first time between 1770 and 1771.

Boat building at the Government dockyard

England Takes Possession
In 1770 the Union Jack was ̃aised on the east coast of ̃tralia, and England ̃ claimed possession ̃w-found land.

̃seph Banks
̃eavour with ̃ist Joseph ̃for the ̃ the ̃t.

Aborigines depicted observing the new white settlement.

A VIEW OF SYDNEY COVE
This idyllic image, drawn by Edward Dayes and engraved by F Jukes in 1804, shows the Aboriginal peoples living peacefully within the infant colony alongside the flourishing maritime and agricultural industries. In reality, by the end of the 18th century they had been entirely ostracized from the life and prosperity of their native land. The first settlement was founded at Port Jackson, renamed Sydney Cove.

First Fleet Ship
This painting by Francis Holman (c.1787) shows three views of the Borrowdale, *one of the fleet's three commercial store ships.*

Scrimshaw
Engraving bone or shell was a skilful way to pass time during long months spent at sea.

Buildings looked impressive but were poorly built.

Convict housing

Governor Phillip's House, Sydney
This grand colonial mansion, flanked by landscaped gardens, was home to Australia's first government.

Barracks housing NSW Rum Corps

Prison Hulks
Old ships, unfit for naval service, were used as floating prisons to house convicts until the mid-19th century.

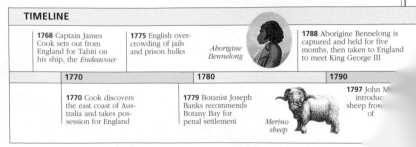

TIMELINE

1768 Captain James Cook sets out from England for Tahiti on his ship, the *Endeavour*

1775 English overcrowding of jails and prison hulks

Aborigine Bennelong

1788 Aborigine Bennelong is captured and held for five months, then taken to England to meet King George III

1770

1780

1790

1770 Cook discovers the east coast of Australia and takes possession for England

1779 Botanist Joseph Banks recommends Botany Bay for penal settlement

Merino sheep

1797 John M introduc sheep fro of

EXPLORING THE COASTLINE

Once the survival of the first settlement was assured, both the government and the free settlers began to look beyond its confines. Faced with a vast, unknown continent and fuelled by desires for knowledge and wealth, they set out to explore the land. The 19th century was a period of exploration, discovery and settlement.

Between 1798 and 1799 the English midshipman Matthew Flinders and surgeon George Bass charted much of the Australian coastline south of Sydney. They also circumnavigated Tasmania, known at that time as Van Diemen's Land *(see p49)*. In 1801 Flinders was given command of the sloop *Investigator* and explored the entire Australian coastline, becoming the first man to successfully circumnavigate the whole continent.

John Batman and local Aboriginal chiefs

EXPLORING THE INTERIOR

Inland New South Wales was opened up for settlement in 1813, when George Blaxland, William Wentworth and William Lawson forged a success-ful route across the Blue Mountains *(see pp170–71)*. In 1824 explorers Hamilton Hume and William Hovell opened up the continent further when they travelled overland from New South Wales to Port Phillip Bay, the present site of Melbourne.

Between 1828 and 1830 Charles Sturt, a former secretary to the New South Wales Governor, led two expeditions along Australia's inland river systems. On his first journey he discovered the Darling River. His second expedition began in Sydney and followed the Murray River to the sea in South Australia. This arduous task left Sturt, like many such explorers before and after him, suffering from ill health for the rest of his life.

Sturt's party shown being attacked by Aborigines on their journey to the Murray River

NEW COLONIES

Individual colonies began to emerge across the continent throughout the 19th century. First settled in 1804, Tasmania became a separate colony in 1825; in 1829 Western Australia became a colony with the establishment of Perth. Originally a colony of free settlers, a labour shortage led to the westward transportation of convicts.

In 1835 a farmer, John Batman, signed a contract with local Aborigines to acquire 250,000 ha (600,000 acres) of land where Melbourne now stands *(see p381)*. His action resulted in a rush for land in the area. The settlement was recognized in 1837, and the separate colony of Victoria was proclaimed in 1851, at the start of its gold rush *(see pp54–5)*. Queensland became a separate colony in 1859.

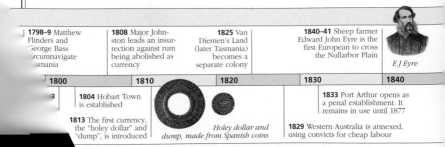

1798–9 Matthew Flinders and George Bass circumnavigate Tasmania	**1808** Major Johnston leads an insurrection against rum being abolished as currency	**1825** Van Diemen's Land (later Tasmania) becomes a separate colony	**1840–41** Sheep farmer Edward John Eyre is the first European to cross the Nullarbor Plain	*E J Eyre*
1800	**1810**	**1820**	**1830**	**1840**
1804 Hobart Town is established			**1833** Port Arthur opens as a penal establishment. It remains in use until 1877	
1813 The first currency, the "holey dollar" and "dump", is introduced	*Holey dollar and dump, made from Spanish coins*		**1829** Western Australia is annexed, using convicts for cheap labour	

A typical colonial house in Hobart Town (now Hobart), Tasmania, during its early days in 1856

South Australia was established in 1836 as Australia's only convict-free colony. Based on a theory formulated by a group of English reformers, the colony was funded by land sales which paid for public works and the transportation of free labourers. It became a haven for religious dissenters, a tradition that still continues today.

CROSSING THE CONTINENT

Edward John Eyre, a sheep farmer who arrived from England in 1833, was the first European to cross the Nullarbor Plain from Adelaide to Western Australia in 1840.

In 1859 the South Australian government, anxious to build an overland telegraph from Adelaide to the north coast, offered a reward to the first person to cross the continent from south to north. An expedition of 20 to 40 men and camels left Melbourne in 1860 under the command of police officer Robert O'Hara Burke and surveyor William Wills. Burke, Wills and two other men travelled from their base camp at Cooper Creek to the tidal mangroves of the Flinders River which they mistook

THE RUM REBELLION

In 1808, the military, under the command of Major George Johnston and John Macarthur (see p127), staged an insurrection known as the Rum Rebellion. At stake was the military's control of the profitable rum trade. Governor William Bligh (1754–1817), target of a mutiny when captain of the *Bounty*, was arrested after he tried to stop rum being used as currency. The military held power for 23 months until government was restored by Governor Lachlan Macquarie.

William Bligh

for the ocean, before heading back south. They returned to the base camp only hours after the main party, who now believed them dead, had left. Burke and Wills died at the base camp from starvation and fatigue.

The crossing from south to north was finally completed by John McDouall Stuart in 1862. He returned to Adelaide sick with scurvy and almost blind.

The return of Burke and Wills to Cooper Creek in 1860

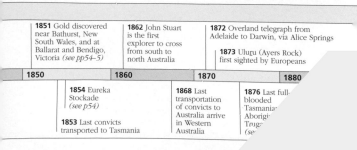

1850	1860	1870	1880
1851 Gold discovered near Bathurst, New South Wales, and at Ballarat and Bendigo, Victoria *(see pp54–5)*	**1862** John Stuart is the first explorer to cross from south to north Australia	**1872** Overland telegraph from Adelaide to Darwin, via Alice Springs	
		1873 Uluṟu (Ayers Rock) first sighted by Europeans	
	1854 Eureka Stockade *(see p54)*	**1868** Last transportation of convicts to Australia arrive in Western Australia	**1876** Last full-blooded Tasmania Aborigi Trug *(se*
1853 Last convicts transported to Tasmania			

The 1850s Gold Rush

19th-century gold decoration

Gold was discovered near Bathurst in New South Wales and at Ballarat and Bendigo in Victoria in 1851. Established towns were almost deserted as men from all over the country, together with immigrants from Europe and China, rushed to the gold fields. Some became extremely wealthy, while others returned empty-handed. By the 1880s, Australia was a prosperous country and cities were lined with ornate architecture, some of which was constructed by the last waves of convict labour. Despite gold found in Western Australia in the 1890s, however, the final decade of the 19th century was a period of depression, when wool prices fell, Victoria's land boom collapsed and the nation suffered a severe drought.

Edward Hargraves
In 1851 Hargraves made his name by discovering gold in Bathurst, New South Wales.

Panning dish

Lamp

Pick axe

Gold Mining Utensils
Mining for gold was initially an unskilled and laborious process that required only a few basic utensils. A panning dish to swill water, a pick axe to loosen rock and a miner's lamp were all that were needed to commence the search.

... took place just ... when miners ... and ... (p434).

DIGGING FOR GOLD

Edwin Stocqueler's painting *Australian Gold Diggings* (1855) shows the varying methods of gold mining and the hard work put in by thousands of diggers in their quest for wealth. As men and their families came from all over the world to make their fortune, regions rich in gold, in particular Victoria, thrived. Previous wastelands were turned into tent settlements and gradually grew into impressive new cities.

Might versus Right *(c.1861)*
ST Gill's painting depicts the riots on the Lambing Flag gold fields in New South Wales in 1861. Chinese immigrants, who came to Australia in search of gold, were met with violent racism by European settlers who felt their wealth and position were in jeopardy.

Tent villages covered the Victoria landscape in the 1850s.

Gold panning was the most popular extraction method.

Prosperity in Bendigo
The buildings of Williamson Street in Bendigo (see p432) display the prosperity that resulted from gold finds in Victoria.

Chinese Miners' Medal
Racism against the Chinese eventually subsided. This medal was given by the Chinese to the district of Braidwood, Victoria, in 1881.

Miners wore hats and heavyweight trousers to protect them from the sun.

The sluice was a trough which trapped gold in its bars as water was flushed through.

Gold Prospecting Camel Team
Just as the gold finds dried up in Victoria, gold was discovered in Western Australia in the 1890s. Prospectors crossed the continent to continue their search.

Souvenir handkerchief of the Australian Federation

FEDERAL BEGINNINGS

Following the economic depression at the end of the 19th century, Australia entered the 20th century on an optimistic note: the federation of its six colonies formed the Australian nation on 1 January 1901. Within the federation, there was one matter on which almost everyone agreed: Australia would remain "European" with strong ties to Britain. One of the first acts of the new parliament was to legislate the White Australia Policy. The Immigration Restriction Act required anyone wishing to emigrate to Australia to pass a dictation test in a European language. Unwanted immigrants were tested in obscure languages such as Gaelic. Between 1901 and 1910 there were nine different governments led by five different prime ministers. None of the three major political groups, the Protectionists, the Free Traders and the Labor Party, had sufficient support to govern in its own right. By 1910, however, voters were offered a clear choice between two parties, Labor and Liberal. The Labor Party won a landslide victory and since then the Australian government has come solely from one of these two parties.

Enlisting poster

WORLD WAR I

When Britain entered World War I in 1914, Australia followed to defend the "mother land". Most Australians supported the war, but they would not accept conscription or compulsory national service.

Australia paid a very high price for its allegiance, with 64 per cent of the 331,781 troops killed or wounded. Memorials to those who fought and died are found throughout the country, ranging from the simple to the impressive such as the Australian War Memorial in Canberra *(see pp200–1)*. World War I was a defining moment in Australia's history. Anzac Day, rather than Australia Day, is felt by many to be the true national day. It commemorates the landing of the Australian and New Zealand Army Corps at Gallipoli in Turkey on the 25th April 1915, for their unsuccessful attempt to cross the Dardanelles and

Labor government publicity poster

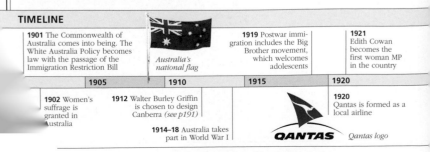

TIMELINE

1901 The Commonwealth of Australia comes into being. The White Australia Policy becomes law with the passage of the Immigration Restriction Bill

Australia's national flag

1919 Postwar immigration includes the Big Brother movement, which welcomes adolescents

1921 Edith Cowan becomes the first woman MP in the country

1905	1910	1915	1920

1902 Women's suffrage is granted in Australia

1912 Walter Burley Griffin is chosen to design Canberra *(see p191)*

1914–18 Australia takes part in World War I

1920 Qantas is formed as a local airline

Qantas logo

link up with the Russians. This was the first battle in which Australian soldiers fought as a national force and, although a failure, they gained a reputation for bravery and endurance. It is an event which many believe determined the Australian character and saw the real birth of the Australian nation.

BETWEEN THE WARS

During the 1920s, Australia, boosted by the arrival of some 300,000 immigrants, entered a period of major development. In 1920 Qantas (Queensland and Northern Territory Aerial Service Ltd) was formed, which was to become the national airline, and made its first international flight in 1934. Building of the Sydney Harbour Bridge began in 1923 *(see pp80–81)*. Australia's population reached 6 million in 1925, but this new optimism was not to last.

In 1929 Australia, along with much of the world, went into economic decline. Wool and wheat prices, the country's major export earners, fell dramatically. By 1931, a third of the

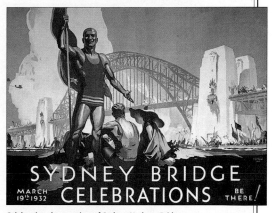

SYDNEY BRIDGE CELEBRATIONS
MARCH 19ᵗʰ 1932   BE THERE!

Celebrating the opening of Sydney Harbour Bridge

country was unemployed. People slept in tents in city parks; swagmen (workers with their possessions on their backs) appeared as men left cities in search of work in the country.

Prices began to increase again by 1933 and manufacturing revived. From 1934 to 1937 the economy improved and unemployment fell. The following year, however, Australia again faced the prospect of war.

WORLD WAR II

Though World War II was initially a European war, Australians again fought in defence of freedom and the "mother land". However, when Japan entered the war, Australians felt for the first time that their national security was at risk. In 1942 Darwin, Broome and Townsville were bombed by the Japanese, the first act of war on Australian soil. The same year two Japanese midget submarines entered Sydney Harbour.

Britain asked for more Australian troops but for the first time they were refused: the men were needed in the

Swagmen during the Great Depression

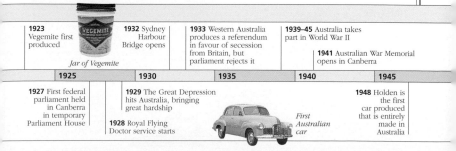

1923 Vegemite first produced

Jar of Vegemite

1932 Sydney Harbour Bridge opens

1933 Western Australia produces a referendum in favour of secession from Britain, but parliament rejects it

1939–45 Australia takes part in World War II

1941 Australian War Memorial opens in Canberra

| 1925 | 1930 | 1935 | 1940 | 1945 |

1927 First federal parliament held in Canberra in temporary Parliament House

1929 The Great Depression hits Australia, bringing great hardship

1928 Royal Flying Doctor service starts

First Australian car

1948 Holden is the first car produced that is entirely made in Australia

Pacific. This was a major shift in Australian foreign policy away from Britain and towards the USA. Australians fought alongside the Americans in the Pacific and nearly 250,000 US troops spent time in Australia during the war. This led, in 1951, to the signing of Australia's first defence treaty with a foreign country: the ANZUS treaty between Australia, New Zealand and the United States.

Again, war affected most Australian communities and towns. Nearly one million of Australia's seven million population went to fight: 34,000 were killed and 180,000 wounded.

Poster promoting travel and tourism in 1950s Australia

POSTWAR IMMIGRATION
The proximity of the fighting in World War II left Australia feeling vulnerable. The future defence of the country was seen to be dependent upon a strong economy and a larger population.

The postwar immigration programme welcomed not only British immigrants but also Europeans. Almost two million

immigrants arrived in Australia in the 20 years following World War II, 800,000 of whom were not British. In 1956, the status of "permanent resident" allowed non-Europeans to claim citizenship. In 1958, the dictation entry test was abolished. Yet until 1966 non-Europeans had to have 15 years' residence before gaining citizenship, as opposed to five years for Europeans.

THE MENZIES ERA
From 1949 until 1966, Prime Minister Robert Menzies "reigned", winning eight consecutive elections. The increasing population and international demand for Australian raw materials during this time provided a high standard of living.

British migrants arriving in Sydney in 1967 as part of the postwar wave of immigration

MABO AND BEYOND
In 1982, Edward Koiki (Eddie) Mabo, a Torres Strait Islander, took action against the Queensland government claiming that his people had ancestral land rights. After a ten-year battle, the High Court ruled that Aborigines and

Edward Koiki Mabo

Torres Strait Islanders may hold native title to land where there has been no loss of traditional connection. This ended the concept of *terra nullius* – that Australia belonged to no one when Europeans arrived there – and acknowledged that Aborigines held valid title to their land. Subsequent legislation has provided a framework for assessing such claims.

TIMELINE

1955 Australian troops sent to Malaya

Neville Bonner

1958 Immigration dictation test abolished

1971 Neville Bonner becomes Australia's first Aboriginal MP

1976 "Advance Australia Fair" becomes national anthem

1979 Severe droughts in the country last three years

1981 Preference given to immigrants with family members already in Australia. Increase in Asian immigration

1955   1960   1965   1970   1975   1980   1985

1965 Australian troops sent to Vietnam as part of their National Service

1956 Melbourne hosts the Olympic Games

1966–72 Demonstrations against the Vietnam War

1967 Referendum on Aborigines ends legal discrimination

1973 Sydney Opera House opens (*see pp84–5*)

Sydney Opera House

1983 Bob Hawke elected as prime minister

1983 America's Cup victory

1986 Proclamation of Australia Act breaks legal ties with Britain

Anti-Vietnam demonstrations as US President Johnson arrives in Australia

In 1972, the Labor Party, under Edward Gough Whitlam, was elected on a platform of social reform. It abolished conscription, introduced free university education, lowered the voting age from 21 to 18 and gave some land rights to Aborigines. In 1974, an immigration policy without any racial discrimination was adopted.

Menzies understood his people's desire for peace and prosperity, and gave Australians conservatism and stability. He did, however, also involve them in three more wars, in Korea (1950), Malaya (1955) and Vietnam (1965). Vietnam was the first time Australia fought in a war in which Britain was not also engaged.

SOCIAL UNREST AND CHANGE

Opposition to conscription and the Vietnam War increased in the late 1960s and led to major demonstrations. At the same time there was concern for issues such as Aboriginal land rights and free education. In 1967, a constitutional referendum was passed by 90.8 per cent of the voters, ending the ban on Aboriginal inclusion in the national census. It also gave power to the federal government to legislate for Aborigines in all states, ending state discriminations.

Prime Minister Whitlam hands over Aboriginal land rights in 1975

THE CHANGING ECONOMY

In 1975, the Liberal leader Malcolm Fraser won the election. Subsequent governments, both Liberal under Fraser (1975–83) and Labor under Bob Hawke and Paul Keating (1983–96), were concerned with economic rather than social agendas. The boom of the 1980s was followed by recession in the 1990s. During this period Australia shifted its focus from Europe towards Asia. The election of Kevin Rudd as prime minister in 2007 marked a return to government for the Labor party after 11 years under Liberal leader John Howard. The new government's first act was a formal apology to indigenous Australians for the pain of past mistreatment. Rudd was toppled as leader of the Labor party in 2010 by Julia Gillard, the country's first female prime minister.

SYDNEY

Central Sydney

This guide divides the centre of Sydney into four distinct areas, and the majority of the city's main sights are contained in these districts. The Rocks and Circular Quay are the oldest part of inner Sydney. The City Centre is the central business district, and to its west lies Darling Harbour, which includes Sydney's well-known Chinatown. The Botanic Gardens and The Domain form a green oasis almost in the heart of the city. To the east are Kings Cross and Darlinghurst, hub of the café culture, and Paddington, an area that still retains its charming 19th-century character.

The Lord Nelson Hotel *is a traditional pub in The Rocks (see p480) which first opened its doors in 1834. Its own specially brewed beers are available on tap.*

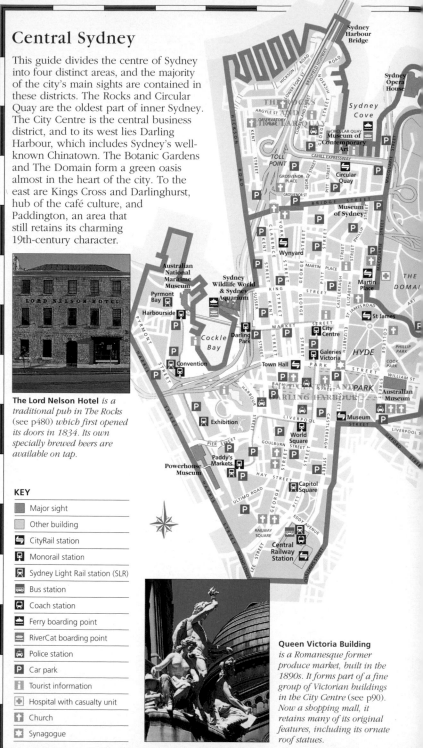

KEY

■	Major sight
■	Other building
🚆	CityRail station
🚝	Monorail station
🚊	Sydney Light Rail station (SLR)
🚌	Bus station
🚍	Coach station
⛴	Ferry boarding point
⛴	RiverCat boarding point
🚓	Police station
P	Car park
i	Tourist information
✚	Hospital with casualty unit
✝	Church
✡	Synagogue

Queen Victoria Building *is a Romanesque former produce market, built in the 1890s. It forms part of a fine group of Victorian buildings in the City Centre (see p90). Now a shopping mall, it retains many of its original features, including its ornate roof statues.*

◁ **Sydneysiders enjoying the sunshine in front of the distinctive Sydney Opera House**

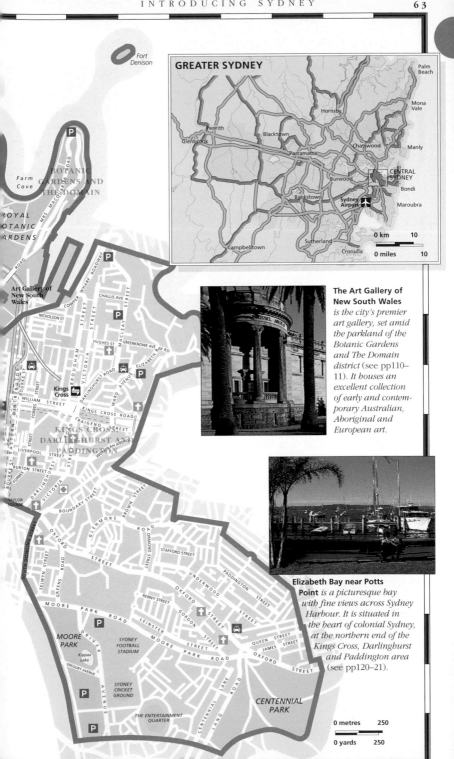

GREATER SYDNEY

Palm Beach

Mona Vale

Hornsby

Manly

Penrith

Blacktown

Chatswood

Glenbrook

Parramatta

CENTRAL SYDNEY

Burwood

Bondi

Bankstown

Sydney Airport

Maroubra

Campbelltown

Sutherland

Cronulla

0 km 10

0 miles 10

Fort Denison

Farm Cove

BOTANIC GARDENS AND THE DOMAIN

ROYAL BOTANIC GARDENS

Art Gallery of New South Wales

NICHOLSON ST

CHALLIS AVE

HUGHES ST

GREENKNOWE AVE

Kings Cross

KINGS CROSS ROAD

WILLIAM STREET

CRAIGEND STREET

KINGS CROSS DARLINGHURST PADDINGTON

LIVERPOOL STREET

BURTON STREET

TAYLOR SQUARE

BOUNDARY STREET

GLENMORE ROAD

BROWN STREET

STAFFORD STREET

UNDERWOOD STREET

PADDINGTON STREET

OXFORD STREET

OXFORD STREET

RENNY STREET

GORDON STREET

LEINSTER STREET

MOORE PARK ROAD

QUEEN STREET

JAMES STREET

OXFORD STREET

MOORE PARK

Kippax Lake

GREGORY AVENUE

SYDNEY FOOTBALL STADIUM

MOORE PARK ROAD

CENTENNIAL PARK

SYDNEY CRICKET GROUND

THE ENTERTAINMENT QUARTER

0 metres 250

0 yards 250

The Art Gallery of New South Wales *is the city's premier art gallery, set amid the parkland of the Botanic Gardens and The Domain district (see pp110–11). It houses an excellent collection of early and contemporary Australian, Aboriginal and European art.*

Elizabeth Bay near Potts Point *is a picturesque bay with fine views across Sydney Harbour. It is situated in the heart of colonial Sydney, at the northern end of the Kings Cross, Darlinghurst and Paddington area (see pp120–21).*

Sydney's Best: Museums and Galleries

Sydney is well endowed with museums and galleries, and, following the current appreciation of social history, much emphasis is placed on the lifestyles of past and present Sydneysiders. Small museums are also a feature of the Sydney scene, with a number of historic houses recalling the colonial days. Most of the major collections are housed in architecturally significant buildings – the Classical façade of the Art Gallery of NSW makes it a city landmark, while the MCA or Museum of Contemporary Art has given new life to a 1950s Art Deco-style building at Circular Quay.

Bima figure, Powerhouse Museum

The Museum of Sydney
includes The Edge of the Trees, an interactive installation (see p92).

THE ROCKS AND
CIRCULAR QUAY

The Museum of Contemporary Art
is Australia's only museum dedicated to exhibiting national and international contemporary art (see p78).

CITY CENTRE
AND DARLING
HARBOUR

The National Maritime Museum
is the home port for HMB Endeavour, *a replica of the vessel that charted Australia's east coast in 1770, with Captain Cook in command* (see pp100–1).

The Powerhouse Museum, *set in a former power station, uses both traditional and interactive displays to explore Australian innovations in science and technology* (see pp102–3).

0 metres	500
0 yards	500

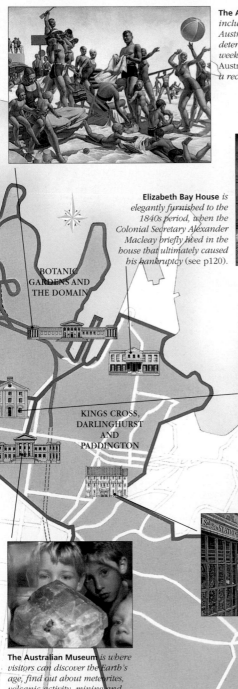

The Art Gallery of New South Wales *includes colonial watercolours in its Australian collection, which, to avoid deterioration, are only shown for a few weeks each year. Charles Meere's Australian Beach Pattern (1940) is a recent work* (see pp110–13).

Elizabeth Bay House *is elegantly furnished to the 1840s period, when the Colonial Secretary Alexander Macleay briefly lived in the house that ultimately caused his bankruptcy* (see p120).

BOTANIC GARDENS AND THE DOMAIN

KINGS CROSS, DARLINGHURST AND PADDINGTON

The Hyde Park Barracks *were originally built by convicts for their own incarceration. They were later home to poor female immigrants. Exhibits recall the daily life of these occupants* (see p114).

The Australian Museum *is where visitors can discover the Earth's age, find out about meteorites, volcanic activity, mining and more with its stunning display of rocks and minerals* (see pp94–5).

The Sydney Jewish Museum *documents the history of the city's Jewish community. Exhibits include reconstructed scenes, such as George Street in 1848, a Jewish business area* (see p121).

Sydney's Best: Architecture

For such a young city, Sydney possesses a great
diversity of architectural styles. They range from the
simplicity of Francis Greenway's Georgian buildings
(see p169) to Jørn Utzon's Expressionist Sydney Opera
House *(see pp84–5)*. Practical colonial structures gave
way to elaborate Victorian edifices such as Sydney
Town Hall. The same passion for detail is seen in
Paddington's terraces. Later, Federation warehouses and
bungalows introduced a uniquely Australian style.

Colonial convict *structures were
simple with shingled roofs, based
on the English homes of the first
settlers. Cadman's Cottage
is an example of this style
(see p78).*

Contemporary
*architecture abounds in
Sydney, including
Governor Phillip Tower.
The Museum of Sydney is
at its base (see p92).*

**THE ROCKS
AND
CIRCULAR
QUAY**

Colonial Georgian *buildings
include St James Church (see
p115). Francis Greenway's
design was adapted to suit
the purposes of a church.*

**American
Revivalism** *took up
the 1890s vogue of
arcades connecting
many different
streets. The Queen
Victoria Building is
a fine example
(see p90).*

Victorian
*architecture
abounds in the city.
Sydney Town Hall
includes a metal
ceiling, installed for
fear that the organ
would vibrate a plaster
one loose (see p93).*

**CITY
CENTRE &
DARLING
HARBOUR**

Contemporary Expressionism's *main
emphasis is roof design and the silhouette.
Innovations were made in sports stadiums
and museums, such as the Australian
National Maritime Museum (see p100–1).*

Interwar Architecture
*encapsulates the spirit of Art Deco,
as seen in the Anzac Memorial in
Hyde Park (see p93).*

0 metres	500
0 yards	500

Modern Expressionism
*includes one of the world's greatest
examples of 20th-century architecture.
The construction of Jørn Utzon's Sydney
Opera House began in 1959. Despite the
architect's resignation in 1966, it was
opened in 1973 (see pp84–5).*

Australian Regency *was popular
during the 1830s. The best-designed
villas were the work of John Verge. The
beautiful Elizabeth Bay House is considered his masterpiece (see p120).*

BOTANIC
GARDENS AND
THE DOMAIN

Early Colonial's
*first buildings, such as
Hyde Park Barracks
(see p114), were mainly
built for the government.*

KINGS CROSS,
DARLINGHURST &
PADDINGTON

Colonial military *buildings were both
functional and ornate. Victoria Barracks,
designed by engineers, is a fine example of a
Georgian military compound (see p124).*

Colonial Grecian *and
Greek Revival were the
most popular styles for
public buildings
designed during the
1820–50 period. The
Darlinghurst Court
House is a particularly
fine example (see p121).*

Victorian iron lace
*incorporated filigree
of cast-iron in prefab-
ricated patterns.
Paddington's verandas
are fine examples of
this 1880s style
(see pp122–3).*

Sydney's Best: Parks and Reserves

Flannel flower

Sydney is almost completely surrounded by national parks and intact bushland. There are also a number of national parks and reserves within Greater Sydney itself. Here, the visitor can gain some idea of how the landscape looked before the arrival of European settlers. The city parks, too, are filled with plant and animal life. The more formal plantings of both native and exotic species are countered by the indigenous birds and animals that have adapted and made the urban environment their home.

One of the highlights of a trip to Sydney is the huge variety of birds to be seen, from large birds of prey such as sea eagles and kites, to the shyer species such as wrens and tiny finches.

Garigal National Park
is made up of rainforest and moist gullies, which provide shelter for superb lyrebirds and sugar gliders.

North Arm Walk
is covered in spring with grevilleas and flannel flowers blooming profusely.

Lane Cove National Park *is an open eucalypt forest dotted with grass trees, as well as fine stands of blue gums and apple gums. The rosella, a type of parrot, is common in the area.*

Bicentennial Park *is situated at Homebush Bay (see p147). The park features a mangrove habitat and attracts many water birds, including pelicans.*

Hyde Park *is situated on the edge of the city centre (see p93). The park provides a peaceful respite from the hectic streets. The native iris is just one of the plants found in the lush gardens. The sacred ibis, a water bird, is often seen.*

Middle Head and Obelisk Bay *are dotted with gun emplacements, tunnels and bunkers built in the 1870s to protect Sydney from invasion. The superb fairy wren lives here, and water dragons can at times be seen basking on rocks.*

North Head *is covered with coastal heathland, with banksias, tea trees and casuarinas dominating the cliff tops. On the leeward side, moist forest surrounds tiny, secluded harbour beaches.*

Grotto Point's paths, winding through the bush to the lighthouse, are lined with bottlebrushes, grevilleas and flannel flowers.

Bradleys Head *is a nesting place for the ringtail possum. Noisy flocks of rainbow lorikeets are also often in residence. The views across the harbour to Sydney are spectacular.*

South Head contains unique plant species such as the sundew.

Nielsen Park is inhabited by the kookaburra, easily identified by its call, which sounds like laughter.

The Domain *features palms and Moreton Bay figs. The Australian magpie, with its black and white plumage, is a frequent visitor (see p109).*

Moore Park is filled with huge Moreton Bay figs which provide an urban habitat for the flying fox.

Centennial Park *contains open expanses and groves of paperbark and eucalypt trees, bringing sulphurcrested cockatoos en masse. The brushtail possum is a shy creature that comes out at night (see p125).*

| 0 kilometres | 4 |
| 0 miles | 2 |

Garden Island to Farm Cove

Waterlily in the Royal Botanic Gardens

Sydney's vast harbour, also named Port Jackson after a Secretary in the British Admiralty who promptly changed his name, is a drowned river valley which was transformed over millions of years. Its intricate coastal geography of headlands and secluded bays can sometimes confound even lifelong residents. This waterway was the lifeblood of the early colony, with the maritime industry a vital source of wealth and supply. The legacies of recessions and booms can be viewed along the shoreline: a representation of a nation where an estimated 70 per cent of the population cling to the coastal cities, especially in the east.

The city skyline *is a result of random development. The 1960s' destruction of architectural history was halted, and towers now stand amid Victorian buildings.*

Two harbour beacons, *known as "wedding cakes" because of their three tiers, are solar powered and equipped with a fail-safe back-up service. There are around 350 buoys and beacons now in operation.*

The barracks for the naval garrison date from 1888.

Garden Island marks a 1940s construction project with 12 ha (30 acres) reclaimed from the harbour.

Sailing on the harbour *is a pastime not exclusively reserved for the rich elite. Of the several hundred thousand pleasure boats registered, some are available for hire while others take out groups of inexperienced sailors.*

0 metres	250
0 yards	250

Mrs Macquaries Chair *is a carved rock seat by Mrs Macquaries Road (see p108). In the early days of the colony this was the site of a fruit and vegetable garden which was farmed until 1805.*

The Andrew (Boy) Charlton Pool *is a favourite bathing spot for inner-city residents, and is named after the 16-year old who won an Olympic gold medal in 1924. It was erected in 1963 on the Domain Baths' site, which had a grandstand for 1,700.*

Woolloomooloo Finger Wharf was a disembarkation point when most travellers arrived by sea.

LOCATOR MAP
See Street Finder, *map 2*

Harry's Café de Wheels, *a snack van, has been a Sydney culinary institution for more than 50 years. Photographs of celebrity customers are pinned to the van, attesting to its fame.*

The Royal Botanic Gardens *display both flowering and non-flowering plants. Here the first trees were planted by the new European colonists; some of these trees survive today (see pp106–7).*

Farm Cove *has long been a mooring place for visiting naval vessels. The land opposite, now the Botanic Gardens, has been continuously cultivated for over 200 years.*

Sydney Cove to Walsh Bay

It is estimated that over 70 km (43 miles) of harbour foreshore have been lost as a result of the massive land reclamation projects carried out since the 1840s. That the 13 islands existing when the First Fleet arrived in 1788 have now been reduced to just eight is a startling indication of rapid and profound geographical transformation. Redevelopments around the Circular Quay and Walsh Bay area from the 1980s have opened up the waterfront for public use and enjoyment, acknowledging it as the city's greatest natural asset. Sydney's environmental and architectural aspirations recognize the need to integrate city and harbour.

Detail from railing at Circular Quay

Conservatorium of Music

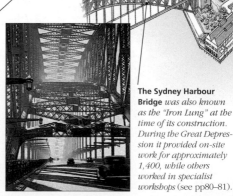

1857 Man O'War Steps

The Sydney Opera House *was designed to take advantage of its spectacular setting. The roofs shine during the day and seem to glow at night. The building appears as a visionary landscape to the onlooker (see pp84–5).*

Government House, a Gothic Revival building, was home to the state's governors until 1996.

Harbour cruises *regularly depart from Circular Quay, taking visitors out and about both during the day and in the evening. They are an incomparable way to see the city and its waterways.*

0 metres	250
0 yards	250

The Sydney Harbour Bridge *was also known as the "Iron Lung" at the time of its construction. During the Great Depression it provided on-site work for approximately 1,400, while others worked in specialist workshops (see pp80–81).*

The Rocks, *settled by convicts and troops in 1788, is one of Sydney's oldest neighbourhoods. Rich in heritage, many of its old sandstone buildings have been restored and house speciality and craft shops.*

The Tank Stream, the colony's first water supply, now runs underground and spills into the quay.

LOCATOR MAP
See Street Finder, *maps 1 & 2*

THE ROCKS
AND CIRCULAR
QUAY

BOTANIC
GARDENS AND
THE DOMAIN

CITY CENTRE
AND
DARLING
HARBOUR

KINGS CROSS,
DARLINGHURST
AND PADDINGTON

Cahill Expressway

Circular Quay, *originally and more accurately known as Semi-Circular Quay, was the last and arguably greatest convict-built structure. Tank Stream mudflats were filled in to shape the quay, and sandstone from The Rocks formed the sea wall.*

The Wharf Theatre *resides on a pier that took six years to build, mostly due to the diversion of labour and materials during World War I. The theatre was opened in 1984.*

The wharves were completed in 1922.

Imports and exports to and from the city were stored in these wharves until 1977.

The wharves' design *included a rat-proof sea wall around the port. This was an urgent response to the 1900 bubonic plague outbreak, attributed to rats on the wharves.*

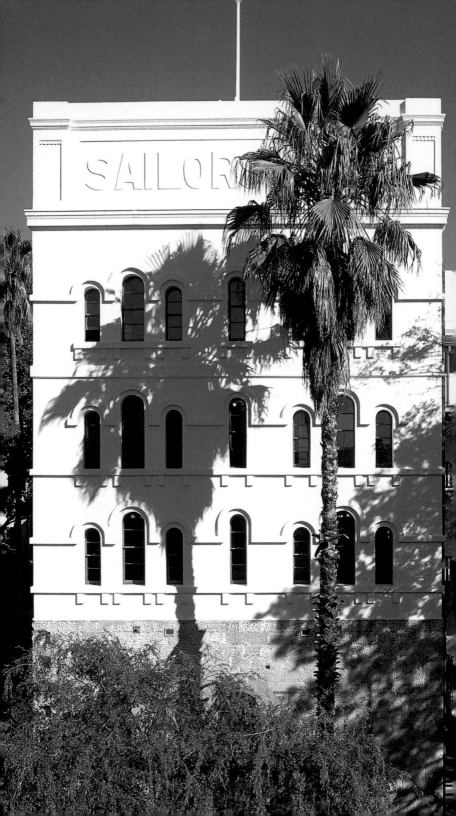

THE ROCKS AND CIRCULAR QUAY

Circular Quay, once known as Semi-Circular Quay, is often referred to as the "birthplace of Australia". It was here, in January 1788, that the First Fleet landed its human freight of convicts, soldiers and officials, and the new British colony of New South Wales was declared. Sydney Cove became a rallying point whenever a ship arrived bringing much-needed supplies from "home". Crowds still gather here whenever there is a national or civic celebration. The Quay and The Rocks

Sculpture on the AMP Building, Circular Quay

are focal points for New Year's Eve festivities. Circular Quay was the setting for huge crowds when, in 1994, Sydney was awarded the year 2000 Olympic Games. The Rocks area offers visitors a taste of Sydney's past, but it is a far cry from the time, less than 100 years ago, when most inhabitants lived in rat-infested slums, and gangs ruled its streets. Now scrubbed and polished, The Rocks forms part of the colourful promenade from the Sydney Harbour Bridge to the spectacular Sydney Opera House.

SIGHTS AT A GLANCE

Museums and Galleries

Justice and Police Museum **15**
Museum of
  Contemporary Art **2**
National Trust Centre **11**
The Rocks
  Discovery Museum **5**
Sailors' Home **4**
Susannah Place **1**

Theatres and Concert Halls

Sydney Opera House
pp84–5 **17**

Historic Streets and Buildings

Cadman's Cottage **3**
Campbell's Storehouses **6**
Customs House **14**
Hero of Waterloo **8**
Macquarie Place **13**
Sydney Harbour Bridge
pp80–81 **7**

Sydney Observatory **10**
Writers' Walk **16**

Churches

Garrison Church **9**
St Philip's Church **12**

GETTING THERE

Circular Quay is the best stop for ferries and trains. Sydney Explorer and bus routes 431, 432, 433 and 434 run regularly to The Rocks, while most buses through the city go to the Quay.

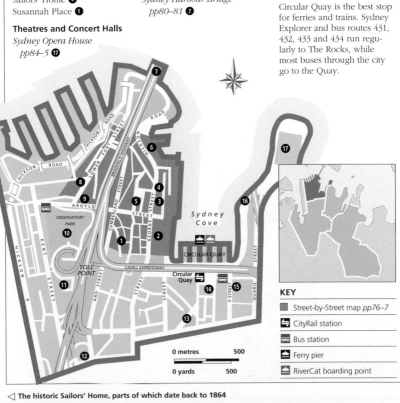

KEY

- Street-by-Street map *pp76–7*
- CityRail station
- Bus station
- Ferry pier
- RiverCat boarding point

◁ The historic Sailors' Home, parts of which date back to 1864

Street-by-Street: The Rocks

Governor Arthur Phillip

Named for the rugged cliffs that were once its dominant feature, this area has played a vital role in Sydney's development. In 1788, the First Fleeters under Governor Phillip's command erected makeshift buildings here, with the convicts' hard labour used to establish more permanent structures in the form of rough-hewn streets. The Argyle Cut, a road carved through solid rock using just hammer and chisel, took 18 years to build, beginning in 1843. By 1900, The Rocks was overrun with disease; the street now known as Suez Canal was once Sewer's Canal. Today, the area is still rich in colonial history and colour.

Hero of Waterloo
Lying beneath this historic pub is a tunnel originally used for smuggling **8**

Hero of Waterloo

WATSON ROAD

ARGYLE STREET

TRINITY AVENUE

LOW

UPPER FORT STREET

BRADFIELD HIGHWAY

CUMBERLAND STREET

GLOUCESTER

★ Sydney Observatory
The first European structure on this prominent site was a windmill. The present museum holds some of the earliest astronomical instruments brought to Australia **10**

HARRINGTON STREET

ARGYLE STREET

PLAY

Garrison Church
Columns in this church are decorated with the insignia of British troops stationed here until 1870. Australia's first prime minister was educated next door **9**

GEORGE STREET

Argyle Cut

Suez Canal

★ Museum of Contemporary Art
The stripped Classical façade belies the contemporary nature of the Australian and international art displayed in an ever-changing programme **2**

Walkway along Circular Quay West foreshore

The Rocks Discovery Museum

Key episodes in The Rocks' history are illustrated by this museum's collection of maritime images and other artifacts ❺

LOCATOR MAP
See Street Finder, map 1

The Rocks Market

is a hive of activity every weekend, offering an eclectic range of craft items and jewellery utilizing Australian icons from gum leaves to koalas *(see p133).*

★ Cadman's Cottage

John Cadman, government coxswain, resided in what was known as the Coxswain's Barracks with his family. His wife Elizabeth was also a significant figure, believed to be the first woman to vote in New South Wales, a right she insisted on ❸

0 metres	100
0 yards	100

KEY

– – – Suggested route

The Overseas Passenger Terminal is where some of the world's luxury cruise liners, including the *QEII*, berth during their stay in Sydney.

STAR SIGHTS

★ Cadman's Cottage

★ Museum of Contemporary Art

★ Sydney Observatory

Old-fashioned Australian goods at the corner shop, Susannah Place

Susannah Place ❶

58–64 Gloucester St, The Rocks.
Map 1 B2. **Tel** (02) 9241 1893. 🚊
Sydney Explorer, 431, 432, 433, 434.
🚢 Circular Quay, Wynyard. ◯
10am–5pm Sat & Sun, Tue–Thu. ◯
Good Fri, 25 Dec. 📷 📷
www.hht.net.au

This terrace of four brick and
sandstone houses dating back
to 1844 has a rare history of
continuous domestic
occupancy from the 1840s
through to 1990. It is now a
museum examining the living
conditions of its former inhabitants. Rather than re-creating
a single period, the museum
retains the renovations carried out by different tenants.

   Built for Edward and Mary
Riley, who arrived from Ireland
with their niece Susannah in
1838, these houses have basement kitchens and backyard
outhouses. Piped water and
sewerage were probably
added by the mid-1850s.

   The terrace escaped the
wholesale demolitions that
occurred after the outbreak of
bubonic plague in 1900, as
well as later clearings of land
to make way for the Sydney
Harbour Bridge (see pp80–81)
and the Cahill Expressway. In
the 1970s it was saved once
again when the Builders
Labourers' Federation imposed
a "green ban" on The Rocks,
temporarily halting all redevelopment work which was des-
tructive to cultural heritage.

Museum of Contemporary Art ❷

Circular Quay West, The Rocks. **Map**
1 B2. **Tel** (02) 9245 2400. 🚊 431, 432,
433, 434, Sydney Explorer. ◯ 10am–
5pm daily. ◯ 25 Dec. ♿ 📷
www.mca.com.au

When Sydney art collector
John Power died in 1943, he
left his entire collection and a
financial bequest to the
University of Sydney. In 1991
the collection, which by then
included works by Hockney,
Warhol, Lichtenstein and
Christo was transferred to this
1950s Art Deco-style building
at Circular Quay West. As well
as showing its permanent
collection, the museum hosts
exhibitions by local and
overseas artists. The MCA
Store sells distinctive gifts by
Australian designers.

Cadman's Cottage ❸

110 George St, The Rocks. **Map** 1 B2.
Tel (02) 9247 5033. 🚊 431, 432,
433, 434. ◯ 9:30am–4:30pm
Mon–Fri, 10am–4:30pm Sat–Sun. ◯
1 Jan, Good Fri, 25 Dec, 31 Dec.

Built in 1816 as barracks for
the crews of the governor's
boats, this sandstone cottage
is Sydney's oldest surviving
dwelling and now serves as
the information centre for the
Sydney Harbour National Park.

   The cottage is named after
John Cadman, a convict who
was transported in 1798 for
horse-stealing. By 1813, he was
coxswain of a timber boat and
later, coxswain of government
craft. He was granted a full
pardon and in 1827 he was
made boat superintendent and
moved to the four-room cottage that now bears his name.

   Cadman married Elizabeth
Mortimer in 1830, another ex-
convict who was sentenced to
seven years' transportation for
the theft of one hairbrush.
They lived in the cottage until
1845. Cadman's Cottage was
built on the foreshore of
Sydney Harbour. Now, as a
result of successive land
reclamations, it is set well
back from the water's edge.

Art Deco-style façade of the Museum of Contemporary Art

Sailors' Home ❹

106 George St, The Rocks. **Map** 1
B2. 🚌 *Sydney Explorer, 339, 340, 431, 432, 433, 434.*

Built in 1864 as lodgings
for visiting sailors, the first
and second floors here were
dormitories, but these were
later divided into 56 cubicles
or "cabins" which were
arranged around open
galleries and lit by four
enormous skylights. At the
time it was built, the Sailors'
Home was a welcome
alternative to the many
seedy inns and brothels
in the area, saving sailors
from the perils of "crimping".
"Crimps" would tempt
newly arrived men into bars
providing much sought-after
entertainment. While drunk,
the sailors would be sold on
to departing ships, waking
miles out at sea and returning
home in debt.

Sailors used the home until
1980. It is now home to the
highly-regarded Sailors' Thai
restaurant and noodle bar.

The Rocks Discovery Museum ❺

Kendall Lane, The Rocks. **Tel** *1800
067 676.* 🚌 *Sydney Explorer, 431,
432, 433, 434.* 🚢 *Circular Quay.*
⭘ *10am–5pm daily.* ● *Good Fri,
25 Dec.* ♿

This fascinating museum, in
a restored 1850s sandstone
coach house, is home to
a unique collection of
archaeological artifacts and
images that detail the story
of The Rocks from the pre-
European days to the present.
There are four permanent
exhibitions which are highly
interactive, making use of
touch screens and audio and
visual technology to bring
the history alive. Some of
the artifacts were found at
the archaeological site on
Cumberland Street.

The Rocks Discovery
Museum has been developed
in close consultation with
local Aboriginal groups, so
that their story of the area
is properly told.

Terrace restaurants at Campbell's Storehouses on the waterfront

Campbell's Storehouses ❻

7–27 Circular Quay West, The Rocks.
Map 1 B2. 🚌 *Sydney Explorer, 431,
432, 433, 434.* ♿

Robert Campbell, a promi-
nent Scottish merchant in
the early days of Sydney,
purchased this land on
Sydney Cove in 1799. In
1802 he began constructing a
private wharf and storehouses
in which to house the tea,
sugar, spirits and cloth he
imported from India.
Campbell was the only
merchant operating in
Australia who managed to
infiltrate the monopoly held
by the British East India
Company. The first five
sandstone bays were built
between 1839 and 1844. A
further seven bays were built
between 1854 and 1861. The
full row of storehouses were
finally completed in 1890,
including a brick upper
storey. Part of the old sea
wall and 11 of the original
stores are still standing. The
pulleys that were used to
raise cargo from the wharf
can be seen near the top of
the preserved buildings.

The area fell into disrepair
during the first half of the
20th century. However, in the
1970s the Sydney Cove
Redevelopment Authority
finalized plans and began
renovating the site. Today the
bond stores contain a range
of fine restaurants catering to
all tastes, from contemporary
Australian to Chinese and
Italian. Their virtually
unimpeded views across
Circular Quay towards the
Sydney Opera House
(see pp84–5) and Sydney
Harbour Bridge *(see pp80–81)*
make these outdoor eating
establishments very popular
with local business people
and tourists alike.

Sydney Harbour Bridge ❼

See pp80–81.

The Hero of Waterloo Inn

Hero of Waterloo ❽

81 Lower Fort St, The Rocks.
Map 1 A2. **Tel** *(02) 9252 4553.* 🚌
431, 432, 433, 434. ⭘ *10am–11pm
Mon–Wed, 10am–11:30pm
Thu–Sat, 10am–10pm Sun.*
● *Good Fri, 25 Dec.* ♿ *limited.*

This picturesque old inn is
especially welcoming in the
winter with its log fires.

Built in 1844, this was a
favourite drinking place for
the nearby garrison's soldiers.
Some sea captains were said
to use the hotel to recruit.
Patrons who drank too much
were pushed into the cellars
via a trapdoor. Tunnels then
led to the wharves and on to
waiting ships.

Sydney Harbour Bridge **❼**

Completed in 1932, the construction of the Sydney Harbour Bridge was an economic feat, given the depressed times, as well as an engineering triumph. Prior to this, the only links between the city centre on the south side of the harbour and the residential north side were by ferry or a circuitous 20-km (12-mile) road route which involved five bridge crossings. The single-span arch bridge, colloquially known as the "Coathanger", took eight years to build, including the railway line. The bridge was manufactured in sections on the latter-day Luna Park site. Loans for the total cost of approximately 6.25 million old Australian pounds were eventually paid off in 1988.

Ceremonial scissors

The 1932 Opening
The ceremony was disrupted when zealous royalist Francis de Groot rode forward and cut the ribbon, in honour, he claimed, of King and Empire.

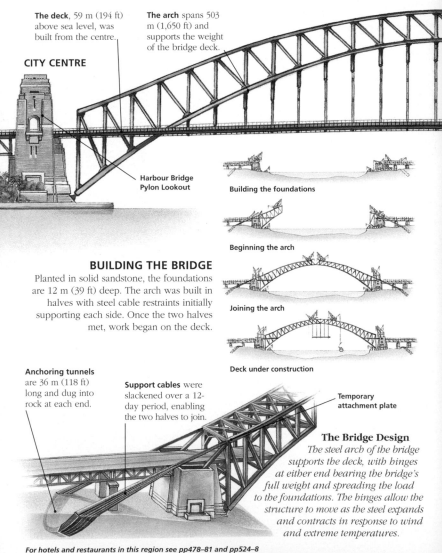

The deck, 59 m (194 ft) above sea level, was built from the centre.

The arch spans 503 m (1,650 ft) and supports the weight of the bridge deck.

CITY CENTRE

Harbour Bridge Pylon Lookout

Building the foundations

Beginning the arch

BUILDING THE BRIDGE
Planted in solid sandstone, the foundations are 12 m (39 ft) deep. The arch was built in halves with steel cable restraints initially supporting each side. Once the two halves met, work began on the deck.

Joining the arch

Deck under construction

Anchoring tunnels are 36 m (118 ft) long and dug into rock at each end.

Support cables were slackened over a 12-day period, enabling the two halves to join.

Temporary attachment plate

The Bridge Design
The steel arch of the bridge supports the deck, with hinges at either end bearing the bridge's full weight and spreading the load to the foundations. The hinges allow the structure to move as the steel expands and contracts in response to wind and extreme temperatures.

For hotels and restaurants in this region see pp478–81 and pp524–8

BridgeClimb

Thousands of people have enjoyed the spectacular bridge-top views after a 3.5-hour guided tour up ladders, catwalks and finally the upper arch of the bridge.

Over 150,000 vehicles cross the bridge each day, about 15 times as many as in 1932.

Bridge Workers

The bridge was built by 1,400 workers, 16 of whom were killed in accidents during construction.

NORTH SHORE

Maintenance

Painting the bridge has become a metaphor for an endless task. Approximately 30,000 litres (6,593 gal) of paint are required for each coat, enough to cover an area equivalent to 60 soccer pitches.

The vertical hangers support the slanting crossbeams which, in turn, carry the deck.

Paying the Toll

The initial toll of sixpence helped pay off the construction loan. The toll is now used for maintenance and to pay for the 1992 Sydney Harbour Tunnel.

FATHER OF THE BRIDGE

Chief engineer Dr John Bradfield shakes the hand of the driver of the first train to cross the bridge. Over a 20-year period, Bradfield supervised all aspects of the bridge's design and construction. At the opening ceremony, the highway linking the harbour's south side and northern suburbs was named in his honour.

A FLAGPOLE ON THE MUDFLATS

The modest flagpole on Loftus Street, near Customs House, flies a flag, the Union Jack, on the spot where Australia's first ceremonial flag-raising took place. On 26 January 1788, Captain Arthur Phillip hoisted the flag to declare the foundation of the colony. A toast to the king was drunk and a musket volley fired. On this date each year, the country marks Australia Day with a national holiday *(see p43)*. In 1788, the flagpole was on the edge of mudflats on Sydney Cove. Today, due to land reclamations, it is set back from the water's edge.

The Founding of Australia by Algernon Talmage

Garrison Church ❾

Cnr Argyle & Lower Fort sts, Millers Point. **Map** 1 A2.
Tel *(02) 9247 1268.* 431, 433.
9am–6pm daily.

Officially named the Holy Trinity Church, this was dubbed the Garrison Church because it was the colony's first military church.

Henry Ginn designed the church and, in 1840, the foundation stone was laid. In 1855, it was enlarged to hold up to 600 people. Regimental plaques hanging along interior walls recall the church's military associations. A museum contains Australian military and historical items.

Other features to look out for are the brilliantly coloured east window and the carved red cedar pulpit.

East window, Garrison Church

Sydney Observatory ❿

Watson Rd, Observatory Hill, The Rocks. **Map** 1 A2. ***Tel*** *(02) 9921 3485.*
Sydney Explorer, 343, 431, stop 22.
10am–5pm daily. **Night viewings** call to book. 25 Dec.
www.sydneyobservatory.com.au

In 1982 this domed building, which had been a centre for astronomical observation and research for almost 125 years, became the city's astronomy museum. It has interactive displays and games, along with night sky viewings; it is essential to book for these.

The building began life in the 1850s as a time-ball tower. At 1pm daily, the ball on top of the tower dropped to signal the correct time. At the same time, a cannon was fired at Fort Denison. This custom continues today *(see p108)*.

During the 1880s Sydney Observatory became known around the world when some of the first astronomical photographs of the southern sky were taken here. From 1890 to 1962 the observatory mapped some 750,000 stars as part of an international project that resulted in an atlas of the entire night sky.

National Trust Centre ⓫

Observatory Hill, Watson Rd, The Rocks. **Map** 1 A3. ***Tel*** *(02) 9258 0123.* Sydney Explorer, 343, 431, 432, 433, 434. 9am–5pm Tue–Fri. **Gallery** 11am–5pm Tue–Sun. Public hols.
www.nsw.nationaltrust.org.au

The buildings that form the headquarters of the National Trust of Australia, date from 1815, when Governor Macquarie chose the site for a military hospital. Today they house a café, a National Trust shop and the SH Ervin Gallery, with changing exhibitions throughout the year, designed to explore the richness and diversity in Australian art.

St Philip's Church ⓬

3 York St (enter from Jamison St). **Map** 1 A3. ***Tel*** *(02) 9247 1071.*
George St routes. 9am–5pm Tue–Fri. 26 Jan. Phone first.
1pm Wed, 8am, 10am, 6:15pm Sun, 4pm 1st & 3rd Sun of month.
www.stphilips-sydney.org.au

This Victorian Gothic church may seem overshadowed in its modern setting, yet when it was first built, the square tower was a local landmark.

Begun in 1848, St Philip's is by Edmund Blacket. In 1851 work was disrupted when its stonemasons left for the gold fields, but by 1856 the building was finally completed.

A peal of bells was donated in 1888 to mark Sydney's centenary and they still announce the services each Sunday.

Interior and pipe organ of St Philip's Church

Macquarie Place ⓭

Map 1 B3. 🚌 *Circular Quay routes.*

Governor Macquarie created this park in 1810 on what was once the vegetable garden of the first Government House. The sandstone obelisk, designed by Francis Greenway *(see p169)*, was erected in 1818 to mark the starting point for all roads in the colony. The gas lamps recall the fact that this was also the site of the city's first street lamp in 1826.

Also in this area are the remains of the bow anchor and cannon from HMS *Sirius*, flagship of the First Fleet. The statue of Thomas Mort, a successful 19th-century industrialist, is today a marshalling place for the city's somewhat kamikaze bicycle couriers.

Customs House ⓮

31 Alfred St, Circular Quay. **Map** 1 B3. **Tel** (02) 9242 8595. 🚌 *Circular Quay routes.* ⬜ *8am–7pm Mon–Fri, 10am–4pm Sat, 12pm–4pm Sun.* 🅿️ ♿ 🖥️ 🍴 **www.**
sydneycustomshouse.com.au

Colonial architect James Barnet designed this 1885 sandstone Classical Revival building on the same site as a previous Customs House. Its recalls the bygone days when trading ships berthed at Circular Quay. The building stands near the mouth of Tank Stream, the fledgling colony's freshwater supply. Among its many fine features are tall veranda columns made out of polished granite, a finely sculpted coat of arms and an elaborate clock face, added in 1897, which features a pair of tridents and dolphins.

A complete refurbishment was completed in 2005. Facilities include a City Library with a reading room and exhibition space, and an open lounge area with an international newspaper and magazine salon, internet access and bar. On the roof, Café Sydney offers great views.

**Detail from
Customs House**

**Montage of criminal "mug shots",
Justice and Police Museum**

Justice and Police Museum ⓯

Cnr Albert & Phillip sts. **Map** 1 C3. **Tel** (02) 9252 1144. 🚌 *Circular Quay routes.* ⬜ *10am–5pm Sat & Sun (open daily in Jan).* ⚫ *Good Fri, 25 Dec.* 🅿️ 🎫 🖼️ ♿ *limited.* **www.**hht.net.au

The buildings housing this museum originally comprised the Water Police Court, designed by Edmund Blacket in 1856, the Water Police Station, designed by Alexander Dawson in 1858, and the Police Court, designed by James Barnet in 1885. Here the rough-and-tumble underworld of quayside crime, from the petty to the violent, was dealt swift and, at times, harsh justice. The museum exhibits illustrate that turbulent period, as they re-create legal and criminal history.

Formalities of the late-Victorian legal proceedings can be easily imagined in the fully restored courtroom. Menacing implements from knuckledusters to bludgeons are displayed as the macabre relics of notorious crimes. Other interesting aspects of policing, criminality and the legal system are highlighted in special changing exhibitions. The musuem powerfully evokes the realities of Australian policing and justice.

Writers' Walk ⓰

Circular Quay. **Map** 1 C2. 🚌 *Circular Quay routes.*

This series of plaques is set in the pavement at regular intervals between East and West Circular Quay. It gives the visitor the chance to ponder the observations of famous Australian writers, both past and present, on their home country, as well as the musings of some noted literary visitors.

Each plaque is dedicated to a particular writer, consisting of a personal quotation and a brief biographical note. Australian writers in the series include the novelists Miles Franklin and Peter Carey, poets Oodgeroo Noonuccal and Judith Wright *(see pp34–5)*, humorists Barry Humphries and Clive James, and the influential feminist writer Germaine Greer. Among the international writers included who visited Sydney are Mark Twain, Charles Darwin and Joseph Conrad.

Strolling along a section of the Writers' Walk at Circular Quay

Sydney Opera House ⑰

No other building on earth looks like the Sydney Opera House. Popularly known as the "Opera House" long before the building was complete, it is, in fact, a complex of theatres and halls linked beneath its famous shells. Its birth was long and complicated. Many of the construction problems had not been faced before, resulting in an architectural adventure which lasted 14 years. An appeal fund was set up, eventually raising A$900,000, while the Opera House Lottery raised the balance of the A$102 million final cost. Today it is the city's most popular tourist attraction, as well as one of the world's busiest performing arts centres.

Advertising poster

★ Opera Theatre
Mainly used for opera and ballet, this 1,507-seat theatre is big enough to stage grand operas such as Verdi's Aïda.

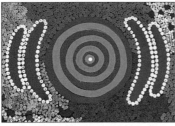

Detail of The Possum Dreaming *(1988)*
The mural in the Opera Theatre foyer is by Michael Tjakamarra Nelson, an artist from the central Australian desert.

The Opera Theatre's ceiling and walls are painted black to focus attention on the stage.

Opera House Walkway
Extensive public walkways around the building offer the visitor views from many different vantage points.

Northern Foyers
The Utzon Room and the large northern foyers of the Opera Theatre and Concert Hall have spectacular views over the harbour and can be hired for conferences, lunches, parties and weddings.

STAR FEATURES

★ Concert Hall

★ Opera Theatre

★ The Roofs

For hotels and restaurants in this region see pp578–81 and pp524–8

★ **Concert Hall**
This is the largest hall, with seating for 2,690. It is used for symphony, choral, jazz, folk and pop concerts, chamber music, opera, dance and everything from body building to fashion parades.

VISITORS' CHECKLIST

Bennelong Point. **Map** 1 C2. **Tel** (02) 9250 7111. **Box office** (02) 9250 7777. ⬛ Sydney Explorer, 111, 311, 380, 389, 392, 394, 396, 397, 399, 890. ⬛ 🚢 Circular Quay. ⬤ tours and performances. ⬤ Good Fri, 25 Dec. ♿ limited (02) 9250 7777. 📷 9am–5pm, call (02) 9250 7209. TTY for hearing impaired 9250 7347. 🔢 🖥 📱 www.sydneyoperahouse.com

The Monumental Steps and forecourt are used for outdoor performances.

Guillaume at Bennelong
This is one of the finest restaurants in Sydney (see p528).

The Playhouse, seating almost 400, is ideal for intimate productions, while also able to present plays with larger casts.

★ **The Roofs**
Although apocryphal, the theory that Jørn Utzon's arched roof design came to him while peeling an orange is enchanting. The highest point is 67 m (221 ft) above sea level.

Detail of Utzon's Tapestry *(2004)*
Jørn Utzon's original design for this Gobelin-style tapestry, which hangs floor to ceiling in the refurbished Utzon Room, was inspired by the music of Carl Philipp Emanuel Bach.

View from Harbourside Shopping Centre looking east towards the city

SIGHTS AT A GLANCE

CITY CENTRE
AND DARLING HARBOUR

George Street, Australia's first thoroughfare, was originally lined with mud and wattle huts, but following the gold rush shops and banks came to dominate the area. The city's first skyscraper, Culwulla Chambers, was completed in 1913. Hyde Park, on the edge of the city centre, was once a racecourse, attracting gambling taverns to Elizabeth Street. Today it provides a peaceful oasis,

Mosaic floor detail, St Mary's Cathedral

while the city's commercial centre is an area of department stores and arcades. The country's industrial age began in Darling Harbour in 1815 with the opening of a steam mill, but later the area became rundown. In the 1980s, it was the site of a massive urban redevelopment project. Today, Darling Harbour contains many fine museums and other attractions.

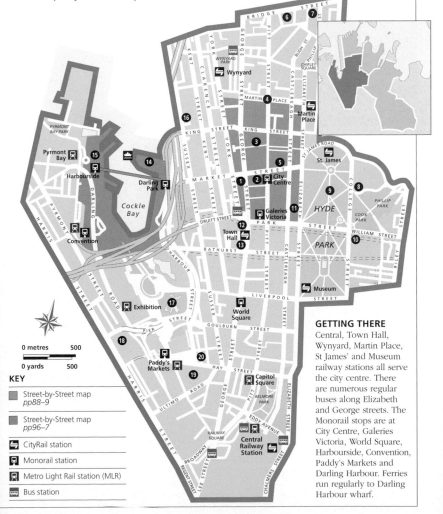

GETTING THERE

Central, Town Hall, Wynyard, Martin Place, St James' and Museum railway stations all serve the city centre. There are numerous regular buses along Elizabeth and George streets. The Monorail stops are at City Centre, Galeries Victoria, World Square, Harbourside, Convention, Paddy's Markets and Darling Harbour. Ferries run regularly to Darling Harbour wharf.

KEY

- Street-by-Street map *pp88–9*
- Street-by-Street map *pp96–7*
- CityRail station
- Monorail station
- Metro Light Rail station (MLR)
- Bus station

0 metres 500
0 yards 500

Street-by-Street: City Centre

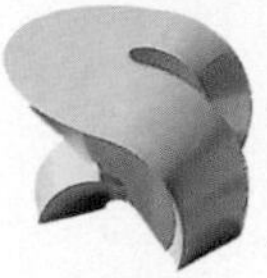

Although closely rivalled by Melbourne, Sydney is the business and commercial capital of Australia. Vibrant by day, at night the streets are far less busy when office workers and shoppers have gone home. The comparatively small city centre of this **Sculpture outside the MLC Centre** sprawling metropolis seems to be almost jammed into a few city blocks. Because Sydney grew in such a haphazard fashion, with many of today's streets following tracks from the harbour originally made by bullocks, there was no allowance for the expansion of the city into what has become a major international centre. A colourful night scene of cafés, restaurants and theatres is emerging, however, as more people return to the city centre to live.

★ Queen Victoria Building
Taking up an entire city block, this 1898 former produce market was lovingly restored in 1986 and is now a shopping mall ❶

State Theatre
A gem from the golden age of movies, this 1929 cinema was once hailed as "the Empire's greatest theatre". It now hosts live concerts too ❷

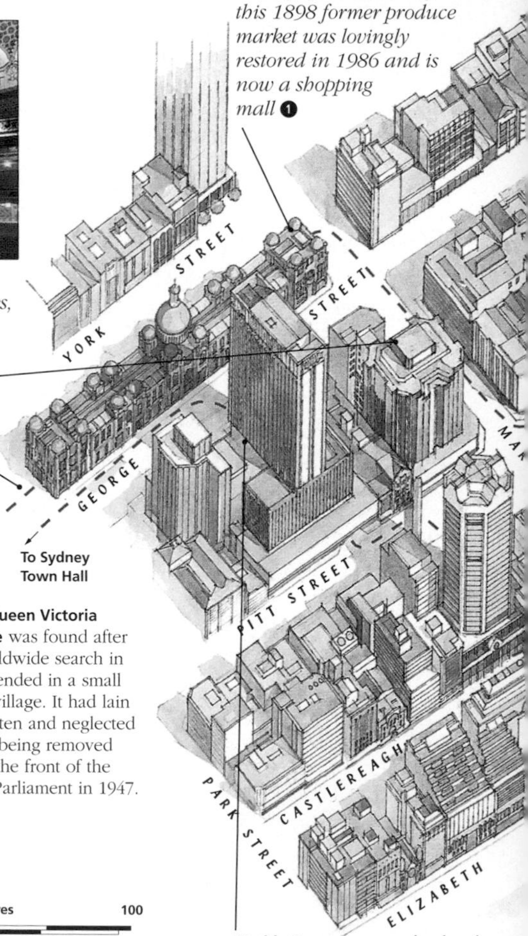

To Sydney Town Hall

The Queen Victoria Statue was found after a worldwide search in 1983 ended in a small Irish village. It had lain forgotten and neglected since being removed from the front of the Irish Parliament in 1947.

STREET labels: YORK, GEORGE, STREET, PITT STREET, PARK STREET, CASTLEREAGH, ELIZABETH, MARKET

STAR SIGHTS

- ★ Sydney Tower
- ★ Martin Place
- ★ Queen Victoria Building

0 metres	100
0 yards	100

KEY

━ ━ ━ Suggested route

Marble Bar was once a landmark bar in the 1893 Tattersalls hotel. It was re-erected in the Sydney Hilton in 1973, and again in 2005 when the hotel was rebuilt.

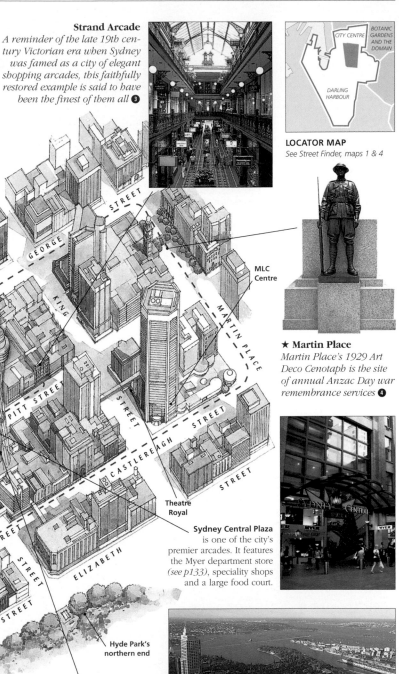

Strand Arcade
A reminder of the late 19th century Victorian era when Sydney was famed as a city of elegant shopping arcades, this faithfully restored example is said to have been the finest of them all ❸

LOCATOR MAP
See Street Finder, maps 1 & 4

MLC
Centre

★ **Martin Place**
Martin Place's 1929 Art Deco Cenotaph is the site of annual Anzac Day war remembrance services ❹

Sydney Central Plaza
is one of the city's premier arcades. It features the Myer department store *(see p133)*, speciality shops and a large food court.

Theatre
Royal

Hyde Park's
northern end

★ **Sydney Tower**
The tower tops the city skyline, giving a bird's eye view of the whole of Sydney. It rises 305 m (1,000 ft) above the ground and can be seen from as far away as the Blue Mountains ❺

Queen Victoria Building ❶

455 George St. **Map** 1 B5. *Tel (02) 9264 9209.* 🚌 *George St routes.* ◻ *9am–6pm Mon–Wed, 9am–9pm Thu, 9am–6pm Fri & Sat, 11am–5pm Sun; 11am–5pm public hols.* ♿ ⬛ See **Shopping** *pp132–7.* **www.**qvb.com.au

French designer Pierre Cardin called the Queen Victoria Building "the most beautiful shopping centre in the world". Yet this ornate Romanesque building, better known as the QVB, began life as the Sydney produce market. Completed to the design of City Architect George McRae in 1898, the dominant features are the central copper dome and the glass roof which lets in a flood of natural light.

The market closed at the end of World War I. By the 1950s, the building was threatened with demolition.

Ornately decorated Gothic foyer of the State Theatre

Refurbished at a cost of over A\$75 million, the QVB re-opened in 1986 as a shopping gallery with more than 190 shops. A wishing well incorporates a stone from Blarney Castle, a sculpture of Islay, Queen Victoria's dog and a statue of the queen herself.

Inside the QVB, suspended from the ceiling, is the Royal Clock. Designed in 1982 by Neil Glasser, it features part of Balmoral Castle above a copy of the four dials of Big Ben. Every hour, a fanfare is played with a parade depicting various English monarchs.

State Theatre ❷

49 Market St. **Map** 1 B5. *Tel (02) 9373 6852.* 🚌 *George St routes.* **Box office** ◻ *9am–5:30pm Mon–Fri.* ⬤ *Good Friday, 25 Dec.* ♿ ⬛ *(bookings necessary).* **www.**statetheatre.com.au

When it opened in 1929, this cinema was hailed as the finest that local craftsmanship could achieve. The State Theatre is one of the best

Roof detail, Queen Victoria Building

examples of ornate period cinemas in Australia.

Its Baroque style is evident in the foyer, with its high ceiling, mosaic floor, marble columns and statues. The auditorium is lit by a 20,000-piece chandelier. The beautiful Wurlitzer organ (under repair) rises from below stage before performances. The theatre is now one of the city's special events venues.

Strand Arcade ❸

412–414 George St. **Map** 1 B5. *Tel (02) 9232 4199.* 🚌 *George St routes.* ◻ *9am–5:30pm Mon–Wed & Fri, 9am–9pm Thu, 9am–4pm Sat, 11am–4pm Sun.* ⬤ *25, 26 Dec, some public hols.* ♿ See **Shopping** *pp132–7.* **www.**strandarcade.com.au

Victorian Sydney was a city of grand shopping arcades. The Strand, joining George and

Pitt Street entrance to the majestic Strand Arcade

Pitt streets and designed by English architect John Spencer, was the finest of all. Opened in April 1892, it was lit by natural light pouring through the glass roof and the chandeliers, each carrying 50 jets of gas as well as 50 lamps.

After a fire in 1976, the building was restored to its original Victorian splendour. Enjoy its shopping and beautiful coffee shops.

Martin Place ❹

Map 1 B4. 🚌 *George St & Elizabeth St routes.* 🚇 *Martin Place.*

This plaza was opened in 1891 and made a traffic-free precinct in 1971. It is busiest at lunchtime as city workers enjoy their sandwiches while watching free entertainment in the amphitheatre near Castlereagh Street.

Every Anzac Day *(see p42)* the focus moves to the Cenotaph at the George Street end. Past and present service personnel attend a dawn service and wreath-laying ceremony, followed by a march past. The shrine, by Bertram MacKennal, was unveiled in 1929.

On the southern side of the Cenotaph is the façade of the Renaissance-style General Post Office, considered to be the finest building by James Barnet, colonial architect in 1866.

A stainless steel sculpture of upended cubes, the Dobell Memorial Sculpture, is a tribute to Australian artist William Dobell, created by Bert Flugelman in 1979.

Sydney Tower ❺

With a design capable of withstanding earthquakes and extreme wind, Sydney Tower was conceived as part of the original 1970s Centrepoint shopping centre, but was not completed until 1981. About one million people per year admire the stunning views. On the podium level, visitors enjoy a multimedia journey around Australia on a virtual adventure ride called Oztrek. Those with a head for heights can also venture outside the tower on a skywalk tour.

VISITORS' CHECKLIST

100 Market St. **Map** 1 B5. *Tel* (02) 9333 9222. 🚌 *Sydney Explorer, all city routes.* 🚢 *Darling Harbour.* 🚇 *St James, Town Hall.* 🚉 *City Centre.* ⭘ *9am–10:30pm daily.* **Last entry:** *45 mins before closing.* ⭘ *25 Dec.* ♿ 🚼 🎬 🛍 🍴 **www**.sydneytower.com.au

Observation Level
Views from Level 4 stretch north to Pittwater, Botany Bay to the south, west to the Blue Mountains, and along the harbour out to the open sea.

The turret's nine levels, with room to hold almost 1,000 people at a time, include two revolving restaurants, a coffee shop and the Observation Level.

The windows comprise three layers. The outer has a gold dust coating. The frame design prevents panes falling outwards.

The 30-m (98-ft) spire completes the total 305 m (1,000 ft) of the tower's height.

The water tank holds 162,000 l (35,500 gal) and acts as an enormous stabilizer on very windy days.

Skywalk

Level 4: Observation

Level 3: Coffee shop

Level 2: Buffet restaurant

Level 1: A la carte restaurant

The 56 cables weigh seven tonnes each. If laid end to end, they would reach from New Zealand to Sydney.

The shaft is designed to withstand wind speeds expected only once in 500 years, and earthquakes.

The stairs are two separate, fireproofed emergency escape routes with 1,504 steps.

Double-decker lifts can carry up to 2,000 people per hour. At full speed, a lift takes only 40 seconds to ascend the 76 floors to the Observation Level.

Construction of Turret
The nine turret levels were erected on the roof of the base building, then hoisted up the shaft using hydraulic jacks.

Oztrek is a unique virtual reality ride across Australia, with a 180° cinema, 3D technology and real motion seating.

New Year's Eve
Visitors flock to Sydney's highest observation deck to watch the fireworks over the city and Harbour Bridge.

Lands Department Building

23 Bridge St. **Map** 1 B3. 🚌 *325, George St routes.* ⬜ *only 2 weeks in the year.* ♿

Designed by the colonial architect James Barnet, this three-storey Classical Revival sandstone edifice was built between 1877 and 1890. Pyrmont sandstone was used for the exterior, as it was for the GPO building.

All the decisions about the subdivision of much of rural eastern Australia were made in the offices within. Statues of explorers and legislators who "promoted settlement" fill 23 of the façade's 48 niches; the remainder are still empty. The luminaries include the explorers Hovell and Hume, Sir Thomas Mitchell, Blaxland, Lawson and Wentworth, Ludwig Leichhardt, Bass, Matthew Flinders and botanist Sir Joseph Banks.

The Lookout on Level 3 of the Museum of Sydney

Museum of Sydney

Cnr Phillip & Bridge sts. **Map** 1 B3. *Tel (02) 9251 5988.* 🚌 *Circular Quay routes.* ⬜ *9:30am–5pm daily.* ⬤ *Good Fri, 25 Dec.* 🎫 📷 📱 ♿ 🍴 🖥

Situated at the base of Governor Phillip Tower, the Museum of Sydney is a modern museum built on a historic site and details the history of Sydney from 1788 to the present. Its many attractions include the archaeological remains of the

The imposing sandstone edifice of the Lands Department Building

colony's first Government House, as well as exhibits that explore the evolution of Sydney over two centuries and honour the original Cadigal people.

Indigenous Peoples
This gallery explores the culture, history, continuity and place of Sydney's original inhabitants. The collectors' chests hold items of daily use such as flint and ochre. In the square outside the complex, the *Edge of the Trees* sculptural installation symbolizes the first contact between the Aborigines and Europeans. Inscribed in the wood are signatures of First Fleeters and names of botanical species in native languages and Latin.

History of Sydney
Outside the museum, a paving pattern outlines the site of the first Government House. The original foundations, below street level, can be seen through a window. A segment of wall has now been reconstructed using the original sandstone.

The Colony display on Level 2 focuses on Sydney during the critical decade of the 1840s: convict transportation ended, the town officially became a city and then suffered economic depression. On Level 3, 20th century Sydney is explored against a panorama of images.

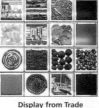

Display from Trade Exhibition on Level 2

St Mary's Cathedral

St Marys Rd. **Map** 1 C5. *Tel (02) 9220 0400.* 🚌 *Elizabeth St routes.* ⬜ *6:30am–6pm Mon–Fri, 6:30am–7pm Sat–Sun.* ♿ *with advance notice.* 🎫 *noon Sun.* **www**.sydney.catholic.org.au

Although Catholics arrived with the First Fleet, the celebration of Mass was at first prohibited as it was feared priests would provoke civil strife among the colony's Irish Catholic population. It was not until 1820 that the first Catholic priests were officially appointed and services were permitted. In 1821, Governor Macquarie laid the foundation stone for St Mary's Chapel on the first land granted to the Catholic Church in Australia.

The initial section of this Gothic Revival-style cathedral was opened in 1882 and completed in 1928, but without the twin southern spires originally proposed by the architect William Wardell. By the entrance are statues of Australia's first cardinal, Moran, and Archbishop Kelly, who laid the stone for the final stage in 1913. They were sculpted by Bertram MacKennal, also responsible for the Martin Place Cenotaph *(see p89)*. The crypt's terrazzo mosaic floor took 15 years to complete.

Hyde Park ❾

Map 1 B5. 🚃 *Elizabeth St routes.*

Hyde Park was named after its London equivalent by Governor Macquarie in 1810. The fence around the park marked the outskirts of the township. Once an exercise field for garrison troops, it later incorporated a racecourse and a cricket pitch. Though much smaller today than the original park, it is still a quiet haven in the middle of the bustling city centre, with many notable features.

The 30-m (98-ft) high Art Deco Anzac Memorial commemorates Australians who have died for their country. Opened in 1934 it now includes a military exhibition downstairs.

Sandringham Garden, filled with mauve wisteria, is a memorial to kings George V and George VI, opened by Queen Elizabeth II in 1954.

The bronze and granite Archibald Fountain commemorates the French and Australian World War I alliance. It was completed by François Sicard in 1932 and donated by JF Archibald, one of the founders of the popular *Bulletin* literary magazine.

The *Emden* Gun, on the corner of College and Liverpool Streets, commemorates a World War I naval action. HMAS *Sydney* destroyed the German raider *Emden* off the Cocos Islands on 9 November 1914, and 180 crew members were taken prisoner.

Australian Museum ❿

See pp94–5.

Great Synagogue ⓫

187 Elizabeth St, entrance at 166 Castlereagh St. **Map** 1 B5. **Tel** *(02) 9267 2477.* 🚃 *394, 396, 380, 382.* 🕐 *for services and tours only.* ♿ *by arrangement.* ⬤ *public and Jewish hols.* ▨ 🎫 *noon Tue & Thu.* **www**.greatsynagogue.org.au

The longest established Jewish Orthodox congregation in Australia assembles in this synagogue (consecrated in 1878). Although Jews had arrived with the First Fleet, worship did not commence until the 1820s. With its carved porch columns and wrought-iron gates, the synagogue is perhaps the finest work of Thomas Rowe, architect of Sydney Hospital (*see p113*). The interior features a stunning panelled ceiling.

Candelabra in the Great Synagogue

Sydney Town Hall ⓬

483 George St. **Map** 4 E2. **Tel** *(02) 9265 9333.* 🚃 *George St routes.* 🕐 *8:30am–6pm Mon–Fri.* ⬤ *public hols.* ♿ **www**.cityofsydneyvenues.com.au

The steps of Sydney Town Hall have been a favourite meeting place since it opened in 1869. Walled burial grounds originally covered the site.

Grand organ in Centennial Hall

It is a fine example of High Victorian architecture. The original architect, JH Wilson, died during its construction, as did several of the architects who followed. The vestibule, an elegant salon with stained glass and a crystal chandelier, is the work of Albert Bond. The clock tower was completed by the Bradbridge brothers in 1884. From 1888–9, other architects designed Centennial Hall, with its imposing 19th-century Grand Organ with over 8,500 pipes.

Some people believe this became Sydney's finest building by accident, as each architect strove to outdo similar buildings in Manchester and Liverpool. Today, it makes a good venue for concerts.

St Andrew's Cathedral ⓭

Sydney Square, cnr George & Bathurst sts. **Map** 4 E3. **Tel** *(02) 9265 1661.* 🚃 *George St routes* 🕐 *contact the cathedral for opening times.* ♿ 🎫 **www**.cathedral.sydney.anglican.asn.au

While the foundation stone for the country's oldest cathedral was laid in 1819, the building was not consecrated until 1868. The Gothic Revival design, by Edmund Blacket, was inspired by York Minster in England. Inside are memorials to Sydney pioneers, a 1539 Bible and beads made from olive seeds collected in the Holy Land.

The southern wall includes stones from London's St Paul's Cathedral, Westminster Abbey and the House of Lords.

Game in progress on the giant chessboard in Hyde Park

Australian Museum 🔟

Model head of
Tyrannosaurus rex

The Australian Museum, the nation's leading natural science museum, founded in 1827, was the first museum established and remains the premier showcase of Australian natural history. The main building, an impressive sandstone structure with a marble staircase, faces Hyde Park. Architect Mortimer Lewis was forced to resign his position when building costs began to far exceed the budget. Construction was completed in the 1860s by James Barnet. The collection provides a journey across Australia and the near Pacific, covering biology, and natural and cultural history. Australian Aboriginal traditions are celebrated in a community access space that is also used for dance and other performances every Sunday.

Museum Entrance
The façade features massive Corinthian square pillars or piers.

Planet of Minerals
This section features a walk-through recreation of an underground mine with a display of gems and minerals.

Rhodochrosite **Cuprite**

Mesolite with green apophyllite

Education Centre

Chapman Mineral Collection

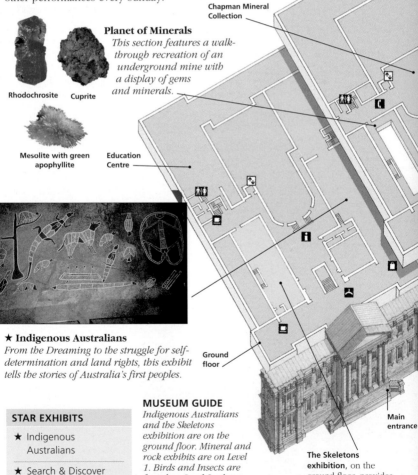

★ **Indigenous Australians**
From the Dreaming to the struggle for self-determination and land rights, this exhibit tells the stories of Australia's first peoples.

Ground floor

Main entrance

The Skeletons exhibition, on the ground floor, provides a different perspective on natural history.

MUSEUM GUIDE

Indigenous Australians and the Skeletons exhibition are on the ground floor. Mineral and rock exhibits are on Level 1. Birds and Insects are found on Level 2, along with Kidspace, Surviving Australia and Dinosaurs.

STAR EXHIBITS

- ★ Indigenous Australians
- ★ Search & Discover
- ★ Kidspace

★ **Search & Discover**
Sydneysiders bring bugs, rocks and bones here for identification. The public can also access electronic archives for research.

VISITORS' CHECKLIST

6 College St. **Map** 4 F3.
Tel 9320 6000. 🚌 Sydney
Explorer, 323, 324, 325, 327,
389. 🚉 Museum, Town Hall.
🕙 9:30am–5pm daily. ⬤ 25
Dec. 🎟️ 📷 ♿ ✂️ 🍴 🛍️ 🎁
www.austmus.gov.au

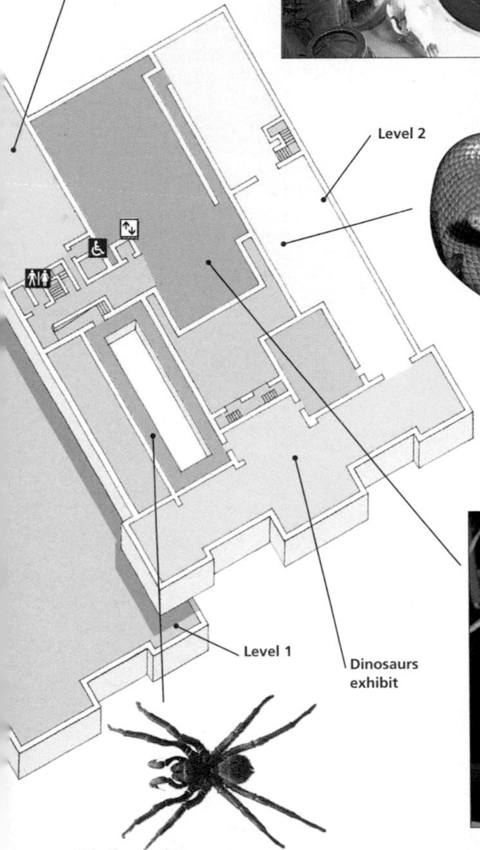

Level 2

Level 1

Dinosaurs exhibit

Surviving Australia
This exhibit explores wild Australia, including this venomous Speckled Brown Snake as well as sharks, crocodiles and other dangerous animals.

Birds and Insects
Australia's most poisonous spider, the male of the funnel-web species, dwells exclusively in the Greater Sydney region.

★ **Kidspace**
This mini museum has been designed especially for children aged five and under to investigate the natural world, with five "pods" – Bugs, Marine, Volcano, Observation and Imagination – to explore.

KEY TO FLOORPLAN

- ☐ Plants and Minerals
- ☐ Kidspace
- ☐ Birds and Insects exhibition
- ☐ Indigenous Australians
- ☐ The Skeleton exhibition
- ☐ Australian Environments
- ☐ Surviving Australia
- ☐ Temporary exhibition space
- ☐ Non-exhibition space

"WELCOME STRANGER" GOLD NUGGET CAST

In 1869, the largest gold nugget ever found in Australia was discovered in Victoria. It weighed 71.06 kg (156 lb). The museum holds a cast of the original in a display examining the impact of the gold rush, when the Australian population doubled in ten years.

←— 67.5 cm (26½ in) wide —→

Street-by-Street: Darling Harbour

Carpentaria lightship, National Maritime Museum

Darling Harbour was New South Wales' bicentennial gift to itself. This imaginative urban redevelopment, close to the heart of Sydney, covers a 54-ha (133-acre) site that was once a busy industrial centre and international shipping terminal catering for the developing local wool, grain, timber and coal trades. In 1984 the Darling Harbour Authority was formed to examine the area's commercial options. The resulting complex opened in 1988, complete with the Australian National Maritime Museum and Sydney Aquarium, two of the city's tourist highlights. Free outdoor entertainment, appealing to children in particular, is a regular feature, and there are many shops, waterside cafés and restaurants, as well as several major hotels overlooking the bay (www.darlingharbour.com.au).

Harbourside Complex offers restaurants and cafés with superb views over the water to the city skyline. There is also a wide range of speciality shops, selling unusual gifts and other items.

The Sydney Convention and Exhibition Centre complex presents an alternating range of international and local trade shows displaying everything from home decorating suggestions to bridal wear.

DARLING DRIVE

WESTERN DISTRIBUTOR

WESTERN DISTRIBUTOR

The Tidal Cascades sunken fountain was designed by Robert Woodward, also responsible for the El Alamein Fountain (*see p120*). The double spiral of water and paths replicates the circular shape of the Convention Centre.

IMAX large-screen cinema

Chinese Garden of Friendship

The Chinese Garden of Friendship is a haven of peace and tranquillity in the heart of Sydney. Its landscaping, with winding pathways, waterfalls, lakes and pavilions, offers an insight into the rich culture of China.

STAR SIGHTS

★ Sydney Aquarium

★ Australian National Maritime Museum

For hotels and restaurants in this region see pp478-81 and pp524-8

Pyrmont Bridge opened in 1902 to service the busy harbour. It is the world's oldest swingspan bridge and opens for vessels up to 14 m (46 ft) tall. The monorail track above the walkway also opens up for even taller boats.

LOCATOR MAP
See Street Finder, maps 3 & 4

Swingspan supports for Pyrmont Bridge are sunk 10 m (33 ft) below the harbour floor.

Star City Casino

★ **Australian National Maritime Museum**
Compelling exhibits detail the nation's seafaring history before and after European settlement ⑮

The *Vampire* destroyer (1959) is the largest in the vessel fleet moored outside the museum.

King Street Wharf →

Wharf for harbour cruise departures

★ **Sydney Aquarium**
The aquatic life of Sydney Harbour, the open ocean and the Great Barrier Reef is displayed in massive tanks which can be seen from underwater walkways ⑭

| 0 metres | 100 |
| 0 yards | 100 |

KEY

– – – Suggested route

Cockle Bay Wharf is vibrant and colourful, and is an exciting food and entertainment precinct.

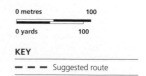

Sydney Aquarium & Wildlife World ⓮

Aquarium Pier, Darling Harbour. **Map** 4 D2. ***Tel*** *(02) 8251 7800 (Aquarium), (02) 9333 9288 (Wildlife World).* *Sydney Explorer.* *Darling Harbour.* *Town Hall.* *Darling Park.* *9am–10pm daily (last adm 9pm).*
www.sydneyaquarium.com.au
www.sydneywildlifeworld.com.au

Located adjacent to each other on Darling Harbour are the fascinating Sydney Aquarium and Sydney Wildlife World.

The aquarium contains more than 12,000 animals from approximately 650 species, held in a series of re-created marine environments. For many visitors, the highlight is a walk "on the ocean floor", passing through two floating oceanaria with 165 m (541 ft) of acrylic underwater tunnels. These allow close observation of sharks, stingrays and schools of many types of fish. Other exhibits include a Great Barrier Reef display, a collection of sharks, and a Touch Pool, where visitors may touch marine invertebrates such as sea urchins and tubeworms.

Wildlife World offers an authentic Australian wildlife experience, with more than 100 native species in nine different habitats. Highlights include the koala sanctuary and the interactive bird show.

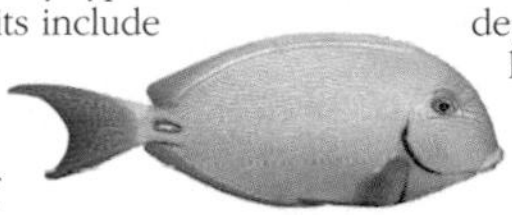
A tang fish in the Great Barrier Reef display

Australian National Maritime Museum ⓯

See pp100–1.

King Street Wharf ⓰

Lime St, between King and Erskine sts. **Map** 4 D1. *Darling Park.* *Darling Harbour.*
www.ksw.com.au

Journalists from nearby newspaper offices and city workers flock to this harbourside venue, which combines an aggressively modern glass and steel shrine to café society with a working wharf. Passengers arrive and depart in style on harbour cruises, ferries, water taxis and rivercats. The complex is flush with bars that vie for the best views, and restaurants including Thai, Japanese, Italian and Modern Australian. Midway along the wharf is the Pumphouse boutique brewery with more than 50 beers, including several of their own creations. This is not just a party circuit, there are also residents here in low-rise apartments set back from the water.

Night lights at King Street Wharf, Darling Harbour

Chinese Garden ⓱

Darling Harbour. **Map** 4 D3. ***Tel*** *(02) 9240 8888.* *Sydney Explorer.* *Haymarket.* *Darling Harbour.* *9:30am–5pm daily.* *Good Fri, 25 Dec.* *about 60 per cent.*
www.chinesegarden.com.au

Known as the Garden of Friendship, the Chinese Garden was built in 1984. It is a tranquil refuge from the city streets. The garden's design was a gift to Sydney from its Chinese sister city of Guangdong. The Dragon Wall is in the lower section beside the lake. It has glazed carvings of two dragons, one representing Guangdong province and the other the state of New South Wales. In the

Structuralist design of the Sydney Aquarium and Pier

For hotels and restaurants in this region see pp478–81 and pp524–8

Twin Pavilion in the Chinese Garden, decorated with carved flowers

centre of the wall, a carved pearl, symbolizing prosperity, is lifted by the waves. The lake is covered with lotus and water lilies for much of the year and a rock monster guards against evil. On the other side of the lake is the Twin Pavilion. Waratahs (New South Wales' floral symbol) and flowering apricots are carved into its woodwork in Chinese style, and are also planted at its base.

A tea house at the top of the stairs in the Tea House Courtyard serves Chinese and Western light refreshments.

Powerhouse Museum ⑱

See pp102–3.

Paddy's Markets ⑲

Cnr Thomas & Hay sts, Haymarket.
Map 4 D4. **Tel** *1300 361 589.*
Sydney Explorer. Paddy's
Market. ○ *9am–5pm Wed–Sun &
public hols.* ● *25 Apr, 25 Dec.*
See also **Shopping** *pp128–31.*
www.paddysmarkets.com.au

The Haymarket district, near Chinatown, is home to Paddy's Markets, Sydney's

oldest and best-known market. It has been in this area, on a number of sites, since 1869 (with only one five-year absence). The origin of the name is uncertain, but is believed to have come from either the Chinese who originally supplied much of its produce, or the Irish who were among their main customers.

Once the shopping centre for the inner-city poor, Paddy's Markets is now an integral part of the Market City Shopping Centre, which includes cut-price fashion outlet stores, an Asian food court and a cinema complex. Yet despite this transformation, the familiar clamour, smells and chaotic bargain-hunting atmosphere of the original marketplace remain. Every weekend the market is filled with up to 800 stalls selling everything from fresh produce to electrical products, homewares, leather goods, and pets, including rabbits, puppies and chickens,

Chinatown ⑳

Dixon St Plaza, Sydney. **Map** 4 D4.
Haymarket.

Originally concentrated around Dixon and Hay streets, Chinatown is now expanding to fill Sydney's Haymarket area, stretching as far west as Harris Street, south to Broadway and east to Castlereagh Street. It is close to the Sydney Entertainment Centre, where some of the world's best-known rock and pop stars perform in concert and many indoor sporting events are held *(see p142).*

For years, Chinatown was little more than a run-down district at the edge of the city's produce markets, where many Chinese immigrants worked at traditional businesses. Today, Dixon Street, its main thoroughfare, has been spruced up to equal many of the other popular Chinatowns around the world. There are authentic-looking street lanterns and archways, and a new wave of Asian immigrants fills the now upmarket restaurants.

Chinatown is a distinctive area and now home to a new wave of Sydney's Asian population and vibrant Chinese New Year celebrations. There are excellent greengrocers, traditional herbalists and butchers' shops with wind-dried ducks hanging in their windows. Asian jewellers, clothes shops and confectioners fill the arcades. There are also two Chinese-language cinema complexes.

Chinese food products in Chinatown

Traditional archway entrance to Chinatown in Dixon Street

Australian National Maritime Museum ⑮

1602 Willem Blaeu Celestial Globe

Bounded as it is by the sea, Australia's history is inextricably linked to maritime traditions. The museum displays material in a broad range of permanent and temporary thematic exhibits, many with inter-active elements. As well as artifacts relating to the enduring Aboriginal maritime cultures, the exhibits survey the history of European exploratory voyages in the Pacific, the arrival of convict ships, successive waves of migration, water sports and recreation, and naval life. Historic vessels on show at the wharf include a flimsy Vietnamese refugee boat, sailing, fishing and pearling boats, a navy patrol boat and a World War II commando raider.

Museum Façade
The billowing steel roof design by Philip Cox suggests both the surging sea and the sails of a ship.

Passengers
The model of the Orcades reflects the grace of 1950s liners. This display also charts harrowing sea voyages made by migrants and refugees.

Eora – First People traces the seafaring traditions of Aboriginal peoples and Torres Strait Islanders.

The Tasman Light was used in a Tasmanian lighthouse.

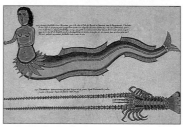

★ Navigators
This 1754 engraving of an East Indian sea creature is a European vision of the un-charted, exotic "great south".

The *Sirius* anchor is from a 1790 wreck off Norfolk Island.

Main entrance (sea level)

The Navy exhibit examines naval life in war and peace, as well as the history of colonial navies.

Linked by the Sea honours enduring links between the US and Australia. American traders stopped off in Aust-ralia on their way to China.

KEY TO FLOORPLAN

- ☐ Navigators and Eora – First People
- ☐ Passengers
- ☐ Commerce
- ☐ Watermarks
- ☐ Navy
- ☐ Linked by the Sea: USA Gallery
- ☐ Temporary exhibitions
- ☐ Non-exhibition space

STAR EXHIBITS

- ★ Eora – First People
- ★ Watermarks
- ★ HMAS Vampire

For hotels and restaurants in this region see pp478–81 and pp524–8

Commerce

This 1903 Painters' and Dockers' Union banner was carried by waterfront workers in marches. It shows the Niagara *entering the dry dock at Cockatoo Island.*

★ Watermarks

This 1960s poster for Bondi beach is part of the museum's Watermarks – adventure, sport and play exhibition. The displays, including fully-rigged boats and profiles of world champion scullers and swimmers, celebrate Australia's love affair with the water.

Upper level

Gallery One

A replica of Captain Cook's *Endeavour* is based at the museum.

Lighthouse

Sailors were guided by this 1874 lighthouse for over a century. It was rebuilt complete with original kerosene lamp.

HMAS *Onslow* (Oberon-class submarine)

The Wharf for Visiting Vessels is currently under construction and is due to be completed in 2011.

★ Vampire

The museum's largest vessel is the 1959 Royal Australian Navy destroyer, whose insignia is shown here. Tours of "The Bat" are accompanied by simulated battle action sounds.

VAMPIRE

AUDAMUS

MUSEUM GUIDE

The Watermarks, Navy and Linked by the Sea: USA Gallery exhibits are located on the main entrance level (sea level). The Eora – First People, Navigators, Passengers and Commerce sections are found on the first level.

Powerhouse Museum ⑱

This former power station, completed in 1902 to provide power for Sydney's tramway system, was redesigned to cater for the needs of an interactive, hands-on museum. Revamped, the Powerhouse opened in 1988. The early collection was held in the Garden Palace where the 1879 international exhibition of invention and industry from around the world was held. Few exhibits survived the devastating 1882 fire, and today's huge and ever-expanding collection was gathered after this disaster. The building's monumental scale provides an ideal context for the epic sweep of ideas encompassed within: everything from the realm of space and technology to the decorative and domestic arts. The museum emphasizes Australian innovations and achievements, celebrating both the extraordinary and the everyday.

Silver cricket trophy

What's It Like to Live in Space?
Find out how astronauts live and work in space and experience weightlessness in the zero gravity space lab.

Level 2

Thinkspace
This is a state-of-the-art digital studio for the exploration of sound and music projects.

★ Experimentations
Explore the principles of pressure, temperature, electricity, magnetism, light, gravity, motion and chemistry in this exciting interactive exhibit.

Level 1

Cyberworlds: Computers and Connections
These toy robots are part of an interactive exploration of the past, present and future of computers.

Ecologic, discover the science behind global warming and what can be done to prevent it.

MUSEUM GUIDE

*The museum is housed in two buildings: the former power-
house and the Neville Wran building. There are over 20
exhibitions on four levels, descending from Level 4. The shop,
entrance and temporary exhibits are
on Level 3. Level 2 has thematic
exhibits. Level 1 has
displays on space,
transport and
computers.*

Level 4

VISITORS' CHECKLIST

500 Harris St, Ultimo. **Map** 4 D4.
Tel 9217 0111. 449, 501.
Darling Harbour. Central.
Paddy's Markets.
10am–5pm daily. 25 Dec.
www.power
housemuseum.com

★ **Boulton & Watt Engine**
*The oldest surviving rotative
steam engine in the world, it
powered a London brewery for
102 years from 1875. It is
regularly put into operation
in the museum.*

Level 3

The Neville Wran Building, a
1980s addition, is based on
the design of grand exhibition
halls and railway stations of
the 19th century.

KEY TO FLOORPLAN

- Temporary exhibitions
- Social History & Design
- Science & Technology
- Non-exhibition space

**Main
entrance**

STAR EXHIBITS

★ Experimentations

★ Boulton & Watt
Engine

★ Locomotive No. 1

★ **Locomotive No. 1**
*Robert Stephenson built this locomo-
tive in England in 1854. It hauled
the first train in New South Wales
in 1855. Using models and voices,
the display re-creates a 19th-century
day trip for a group of Sydneysiders.*

BOTANIC GARDENS
AND THE DOMAIN

Wooden angel, St James' Church

This tranquil part of Sydney can seem a world away from the bustle of the city centre. It is rich in the remnants of Sydney's convict and colonial past: the site of the first farm and the boulevard-like Macquarie Street where the barracks, hospital, church and mint – bastions of civic power – are among the oldest surviving public buildings in Australia. This street continues to assert its dominance today as the location of the state government of New South Wales.

The Domain, an open, grassy space, was originally set aside by the colony's first governor for his private use. Today it is filled with joggers and touch footballers sidestepping picnickers and sunbathers. In January, during the Festival of Sydney, it hosts free outdoor concerts. The Royal Botanic Gardens has for almost 200 years collected, grown, researched and conserved plants from Australia and the rest of the world. The result is a parkland of great diversity and beauty.

SIGHTS AT A GLANCE

Historic Streets and Buildings
Conservatorium of Music ❷
Hyde Park Barracks Museum ⓫
The Mint ❿
Parliament House ❽
State Library of New South Wales ❼
Sydney Hospital ❾

Museums and Galleries
Art Gallery of New South Wales pp110–13 ❺

Churches
St James' Church ⓬

Islands
Fort Denison ❹

Monuments
Mrs Macquaries Chair ❸

Parks and Gardens
The Domain ❻
Royal Botanic Gardens pp106–7 ❶

GETTING THERE
Visit on foot, if possible. St James' and Martin Place train stations are close to most of the sights. The 311 bus from Circular Quay runs near the Art Gallery of NSW. The Sydney Explorer also stops at several sights.

0 metres	500
0 yards	500

KEY

▦ Royal Botanic Gardens *pp106–7*

🚪 CityRail station

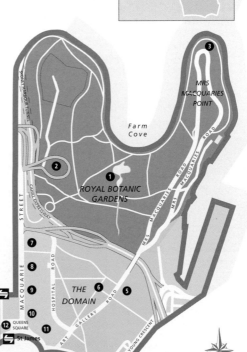

◁ **Succulents and cacti from the Succulent Garden in the Royal Botanic Gardens**

Royal Botanic Gardens ➊

Statue in the Botanic Gardens

The Royal Botanic Gardens, a 30-ha (75-acre) oasis in the heart of the city, occupies a superb position, wrapped around Farm Cove at the harbour's edge. Established in 1816 as a series of pathways through shrubbery, it is the oldest scientific institution in the country and houses an outstanding collection of plants from Australia and overseas. A living museum, the gardens are also the site of the first farm in the fledgling colony. Fountains, statues and monuments are today scattered throughout. The diversity is amazing: there are thousands of trees, stands of bamboo, a cactus garden, a rainforest walk, one of the world's finest collections of palms, a herb garden and a garden containing rare and threatened plant species.

LOCATOR MAP
See Street Finder, maps 1 & 2

Government House (1897)

★ **Palm Grove**
Begun in 1862, this cool summer haven is one of the world's finest outdoor collections of palms. There are about 180 species in the grove.

Conservatorium of Music *(see p108)*

★ **Herb Garden**
Herbs from around the world used for a wide variety of purposes – culinary, medicinal and aromatic – are on display here. A sensory fountain and a sundial modelled on the celestial sphere are also features.

| 0 metres | 200 |
| 0 yards | 200 |

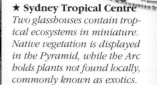

★ **Sydney Tropical Centre**
Two glasshouses contain tropical ecosystems in miniature. Native vegetation is displayed in the Pyramid, while the Arc holds plants not found locally, commonly known as exotics.

Macquarie Wall
In 1810, work began on this 290-m (950-ft) long wall intended to separate the convict domain from the town's "respectable Class of Inhabitants". Only a small section remains standing today.

Mrs Macquaries Chair, where the governor's wife liked to watch the harbour, is marked by a rock ledge seat *(see p108).*

Mrs Macquaries Road

Choragic Monument *(1870)*
This sandstone replica of the marble monument by Lysicrates in Athens was sculpted by Walter McGill.

The Fleet Steps met those disembarking from ships in Farm Cove.

Andrew (Boy) Charlton Pool is a popular spot for inner-city swimming and sunbathing.

★ **Australia's First Farm**
Some oblong beds in the Middle Garden follow the direction of the first furrows ploughed in the colony.

National Herbarium of New South Wales
Over one million dried plant specimens document biological diversity. Discovery and study of new plants aims to slow down the extinction rate of entire species

Wollemi Pine

STAR FEATURES

★ Australia's First Farm

★ Herb Garden

★ Palm Grove

★ Sydney Tropical Centre

Conservatorium of Music ❷

Macquarie St. **Map** 1 C3. **Tel** (02) 9351 1222. 🚌 Sydney Explorer, Circular Quay routes. 🕐 9am–5pm Mon–Fri, 9am–4pm Sat, public areas only. Phone for details of concerts. 🚻 🅿 public holidays, Easter Sat, 24 Dec–2 Jan. 🎦 phone 9351-1296 for details.

When it was finished in 1821, this striking castellated Colonial Gothic building was meant to be the stables and servants' quarters for Government House, but construction of the latter was delayed for almost 25 years. That stables should be built in so grand a style, and at such great cost, brought forth cries of outrage and led to bitter arguments between the architect, Francis Greenway (see p169), and Governor Macquarie – and a decree that all future building plans be submitted to London.

Between 1908 and 1915 "Greenway's folly" underwent a dramatic transformation. A concert hall, roofed in grey slate, was built on the central courtyard and the building in its entirety was converted for the use of the Sydney Conservatorium of Music.

Recently added facilities include a café, which holds lunchtime concerts during the school term and an upper level with great harbour views. "The Con" continues to be a training ground for future musicians and a great place to visit.

Resting on the carved stone seat of Mrs Macquaries Chair

Mrs Macquaries Chair ❸

Mrs Macquaries Rd. **Map** 2 E2. 🚌 Sydney Explorer, 111. 🚻 🎦

The Scenic Mrs Macquaries Road winds alongside much of what is now the city's Royal Botanic Gardens, stretching from Farm Cove to Woolloomooloo Bay and back again. The road was built in 1816 at the instigation of Elizabeth Macquarie, wife of the Governor. In the same year, a stone bench, inscribed with details of the new road and its commissioner, was carved into the rock at the point where Mrs Macquarie would often stop to rest and admire the view on her daily stroll. Although today the outlook is much changed, it is just as arresting, taking in the broad sweep of the harbour with all its landmarks.

Rounding the cove to the west leads to Mrs Macquaries Point. These lawns are a popular picnic spot with Sydneysiders, particularly at sunset.

Fort Denison ❹

Sydney Harbour. **Map** 2 E1. **Tel** (02) 9247 5033. 🚢 Circular Quay. 🕐 daily tours: for prices and times contact 9247 5033, or email: cadman.cottage@environment.nsw. gov.au. 🕐 25 Dec. 🎦 🍴 🎦

First named Rock Island, this prominent, rocky outcrop in Sydney Harbour was also dubbed "Pinchgut". This was probably because of the meagre rations given to convicts who were confined there as punishment. It had a grim history of incarceration in the early years of the colony.

In 1796, the convicted murderer Francis Morgan was hanged on the island in chains. His body was left to rot on the gallows for three years as a warning to the other convicts.

Between 1855 and 1857, the Martello tower (the only one in Australia), gun battery and barracks that now occupy the island were built as part of Sydney's defences. The site was renamed after the governor of the time. The gun, still fired at 1pm each day, helped mariners to set their ships' chronometers accurately.

Today the island is the perfect setting for watching the many harbour activities, such as the New Year fireworks displays (see p41). To explore Fort Denison, book one of the tours from Cadman's Cottage.

Fort Denison in 1907

Art Gallery of New South Wales ❺

See pp110–11.

Conservatorium of Music at the edge of the Royal Botanic Gardens

The Domain ⑥

Art Gallery Rd. **Map** 1 C4. 🚌
Sydney Explorer, 111, 411. ♿

The tens of thousands of people who swarm to the January concerts and other Festival of Sydney events in The Domain are part of a long-standing tradition. They come equipped with picnic baskets and blankets to enjoy the ongoing entertainment.

Once the governor's private park, this extensive space is now public and has long been a rallying point for crowds of Sydneysiders whenever emotive issues of public importance have arisen. These have included the attempt in 1916 to introduce military conscription and the sudden dismissal of the elected federal government by the then governor-general in 1975.

From the 1890s, part of The Domain was also used as the Sydney version of "Speakers' Corner". Today, you are more likely to see joggers or office workers playing touch football in their lunch hours, or simply enjoying the shade.

Harbour view from The Domain

State Library of New South Wales ⑦

Macquarie St. **Map** 4 F1. **Tel** (02) 9273 1414. 🚌 *Sydney Explorer, Elizabeth St routes.* ◗ *9am–9pm Mon–Fri, 11am–5pm Sat & Sun.* ◗ *most public hols, Mitchell Library closed Sun.* ♿ 📷 🖥 🛍
www.sl.nsw.gov.au

The state library is housed in two separate buildings connected by a passageway and a glass bridge. The older building, the Mitchell Library

Mosaic replica of the Tasman Map, State Library of New South Wales

wing (1910), is a majestic sandstone edifice facing the Royal Botanic Gardens *(see pp106–7)*. Huge stone columns supporting a vaulted ceiling frame the impressive vestibule. On the vestibule floor is a mosaic replica of an old map illustrating the two voyages made to Australia by Dutch navigator Abel Tasman in the 1640s *(see p49)*. The two ships of the first voyage are shown off the south coast, the two from the second voyage are seen to the northwest. The original Tasman Map is held in the Mitchell Library as part of its collection of historic Australian paintings, books, documents and pictorial records.

The Mitchell wing's vast reading room, with its huge skylight and oak panelling, is just beyond the main vestibule. There is also an attractive contemporary structure that faces Macquarie Street *(see pp114–15)*. This area houses the State Reference Library. Beyond the Mitchell wing is the Dixson Gallery, housing cultural and historical exhibitions which change regularly.

Outside the library, facing Macquarie Street, is a statue of the explorer Matthew Flinders, who first ventured into central Australia *(see pp52–3)*. On the windowsill behind him is a statue of his travelling companion, his cat, Trim.

Malby's celestial globe, Parliament House

Parliament House ⑧

Macquarie St. **Map** 4 F1. **Tel** (02) 9230 2111. 🚌 *Sydney Explorer, Elizabeth St routes.* 🚇 *Martin Place.* ◗ *9:30am–4:30pm Mon–Fri.* ◗ *public hols.* ♿ 📷 (02) 9230 3444 to book.
www.parliament.nsw.gov.au

The central section of this building, which houses the State Parliament, is part of the original Sydney Hospital built from 1811–16 *(see p113)*. It has been a seat of government since 1829 when the newly appointed Legislative Council first held meetings here. The building was extended twice during the 19th century and again during the 1970s and 1980s. The current building contains the chambers for both houses of state parliament, as well as parliamentary offices.

Parliamentary memorabilia is on view in the Jubilee Room, as are displays showing Parliament House's development and the legislative history of the state.

The corrugated iron building with a cast-iron façade tacked on at the southern end was a prefabricated kit from England. In 1856, this dismantled kit became the chamber for the new Legislative Council. Its packing cases were used to line the chamber; the rough timber can still be seen.

Art Gallery of New South Wales ❺

Established in 1874, the art gallery has occupied its present imposing building since 1897. Designed by the Colonial Architect WL Vernon, the gallery doubled in size following 1988 building extensions. Two equestrian bronzes – *The Offerings of Peace* and *The Offerings of War* – greet the visitor on entry. The gallery itself houses some of the finest works of art in Australia, with permanent collections of Australian, Aboriginal, European, Asian and Contemporary art. The Yiribana Gallery is the largest in the world to exclusively exhibit Aboriginal and Torres Strait Islander art and culture. Free guided tours take place daily, covering Aboriginal art, highlights of the collection or major exhibitions.

Lower Level 3

Mars and the Vestal Virgin *(1638)*
This oil on canvas by Parisian painter Jacques Blanchard (1600–38) depicts Mars's encounter with a Vestal Virgin, who subsequently gave birth to Romulus and Remus, founders of Rome.

Sunbaker *(1937)*
Max Dupain's iconic, almost abstract, Australian photograph of hedonism and sun worship uses clean lines, strong light and geometric form. The image's power lies in its simplicity.

Sofala *(1947)*
Russell Drysdale's visions of Australia show "ghost" towns laid waste by devastating natural forces such as drought.

GALLERY GUIDE
There are five levels. The Upper Level and Lower Level 1 host temporary exhibitions. The Ground Level has European and Australian works. On Lower Level 2 are the Contemporary Galleries, which house the most extensive collection of modern art in the country. The Yiribana Aboriginal Gallery is on Lower Level 3.

STAR EXHIBITS

★ The Golden Fleece

★ Pukumani Grave Posts

Ground Level

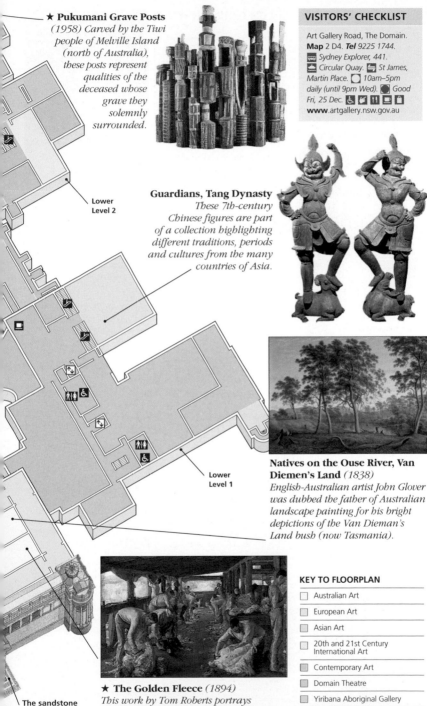

★ **Pukumani Grave Posts**
(1958) Carved by the Tiwi people of Melville Island (north of Australia), these posts represent qualities of the deceased whose grave they solemnly surrounded.

Guardians, Tang Dynasty
These 7th-century Chinese figures are part of a collection highlighting different traditions, periods and cultures from the many countries of Asia.

Lower
Level 2

Natives on the Ouse River, Van Diemen's Land *(1838)*
English-Australian artist John Glover was dubbed the father of Australian landscape painting for his bright depictions of the Van Dieman's Land bush (now Tasmania).

Lower
Level 1

The sandstone
entrance was
added in 1909.

★ **The Golden Fleece** *(1894)*
This work by Tom Roberts portrays the vanished tradition of manual shearing, and captures the heroic quality of the men.

KEY TO FLOORPLAN

- ☐ Australian Art
- ☐ European Art
- ☐ Asian Art
- ☐ 20th and 21st Century International Art
- ☐ Contemporary Art
- ☐ Domain Theatre
- ☐ Yiribana Aboriginal Gallery
- ☐ Temporary exhibition space
- ☐ Non-exhibition space

Exploring the Art Gallery's Collection

The gallery's early focus was on Australian and British art, and these areas continue to be well represented. Aboriginal art began to be added to the collection during the 1940s, with strong acquisition programmes in recent decades. The Contemporary Galleries are an exciting addition, with both international and Australian pieces on display. The gallery stages major temporary exhibitions, and the annual Archibald, Wynne and Sulman prizes always entertain and usually stir controversy.

Grace Cossington Smith's *The Curve of the Bridge* (1928–9)

AUSTRALIAN ART

Among the most important colonial works is John Glover's *Natives on the Ouse River, Van Diemen's Land* (1838), an image of doomed Tasmanian Aborigines. The old wing holds paintings from the Heidelberg school of Australian Impressionism. *Departure of the Orient – Circular Quay* (1888) by Charles Conder and Tom Roberts's *The Golden Fleece* (1894) hang near the equally iconic *Fire's On* (1891) by Arthur Streeton.

Australia was slow to take up Modernism. *Implement Blue* (1927) by Margaret

Preston is an emphatic statement of its period. Some of Sidney Nolan's most powerful paintings exploiting myths and landscapes of Australia include *Hare in a Trap* (1946) and *Central Australia* (1950). There are also fine holdings of William Dobell, Russell Drysdale, Grace Cossington Smith and Brett Whiteley *(see p34).*

YIRIBANA ABORIGINAL GALLERY

This gallery opened in 1994 and exhibits works by Aboriginal and Torres Strait Islanders. The name Yiribana implies a multiplicity of directions, reflecting the diversity of a collection representing artists from many different communities, including Emily Kam Ngwarray, John Mawurndjul and Pedro Wonaeamirri. Most of the works were produced after 1945 yet depict stories dating back thousands of years.

The gallery received an important gift of 24 paintings on bark and works on paper from the Commonwealth Government's 1948 expedition to Arnhem Land. Between 1959 and 1962 more works and a set of Pukumani grave posts were also acquired.

***Three Bathers,* an Ernst Ludwig Kirchner painting from 1913**

EUROPEAN ART

Among the Old Masters are some significant Italian works. Hogarth, Turner and Joshua Reynolds are represented, as are Neo-Classical works such as *The Visit of the Queen of Sheba to King Solomon* (1884–90) by Edward Poynter. *Chaucer at the Court of Edward III* (1845–51) by Ford Madox Brown is the most commanding Pre-Raphaelite painting.

Impressionists and Post-Impressionists are represented by Pissarro, Cézanne and Monet, as well as Bonnard, Kandinsky and Braque. *Old Woman in Ermine* (1946) by Max Beckmann and *Three Bathers* (1913) by Ernst Ludwig Kirchner are strong examples of German Expressionism. The gallery's first Picasso, *Nude in a Rocking Chair* (1956), was bought in 1981.

PHOTOGRAPHY

There are 4,500 photographs in the collection, celebrating the extraordinary diversity of the medium. The majority are Australian and half date from 1980 onwards. Major holdings of a wide variety of artists include Micky Allan, Mark Johnson, Max Pam, Lewis Morley, Tracey Moffatt and Bill Henson. Australian Pictorialism, as represented by Harold Cazneaux, is also a particular strength, as is the Modernism and postwar photodocumentary of artists such as Olive Cotton and Max Dupain.

Brett Whiteley's vivid *The Balcony (2)* from 1975

ASIAN ART

The Asian collections offer one of the largest pan-Asian displays of art in the southern hemisphere, including exquisite calligraphy, traditional and modern paintings, textiles, porcelain and an extraordinary legacy of Buddhist art. The galleries occupy two levels; the lower level displays the art of East Asia – China, Korea and Japan; the upper level displays the art of South and South-East Asia and changing exhibitions.

PRINTS AND DRAWINGS

This collection represents the European tradition from the High Renaissance to the 19th and 20th centuries, with work by Rembrandt, Constable, William Blake, Edvard Munch and Egon Schiele. A strong bias towards Sydney artists of the past 100 years has resulted in an exceptional gathering of work by Thea Proctor, Norman and Lionel Lindsay and Lloyd Rees.

Egon Schiele's *Poster for the Vienna Secession* (1918)

CONTEMPORARY ART

The Contemporary Galleries present the most comprehensive collection of contemporary artworks in Australia. Leading international and Australian artists represented include Sol Lewitt, Ugo Rondinone, Urs Fischer, Richard Long, Gilbert and George, Vanessa Beecroft, Christo and Jeanne-Claud, Jeff Koons and Bill Viola.

Il Porcellino, the bronze boar in front of Sydney Hospital

Sydney Hospital ❾

Macquarie St. **Map** 1 C4.
Tel *(02) 9382 7111.* 🚌 *Sydney Explorer, Elizabeth St routes.* ⬜ *daily.* 🎟 *for tours.* ♿ 🎫 *book in advance.*

This imposing collection of Victorian sandstone buildings stands on the site of what was once the central section of the original convict-built Sydney Hospital. It was known locally as the Rum Hospital because the builders were paid by being allowed to import rum for resale. Both the north and south wings of the Rum Hospital survive as Parliament House *(see p109)* and the Sydney Mint. The central wing was demolished in 1879 and the new hospital, which is still operational, was completed in 1894.

The Classical Revival building boasts a Baroque staircase and elegant stained-glass windows in its central hall. Florence Nightingale approved the design of the 1867 nurses' wing. In the inner courtyard, there is a brightly coloured Art Deco fountain (1907), somewhat out of place among the surrounding heavy stonework.

At the front of the hospital sits a bronze boar called *Il Porcellino*. It is a replica of a 17th-century fountain in Florence's Mercato Nuovo. Donated in 1968 by an Italian woman whose relatives had worked at the hospital, the statue is an enduring symbol of the friendship between Italy and Australia. Like his Florentine counterpart, *Il Porcellino* is supposed to bring good luck to all those who rub his snout. Coins tossed in the pool at his feet for luck and fortune are collected for the hospital.

Stained glass at Sydney Hospital

The Mint ❿

10 Macquarie St. **Map** 1 C5. ***Tel*** *(02) 8239 2288.* 🚌 *Sydney Explorer, Elizabeth St routes.* ⬜ *9am–5pm Mon–Fri.* ⬤ *Good Fri, 25 Dec.* 📷 ♿ *ground floor only.* ⬜ *www.*hht.net.au

The gold rushes of the mid-19th century transformed colonial Australia *(see pp54–5)*. The Sydney Mint opened in 1854 in the south wing of the Rum Hospital in order to turn recently discovered gold into bullion and currency. This was the first branch of the Royal Mint to be established outside London, but it was closed in 1927 as it was no longer competitive with the mints in Melbourne *(see p387)* and Perth *(see p305)*. The Georgian building then went into decline after it was converted into government offices.

The Mint's artifacts are now in the Powerhouse Museum *(see pp102–3)*. The head office of the Historic Houses Trust of NSW is now located here and you can look through the front part of the building.

Hyde Park Barracks Museum ⑪

Queens Square, Macquarie St. **Map** 1
C5. **Tel** (02) 8239 2311. 🚇 St James,
Martin Place. 🕙 9:30am–5pm daily.
⬤ Good Fri, 25 Dec. 🎫 ♿ ground
floor only. 🎧 on request. 🖥
www.hht.net.au

Described by Governor
Macquarie as "spacious" and
"well-aired", the beautifully
proportioned barracks are the
work of Francis Greenway
and are considered his
masterpiece (see p169). They
were completed in 1819 by
convict labour and designed
to house 600 convicts. Until
that time convicts had been
forced to find their own lodgings after their day's work.
Subsequently, the building

**Replica convict hammocks on the
third floor of Hyde Park Barracks**

then housed, in turn, young
Irish orphans and single
female immigrants, before it
later became courts and legal
offices. Refurbished in 1990,

the barracks reopened as a
museum on the history of the
site and its occupants. The
displays include a room
reconstructed as convict quarters of the 1820s, as well as
pictures, models and artifacts.
Many of the objects recovered
during archaeological digs at
the site and now on display
survived because they had
been dragged away by rats to
their nests; today the rodents
are acknowledged as valuable
agents of preservation.

The Greenway Gallery on
the first floor holds varied
exhibitions on history and
culture. Elsewhere, the
Barracks Café, which incorporates the original cell area,
offers views of the courtyard,
today cool and attractive but
in the past the scene of brutal
convict floggings.

MACQUARIE STREET

Described in the 1860s as one of the gloomiest
streets in Sydney, this could now claim to be
the most elegant. Open to the harbour breezes
and the greenery of The Domain, a stroll down
this tree-lined street is a pleasant way to view
the architectural heritage of Sydney.

This wing of
the library was
built in 1988
and connected
to the old
section by a
glass walkway.

The Mitchell Library
wing's portico (1906) has
Ionic columns.

Parliament House was
once the convict-built Rum
Hospital's northern wing.

1. STATE LIBRARY OF NSW (1906–41)

2. PARLIAMENT HOUSE (1811–16)

The roof of The
Mint has now been
completely restored to
replicate the original
wooden shingles in
casuarina (she-oak).

The Mint, like its twin,
Parliament House, has
an unusual double-
colonnaded, two-storeyed
veranda.

**Hyde Park
Barracks Café**

4. THE MINT (1816)

St James' Church

179 King St. **Map** 1 B5. **Tel** (02)
8227 1300. St James, Martin
Place. 10am–4pm Mon–Fri,
9am–1pm Sat, 7:30am–5pm Sun.
Concerts 1:15pm Wed (free).

This fine Georgian building, constructed by convict labour, was originally designed as a courthouse in 1819. The architect, Francis Greenway, had to build a church instead when plans to construct a cathedral on George Street were abandoned. Greenway designed a simple yet elegant church. Consecrated in 1824, it is the city's oldest church. Many additions were carried out, including designs by John Verge in which the pulpit faced the high-rent pews, while convicts and the military sat directly behind the preacher where the service was inaudible. A Children's Chapel was created in 1929. Prominent members of early 19th-century society, many of whom died violently, are honoured with marble tablets. These tell the stories of luckless explorers, the governor's wife dashed to her death from her carriage, and shipwreck victims.

Detail from the Children's Chapel mural in the St James' Church crypt

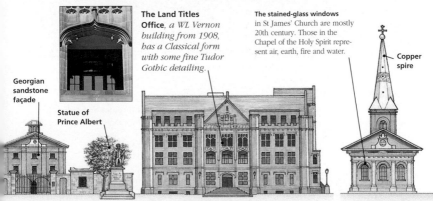

The lamps hanging over the gateways of Parliament House are reproductions of the 19th-century gas lamps that used to stand here.

Corrugated iron and cast-iron façade

The entrance stairs *of Pyrmont sandstone have set the tone for all renovations. The stone, quarried in colonial times, must be matched exactly.*

Arcaded stone verandas with ornate balustrading

Arched sandstone bridges

LOCATOR MAP

3. SYDNEY HOSPITAL *(1868–94)*

The Land Titles Office, *a WL Vernon building from 1908, has a Classical form with some fine Tudor Gothic detailing.*

The stained-glass windows in St James' Church are mostly 20th century. Those in the Chapel of the Holy Spirit represent air, earth, fire and water.

Georgian sandstone façade

Statue of Prince Albert

Copper spire

5. HYDE PARK BARRACKS MUSEUM *(1817–19)*   **6. LAND TITLES OFFICE** *(1908–13)*   **7. ST JAMES'** *(1820)*

The front entrance to a lovingly restored Victorian terrace house in Paddington

SIGHTS AT A GLANCE

Historic Streets and Buildings
Darlinghurst Court House **7**
Elizabeth Bay House **3**
The Entertainment Quarter **16**
Five Ways **8**
Juniper Hall **10**
Old Gaol, Darlinghurst **6**
Paddington Street **14**

Paddington Town Hall **11**
Paddington Village **9**
Victoria Barracks **12**
Victoria Street **2**

Parks and Gardens
Beare Park **4**
Centennial Park **15**

Museums and Galleries
Sydney Jewish Museum **5**

Monuments
El Alamein Fountain **1**

Markets
Paddington Markets **13**

KINGS CROSS, DARLINGHURST AND PADDINGTON

Façade detail,
Del Rio *(see p119)*

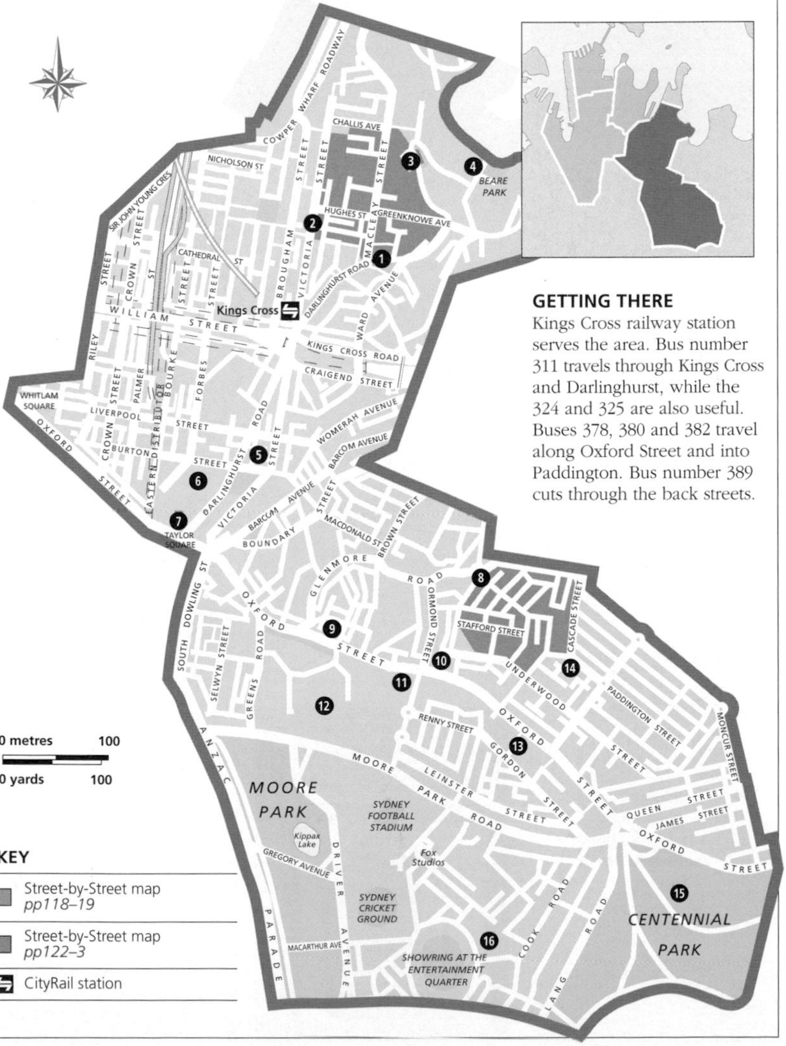

Sydney's Kings Cross and Darlinghurst districts are still remembered for their 1920s gangland associations. However, both areas are now cosmopolitan and densely populated parts of the city. Kings Cross has a thriving café society, in spite of the nearby red light district. Darlinghurst comes into its own every March, during the flamboyant Gay and Lesbian Mardi Gras parade. The Victorian terraces of Paddington are still admired for their wrought-iron "lace" verandas. Paddington is also famed for its fine restaurants, galleries and antiques shops. On Saturdays, people flock to Paddington Markets, spilling out into the pubs and cafés of the surrounding area.

GETTING THERE

Kings Cross railway station serves the area. Bus number 311 travels through Kings Cross and Darlinghurst, while the 324 and 325 are also useful. Buses 378, 380 and 382 travel along Oxford Street and into Paddington. Bus number 389 cuts through the back streets.

KEY

Street-by-Street map pp118–19	
Street-by-Street map pp122–3	
CityRail station	

Map labels: COWPER WHARF ROADWAY, CHALLIS AVE, NICHOLSON ST, STREET, STREET, BEARE PARK, HUGHES ST, GREENKNOWE AVE, MACLEAY STREET, CATHEDRAL ST, BROUGHAM STREET, DARLINGHURST ROAD, VICTORIA STREET, WARD AVENUE, SIR JOHN YOUNG CRES, STREET, CROWN ST, RILEY STREET, Kings Cross, WILLIAM STREET, KINGS CROSS ROAD, CRAIGEND STREET, WHITLAM SQUARE, PALMER STREET, FORBES STREET, BOURKE STREET, LIVERPOOL STREET, CROWN STREET, BURTON STREET, EASTERN DISTRIBUTOR, DARLINGHURST ROAD, VICTORIA STREET, WOMERAH AVENUE, BARCOM AVENUE, TAYLOR SQUARE, BOUNDARY STREET, BARCOM AVENUE, BROWN STREET, MACDONALD ST, GLENMORE ROAD, ORMOND STREET, STAFFORD STREET, UNDERWOOD, CASCADE STREET, SOUTH DOWLING ST, SELWYN STREET, OXFORD STREET, GREENS ROAD, STREET, RENNY STREET, GORDON STREET, OXFORD STREET, PADDINGTON STREET, MONCUR STREET, LEINSTER STREET, QUEEN STREET, JAMES STREET, OXFORD STREET, MOORE PARK, SYDNEY FOOTBALL STADIUM, Kippax Lake, GREGORY AVENUE, MOORE PARK ROAD, DRIVER AVENUE, Fox Studios, SYDNEY CRICKET GROUND, ANZAC PARADE, MACARTHUR AVE, SHOWING AT THE ENTERTAINMENT QUARTER, COOK ROAD, LANG ROAD, CENTENNIAL PARK

0 metres 100
0 yards 100

Street-by-Street: Potts Point

Beare Park fountain detail

The substantial Victorian houses filling the streets of this old suburb are excellent examples of the 19th-century concern with architectural harmony. New building projects were designed to enhance rather than contradict the surrounding buildings and general streetscape. Monumental structures and fine details of moulded stuccoed parapets, cornices and friezes, even the spandrels in herringbone pattern, are all integral parts of a grand suburban plan. (This plan included an 1831 order that all houses cost at least £1,000.) Cool, dark verandas extend the street's green canopy of shade, leaving an impression of cold drinks enjoyed on summer days in fine Victorian style.

The McElhone Stairs were preceded by a wooden ladder that linked Woolloomooloo Hill, as Kings Cross was known, to the estate far below.

Horderns Stairs

These villas, from the Georgian and Victorian eras, can be broadly labelled as Classical Revival and are fronted by leafy gardens.

VICTORIA STREET

TUSCULUM STREET

MANNING STR

Kings Cross Station

HUGHES STREET

★ Victoria Street
From 1972–4, residents of this historic street fought a sometimes violent battle against developers wanting to build high-rise towers, motels and blocks of flats ❷

Werrington, a mostly serious and streamlined building, also has flamboyant Art Deco detailing which is now hidden under brown paint.

MACLEAY STREET

GREENKN

ELIZABE

Tusculum Villa was just one of a number of 1830s houses subject to "villa conditions". All had to face Government House, be of a high monetary value and be built within three years.

STAR SIGHTS

★ Elizabeth Bay House

★ Victoria Street

Challis Avenue is a fine and shady complement to nearby Victoria Street. This Romanesque group of terrace houses has an unusual façade, with arches fronting deep verandas and a grand ground floor colonnade.

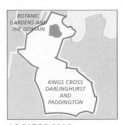

LOCATOR MAP
See Street Finder, map 2

Rockwall, a symmetrical and compact Regency villa, was built to the designs of the architect John Verge in 1830–37.

Landmark Hotel

Del Rio is a finely detailed high-rise apartment block. It clearly exhibits the Spanish Mission influence that filtered through from California in the first quarter of the 20th century.

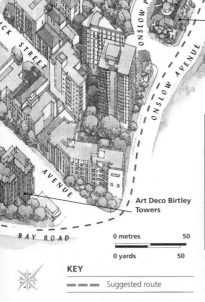

The Arthur McElhone Reserve

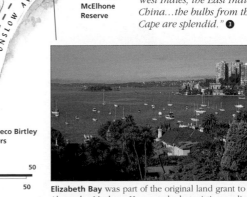

★ **Elizabeth Bay House**
A contemporary exclaimed over the beauty of the 1830s garden: "Trees from Rio, the West Indies, the East Indies, China…the bulbs from the Cape are splendid." ❸

Art Deco Birtley Towers

0 metres 50
0 yards 50

KEY

- - - Suggested route

Elizabeth Bay was part of the original land grant to Alexander Macleay. He created a botanist's paradise with ornamental ponds, quaint grottoes and promenades winding all the way down to the harbour.

El Alamein Fountain, commemorating the World War II battle

El Alamein Fountain ❶

Fitzroy Gardens, Macleay St, Potts Point. **Map** 2 E5. 🚌 *222, 311.*

This dandelion of a fountain in the heart of the Kings Cross district has a reputation for working so spasmodically that passers-by often murmur facetiously, "He loves me, he loves me not." Built in 1961, it commemorates the Australian army's role in the siege of Tobruk, Libya, and the battle of El Alamein in Egypt during World War II. At night, when it is brilliantly lit, the fountain looks surprisingly ethereal.

Victoria Street ❷

Potts Point. **Map** 5 B2. 🚌 *311, 324, 325, 389.*

At the Potts Point end, this street of 19th-century terrace houses, interspersed with a few incongruous-looking high-rise blocks, is, by inner-city standards, almost a boulevard. The gracious street you see today was once at the centre of a bitterly fought conservation struggle, one which almost certainly cost the life of a prominent heritage campaigner.

In the early 1970s, many residents, backed by the "green bans" put in place by the Builders' Labourers Federation of New South Wales, fought to prevent demolition of old buildings for high-rise

development. Juanita Nielsen, heiress and publisher of a local newspaper, vigorously took up the conservation battle. On 4 July 1975, she disappeared without trace. An inquest into her disappearance returned an open verdict.

As a result of the actions of the union and residents, most of Victoria Street's superb old buildings still stand. Ironically, they are now occupied not by the low-income residents who fought to save them, but by the well-off professionals who eventually displaced them.

Elizabeth Bay House ❸

7 Onslow Ave, Elizabeth Bay. **Map** 2 F5. **Tel** (02) 9356 3022. 🚌 *Sydney Explorer, 311.* ⏱ *10am–4:30pm Tue–Sun.* ⬤ *Good Fri, 25 Dec.* 📷 🎦 ♿ *groundfloor.* **www**.hht.net.au

Elizabeth Bay House contains the finest colonial interior on display in Australia. It is a potent expression of how the depression of the 1840s cut short the 1830s' prosperous optimism. Designed in Greek Revival style by John Verge, it was built for Colonial Secretary Alexander Macleay, from 1835–39. The oval saloon with its dome and cantilevered staircase is recognized as Verge's masterpiece. The exterior is less satisfactory, as the intended colonnade and portico were not finished owing to a crisis in Macleay's financial affairs.

Juanita Nielsen

The present portico dates from 1893. The interior is furnished to reflect Macleay's occupancy from 1839–45, and is based on inventories drawn up in 1845 for the transfer of the house and contents to his son, William Sharp. He took the house in return for paying off his father's debts, leading to a rift that was never resolved.

Macleay's original 22-ha (55-acre) land grant was subdivided for flats and villas from the 1880s to 1927. In the 1940s, the house itself was divided into 15 flats. In 1942, the artist Donald Friend saw the ferry *Kuttabul* hit by a torpedo from a Japanese midget submarine from his flat's balcony.

The house was restored and opened as a museum in 1977. It is a property of the Historic Houses Trust of NSW.

The sweeping staircase under the oval dome, Elizabeth Bay House

Beare Park ❹

Ithaca Rd, Elizabeth Bay. **Map** 2 F5. 🚌 *311, 350.*

Originally a part of the Macleay Estate, Beare Park is now encircled by a jumble of apartment blocks.

A refuge from hectic Kings Cross, it is one of only a few parks serving a populated area. Shaped like a natural amphitheatre, the park has glorious views of Elizabeth Bay.

The family home of JC Williamson, a famous theatrical entrepreneur who came to Australia from America in the 1870s, formerly stood at the eastern extremity of the park.

Star of David in the lobby of the Sydney Jewish Museum

Sydney Jewish Museum [5]

148 Darlinghurst Rd, Darlinghurst. **Map** 5 B2. ***Tel*** *(02) 9360 7999.* 🚌 *Sydney, Bondi & Bay Explorer, 311, 389.* ○ *10am–4pm Sun–Thu, 10am–2pm Fri.* ● *Sat, Jewish hols.* 👂 ♿ 🖐 **www**.sydneyjewishmuseum.com.au

Sixteen Jewish convicts were on the First Fleet, and many more were to be transported before the end of the convict era. As with other convicts, most would endure and some would thrive, seizing all the opportunities the colony had to offer.

The Sydney Jewish Museum relates stories of Australian Jewry within the context of the Holocaust. The ground floor display explores present-day Jewish traditions and culture within Australia. Ascending the stairs to the mezzanine levels 1–6, the visitor passes through chronological and thematic exhibitions which unravel the tragic history of the Holocaust.

From Hitler's rise to power and *Kristallnacht*, through the evacuation of the ghettos and the Final Solution, to the ultimate liberation of the infamous death camps and Nuremberg Trials, the harrowing events are graphically documented. This horrific period is recalled using photographs and relics, some exhumed from mass graves, as well as audiovisual exhibits and oral testimonies.

Holocaust survivors act as guides and their presence, bearing witness to the recorded events, lends considerable power and moving authenticity to the exhibits in the museum.

Old Gaol, Darlinghurst [6]

Cnr Burton & Forbes sts, Darlinghurst. **Map** 5 A2. ***Tel*** *(02) 9339 8744.* 🚌 *378, 380, 382, 389.* ○ *9am–5pm Mon–Fri.* ● *public hols.* ♿

Originally known as the Woolloomooloo Stockade and later as Darlinghurst Gaol, this complex is now the National Art School. It was constructed over a 20-year period from 1822.

Surrounded by walls almost 7 m (23 ft) high, the cell blocks radiate from a central roundhouse. The jail is built of stone quarried on the site by convicts which was then chiselled by them into blocks.

No fewer than 67 people were executed here between 1841 and 1908. Perhaps the most notorious hangman was Alexander "The Strangler" Green, after whom Green Park, outside the jail, is thought to have been named. Green lived near the park until public hostility forced him to live in relative safety inside the jail.

Some of Australia's most noted artists, including Frank Hodgkinson, Jon Molvig and William Dobell, trained or taught at the art school which was established here in 1921.

Beare Park, a quiet inner-city park with harbour views

The former Governor's house, Old Gaol, Darlinghurst

Darlinghurst Court House [7]

Forbes St, Darlinghurst. **Map** 5 A2. ***Tel*** *(02) 9368 2947.* 🚌 *378, 380, 382.* ○ *Feb–Dec: 10am–4pm Mon–Fri & Sun.* ● *Jan, mid-Dec, public hols.* ♿ 🖐 *groups only.*

Abutting the grim old gaol, to which it is connected by underground passages, and facing tawdry Taylor Square, this unlikely gem of Greek Revival architecture was begun in 1835 by colonial architect Mortimer Lewis. He was only responsible for the central block of the main building with its six-columned Doric portico with Greek embellishments. The side wings were not added until the 1880s.

The Court House is still used by the state's Supreme Court, mainly for criminal cases, and these are open to the public.

Street-by-Street: Paddington

Paddington began to flourish in the 1840s, when the decision was made to build the Victoria Barracks. At the time much of it was "the most wild looking place… barren sandhills with patches of scrub, hills and hollows galore." The area began to fill rapidly, as owner builders bought into the area and built rows of terrace houses, many very narrow because of the lack of building regulations. After the Depression, most of the district was threatened with demolition, but was saved and restored by the large influx of postwar migrants.

Victorian finial in Union Street

★ **Five Ways**
This shopping hub was established in the late 19th century on the busy Glenmore roadway trodden out by bullocks ⑧

Duxford Street's terrace houses in toning pale shades constitute an ideal of town planning: the Victorians preferred houses in a row to have a pleasingly uniform aspect.

"Gingerbread" houses can be seen in Broughton and Union streets. With their steeply pitched gables and fretwork bargeboards, they are typical of the rustic Gothic Picturesque architectural style.

The London Tavern opened for business in 1875, making it the suburb's oldest pub. Like many of the pubs and delicatessens in this well-serviced suburb, it stands at the end of a row of terraces.

STAR SIGHTS

★ Five Ways

★ Paddington Street

KEY

– – – Suggested route

The Sherman Gallery is housed in a strikingly modern building. It is designed to hold Australian and international contemporary sculpture and paintings. Suitable access gates and a special in-house crane enable the movement of large-scale artworks, including textiles.

LOCATOR MAP
See Street Finder, maps 5 & 6

Paddington's streets are a treasure trove of galleries, bars and restaurants. A wander through the area should prove an enjoyable experience.

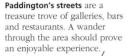

Warwick, built in the 1860s, is a minor castle lying at the end of a row of humble terraces. Its turrets, battlements and assorted decorations, in a style somewhat fancifully described as "King Arthur", even adorn the garages at the rear.

Windsor Street's terrace houses are, in some cases, a mere 4.5 m (15 ft) wide.

Street-making in Paddington's early days was often an expensive and complicated business. A cascade of water was dammed to build Cascade Street.

0 metres 50
0 yards 50

★ Paddington Street
Under the established plane trees, some of Paddington's finest Victorian terraces exemplify the building boom of 1860–90. Over 30 years, 3,800 houses were built in the suburb ⓮

Pretty cast-iron balcony, the typical architecture of Paddington

Five Ways ❽

Cnr Glenmore Rd & Heeley St.
Map 5 C3. 389.

At this picturesque intersection, where three streets cross on Glenmore Road, a shopping hub developed by the tramline that ran from the city to Bondi Beach *(see p126)*. On the five corners stand 19th- and early 20th-century shops, one now a restaurant.

Much of the architecture in Paddington features decorative cast-iron "lacework" balconies, using mixed Victorian and Classical Revival styles. Streets lined with pretty houses make this one of Sydney's most desirable areas.

Paddington Village ❾

Cnr Gipps & Shadforth sts. **Map** 5 C3. 378, 380, 382.

Paddington began its life as a working-class suburb of Sydney. The community mainly consisted of the carpenters, quarrymen and stonemasons who supervised the convict gangs that built the Victoria Barracks in the 1840s.

The 19th-century artisans and their families occupied a tight huddle of spartan houses crowded into the area's narrow streets. A few of these houses still remain. Like the barracks, these dwellings and surrounding shops and hotels were built of locally quarried stone.

The terraces of Paddington Village are now a popular address with young, up-and-coming Sydneysiders.

Juniper Hall ❿

250 Oxford St. **Map** 5 C3. 378, 380, 382. ◯ *closed to the public.*

The emancipist gin distiller Robert Cooper built this superb example of colonial Georgian architecture for his third wife, Sarah. He named it after the main ingredient of the gin that made his fortune.

Completed in 1824, the two-storey home is the oldest dwelling still standing in Paddington. It is probably also the largest and most extravagant house ever built in the suburb. It had to be: Cooper already had 14 children when he declared that Sarah would have the finest house in Sydney. Once resident in the new house, he subsequently fathered 14 more.

Juniper Hall was saved from demolition in the mid-1980s and has been restored. Now under the auspices of the National Trust, the building is used as private offices.

Paddington Town Hall ⓫

Cnr Oxford St & Oatley Rd.
Map 5 C3. 378, 380, 382. ◯ *10am–4pm Mon–Fri.* ◯ *public hols.*

Paddington Town Hall was completed in 1891. A design competition was won by local architect JE Kemp. The Classical Revival building still dominates the area.

No longer a centre of local government, the building now houses a cinema, library and a large ballroom.

Paddington Town Hall

The archway at the Oxford Street entrance to Victoria Barracks

Victoria Barracks ⓬

Oxford St. **Map** 5 B3. **Tel** *(02) 9339 3330.* 378, 380, 382. **Museum** ◯ *10am–12:30pm Thu; 10am–3:45pm Sun.* ◯ *Sun.* ◯ *25 Dec.* ◯ **Parade & tour:** *10am Thu (phone 9339 3170 to book).*

Victoria Barracks is the largest and best-preserved group of late Georgian architecture in Australia, covering almost 12 ha (30 acres). They are widely considered to be one of the best examples of a military barracks in the world.

Designed by the colonial engineer Lieutenant Colonel George Barney, the barracks were built between 1841 and 1848 using local sandstone quarried by convict labour. Originally intended to house 800 men, they have been in continuous use ever since and still operate as a centre of military administration.

The main block is 225 m (740 ft) long and has symmetrical two-storey wings with cast-iron verandas flanking a central archway. The perimeter walls have foundations 10 m (40 ft) deep in places. A former gaol block now houses a military museum. The tour leaves with military precision at 10am on Thursdays.

Paddington Markets ⓭

395 Oxford St. **Map** 6 D4. **Tel** *(02) 9331 2923.* 378, 380, 382. ◯ *10am–4pm Sat.* ◯ *25 Dec.* ◯ See **Shopping** *p133.* **www**.paddingtonmarkets.com.au

This market, which began in 1973 as Paddington Bazaar, takes place every Saturday, come rain or shine, in the

For hotels and restaurants in this region see pp478–81 and pp524–8

grounds of Paddington Village Uniting Church. It is probably the most colourful in Sydney – a place to meet and be seen as much as to shop. Stallholders come from all over the world and young designers, hoping to launch their careers, display their wares. Other offerings are jewellery, pottery and other arts and crafts, as well as new and second-hand clothing. Whatever you are looking for you are more than likely to find it here.

Paddington Street terrace house

Paddington Street ⓮

Map 6 D3. 🚌 *378, 380, 382.*

With its huge plane trees shading the road and fine terrace houses on each side, Paddington Street is one of the oldest and loveliest of the suburb's streets.

Paddington grew rapidly as a commuter suburb in the late 19th century and most of the terraces were built for renting to Sydney's artisans. They were decorated with iron lace, Grecian-style friezes, worked parapets and cornices, pilasters and scrolls.

By the 1900s, the terraces became unfashionable and people moved out to newly emerging "garden suburbs". In the 1960s, however, their architectural appeal came to be appreciated again and the area was reborn.

Paddington Street now has a chic atmosphere where small art galleries operate out of quaint and grand shopfronts.

Centennial Park ⓯

Map 6 E5. **Tel** *(02) 9339 6699.*
🚌 *Clovelly, Coogee, Maroubra, Bronte, Randwick, City, Bondi Beach & Bondi Junction routes, Bondi Explorer Bus.* ⭕ *permanently, but cars permitted only between sunrise and sunset.* ♿ 🍴 ▣
🎁 *upon request.*
www.centennialparklands.com.au

Entering this 220-ha (544-acre) park through one of its sandstone and wrought-iron gates, the visitor may wonder how such an extensive and idyllic place has survived so close to the centre of the city. Formerly a common, Centennial Park was dedicated "to the enjoyment of the people of New South Wales forever" in 1888 as part of the centenary of the foundation of the colony. On 1 January 1901, 100,000 people gathered here to witness the Commonwealth of Australia come into being, when the first Australian federal ministry was sworn in by the first governor-general *(see p56)*.

The park boasts landscaped lawns, a rose garden, statues and a coordinated series of walks. Once the source of the city's water supply, the swamps are home to many species of waterbirds. Picnickers, painters, runners, cyclists, skaters and horse-riders all share this vast park. Equipment hire is available, as well as barbecues and a scenic café and restaurant. An adjacent golf course with a large driving range, and tennis courts offer even more sporting opportunities.

The Entertainment Quarter ⓰

Lang Rd, Moore Park. **Tel** *8117 6700.* **Map** 5 C5. 🚌 *339, 355.* ⭕ *many retail shops open 10am–10pm.* **www**.eqmoorepark.com.au

There is a vibrant atmosphere in the Entertainment Quarter, which is located next door to the working studios that produced some very famous movies, such as *The Matrix* and *Moulin Rouge*.

There are 16 cinema screens where you can watch the latest movies, and at the La Premiere cinema you can enjoy your movie with wine and cheese, sitting on comfortable sofas. There are four live-entertainment venues which regularly feature the latest local and international acts. You can also enjoy bungy trampolining, bowling or seasonal ice-skating, and children love the play areas. There are many restaurants, cafés and bars offering a range of snacks, meals and drinks.

Every Wednesday you can savour the fresh produce at the Farmers Market. More than 100 stalls feature regional products, with many offering free tastings.

The weekend market consists of the Farmers Market on Saturday and the merchandise market, with its eclectic range of stalls, on Sunday. Shops are open until late every day, and there is a good selection of products. There is plenty of undercover parking and the Entertainment Quarter is a pleasant stroll from the Paddington end of Oxford Street.

The lush green expanse of Centennial Park

Further Afield

Beyond Sydney's inner city, around the harbour shores, are picturesque suburbs, secluded beaches and historic sights. Taronga Zoo, just a short ferry ride from the city, shelters 400 animal species. To the north is the beautiful landscape of Ku-ring-gai Chase National Park. Manly is the city's northern playground, while Bondi is its eastern counterpart. Further west at Parramatta are sites that recall and evoke the first days of European settlement.

KEY

- ▦ Central Sydney
- ▫ Greater Sydney
- ③ Metroad (city) route
- ▬ Highway
- ▬ Major road

SIGHTS WITHIN GREATER SYDNEY

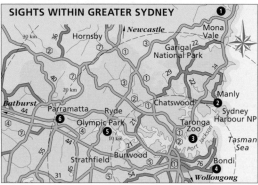

10 km = 6 miles

Ku-ring-gai Chase National Park ❶

McCarrs Creek Rd, Church Point.
🛈 Kalkari Discovery Centre (02)
9472 9300. ◯ 10am–4pm Mon–Fri,
10am–5pm Sat–Sun. ● 25 Dec.

Ku-ring-gai Chase National Park lies on Sydney's northernmost outskirts, 30 km (19 miles) from the city, and covers 15,000 ha (37,000 acres). It is bounded to the north by Broken Bay, at the mouth of the Hawkesbury River, with its eroded valleys formed during the last Ice Age. Sparkling waterways and golden beaches are set against the backdrop of the national park. Picnicking, bushwalking, surfing, boating and windsurfing are popular with visitors.

The Hawkesbury River curls around an ancient sandstone landscape rich in Aboriginal rock art. The national park has literally hundreds of Aboriginal art sites, the most common being rock engravings thought to be 2,000 years old. They include whales up to 8 m (26 ft) long, sharks, wallabies and echidnas, as well as ancestral spirits.

Manly ❷

🚢 Manly. **Oceanworld Manly** West
Esplanade. **Tel** (02) 8251 7877. ◯
10am–5:30pm daily. ● 25 Dec. 🏷
🌐 www.oceanworld.myfun.com.au

If asked to suggest a single excursion outside the city, most Sydneysiders would nominate the 11-km (7-mile) ferry ride from Circular Quay to Manly. This narrow stretch of land lying between the harbour and the ocean was named by Governor Phillip, even before the township of

Brass band playing on The Corso,
Manly's esplanade

Sydney got its name, for the impressive bearing of the Aboriginal men.

To the right of Manly wharf are shops, restaurants and bars on the adjacent pier and, on the left, the tranquil harbourside beach known as Manly Cove. **Oceanworld Manly** is at the far end of Manly Cove, where visitors can see sharks, giant stingrays and other species in an underwater viewing tunnel. You can also dive with the sharks.

The Corso is a lively pedestrian thoroughfare that leads to Manly's ocean beach, popular with sunbathers, with its promenade lined by towering Norfolk pines.

Taronga Zoo ❸

Bradley's Head Rd, Mosman.
Tel (02) 9969 2777. 🚢 from Circular
Quay. 🚌 247 from Wynard. ◯
9am–5pm daily. 🏷 🗐 🚻 🖵
www.taronga.org.au

Taronga opened in 1916 in its idyllic harbourside location, with sweeping views across the water. It is home to 2,000 animals, and the protection and preservation of endangered creatures is at the heart of the zoo's prolific conservation programmes. Free daily presentations include a Free Flight Bird Show, while the Great Southern Ocean exhibit emulates the natural habitats of a superb range of marine life. Zoo volunteers allow visitors to view close-up and even touch some of the animals.

Crescent-shaped Bondi Beach, Sydney's most famous beach, looking towards North Bondi

Bondi Beach ❹

🚌 380, 382, 381.

This long crescent of golden sand (it is approximately a kilometre long) has long drawn the sun and surf set *(see pp144–5)*. The word *bondi* is Aboriginal for "water breaking over rocks". Surfers visit from far and wide in search of the perfect wave, and inline skaters hone their skills on the promenade.

People also seek out Bondi for its trendy seafront cafés and cosmopolitan milieu as much as for the world-famous beach. The pavilion, built in 1928 as changing rooms, is now a busy venue for festivals, plays, films and arts and crafts displays.

Sydney Olympic Park ❺

Sydney Olympic Park. *Tel* 9714 7888.
🚊 Olympic Park. **Visitors' Centre**
1 Showground Rd. ⬤ 9am–5pm daily. ⬤ Good Fri, 25 Dec, 26 Dec, 1 Jan. ⬤ ⬤ ⬤ **www**.
sydneyolympicpark.com.au

Once host to the 27th Summer Olympic Games and Paralympic Games, Sydney Olympic Park is situated at Homebush Bay. Visitors can buy a ticket for a guided tour of the park or the main Olympic Stadium. Bicycles can also be hired. There is a tour of the wetlands of Bicentennial

Park as well as Breakfast with the Birds – breakfast after a morning of birdwatching. All tickets for tours can be bought at the Visitors' Centre. Other facilities include the Aquatic Centre with a water-park, and a Tennis Centre. There is also a market on the fourth Sunday of every month.

Parramatta ❻

🚉 Parramatta. 🚢 Parramatta.
ℹ️ 346a Church St (02) 8839 3311.

The fertile soil of this Sydney suburb resulted in its foundation as Australia's first rural settlement, celebrating its first wheat crop in 1789. **Elizabeth Farm**, dating from 1793, is the oldest surviving home in Australia. Once the home of John Macarthur, the farm played a major role in

breeding merino sheep, so vital to the country's economy *(see p51)*. The house is now a museum, detailing the lives of its first inhabitants until 1850.

Old Government House in Parramatta Park is the oldest intact public building in Australia, built in 1799. The Doric porch, added in 1816, is attributed to Francis Greenway *(see p169)*. A collection of early 19th-century furniture is housed inside. St John's Cemetery on O'Connell Street is the final resting place of many of the First Fleet's settlers *(see p50)*.

🏛 **Elizabeth Farm**
70 Alice St, Rosehill. *Tel* (02) 9635 9488. ⬤ 10am–5pm daily. ⬤
Good Fri, 25 Dec. ⬤ ⬤ ⬤ ⬤ ⬤

🏚 **Old Government House**
Parramatta Park (entry by Macquarie St). *Tel* (02) 9635 8149. ⬤ daily.
⬤ Good Fri, 25 Dec. ⬤ ⬤

Drawing room in Old Government House in Parramatta

GETTING AROUND SYDNEY

The best way to see the city's sights and attractions is on foot, coupled with public transport. Buses and trains serve the suburbs and outlying areas as well as the inner city. Passenger ferries provide a fast and scenic means of travel between the city and the many

Sydney taxi company sign

harbourside suburbs. Most visitors will find it best to invest in a combined ticket that includes all three modes of public transport. On Sundays, families with at least one adult and child enjoy unlimited travel on Sydney's public buses, trains and ferries for a flat fare of A$2.50 per person.

DRIVING IN SYDNEY

Driving is not the ideal way to get around Sydney: the city road network is confusing, traffic is congested and parking can be expensive. If using a car, it is best to avoid the peak hours (about 7:30–9:30am and 4–7:30pm).

Overseas visitors can use their usual driving licences to drive in Sydney, but must have proof that they are simply visiting and keep the licence with them when driving.

Parking in Sydney is strictly regulated, with fines for any infringements. Vehicles can be towed away if parked illegally. Contact the **RTA's Transport Management Centre** if this happens. There are many car parks in and around the city. Also look for blue and white "P" signs or metered parking zones, many of which apply seven days a week, but it varies from council to council.

TAXIS

Taxis are plentiful in the city: there are many taxi ranks and taxis are often found outside large hotels. Meters indicate the fare plus any extras, such as booking fees and waiting time. A 20 per cent tarif applies from 10pm. It is customary to round the fare

up to the next dollar. A fleet of taxis caters for disabled passengers, including those in wheelchairs. Book these with any major taxi company.

Cycling in Centennial Park

SYDNEY BY BICYCLE

While cycling is permitted on all city and suburban roads, visitors are advised to stay within designated cycling tracks or areas with light motor traffic. Centennial Park is a popular cycling spot. Helmets are compulsory by law. Those who wish to take advantage of Sydney's undulating terrain can seek advice from **Bicycle New South Wales**. Bicycles are permitted on CityRail trains *(see p130)* but you may have to pay an extra fare.

TRAMS

In 1997, Sydney reintroduced trams to its transport system, after an absence of 36 years. Sydney Light Rail's fleet of

seven trams journey around the downtown area, from Central Station *(see p130)* to Lilyfield via Pyrmont, taking in a large proportion of the area's sights *(see pp76–7)*. Purchase tickets at Central Station.

COMPOSITE TICKETS

Sydney's transport is good value, particularly with one of the composite tickets available from **Sydney Buses Transit Shop** or railway stations. TravelTen tickets, also available from newsagents and convenience stores, entitle you to make ten bus journeys. MyMulti weekly travel passes allow unlimited seven-day travel on Sydney's buses, trains and government ferries within stipulated zones. Fortnightly train passes are also available.

A BusTripper allows one day's unlimited travel on regular buses. A MyMulti Day Pass allows one day's unlimited travel on trains, buses and ferries.

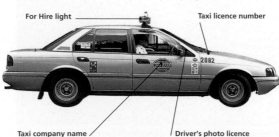

For Hire light

Taxi licence number

Taxi company name

Driver's photo licence

Travelling by Bus

Sydney buses provide a punctual service that links up conveniently with the city's rail and ferry systems. As well as covering city and suburban areas, there are two excellent sightseeing buses – the Sydney Explorer and the Bondi Explorer. The **Transport Infoline** can advise you on routes, fares and journey times for all Sydney buses. Armed with the map printed on the inside back cover of this book and a composite ticket, you can enjoy travelling about the city without the difficulties and expense of city parking.

USING SYDNEY BUSES

Route numbers and journey destinations are displayed on the front, back and left side of all Sydney buses. An "X" in front of the number means that it is an express bus. Many buses also feature electronic displays that scroll to show the areas the bus travels through. When you see your bus approaching, raise your arm to signal to the driver that you want the bus to stop. Most buses now have stepless entries, which allow less mobile passengers and people with strollers to board with ease. Buses also have priority seating areas at the front for disabled, elderly or less mobile passengers. Signs indicate where these seats are; on some buses priority seats are in red.

Single-journey tickets can be purchased on board regular buses from the driver. Try to have coins ready as drivers are not always able to change large notes. You will be given a ticket valid for that journey only. Buses with a "pre-pay" sign require you to buy a ticket or travel pass before you board. You must have pre-paid tickets to board buses in the city centre. These are available at main bus stops, convenience stores and newsagents. Insert pre-purchased tickets into the ticket reader when you board. If using a TravelTen ticket or TravelPass, it must also be inserted into the automatic stamping machine as you board. If sharing a TravelTen ticket, insert it into the machine once for each person travelling.

When you wish to alight, press one of the stop buttons well before the bus reaches your stop. The doors are

Automatic stamping machine for validating composite tickets

electronic and can only be opened by the bus drivers.

Note that eating, drinking, smoking and playing music are prohibited on Sydney buses.

BUS STOPS

Bus stops are indicated by yellow and black signs displaying a profile of a bus. Below this symbol, the numbers of all buses along the route are clearly listed.

Timetables are usually found at main bus stops. Public holidays follow the Sunday timetable. While bus stop timetables are kept as up-to-date as possible, it is best to carry a current timetable with you. These are available from Sydney Buses Transit Shops, as well as some tourist information facilities.

SIGHTSEEING BY BUS

Two Sydney bus services, the red double-decker Sydney Explorer and the Bondi Explorer, offer flexible sightseeing with commentaries. The Sydney Explorer covers a 32-km (20-mile) circuit and stops at 26 of the city's most popular attractions. The Bondi Explorer travels through a number of Sydney's eastern suburbs, taking in much of the area's coastal scenery.

The red Sydney Explorer buses run daily every 15 to 20 minutes, the Bondi route every 30 to 45 minutes. The great advantage of these services is that you can explore at will, getting on and off the buses as often as you wish in the course of a day. Explorer bus stops are clearly marked. Tickets for both Explorer buses are valid for 24 or 48 hours and can be bought when boarding a bus. Tickets are also available from Sydney Buses Transit Shops.

The best way to make the most of your journey is to choose the sights you most want to see and plan a basic itinerary. Be sure to note the various opening times of museums, art galleries and shops; the bus drivers can often advise you about these.

City sightseeing on the open-top Sydney Explorer

Travelling by Train and Monorail

CityRail logo

As well as the key link between the city and suburbs, Sydney's railway network also serves a large part of the central business district and reaches out to Newcastle to the north, Lithgow to the west, Nowra to the south and Goulburn to the southeast. CityRail's double-decker trains operate on 16 major lines. The City Circle loop stops as Central, Town Hall, Wynyard, Circular Quay, St James and Museum stations. Most suburban lines pass through Central and Town Hall.

Pedestrian concourse outside Central Railway Station

FINDING YOUR WAY AROUND CITYRAIL

Part of state rail, Sydney's CityRail system is mainly used by commuters. It is the most efficient and economical way to travel to and from the suburbs such as Parramatta. The system is easy to follow and **CityRail Information** will offer all details of services and timetables.

Trains run from 4:15am until after 1:30am. When using trains at night: stand in the "Nightsafe" areas and only use carriages near the train guard, marked by a blue light.

USING THE CITYRAIL ROUTE MAP

The 16 CityRail lines are colour-coded and route maps are displayed at all CityRail stations and inside train carriages. Simply trace the line from where you are to your destination, noting if and where you need to change and make connections.

Note that the distances shown on the CityRail map are not to the correct scale.

COUNTRY AND INTER-URBAN TRAINS

State rail has **Countrylink Travel Centres** throughout the city, which provide information about rail and coach services and also take ticket bookings (see their website).

Inter-urban trains run to a variety of areas, including the Blue Mountains (*see pp170–73*), Wollongong (*see p186*) and Newcastle (*see p169*).

SIGHTSEEING BY MONORAIL

More novel than practical, Sydney's Monorail runs along a scenic loop through

Monorail leaving the city centre, backed by Sydney Tower

central Sydney, Chinatown and Darling Harbour. Although it only covers a short distance, the Monorail can be a convenient way to travel from the city centre to Darling Harbour.

It runs from 7am–10pm Monday to Thursday, 7am to midnight on Friday and Saturday, and 8am to 10pm on Sunday. Trains run every 3–5 minutes and the full circuit takes about 15 minutes. Ticket machines are found at each station. They accept most Australian notes and coins and give change.

A Monorail Day Pass allows unlimited rides for an entire day. It can be bought from any of the Monorail information booths.

USEFUL ADDRESSES

CityRail Information
Central Railway Station
Map 4 E5.
Tel (02) 131500.
Circular Quay Railway Station
Map 1 B3.
Tel (02) 9224 3553.
www.cityrail.info

Countrylink Travel Centres
Central Railway Station
Sydney Terminal.
Map 4 E5.
Tel (02) 132232.
www.countrylink.info

Metro Light Rail & Monorail
Tel (02) 8584 5288.
www.metrotransport.com.au

THE METRO LIGHT RAIL

The MLR is Sydney's most recent transport development and is designed to link Central Railway Station with Glebe and Lilyfield, via Darling Harbour. These efficient and environmentally friendly trains offer a quicker and quieter means of travelling around parts of the city. Tickets are available on board from the conductor.

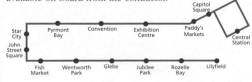

Travelling by Ferry and Water Taxi

For more than a century, Sydney ferries have been a picturesque, as well as a practical, feature of the Sydney scene. Today, they are as popular as ever. Travelling by ferry is both a pleasure and an efficient way to journey between Sydney's various harbour suburbs. Sightseeing cruises are operated by various private companies as well as by Sydney Ferries Corporation *(see p128)*. Water taxis can be a convenient and fast alternative, although they are more expensive.

A water taxi on Sydney Harbour

Sydney ferries coming and going at Circular Quay Ferry Terminal

WATER TAXIS

Small, fast taxi boats are available for hire to carry passengers around the harbour. You can flag them down like normal road cabs if you spot one cruising for a fare. Try King Street Wharf or Circular Quay, near the Overseas Passenger Terminal.

Water taxis will pick up and drop off passengers at any navigable pier. However, they are certainly not cheap. Rates vary, depending on the distance, with some drivers charging for the boat (about $60) or a fee per person (about $15 for a short trip).

USING SYDNEY'S FERRIES

There is a steady procession of State Transit Sydney Ferries traversing the harbour between 6am and midnight daily. They service most of Sydney Harbour, Manly and also several stops along the Parramatta River.

Staff at the **Sydney Ferries Information Office**, open 7am–6pm daily, will answer passenger queries and provide ferry timetables.

All ferry journeys start at the Circular Quay Ferry Terminal. Electronic destination boards at the entrance to each wharf indicate the wharf from which your ferry will leave, and also give departure times and all stops made en route. Tickets and TravelPasses can be bought from the ticket booths that are located on each wharf. On some ferries, tickets can be purchased on board.

Manly's ferry terminal is serviced both by regular ferries and a fast ferry service which operates during peak hours from Monday to Friday. Tickets and information can be obtained from the ticket windows in the centre of the terminal.

SIGHTSEEING BY FERRY

Sydney Ferries has a variety of well-priced cruises which take in the history and sights of Sydney Harbour. They are a cheap alternative to the commercial harbour cruises. There are morning, afternoon and evening tours, all with a commentary throughout. The day cruises show aspects of the city that are rarely seen, while the evening cruises offer spectacular views of the sun setting over the city's landmarks at sunset. Food and drink are available on board, but passengers may bring their own.

The **Australian Travel Specialists** has information on all river and harbour cruises from Circular Quay and Darling Harbour.

USEFUL INFORMATION

Australian Travel Specialists
Wharf 6, Circular Quay;
Harbourside Shopping Centre, Darling Harbour. **Map** 1 B3, 3 C2.
Tel (02) 9211 3192.
www.atstravel.com.au

Sydney Ferries Lost Property
Wharf 3, Circular Quay. **Map** 1 B3.
Tel (02) 9207 3101; 131 500 (timetable information).
www.sydneyferries.info

Water Taxi Companies
Harbour Taxi Boats
Tel (02) 9955 1155.
Sydney Harbour Water Taxis
Tel (02) 9299 0199.
Water Taxis Combined
Tel (02) 9555 8888.
www.watertaxis.com.au

Electronic destination board for all ferries leaving Circular Quay

SHOPPING IN SYDNEY

For most travellers, shopping can be as much of a voyage of discovery as sightseeing. The variety of shops in Sydney is wide and the quality of goods is high. The city has two good quality department stores, many elegant arcades and shopping galleries, as well

Souvenir boomerangs

as several popular weekly and monthly markets. The range of merchandise available is vast and local talent is promoted. Nor does the most interesting shopping stop at the city centre; there are several "satellite" alternatives within close proximity.

A jumble of bric-a-brac in a typical Sydney junk shop

SHOPPING HOURS

Most shops are open from 9am to 5:30pm every day, though some may close early on Saturdays and Sundays. High-end boutiques open from 10am to 6pm. On Thursdays, most shops stay open until 9pm. Most shops in Chinatown are open late every evening and on Sundays.

HOW TO PAY

Major credit cards are accepted almost everywhere. You will need identification, such as a passport or driver's licence, when using traveller's

cheques. Department stores will exchange goods or refund your money if you are not satisfied, provided you have kept your receipt. Other stores will only refund if an item is faulty. There is also a 10 per cent Goods and Services Tax (GST) which is almost always included in the marked price.

SALES

Many shops conduct sales all year round. The big department stores of **David Jones** and **Myer** have two gigantic and chaotic clearance sales every year. The post-Christmas sales start on 26 December and last into January. The other major sale time starts in June in the lead up to the end of the financial year.

TAX-FREE SALES

Duty-free shops are found in the centre of the city as well as at Kingsford Smith Airport *(see p582)*. You can save 10 per cent on goods such as perfume, jewellery and watches, and up to 30 per cent on alcohol at duty-free shops but you must show your passport and onward ticket. Some stores

will also deliver your goods to the airport to be picked up on departure. Duty-free items must be kept in their sealed bags until you leave the city.

You can claim back the GST paid on most goods, purchased for (or in a single transaction of) A$300 or more, at the airport.

Chifley Tower, with the Chifley Plaza shopping arcade at its base

ARCADES AND MALLS

Arcades and shopping malls in Sydney range from the ornately Victorian to modern marble and glass. The Queen Victoria Building *(see p90)* is Sydney's most palatial shopping space. Four levels contain more than 200 shops.

The elegant Strand Arcade *(see p90)* was originally built in 1892. Jewellery, lingerie, high fashion, antiques and fine cafés are its stock in trade.

Pitt Street Mall has several shopping centres including **Westfield Sydney** and **Sydney Central Plaza**, which feature upmarket stores.

Next door to the Hilton, **The Galeries** houses the fantastic Kinokuniya bookstore, which sells Australian and American imprints, as well as Chinese and Japanese language books.

Gleebooks, popular with students and Glebe locals *(see pp134–5)*

Both the **MLC Centre** and nearby **Chifley Plaza** cater to the prestige shopper. Gucci, Cartier and Tiffany & Co. are just some of the shops found in these arcades.

Harbourside Shopping Centre has dozens of shops selling articles of fine art, jewellery and Australiana, along with a range of waterfront restaurants.

Further afield, the new **Westfield Bondi Junction** complex is only a 15-minute train ride from the centre of Sydney. It offers more than 440 stores, as well as bars, restaurants and an 11-screen cinema. The only problem is having the time and energy to make your way through this large centre, which can be filled with local shoppers on a wet weekend.

BEST OF THE DEPARTMENT STORES

The spring floral displays and Christmas windows at **David Jones** are legendary, as is the luxurious perfumery and cosmetics hall on the ground floor. The store spreads out in two buildings, across the road from each other on Market and Elizabeth streets. The food hall is famous for its gourmet fare and fine wines. **Myer** has a ground floor packed with makeup and accessories, including a large MAC counter. Both stores sell women's clothing, lingerie, menswear, baby goods, children's clothes, toys, stationery, kitchenware, furniture, china crystal and silver.

Part of the spring floral display in David Jones department store

Canopy over the harbourside Rocks Market

MARKETS

Scouring markets for the cheap, the cheerful and the unusual has become a popular pastime in Sydney. **Balmain Market**, held each Saturday, includes a food hall selling Japanese, Thai and Indian dishes. The **Bondi Beach Market** on Sundays is known for its trendy second-hand clothing. The Saturday **Glebe Market** is a treasure-trove for the junk shop enthusiast and canny scavenger. The market is bright and popular with the inner-city grunge set.

The Rocks Market, held all weekend under a canopy, has around 140 stalls. Posters, lace, stained glass and leather are among the goods. You can watch a sculptor making art out of stone or have your portrait sketched in charcoal.

Sydney Fish Market is the place to go for fresh seafood. You can choose from more than 100 species, both live and prepared. Above the market, the Sydney Seafood School offers lessons in preparing and serving seafood. **The Good Living Growers' Market** sells everything you need for a gourmet feast, and is where you will find native Australian bushfoods, such as lemon myrtle linguini, dried bush tomatoes, nutty wattleseed and pepperberries.

The **Sydney Opera House Market** on Sundays displays an eclectic mix of arts and crafts in a spectacular setting next to the Opera House.

Other good markets are Paddy's Markets *(see p99)*, Fox Studio Markets *(see p125)* and Paddington Markets *(see p125)*.

Paddy's Markets *(see p99)*, Fox Studio Markets *(see p125)* and Paddington Markets *(see p125)*.

DIRECTORY

ARCADES AND MALLS

Chifley Plaza
2 Chifley Square. **Map** 1 B4.
Tel (02) 9221 6111.
www.chifleyplaza.com.au

The Galeries
2 Park St. **Map** 4 E2.
Tel (02) 9261 0456.
www.thegaleries.com

Harbourside Shopping Centre
Darling Harbour. **Map** 3 C2.
Tel (02) 9281 3999.
www.harbourside.com.au

MLC Centre
19–29 Martin Place. **Map** 1 B4.
Tel (02) 9224 8333.
www.mlccentre.com.au

Sydney Central Plaza
100 Market St. **Map** 4 E2.
Tel (02) 8224 2000.

Westfield
500 Oxford St, Bondi Junction.
Tel (02) 9947 8000;
Cnr Pitt St & Market St, Sydney.
Tel (02) 8236 9200. **Map** 4 E2.

DEPARTMENT STORES

David Jones
Cnr Elizabeth & Castlereagh sts.
Map 1 B5. *Tel* (02) 9266 5544.
www.davidjones.com.au

Myer
436 George St. **Map** 1 B5.
Tel (02) 9238 9111.
www.myer.com.au

MARKETS

Balmain Market
Cnr Darling St & Curtis Rd, Balmain.

Bondi Beach Market
Bondi Beach Public School,
Campbell Parade, North Bondi.

Glebe Market
Glebe Public School, Glebe Point
Rd, Glebe. **Map** 3 B5.

Sydney Fish Market
Cnr Pyrmont Bridge Rd & Bank
St, Blackwattle Bay. **Map** 3 B2.

Sydney Opera House Market
Western Boardwalk, Sydney Opera
House. **Map** 1 C2.

The Good Living Growers' Market
Pyrmont Bay Park. **Map** 3 C1

The Rocks Market
George St, The Rocks. **Map** 1 B2.

Specialist Shopping in Sydney

Sydney offers an extensive range of gift and souvenir ideas, from unset opals and jewellery to Aboriginal art and hand-crafted souvenirs. Museum shops, such as at the Museum of Sydney *(see p92)* and the Art Gallery of NSW *(see pp110–13)*, often have specially commissioned items that make great presents or reminders of your visit.

ONE-OFFS

Specialist shops abound in Sydney – some practical, some eccentric, others simply indulgent. **Wheels & Doll Baby** designs clothes that are the perfect mix of 1950s chic, rock'n'roll and Hollywood glamour. **The Hour Glass** stocks traditional-style watches, while designer sunglasses such as Armani and Jean Paul Gaultier can be found at **The Looking Glass**.

For a touch of celebrity glamour, **Napoleon Perdis Cosmetics** sells a huge array of make-up and bears the name of Australia's leading make-up artist to the "stars". Or, for some eclectic fashion and homewares, try a branch of **Orson & Blake**, the one in Surry Hills has a good café.

AUSTRALIANA

Australiana has become more than just a souvenir genre; it is now an art form in itself. **Done Art and Design** has distinctive prints by Ken and Judy Done on a wide range of clothes, swimwear and accessories, while at **Weiss Art** you will find tasteful, mainly black and white, minimalist designs on clothes, umbrellas, baseball caps and cups. The **Art Gallery of NSW** store stocks a wide range of Australian art books, prints, posters and giftware. The Queen Victoria Building *(see p90)* is dominated by shops selling Australiana: souvenirs, antiques, art and crafts.

The Australian Museum *(see pp94–5)* has a small shop on the ground floor. It sells slightly unusual gift items such as native flower presses, bark paintings and Australian animal puppets, puzzles and games, as well as a collection of jewellery made from Australian minerals and products featuring Aboriginal designs.

BOOKS

The larger chains such as **Dymocks** and **Angus & Robertson's Bookworld** have a good range of guide books and maps on Sydney. For more eclectic browsing, try **Abbey's Bookshop**, **Ariel** and **Gleebooks**, while **Berkelouw Books** has three floors of new, second-hand and rare books. **The Bookshop Darlinghurst** specializes in gay and lesbian fiction and non-fiction. The State Library of NSW *(see p109)* bookshop has a good choice of Australian books, particularly on history.

MUSIC

Several specialist music shops of international repute can be found in Sydney. **Red Eye Records** is for the streetwise, with its collectables, rarities, alternative music and concert tickets. **Central Station Records and Tapes** has mainstream grooves, plus rap, hip hop and cutting edge dance music. **Birdland** has a good stock of blues, jazz, soul and avant-garde. **The Recordstore** specializes in vinyl records of many styles, including breakbeat, drum 'n' bass, dubstep and hip hop. **Waterfront** specializes in world and left-of-centre music and **Utopia Records** in hard rock and heavy metal. **Michael's Music Room** sells classical music, specializing in historical and contemporary opera recordings.

ABORIGINAL ART

Traditional paintings, fabric, jewellery, boomerangs, carvings and cards can be bought at the **Aboriginal and Pacific Art**. You can find tribal artifacts from Aboriginal Australia at several shops in the Harbourside Shopping Centre, Darling Harbour. The **Coo-ee Aboriginal Art Gallery** boasts a large selection of limited edition prints, hand-printed fabrics, books and Aboriginal music.

The long-established **Hogarth Galleries Aboriginal Art Centre** has a fine reputation and usually holds work by Papunya Tula and Balgo artists and respected painters such as Clifford Possum Tjapaltjarri *(see p30)*. Works by urban indigenous artists can be found at the **Boomalli Aboriginal Artists' Cooperative**.

OPALS

Sydney offers a variety of opals in myriad settings. **Flame Opals** is a family run store, selling stones from all the major Australian opal fields. At **Opal Fields** you can view a museum collection of opalized fossils, before buying from the wide range of gems. **Giulian's** has unset opals, including blacks from Lightning Ridge, whites from Coober Pedy and boulder opals from Quilpie.

JEWELLERY

Long-established Sydney jewellers with 24-carat reputations include **Fairfax & Roberts** and **Hardy Brothers**. World-class pearls are found in the waters off the northwestern coast of Australia. Rare and beautiful examples can be found at **Paspaley Pearls**.

The Family Jewels has been attracting jewellery buyers to its Paddington store since the 1980s. **Dinosaur Designs** made its name with colourful, chunky resin jewellery, while at **Love & Hatred**, jewelled wrist cuffs, rings and crosses recall lush medieval treasures.

Jan Logan is an iconic Australian jewellery designer, with stores in Melbourne, Hong Kong and London, as well as Sydney. Choose from beautiful and unusual contemporary pieces, otherwise the shop also carries antiques.

DIRECTORY

ONE-OFFS

The Hour Glass
142 King St.
Map 1 B5.
Tel 9221 2288.

The Looking Glass
Queen Victoria Building.
Map 1 B5.
Tel 9261 4997.

Napoleon Perdis Cosmetics
74 Oxford St,
Paddington.
Tel 9331 1702.
Map 5 A2.
www.
napoleoncosmetics.com

Orson & Blake
83–85 Queen St,
Woollahra.
Map 6 E4.
Tel 9326 1155.
Also at:
483 Riley St, Surry Hills.
Map 4 F5.
Tel 8399 2525.
www.
orsanandblake.com.au

Wheels & Doll Baby
259 Crown St,
Darlinghurst.
Map 5 A2.
Tel 9361 3286.

AUSTRALIANA

Art Gallery of NSW
Art Gallery Road,
The Domain.
Map 2 D4.
Tel 9225 1744.

Done Art and Design
123 George St,
The Rocks.
Map 1 B2.
Tel 9251 6099.
One of several branches.

Weiss Art
85 George St,
The Rocks.
Map 1 B2.
Tel 9241 3819.

BOOKS

Abbey's Bookshop
131 York St.
Map 1 A5.
Tel 9264 3111.

Angus & Robertson's Bookworld
Pitt St Mall, Pitt St.
Map 1 B5.
Tel 9235 1188.
One of many branches.

Ariel
42 Oxford St, Paddington.
Map 5 B3.
Tel 9332 4581.

Berkelouw Books
19 Oxford St,
Paddington.
Map 5 B3.
Tel 9360 3200.
Also at:
70 Norton St, Leichhardt.
Tel 9560 3200.
www.berkelouw.com.au

The Bookshop Darlinghurst
207 Oxford St,
Darlinghurst.
Map 5 A2.
Tel 9331 1103.

Dymocks
424 George St.
Map 1 B5.
Tel 9235 0155.
One of many branches.

Gleebooks
49 Glebe Point Rd, Glebe.
Map 3 B5.
Tel 9660 2333.

MUSIC

Birdland
231 Pitt St. **Map** 1 B5.
Tel 9267 6881.

Central Station Records and Tapes
46 Oxford St, Darlinghurst.
Map 4 F4.
Tel 9361 5222.

Michael's Music Room
Shop 17, Town Hall
Square. **Map** 4 E3.
Tel 9267 1351.

The Recordstore
255B Crown St,
Darlinghurst.
Map 5 A2.
Tel 9380 8223.

Red Eye Records
66 King St,
Sydney.
Map 1 B5.
Tel 9299 4233.

Utopia Records
233 Broadway,
Chippendale.
Map 3 B5.
Tel 9571 6662.

Waterfront
Online sales only.
Tel 9283 9301.
www.waterfrontrecords.
com

ABORIGINAL ART

Aboriginal and Pacific Art
2 Danks St,
Waterloo.
Tel 9699 2211.

Boomalli Aboriginal Artists' Cooperative
191 Parramatta Rd,
Annandale.
Map 3 A5.
Tel 9560 2541.

Coo-ee Aboriginal Art Gallery
31 Lamrock Ave, Bondi
Beach.
Tel 9300 9233.

Hogarth Galleries Aboriginal Art Centre
7 Walker Lane,
off Brown St,
Paddington.
Map 5 C3.
Tel 9360 6839.

OPALS

Flame Opals
119 George Street,
The Rocks.
Map 1 B2.
Tel 9247 3446.

Giulian's
2 Bridge St.
Map 1 B3.
Tel 9252 2051.

Opal Fields
190 George St,
The Rocks.
Map 1 B2.
Tel 9247 6800.
One of two branches.

JEWELLERY

Dinosaur Designs
Level 1,
Strand Arcade.
Map 1 B5.
Tel 9223 2953.
One of several branches.

Fairfax & Roberts
44 Martin Place.
Map 1 B4.
Tel 9232 8511.

The Family Jewels
393a Oxford St,
Paddington.
Map 5 D3.
Tel 9331 3888.

Hardy Brothers
60 Castlereagh St.
Map 1 B5.
Tel 9232 2422.

Jan Logan
36 Cross St,
Double Bay.
Tel 9363 2529.

Love & Hatred
Strand Arcade.
Map 1 B5.
Tel 9233 3441.

Paspaley Pearls
2 Martin Place.
Map 1 A4.
Tel 9232 7633.

Clothes and Accessories

Australian style was once an oxymoron. Sydney now offers a plethora of chic shops as long as you know where to look. Top boutiques sell both men's and women's clothing, as well as accessories. The city's "smart casual" ethos, particularly in summer, means there are plenty of luxe but informal clothes available.

AUSTRALIAN FASHION

A number of Sydney's fashion designers have attained a global profile, including **Collette Dinnigan** and **Akira Isogawa**. Dinnigan's is filled with lacy evening gowns whereas Japanese-born Isogawa makes artistic clothing for women and men.

Young jeans labels such as **Tsubi** (for men and women) and **Sass & Bide** (women only) have also shot to fame, with celebrities wearing their denims. Nearby is **Scanlan & Theodore**, a stalwart of the Australian fashion scene.

Other shops are **Dragstar**, with its selection of retro women's and children's clothing, such as bright sundresses and minis. The quirky **Capital L** boutique houses the hottest names in Aussie fashion, while **Zimmermann** offers women's and girls' clothes and is famous for its swimwear. **Lisa Ho** is the place to go for a frock, with designs ranging from pretty sundresses to glam gowns. Head to **Farage Man & Farage Women** for quality suits and shirts.

High-street clothing can be found in and around Pitt Street Mall and Bondi Junction. Here you will find both international and homegrown fashion outlets. **Sportsgirl** sells funky clothes that appeal to both teens and adult women. The **Witchery** stores are a favourite among women for their stylish designs. **Just Jeans** doesn't just sell jeans; it stocks the latest trends for men and women.

General Pants has funky street labels such as One Teaspoon and Just Ask Amanda. Surry Hills is the place for discount and vintage clothing; check out **Zoo Emporium**. New designers try out their wares in Bondi, Glebe and Paddington markets (see p133).

INTERNATIONAL LABELS

Many Sydney stores sell designer imports. For the best ranges, visit **Belinda** – a women's and men's boutique – as well as others in Double Bay such as **Varese** for stylish shoes. In **Robby Ingham Stores** you will find women's and men's ranges including Chloé, Paul Smith and Comme des Garçons. **Cosmopolitan Shoes** stocks labels such as Dolce & Gabbana, Sonia Rykiel, Dior and Jimmy Choo. **Hype DC** also offers all the latest ranges. New Zealand designers **Zambesi** offer their own designs for women and men as well as a range of Martin Margiela pieces.

LUXURY BRANDS

Many visitors like to shop for international labels such as **Gucci** and **Louis Vuitton**. You will find both in Castlereagh Street, along with **Chanel** and **Versace**. The Queen Victoria Building (see p90) is home to **Bally**, and Martin Place has resident designer A-listers such as **Prada** and **Armani**. **Diesel** is further afield on Oxford Street.

SURF SHOPS

For the latest surf gear, look no further than Bondi where the streets are lined with shops selling clothing, swimwear as well as boards of all sizes to buy and hire. Serious surfers and novices should check out **Surf Culture** for boards, as well as **Bondi Surf Co**. Besides selling its own beachwear label, **Rip Curl** also sells Australian brands such as Tigerlily and Billabong. **Labyrinth** and **The Big Swim** are hugely popular swimwear shops packed with bikinis by designers including Jet and Seafolly.

CLOTHES FOR CHILDREN

Department stores, **David Jones** and **Myer** (see p133), are one-stop shops for children's clothes, from newborn to teenage. Look out for good quality

SIZE CHART

Women's clothes

Australian	6	8	10	12	14	16	18	20
American	4	6	8	10	12	14	16	18
British	6	8	10	12	14	16	18	20
Continental	38	40	42	44	46	48	50	52

Women's shoes

Australian	6–6½	7	7½–8	8½	9–9½	10	10½–11	
American	5	6	7	8	9	10	11	
British	3	4	5	6	7	8	9	
Continental	36	37	38	39	40	41	42	

Men's suits

Australian	44	46	48	50	52	54	56	58
American	34	36	38	40	42	44	46	48
British	34	36	38	40	42	44	46	48
Continental	44	46	48	50	52	54	56	58

Men's shirts

Australian	36	38	39	41	42	43	44	45
American	14	15	15½	16	16½	17	17½	18
British	14	15	15½	16	16½	17	17½	18
Continental	36	38	39	41	42	43	44	45

Men's shoes

Australian	7	7½	8	8½	9	10	11	12
American	7	7½	8	8½	9½	10½	11	11½
British	6	7	7½	8	9	10	11	12
Continental	39	40	41	42	43	44	45	46

Australian labels such as Fred Bare and Gumboots. Mambo, Dragstar and Zimmermann also sell fun and unusual kidswear.

ACCESSORIES

The team behind **Dinosaur Designs** are some of Australia's most celebrated designers. They craft chunky bangles, necklaces and rings, and also bowls, plates and vases, from jewel-coloured resin. **Collect**, the retail outlet of Object Gallery, is another place to look for handcrafted jewellery, scarfs, textiles, objects, ceramics and glass by leading and emerging Australian designers. At the **Art Gallery of NSW** (*see pp134*) you can find brooches and bags featuring designs by Australian artists such as Brett Whiteley. In her plush store, **Jan Logan** sells exquisite jewellery, using all kinds of precious and semi-precious stones.

Australian hat designer, **Helen Kaminski**, uses fabrics, raffia, straw, felt and leather to make hats and bags. In a different style altogether, **Crumpler** use high-tech fabrics to make bags that will last a century. And in a street of designer names, **Andrew McDonald**'s little studio shop doesn't cry for attention, but he does sell handcrafted shoes for men and women.

DIRECTORY

AUSTRALIAN FASHION

Akira Isogawa
12A Queen St, Woollahra.
Map 6 E4. **Tel** 9361 5221.

Capital L
333 South Dowling St,
Darlinghurst. **Map** 5 A3.
Tel 9361 0111.

Collette Dinnigan
33 William St,
Paddington. **Map** 6 D3.
Tel 9360 6691.

Dragstar
535A King St, Newtown.
Map 1 B4. **Tel** 9550 1243.

Farage Man & Farage Women
Shops 54 & 79, Level 1
Strand Arcade. **Map** 1 B5.
Tel 9231 3479.

General Pants
Queen Victoria Building.
Map 4 E2. **Tel** 9264 2842.

Just Jeans
Mid City Centre, Pitt St.
Map 4 E2. **Tel** 9223 8349.

Lisa Ho
2a–6a Queen St,
Woollahra. **Map** 6 D4.
Tel 9360 2345.

Sass & Bide
132 Oxford St,
Paddington. **Map** 5 B3.
Tel 9360 3900.

Scanlan & Theodore
122 Oxford St,
Paddington. **Map** 5 B3.
Tel 9380 9388.

Sportsgirl
Shop 2047, Westfield
Sydney, 188 Pitt St. **Map**
1 B5. **Tel** 9223 8255.

Tsubi
16 Glenmore Rd,
Paddington. **Map** 5 B3.
Tel 9361 6291.

Witchery
Shop 09, Chifley Plaza, 2
Chiffley Sq. **Map** 1 C4.
Tel 9232 4102.

Zimmermann
2–16 Glenmore Rd,
Paddington. **Map** 5 B3.
Tel 9357 4700.

Zoo Emporium
180B Campbell St, Surry
Hills. **Tel** 9380 5990.

INTERNATIONAL LABELS

Belinda
39 & 29 William St,
Paddington. **Map** 6 D3.
Tel 9380 8728.

Cosmopolitan Shoes
Cosmopolitan Centre,
Knox St, Double Bay.
Tel 9362 0510.

Hype DC
Cnr Market St &
Pitt St Mall. **Map** 1 B5.
Tel 9221 5688.

Robby Ingham Stores
424–426 Oxford St,
Paddington. **Map** 6 D4.
Tel 9332 2124.

Varese
45 Cross St,
Double Bay.
Tel 9328 6015.

Zambesi
5 Glenmore Rd,
Paddington. **Map** 5 B3.
Tel 9331 1140.

LUXURY BRANDS

Armani
4 Martin Place.
Map 1 B4. **Tel** 8233 5888.

Bally
Ground floor, Queen
Victoria Building.
Map 1 B5. **Tel** 9267 3887.

Chanel
70 Castlereagh St.
Map 1 B5. **Tel** 9233 4800.

Diesel
408–410 Oxford St,
Paddington. **Map** 6 D4.
Tel 9331 5255.

Gucci
MLC Centre, 15–25
Martin Place. **Map** 1 B4.
Tel 9232 7565.

Louis Vuitton
63 Castlereagh St.
Map 1 B5.
Tel 1300 883 880.

Prada
44 Martin Place. **Map** 1
B4. **Tel** 9231 3929.

Versace
161 Elizabeth St.
Map 1 B5.
Tel 9267 3232.

SURF SHOPS

The Big Swim
74 Campbell Parade, Bondi
Beach. **Tel** 9365 4457.

Bondi Surf Co.
72–76 Campbell Parade,
Bondi Beach.
Tel 9365 0870.

Labyrinth
30 Campbell Parade,
Bondi Beach.
Tel 9130 5091.

Rip Curl
82 Campbell Parade,
Bondi Beach.
Tel 9130 2660.

Surf Culture
40 Bronte Rd, Bondi
Junction.
Tel 9389 5477.

CLOTHES FOR CHILDREN

David Jones
Cnr Elizabeth & Market
sts. **Map** 1 B5.
Tel 9266 5544.

Myer
436 George St. **Map** 1 B5.
Tel 9238 9111.

ACCESSORIES

Andrew McDonald
58 William St, Paddington.
Map 6 D3.
Tel 9358 6793.

Art Gallery of NSW
Art Gallery Rd,
The Domain. **Map** 2 D4.
Tel 9225 1744.

Collect
417 Bourke St, Surry Hills.
Map 5 A3. **Tel** 9361 4511.

Crumpler
Ground floor, Strand
Arcade. **Map** 1 B5.
Tel 9222 1300.

Dinosaur Designs
See pp134–5.

Helen Kaminski
Shop 3, Four Seasons
Hotel, 199 George St.
Map 1 B3. **Tel** 9251 9850.

Jan Logan
36 Cross St, Double Bay.
Tel 9363 2529.

ENTERTAINMENT IN SYDNEY

Sydney has the standard of entertainment and nightlife you would expect from a cosmopolitan city. Everything from opera and ballet at Sydney Opera House to Shakespeare productions in the Royal Botanic Gardens is on offer. Venues such as the Capitol, Her Majesty's Theatre and the Theatre Royal play host to the latest musicals, while Sydney's many smaller theatres are home to interesting fringe theatre,

A Wharf Theatre production poster

modern dance and rock and pop concerts. Pub rock thrives in the inner city and beyond; and there are many nightspots for jazz, dance and alternative music. Movie buffs are well catered for with film festivals, art-house films and foreign titles, as well as the latest Hollywood blockbusters. One of the features of harbourside living is the free outdoor entertainment, which is very popular with children.

The Sydney Theatre on Hickson Road, Walsh Bay

INFORMATION

For details of events in the city, you should check the daily newspapers first. They carry cinema, and often arts and theatre, advertisements daily. The most comprehensive listings appear in the *Sydney Morning Herald*'s "Metro" guide every Friday. The *Daily Telegraph* has a daily gig guide, with opportunities to win free tickets to special events. The *Australian*'s main arts pages appear on Fridays, and all the papers review new films in weekend editions.

Tourism NSW information kiosks have free guides and the quarterly *What's on in Darling Harbour*. Kiosks are found at Town Hall, Circular Quay and Martin Place. *Where Magazine* is available at the airport and the **Sydney Visitor Centre** at The Rocks. Hotels also offer free guides, or try **www. sydney.citysearch.com.au**.

Music fans are well served by the free weekly guides *Drum Media*, *3-DWorld* and *Brag*, found at video and music shops, pubs and clubs.

Many venues have leaflets about forthcoming attractions, while the major venues have information telephone lines and websites.

BUYING TICKETS

Some of the most popular operas, shows, plays and ballets in Sydney are sold out months in advance. While it is better to book ahead, many theatres do set aside tickets to be sold at the door on the night.

You can buy tickets from the box office or by telephone. Some orchestral performances do not admit children under seven, so check with the box office before buying. If you make a phone booking using a credit card, the tickets can be mailed to you.

Alternatively, tickets can be collected from the box office

half an hour before the show. The major agencies will take overseas bookings.

Buying tickets from touts is not advisable, if you are caught with a "sold on" ticket you will be denied access to the event. If all else fails, hotel concierges have a reputation for being able to secure hard-to-get seats.

CHOOSING SEATS

If booking in person at either the venue or the agency, you will be able to look at a seating plan. Be aware that in the State Theatre's stalls, row A is the back row. In Sydney, there is not as much difference in price between stalls and dress circle as in other cities.

If booking by phone with one of the agencies, you will only be able to get a rough idea of where your seats are. The computer will select the "best" tickets.

The annual Gay and Lesbian Mardi Gras Festival's dog show (*see p42*)

BOOKING AGENCIES

Sydney has two main ticket agencies: **Ticketek** and **Ticketmaster**. Between them, they represent all the major entertainment and sporting events. Ticketek has more than 60 outlets throughout NSW and the ACT, open from 9am to 5pm weekdays, and Saturdays from 9am to 4pm. Opening hours vary between agencies and call centres, so check with Ticketek to confirm. Phone bookings: 8:30am–10pm, Monday to Saturday, and 8:30am–5pm Sunday. For Internet bookings, visit their website.

Ticketmaster outlets are open 9am–5pm Monday to Friday. Phone bookings: 9am–9pm Monday to Saturday and 10am-5pm Sunday. Agencies accept traveller's cheques, bank cheques, cash, Visa, MasterCard (Access) and Amex. Some agencies do not accept Diners Club. A booking fee applies, plus a postage and handling charge if tickets are mailed out. There are generally no refunds (unless a show is cancelled) or exchanges. If one agency has sold out its allocation for a show, it is worth checking with another.

A busker at Circular Quay

DISCOUNT TICKETS AND FREE ENTERTAINMENT

Tuesday is budget-price day at most cinemas. Some independent cinemas have special prices throughout the week. The Sydney Symphony Orchestra and Opera Australia *(see p140)* offer a special Student Rush price to full-time students under 28 but only if surplus tickets are available. These can be bought on the day of the performance, from the box office at the venue.

Outdoor events are especially popular in Sydney, and many are free *(see pp40–3)*. Sydney Harbour is a splendid setting for the fabulous New Year's Eve fireworks, with a display at 9pm for families as well as the midnight display.

The Spanish firedancers *Els Comediants* at the Sydney Festival

The Sydney Festival in January is a huge extravaganza of performance and visual art. Various outdoor venues in the Rocks, Darling Harbour and in front of the **Sydney Opera House** *(see pp84-5)* feature events to suit every taste, including musical productions, drama, dance, exhibitions and circuses. The most popular free events are the symphony and jazz concerts held in the Domain. Also popular are the Darling Harbour Circus and Street Theatre Festival at Easter, and the food and wine festival held in June at Manly Beach.

DISABLED VISITORS

Many older venues were not designed with the disabled visitor in mind, but this has been redressed in most newer buildings. It is best to phone the box office beforehand to request special seating and

Publicity shot of the Australian Chamber Orchestra *(see p140)*

other needs or call **Ideas Inc**, who have a list of Sydney's most wheelchair-friendly venues. The Sydney Opera House has disabled parking, wheelchair access and a loop system in the Concert Hall for the hearing impaired. The website of the **Access Foundation**, is another source of disability information.

Performing Arts and Cinema

Sydney has a wealth of orchestral, choral, chamber and contemporary music from which to choose, and of course every visitor should enjoy a performance of some kind at the Sydney Opera House. There is also a stimulating range of musicals, classic plays and Shakespeare by the Sea, as well as contemporary, fringe, experimental theatre and comedy. Prominent playwrights include David Williamson, Debra Oswald, Brendan Cowell, Stephen Sewell and Louis Nowra. Australian film-making has also earned an excellent international reputation. A rich variety of both local and foreign films are screened throughout the year.

CLASSICAL MUSIC

Much of Sydney's orchestral music and recitals are the work of the famous **Sydney Symphony Orchestra (SSO)**. Numerous concerts are given, mostly in the Sydney Opera House Concert Hall (see pp84–5), the **City Recital Hall** and the **Sydney Town Hall**.

The **Australian Chamber Orchestra** also performs at the Opera House and City Recital Hall, and has won high acclaim for its creativity. The **Australia Ensemble** is the resident chamber music group at the University of New South Wales.

Many choral groups and ensembles book St James' Church (see p115) for their performances because of its atmosphere and acoustics.

Formed in 1973, the respected **Sydney Youth Orchestra** stages performances in major concert venues. The **Australian Youth Choir** is booked for many private functions, but if you are lucky, you may catch one of their major annual performances.

Comprising the 120-strong Sydney Philharmonia Symphonic Choir and the 40-member Sydney Philharmonia Motet Choir, the **Sydney Philharmonia Choirs** are the city's finest.

One of Sydney's most impressive vocal groups is the **Café of the Gate of Salvation**, which has been described as an "Aussie blend of a capella and gospel".

Originally specialized in chamber music, **Musica Viva** now presents string quartets, jazz, piano groups, percussionists, soloists and international avant-garde artists as well.

Synergy is one of Australia's foremost percussion quartets. Its innovative performance style spans traditional and contemporary percussion from around the world.

COMEDY

Sydney's most established comedy venue, the **Comedy Store** is known for its themed nights. Tuesday is open-mic night; Wednesday, new comics; Thursday, cutting edge; Friday and Saturday are reserved for the best of the best. Monday is comedy night at **The Old Manly Boatshed**, where both local and visiting comics perform. Monday is also comedy night at the **Bridge Hotel**, where live entertainment is offered most nights of the week.

DANCE

The **Australian Ballet** has two seven-week Sydney seasons at the Opera House: one in March/April, the other in November/December. **Sydney Dance Company** is the city's leading modern dance group. Productions are mostly staged at the Sydney Opera House.

Bangarra Dance Theatre uses traditional Aboriginal and Torres Strait Islander dance and music as its inspiration. The startling and original **Legs on the Wall** are a physical theatre group, brilliantly combining circus and aerial techniques with dance and narrative, often performed while suspended from skyscrapers.

OPERA

In 1956, the Australian Opera (now called **Opera Australia**) was formed. It presented four Mozart productions in its first year. But it was the opening of the Sydney Opera House in 1973 that heralded new public interest. Opera Australia's summer season is held from early January to early March; the winter season from June to the end of October. Every year at the popular Opera in The Domain, members of Opera Australia perform excerpts from famous pieces.

THEATRE

Sydney's larger, mainstream musicals are staged at the **Theatre Royal**, the opulent **State Theatre** (see p90) and the **Capitol Theatre**. The **Star City** entertainment and casino complex boasts two theatres, the Showroom, and the first-rate Lyric Theatre.

Smaller venues also offer a range of interesting plays and performances. These include the **Seymour Theatre Centre**, the **Belvoir Street Theatre** and the **Ensemble Theatre**. The **Stables Theatre** specializes in works by new Australian playwrights, while the new **Parade Theatre** at the National Institute of Dramatic Arts (NIDA) showcases work by NIDA's students. The well-respected **Sydney Theatre Company (STC)** has just introduced an ensemble of actors, employed full time, who will perform a minimum of two plays each season. Most STC productions are performed at **The Wharf**.

The **Bell Shakespeare Company** productions are ideal for the young or the more wary theatre-goers. The **Australian Shakespeare Company** performs *The Wind in the Willows* in the Royal Botanic Gardens every year in January.

The **Sydney Festival** provides an enjoyable celebration of original, often quirky, Australian theatre, dance, music and visual arts.

FILM

The city's main commercial cinema, the **Greater Union Hoyts Village Complex**, is on George Street. A similar multiplex is in the Fox Studios Entertainment Quarter *(see p125)*. The **IMAX Theatre** in Darling Harbour has a giant, 8-storey screen showing 2D and 3D films.

Cinephiles flock to **Palace Cinemas** on Norton Street and **Dendy Cinema** at Circular Quay. **Cinema Paris** shows arthouse and indie films, as well as many Bollywood productions. The **Reading Cinema** regularly shows the latest Chinese films.

Most foreign films are shown in the original language with English subtitles. The latest screenings are usually at 9:30pm, although most major cinemas run later shows. Commercial cinema houses offer half-price tickets on Tuesday, while Palace does so on Monday. The Sydney Film Festival is one of the highlights of the city's calendar *(see p43)*. The main venue is the State Theatre. The **Flickerfest International Short Film Festival** is held at the Bondi Pavilion Amphitheatre at Bondi Beach in early January. It screens shorts and animated films. In February, **Tropfest** shows local short films.

Run by Queer Screen, the **New Mardi Gras Film Festival** starts mid-February for 15 days.

DIRECTORY

CLASSICAL MUSIC

Australia Ensemble
Tel 9385 4872.
www.ae.unsw.edu.au

Australian Chamber Orchestra
www.aco.com.au

Australian Youth Choir
www.niypaa.com.au

Café of the Gate of Salvation
www.cafeofthegateof
salvation.com.au

City Recital Hall
Angel Place. **Map** 1 B4.
Tel 8256 2222.
www.cityrecitalhall.com

Musica Viva
www.mva.org.au

Sydney Philharmonia Choirs
Tel 9251 2024. www.
sydneyphilharmonia.com.au

Sydney Symphony Orchestra
Tel 8215 4600. www.
sydneysymphony.com

Sydney Town Hall
483 George Street.
Map 4 E2. *Tel* 9265 9333.

Sydney Youth Orchestra
Tel 9251 2422.
www.syo.com.au

Synergy
Tel 9703 2008. www.
synergypercussion.com

COMEDY

Bridge Hotel
135 Victoria Rd, Rozelle.
Tel 9810 1260.
www.bridgehotel.com.au

Comedy Store
Entertainment Quarter,
Driver Ave, Moore Park.
Map 5 C5. *Tel* 9357 1419.
www.comedystore.com.au

The Old Manly Boatshed
40 The Corso, Manly.
Tel 9977 4443. www
oldmanlyboatshed.com.au

DANCE

Australian Ballet
Tel 9252 5500. www.
australianballet.com.au

Bangarra Dance Theatre
Tel 9251 5333.
www.bangarra.com.au

Legs on the Wall
Tel 9560 9479. www.
legsonthewall.com.au

Sydney Dance Company
www.sydneydance.com.au

OPERA

Opera Australia
Tel 9699 1099. www.
opera-australia.org.au

THEATRE

Australian Shakespeare Company
Tel 8676 7511. www.
australianshakespeare
company.com.au

Bell Shakespeare Company
Tel 8298 9000. www.
bellshakespeare.com.au

Belvoir St Theatre
25 Belvoir St, Surry Hills.
Tel 9699 3444.
www.belvoir.com.au

Capitol Theatre
13 Campbell St, Haymarket.
Map 4 E4.
Tel 9320 5000.
www.capitoltheatre.com.au

Ensemble Theatre
78 McDougall St,
Kirribilli. **Box office**
Tel 9929 0644.
www.ensemble.com.au

Parade Theatre
215 Anzac Parade,
Kensington. **Map** 5 B4
Tel 9697 7600.
www.nida.edu.au

Seymour Theatre Centre
Cnr Cleveland St & City Rd,
Chippendale.
Tel 9351 7940. www.
seymour.usyd.edu.au

Stables Theatre
10 Nimrod St, Kings
Cross. **Map** 5 B1.
Tel 9361 3817. www.
griffintheatre.com.au

Star City
80 Pyrmont St,
Pyrmont. **Map** 3 B1.
Tel 9777 9000.
www.starcity.com.au

State Theatre
49 Market St. **Map** 1 B5.
Tel 9373 6852. www.
statetheatre.com.au

Sydney Festival
Tel 8248 6500. www.
sydneyfestival.org.au

Sydney Theatre Co
Tel 9250 1777. www.
sydneytheatre.com.au

Theatre Royal
MLC Centre, King St.
Map 1 B5.
Tel 9224 8444.

The Wharf

Pier 4, Hickson Rd, Walsh
Bay. **Map** 1 A1.
Tel 9250 1777. www.
sydneytheatre.com.au

FILM

Cinema Paris
Entertainment Quarter,
Driver Ave, Moore Park.
Map 5 C5. *Tel* 9332 1633.
www.hoyts.com.au

Dendy Cinema
Shop 9/2, East Circular
Quay. **Map** 1 C2.
Tel 9247 3800.
www.dendy.com.au

Flickerfest
www.flickerfest.com.au

Greater Union Hoyts Village Complex
505–525 George St.
Map 4 E3. *Tel* 9273 7431.
www.greaterunion.com.au

IMAX Theatre
Southern Promenade,
Darling Harbour.
Map 4 D3. *Tel* 9281
3300. www.imax.com.au

New Mardi Gras Festival
www.queerscreen.com.au

Palace Cinemas
Palace Norton Street
Cinema
99 Norton St, Leichhardt.
Tel 9550 0122.

Reading Cinema
Level 3, Market City, 9 Hay
St, Haymarket. **Map** 4 E4.
Tel 9280 1202. www.
readingcinemas.com.au

Tropfest
www.tropfest.com

Music Venues and Nightclubs

Sydney attracts some of the biggest names in modern music all year round. Venues range from the cavernous Sydney Entertainment Centre to small and noisy back rooms in pubs. Visiting international DJs frequently play sets at Sydney clubs. Some venues cater for a variety of music tastes – rock and pop one night, jazz, blues or folk the next. There are several free weekly gig guides available, including *Drum Media*, *3-D World* and *Brag (see p138)*, which tell you what is on.

GETTING IN

Tickets for major shows are available through booking agencies such as Ticketek and Ticketmaster *(see p138)*. Prices vary considerably, depending on the shows that are going to take place. You may pay from A$30 to A$70 for a gig at the Metro, but over A$150 for seats for a Rolling Stones concert. **Moshtix** also sells tickets for smaller venues across Sydney and their website gives a good idea of the various venues and what is on. Buying online also prevents you from having to queue early for tickets from the door.

You can also pay at the door on the night at most places, unless the show is sold out. Nightclubs often have a cover charge, but some venues will admit you free before a certain time in the evening or on weeknights.

Most venues serve alcohol, so shows are restricted to those at least 18 years of age. This is the usual case unless a gig is specified "all ages". It is advisable that people under 30 years old carry photo identification, such as a passport or driver's licence, because entry to some establishments is very strict. You are also not allowed to carry any kind of bottle into most nightclubs or other venues. Similarly, any cameras and recording devices are usually prohibited.

Dress codes vary, but generally shorts (on men) and flip flops are not welcome. Wear thin layers, which you can remove when you get hot, instead of a coat, and avoid carrying a big bag, because many venues do not have a cloakroom.

ROCK, POP AND HIP HOP

Pop's big names and famous rock groups perform at the **Sydney Entertainment Centre**, **Acer Arena**, **Hordern Pavilion** and sports grounds such as the Sydney Football Stadium at **Sydney Olympic Park** *(see p127)* in Homebush Bay. More intimate locations include the **State Theatre** *(see p90)*, **Enmore Theatre** and Sydney's best venue, **The Metro Theatre**. Hip hop acts usually play in rock venues rather than in nightclubs. You are almost as likely to find a crew rapping or as a band strumming and drumming at the Metro Theatre, the **Gaelic Club** or the **@Newtown**. It is not unusual to catch a punk, garage or electro-folk band at **Spectrum** or the **Annandale Hotel** on Parramatta Road.

Pub rock is a constantly changing scene in Sydney. Weekly listings appear on Fridays in the "Metro" section of the *Sydney Morning Herald* and in the street press *(see p138)*. Music stores are also full of flyers for gigs at the Metro Theatre and Gaelic Club, where international and Australian acts perform every week. These shows usually sell out very quickly.

JAZZ, FOLK AND BLUES

For many years, the first port of call for any jazz, funk, groove or folk enthusiast has been **The Basement**. Visiting luminaries play some nights, talented but struggling local musicians others, and the line-ups now also include increasingly popular world music and hip-hop bands. **505**, in Surry Hills, features live jazz, reggae, gypsy, latin, funk and folk styles Monday to Saturday. Experimental jazz is offered on Fridays and Saturdays at the **Seymour Theatre Centre** *(see p141)*. **The Vanguard**, a newer venue, also offers dinner and show deals, as well as show-only tickets, and has been drawing an excellent roster of jazz, blues and roots talent. Annandale's **Empire Hotel** is Sydney's official home of the blues, while the **Cat & Fiddle Hotel** in Balmain is the place to go for acoustic music and folk.

HOUSE, BREAKBEATS AND TECHNO

Sydney's long-time super club, **Home Sydney** in Cockle Bay, features three levels and a gargantuan sound system. Friday night is the time to go, as the DJs present a pulsating mix of house, trance, drum and bass and breakbeats. A mainstream crowd flocks to the nearby **Bungalow 8** on King Street Wharf. Once the sun has set, house DJs turn the place into a club. At the swank **Tank** on Bridge Lane, the emphasis is on pure house music and the decor is a throwback to Studio 54 in New York. The dance floor at the **Iguana** bar in Potts Point is packed until late every night.

For something a little more hip, try **Candy's Apartment** on Bayswater Road, or head a few doors down the street to **Hugo's Lounge**, three-time Nightclub of the Year winner. For the best of House, presented by Paul Strange, go to the **Arthouse Hotel** on Saturday nights. It is located in the 1836, heritage School of Arts Building next to the Hilton Hotel. Down the road, **Q Bar**, one of many bars in the Exchange Hotel on Oxford Street, Darlinghurst, has arcade games for when you need a breather from strutting your stuff. Or sample the low-ceilinged **Chinese Laundry** on Sussex Street, which you'll find tucked under the gentrified pub, Slip Inn.

GAY AND LESBIAN PUBS AND CLUBS

Sunday night is the big night for many of Sydney's gay community, although there is plenty of action throughout the week. A number of venues have a gay or lesbian night on one night of the week and attract a mainstream crowd on the other nights. Wednesday is lesbian night at the **Bank Hotel** in Newtown. **The Polo Lounge**, situated on the top floor of the Oxford Hotel, has great views of the city's skyline. Catch live music at the first-floor supper club.

ARQ on Flinders Street is the largest of the gay clubs, with pounding commercial house music. The main dance floor is overlooked by a mezzanine for watching the writhing mass of bodies below. **Midnight Shift** on Oxford Street is for men only, and **Stonewall** plays camp anthems and is patronized mostly by men and their straight female friends. At the **Flinders Hotel**, one of Sydney's longest running gay venues, the entertainment depends on which night of the week you are visiting.

The **Colombian** is the best of the Oxford Street bars, with a mock Central American jungle and large windows that open out to the street. The **Oxford Hotel** and its upper-level cocktail bars are popular too. The **Imperial Hotel** has drag shows on most nights of the week. The **Oxford Art Factory** in Darlinghurst has live music as well as burlesque and cabaret evenings.

DIRECTORY

ROCK, POP AND HIP HOP

Acer Arena
Homebush Bay.
Tel 8765 4321.
www.acerarena.com.au

Annandale Hotel
17–19 Parramatta Rd,
Annandale.
Tel 9550 1078. **www.**
annandalehotel.com

Enmore Theatre
130 Enmore Rd,
Newtown.
Tel 9550 3666.
www.
enmoretheatre.com.au

Gaelic Club
64 Devonshire St, Surry
Hills. *Tel 9211 1687.*
www.thegaelic.com

Hordern Pavilion
Driver Ave, Moore Park.
Map 5 C5.
Tel 9921 5333.
www.playbillvenues.com

The Metro Theatre
624 George St.
Map 4 E3.
Tel 9550 3666.
www.metrotheatre.com.au

Moshtix
Tel 9209 4614.
www.moshtix.com.au

@Newtown
52 Enmore Rd, Newtown.
Tel 9557 5044.
www.atnewtown.com.au

Spectrum
34 Oxford St,
Darlinghurst. **Map** 4 F4.
www.pashpresents.com

State Theatre
49 Market St.
Map 1 B5.
Tel 9373 6852.
www.statetheatre.com.au

Sydney Entertainment Centre
Harbour St, Haymarket.
Map 4 D4.
Tel 9320 4200.
www.sydentcent.com.au

Sydney Olympic Park
Homebush Bay.
Tel 9714 7888.
www.sydneyolympicpark.
nsw.gov.au

JAZZ, FOLK AND BLUES

505
280 Cleveland St,
Surry Hills.
www.venue505.com

The Basement
29 Reiby Place.
Map 1 B3.
Tel 9251 2797. **www.**
thebasement.com.au

Cat & Fiddle Hotel
456 Darling St, Balmain.
Tel 9810 7931.
www.thecatandfiddle.net

Empire Hotel
Cnr Johnston St &
Paramatta Rd, Annandale.
Tel 9557 1701.
www.empirelive.com.au

Seymour Theatre Centre
Cnr Cleveland St & City
Rd, Chippendale.
Tel 9351 7940.

The Vanguard
42 King St, Newtown.
Tel 9557 7992. **www.**
thevanguard.com.au

HOUSE, BREAKBEATS AND TECHNO

The Arthouse Hotel
275 Pitt St. **Map** 1 B5.
Tel 9284 1200.

Bungalow 8
The Promenade,
King St Wharf.
Tel 9299 4660.

Candy's Apartment
22 Bayswater Rd,
Kings Cross. **Map** 5 B1.
Tel 9380 5600.
www.candys.com.au

Chinese Laundry
Slip Inn 111 Sussex St.
Map 1 A3. *Tel 8295 9950.*

Home Sydney
101 Cockle Bay Wharf,
Darling Harbour.
Map 4 D2.
Tel 9266 0600.
http://homesydney.com

Hugo's Lounge
Level 1, 33 Bayswater Rd,
Kings Cross. **Map** 5 B1.
Tel 9357 3399.

Iguana
13–15 Kellett St, Potts
Point. *Tel 9357 2609.*

Q Bar at the Exchange Hotel
Level 2, 44 Oxford St,
Darlinghurst. **Map** 4 F4.
Tel 9360 1375.

Tank
3 Bridge Lane.
Tel 9240 3000.

GAY AND LESBIAN CLUBS AND PUBS

ARQ
16 Flinders St, Taylor
Square. **Map** 5 A2.
Tel 9380 8700.

Bank Hotel
324 King St, Newtown.
Tel 8568 1988.

Colombian
Cnr Oxford and Crown
Sts, Surfs Hills. **Map** 5 A2.
Tel 9360 2151.

The Flinders Hotel
63 Flinders St,
Darlinghurst. **Map** 5 A2.
Tel 9356 3622.

Imperial Hotel
35 Erskineville Rd,
Erskineville.
Tel 9519 9899.

Midnight Shift
85 Oxford St, Darlinghurst.
Map 5 A2.
Tel 9360 4319.

Oxford Art Factory
38–46 Oxford St,
Darlinghurst. **Map** 5 A2.
Tel 9332 3711.

Oxford Hotel
134 Oxford St,
Darlinghurst. **Map** 5 A2.
Tel 9331 3467.

The Polo Lounge and Supper Club
134 Oxford St,
Darlinghurst. **Map** 5 A2.
Tel 9331 3467.

Stonewall
175 Oxford St,
Darlinghurst. **Map** 5 A2.
Tel 9360 1963.

Sydney's Beaches

Being a city built around the water, it is no wonder that many of Sydney's recreational activities involve the sand, sea and sun. There are many harbour and surf beaches in Sydney, most of them accessible by bus (*see p129*). Even if you're not a swimmer, the beaches offer a chance to get away from it all for a day or weekend and enjoy the fresh air and relaxed way of life.

Scuba diving at Gordons Bay

SWIMMING

You can swim at either harbour or ocean beaches. Harbour beaches are generally smaller and sheltered. Popular ones are Camp Cove, Shark Bay and Balmoral Beach.

At the ocean beaches, surf lifesavers in their red and yellow or blue caps are on duty. Swimming rules are strongly enforced. Surf lifesaving carnivals are held throughout the summer. Call **Surf Life Saving NSW** for a calendar. Well-patrolled, safer surf beaches include Bondi, Manly and Coogee.

The beaches can become polluted, especially after heavy rain. The **Beach Watch and Harbour Watch Info Line** provides information.

SURFING

Surfing is more a way of life than a leisure activity for some Sydneysiders. If you're a beginner, try Bondi, Bronte, Palm Beach or Collaroy.

Two of the best surf beaches are Maroubra and Narrabeen. Bear in mind that local surfers know one another well and do not take kindly to "intruders" who drop in on their waves. To hire a surfboard, try Bondi Surf Co on Campbell Parade, Bondi Beach, or Aloha Surf on Pittwater Road, Manly. If you would like to learn, there are two schools: **Manly Surf School** and **Lets Go Surfing** at Bondi Beach. They also hire out boards and wetsuits.

WINDSURFING AND SAILING

There are locations around Sydney suitable for every level of windsurfer. Boards can be hired from **Balmoral Windsurfing, Sailing & Kayaking School & Hire**.

Good spots include Palm Beach, Narrabeen Lakes, La Perouse, Brighton-Le-Sands and Kurnell Point (for beginner and intermediate boarders) and Long Reef Beach, Palm Beach and Collaroy (for more experienced boarders).

One of the best ways to see the harbour is while sailing. A sailing boat, including a skipper, can be hired for the afternoon from the **East Sail** sailing club. The sailing club has two-day courses and also hires out sailing boats and motor cruisers to experienced sailors.

SCUBA DIVING

The great barrier reef it may not be, but there are some excellent dive spots around Sydney, especially in winter when the water is clear, if a little cold. Favoured spots are Shelly Beach, Gordons Bay and Camp Cove.

Pro Dive Coogee offers a complete range of courses, escorted dives, introductory dives for beginners, and hire equipment. **Dive Centre Manly** also runs courses, hires equipment and conducts boat dives seven days a week.

DIRECTORY

Balmoral Windsurfing and Kitesurfing School
Balmoral Sailing Club, Balmoral Beach. *Tel* 9960 5344.
www.sailboard.net.au

Beach Watch Info Line
Tel 1800 036 677.

Dive Centre Manly
10 Belgrave St, Manly. *Tel* 9977 4355. www.divesydney.com.au
Also at Bondi and City.

East Sail
d'Albora Marinas, New Beach Rd, Rushcutters Bay. *Tel* 9327 1166.
www.eastsail.com.au

Lets Go Surfing
128 Ramsgate Ave, North Bondi. *Tel* 9365 1800.
www.letsgosurfing.com.au

Manly Surf School
North Steyne Rd, Manly.
Tel 9977 6977.
www.manlysurfschool.com

Pro Dive Coogee
27 Alfreda St, Coogee.
Tel 1 800 820 820.
www.prodive.com

Surf Life Saving NSW
Tel 9471 8000.
www.surflifesaving.com.au

Rock baths and surf lifesaving club at Coogee Beach

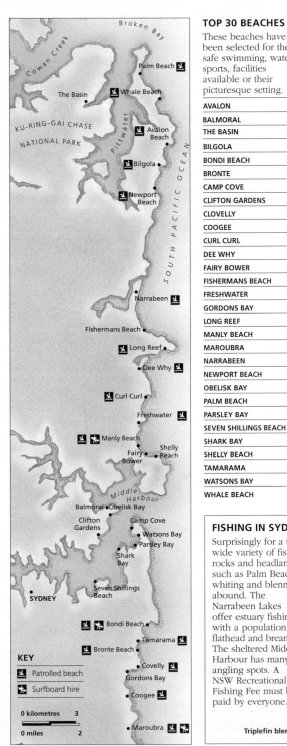

TOP 30 BEACHES

These beaches have been selected for their safe swimming, water sports, facilities available or their picturesque setting.

	SWIMMING POOL	SURFING	WINDSURFING	FISHING	SCUBA DIVING	PICNIC/BARBECUE	RESTAURANT/CAFE
AVALON	★	★	★	★		★	
BALMORAL	★		★	★	★	★	★
THE BASIN	★					★	
BILGOLA							
BONDI BEACH	★	★		★	★	★	★
BRONTE	★	★		★	★	★	★
CAMP COVE					★		
CLIFTON GARDENS	★		★	★	★	★	
CLOVELLY				★	★	★	★
COOGEE	★		★	★	★	★	★
CURL CURL	★	★		★			
DEE WHY	★	★		★	★	★	★
FAIRY BOWER					★		
FISHERMANS BEACH		★	★	★	★		
FRESHWATER	★	★		★	★	★	
GORDONS BAY					★	★	
LONG REEF		★	★	★	★		
MANLY BEACH	★	★			★	★	★
MAROUBRA		★	★	★	★	★	★
NARRABEEN	★	★		★		★	
NEWPORT BEACH	★	★	★	★		★	
OBELISK BAY							
PALM BEACH	★	★	★	★		★	★
PARSLEY BAY						★	
SEVEN SHILLINGS BEACH	★					★	
SHARK BAY	★					★	★
SHELLY BEACH					★	★	★
TAMARAMA		★	★	★	★	★	★
WATSONS BAY	★				★		★
WHALE BEACH	★	★	★	★		★	★

KEY

![Patrolled beach] Patrolled beach

![Surfboard hire] Surfboard hire

0 kilometres   3

0 miles   2

FISHING IN SYDNEY

Surprisingly for a thriving city port, there is a wide variety of fish to be caught. From the rocks and headlands of the northern beaches, such as Palm Beach and Bilgola, tuna, whiting and blenny abound. The Narrabeen Lakes offer estuary fishing, with a population of flathead and bream. The sheltered Middle Harbour has many angling spots. A NSW Recreational Fishing Fee must be paid by everyone.

Triplefin blenny

SPORTING SYDNEY

Throughout Australia sport is a way of life and Sydney is no exception. On any day you'll see locals on golf courses at dawn, running on the streets keeping fit, or having a quick set of tennis after work. At weekends, during summer and winter, there is no end to the variety of sports you can watch. Thousands gather at the Sydney Football Stadium and Sydney Cricket Ground every weekend while, for those who cannot make it, sport reigns supreme on weekend television.

CRICKET

During the summer months Test cricket and one-day internationals are played at the Sydney Cricket Ground (SCG). Tickets for weekday sessions of the Tests can often be bought at the gate, although it is advisable to book well in advance (through **Ticketek**) for weekend sessions of Test matches and for all the one-day international matches.

Australia versus the All Blacks

RUGBY LEAGUE AND RUGBY UNION

The popularity of rugby league knows no bounds in Sydney. This is what people refer to as "the footie". There are three major competition levels: local, State of Origin – which matches Queensland against New South Wales – and Tests. The "local" competition fields teams from all over Sydney as well as Newcastle, Canberra, Perth, Brisbane, Melbourne, the Gold Coast, Far North Queensland and Auckland, New Zealand.

These matches are held all over Sydney, but the Telstra Stadium at Sydney Olympic Park is by far the biggest venue. Tickets for State of Origin and Test matches often sell out immediately. Call Ticketek to check availability.

Rugby union is the second most popular football code. Again, matches at Test level sell out very quickly. For some premium trans-Tasman rivalry, catch a Test match between Australia's "Wallabies" and the New Zealand "All Blacks". Phone Ticketek for details.

GOLF AND TENNIS

Golf enthusiasts need not do without their round of golf. There are many courses throughout Sydney where visitors are welcome at all times. These include **Moore Park**, **St Michael's** and **Warringah** golf courses. It is sensible to phone beforehand for a booking, especially at weekends.

Tennis is another favoured sport. Courts available for hire can be found all over Sydney. Many centres also have floodlit courts available for night time. Try **Cooper Park** or **Parkland Sports** Centre.

Playing golf at Moore Park, one of Sydney's public courses

AUSTRALIAN RULES FOOTBALL

Although not as popular as in Melbourne, "Aussie Rules" has a strong following in Sydney. The local team, the Sydney Swans, plays its home games at the Sydney Cricket Ground during the season. Check a local paper for details.

Rivalry between the Sydney supporters and their Melbourne counterparts is always strong. Busloads of diehard fans from the south arrive to cheer on their teams. Tickets can usually be bought at the ground on the day of the game.

BASKETBALL

Basketball has grown in popularity as both a spectator and recreational sport in recent years. Sydney has male and female teams competing in the National Basketball League. The games, held at the Sydney Entertainment

One-day cricket match between Australia and the West Indies, SCG

Aerial view of the Sydney Football Stadium at Moore Park

Centre, Haymarket, have much of the pizzazz, colour and excitement of American basketball. Tickets can be purchased by phone or on the internet from Ticketek.

CYCLING AND INLINE SKATING

Sydney boasts excellent, safe locations for the whole family to go cycling. One of the most frequented is Centennial Park *(see p128)*. You can hire bicycles and safety helmets from **Centennial Park Cycles** and also from **Inner City Cycles** in Glebe, where you can hire out equipment by the day or by the week.

Another popular pastime in summer is inline skating. **Rollerblading.com** runs tours starting at Milsons Point to all parts of Sydney. If you are a little unsteady on your feet, they offer private and group lessons. Or keep both feet firmly on the ground and watch skateboarders and inline skaters practising their moves at the ramps at Bondi Beach *(see p145)*.

Inline skaters enjoying a summer evening on the city's streets

HORSE RIDING

For a leisurely ride, head to Centennial Park or contact the **Centennial Parklands Equestrian Centre**. They will give you details of the four riding schools that operate in the park. **Samarai Park Riding School** conducts trail rides through Ku-ring-gai Chase National Park *(see p126)*.

Further afield, you can enjoy the magnificent scenery of the Blue Mountains *(see pp170–71)* on horseback. The **Megalong Australian Heritage Centre** has trail rides from one hour to an overnight ride. All levels of experience are catered for.

Horse riding in one of the parks surrounding the city centre

ADVENTURE SPORTS

Sydney offers a wide range of adventure sports for those seeking a more active and thrill-filled time. You can participate in guided bush-walking, mountain biking, canyoning, rock climbing and abseiling expeditions in the nearby Blue Mountains National Park. The **Blue Mountains Adventure Company** runs one-day or multi-day courses and trips for all standards of adventurer.

DIRECTORY

Blue Mountains Adventure Company
84a Bathurst Rd, Katoomba.
Tel 4782 1271.
www.bmac.com.au

Centennial Park Cycles
50 Clovelly Rd, Randwick.
Tel 9398 5027.
www.cyclehire.com.au

Centennial Parklands Equestrian Centre
Cnr Lang & Cook Rds, Moore Park. **Map** 5 D5.
Tel 9332 2809.
www.cpequestrian.com.au

Cooper Park Tennis Courts
Off Suttie Rd, Double Bay.
Tel 9389 3100.

Inner City Cycles
151 Glebe Point Road, Glebe.
Map 3 B5. *Tel* 9660 6605.

Megalong Australian Heritage Centre
Megalong Valley Rd, Megalong Valley. *Tel* 4787 8188.

Moore Park Golf Club
Cnr Cleveland St & Anzac Parade, Moore Park. **Map** 5 B5.
Tel 9663 1064.

Parkland Sports
Lang Rd, Moore Park.
Tel 9662 7033.

Rollerblading.com
Tel 0411 872 022.
www.rollerblading.com.au/
rollerbladingsydney

St Michael's Golf Club
Jennifer St, Little Bay.
Tel 9311 0068.
www.stmichaelsgolf.com.au

Samarai Park Riding School
90 Booralie Rd, Terrey Hills.
Tel 9450 1745.

Ticketek
Tel 13 28 49.
www.ticketek.com.au

Warringah Golf Club
397 Condamine St, North Manly.
Tel 9905 4028.

SYDNEY STREET FINDER

The page grid superimposed on the *Area by Area* map below shows which parts of Sydney are covered in this *Street Finder*. Map references given for all sights, shops and entertainment venues described in this guide refer to the maps in this section. All the major sights are clearly marked so they are easy to locate. The key,

set out below, indicates the scale of the maps and shows what other features are marked on them, including railway stations, bus terminals, ferry boarding points, taxi ranks, emergency services, post offices and tourist information centres. Map references are also given for hotels *(see pp478–517)* and restaurants *(see pp524–63)*.

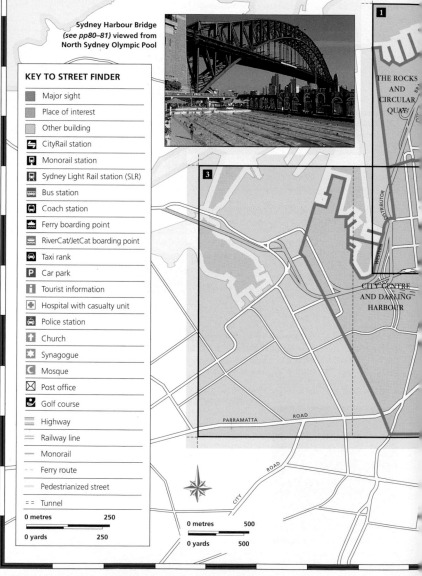

Sydney Harbour Bridge
(see pp80–81) viewed from
North Sydney Olympic Pool

KEY TO STREET FINDER

■	Major sight
■	Place of interest
□	Other building
🚉	CityRail station
Ⓜ	Monorail station
Ⓡ	Sydney Light Rail station (SLR)
🚌	Bus station
🚍	Coach station
⛴	Ferry boarding point
〰	RiverCat/JetCat boarding point
🚕	Taxi rank
P	Car park
ℹ	Tourist information
✚	Hospital with casualty unit
🚔	Police station
✝	Church
✡	Synagogue
Ⓒ	Mosque
✉	Post office
⛳	Golf course
═	Highway
⚌	Railway line
—	Monorail
--	Ferry route
▬	Pedestrianized street
═ ═	Tunnel

0 metres	250
0 yards	250

0 metres	500
0 yards	500

THE ROCKS AND CIRCULAR QUAY

CITY CENTRE AND DARLING HARBOUR

PARRAMATTA   ROAD

ROAD

CITY

Sundial in the Royal Botanic Gardens *(see pp106–7)*

Statues on the Art Deco Anzac
Memorial in Hyde Park *(see p93)*

Enjoying coffee outside a café in
Darlinghurst *(see pp526–7)*

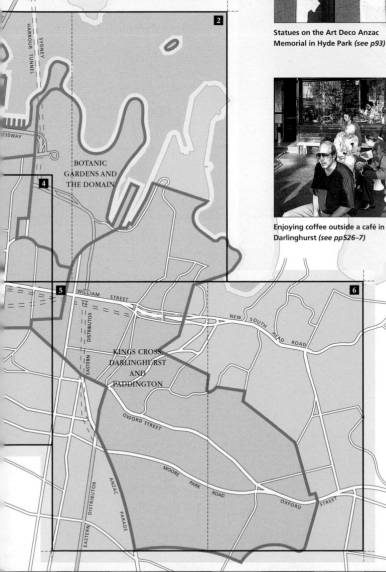

BOTANIC
GARDENS AND
THE DOMAIN

KINGS CROSS,
DARLINGHURST
AND
PADDINGTON

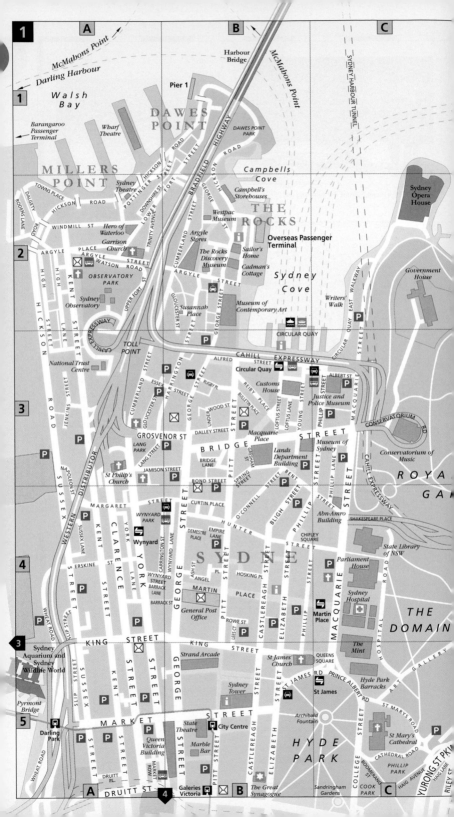

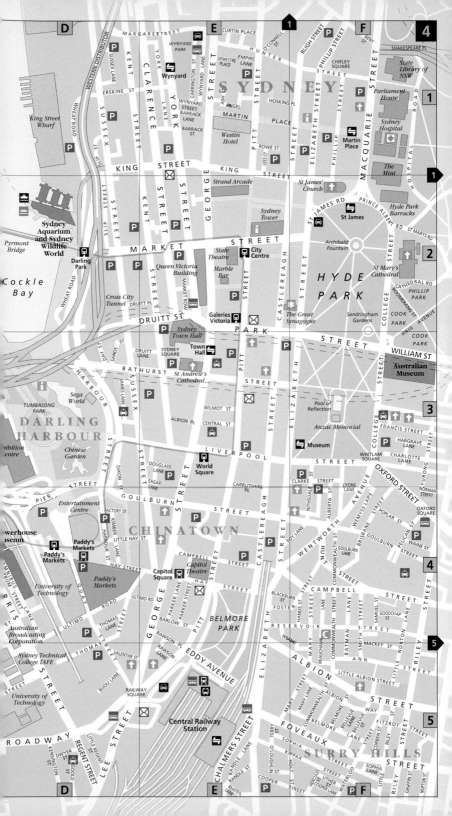

NEW SOUTH
WALES AND ACT

New South Wales and ACT at a Glance

This southeastern corner of the continent, around Sydney Cove, was the site of the first European settlement in the 18th century and today it is the most densely populated and varied region in Australia, and home to its largest city, Sydney *(see pp60–155)*, as well as Canberra, the nation's capital. It also contains the country's highest mountain, Mount Kosciuszko. In the east there are farmlands and vineyards, the Blue Mountains and the ski resorts of the Snowy Mountains. To the west is a desert landscape. The coastline is tropically warm in the north, cooler in the south.

Broken Hill *is one of the few 19th-century mining towns in Australia that continues to survive on its mineral resources* (see p181). *It is also the location of the Royal Flying Doctor Service headquarters, and tours detailing the history of the service are popular with visitors.*

**THE BLUE
MOUNTAINS AND
BEYOND**
(see pp164–81)

Bourke's *major attraction is its remote location. Irrigated by the Darling River, the town is also a successful agricultural centre* (see p181). *A lift-up span bridge crosses the river.*

Mount Kosciuszko, *in Kosciuszko National Park, is Australia's highest mountain. Panoramic views of the Snowy Mountains can be found at the Mount Kosciuszko Lookout, accessible via a walking trail or a chairlift* (see pp160–61).

◁ **The Breadknife rock formation in the Warrumbungle National Park north of Dubbo, New South Wales**

Tenterfield's School of Arts *building has a proud history as the site of Sir Henry Parkes' Federation speech in 1889, which was followed, 12 years later, by the founding of the Commonwealth of Australia (see p56). A museum in the town details the event.*

Tamworth *is the heart of Australian country music. The Golden Guitar Hall, fronted by a model guitar, holds concerts (see p177).*

The Three Sisters *rock formation is the most famous sight within the Blue Mountains National Park. At night it is floodlit for a spectacular view (see pp170–71).*

0 kilometres 100

0 miles 100

**CANBERRA
AND ACT**
(see pp190–207)

Windsor *is one of the best preserved 19th-century towns in the state. The Macquarie Arms Hotel is considered to be the oldest operational hotel in Australia (see p168).*

**THE SOUTH
COAST AND
SNOWY
MOUNTAINS**
(see pp182–9)

Canberra *was designed as the new national capital in 1912 by architect Walter Burley Griffin. Anzac Parade offers fine views of New Parliament House, atop Capital Hill (see pp194–5).*

The Snowy Mountains

The Snowy Mountains stretch 500 km (310 miles) from Canberra to Victoria. Formed more than 250 million years ago, they include Australia's highest mountain, Mount Kosciuszko, and the country's only glacial lakes. In summer, wildflowers carpet the meadows; in winter, snow gums bend beneath the cold winds. The Snowy Mountains are preserved within the Kosciuszko National Park and are also home to two of Australia's largest ski resorts, Thredbo and Perisher. The Snowy Mountains Scheme dammed four rivers to supply power to much of inland eastern Australia *(see p183)*.

The Snowy Mountains *are home to the Kosciuszko National Park which was declared a World Biosphere Reserve by UNESCO in 1997.*

The Snowy River *rises below Mount Kosciuszko and is now damned and diverted to provide hydroelectricity for Melbourne and Sydney as part of the Snowy Mountains Scheme.*

Blue Lake is a spectacular glacial lake, one of only a few in the country, which lies in an ice-carved basin 28 m (90 ft) deep.

Seaman's Hut, built in honour of a skier who perished here in 1928, has saved many lives during fierce blizzards.

The Alpine Way offers a spectacular drive through the mountains, best taken in spring or summer, via the Thredbo River Valley.

Geehi River

Snowy River

Perisher
Valley •

MOUNT KOSCIUSZKO
▲
2,228 m (7,310 ft)

Alpine Way

Thredbo

Dead Horse Gap is a striking pass named after a group of "brumbies" (wild horses) that perished in a snow drift here during the 19th century.

PROMINENT PEAKS OF THE SNOWY MOUNTAINS

Mount Kosciuszko is Australia's highest mountain, and may be approached by gentle walks across alpine meadows from Thredbo or from Charlottes Pass. Mount Townsend is only slightly lower but, with a more pronounced summit, is often mistaken for its higher and more famous neighbour.

Charlottes Pass *marks the start of the summit walk to Mount Kosciuszko. It was named after Charlotte Adams, who, in 1881, was the first European woman to climb the peak.*

| 0 kilometres | 5 |
| 0 miles | 5 |

KEY

▬	Major road
▭	Minor road
▪▪▪	Walking trail
⛷	Ski trail
⛺	Camp site
ℹ	Tourist information
※	Viewpoint

Downhill and cross-country skiing *and snow-boarding are popular in the Snowy Mountains between June and September.*

VISITORS' CHECKLIST

ℹ *Kosciusko Road, Jindabyne* (02) 6450 5600. **www**.snowy mountains.com.au **Perisher Valley www**.perisherblue.com.au **Charlotte Pass www**.charlotte pass.com.au **Yarrangobilly** 🛗 ☑ 🅿 ⭕ *9am–5pm daily.*

FLORA AND FAUNA

The Snowy Mountains are often harsh, windswept and barren, yet myriad flowers, trees and wildlife have evolved to survive all seasons. Almost all species here are unique to the alpine regions of Australia.

Silver snow daisies, *with their white petals and yellow centres, are the most spectacular of all the alpine flowers en masse.*

Mountain plum pine *is a natural bonsai tree, which grows slowly and at an angle. The pygmy possum feeds on its berries.*

Sphagnum moss *surrounds the springs, bogs and creeks in the highest regions, and helps to protect primitive alpine plants.*

Corroboree frogs *live only in the fragile sphagnum moss bogs of the region.*

Thredbo River was once known as the Crackenback River by stockmen who thought the ranges rising on either side of the valley were steep enough to break a man's back.

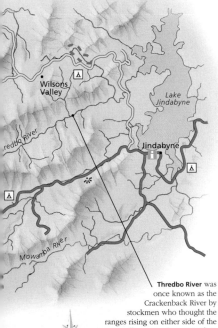

Mountain pygmy possums *live under the snow, high up in the mountains.*

The Yarrangobilly Caves, *about 130 km (80 miles) north of Thredbo, are a system of 70 limestone caves formed 750,000 years ago. They contain magnificent white columns, cascading frozen waterfalls and delicate underground pools.*

Brown and rainbow trout, *both introduced species, thrive in the cool mountain streams.*

Wines of New South Wales and ACT

New South Wales and ACT were the cradle of Australian wines. A small consignment of vines was on board the First Fleet when it landed at Sydney Cove in January 1788 *(see pp50–51)*, and this early hope was fulfilled in the steady development of a successful wine industry. New South Wales is now the home of many fine wineries with an international reputation. The state is currently in the vanguard of wine industry expansion, planting new vineyards and developing established districts to meet steadily rising domestic and export demand.

Rosemount Chardonnay

LOCATOR MAP

☐ *New South Wales wine regions*

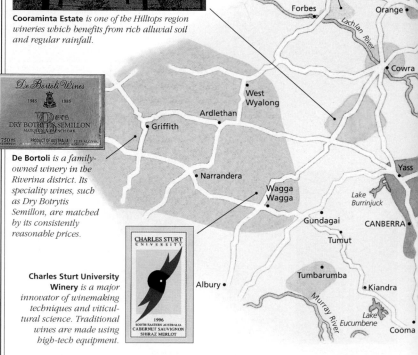

Sand Hills Vineyard *in the Lachlan Valley near Forbes produces both traditional and modern wines. Shiraz reds along with classic dry whites, such as Chardonnay, are particularly good.*

Cooraminta Estate *is one of the Hilltops region wineries which benefits from rich alluvial soil and regular rainfall.*

De Bortoli *is a family-owned winery in the Riverina district. Its speciality wines, such as Dry Botrytis Semillon, are matched by its consistently reasonable prices.*

Charles Sturt University Winery *is a major innovator of winemaking techniques and viticultural science. Traditional wines are made using high-tech equipment.*

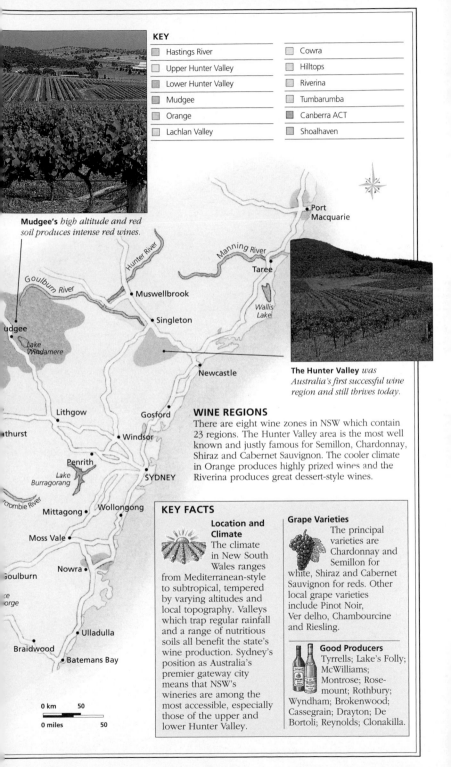

KEY

▨ Hastings River	▨ Cowra
▨ Upper Hunter Valley	▨ Hilltops
▨ Lower Hunter Valley	▨ Riverina
▨ Mudgee	▨ Tumbarumba
▨ Orange	▨ Canberra ACT
▨ Lachlan Valley	▨ Shoalhaven

Mudgee's *high altitude and red soil produces intense red wines.*

The Hunter Valley *was Australia's first successful wine region and still thrives today.*

WINE REGIONS

There are eight wine zones in NSW which contain 23 regions. The Hunter Valley area is the most well known and justly famous for Semillon, Chardonnay, Shiraz and Cabernet Sauvignon. The cooler climate in Orange produces highly prized wines and the Riverina produces great dessert-style wines.

KEY FACTS

Location and Climate

The climate in New South Wales ranges from Mediterranean-style to subtropical, tempered by varying altitudes and local topography. Valleys which trap regular rainfall and a range of nutritious soils all benefit the state's wine production. Sydney's position as Australia's premier gateway city means that NSW's wineries are among the most accessible, especially those of the upper and lower Hunter Valley.

Grape Varieties

The principal varieties are Chardonnay and Semillon for white, Shiraz and Cabernet Sauvignon for reds. Other local grape varieties include Pinot Noir, Ver delho, Chambourcine and Riesling.

Good Producers

Tyrrells; Lake's Folly; McWilliams; Montrose; Rosemount; Rothbury; Wyndham; Brokenwood; Cassegrain; Drayton; De Bortoli; Reynolds; Clonakilla.

0 km 50

0 miles 50

THE BLUE MOUNTAINS AND BEYOND

T*hink of northern New South Wales and vibrant colours spring to mind. There are the dark blues of the Blue Mountains; the blue-green seas of the north coast; the verdant green of the rainforests near the Queensland border; and the gold of the wheat fields. Finally, there are the reds and yellows of the desert in the far west.*

Ever since English explorer Captain James Cook claimed the eastern half of Australia as British territory in 1770 and named it New South Wales, Sydney and its surroundings have been at the forefront of Australian life.

On the outskirts of Sydney, at Windsor and Richmond, early convict settlements flourished into prosperous farming regions along the fertile Hawkesbury River. The barrier of the Blue Mountains was finally penetrated in 1812, marking the first spread of sheep and cattle squatters north, west and south onto the rich plains beyond. In the middle of the 19th century came the gold rush around Bathurst and Mudgee and up into the New England Tablelands, which led to the spread of roads and railways.

Following improved communications in the late 19th and early 20th centuries, northern New South Wales now contains more towns, a denser rural population and a more settled coastline than anywhere else in the country. Fortunately, all this development has not robbed the region of its natural beauty or assets. From the grand and daunting wilderness of the Blue Mountains to the blue waters and surf of Byron Bay, the easternmost point in Australia, the region remains easy to explore and a delight to the senses. It is most easily divided into three parts: the coastline and mild hinterland, including the famous Hunter Valley vineyards; the hills, plateaus and flats of the New England Tablelands and Western Plains with their rivers, national parks and thriving farming areas; and the remote, dusty Outback, west of the vast Great Dividing Range.

The combination of urban civilization, with all the amenities and attractions it offers, and the beautiful surrounding landscape, make this region a favourite holiday location with locals and tourists all year round.

Cape Byron lighthouse on Australia's most easterly point

◁ **The Three Sisters rock formation in the Blue Mountains National Park, seen from Echo Point**

Exploring the Blue Mountains and Beyond

Distances can be long in northern New South Wales so the extent of any exploration will depend on the time available. Within easy reach of Sydney are historic gold rush towns such as Windsor and those between Bathurst and Mudgee, the cool retreats of the Blue Mountains, and the gentle, green hills of the Hunter Valley and its vineyards. The north coast and its hinterland are best explored as part of a touring holiday sbetween Sydney and the Queensland capital, Brisbane, or as a short break to the beaches and fishing areas around Port Macquarie, Taree and Coffs Harbour.

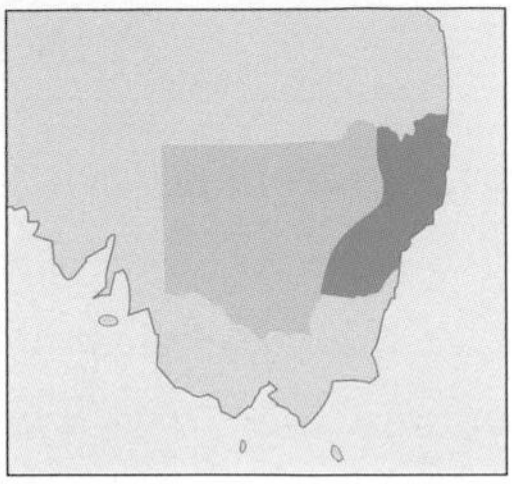

KEY

The Blue Mountains and Beyond

West of the Divide pp180–81

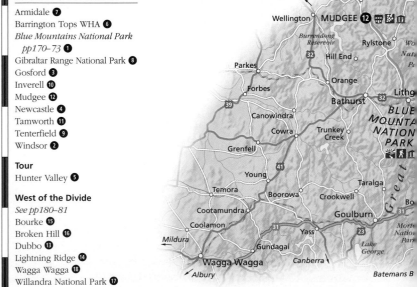

Impressive Three Sisters rocks in the Blue Mountains National Park

SIGHTS AT A GLANCE

Armidale [7]
Barrington Tops WHA [6]
Blue Mountains National Park pp170–73 [1]
Gibraltar Range National Park [8]
Gosford [3]
Inverell [10]
Mudgee [12]
Newcastle [4]
Tamworth [11]
Tenterfield [9]
Windsor [2]

Tour
Hunter Valley [5]

West of the Divide
See pp180–81
Bourke [15]
Broken Hill [16]
Dubbo [13]
Lightning Ridge [14]
Wagga Wagga [18]
Willandra National Park [17]

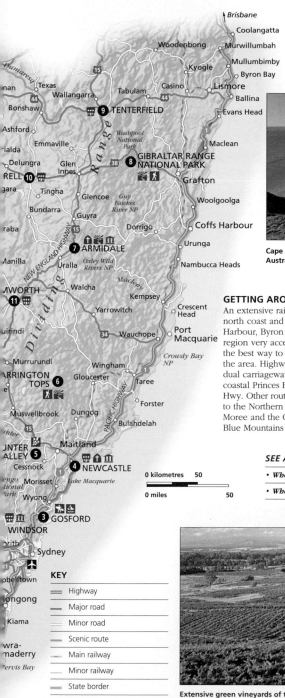

**Cape Byron, Byron Bay; mainland
Australia's easternmost point**

GETTING AROUND

An extensive rail and bus network up the
north coast and to major towns such as Coffs
Harbour, Byron Bay and Armidale makes this
region very accessible. However, a car is still
the best way to see the natural highlights of
the area. Highways are good, although rarely
dual carriageway, with the exception of the
coastal Princes Hwy and parts of the Hume
Hwy. Other routes are the New England Hwy
to the Northern Tablelands, the Newell Hwy to
Moree and the Great Western Hwy through the
Blue Mountains to Bathurst.

SEE ALSO

• **Where to Stay** pp482–3

• **Where to Eat** pp528–31

0 kilometres 50

0 miles 50

KEY

═══ Highway

─── Major road

···· Minor road

── Scenic route

┅┅ Main railway

─── Minor railway

═══ State border

Extensive green vineyards of the Hunter Valley

Blue Mountains National Park ❶

See pp170–73.

Windsor ❷

🏯 *1,850.* 🚉 🚌 📧 ℹ️ *Windsor St, Clarington (02) 4578 0233.* **www.**hawkesburytourism.com.au

Windsor was named by Governor Macquarie and this well-preserved colonial settlement is one of the five "Macquarie towns". Established on the banks of the Hawkesbury River in 1794, the town provided farmers with both fertile land and the convenience of river transport.

In the centre of town, St Matthew's Church, designed by Francis Greenway, is a fine example of Georgian colonial architecture and is considered to be his most successful work. Other buildings of interest include the Macquarie Arms, which claims to be Australia's oldest hotel, and the **Hawkesbury Museum**, set in a Georgian residence. The museum chronicles Windsor's early colonial history.

🏛 Hawkesbury Museum
8 Baker St, Windsor. **Tel** *(02) 4560 4655.* ⬜ *Wed–Mon (phone to check hours).* ⬤ *Good Fri, 25 Dec.* 📷

Environs
One of the other five "Macquarie towns" is Richmond, which lies 6 km (3.5 miles) west of Windsor. This attractive

St Matthew's Church in Windsor, designed by Francis Greenway

settlement was established five years earlier, in 1789. The farmstead of Mountainview, built in 1804, is one of the oldest surviving homes in the country.

Gosford ❸

🏯 *155,000.* 🚉 🚌 📧 ⛴ ℹ️ *1300 130 708, (02) 4343 4444.* **www.**visitcentralcoast.com.au

Gosford is the principal town of the popular holiday region known as the Central Coast, and provides a good base for touring the surrounding area. The rural settlements that once dotted this coastline have now evolved into one continuous beachside suburb, stretching as far south as Ku-ring-gai Chase National

A kangaroo at the Forest of Tranquility

Park *(see p126).* Gosford itself sits on the calm northern shore of Brisbane Waters, an excellent spot for sailing and other recreational activities. The nearby coastal beaches are renowned for their great surf, clear lagoons and long stretches of sand. The beaches here are so numerous that it is still possible to find a deserted spot in any season except high summer. The **Forest of Tranquility – Australian Rainforest Sanctuary** is located in a valley of subtropical and temperate rainforest. There are undercover picnic areas, play areas, barbecue facilities, a kiosk and Function Centre, in addition to 5 km (3 miles) of beautiful rainforest walks.

The **Australian Reptile Park** is home to many types of reptiles, including crocodiles, massive goannas, snakes and other species. The park offers wildlife shows such as crocodile feeding, venomous snake and spider milking and a picnic area where you can hand-feed the friendly kangaroos that share the grassy space.

Memorial Park, located in the town of The Entrance, is a short drive north of Gosford. See dozens of pelicans vying for fish from the human feeders at the free pelican feeding show that takes place at 3:30pm daily on the waterfront. The show also provides visitors with an

Entrance to the Australian Reptile Park

For hotels and restaurants in this region see pp482–3 and pp528–31

entertaining and educational commentary about the area's pelicans, birds and marine life.

🦋 Forest of Tranquility – Australian Rainforest Sanctuary
Ourimbah Creek Rd, Ourimbah.
Tel (02) 4362 1855. ⬜ 10am–5pm Sat & Sun. ⬤ 25 Dec. 📷 🚻 limited. www.forestoftranquility.com

🦋 Australian Reptile Park
Pacific Hwy, Somersby. *Tel* (02) 4340 1022. ⬜ 9am–5pm daily. ⬤ 25 Dec. 📷 🚻 www.reptile park.com.au

Environs
There are several national parks within a short distance of Gosford. Bouddi National Park is one of the most diverse reserves in the state, with sandstone cliffs, secluded beaches and coastal heaths blanketed in wildflowers. Also worth a visit is the Bulgandry Aboriginal site in Brisbane Waters National Park, which has rock engravings of human and animal figures dating back thousands of years.

Newcastle ❹

🏚 140,000. ✈ 🚇 🚌 🚢
ℹ 361 Hunter St, 1800 654 558.
www.visitnewcastle.com.au

One visitor to Newcastle, Australia's second-oldest city, remarked in the 1880s: "To my mind the whole town appeared to have woke up in fright at our arrival and to have no definite ideas of a rendezvous whereat to rally." The chaos to which he referred was largely the result of the city's reliance on coal mining and vast steel works. Building progressed only as profits rose with no planning.

Today this chaos only adds to Newcastle's charm. The city curls loosely around a splendid harbour and its main streets rise randomly up the surrounding hills. Industry is still the mainstay, but this does not detract from the city's quaint beauty. The main thoroughfare of Hunter Street has many buildings of diverse architectural styles. The Courthouse follows a style known as Late Free Classical; the

Italianate post office in Newcastle

Court Chambers are High Victorian; the post office was modelled on Palladio's Basilica in Venice and the town's cathedral, Christ Church, is an elaborate and impressive example of Victorian Gothic.

The modern **Newcastle Region Art Gallery** houses works by some of the country's most prominent 19th- and 20th-century artists, including the Newcastle-born William Dobell, Arthur Boyd and Brett Whiteley *(see pp34–5)*.

Queens Wharf is the main attraction of the harbour foreshore. It was redeveloped during the 1980s as part of a bicentennial project. There are splendid views from its promenade areas and outdoor

cafés. On the southern side of the harbour, Nobbys Lighthouse sits at the end of a long causeway; the vista back over old Newcastle makes the brief walk worthwhile.

Further on lies **Fort Stratchley**, built originally to repel the coal-seeking Russians in the 1880s. Despite constant surveillance, the fort did not open fire until the 1940s, when the Japanese shelled Newcastle during World War II. Good surfing beaches lie on either side of the harbour's entrance.

🏛 Newcastle Region Art Gallery
Cnr Darby & Laman sts.
Tel (02) 4974 5100. ⬜ 10am–5pm Tue–Sun. ⬤ 25 Dec, Good Fri. 🚻

🏰 Fort Scratchley
Nobbys Rd. *Tel* (02) 4929 3066.
Museum ⬜ 10:30am–4pm Tue–Fri.
Fort & Tunnels ⬜ noon–4pm Sat & Sun. ⬤ Good Fri, 25 Dec. 📷 🚻

Environs
Four times the size of Sydney Harbour *(see pp74–103)*, Lake Macquarie lies 20 km (12 miles) south of Newcastle. The lake's vast size facilitates nearly every kind of watersport imaginable. On the western shore, at Wangi Wangi, is Dobell House, once home to the renowned local artist, William Dobell.

FRANCIS GREENWAY, CONVICT ARCHITECT

Australian $10 notes once bore the portrait of the early colonial architect Francis Greenway. This was the only currency in the world to pay tribute to a convicted forger. Greenway was transported from England to Sydney in 1814 to serve a 14-year sentence for his crime. Under the patronage of Governor Lachlan Macquarie, who appointed him Civil Architect in 1816, Greenway designed more than 40 buildings, of which 11 still survive today. He received a full King's Pardon in 1819, but soon fell out of favour because he charged exorbitant fees for his architectural designs while still on a government salary. Greenway eventually died in poverty in 1837.

Francis Greenway (1777–1837)

Blue Mountains National Park ❶

Kookaburra

The landscape of the Blue Mountains was more than 250 million years in the making as sediments built up then were eroded, revealing sheer cliff faces and canyons. Home to Aboriginal communities for an estimated 14,000 years, the rugged terrain proved, at first, a formidable barrier to white settlers *(see p172)*, but since the 1870s it has been a popular holiday resort. The mountains get their name from the release of oil from the eucalyptus trees which causes a blue haze. Excellent drives and walking trails allow for easy exploration of the region.

The Cathedral of Ferns is an area of green foliage set amid streams, resembling tropical rainforest.

Mount Wilson
A basalt cap, the result of a now extinct volcano, provides the rich soil for the gardens of this attractive summer retreat.

The Zig Zag Railway is a steam train line between Sydney and Lithgow.

FLORA AND FAUNA IN THE BLUE MOUNTAINS

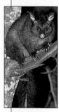

Possum

Many flora and fauna species which are unique to Australia can be easily seen in the Blue Mountains. For example, the superb lyrebird is a fan-tailed bird found in the forests, distinguishable by its high-pitched cry. The sassafras (*Doryphora sassafras*) tree is one of the species of the warm temperate rainforest and produces tiny white flowers. The shy brushtail possum seeks shelter in the woodlands by day and forages at night.

MUDGEE

Lithgow

Bells Line of Road

Bell

Hartley

Mount Victoria

Blackheath

Jenolan Caves Road

Hampton

JENOLAN STATE FOREST

Jenolan Caves
Nine spectacular limestone caves are open to the public; stalactites and stalagmites can be seen in beautiful and striking formations.

Katoomba is the largest town in the vicinity of the national park and has a full range of accommodation for tourists.

Mount Tomah Botanic Garden
Cool-climate species from around the
world are grown here, including
rhododendrons from the Himalayas.

Wentworth Falls
This waterfall is evidence of
a massive slip in the escarp-
ment. Pockets of rainforest
thrive along its edges.

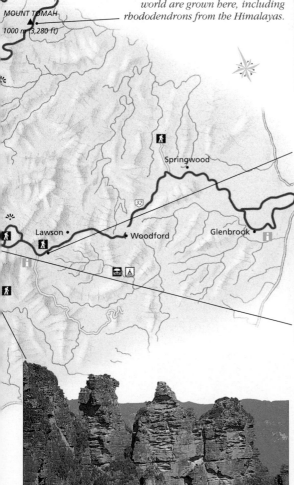

Leura
Elegant old residences such
as the Leura Mansion are
features of this pretty village.

KEY

▬▬	Major road
═	Minor road
🚶	Walking trail start-point
🄸	Tourist information
▪▪	Railway
🄰	Camp site
🏕	Picnic area
☀	Viewpoint

Three Sisters
Erosion has formed this spectacular rock formation.
Aboriginal legend has it that the rock is in fact three sisters,
imprisoned by their father to protect them from a bunyip.

Exploring the Blue Mountains

The Blue Mountains, reaching 1,100 m (3,600 ft) above sea level at their highest point, at first made the early colonists virtual prisoners of the Sydney Cove area. Many settlers were convinced that plains suitable for grazing and crops would be found beyond the mountains, but attempts to reach the imagined pastures repeatedly failed. In 1813, however, three farmers, Gregory Blaxland, William Lawson and William Charles Wentworth, set out on a well-planned mission, following the ridge between the Grose and Cox rivers, and emerged successfully on the western side of the mountains. The construction of roads and a railway made the mountains an increasingly attractive destination, and resorts and country homes were soon established. In 1959, the Blue Mountains National Park was gazetted, ensuring the preservation of the large tracts of remaining wilderness.

🏛 Norman Lindsay Gallery and Museum

14 Norman Lindsay Crescent, Faulconbridge. *Tel (02) 4751 1067.* ☐ *10am–4pm daily.* ● *25 Dec.* ☑ 🖼 🚻
www.normanlindsay.com.au

Norman Lindsay, one of Australia's most recognized artists, inspired considerable controversy during his lifetime with his sumptuous nudes and risqué novels. Born in 1879, he bought his mountain retreat in 1913 and set about producing an enormous body of work, much of which reflects his rejection of the moral and sexual restraints of his era.

His beautifully preserved home is now a gallery for his many paintings, cartoons, mythological garden sculptures and children's books. There is a whole room devoted to *The Magic Pudding*, a perennial favourite. There is also a re-creation of the interior of his original studio, and a peaceful garden set amid the mountain bushland.

Leura

🛈 Echo Point, Katoomba. *Tel 1300 653 408.* ☐ *first Sunday of the month.*

This small town on the Great Western Highway, with its European gardens and Art Deco architecture, recalls the elegance of life in the 1920s. Its secluded, tree-lined main street is a magnet for fine art galleries, cafés, shops and upmarket restaurants.

Six km (3.5 miles) from Leura, Everglades House is an Art Deco fantasy of curves, balconies and rose-pink walls. The Everglades gardens are considered classic examples of cool-climate design from the 1930s. They include a shaded alpine garden, a grotto pool, rhododendron stands, an arboretum and peacocks roaming around the grounds.

Some other gardens in the area are opened to the public during the Leura Garden Festival each October *(see p41)*

Visitors can get an overview of the surrounding landscape by taking the Cliff Drive to Katoomba. The lookout at Sublime Point, at the end of Sublime Point Road, also provides startling views across the Jamison Valley.

Scenic Skyway ride over the Blue Mountains from Katoomba

Katoomba

🛈 Echo Point, Katoomba. *Tel 1300 653 408.* www.visitbluemountains.com.au

Katoomba is the bustling tourism centre of the Blue Mountains and a good base from which to explore the mountains. However, it still manages to retain a veneer of its gracious former self, when it first attracted wealthy Sydneysiders in need of mountain air during the 1870s. The Paragon Café, with its dark-wood panelling and mirrored walls, is a reminder of these glory days, as are the imposing guesthouses with their fresh air and beautiful views across the Jamison Valley.

Within a few minutes' drive of the town are the region's most popular attractions. Echo Point is home to a large information centre and lookout, with views across to the imposing bulk of Mount Solitary and the most famous of icons, the Three Sisters *(see pp170–71)*. A short walk leads down to this striking rock formation, while further on the Giant Staircase – steps hewn out of the rock face –

Picturesque tree-lined Main Street in Leura

curls around its eastern side. Beyond the Staircase is the Leura Forest, which is a warm temperate rainforest.

On the western side of town the world's first glass-floor Skyway, 270 m (885 ft) above the valley floor, departs regularly. The Scenic Skyway traverses 205 m (670 ft) above the mountains, while the Scenic Railway offers a nerve-wracking plummet down a mountain gorge. Reputed to be the steepest rail track in the world, it was originally built in the 1880s to transport miners down to the valley's rich coal deposits.

Blackheath
🏠 4,100. 🚹 Govetts Leap Rd.
Tel (02) 4787 8877.
Blackheath is a small village that offers a quieter prospect than many of the busy mountain towns further east. The excellent standard of restaurants and accommodation available in the town often induces visitors to stay one or two nights here, rather than make the return to Sydney the same day. But the real draw of this area is the chance to explore the mist-enshrouded rifts and ravines of the beautiful Grose Valley.

The best place to start is the Heritage Centre, 3 km (2 miles) from Blackheath along Govetts Leap Road. Displays document the geological, Aboriginal and European histories of the region and local flora and fauna, while park officers are available to offer advice on the best walks in the area. Govetts Leap, with its heady views across Grose Valley, provides a point of orientation and is the starting place for a number of tracks. A clifftop track leads off in a southerly direction past Bridal Falls, the highest waterfalls in the Blue Mountains, and through stretches of exposed mountain heathland.

A steep and arduous 8-hour return trek into the valley leads to Blue Gum Forest. Walk through the dense covered forest with towering blue gum, Eucalyptus trees. The Grand Canyon is a destination only for the fit – this 5-hour walk, through

Eroded gorge in Grose Valley, near the town of Blackheath

deep gorges and sandstone canyons, sheds some light on the geological mysteries of the mountains.

🦇 Jenolan Caves
Jenolan Caves Rd. **Tel** (02) 6359 3311.
🕐 9am–5pm daily. 🅿️ 🚻 to small section of Orient and Chifley caves.
www.jenolancaves.org.au
The Jenolan Caves lie southwest of the mountain range. The Great Western Highway passes the grand old hotels of Mount Victoria before a south turn is taken at Hartley, the centre of the first grazing region established by Blaxland, Lawson and Wentworth from 1815 onwards. The southern stretch of the road, cutting across the escarpment of Kanimbla Valley, is one of the

Limestone formations in the Jenolan Caves

most scenic in the mountains. The Jenolan Caves were first discovered in 1838 and are remarkable for their complexity and accessibility. More than 300 subterranean chambers were formed in a limestone belt that was deposited more than 300 million years ago. The nine caves open to the public have a variety of delicate limestone formations, pools and rivers, including the ominously named Styx River.

🌿 Mount Tomah Botanic Gardens
Bells Line of Road. **Tel** (02) 4567 2154. 🕐 Mar–Sep: 10am–4pm daily, Oct–Feb: 10am–5pm daily.
🔵 25 Dec. 🅿️ 🚻
Mount Tomah lies along the Bells Line of Road, a quiet but increasingly popular route with tourists to the area.

Tomah takes its name from an indigenous word for "fern". The Botanic Gardens were set up as an annex to Sydney's Royal Botanic Gardens (see pp106–7) in order to house species that would not survive the coastal conditions. Of special interest are the southern hemisphere plants which developed in isolation once Australia broke away from Gondwanaland (see p23).

The overall layout of the gardens is a feat of engineering, and the views across Grose Valley are breathtaking.

A Tour of the Hunter Valley [5]

The first commercial vineyards in Australia were established on the fertile flats of the Hunter River in the 1830s. Originally a specialist area for fortified wines, Tyrell's helped shift the focus towards new, high-quality modern wines. February and March are busy months with the Harvest Festival taking place from March to May and the Jazz in the Vines festival in October. With beautiful scenery and 74 wineries, mostly open daily, the Hunter Valley is one of the top tourist destinations in New South Wales.

Lake's Folly [3]
Max Lake started this vineyard in the 1960s, successfully growing Cabernet Sauvignon grapes in the Hunter Valley for the first time since the 1900s.

Rothbury Estate [4]
Cask Hall was the vision of the late wine writer Len Evans. The vineyard's wines are now world famous, as are its concerts.

Tyrrells' Vineyards [5]
The Tyrrell family has been making wine here since 1858. An outdoor tasting area gives views over the vineyards.

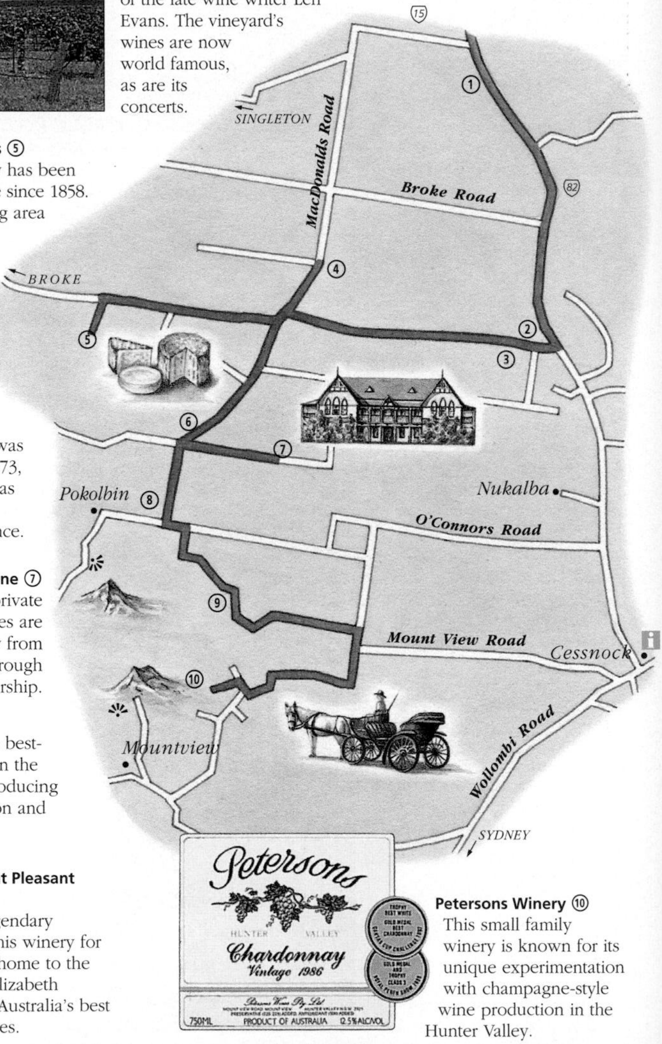
15
SINGLETON
MacDonalds Road
Broke Road
82
BROKE
Pokolbin
Nukalba
O'Connors Road
Mount View Road
Cessnock
Mountview
Wollombi Road
SYDNEY
Petersons
HUNTER VALLEY
Chardonnay
Vintage 1986
750ML PRODUCT OF AUSTRALIA 12.5%ALC/VOL

Brokenwood [6]
The first vintage was picked here in 1973, and this winery has attracted a loyal following ever since.

Tamburlaine [7]
A small private producer – wines are available only from the winery or through winery membership.

Lindemans [8]
This is one of the best-known wineries in the Hunter Valley, producing legendary Semillon and Shiraz wines.

McWilliams Mount Pleasant Winery [9]
Phil Ryan, the legendary winemaker, ran this winery for many years. It is home to the Mount Pleasant Elizabeth Semillon, one of Australia's best quality white wines.

Petersons Winery [10]
This small family winery is known for its unique experimentation with champagne-style wine production in the Hunter Valley.

Rothbury ①
An early morning champagne breakfast and hot-air balloon flight over the Hunter Valley from this town are a luxurious way to start a day touring the wineries.

The Hunter Valley Wine Society ②
This group organizes wine tastings from many local vineyards and offers excellent advice for the novice. Shiraz and Semillon are the two most recognizable Hunter Valley styles.

0 kilometres   5

0 miles   5

KEY

▬ Tour route

═ Other road

☆ Viewpoint

TIPS FOR DRIVERS

Tour length: 60 km (37 miles). While there are no limits on the numbers of wineries that can be visited, three or four in one day will give time to taste and discuss the wines leisurely. Don't forget Australia's strict drink-driving laws (see p589).

Starting point: Cessnock is the gateway to the Hunter Valley and is home to its major visitors' centre.

Stopping-off points: Apart from the picnic areas and restaurants at the wineries, Pokolbin has plenty of cafés, a general store and a bush picnic area. The Mount Bright lookout gives a panoramic view over the region.

Panoramic mountain view from Barrington Tops

Barrington Tops World Heritage Area ⑥

🚉 Gloucester. ℹ️ 27 Denison St, Gloucester (02) 6558 1408. ☐ daily. **www**.gloucester.org.au

Flanking the north of the Hunter Valley is the mountain range known as the Barringtons. One of the highest points in Australia, its high country, the "Barrington Tops", reaches 1,550 m (5,080 ft), and light snow is common in winter. The rugged mountains, cool-climate rainforest, gorges, cliffs and waterfalls make Barrington Tops a paradise for hikers, campers, birdwatchers and climbers. Its 280,000 ha (690,000 acres) of forest, with 1,000-year-old trees, are protected by the Barrington Tops National Park. The rainforest was declared a World Heritage Area in 1986 and a Wilderness Area in 1996 as part of the Central Eastern Rainforest Reserves *(see pp26–7).*

Barrington Tops has been a favourite weekend escape for Sydney-siders for more than 100 years. Tourist operators organize environmentally friendly 4WD trips into the heart of the wild forests, with camping along the Allyn River, hiking trails at Telegherry and Jerusalem Creek and swimming in the rock pool at Lady's Well.

Barrington Tops is best reached through Dungog or from Gloucester.

Spinning wheel from the Armidale Folk Museum

Armidale ⑦

🏚 22,000. ✈ 🚉 🚌 🚏 ℹ️ 82 Marsh St 1800 627 736. ☐ daily. **www**.armidaletourism.com.au

Lying in the heart of the New England Tablelands, Armidale is a sophisticated university city surrounded by some of the state's most magnificent national parks, while concerts, plays, films and lectures fill its many theatres, pubs and university halls.

Some 35 buildings in Armidale are classified by the National Trust, testament to the land booms of the 19th century, including the town hall, courthouse and St Peter's Anglican Cathedral. The **New England Regional Art Museum** holds the A$20 million Howard Hinton and Chandler Coventry collections, with many works by Australian artists, including Tom Roberts and Norman Lindsay *(see p34).* To the east of Armidale is the 90-ha (220-acre) **Oxley Wild Rivers National Park**, containing the 220-m (720-ft) high Wollomombi Gorge, one of the highest waterfalls in Australia.

🏛 **New England Regional Art Museum**
Kentucky St. **Tel** (02) 6772 5255.
☐ 10am–5pm Tue–Sun.
● 1 Jan, Good Fri, 25 Dec. 🖼 👍

🌿 **Oxley Wild Rivers National Park**
145 Miller St, Armidale. **Tel** (02) 6738 9100. ☐ Mon–Fri. 👍 limited.

Wilderness stream in Gibraltar Range National Park

Gibraltar Range National Park ❽

Gwydir Hwy. *Tel (02) 6732 5133.* ☐ daily. 🅿 only for camping and facilities. ♿ **www**. nationalparks.nsw.gov.au

Situated 70 km (43 miles) east of Glen Innes, Gibraltar Range National Park is known for its giant rocky tors towering 1,200 m (4,000 ft) above sea level, surrounded by heath and swamp land. The area is at its most beautiful in the summer, when wild-flowers such as waratahs and Christmas bells bloom. The park also has good walking trails and camping facilities.

Gibraltar Range National Park is linked to Washpool National Park by a 40-km (25-mile) World Heritage walk. Washpool has visitor facilities at Coombadjha Creek but wilderness walking is its main feature.

Glen Innes and its surround-ing villages of Glencoe, Ben Lomond and Shannon Vale are known as Australia's "Celtic Country". Settled by Scottish, Welsh, Irish and Corn-ish immigrants in 1852, the

area's heritage is celebrated by the annual Australian Celtic Festival *(see p42)*. The town's Standing Stones are a traditional monument to all Celtic settlers.

Sapphire mining remains a major industry. Public digging, known as "fossicking", for sapphires, topaz, garnet and beryl is still possible near the mining villages of Emmaville and Torrington. Glen Innes hosts a gem and mineral fair in September each year.

Tenterfield ❾

🏠 3,500. ✈ 🚌 🚏 **ℹ**157 Rouse St (02) 6736 1082.

The rural town of Tenter-field, to the north of the New England Tablelands, occupies a special place in Australian history. Often described as the "Birthplace of Our Nation", it was at the town's School of Arts building on 24 October 1889 that local politician and towering figure of 19th-century

Plaque celebrating Henry Parkes' speech

Australian politics, Sir Henry Parkes, made his historic "One Nation" speech. The address explained his vision of all the colonies in Australia uniting to form one country. Parkes' Tenterfield address led to a popular movement of support, resulting in Australian Federation on 1 January 1901 *(see p56)*. The School of Arts was the first building to be acquired by the New South Wales National Trust because of its political and historic importance.

Other historic buildings in this small town include the Victorian mansion Stannum House, the bluestone saddlers' shop (made famous in the song "Tenterfield Saddler"), and the restored courthouse with its glass ceiling.

Also not to be missed are Bald Rock and Boonoo Boonoo, which are about 40 km (25 miles) north of Tenter-field. Bald Rock is the second biggest monolith in Australia after Uluru *(see pp286–9)* and the largest exposed granite rock, dating back to the Lower Triassic period which was over 200 million years ago. It is 750 m (2,460 ft) long and approxi-mately 200 m (650 ft) high. It offers magnificent views of volcanic ranges to the east, Girraween National Park in Queensland to the north and Mount McKenzie to the south. Boonoo Boonoo Falls cascade 210 m (690 ft) into the gorge below, ideal for swimming, and surrounded by rainforest bathed in moisture from the falls.

Tenterfield's School of Arts building

For hotels and restaurants in this region see pp482–3 and pp528–31

Inverell ⓾

🏃 *11,000.* ☒ 🚌 🚌 ℹ️ *Water Towers Complex, Campbell St (02) 6728 8161.* **www**.inverell-online.com.au

Inverell is known as "Sapphire City" because so many of the world's sapphires are mined in the area. Many of the buildings in the main street were built during the 1880s mining boom and are well preserved. The **Inverell Pioneer Village** features buildings gathered from around the district and relocated to create this tourist theme town.

Just south of Inverell lies the mighty Copeton Dam. Whitewater rafting below the dam on the wild Gwydir River is an exhilarating experience.

🚗 **Inverell Pioneer Village**
Tingha Rd, Inverell. **Tel** (02) 6722 1717. ◯ 10am–4pm Tue–Sun. ● Good Fri, 25 Dec. 🏛️ &

Tamworth ⓫

🏃 *36,000.* ☒ 🚌 🚌 🚌 ℹ️ *cnr Murray & Peel sts (02) 6755 4300.* **www**.visittamworth.com

Tamworth is a thriving rural city, located at the centre of fertile agricultural plains. Yet despite its history, fine old buildings and claim to fame as the first Australian city with electric street lighting, it remains best known as Australia's country music capital.

Every January, thousands of country music fans and performers flock here for the ten-day Country Music Festival, which includes country music, blue grass, busking, bush ballads, harmonica playing and the Golden Guitar Awards *(see p41).* Reflecting the city's main interest there is the Tamworth Information Centre built in the shape of a horizontal guitar, the Country Music Gallery of Stars, where Australia's country music greats are immortalized in wax, the Roll of Renown dedicated to musicians who have made a major contribution to the industry and the Country Music Hands of Fame cornerstone.

Tamworth's other source of fame is as the equestrian centre of Australia. The Quarter Horse Association and Appaloosa Association are based here, and rodeos and show-jumping events are held here.

Mudgee ⓬

🏃 *8,500.* 🚌 🚌 *Lithgow.* ℹ️ *84 Market St (02) 6372 1020.* **www**.mudgee.org

Mudgee is a magnificent old rural town with gardens and grand buildings, many of which are protected by the National Trust.

Situated on the banks of the Cudgegong River, the town was first settled by William Lawson, who discovered its good grazing country in 1821. The settlement was surveyed and planned in 1824 by Robert Hoddle. The design was so successful that he copied Mudgee's grid layout 14 years later for the city of Melbourne *(see pp382–3).* Historic buildings not to be missed include the Regent Theatre on Church Street, the many churches, banks and civic buildings on Market Street,

Sheep grazing under a tree in the Mudgee region

the railway station and the restored West End Hotel that now houses the excellent Colonial Inn Museum.

Mudgee is also famous for its surrounding wineries and the Mudgee Wine Festival held each September *(see p40).* From the surrounding countryside come local gourmet foods such as yabbies, trout, lamb, peaches and asparagus.

Environs
During the 1850s and 1860s, gold was discovered to the south of Mudgee, bringing thousands of hopeful prospectors to the region *(see pp54–5).* The villages of Hill End, Hargraves, Windeyer and Sofala once had populations of more than 20,000 each, but became ghost towns once the boom was over. Hill End is the most famous of these and is now classed as a Living Historic Site with almost all of its buildings dating back to the 1870s. The creeks of Windeyer continued to yield alluvial gold until the 1930s. Panning for gold in the river is a popular tourist activity.

One of Australia's most famous writers, Henry Lawson, hailed from the region *(see p35),* and Gulgong, a quaint gold rush village famous for being depicted on the original A$10 note, contains the **Henry Lawson Centre**.

🏛️ **Henry Lawson Centre**
147 Mayne St, Gulgong. **Tel** (02) 6374 2049. ◯ 10am–3:30pm Wed–Sat, 10am–1pm Sun–Tue. ● Good Fri, 25 Dec. 🏛️

Tamworth Information Centre, fronted by a huge golden guitar

Northern New South Wales Coastline

The northern New South Wales coastline is known for its mix of natural beauty, mild climate and good resorts. Australia's most easterly mainland point, Byron Bay, is an attractive, up-market resort which is enhanced by its unspoiled landscape and outstanding beaches. Elsewhere, clean and isolated beaches directly abut rainforest, with some national parks and reserves holding World Heritage status *(see pp26–7)*. Sugar cane and bananas are commonly grown in the region.

Coffs Harbour *is one of the most popular tourist destinations in New South Wales. Surrounded by excellent beaches, there is also an attractive man-made harbour and a range of top-quality tourist facilities.*

Red Cliff Beach ④

🌊 🏄 🛟 🚻 ⛺

Adjacent to the beautiful Yuraygir National Park, Red Cliff is one of several sandy, isolated beaches in the immediate vicinity.

Moonee Beach ⑤

🌊 🏄 🛟 🚻 ⛺

A creek meandering through bush country to the ocean offers perfect opportunities for safe swimming, picnics and camping.

Urunga ⑥

🌊 🏄 🏊 🛟 🚻

Two rivers, the Bellingen and the Kalang, reach the ocean in this picturesque beach resort. Its safe waters make it a particularly popular holiday site for families.

Arakoon ⑨

🌊 🏄 🛟

This picturesque headland is part of a state recreation area. Nearby is Trial Bay Gaol, a progressive 19th-century prison that re-opened during World War I to house prisoners of war from various countries.

Third Headland Beach ⑦

🌊 🛟 🚻 ⛺

Like its neighbour Hungry Head Beach, 5 km (3 miles) north, Third Headland is a popular surfing beach with strong waves hitting the headland cliffs.

Grafton *is a quaint 19th-century rural town, with elegant streets and riverside walks. The town is best known for its abundance of jacaranda trees, whose striking purple blooms are celebrated in a festival each October* (see p41).

★ Crowdy Bay ⑫

🌊 🏄 🏊 🛟 🚻

Part of a national park, Crowdy Bay's lagoons, forests and swamps are abundant with native wildlife here. Coarse-fishing is a popular activity from the sea's edge.

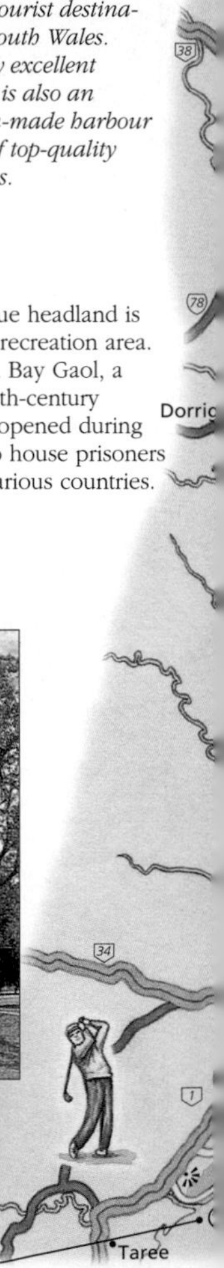
38
78
Dorrig
34
1
Taree
NEWCASTLE
SYDNEY

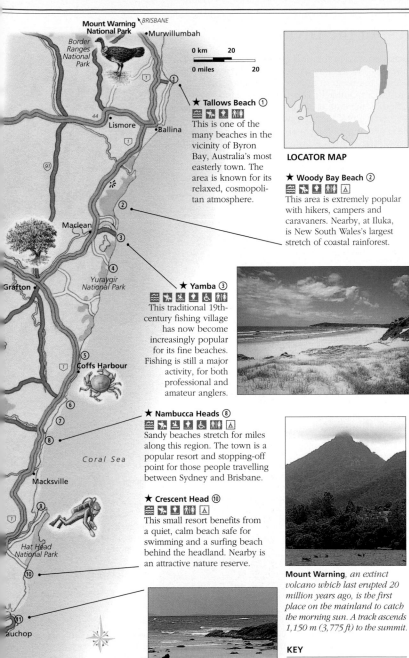

Brisbane

Mount Warning National Park
•Murwillumbah

Border Ranges National Park

0 km 20

0 miles 20

Lismore •Ballina

LOCATOR MAP

★ Tallows Beach ①

This is one of the many beaches in the vicinity of Byron Bay, Australia's most easterly town. The area is known for its relaxed, cosmopolitan atmosphere.

★ Woody Bay Beach ②

This area is extremely popular with hikers, campers and caravaners. Nearby, at Iluka, is New South Wales's largest stretch of coastal rainforest.

Maclean

Yuraygir National Park

Grafton•

★ Yamba ③

This traditional 19th-century fishing village has now become increasingly popular for its fine beaches. Fishing is still a major activity, for both professional and amateur anglers.

Coffs Harbour

★ Nambucca Heads ⑧

Sandy beaches stretch for miles along this region. The town is a popular resort and stopping-off point for those people travelling between Sydney and Brisbane.

Coral Sea

Macksville

★ Crescent Head ⑩

This small resort benefits from a quiet, calm beach safe for swimming and a surfing beach behind the headland. Nearby is an attractive nature reserve.

Hat Head National Park

Mount Warning, *an extinct volcano which last erupted 20 million years ago, is the first place on the mainland to catch the morning sun. A track ascends 1,150 m (3,775 ft) to the summit.*

auchop

★ Port Macquarie ⑪

Established as a penal settlement in 1821, the port only became successful in the 1970s. Its fine climate makes it a popular resort.

KEY

▬	Highway
▬	Major road
▭	Minor road
↝	River
✼	Viewpoint

West of the Divide

In stark contrast to the lush green of the Blue Mountains and the blue waters of the New South Wales coastline, the western region of the state is archetypal of Australia's Outback. This dusty, dry landscape, parched by the sun, is an understandably remote area, dotted with a few mining towns and national parks. Dubbo and Wagga Wagga are the main frontier towns, but anything beyond is commonly referred to as "Back o' Bourke" and ventured into by only the most determined of tourists. Even the most adventurous should avoid the area in high summer.

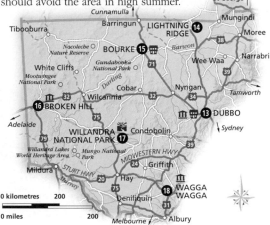

LOCATOR MAP

■ West of the Divide

□ The Blue Mountains *pp164–79*

SIGHTS AT A GLANCE

Bourke **15**
Broken Hill **16**
Dubbo **13**
Lightning Ridge **14**
Wagga Wagga **18**
Willandra National Park **17**

KEY

— Major road
═ Minor road
– – Track
— Main railway
— Regional border

Dubbo **13**

🏙 *39,500.* ✈ 🚉 🚌 🚍 ⓘ *cnr Newell Hwy & Macquarie St (02) 6801 4450.*
www.dubbotourism.com.au

Dubbo is located at the geographical heart of the state and is the regional capital of western New South Wales. The area was first noted for its rich agricultural potential in 1817 by explorer John Oxley, sited as it is on the banks of the Macquarie River. The city has since grown into a rural centre producing $45 million worth of food and agricultural goods annually.

Dubbo also has a strong colonial history and period architecture. Among the more interesting buildings are the 1876 Dubbo Museum, with its ornate ceilings and cedar staircase, the 1890 Italianate courthouse and the 1884 Macquarie Chambers, with their Tuscan columns and terracotta tiles.

At the **Old Dubbo Gaol**, visitors can hear the tragic story of Jacky Underwood, an Aborigine hung for his part in the Breelong massacre of 1900, when eleven white settlers were killed. Dubbo magistrate Rolf Boldrewood drew on the characters of the gaol's inmates to write the classic novel *Robbery Under Arms (see p34).*

The most popular sight in Dubbo is the **Western Plains**

Rhinoceros in Western Plains Zoo

Zoo, 5 km (3 miles) from the town. The zoo's emphasis is on breeding endangered species. Visitors can see over 1,000 animals living freely.

🏛 **Old Dubbo Gaol**
Macquarie St. **Tel** *(02) 6801 4460.*
⏱ *9am–4:30pm daily.* ● *Good Fri, Dec 25.* 📷

🦋 **Western Plains Zoo**
Obley Rd. **Tel** *(02) 6882 5888.*
⏱ *9am–5pm daily.* 📷 ♿ ▯

Lightning Ridge **14**

🏙 *5,000.* ✈ ⓘ *Morilla St (02) 6829 1670.*

Lightning Ridge is a small mining village and home of the treasured black opal – a rare dark opal shot with red, blue and green. Gem enthusiasts from around the world come to try their luck on the opal fields. The town is also famous for its hearty welcome to visitors, unusual within mining communities, and its mine tours, plethora of opal shops and hot bore spas.

Bourke ⓯

🏚 3,000. ✕ 🚃 🚌
ℹ️ 24 Anson St (02) 6872 1222.
www.visitbourke.com

Situated on the Darling River, part of Australia's longest river system, Bourke is a colourful town that was once the centre of the world's wool industry. It still produces 25,000 bales per year.

Bourke's heyday is evident in the colonial buildings and the old weir, wharf, lock and lift-up span bridge which recall the days of the paddle-steamer trade to Victoria (*see p431*). The town's cemetery tells something of Bourke's history: Afghan camel drivers who brought the animal to Australia from the Middle East in the 19th century are buried here.

Broken Hill ⓰

🏚 21,000. ✕ 🚃 🚌 🚌 ℹ️ cnr
Blende and Bromide sts (08) 8088
9700. **www**.visitbrokenhill.com.au

The unofficial centre of Outback New South Wales, Broken Hill is a mining city perched on the edge of the deserts of inland Australia. The town was established in 1883, when vast deposits of zinc, lead and silver were discovered in a 7-km (4-mile) long "Line of Lode" by the then-fledgling company, Broken Hill Pty Ltd. Broken Hill has since grown into a major town and BHP has become Australia's biggest corporation.

Broken Hill's now declining mining industry is still evident; slag heaps are piled up, there

are more pubs per head than any other city in the state and streets are named after metals.

Surprisingly, Broken Hill also has more than 20 art galleries featuring desert artists. The city is also the base of the Royal Flying Doctor Service (*see p257*) and School of the Air.

To the northwest of Broken Hill is **Silverton**, once a thriving silver mining community and now a ghost town. It is popular as a location for films, such as *Mad Max* and *Priscilla, Queen of the Desert*.

Willandra National Park ⓱

ℹ️ 200 Yambil St, Griffith (02) 6966
8100. ⭕ daily. 🌑 in wet weather.
🅿️ ♿ to homestead.
www.nationalparks.nsw.gov.au

Willandra National Park, on the edge of a riverine plain, has significant wildlife and historic values. The park covers part of the once

prosperous Willandra Sheep Station and contains the homestead and shearing complexes of the former station. The homestead overlooks peaceful Willandra Creek, where grasslands and creek beds are home to kangaroos, emus and ground-nesting birds.

Wagga Wagga ⓲

🏚 57,000. ✕ 🚃 🚌
ℹ️ Tarcutta St, 1300 100 122.
www.tourismwaggawagga.com.au

Named by its original inhabitants, the Widadjuri people, as "a place of many crows", Wagga Wagga has grown into a large, modern city serving the surrounding farming community. It has won many accolades for its wines and the abundance of gardens has earned it the title of "Garden City of the South".

The large Botanic Gardens and the Wagga Historical Museum are well worth a visit. The Widadjuri track is a popular walk along the Murrumbidgee River banks.

Environs

The gentle town of **Gundagai**, nestling beneath Mount Parnassus on the banks of the Murrumbidgee River, has been immortalized in the bush ballad "Along the Road to Gundagai". More tragic is Gundagai's place in history as the site of Australia's greatest natural disaster when floods swept away the town in 1852.

MUNGO WORLD HERITAGE AREA

Lake Mungo is an area of great archaeological significance. For 40,000 years, it was a 10-m (33-ft) deep lake, around which Aborigines lived. The lake then dried up, leaving its eastern rim as a wind-blown sand ridge known as the Walls of China. Its age was determined in the 1960s when winds uncovered an Aboriginal skeleton known as Mungo Man. Lake Mungo has been protected as part of the Willandra Lakes World Heritage Area since 1981 (*see pp26–7*).

Walls of China sand ridges

Historic pub in the ghost town of Silverton, near Broken Hill

THE SOUTH COAST AND SNOWY MOUNTAINS

Although the busiest highway in Australia runs through southern New South Wales, the area remains one of the most beautiful in the country. Its landscape includes the Snowy Mountains, the surf beaches of the far south, the historic Southern Highland villages and the farming towns of the Murray and Murrumbidgee plains.

Ever since European settlers crossed the Blue Mountains in 1812 *(see p172)*, the southern plains of New South Wales around Goulburn, Yass and Albury have been prime agricultural land. Yet the wilderness of the Snowy Mountains to the east and the steep escarpment which runs the length of the beautiful South and Sapphire coasts, from Wollongong to the Victoria border, has never been completely tamed. Today, the splendour of southern New South Wales is protected by a number of large national parks.

The great Snowy Mountains offer alpine scenery at its best. In summer, the wildflower-scattered meadows, deep gorges and cascading mountain creeks seem to stretch endlessly into the distance; in winter, the jagged snow-capped peaks and twisted snow gums turn this summer walking paradise into a playground for keen downhill and cross-country skiers.

The area also has a long and colourful cultural heritage: Aboriginal tribes, gold diggers and mountain cattlemen have all left their mark here. During the 1950s and 1960s, the region became the birthplace of multicultural Australia, as thousands of European immigrants came to work on the Snowy Mountains Scheme, an engineering feat which diverted the flow of several rivers to provide hydroelectricity and irrigation for southeastern Australia.

But southern New South Wales is more than just landscapes; civilization is never far away. There are excellent restaurants and hotels along the coast, Wollongong is an industrial city and the gracious towns of the Southern Highlands offer historic attractions.

Snowy Mountains landscape in autumn

◁ **Red rocks and blue waters of the Sapphire Coast at Merimbula Wharf**

Exploring the South Coast and Snowy Mountains

The Great Dividing Range, which runs from the Blue Mountains *(see pp170–73)* down to the Snowy Mountains and into Victoria, divides the region into three areas. There is the coastal strip, a zone of beautiful beaches, which starts at Wollongong and runs south for 500 km (310 miles) to Eden, hemmed in by the rising mountain range to its west. On the range lie the Southern Highlands, Mount Kosciuszko and the Snowy Mountains. West of the range are the farming plains of the Murrumbidgee River.

Waterfall in the beautiful Morton National Park

Golden inlet at Ben Boyd National Park, on the southern tip of New South Wales

GETTING AROUND

A car is essential to do full justice to this region; with the Hume Hwy providing excellent access to the Southern Highlands and the western farming towns. Wollongong and the southern beaches are linked from Sydney to the Victoria border by the coastal Princess Hwy. From Canberra, the Monaro Hwy is the best route to the Snowy Mountains. From Bega to the east or Gundagai and Tumut in the west, take the Snowy Mountains Hwy. A train service between Sydney and Canberra stops at the Southern Highlands and Hume Hwy towns, while the coastal resorts are serviced by buses from both Sydney and Melbourne.

SEE ALSO

- *Where to Stay* pp484–5

- *Where to Eat* pp531–2

0 kilometres 25

0 miles 25

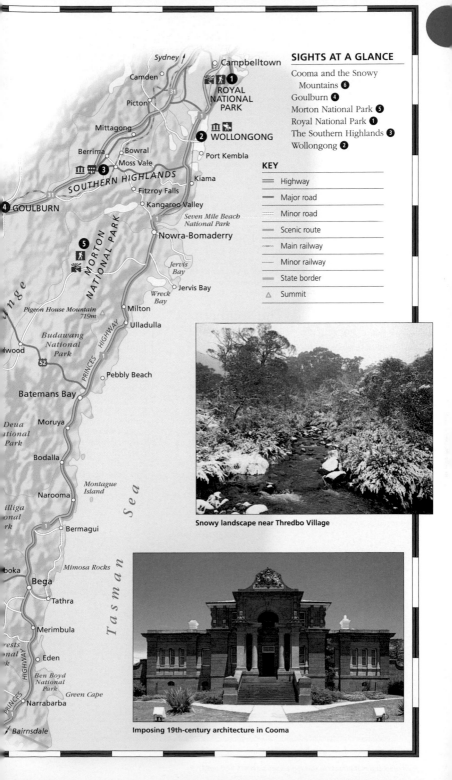

Sydney

Campbelltown

Camden

ROYAL
NATIONAL
PARK

Picton

Mittagong

WOLLONGONG

Berrima   Bowral

Port Kembla

Moss Vale

SOUTHERN HIGHLANDS   Kiama

Fitzroy Falls

GOULBURN   Kangaroo Valley

Seven Mile Beach
National Park

MORTON NATIONAL PARK

Nowra-Bomaderry

Jervis
Bay

Wreck
Bay   Jervis Bay

nge

Pigeon House Mountain
719m   Milton

Budawang
National
Park   Ulladulla

dwood   52

PRINCES HIGHWAY

Pebbly Beach

Batemans Bay

Deua
ational
Park   Moruya

Bodalla

Narooma   Montague
Island

illiga
onal
rk   Bermagui

Mimosa Rocks

boka

Bega

Tathra

Merimbula

rests
nal
k   Eden

Ben Boyd
National
Park   Green Cape

PRINCES   Narrabarba

Bairnsdale

Tasman Sea

SIGHTS AT A GLANCE

Cooma and the Snowy
  Mountains **6**
Goulburn **4**
Morton National Park **5**
Royal National Park **1**
The Southern Highlands **3**
Wollongong **2**

KEY

═══	Highway
──	Major road
····	Minor road
──	Scenic route
╫╫	Main railway
┄┄	Minor railway
──	State border
△	Summit

Snowy landscape near Thredbo Village

Imposing 19th-century architecture in Cooma

Royal National Park **❶**

🚉 *Loftus, then tram to Audley (Sun public hols only).* 🚢 *Bundeena from Cronulla.* 🛈 *Sir Bertram Stevens Drive, Audley (02) 9542 0648.* 🖥
www.nationalparks.nsw.gov.au

Designated a national park in 1879, the "Royal" is the oldest national park in Australia and the oldest in the world after Yellowstone in the USA. It covers 16,500 ha (37,000 acres) of spectacular landscape.

To the east, waves from the Pacific Ocean have undercut the sandstone and produced coastal cliffs, interspersed by creeks, waterfalls, lagoons and beaches. Sea eagles and terns nest in caves at the Curracurrang Rocks. Heath vegetation on the plateau merges with woodlands on the upper slopes and rainforest in the gorges. The park is ideal for bushwalking, swimming and bird-watching.

Wollongong **❷**

🏨 *280,000.* 🚉 🚆 🚌
🛈 *93 Crown St (02) 4227 5545.*
www.tourismwollongong.com.au

The third largest city in the state, Wollongong is situated on a coastline of beautiful surf beaches. Mount Kembla and Mount Keira provide a backdrop to the city. Originally a coal and steel industrial city – the BHP steel mill at Port Kembla is still a major employer – Wollongong is fast building a reputation as a leisure centre. Northbeach is the most famous of its 17 surf beaches. Flagstaff Point, with its lighthouse, boat harbour, beach views and seafood restaurants, is popular with visitors. Fresh seafood is also on offer at the fish market in Wollongong harbour. The city boasts Australia's largest regional art gallery, and the Nan Tien Temple, the largest Buddhist temple in the southern hemisphere, built for Sydney's Chinese community.

Figure in Nan Tien Temple

The Southern Highlands **❸**

🚆 🚉 *Bowral, Moss Vale, Mittagong, Bundanoon.* 🛈 *62–70 Main St, Mittagong (02) 4871 2888.*
www.southern-highlands.com.au

Quaint villages, country guesthouses, homesteads and beautiful gardens are scattered across the lush landscape of the Southern Highlands. The region has been a summer retreat for Sydneysiders for almost 100 years. Villages such as Bowral, Moss Vale, Berrima and Bundanoon are also ideal places in the winter for pottering around antiques shops, dining on hearty soups, sitting by open fires and taking bush walks and country drives. The region's gardens are renowned for their blaze of colours in the spring and autumn. The Corbett Gardens at Bowral are a showpiece during its Tulip Festival *(see p40).* Bowral is also home to the **Bradman Museum**, where a fascinating collection of photos and cricketing memorabilia commemorates the town's famous son, cricketer Sir Donald Bradman. Bradman is said to have first showed signs of greatness as a child, hitting a golf ball against a water tank stand with a stump-wide strip of wood.

Visiting the village of Berrima is like stepping back in time. The settlement, now home to an abundance of antiques and craft shops, is one of the most unspoilt examples of a small Australian town of the 1830s.

Popular walks in the area include Mount Gibraltar, Carrington Falls, the magnificent Fitzroy Falls at the northern tip of Morton National Park and the majestic Kangaroo Valley. The five Wombeyan Caves, west of the

Fishing boats moored along Wollongong Harbour

Impressive peak of Pigeon House in Morton National Park

town of Mittagong, form an imposing underground limestone cathedral.

🏛 Bradman Museum

St Jude St, Bowral. *Tel (02) 4862 1247.* ◯ 10am–5pm daily. ● 25 Dec. ▨ 🔥 ▢

Sandstone house in Goulburn

Goulburn ❹

🏚 24,500. 🚉 🏠 🚌 🛈 *201 Sloane St (02) 4823 4492.*

Goulburn is at the heart of the Southern Tablelands, with its rich pastoral heritage. Proclaimed in 1863, the town's 19th-century buildings, such as the courthouse, post office and railway station, are testament to the continuing prosperity of the district.

The Big Merino, a giant, hollow concrete sheep, marks Goulburn as the "fine wool capital of the world".

Environs

The town of **Yass** is known for its fine wool and cool-climate wines. Worth a visit is the historic Cooma Cottage, now owned by the National Trust. It was once the home of Australian explorer Hamilton Hume, between 1839 and 1873.

Morton National Park ❺

🚉 Bundanoon. 🚌 Fitzroy Falls. 🛈 Fitzroy Falls (02) 4422 2346.

Morton National Park stretches along the rugged hinterland from north of the Shaolhavern Valley to the Ulladulla area. Fitzroy Falls are at the northern end of the park. At Bundanoon, magnificent sandstone country can be explored.

To the south, views of the coastline and Budawang wilderness can be found at Little Forest Plateau and the top of Pigeon House Mountain.

Cooma and the Snowy Mountains ❻

🏚 8,000. ✈ 🏠 🚌 🛈 *119 Sharp St (02) 6450 1742, 1800 636 525.* www.visitcooma.com.au

Colourful Cooma has a rich history as a cattle, engineering and ski town. During the construction of the Snowy Mountains Scheme *(see p183)*, Cooma was also the weekend base for the thousands of immigrants working up in the mountains during the week. Stories surviving from this era include tales of frontier-like shootouts in the main street, interracial romances and bush mountain feats. However, Cooma is now a sleepy rural town that acts as the gateway to the Snowy Mountains and the southern ski slopes.

The modern resort town of Jindabyne on Lake Jindabyne is home to the Kosciuszko National Park information centre, a myriad of ski shops and lodges, and plenty of nightlife. The two major ski resorts are Thredbo Village along the Alpine Way and the twin resort of Perisher Blue, linked by the ski tube train to Lake Crackenback and the Blue Cow ski fields. Take the chairlift from Thredbo in summer to walk to the summit of Australia's highest mountain, Mount Kosciuszko *(see p160)*, or simply to stroll among the wildflowers and snow gums in the alpine meadows. Another recommended walk is to Blue Lake and the Cascades from Dead Horse Gap. Lake Eucumbene and the Thredbo and Eucumbene rivers offer excellent fly-fishing.

Environs

The ghost settlement of **Kiandra** has a marked historic walking trail detailing the gold rush era in the town *(see pp54–5)*. Nearby is the gentle ski resort of Mount Selwyn and the spectacular Yarrangobilly Caves with their underground walks set among limestone stalactites and stalagmites.

Resort town of Jindabyne in the Snowy Mountains

The South Coast

From Nowra to the border with Victoria, the south coast of New South Wales is a magical mix of white sand beaches, rocky coves and coastal bush covered with spotted gums and wattles, and alive with a variety of birds. The coastline is rich in Aboriginal sites, fishing villages and unspoilt beach settlements. The 400 km (250 miles) of coast are divided into three distinct areas – the Shoalhaven Coast to the north, the Eurobodalla ("Land of Many Waters") Coast in the centre and the Sapphire Coast in the far south.

Whale Museum harpoon gun

Ulladulla *is a small fishing village flanked by the dovecote-shaped peak of Pigeon House Mountain in the Morton-Budawang National Park. A bushwalk offers breathtaking coastal views.*

Central Tilba *is a delightful historic farming village, backed by the 800-m (2,600-ft) Mount Dromedary. The town itself is famous for its weatherboard cottages and shops, now housing some of the region's finest cafés and arts and crafts shops, and its cheese and wine. The cheese factory and wineries are all open to visitors.*

★ Horseshoe Bay Beach, Bermagui ⑦
Writer Zane Grey brought fame to this tiny game fishing town with his tales of marlin fishing.

★ Merimbula Beach ⑩
The tourist centre of the Sapphire Coast is famous for its oysters, deep-sea fishing and surrounding white sandy beach.

★ Eden ⑪
Set on the deep Twofold Bay, this was once a whaling station. It is now the centre of whale-watching on the south coast during spring. It is also a major tuna fishing town and centre for the local timber industry.

Nowra *is the town centre of the beautiful Shoalhaven Coast, near the mouth of the Shoalhaven River. The name means "black cockatoo" in the local Aboriginal language. Nearby are the resorts of Culburra and Shoalhaven Heads, adjacent to Seven Mile Beach National Park.*

Deua National Park

Moruya

Bodalla

Central Tilba

Bega

ORBOST

0 kilometres   25

0 miles   25

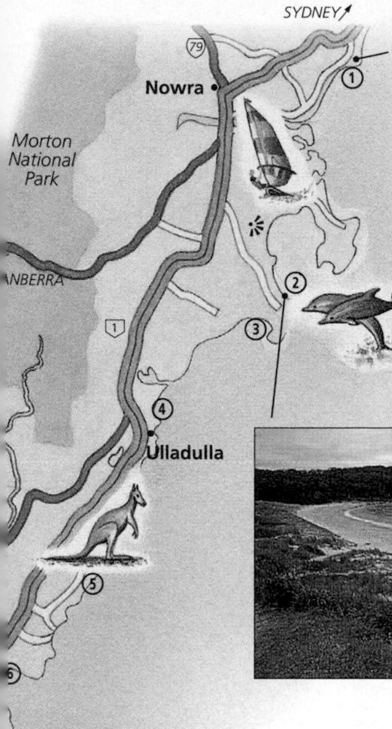
SYDNEY
79
Nowra
Morton National Park
1
Ulladulla

★ Shoalhaven Heads 1

🏄 🌊 🛟 🚻 ⛺

At the mouth of the Shoalhaven River, this beach resort is at the heart of a popular holiday area. Sailing and windsurfing on the river are popular activities among the locals.

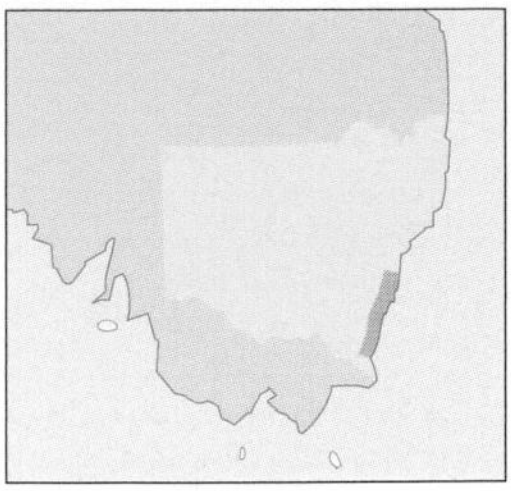

LOCATOR MAP

★ Jervis Bay 2

🌊 🛟 🚻 ⛺

This is one of the most beautiful natural harbours in Australia, famous for its naval bases, national park, tiny settlements of Husskinson and Vincentia, and some of the whitest beaches and crystal clear waters in the world.

Wreck Bay 3

🌊 🛟

This area, within Jervis Bay National Park, abounds with Aboriginal history. The cultural centre offers walkabout tours of local bushlife and archaeology. Nearby Cave Beach is one of the region's most popular for its secluded location.

Lake Conjola 4

🌊 🚻 ⛺

This lake, 10 km (6 miles) north of Ulladulla, is one of many lakes in the region popular with canoeists. Camp sites are also available.

Batemans Bay 6

🏄 🌊 🛟 🚻 ⛺

The Clyde River enters the sea here, marking the start of the Eurobodalla coastline with its rivers, lakes and chain of heavenly quiet beaches popular with Canberrans.

Mimosa Rocks 8

🛟 ⛺

This coastal park, just off the south coast road, offers exceptional bushwalking opportunities and idyllic beaches. Secluded camp sites, with minimum facilities, are popular with families and anglers.

Tathra Beach 9

🏄 🌊 🛟 🚻 ⛺

This tiny fishing village and holiday haven includes a maritime museum, housed in a 150-year-old wharf building.

Ben Boyd National Park 12

🌊 🛟 ⛺

Camping, bushwalks and fine beaches are all features of this park. Temperate rainforests begin to take over the landscape in the surrounding region. The ascent to Mount Imlay offers panoramic views of the coast.

★ Pebbly Beach 5

🏄 🌊 🛟

Set within Murramarang National Park, this beach is famous for its tame kangaroos which sometimes venture into the water at dusk and dawn, and have been seen to "body surf".

KEY

- Highway
- Major road
- Minor road
- River
- Viewpoint

CANBERRA AND AUSTRALIAN CAPITAL TERRITORY

L *ocated within New South Wales, some 300 km (185 miles) southwest of Sydney, Canberra is Australia's capital and its political heart-land. The city was planned in 1908 as the new seat of federal parliament to end rivalry between Sydney and Melbourne. The surrounding Australian Capital Territory features bush and mountain terrain.*

Canberra was once little more than a sheep station on the edge of the Molonglo River. American architect Walter Burley Griffin won an international competition to design the city. He envisaged a spacious, low-level, modern city, with its major buildings centred on the focal point of Lake Burley Griffin. Canberra (its name is based on an Aboriginal word meaning "meeting place") is a city of contradictions. It consists of more than just politics, diplomacy and monuments. Lacking the traffic and skyscrapers of Australia's other main cities, it has a serenity and country charm suited to strolling around the lake, bush driving and picnicking.

Canberra is the national capital and the centre of political and administrative power in Australia, yet it is also a rural city, ringed by gum trees, with the occasional kangaroo seen hopping down its suburban streets. The city holds the majority of the nation's political,

literary and artistic treasures, and contains important national institutions such as the High Court of Australia, the Australian National University and the Australian War Memorial, but it has a population of fewer than 400,000. These contradictions are the essence of the city's attraction. Canberra's hidden delights include Manuka's elegant cafés *(see pp533–4)*, excellent local wines and sophisticated restaurants. Special events include the annual spring flower festival, Floriade, which turns the north shore of the lake into a blaze of colour, and the spectacular hot-air ballooning festival in April.

Outside the city lie the region's natural attractions. Tidbinbilla Nature Reserve is home to wild kangaroos, wallabies, emus, koalas and platypuses. The Murrumbidgee River is excellent for canoeing, and the wild Namadgi National Park has bush camping, Aboriginal art sites, alpine snow gums and mountain creeks for trout fishing.

Hot-air ballooning festival over Lake Burley Griffin, near the National Library of Australia

◁ **The imposing flag-topped Parliament House in Canberra**

Exploring Canberra and ACT

Central Canberra lies around Lake Burley Griffin, framed by the city's four hills – Black Mountain and Mount Ainslie to the north and Capital Hill and Red Hill to the south. Most of Canberra's main sights are accessible from the lake. Scattered throughout the northern suburbs are other places of interest such as the Australian Institute of Sport. To the south lies the wilderness and wildlife of Namadgi National Park.

View of Canberra from Mount Ainslie

SIGHTS AT A GLANCE

Historic Streets and Buildings
Australian War Memorial
   pp200–1 **8**
Black Mountain Tower **10**
Civic Square **7**
Government House **3**
Mugga-Mugga **14**
Royal Australian Mint **2**
Yarralumla **5**

Parks and Gardens
Australian National Botanic
   Gardens **9**
Namadgi National Park p207 **18**
Red Hill **1**

Modern Architecture
Parliament House pp198–9 **4**

Museums and Galleries
Australian Institute of Sport **12**
Canberra Deep Space
   Communication Complex **16**
National Gallery pp202–3 **6**
National Museum of Australia **13**

**Aquariums and Nature
Reserves**
National Zoo and Aquarium **11**
Tidbinbilla Nature Reserve **17**

Rivers
Murrumbidgee River **15**

0 kilometres   1

0 miles   1

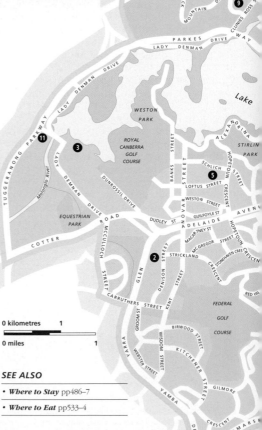

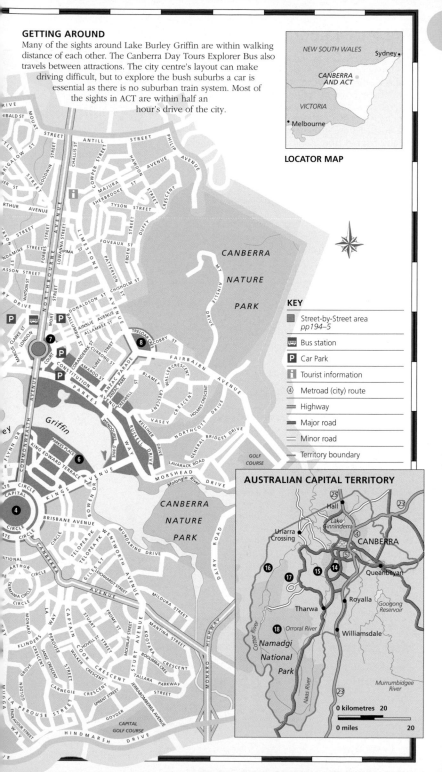

GETTING AROUND

Many of the sights around Lake Burley Griffin are within walking distance of each other. The Canberra Day Tours Explorer Bus also travels between attractions. The city centre's layout can make driving difficult, but to explore the bush suburbs a car is essential as there is no suburban train system. Most of the sights in ACT are within half an hour's drive of the city.

LOCATOR MAP

NEW SOUTH WALES · Sydney

CANBERRA AND ACT

VICTORIA

· Melbourne

KEY

- Street-by-Street area *pp194–5*
- Bus station
- P Car Park
- Tourist information
- ④ Metroad (city) route
- Highway
- Major road
- Minor road
- Territory boundary

AUSTRALIAN CAPITAL TERRITORY

Hall

Lake Ginninderra

Uriarra Crossing

CANBERRA

Queanbeyan

Royalla

Googong Reservoir

Tharwa

Orroral River

Williamsdale

Cotter River

Namadgi National Park

Naas River

Murrumbidgee River

0 kilometres 20

0 miles 20

The Parliamentary Triangle

Canberra's major monuments, national buildings and
key attractions are all situated around Lake Burley
Griffin within the Parliamentary Triangle. Designed to
be the focal point of Canberra's national activities by
the architect Walter Burley Griffin *(see p197)*, the Parliamentary Triangle has Capital Hill at its apex, topped by
Parliament House. Commonwealth Avenue and Kings
Avenue fan out from Capital Hill, cross the lake and
end at Parkes Way. Running at a
right angle from the base
of the triangle is Anzac Parade,
which leads to the Australian
War Memorial *(see pp200–1)*
and completes the basic
symmetry of Burley
Griffin's plan.

★ Parliament House
*Completed in 1988, this is
one of the world's most
impressive parliamen-
tary buildings* ❹

Capital Hill

Questacon is an action-
packed science and technology centre with hundreds
of hands-on displays.

Kings Avenue

**★ National Gallery
of Australia**
*This impressive art gallery
contains an excellent
collection of
Australian
colonial and
Aboriginal art, as well
as many significant
European works* ❻

**Museum of Australian
Democracy**
*This was the first parliamen-
tary building in the new
capital. Built in 1927, it
remained as the centre of
Australian politics until 1988.
It is now open to the public.*

**The High Court
of Australia** is the
highest court of justice
in the country.

Blundell's Cottage
*Built in 1858, this
is a fine example
of an early colonial
cottage typical of remote
farming life of the time.*

STAR SIGHTS

★ Australian War
Memorial

★ National Gallery of
Australia

★ Museum of Australian
Democracy

Lake Burley Griffin
This artificial lake was created by damming the Molonglo River in 1963. The water feature was central to Walter Burley Griffin's elegant design for Canberra.

CANBERRA

Lake Burley Griffin

LOCATOR MAP

The National Library is the country's largest and includes Captain Cook's original journals.

Commonwealth Avenue

The Captain Cook Memorial Jet in the middle of Lake Burley Griffin spurts water to a height of 137 m (450 ft).

Commonwealth Park is ablaze with colour during September and October when it is home to the city's annual spring flower festival, Floriade *(see p41).*

Parkes Way

St John the Baptist Church and Schoolhouse were built in 1844 and are two of Canberra's oldest buildings.

★ **Australian War Memorial**
The nation's tribute to its 102,000 war dead is also a remarkable museum ❽

The Australian American Memorial was given to Australia by the United States as a thank you for the Pacific alliance during World War II *(see pp57–8).*

Anzac Parade
Eleven memorials line the boulevard, commemorating Australia's war efforts in the 20th century.

| 0 metres | 500 |
| 0 yards | 500 |

Exploring the Parliamentary Triangle

Canberra, with its still lake and impressive national monuments and institutions, can at first glance appear cold and somewhat forbidding to visitors. But venture inside the various buildings dotted around Lake Burley Griffin within the Parliamentary Triangle, and a treasure trove of architecture, art, history and politics will be revealed. The lake itself, surrounded by gardens, cycle paths and outdoor sculptures and memorials, is a picturesque location for relaxing picnics and leisurely strolls. Exploring the entire Parliamentary Triangle can take one or two days. It is, however, more easily tackled by dividing it into two parts, taking in first the north and then the south of the lake.

🏛 Museum of Australian Democracy

King George Terrace, Parkes.
Tel *(02) 6270 8222.* 🕐 *9am–5pm daily.* ● *25 Dec.* 📶 🔥 🖊 🖥
www.oph.gov.au
Built in 1927 as the first parliamentary building in the new national capital, Old Parliament House was the centre of Australian politics for more than 60 years. It was replaced by the new Parliament House in 1988 *(see pp198–9).*

This building has witnessed many historic moments: Australia's declaration of war in 1939; news of the bombing of Australia's northern shores by the Japanese in 1942; the disappearance and presumed drowning of Prime Minister Harold Holt in 1967 and the dismissal of the Whitlam government by Sir John Kerr in 1975 *(see pp58–9).*

Today the building is home to the Museum of Australian Democracy, which includes several historical exhibitions.

Visitors can explore the Kings Hall, the old House of Representatives and Senate chambers, and see the peephole in the wall of the prime minister's office, discovered during renovations. The National Portrait Gallery's main collection is also held in the museum.

Blundell's Cottage

🛖 Blundell's Cottage

Wendouree Drive, Parkes.
Tel *(02) 6272 2900.* 🕐 *10–11:30am, noon–4pm Thu & Sat.* ● *25 Dec.*
📶 **www.**nationalcapital.gov.au
This small sandstone farmhouse was built in 1858 by the Campbell family, owners

of a large farming property at Duntroon Station, for their head ploughman. It was later occupied by bullock driver George Blundell, his wife, Flora, and their eight children.

This excellent example of a colonial cottage conveys the remoteness of early farming life. The cottage once looked out over sheep paddocks, but these were flooded by Lake Burley Griffin *(see pp194–5).*

🏛 National Capital Exhibition

Commonwealth Park.
Tel *(02) 6272 2902.* 🕐 *9am–5pm Mon–Fri, 10am–4pm Sat & Sun.*
● *25 Dec.* 🔥 🖊 🖥 **www.**
nationalcapital.gov.au
The rotunda housing the National Capital Exhibition, north of Lake Burley Griffin at Regatta Point, is recommended as a starting point for any tour of Canberra. Inside are models, videos and old photographs showing the history and growth of Canberra as the federal capital of Australia. These provide a good orientation of the city.

From the windows of the rotunda is a clear view of Lake Burley Griffin, the Parliamentary Triangle and the Captain Cook Memorial Jet, National Carillion and Globe. The jet fountain and bronze, copper and enamel globe on the edge of the lake were part of the 1970 bicentennial commemoration of the claiming of the east coast of Australia by British navy officer Captain James Cook in

Neo-Classical façade of the Museum of Australian Democracy and its impressive forecourt

1770 *(see p46)*. The elegant fountain lifts a column of water 147 m (480 ft) out of the lake from 11am until 2pm, provided the weather is not too windy. The National Carillon has 55 bronze bells and there are regular recitals.

🏛 National Library of Australia

Parkes Place, Parkes. *Tel* (02) 6262 1111. ◯ *9am–9pm Mon–Thu, 9am–5pm Fri–Sat, 1:30–5pm Sun.* ⬤ *Good Fri, 25 Dec.* 🔵 📷 ▣ www.nla.gov.au

This five-storey library, considered to be an icon of 1960s architecture, is the repository of Australia's literary and documentary heritage. Containing more than 7 million books, as well as copies of most newspapers and magazines published in Australia, thousands of tapes, manuscripts, prints, maps and old photographs, it is the nation's largest library and leading research centre. There are also historic items in a rotating display such as Captain Cook's original journal from his *Endeavour* voyages.

Leonard French stained glass

The building, designed by Sydney architect Walter Bunning (1912–1977) and completed in 1968, includes some notable works of art. Foremost are the modern stained-glass windows by Australian architect and artist Leonard French (1928–), made of Belgian chunk glass and depicting the planets. There are also the Australian life tapestries by French artist Mathieu Mategot.

🏛 Questacon – The National Science and Technology Centre

Cnr King Edward Terrace & Parkes Place, Parkes. *Tel* (02) 6270 2800. ◯ *9am–5pm daily.* ⬤ *25 Dec.* 📷 🔵 www.questacon.edu.au

With 200 hands-on exhibits in six different galleries arranged around the 27-m (90-ft) high cylindrical centre of the building, science need never be dull again. A must for anyone visiting Canberra,

Questacon demonstrates that science can be fascinating, intriguing, fun and an everyday part of life.

Visitors can freeze their shadow to a wall, play a harp with no strings, experience an earthquake and feel bolts of lightning. You can also enjoy giant slides and a roller coaster simulator, and there are also regular science demonstrations and special lectures.

🏛 High Court of Australia

Parkes Place, Parkes. *Tel* (02) 6270 6811. ◯ *9:45am–4pm Mon–Fri, noon–4pm Sun.* ⬤ *public hols.* 🔵 ▣ www.hcourt.gov.au

British and Australian legal traditions are embodied in this imposing lakeside structure, opened in 1980 by Queen Elizabeth II. The High Court is centred on a glass public hall, designed to instil respect for the justice system. Two murals by artist Jan Sensbergs look at the Australian constitution, the role of the Federation and the significance of the High Court. There are three courtrooms, and chambers for the Chief Justice and six High Court judges. Sittings are open to the public. On one side of the ramp at the entrance is a sculpture of a waterfall made out of granite.

It is intended to convey how the decisions of this legal institution trickle down to all Australian citizens.

Jan Sensbergs mural in the High Court

🔒 St John the Baptist Church and Schoolhouse Museum

Constitution Ave, Reid. *Tel* (02) 6248 8399. ◯ *10am–noon Wed, 2–4pm Sat, Sun.* ⬤ *Good Fri, 25 Dec.* 📷 🔵 www.stjohnscanberra.org

Built in 1844 of local bluestone and sandstone, the Anglican church of St John the Baptist and its adjoining schoolhouse are Canberra's oldest surviving buildings. They served the pioneer farming families of the region. Memorials on the walls of the church commemorate many early settlers, including statesmen, scientists and scholars.

Within the schoolhouse is a museum containing various 19th-century memorabilia.

WALTER BURLEY GRIFFIN

In 1911, the Australian government, then located in Melbourne, decided on Canberra as the best site for a new national capital. An international competition for a city plan was launched, and the first prize was awarded to a 35-year-old American landscape architect, Walter Burley Griffin. Influenced by the design of Versailles, his plan was for a garden city, with lakes, avenues and terraces rising to the focal point of Parliament House atop Capital Hill. On 12 March 1913, a

Walter Burley Griffin

foundation stone was laid by Prime Minister Andrew Fisher, but bureaucratic arguments and then World War I intervened. By 1921, little of Canberra had begun to be constructed, and Burley Griffin was dismissed from his design post. He stayed in Australia until 1935, when, reduced to municipal designs, he left for India. He died there in 1937, although his original vision lives on in the ever-expanding city of Canberra.

Red Hill ❶

Via Mugga Way, Red Hill.

One of the highlights of a visit to Canberra is a drive to the top of Red Hill, which offers excellent views over Lake Burley Griffin,

Panoramic view of Canberra from Red Hill

Parliament House, Manuka and the embassy suburb of Yarralumla *(see p200)*. Behind Red Hill stretch the southern suburbs of Canberra, with the beautiful green of the Brinda-bella Ranges to the west.

An alternative view of Canberra, offering a better understanding of Walter Burley Griffin's carefully planned city design, can be seen from the top of Mount Ainslie, on the north side of the lake behind the Australian War Memorial *(see pp200–1)*.

Royal Australian Mint ❷

Denison St, Deakin. **Tel** *(02) 6202 6800 or 1 300 652 020.* 📮 *30, 31.* 🕐 *9am–4pm Mon–Fri, 10am–4pm Sat–Sun, public hols.* 🚫 *Good Fri, 25 Dec.* ♿ **www**.ramint.gov.au

The Royal Australian Mint is the sole producer of Australia's circulating coin currency as well as being the country's national mint. It has produced over 11 billion circulating coins and today has the capacity to mint over two million coins per day, or over 600 million per year. The Mint is dedicated to commemorating Australia's

Parliament House ❹

Parliament House is the meeting place of Australia's Parliament and the focal point of Australia's democracy. Opened in 1988, the building on Capital Hill is the third home of the Federal Parliament since 1901. The building is set on a 32-hectare (80-acre) site and is the focal point of Canberra. Its architecture reflects Australia's commitment to open government.

The steel flagpole reaches a height of 81 m (256 ft) and weighs 220 tonnes.

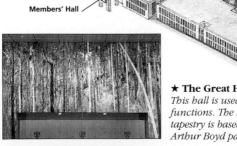

Members' Hall

House of Representatives Chamber
This chamber accommodates the 150 elected members of the House of Representatives.

★ The Great Hall
This hall is used for state functions. The 20-m (65-ft) tapestry is based on an Arthur Boyd painting.

culture and history through its numismatic programme. When touring the Mint you can see the history of Australian currency as well as how coins are made. You can even view the coins coming off the presses.

Government House ❸

Dunrossil Drive, Yarralumla. **Tel** (02) 6283 3533. ⬭ various dates – phone ahead to check. 🖼 🎥 obligatory.

Government House has been the official residence of the Governor General, the representative of the monarch in Australia, since 1927. The

Elegant façade and front grounds of Government House

house was once part of a large sheep station called Yarralumla, which was settled in 1828, and is now where heads of state and the Royal Family stay when visiting Australia.

The house is closed to the public, except on special open days; however, a lookout point on Lady Denman Drive offers good views of the residence and the large gardens.

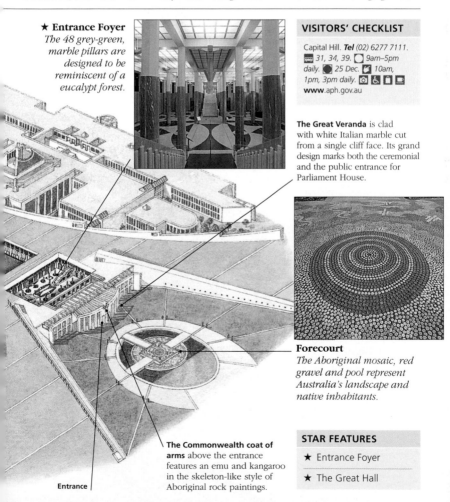

★ **Entrance Foyer**
The 48 grey-green, marble pillars are designed to be reminiscent of a eucalypt forest.

VISITORS' CHECKLIST

Capital Hill. **Tel** (02) 6277 7111. 🚌 31, 34, 39. ⬭ 9am–5pm daily. ● 25 Dec. 🎥 10am, 1pm, 3pm daily. 🅿️ ♿ 🚻 🛍️ 🎦 **www**.aph.gov.au

The Great Veranda is clad with white Italian marble cut from a single cliff face. Its grand design marks both the ceremonial and the public entrance for Parliament House.

Forecourt
The Aboriginal mosaic, red gravel and pool represent Australia's landscape and native inhabitants.

The Commonwealth coat of arms above the entrance features an emu and kangaroo in the skeleton-like style of Aboriginal rock paintings.

Entrance

STAR FEATURES

★ Entrance Foyer

★ The Great Hall

Yarralumla ❺

Yarralumla. 🏛 (02) 6205 0044.
🚌 901, 31. 📞 for embassy open
days. ♿ variable. 🎫

The suburb of Yarralumla, on
the edge of Capital Hill, is
home to more than 80 of
Australia's foreign embassies
and diplomatic residences. A
drive through the tree-lined
streets gives a fascinating view
of the architecture and cultures of each country represented, as embodied in their
embassies and grand ambas-
sadorial residences.

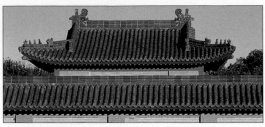

The traditional style of the Chinese Embassy in Yarralumla

Distinctive buildings include
the vast Chinese Embassy at
No. 15 Coronation Drive, with
its red columns, dragon statues and pagoda-shaped roofs.

On Moonah Place, the Indian
Embassy has pools, a shallow
moat and a white temple
building in the Mogul architectural style, with a gold spire on

Australian War Memorial ❽

The Australian War Memorial was built
to commemorate all Australians who
have died while serving their country. The
Roll of Honour and the symbolic Tomb
of the Unknown Australian Soldier serve
as a reminder of the horror and sadness
of war. The Anzac Hall is the stage for
sound and light shows, one of which
recreates a bombing raid over Germany.

Façade of the Australian War Memorial

STAR FEATURES

★ Roll of Honour

★ Tomb of the
   Unknown Soldier

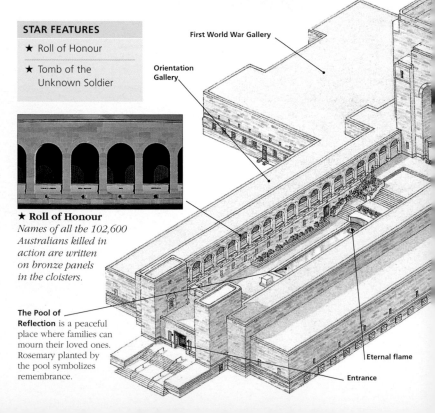

First World War Gallery

Orientation
Gallery

★ Roll of Honour
Names of all the 102,600
Australians killed in
action are written
on bronze panels
in the cloisters.

The Pool of
Reflection is a peaceful
place where families can
mourn their loved ones.
Rosemary planted by
the pool symbolizes
remembrance.

Eternal flame

Entrance

top. The High Commission of Papua New Guinea on Forster Crescent is built as a Spirit House, with carved totem poles outside; the Mexican Embassy on Perth Avenue boasts a massive replica of the Aztec Sun Stone.

Just across Adelaide Avenue is The Lodge, the official residence of the Australian prime minister and his family.

National Gallery of Australia ➏

See pp202–3.

Civic Square ➐

Civic Centre. 🚍 *many routes.*

The commercial heart of Canberra is the Civic Centre, on the north side of Lake Burley Griffin close to the northwest corner of the Parliamentary Triangle *(see pp194–5).* It is the centre of many administrative, legal and local government functions in Canberra, as well as having the highest concentration of offices and private

Ethos Statue, Civic Square

sector businesses. It is also the city's main shopping area. The central Civic Square, as envisaged by Walter Burley Griffin in his original city plan, is a common meeting place and relaxing area. It is dominated by the graceful bronze statue of Ethos, by Australian sculptor Tom Bass, located at the entrance of the ACT Legislative Assembly. In the adjacent Petrie Plaza is a traditional carousel, a much-loved landmark among the citizens of Canberra.

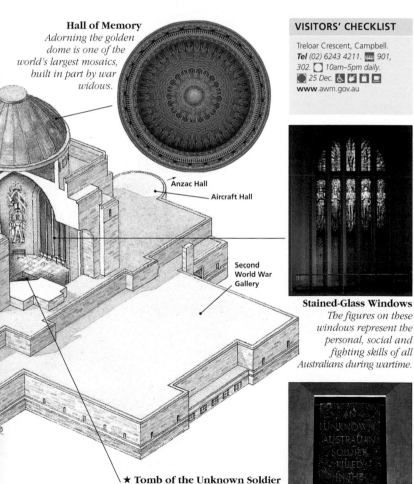

Hall of Memory
Adorning the golden dome is one of the world's largest mosaics, built in part by war widows.

Anzac Hall

Aircraft Hall

Second World War Gallery

VISITORS' CHECKLIST

Treloar Crescent, Campbell.
Tel (02) 6243 4211. 🚍 901, 302. ⏱ 10am–5pm daily.
⬤ 25 Dec. ♿ 🎫 📷 🎥 💻
www.awm.gov.au

Stained-Glass Windows
The figures on these windows represent the personal, social and fighting skills of all Australians during wartime.

★ **Tomb of the Unknown Soldier**
Beneath this red marble slab is buried an unknown Australian soldier who died during World War I. He symbolizes all Australians who have been killed while serving their country.

National Gallery of Australia ⑥

Australian society is diverse, multicultural and vibrant, and the 100,000 works of art owned by the National Gallery of Australia reflect the spirit of the country. The National Gallery opened in 1982, and the core of its collection consists of Australian art, from European settlement to present day, by some of its most famous artists, such as Tom Roberts, Arthur Boyd, Sidney Nolan and Margaret Preston *(see p34)*. The oldest art in Australia is that of its indigenous inhabitants *(see pp32–3)*, and the Aboriginal art collection offers fine examples of both ancient and contemporary works. The gallery's Asian and international collections are also growing. Modern sculptures are on display in the gardens.

Upper level

★ In a Corner on the MacIntyre
(1895) Tom Roberts' depiction of this country's bushland is painted in the fractured light style of the Australian School of Impressionists.

STAR EXHIBITS

- ★ In a Corner on the MacIntyre
- ★ The Aboriginal Memorial

Native Fuchsia *(1925)*
This painting is typical of the hand-coloured woodblock techniques of artist Margaret Preston, best known for depicting Australian flowers.

Lower level entrance

SCULPTURE GARDEN

The National Gallery makes the most of its picturesque, lakeside gardens as the site for an impressive collection of sculptures, from classical, such as Aristide Maillol's *The Mountain*, to modern. Two of the best known and loved contemporary sculptures in the garden are *Cones* by Bert Flugelman and *The Pears* by George Baldessin.

The Mountain by Aristide Maillol

GALLERY GUIDE

The National Gallery is easily visited within two hours, although an excellent one-hour tour of the highlights is offered twice daily. On the lower level is the Aboriginal art collection, which is not to be missed, and the Impressionism to Pop collections. Also highly recommended, on the upper level, is the extensive Australian art collection. Touring "blockbuster" art shows are hung in rooms in what is actually a later addition to the original building.

Prince Shotoku Praying to Buddha
(c.1300) This statue, in the Asian art rooms, is from the Kamakura period. It depicts the two-year-old prince who, in the 6th century AD, went on to become a founding father of the Japanese state.

VISITORS' CHECKLIST

Parkes Place. *Tel* (02) 6240 6502. (02) 6240 6501. 34. 10am–5pm daily. 25 Dec. special exhibitions.

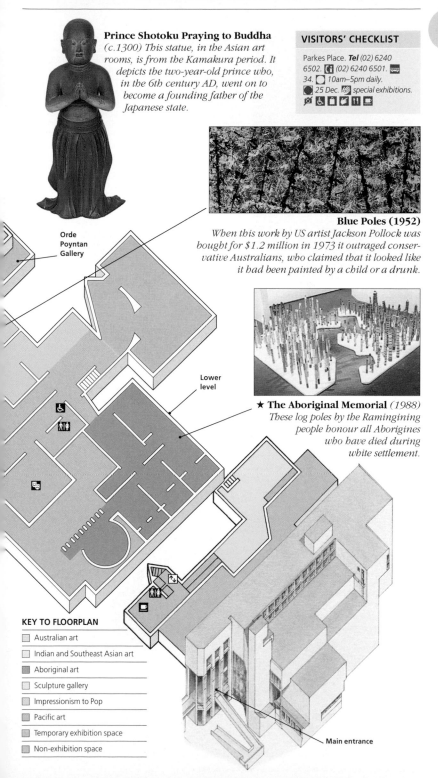

Orde Poyntan Gallery

Blue Poles (1952)
When this work by US artist Jackson Pollock was bought for $1.2 million in 1973 it outraged conservative Australians, who claimed that it looked like it had been painted by a child or a drunk.

Lower level

★ **The Aboriginal Memorial** (1988)
These log poles by the Ramingining people honour all Aborigines who have died during white settlement.

KEY TO FLOORPLAN

☐ Australian art

☐ Indian and Southeast Asian art

☐ Aboriginal art

☐ Sculpture gallery

☐ Impressionism to Pop

☐ Pacific art

☐ Temporary exhibition space

☐ Non-exhibition space

Main entrance

Rock Garden section of the Australian National Botanic Gardens

Australian National Botanic Gardens 🟒

Clunies Ross St, Acton. *Tel* (02) 6250 9450. ⬜ Feb–Dec: 8:30am–5pm daily, Jan: 8:30am–6pm Mon–Fri, 8:30am–8pm Sat & Sun. ⬤ 25 Dec. ♿ 🗐 🖥 www.anbg.gov.au

On the slopes of Black Mountain, the Australian National Botanic Gardens hold the finest scientific collection of native plants in the country. Approximately 90,000 plants of more than 5,000 species are featured in its displays.

The Rainforest Gully, one of the most popular attractions, features plants from the rainforests of eastern Australia. One fifth of the nation's eucalypt species are found on the Eucalypt Lawn. The Aboriginal Trail is a self-guided walk that details how Aborigines have utilized plants over thousands of years.

Black Mountain Tower 🔟

Black Mountain Drive, Acton. *Tel* 1800 806 718. ⬜ 9am–10pm daily. 🗺 ♿ 🖥

Known affectionately by locals as "the giant syringe", the Black Mountain Tower soars 195 m (640 ft) above the summit of Black Mountain. The tower houses state-of-the-art communications equipment, such as television transmitters and cellular phone bases. The tower also features an exhibition on the history of telecommunications in Australia, from its first telegraph wire in Victoria in 1854 to the 21st century.

There are three viewing platforms at different levels offering spectacular 360° views of Canberra and the surrounding countryside. There is also a revolving restaurant. In 1989, Black Mountain Tower was made a member of the World Federation of Great Towers, which includes such buildings as the Empire State Building in New York.

National Zoo and Aquarium 1️⃣1️⃣

Lady Denman Drive, Scrivener Dam. *Tel* (02) 6287 8400. ⬜ 10am–5pm daily. ⬤ 25 Dec. ♿ 🗐 by arrangement. 🖥 🎬 www.nationalzoo.com.au

A wonderful collection of Australia's fish, from native freshwater river fish to brilliantly coloured cold sea, tropical and coral species are on display in the National Zoo and Aquarium. This is Australia's only combined zoo and aquarium. There are about 20 aquariums on show, including a number of smaller tanks containing freshwater and marine animals. They have some eight different species of shark on display.

The 9-ha (22-acre) landscaped grounds of the adjacent Zoo have excellent displays of numerous native

animals including koalas, wombats, dingoes, fairy penguins, Tasmanian devils, emus and kangaroos. As well as the native residents of the zoo there are many favourites from all over the world, including several big cats (the zoo has the largest collection of big cats in the country), primates, giraffes and African antelopes.

The zoo also organizes "Meet a Cheetah" encounters. Under the supervision of a keeper, you will enter the cheetah enclosure and actually be able to touch and pat the animals. For even more close encounters, there is the two-hour ZooVenture tour, which would appeal to those animal lovers who want to enjoy a more hands-on behind-the-scenes kind of experience. Both this tour and "Meet a Cheetah" have age and height restrictions, and must be booked well in advance of your visit.

Australian Institute of Sport 1️⃣2️⃣

Leverrier Crescent, Bruce. *Tel* (02) 6214 1010. 🚌 80. ⬜ **Tours** 10am, 11:30am, 1pm, 2:30pm daily. ⬤ 25 Dec. 🗺 ♿ 🗐 obligatory. www.ais.org.au

Australian Olympic medallists are often on hand to show visitors around the world-class Australian Institute of Sport (AIS). This is the national centre of Australia's sports efforts. Here you can see where the athletes sleep, train and eat. You can see how your fitness levels compare and test your sporting skills. There is also an exhibition of interactive sports displays, the Sportex exhibition, which includes themes such as "Heroes and Legends" and "How do you measure up?" Athletes also take visitors on guided tours around the amazing facilities. A shop and a café are also open to visitors.

Turtle in the National Aquarium

The *Harvest of Endurance* scroll, depicting the 1861 Lambing Flat Riots, in the National Museum of Australia

National Museum of Australia ⑬

Lawson Crescent, Acton Peninsula.
Tel (02) 6208 5000. ▦ 34. ◯
9am–5pm daily. ● 25 Dec.
♿ 🅿 by arrangement. 🎞
(special exhibitions). 🖵 🖸
www.nma.gov.au

Established by an Act of Parliament in 1980, the National Museum of Australia moved to its permanent home on the Acton Peninsula in early 2001. It shares its location with the Australian Institute of Aboriginal and Torres Strait Islander Studies. The innovative, purpose-built facility quickly became an architectural landmark. Its unique design was inspired by the idea of a jigsaw puzzle.

Before beginning a tour of the museum, visitors can experience an audiovisual introduction to the museum in the Circa, a novel rotating cinema. A huge, three-dimensional map of Australia is visible from three floors. Using digital animation and interactive media stations, it helps to place the displays in their geographical context.

The permanent exhibitions explore the people, events and issues that have shaped and influenced the country. The museum's aim is to be a focus for sharing stories and promoting debate, and interactive displays involve visitors by inviting their contributions.

The **First Australians** gallery is the largest permanent exhibition and relates the stories and experiences of Aboriginal and Torres Strait Islander people. It not only illuminates their history but also deals frankly with contemporary social issues. Displays include Central Australian desert art, stone tools and Aboriginal jewellery made from Tasmanian seashells and a Torres Island outrigger canoe. **Creating A Country** uses

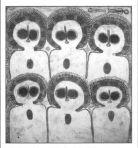

Untitled by Charlie Alyungurra, in the First Australians gallery

more than 700 props and artifacts to look at the way symbols help to define a sense of national identity. Exhibits include the kangaroo, as well as official symbols, such as the flag and Anzac Day. The **Australian Journeys** exhibition reviews the ways in which immigration has shaped the country. Since 1788 more than

10 million people have arrived in Australia as immigrants, and this gallery uses individual stories, as well as objects from the museum's collection, to look at the remarkable diversity of the Australian experience.

One of the more moving exhibitions is **Eternity**, in which the personal stories of 50 Australians are brought to life. The intention of this unique display is to explore history through emotion. "Your Story", an interactive exhibit, allows visitors to record their own stories, which then become part of the collection. The museum also acknowledges the significance of the land in Australia's identity. In **Old New Land**, the relationship between people and the environment is examined.

The landscaping of the museum is also notable and includes the striking Garden of Australian Dreams, which incorporates many symbols of Australian culture. The Backyard Café spills out into the innovative garden.

In addition, the museum hosts a range of temporary exhibitions. There are also children's galleries and performance spaces, as well as a television broadcast studio.

The Mermaid Coffin by Gaynor Peaty, in Eternity

Further Afield in the ACT

More than 70 per cent of the Australian Capital Territory is bushland. A one-day tour along Tourist Drive 5 provides an opportunity to see native animals in the wild, swim in the majestic Murrumbidgee River, visit a deep-space tracking station, and relax in the lovely gardens of the historic Lanyon Homestead.

Interior of the small stone cottage at Mugga-Mugga

Mugga-Mugga ⓲

8 Narrabundah Lane, Symonston. **Tel** (02) 6239 5607. ◯ 1:30–4:30pm Sat–Sun. ◉ 25 Dec. 🅿

One of Canberra's earliest historic sites, Mugga-Mugga reflects the social and material history of a rural working class family who worked on Duntroon Estate. The site's main feature is a small stone cottage built for the estate's head shepherd in the 1830s. It has been adapted over time, but is still furnished with household items that belonged to the Curley family who moved to Mugga-Mugga in 1913. A galvanized iron garage near the cottage houses an exhibition on the issue of Federation *(see p56)*.

Murrumbidgee River ⓯

ℹ️ *ACT Parks and Conservation Service 13 2281.*

The Murrumbidgee River meets the Cotter River at Casuarina Sands, a beautiful place to fish and canoe. Nearby is Cotter Dam, good for picnics, swimming and camping.

On the bank of the Murrumbidgee River south of Canberra is **Lanyon Homestead**, a restored 1850s home.

On the same property is the Sidney Nolan Gallery, which features the Ned Kelly series of paintings *(see p34)*.

🏛 **Lanyon Homestead**
Tharwa Drive, Tharwa. **Tel** (02) 6235 5677. ◯ 10am–4pm Tue–Sun. ◉ Good Fri, 24 & 25 Dec. 🅿 ♿ 🖼 🍴

Canberra Deep Space Communication Complex ⓰

Via Paddys River Rd (Tourist Drive 5). **Tel** (02) 6201 7880. ◯ 9am–5pm daily. ◉ 25 Dec. ♿ 🖼 📷 🍴 by arrangement. **www**.cdscc.nasa.gov

Canberra Deep Space Communication Complex is managed by the Commonwealth

Scientific and Industrial Research Organization (CSIRO) and the American NASA organization. It is one of only three such deep-space tracking centres in the world linked to the NASA control centre in California. The complex has six satellite dishes, the largest of which measures 70 m (230 ft) in diameter and weighs a hefty 3,000 tonnes.

Visitors to the Space Centre can see a piece of moon rock 3.8 billion years old, examine an astronaut's space suit, learn about the role of the complex during the Apollo moon landings and see pictures sent back from Mars, Saturn and Jupiter.

Emu at Tidbinbilla Nature Reserve

Tidbinbilla Nature Reserve ⓱

Via Paddys River Rd (Tourist Drive 5). **Tel** 13 2281. ◯ 9am–5pm daily (to 4:30pm in winter). ◉ 25 Dec. 🖼 ♿ limited. 🍴

The tranquil Tidbinbilla Nature Reserve, with its 5,450 ha (13,450 acres) of forests, grasslands, streams and mountains, is a paradise for wildlife lovers. Kangaroos and their joeys bask in the sun, emus strut on the grassy flats, platypuses swim in the creeks, koalas thrive on the eucalypt branches and bower birds and superb lyrebirds can be seen in the tall forests.

The reserve is set at the end of a valley. Visitors hike up to Gibraltar Rock or take a night stroll with a ranger to see sugar gliders and possums. The Birrigai Time Trail is a 3-km (2-mile) walk through various periods of history. The visitors' centre features Aboriginal artifacts and pioneer relics.

Tracking dishes known as "antenna" at the Canberra Space Complex

For hotels and restaurants in this region see pp486–7 and pp533–4

Namadgi National Park ⑱

Namadgi National Park covers almost half of the Australian Capital Territory. It is a beautiful, harsh landscape of snow, mountains, river valleys and Aboriginal rock art. Only 35 km (22 miles) south of Canberra, Namadgi is remote and solitary. Many days could be spent exploring the park, but even a day's walking will reward you with breathtaking views of the country.

0 km   2

0 miles   2

Corin Dam stores high-quality water from the Cotter River, sourced in the Bimberi Wilderness.

Visitors' Centre
Trail maps of the park and information on ranger-guided walks are available here.

Nursery Swamp

Booromba Rocks

Orroral Bush Camp Site
Camping out in this wild, bush setting amid the wildlife is an experience not to be missed.

Mount Clear is one of three camping grounds in the park.

KEY

— Major road

— Minor road

-- Walking trail

— River

ℹ️ Tourist information

🚻 Picnic area

🅰️ Camp site

🌿 Viewpoint

Yankee Hat
Ancient Aboriginal rock art thought to date back thousands of years has been discovered in this area.

QUEENSLAND

Queensland at a Glance

Australia's second-largest state encompasses some
1,727,000 sq km (667,000 sq miles) and is the country's
most popular tourist destination, after Sydney, due to its
tropical climate. Brisbane, the state capital, is a modern
city, with skyscrapers looking out over the Brisbane
River. The southern coastline is a haven for surfers and
is the region that most typifies the nation's beach culture.
Further north is the Great Barrier Reef, one of the
natural wonders of the world. Inland, cattle stations and
copper mines generate Queensland's wealth. The Far
North remains remote and unspoiled, with rainforests
and savannah land abundant with native wildlife.

Cairns *is Queensland's most
northerly city and is a popular
boarding point for touring the
Great Barrier Reef. The city's
hub is its esplanade, lined
with cafés (see p254).*

NORTHERN
AND OUTBACK
QUEENSLAND
(see pp248-57)

Mount Isa *is Queensland's
largest inland city and revolves
almost entirely around its
copper, zinc and lead mining
industries (see p257).*

```
0 kilometres      150
|————————————————|
0 miles           150
```

Longreach *is in the heart
of Queensland's Outback,
and its most popular sight
is the Stockman's Hall of
Fame, documenting
Australia's Outback
history. Longreach is also
the site of Qantas' original
hangar (see p257).*

◁ **Fairy basslets among the coral in the Great Barrier Reef**

The Great Barrier Reef *is the largest coral reef in the world. Hundreds of islands scatter the coastline, but only a few are developed for tourists, who come here to dive among the coral and tropical fish (see pp212–17).*

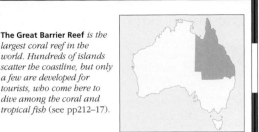

Maryborough *is known for its Queenslander houses, their wide verandas shading residents from the tropical sun (see p241).*

Brisbane, *the state capital, is a highly modern yet relaxing city. Skyscrapers blend with older edifices, such as the impressive City Hall (see pp218–33).*

SOUTH OF
TOWNSVILLE
(see pp234–47)

Surfers Paradise *is the main city of the Gold Coast region and more than lives up to its name. Chic hotels, pulsating nightclubs, high fashion stores and beach poseurs can all be found here (see p239).*

The Great Barrier Reef

Coral reefs are among the oldest and most primitive forms of life, dating back at least 500 million years. Today, the Great Barrier Reef is the largest reef system in the world, covering 2,000 km (1,250 miles) from Bundaberg to the tip of Cape York and an area of approximately 350,000 sq km (135,000 sq miles). Between the outer edges of the reef and the mainland, there are more than 2,000 islands and almost 3,000 separate reefs, of differing types. On islands with a fringing reef, coral can be viewed at close hand, although the best coral is on the outer reef, about 50 km (30 miles) from the mainland.

Saddled butterfly fish

LOCATOR MAP

The channel of water between the inner reef and Queensland's mainland is often as deep as 60 m (200 ft) and can vary in width between 30 km (20 miles) and 60 km (40 miles).

Coral is formed by tiny marine animals called polyps. These organisms have an external "skeleton" of limestone. Polyps reproduce by dividing their cells and so becoming polyp colonies.

Fringing reefs *surround islands or develop off the mainland coast as it slopes away into the sea.*

TYPICAL SECTION OF THE REEF

In this typical section of the Great Barrier Reef, a deep channel of water runs close to the mainland. In shallower water further out are a variety of reef features including coral cays, platform reefs and lagoons. Further out still, where the edge of the continental shelf drops off steeply, is a system of ribbon reefs.

Platform reef

Platform reefs *form in shallow water, growing outwards in a circle or oval rather than upwards in a wall.*

Coral cays are sand islands, formed when reef skeletons and other debris such as shells are exposed to the air and gradually ground down by wave movement into fine sand.

Queensland's tropical rainforest *is moist and dense, thriving on the region's heavy, monsoon-like rains and rich soil.*

Tidal flats consist of either dead or dying coral, since coral cannot survive exposure to air for an extended period of time.

Coral on the outer reef is built up in "walls" on ancient limestone bases. The coral survives down to a depth of about 30 m (100 ft), where enough sunlight penetrates the water and the temperature is above 17.5°C (65°F).

Ribbon reefs *are narrow strips that occur only in the north along the edge of the continental shelf. Exactly why they form here remains a mystery to marine biologists.*

HOW THE REEF WAS FORMED

The growth of coral reefs is dependent on sea level, as coral cannot grow above the water line or below 30 m (100 ft). As sea level rises, old coral turns to limestone, on top of which new coral can build, eventually forming barrier reefs. The Great Barrier Reef consists of thousands of separate reefs and is comparatively young, most of it having formed since the sea level rose after the end of the last Ice Age. An outer reef system corresponds with Queensland's continental shelf. Reef systems nearer the mainland correspond with submerged hills.

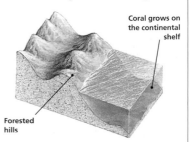

Coral grows on the continental shelf

Forested hills

1 Approximately 18,000 years ago, during the last Ice Age, waters were low, exposing a range of forested hills. Coral grew in the shallow waters of the continental shelf.

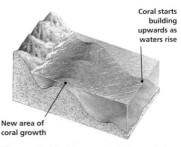

Coral starts building upwards as waters rise

New area of coral growth

2 Approximately 9,000 years ago, following the last Ice Age, the water level rose to submerge the hills. Coral began to grow in new places.

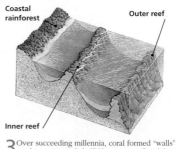

Coastal rainforest

Outer reef

Inner reef

3 Over succeeding millennia, coral formed "walls" on the continental shelf (the outer reef), while an array of fringing and platform reefs, coral cays and lagoons formed around the former hills (the inner reef).

Life on the Great Barrier Reef

Blue-faced angelfish

More than 2,000 species of fish and innumerable species of hard and soft coral are found in the waters of the Great Barrier Reef. The diversity of life forms is extraordinary, such as echinoderms (including sea urchins), crustaceans and sponges. There is also an array of invertebrates, such as the graceful sea slug, some 12 species of sea grasses and 500 types of algae. The reef islands and coral cays support a wonderfully colourful variety of tropical birdlife. This environment is protected by the Great Barrier Reef Marine Park Authority, established by an Act of Parliament in 1975.

Diving amid the dazzling colours and formations of soft coral.

Hard coral is formed from the outer skeleton of polyps *(see p204)*. The most common species is staghorn coral.

Soft coral has no outer skeleton and resembles the fronds of a plant, rippling in the waves.

Wobbegongs *are members of the shark family. They sleep during the day under rocks and caves, camouflaged by their skin tones.*

Manta rays are huge fish, measuring up to 6 m (20 ft) across. Despite their size, they are gentle creatures that are happy to swim close to divers.

Potato cod are known for their friendly demeanour and are often happy to swim alongside divers.

Great white sharks are occasional visitors to the reef, although they usually live in the open ocean and swim in schools.

Giant clams, which are large bivalves, are sadly a gourmet delicacy. Australian clams are now protected by law to save them from extinction.

The sea bed of the Barrier Reef is 60 m (195 ft) deep at its lowest point.

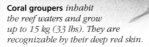

Coral groupers *inhabit the reef waters and grow up to 15 kg (33 lbs). They are recognizable by their deep red skin.*

THE FRAGILE REEF

Ecotourism is the only tourism that is encouraged on the Great Barrier Reef. The important thing to remember when on the reef is to look but not touch. Coral is easily broken; avoid standing on it and be aware that the taking of coral is strictly forbidden and carefully monitored. Camping on the reef's islands requires a permit from the Great Barrier Reef Marine Park Authority.

Beaked coralfish *are abundant and some of the most attractive fish of the Barrier Reef. They often swim in pairs, in shallow waters and around coral heads.*

Gobies feed on sand, ingesting the organic matter. They are found near the shoreline.

Blenny

Butterfly fish

THE REEF AS A MARINE HABITAT

Hard corals are the building blocks of the reef. Together with soft corals, they form the "forest" within which the fish and other sea creatures dwell.

Schultz pipefish

Goatfish

Clown anemonefish have an immunity to the stinging tentacles of sea anemones, among which they reside.

Batfish *swim in large groups and colonize areas of the reef for long periods before moving on elsewhere. They mainly feed on algae and sea jellies.*

Moray eels grow to 2 m (6 ft) in length, but are gentle enough to be hand-fed by divers.

The crown of thorns starfish *feeds mainly on staghorn coral. In the 1960s, a sudden growth in the numbers of this starfish led to worries that it would soon destroy the whole reef. However, many now believe that such a population explosion is a natural and common phenomenon. It contributes to reef life by destroying old coral and allowing new coral to generate.*

BIRDS OF THE GREAT BARRIER REEF

Gulls, gannets, frigate birds, shearwaters and terns all make use of the rich environment of the islands of the Great Barrier Reef to breed and rear their young, largely safe from mainland predators such as cats and foxes. The number of sea birds nesting on some of the coral cays *(see p204)* is astounding – for example, on the tiny area of Michaelmas Cay, 42 km (26 miles) northeast of Cairns, there are more than 30,000 birds, including herons and boobies. **Red-footed booby**

Activities on the Great Barrier Reef

Fewer than 20 of the Great Barrier Reef's 2,000 islands cater for tourists (see map and table below). Accommodation on the islands ranges from luxury resorts to basic camp sites. To make the most of the coral, take a tourist boat trip to the outer reef; most operators provide glass-bottomed boats or semi-submersibles to view the coral. The best way of seeing the reef, however, is by diving or snorkelling. There are numerous day trips from the mainland to the reef and between the islands.

Ornate butterfly fish

Reef walking *involves walking over dead stretches of the reef at low tide. Wear strong shoes and be very careful to avoid standing on living coral under the water.*

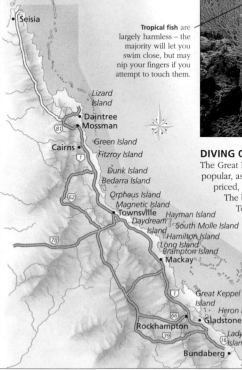

Snorkelling *is one of the most popular activities in the Great Barrier Reef, offering the chance to see beautiful tropical fish at close range.*

THE MAIN ISLANDS

Tropical fish are largely harmless – the majority will let you swim close, but may nip your fingers if you attempt to touch them.

- Seisia

Lizard Island
81
- Daintree
- Mossman
Cairns •
1
Green Island
Fitzroy Island
Dunk Island
Bedarra Island
62
Orpheus Island
Magnetic Island
- Townsville *Hayman Island*
Daydream *South Molle Island*
78 *Island* *Hamilton Island*
Long Island
Brampton Island
- Mackay

DIVING ON THE GREAT BARRIER REEF

The Great Barrier Reef is one of the most popular, as well as one of the more reasonably priced, places to learn to dive in the world. The best places to find dive schools are Townsville or Cairns, although many schools exist along the coast. Some boat trips also offer hand-held dives for complete beginners; some offer night dives.

Great Keppel Island
Heron Island
1
66
- Gladstone
Rockhampton
39
Lady Ellio Island
16
Bundaberg •

KEY

▬▬	Highway
══	Unsealed road

0 km   150

0 miles   150

Heron Island *is one of the few coral cay resorts and is known for its excellent diving. From October to March, turtle-spotting is a popular activity as they make their way up the beach to lay their eggs. Bird-watching is also popular as the island's pisonia trees are home to thousands of birds, including Noddy terns. Guided nature walks around the cay are available.*

Gorgonian fan coral grows in thickets in the deep waters of the Barrier Reef and is recognizable by its orange-yellow colour.

Scuba is an acronym for Self-contained Underwater Breathing Apparatus.

GETTING TO THE TOURIST ISLANDS

Bedarra Island 🚢 *from Dunk Island.* **Brampton Island** ✈ 🚢 *from Mackay.* **Daydream Island** 🚢 *from Shute Harbour.* **Dunk Island** ✈ *from Cairns.* 🚢 *from Mission Beach.* **Fitzroy Island** 🚢 *from Cairns.* **Great Keppel Island** ✈ *from Rockhampton.* **Green Island** 🚢 *from Cairns.* **Hamilton Island** ✈ *from state capitals & Cairns.* 🚢 *from Shute Harbour.* **Hayman Island** 🚢 *from Shute Harbour.* **Heron Island** ✈ 🚢 *from Gladstone.* **Lady Elliot Island** ✈ *from Bundaberg, Hervey Bay.* **Lizard Island** ✈ *from Cairns.* **Long Island** 🚢 *from Shute Harbour.* **Magnetic Island** ✈ 🚢 *from Townsville.* **Orpheus Island** ✈ *from Cairns & Townsville.* **S. Molle Island** 🚢 *from Shute Harbour.*

Hamilton Island *is a popular resort island featuring a wide range of activities, including para-sailing, skydiving, golf, tennis and children's entertainments.*

The Low Isles, *25 km (15 miles) offshore from Port Douglas, are a perfect example of the reef's day-trip opportunities. This glass-bottomed boat offers sunbathing areas, snorkelling, views of reef life and lunch, before returning to the mainland.*

ACTIVITIES ON THE TOURIST ISLANDS
These islands are easily accessible and offer a range of activities.

	DIVING	SNORKELLING	FISHING	DAY TRIPS	BUSHWALKING	WATERSPORTS	FOR CHILDREN
Bedarra Island	●	●	●	●	●	●	
Brampton Island		●	●	●	●	●	
Daydream Island	●	●	●	●	●	●	●
Dunk Island *(see p255)*	●	●	●	●	●	●	●
Fitzroy Island	●	●	●	●	●	●	
Gt Keppel Island		●	●	●	●	●	
Green Island *(see p253)*	●	●	●	●	●	●	
Hamilton Island	●	●	●	●	●	●	●
Hayman Island	●	●	●	●		●	
Heron Island	●	●					●
Lady Elliot Island	●	●					●
Lizard Island	●	●	●	●	●	●	
Long Island	●	●	●	●	●	●	
Magnetic Island *(see p247)*	●	●	●	●	●	●	
Orpheus Island	●	●	●	●	●	●	
South Molle Island	●	●	●	●	●	●	

BRISBANE

Brisbane is the capital of Queensland and, with a population of over 1.6 million, ranks third in size in Australia after Sydney and Melbourne. Situated on the Brisbane River and surrounded by misty blue hills, the city is known for its scenic beauty, balmy climate and friendly atmosphere. Its tropical vegetation is a great attraction, particularly the bougainvillea, poinciana and fragrant frangipani.

In 1823, the Governor of New South Wales, Sir Thomas Brisbane, decided that some of the more intractable convicts in the Sydney penal settlement needed more secure incarceration. The explorer John Oxley was dispatched to investigate Moreton Bay, noted by Captain Cook on his journey up the east coast 50 years earlier. Oxley landed at Redcliffe and thought he had stumbled across a tropical paradise. He was soon disappointed and it was decided to move the colony inland up the Brisbane River. This was mainly due to Brisbane's more reliable water supply and the fact that the river had a bend in it, which made escape more difficult for the convicts.

Free settlers began arriving in 1837, although they were not permitted to move closer than 80 km (50 miles) to the famously harsh penal settlement. This set a pattern of decentralization which is still evident today: Brisbane consists of several distinct communities as well as the central area. The city's growth was rapid and, in 1859, when Queensland became a self-governing colony, Brisbane was duly named as the state capital.

As Queensland's natural resources, including coal, silver, lead and zinc, were developed, so its major city flourished. Brisbane's status as a truly modern city, however, is relatively recent, beginning with a mining boom in the 1960s. Hosting the Commonwealth Games in 1982 and the 1988 World Expo were also milestones, bringing thousands of visitors to the city. Today, Brisbane is a cosmopolitan place boasting some superb restaurants, streetside cafés and a lively arts scene. Yet amid all the high-rises and modernity, pockets of traditional wooden cottages with verandas can still be found. In January 2011, major floods severely damaged homes and businesses in the city.

The Streets Beach swimming lagoon on Brisbane's South Bank with the city's high-rise skyline as a backdrop

◁ An old paddlesteamer on the Brisbane River, set against the city's modern skyline

Exploring Central Brisbane

Brisbane's city centre fits neatly in a U-shaped
loop of the Brisbane River, so one of the best ways to
get acquainted with the city is by ferry. The city
centre can also be easily explored on foot. The streets
follow a grid and are named after British royalty:
queens and princesses run north–south, kings and
princes run east–west. Brisbane's suburbs also have
their own distinct feel: to the east is chic Kangaroo
Point; just west of the centre is trendy Paddington;
while to the northwest Fortitude Valley has a diverse
and multicultural population.

Cenotaph in Anzac Square

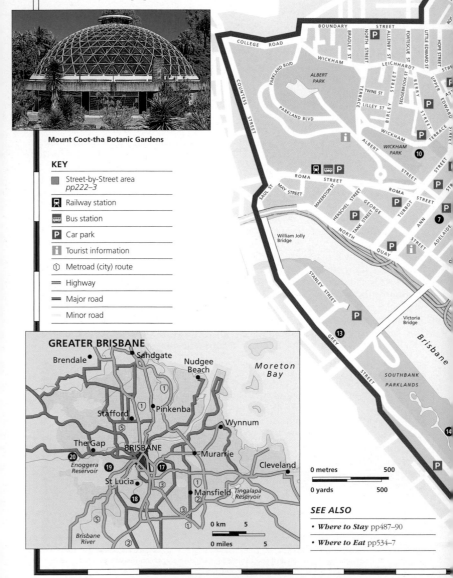

Mount Coot-tha Botanic Gardens

KEY

■	Street-by-Street area *pp222–3*
🚉	Railway station
🚌	Bus station
P	Car park
i	Tourist information
①	Metroad (city) route
=	Highway
—	Major road
—	Minor road

GREATER BRISBANE

Brendale
Sandgate
Nudgee Beach
Moreton Bay
Stafford
Pinkenba
Wynnum
The Gap
BRISBANE
Murarrie
Enoggera Reservoir
St Lucia
Cleveland
Mansfield
Tingalpa Reservoir
Brisbane River

0 km   5
0 miles   5

0 metres   500
0 yards   500

SEE ALSO

- ***Where to Stay*** pp487–90
- ***Where to Eat*** pp534–7

GETTING AROUND

Tours of the city centre are readily available and public transport is cheap and efficient. City centre bus stops are colour-coded for easy route identification and the Free Loop bus does a clockwise and anticlockwise loop around the main city area. The best place for boarding the city's ferries is Riverside Centre.

Street-by-Street: Central Brisbane

Central Brisbane is a blend of glass and
steel high-rises co-existing with graceful
19th-century constructions. The latter fortunately managed to survive the frenzy of demol-
ishing old buildings that took place throughout
the country during the 1970s. Queen Street,
now a pedestrian mall, is the hub of the city.
Reflecting the city's beginnings as a port, most
of the historic buildings are found near the
river. Near the city's first Botanical Gardens, which border Alice Street, many
old pubs have been renovated to cater
for a largely business-lunch clientele.

**Central Brisbane's modern skyline, looming
over the Brisbane River**

Cathedral of St Stephen
*One of the landmarks of
Brisbane's city centre is
this Gothic-style cathedral.
Particularly notable are
its white twin spires* ❷

Elizabeth Arcade
is filled with New
Age, alternative
and bohemian
style bookstores
and retail shops.

★ Commissariat Store Museum
*The original façade of these former 19th-
century granary stores has been preserved,
although the interior is now a museum
detailing Queensland's history* ❸

| 0 metres | | 100 |
| 0 yards | | 100 |

For hotels and restaurants in this region see pp487–90 and pp534–7

The former Coal Board building was erected in the mid-1880s and is an example of the elaborate warehouses that once dominated the city.

Smellie & Co. was a 19th-century hardware merchant housed in this attractive building. Note the Baroque doorway on the eastern side.

Queensland Club

This charming old building has housed the private, men-only Queensland Club since 1884. Panelled wood walls and elegant columns were intended to emulate British gentlemen's clubs.

LOCATOR MAP

KEY

– – – Suggested route

STAR SIGHTS

★ Commissariat Store Museum

★ Parliament House

STREET

ALICE STREET

The Mansions

The Mansions are a row of 1890s three-storey, red brick terrace houses. The arches of lighter coloured sandstone create a distinctive design. Stone cats sit atop the parapets at each end of the building.

★ Parliament House

This stained-glass window depicting Queen Victoria is one of the many beautiful features of this late 19th-century building. Unlike many early parliamentary buildings in Australia, it is still used for its original purpose ❹

South façade of the restored colonial Commissariat Store Museum

General Post Office ❶

261 Queen St. **Tel** 13 13 18.
🚆 Brisbane Central. 🚌 Free Loop.
⛴ Eagle St Pier. ⏰ 7am–6pm
Mon–Fri. ♿

Built between 1871 and
1879, this attractive Neo-
Classical building was erected
to house the city's first official
postal service. It replaced the
barracks for female convicts
which had previously occupied
the site. The building continues to operate as central
Brisbane's main post office.

Post Office Square, oppo-
site the General Post Office,
is a pleasant place to relax,
while looking out over the
landscaped greenery and
fountains of Anzac Square.

Cathedral of St Stephen ❷

249 Elizabeth St. **Tel** (07) 3336 9111.
🚆 Brisbane Central. 🚌 Free Loop.
⛴ Eagle St Pier. ⏰ 8am–6pm
Mon–Fri, 7am–6pm Sat–Sun. ♿ 📷

Early settlers provided
the funds for this lovely
English Gothic-style Catholic
cathedral, designed by noted
colonial architect Benjamin
Backhouse and completed in
1874. The main façade features restored twin spires on
each side of the elaborate
stained-glass windows.

Next door is St Stephen's
Chapel, the original cathedral.
It was designed by AW Pugin,
an English architect who also
worked on London's Houses
of Parliament.

Commissariat Store Museum ❸

115 William St. **Tel** (07) 3221 4198.
🚆 South Brisbane. 🚌 Free Loop.
⛴ North Quay. ⏰ 10am–4pm
Tue–Fri. ⏰ Good Fri, Easter Sun,
25 Dec, 26 Dec. 📷 ♿

The Commissariat Stores,
constructed by convict labour
in 1829, is the only surviving
building from Brisbane's
penal colony days open to
the public. Having been
restored in 2000, it is now
open to visitors and houses
the Royal Historical Society
of Queensland.

Parliament House ❹

Cnr George and Alice sts. **Tel** (07)
3406 7562. 🚆 Brisbane Central.
🚌 1a, 1b, 5, 5b, 5c, 7, 7a, Free
Loop. ⛴ Gardens Point. ⏰ 9am–
4:15pm Mon–Fri (on sitting days).
⏰ public hols. ♿ 📷 obligatory.

Queensland's Parliament
House was designed in
French Renaissance style by

architect Charles Tiffin,
who won an architectural
competition. Begun in 1865, it
was completed in 1868. Tiffin
added features more suited to
Queensland's tropical climate,
such as shady colonnades,
shutters and an arched roof
which is made from Mount
Isa copper (*see p257*). Other
notable features are the cedar
staircases and the intricate
gold leaf detailing on the
Council Chamber ceilings.

The building is still used
for its original purpose and
the public is permitted into
the chambers when parliament
is not in progress. Unlike other
state parliaments, consisting
of an Upper and Lower House,
Queensland has only one
parliamentary body.

Parliament House is also
notable as being the first legislative building in the British
Empire to be lit by electricity.

Interior of the Assembly Chamber
in Parliament House

Brisbane City Botanic Gardens ❺

Alice St. **Tel** (07) 3403 8888.
🚆 Brisbane Central. 🚌 Free Loop.
⛴ Edward St. ⏰ 24 hours. ♿

Brisbane's first Botanic
Gardens on the Brisbane
River are the second oldest
botanic gardens in Australia.
Their peaceful location is a

Mangrove boardwalk in the Botanic Gardens

Arcade and arches of the north façade of Old Government House

welcome haven from the city's high-rise buildings.

In its earliest incarnation, the area was used as a vegetable garden by convicts. It was laid out in its present form in 1855 by the colonial botanist Walter Hill, who was also the first director of the gardens. An avenue of bunya pines dates back to the 1850s, while an avenue of weeping figs was planted in the 1870s.

Hundreds of water birds, such as herons and plovers, are attracted to the lakes dotted throughout the gardens' 18 ha (44 acres). Brisbane River's renowned mangroves are now a protected species and can be admired from a specially built boardwalk.

Old Government House **❻**

Queensland University of Technology Campus, Gardens Point, George St. **Tel** (07) 3138 8005. 🚊 Brisbane Central. 🚌 Free Loop. 🚢 Gardens Point. 🕐 10am–5pm Sun–Fri. 🚻 🖥 www.ogh.qut.edu.au

Home to the National Trust of Queensland since 1973, the state's first Government House was designed by colonial architect Charles Tiffin and completed in 1862. The graceful sandstone building served not only as the state governor's residence, but also as the administrative base and social centre of the state of Queensland until 1910. It was then occupied by the fledgling

University of Queensland. Old Government House reopened in 2009 after renovation. It now has an art gallery dedicated to the works of William Robinson, one of Australia's greatest living landscape artists.

City Hall **❼**

King George Sq. **Tel** (07) 3403 8888. 🚊 Brisbane Central. 🚌 Free Loop. 🚢 Eagle St Pier. 🕐 currently closed for renovation; check website. 🚻 🖥 **Clocktower** 🕐 10am–3pm daily. 🌐 public hols. **Museum of Brisbane** 🕐 10am–5pm daily. www.brisbane.qld.gov.au

Completed in 1930, the Neo-Classical City Hall is home to Brisbane City Council, the largest council in Australia.

Brisbane's early settlement is depicted by a beautiful sculpted tympanum above the main entrance. In the King George Square foyer, some fine examples of traditional craftsmanship are evident in the floor

mosaics, ornate ceilings and woodwork carved from Queensland timbers. City Hall's 92-m (300-ft) Italian Renaissance-style tower gives a panoramic view of the city from a platform at its top. A display of contemporary art and Aboriginal art and ceramics is housed in the Museum of Brisbane.

The attractive King George Square, facing City Hall, continues to resist the encroachment of high-rise office blocks and has several interesting statues, including *Form del Mito* by Arnaldo Pomodoro. The work's geometric forms and polished surfaces, for which this Italian sculptor is noted, reflect the changing face of the city from morning through to night. The bronze *Petrie Tableau*, by Tasmanian sculptor Stephen Walker, was designed for Australia's bicentenary. It commemorates the pioneer families of Brisbane and depicts one of Queensland's earliest explorers, Andrew Petrie, being bid farewell by his family as he departs on an inland expedition.

Façade of City Hall, with its Italian Renaissance clocktower

Customs House ⑧

399 Queen St. *Tel* (07) 3365 8999.
🚆 Brisbane Central. 🚌 Free Loop.
🚤 Riverside. ⬛ 10am–4pm daily.
⬤ public hols. ♿ 📷 Sun. 🍴

Restored by the University of Queensland in 1994, Customs House, with its landmark copper dome and stately Corinthian columns, is now open to the public. Commissioned in 1886, this is one of Brisbane's oldest buildings, predating both City Hall *(see p225)* and the Treasury. Early renovations removed the hall and staircase, but these have now been carefully reconstructed from the original plans. Today, the building is used for numerous civic functions and there is also a restaurant; call ahead for opening times.

Anzac Square ⑨

Ann & Adelaide sts. 🚆 Brisbane Central. 🚌 Free Loop. 🚤 Waterfront Place, Eagle St Pier.

All Australian cities commemorate those who have given their life for their country. Brisbane's war memorial is centred on Anzac Square, an attractive park planted with, among other flora, rare boab (baobab) trees. The Eternal Flame burns in a Greek Revival cenotaph at the Ann Street entrance to the park. Beneath the cenotaph is the Shrine of Memories, containing various tributes and wall plaques to those who gave their lives in war.

Distinctive view of Old Windmill

Old Windmill ⑩

Wickham Terrace. 🚆 Brisbane Central. 🚌 City Sights. ⬤ to public.

Built in 1828, the Old Windmill is one of two buildings still standing in Brisbane from convict days, the old Commissariat Stores being the other survivor *(see p224)*. Originally the colony's first industrial building, it proved unworkable without the availability of trained operators, so it was equipped with treadmills to punish recalcitrant convicts. It later served as a time signal, with a gun fired and a ball dropped each day at exactly 1pm.

The picturesque mill was also chosen as the first television image in Australia in the 1920s. The windmill is not open to the public, but it makes a striking photograph.

St John's Anglican Cathedral ⑪

373 Ann St. *Tel* (07) 3835 2231. 🚆 Brisbane Central. 🚌 Free Loop. 🚤 Riverside Centre. ⬛ 9:30am–4:30pm daily. ♿ 📷

Designed along French Gothic lines in 1888, with the foundation stone laid in 1901, St John's Anglican Cathedral is regarded as one of the most splendid churches in the southern hemisphere. The interior is of Helidon sandstone. On display are numerous examples of local needlework, wood, glass and stone craft. Over 400 cushions depicting Queensland's flora and fauna attract a lot of interest.

It was at the adjacent Deanery in 1859 that Queensland was made a separate colony (it had been part of NSW). The Deanery was the temporary residence of Queenland's first governor.

Nave and altar of St John's Anglican Cathedral

Fortitude Valley and Chinatown ⑫

Brunswick & Ann sts, Fortitude Valley. 🚆 Brunswick St. 🚌 City Sights.

The ship *Fortitude* sailed from England and up the Brisbane River in 1859 with 250 settlers on board, and the name stuck to the valley where they disembarked. For a time the area was the trading centre of the city and some impressive buildings were erected during the 1880s

Greek cenotaph in Anzac Square

For hotels and restaurants in this region see pp487–90 and pp534–7

Entrance to the Pedestrian Hall in Chinatown, Fortitude Valley

and 1890s. It then degenerated into one of Brisbane's seedier areas.

In the 1980s, the city council began to revive the district. It is now the bohemian centre of Brisbane, with some of the city's best restaurants (see pp535–7) . McWhirter's Emporium, an Art Deco landmark, was originally a department store. Shops now occupy the lower levels with apartments above. On weekends, there is also a busy outdoor market in Brunswick Street.

Also within the valley is Brisbane's Chinatown, a bustling area of Asian restaurants, supermarkets, cinemas and martial arts centres. The lions at the entrance to the area were turned around when a *feng shui* expert considered their original position to be bad for business.

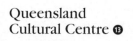

Butterfly at South Bank Parklands

Queensland Cultural Centre ⓫

See pp228–9.

South Bank Precinct ⓮

Brisbane River foreshore, South Bank. ⬛ South Bank. 🚌 12, Adelaide St & George St routes. ⛴ South Bank 1, 2, 3. ♿ Visitors' Centre **Tel** (07) 3867 2051. ◯ 9am–5pm daily. **www**.visitsouthbank.com

The South Bank of the Brisbane River was the site of Expo '88 and is now a 17 ha (42 acres) centre of culture, entertainment and recreation. The area known as the parklands includes the Queensland Performing Arts Centre, the State Library, the Queensland Museum, and Queensland Art Gallery and Gallery of Modern Art (see pp228–9), the Conservatorium, Opera Queensland, two colleges and an exhibition centre. The South Bank area abounds with restaurants, cafés, weekend market stalls and street entertainers. Classical music and pop concerts are also regularly held here. There is even a man-made lagoon with a "real" sandy beach, complete with suntanned lifesavers. South Bank Cinema screens the latest-release movies.

South Bank also features the Wheel of Brisbane, offering breathtaking views of the city, and Goodwill Bridge, a 450-m (1,500-ft) pedestrian and cycle bridge, linking the area with the Botanic Gardens.

Queensland Maritime Museum ⓯

End of Goodwill Bridge, South Bank. **Tel** (07) 3844 5361. ⬛ South Bank. 🚌 174, 175, 203, 204. ⛴ River Plaza, South Bank 3. ◯ 9:30am–4:30pm daily. ◯ Good Fri, 25 Apr (am), 25 Dec, 26 Dec. 🎫 ♿ 📷 **www**.maritimemuseum.com.au

Queensland Maritime Museum lists among its exhibits shipbuilders' models, reconstructed cabins from early coastal steamers and relics from early shipwrecks in the area. In the dry dock, as part of the National Estate, sits HMAS *Diamantina*, a frigate that served during World War II.

A coal-fired tug, *Forceful*, is maintained in running order and cruises with passengers to Moreton Bay two seasons a year. Also on display is the pearling lugger *Penguin* and the bow of a Japanese pleasure boat, a *yakatabume*, donated to Brisbane by Japan after Expo '88.

HMAS *Diamantina* at the Queensland Maritime Museum

Queensland Cultural Centre ⑬

The Queensland Cultural Centre is the hub of
Brisbane's arts scene, with a spectacular setting
on the South Bank. It incorporates the Queensland
Art Gallery, the Gallery of Modern Art (GoMA), the
Queensland Museum, the State Library of Queens-
land and the Queensland Performing Arts Centre.

First established in 1895 and expanded in 2006,
the Queensland Art Gallery has a fine collection
of Australian art, including works by Sidney
Nolan and Margaret Preston, together with Aboriginal art. The international collection includes
15th-century European art and Asian art from the
12th century. Queensland Art Gallery and GoMA
are regarded as one institution and together make
up Australia's second largest public art museum.

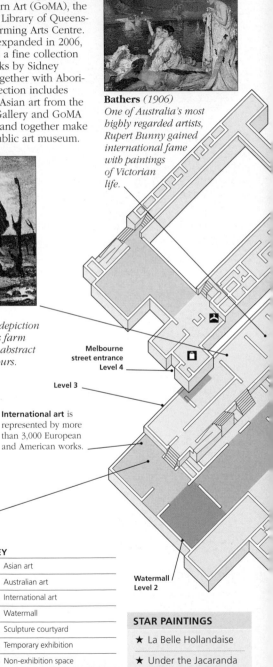

Bathers *(1906)*
*One of Australia's most
highly regarded artists,
Rupert Bunny gained
international fame
with paintings
of Victorian
life.*

Bushfire *(1944)*
*Russell Drysdale is known for his depiction
of harsh Outback life, such as this farm
house destroyed by a fire. It is an abstract
piece with slightly discordant colours.*

Melbourne
street entrance
Level 4

Level 3

International art is
represented by more
than 3,000 European
and American works.

★ La Belle Hollandaise
(1905)
*One of Picasso's transitional
works between his blue and
rose periods, this was
painted during a visit to the
Netherlands. The gallery
paid a then world record
price of £55,000 in 1959 for
the work of a living artist.*

Watermall
Level 2

KEY

■	Asian art
□	Australian art
▨	International art
■	Watermall
□	Sculpture courtyard
▨	Temporary exhibition
□	Non-exhibition space

STAR PAINTINGS

★ La Belle Hollandaise

★ Under the Jacaranda

QUEENSLAND ART GALLERY GUIDE

The collection is housed over three levels. Fine collections of Asian art from the 12th century are found on Level 2. International art begins on Level 2 and moves up to Level 4. Level 3 contains Australian art after 1970. The work in this gallery is complemented by the contemporary art housed in the Gallery of Modern Art. Also of interest is the Watermall's indoor water feature, an acclaimed architectural aspect of the cultural centre.

VISITORS' CHECKLIST

Cnr Melbourne & Grey sts, South Bank. 🚉 *South Brisbane.* 🚌 *174, 175, 203, 204.* 🚊 *South Bank.* **Queensland Art Gallery & GoMA *Tel*** *(07) 3840 7303.* ⬜ *10am–5pm Mon–Fri, 9am–5pm Sat–Sun.* ⬤ *Good Fri, Anzac Day (opens noon), 25 Dec.* ♿ 🅿 📷 ✏ *11am, 1pm, 2pm, Mon–Fri, 11:30am, 1pm, 2:30pm Sat–Sun.* **www**.qag.qld.gov.au

★ Under the Jacaranda
R. Godfrey Rivers' work is part of a collection of Australian art.

The Sculpture Courtyard and surrounding fountains are a pleasant place to relax or enjoy a picnic.

The Watermall's indoor water feature is surrounded by various pieces of art from the gallery's collection.

🏛 Gallery of Modern Art (GoMA)

As Queensland Art Gallery. The architecturally acclaimed GoMA is Australia's largest gallery of modern and contemporary art, focusing on 20th- and 21st-century works from Australia, Asia and the Pacific, with two galleries devoted to contemporary indigenous Australian art.

🏛 Queensland Museum

Tel (07) 3840 7555. ⬜ *9:30am–5pm daily.* ⬤ *Good Fri, 25 Apr (until 1:30pm), 25 Dec.* ♿ 🍴 📷

This imaginative natural history museum is filled with full-scale models, both prehistoric and current. A large-scale model of Queensland's unique dinosaur, the *Muttaburrasaurus*, stands in the foyer.

🏛 State Library of Queensland

Tel (07) 3840 7666. ⬜ *daily.* ⬤ *Good Fri, 25–26 Dec.* ♿ 💻 📷

The State Library houses collections from around the world. Its extensive resources cover all interests and most of its services are free. There are innovative exhibitions, an Indigenous Knowledge Centre and The Edge, a modern digital culture space.

Performers of the acclaimed Queensland Ballet company

🎭 Queensland Performing Arts Centre (QPAC)

Tel 13 62 46. ⬜ *performances only.* ♿ *advise when booking.*

QPAC comprises a main concert hall and three theatres where internationally acclaimed opera, classical music and theatrical productions are staged. The Queensland Ballet is also based here.

River view from Brisbane's Story Bridge

Story Bridge ⑯

Level 1, 170 Main St, Kangaroo Point. *Tel* 1300 254 627.
◯ *daily.* 📷 ✔
www.sbac.net.au

Brisbane's iconic Story Bridge was constructed during the Great Depression, taking five years to build and opening in July 1940. With a bridge already across the Brisbane River, this new bridge was more a means of creating jobs and boosting the city's morale.

The Story Bridge Adventure Climb is a spectacular way to discover Brisbane. Climbs take place several times a day as well as at night. Throughout the two-and-a-half hour experience, the climb leader reveals the history of the bridge and talks about the city's transition from a 19th-century penal settlement to a 21st-century metropolis. At the summit, climbers enjoy views of Brisbane, its river and the surrounding mountains.

Newstead House ⑰

Newstead Park, Breakfast Creek Rd, Newstead. *Tel* (07) 3216 1846.
🚊 *Bowen Hills.* 🚌 *300, 306, 322.*
⛴ *Newstead Point.* ◯ *10am–4pm Mon–Fri, 2–5pm Sun.* ⬤ *Good Fri, 25 Apr, 25–26 Dec.* 📷 ✔ *by arrangement.* **www**.newsteadhouse.com.au

Built in 1846 for Patrick Leslie, one of the first European settlers in the Darling Downs region, Newstead House is the oldest surviving home in Brisbane. This charming building was sold in 1847 to government resident and magistrate, Captain John Wickham.

The centre of the new colony's social life, Newstead House was the scene of lavish parties. A huge fig tree, under which elegant carriages once waited, still graces the drive. In 1939, it became the first Australian house to be preserved by its very own act of parliament. Restored by the Newstead House Trust from 1976, the house is furnished with Victorian antiques.

Decorated Victorian music box in Newstead House

Lone Pine Koala Sanctuary ⑱

Jesmond Rd, Fig Tree Pocket. *Tel* (07) 3378 1366. 🚌 *430, 445.* ⛴ *North Quay.* ◯ *8:30am–5pm daily; 8:30am–4pm on 25 Dec.* ⬤ *until 1:30pm 25 April.* 📷 ✔ ⬤ 🍴 **www**.koala.net

The oldest Koala Sanctuary in Australia, opened in 1927, is now one of Brisbane's most popular tourist attractions. Lone Pine has more than 100 koalas, as well as kangaroos, emus, possums, dingoes, wombats, reptiles and many Australian birds, including various species of parrot. Lone Pine insists that it is more than just a zoo, a claim that is supported by its nationally respected koala breeding programme. For a small fee, visitors can have their photograph taken holding a koala.

A pleasant and scenic way to get to Lone Pine Sanctuary is by ferry. There are daily departures at 10am from Victoria Bridge.

Brisbane Botanic Gardens ⑲

Mt Coot-tha Rd, Toowong.
Tel (07) 3403 2535. 🚌 *333.*
◯ *8am–5pm daily.* ✔

Brisbane Botanic Gardens, in the foothills of Mount Coot-tha Forest Park 8 km (5 miles) from the city centre, were founded in 1976 and feature more than 20,000 specimens, representing 5,000 species, of exotic herbs, shrubs and trees laid out in themed beds. Highlights include eucalypt groves, a Japanese Garden, a Tropical Display Dome, which includes lotus lilies and vanilla orchids, a Lagoon and Bamboo Grove, Fern House, National Freedom Wall (celebrating 50 years of peace) and a large collection of Australian native plants. Many arid and tropical plants, usually seen in greenhouses, thrive in the outdoor setting. Also in the Gardens complex,

Koala at Lone Pine Koala Sanctuary

Lush landscape of the Brisbane Botanic Gardens

the Sir Thomas Brisbane Planetarium is the largest of Australia's planetariums.

Mount Coot-tha Forest Park offers both spectacular views and attractive picnic areas. The Aboriginal name means "place of wild honey", a reference to the tiny bees found in the area. On a clear day, from the summit lookout you can see Brisbane, encircled by the river, Moreton and Stradbroke islands, the Glasshouse Mountains (so named by Captain Cook because they reminded him of the glass furnaces in his native Yorkshire) and the Lamington Plateau backing onto the Gold Coast (see pp238–9). The park also offers easygoing walking trails through the woodland, including Aboriginal trails which detail traditional uses of native plants.

South D'Aguilar National Park ⑳

🚌 385. 🛈 The Gap (07) 3300 4855. ⬤ 9am–4:30pm daily. ⬤ 25–26 & 31 Dec, 1–2 Jan. 🈂

South D'Aguilar National Park, within the D'Aguilar Mountain Range, stretches for more than 50 km (30 miles) north-west of Brisbane city centre. Covering more than 28,500 ha (70,250 acres) of natural bushland and eucalypt forests, the park offers driving routes with breathtaking views over the surrounding countryside. The most scenic driving route is along Mount Nebo Road,

which winds its way through the lush mountains.

Another scenic drive extends from Samford up to the charming mountain village of Mount Glorious and down the other side. It is worth stopping from time to time to hear the distinctive calls of bellbirds and whipbirds.

Six km (4 miles) past Mount Glorious is the Wivenhoe Outlook, with spectacular views down to Lake Wivenhoe, an artificial lake created to prevent the Brisbane River from flooding the city. One km (half a mile) north of Mount Glorious is the entrance to Maiala Recreation Area, where there are picnic areas, some wheelchair accessible, and several walking trails of varying lengths, from short

walks to longer, 8-km (5-mile) treks. These pass through the rainforest, which abounds with animal life. Other excellent walks are at Manorina and at Jolly's Lookout, the oldest formal lookout in the park, which has a good picnic area. Also in the park is the Westridge Outlook, a boardwalk with sweeping views.

The engrossing **Walkabout Creek Wildlife Centre** at the park's headquarters is a re-created large freshwater environment. Water dragons, pythons, water rats, catfish and tiny rainbow fish flourish within these natural surroundings. Visitors also have the chance to see the extraordinary lungfish, a unique species which is equipped with both gills and lungs. The on-site restaurant looks out over the beautiful bush landscape.

About 4 km (2 miles) from the park headquarters is Bellbird Grove, which includes an outdoor Aboriginal collection of bark huts. It has a picnic area and also grassed picnic areas at Ironbark Gully and Lomandra.

🐾 **Walkabout Creek Wildife Centre**
60 Mt Nebo Rd, The Gap. **Tel** (07) 3300 2558. ⬤ 9am–4:30pm daily. ⬤ 25–26 & 31 Dec, 1–2 Jan. 🈂 ⬛ ♿ limited. **www**.walkaboutcreek.com.au

---

Spectacular waterfall in South D'Aguilar National Park

BRISBANE PRACTICAL INFORMATION

Time Off listings guide

Brisbane, built around a serpentine river, takes full advantage of its idyllic subtropical weather. Trendy riverside cafés, heritage trails, miles of boardwalk and a floating walkway, ferries and fast catamaran-style CityCats make Brisbane a relaxed holiday destination. The city offers centrally located five-star hotels, budget inns and historic guesthouses (see pp487–90). There are dining choices in all price ranges, such as silver service at luxury hotels, riverfront cafés, ethnic cuisine and alfresco restaurants, most offering menus based on superb local produce and fresh seafood (see pp535–7). Public transport is reasonably priced and easily accessed. Taxi stands are well signposted, and tourist information centres, identified by the international "I" symbol, are situated throughout the city.

SHOPPING

Brisbane is a shopping heaven, with its hidden arcades, small boutiques, quaint tea shops, lively galleries, pedestrian malls and multi-storied shopping centres. Finding what you are looking for is not difficult as the city is divided into small precincts, each offering a unique shopping experience. The pedestrianized **Queen Street Mall** has 700 speciality stores, including six shopping centres. **Brisbane Arcade**, one of Brisbane's most elegant shopping areas, runs off the Mall. With classic marbled interior and polished wood balustrades, it was opened in 1923 and offers quality jewellers and stylish fashion. Using the river to

The lively art and crafts market on the South Bank, held every weekend

Restored interior of the 19th-century Brisbane Arcade

move from one precinct to another is a convenient and relaxing option. The **Fireworks Gallery** exhibits aboriginal art and local artists, and is just another river stop away at Stratton Street, in Newstead. The **James Street Precinct** in Fortitude Valley has developed around an urban inner-city lifestyle. It is a great place for coffee, small delicatessens, trendy fashion shops, designer boutiques and galleries. Brisbane's weather encourages outdoor markets. The **Riverside Markets** with over 250 stalls are open every Sunday, displaying a huge variety of local arts, crafts, clothes and jewellery. The **South Bank Markets** are held every weekend. Its parklands, man-made beach, cafés and restaurants make the South Bank a great place for a shopping experience.

ENTERTAINMENT

The **Queensland Performing Arts Centre** has an exciting calendar of events, including opera, classical and contemporary dance, and live stage shows. The **La Boite Theatre** in Spring Hill is a 200-seat theatre in the round, and home to one of the oldest production companies in Australia. Brisbane hosts a myriad of music festivals, including the Brisbane River Festival. For live music there are nightclubs in the Fortitude Valley and Caxton Street areas. **Conrad Treasury Brisbane** casino is open 24 hours. Entertainment listings can be found in free magazines such as *This Week in Brisbane* and *Time Off*, which offers a great gig guide. Tickets for most events can be obtained from **Ticketek**.

CityCat ferry service on the Brisbane River

GETTING AROUND

Brisbane is a compact city which can be explored on foot. Maps are available from most hotels and information centres. There are excellent self-guided heritage trails and riverside pathways on both sides of the river.

Public transport in Brisbane includes buses, commuter trains and ferries. The TransLink system allows for use of one ticket for all forms of transport. The river has become one of the main ways of moving about the city. CityCat ferries service some of the most popular locations including South Bank, Eagle Street, Riverside, Dockside, New Farm and Kangaroo Point. The two main points of departure are in Eagle Street.

CityCat ferry sign

The most economical way to travel on all Brisbane's public transport is with a Daily ticket, available from any public transport service. This can offer unlimited travel for a day, or at off-peak times within nominated zones.

Another flexible and economical way to see the city is on a **City Sights Bus Tour**. There is a standard fare and you can get on and off whenever you choose. To get back on a Bus, simply hail one from one of the City Sights' stops and show your ticket.

Brisbane's Free Loop service travels around the centre of the city, with a bus every ten minutes. The Cityxpress buses service the suburbs. All buses stop at the Queen Street Bus Station.

Commercially operated bus companies also offer tours of the city's highlights, as well as to the surrounding areas, including Stradbroke Island, Morcton Bay and Surfers Paradise *(see pp238–9)* and the mountainous hinterland *(see pp240–41)*.

All types of public transport run until midnight, and taxis are plentiful in the city centre at night. Driving is increasingly difficult but there are numerous, well-maintained bike tracks around the city.

City Sights Bus Tour, an easy way to see central Brisbane

SOUTH OF TOWNSVILLE

*S*outhern Queensland is renowned for two distinct features: its fine coastal surfing beaches and, inland, some of the richest farming land in Australia. The area is the centre of the country's beef and sugar industries, and the Burdekin River Delta supports a fertile "salad basin" yielding tomatoes, beans and other small crops. Ports such as Mackay and Gladstone service some rich inland mines.

Recognizing the land's potential, pastoralists followed hard on the heels of the explorers who opened up this region in the 1840s. Sugar production had begun by 1869 in the Bundaberg area and by the 1880s it was a flourishing industry, leading to a shameful period in the country's history. As Europeans were considered inherently unsuited to work in the tropics, growers seized on South Sea Islanders for cheap labour. Called Kanakas, the labourers were paid a pittance, housed in substandard accommodation and given the most physically demanding jobs. Some Kanakas were kidnapped from their homeland (a practice called "blackbirding"), but this was outlawed in 1868 and government inspectors were placed on all Kanakas ships to check that their emigration was voluntary. It was not until Federation in 1901 that the use of island labour stopped but by then some 60,000 Kanakas had been brought to Queensland.

In tandem with this agricultural boom, southern Queensland thrived in the latter half of the 19th century when gold was found in the region. Towns such as Charters Towers have preserved much of their 19th-century architecture as reminders of the glory days of the gold rush. Although much of the gold has been extracted, the region is still rich in coal and has the world's largest sapphire fields. Amid this mineral landscape, there are also some beautiful national parks.

Today, the area is perhaps best known for its coastal features. Surfers from all over the world flock to the aptly named resort of Surfers Paradise, and the white sand beaches of the Gold Coast are crowded throughout the summer months. The region is also the gateway to the southern tip of the Great Barrier Reef and the Whitsunday Islands, and is popular with both locals and visitors.

Beach fishing as dawn breaks in Surfers Paradise

◁ Sandstone Bluff near the entrance of Violet Gorge in the ruggedly beautiful Carnarvon National Park

Exploring South of Townsville

With easy access from Brisbane *(see pp218–33)*, the southern coastline of Queensland is one of the most popular holiday locations in Australia, with its sunny climate, sandy beaches and good surf. Fraser Island is one of the region's undisputed highlights with its vast beaches, cool blue lakes and interior rainforests. Behind the fertile coastal plains are many of the 1850s gold rush "boom towns", while the Capricorn Hinterland, inland from Rockhampton, has the fascinating sapphire gem fields near Emerald and the dramatic sandstone escarpments of the Carnarvon and Blackdown Tableland national parks. To the north of the region is the busy city of Townsville, a major gateway to the Whitsundays and the islands of the Great Barrier Reef *(see pp212–17)*.

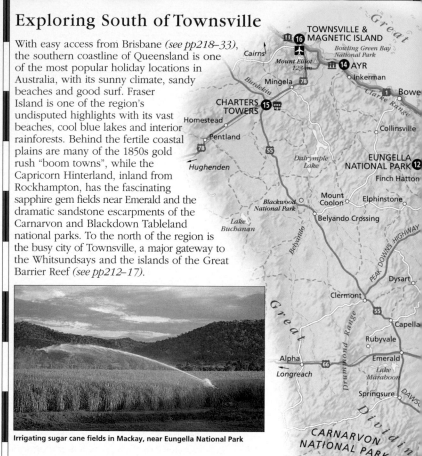

Irrigating sugar cane fields in Mackay, near Eungella National Park

SIGHTS AT A GLANCE

Ayr ⑭
Blackdown Tableland
  National Park ⑩
*Carnarvon National
  Park p245* ⑪
Charters Towers ⑮
Darling Downs ❷
Eungella National Park ⑫
Fraser Island p242 ❻
Gladstone ❽
Hervey Bay ❺
Lamington National Park ❶
Maryborough ❹
Mon Repos Conservation
  Park ❼
Rockhampton ❾
Sunshine Coast Hinterland ❸
Townsville and Magnetic
  Island ⑯
Whitsunday Islands ⑬

SEE ALSO

• **Where to Stay** pp490–92
• **Where to Eat** pp537–8

KEY

═══ Highway
━━━ Major road
┄┄┄ Minor road
╌ ╌ Track
━━━ Scenic route
⊸⊸⊸ Main railway
──── Minor railway
━━━ State border
△   Summit

0 kilometres   100
0 miles   100

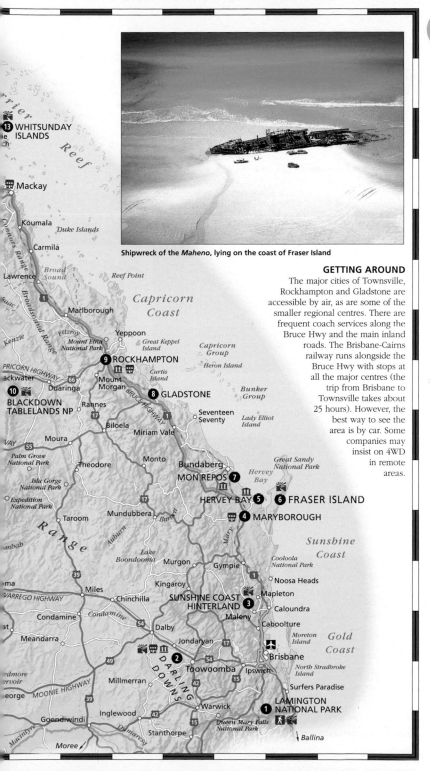

Shipwreck of the *Maheno*, lying on the coast of Fraser Island

WHITSUNDAY ISLANDS 🔟

Mackay

Koumala

Duke Islands

Carmila

Lawrence

Broad Sound

Reef Point

Capricorn Coast

Marlborough

Yeppoon

Great Keppel Island

Mount Etna National Park

Capricorn Group

Heron Island

ROCKHAMPTON 9️⃣

Curtis Island

Duaringa

Mount Morgan

GLADSTONE 8️⃣

BLACKDOWN TABLELANDS NP 🔟

Rannes

Bunker Group

Biloela

Seventeen Seventy

Lady Elliot Island

Moura

Miriam Vale

Monto

Palm Grove National Park

Isla Gorge National Park

Theodore

Bundaberg

MON REPOS 7️⃣

Great Sandy National Park

Hervey Bay

Expedition National Park

Mundubbera

HERVEY BAY 5️⃣   6️⃣ **FRASER ISLAND**

Taroom

Range

MARYBOROUGH 4️⃣

Sunshine Coast

Lake Boondooma

Murgon

Gympie

Cooloola National Park

Miles

Kingaroy

Noosa Heads

Chinchilla

SUNSHINE COAST HINTERLAND 3️⃣

Mapleton

Condamine

Dalby

Maleny

Caloundra

Meandarra

Jondaryan

Caboolture

Moreton Island

Gold Coast

DARLING DOWNS 2️⃣

Toowoomba

Ipswich

Brisbane

North Stradbroke Island

Millmerran

Surfers Paradise

Inglewood

Warwick

LAMINGTON NATIONAL PARK 1️⃣

Goondiwindi

Stanthorpe

Queen Mary Falls National Park

Ballina

Moree

GETTING AROUND

The major cities of Townsville, Rockhampton and Gladstone are accessible by air, as are some of the smaller regional centres. There are frequent coach services along the Bruce Hwy and the main inland roads. The Brisbane-Cairns railway runs alongside the Bruce Hwy with stops at all the major centres (the trip from Brisbane to Townsville takes about 25 hours). However, the best way to see the area is by car. Some companies may insist on 4WD in remote areas.

Southern Queensland Coastline

Movie World entrance sign on the Gold Coast

An hour's drive either north or south of Brisbane, the southern Queensland coast is Australia's most popular beach playground. The famous Gold Coast extends 75 km (45 miles) south of Brisbane and is a flashy strip of holiday apartments, luxury hotels, shopping malls, nightclubs, a casino and, above all, 42 km (25 miles) of golden sandy beaches. To the north, the Sunshine Coast is more restrained and elegant. Inland, the Great Dividing Range provides a cool alternative to the hot coastal climate, with flourishing arts and crafts communities, superb bushwalking and wonderful panoramas.

Burleigh Heads National Park *is a tiny park which preserves the dense eucalypt forests that once covered the entire region. The nutritious volcanic soil stemming from Mount Warning, 30 km (20 miles) southwest of the park, allows the rainforest to thrive.*

The Gold Coast *has three theme parks. Sea World has dolphin, sea lion and penguin displays; Warner Bros. Movie World features stunts and tours of replica film sets; Dreamworld fairground park has wildlife such as Bengal tigers. There are also two water parks: Wet 'n' Wild® and Whitewater World.*

Australia Zoo *began life as a small, four-acre park known as Beerwah Reptile Park. Its founder, Steve "the Croc Hunter" Irwin, became a household name and today the zoo is a 70-acre entertainment mecca with more than 1,000 animals.*

Tewantin [2]

⛑

This well-known town is in the heart of the Sunshine Coast area, with spectacular sunsets and beautiful beaches. It is also the ferry access point to Cooloola National Park.

MARYBOROUGH

Maroochydore Beach [5]

🏄 🌊 🏊 ⛑ ♿ 🚻

An ocean beach and the Maroochy river front make the main commercial centre of the Sunshine Coast a popular holiday destination, with good hotels and restaurants.

Mooloolaba Wharf [6]

🏄 🌊 🏊 ⛑ ♿

The wharf at Mooloolaba is a popular tourist development. Underwater World, said to be the largest oceanarium in the southern hemisphere, contains crocodiles and barramundi.

Bulcock Beach, Caloundra [7]

🌊 🏊 ⛑ ♿ 🚻

The central location of sandy Bulcock Beach means it is often crowded with tourists and families. Nearby Golden Beach and Shelly Beach are also beautiful, but quieter.

Moreton Bay [8]

🌊 🏊 ⛑ ♿ 🚻

This is the access point to some 370 offshore islands, the most popular being Moreton, Bribie and South Stradbroke. Fishing, bird-watching and boating are the main activities.

Coolangatta [12]

🏄 🌊 🏊 ⛑ ♿ 🚻

On the Queensland–New South Wales border, Coolangatta has some of the best surfing waters in the area, but relatively uncrowded beaches. Surfing tuition and boards for hire are available here.

Key to Symbols *see back flap*

★ **Cooloola National Park** ①

Attractive lakes and sclerophyll woodland abound in this area. A 60-km (35-mile) 4WD to Rainbow Beach passes the Teewah Coloured Sands, produced by natural chemicals.

LOCATOR MAP

★ **Noosa Heads, Main Beach** ③

Extraordinary natural beauty, a north-facing beach and an extensive river system have combined to make Noosa a fashionable holiday resort.

★ **Noosa National Park** ④

Consisting of 380 ha (940 acres) of headland surrounded by coastline containing secluded coves, this national park is inhabited with koalas.

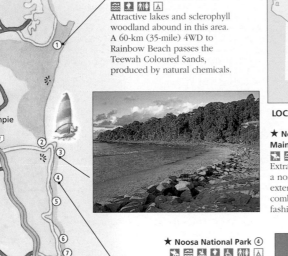

★ **Sanctuary Cove** ⑨

Situated on Hope Island, the glamorous resort of Sanctuary Cove is aimed particularly at golfers and includes two luxury golf courses.

★ **South Stradbroke Island Beach** ⑩

This unspoiled sand island offers peaceful but relatively basic accommodation. Catching crabs and bird-watching are popular activities.

0 kilometres   20

0 miles   20

★ **Surfers Paradise Beach** ⑪

This is the focal point of the Gold Coast with block after block of high-rise developments and a range of entertainment options for visitors.

KEY

 Highway

Major road

Minor road

River

Viewpoint

• ympie

• Caloundra

Australia Zoo

• Caboolture

Moreton Island

• Redcliffe

BRISBANE

North Stradbroke Island

Coomera

Burleigh Heads National Park •

BYRON BAY ↓

Lamington National Park ❶

📷 *Canungra.* ℹ️ *Park Ranger Office (07) 5544 0634.* ⏰ *daily.*

Lamington National Park, set within the McPherson Mountain Range, is one of Queensland's most popular parks. Declared in 1915, it contains 200 sq km (78 sq miles) of thick wooded country, with more than 160 km (100 miles) of walking tracks through subtropical rainforests of hoop pine, black booyongs and strangler figs. The highest ridges in the park reach more than 1,000 m (3,280 ft) and are lined with Antarctic beech trees – the most northerly in Australia. Some 150 species of birds, such as the Albert's lyrebird, make bird-watching a popular pastime. The global importance of the area was recognized in 1994, when Lamington was declared a World Heritage Area.

Stunning king parrot

Nearby Macrozamia National Park has macrozamia palms (cycads) – one of the oldest forms of vegetation still growing in the world.

Darling Downs ❷

📷 *Toowoomba.* 🚌 *Toowoomba.* ℹ️ *Toowoomba (07) 4639 3797.*

Only 90 minutes' drive from Brisbane, stretching west of the Great Dividing Range, is the fertile country of the Darling Downs. The first area to be settled after Brisbane, the region encompasses some of the most productive agricultural land in Australia, as well as one of the most historic areas in Queensland.

Toowoomba is the main centre of the Downs and is also one of Queensland's biggest cities. Early settlers transformed this one-time swamp into the present "Garden City", famous for its jacarandas and Carnival of Flowers *(see p40)*.

About 45 km (28 miles) northwest of Toowoomba along the Warrego Hwy is the **Jondaryan Woolshed**. Built in 1859 to handle 200,000 sheep in one season, it has now been restored as a working memorial to the early pioneers of the district.

South of Toowoomba is Warwick, the oldest town in Queensland after Brisbane and known for its roses and its 19th-century sandstone buildings. It also claims one of the oldest rodeos in Australia, dating from 1857 when £50 (a year's pay) was wagered on the outcome of the riding contest. Today the rodeo follows the Rose and Rodeo Festival in October and offers prize money of more than A$70,000 *(see p41)*.

About 60 km (40 miles) south of Warwick and 915 m (3,000 ft) above sea level, Stanthorpe actively celebrates its freezing winter temperatures with the Brass Monkey Season *(see p43)*.

The town is at the heart of the Granite Belt, one of Queensland's few wine regions *(see p37)*.

Near Warwick, Queen Mary Falls National Park is a 78-ha (193-acre) rainforest park with picnic areas and a 40-m (130-ft) waterfall.

🏛️ **Jondaryan Woolshed**
Evanslea Rd, Jondaryan. **Tel** *(07) 4692 2229.* ⏰ *10am–4pm daily.* 🚫 *Good Fri, 25 Dec.* 🎦 ♿ **www.**jondaryanwoolshed.com

Sunshine Coast Hinterland ❸

🚌 *Bus link at Landsborough station.* ℹ️ *Cnr 6th Ave & Melrose Pde, Maroochydore (07) 5448 9088.*

To the west of the Sunshine Coast is the Blackall Range. The area has become a centre for artists and artisans, with numerous guesthouses and some fine restaurants. The most attractive centres are

Waterfall in Queen Mary Falls National Park, Darling Downs

For hotels and restaurants in this region see pp490–92 and pp537–8

The Glasshouse Mountains, a Queensland landmark on the hinterland of the Sunshine Coast

Montville and Maleny. The drive from Maleny to Mapleton is one of the most scenic in the region, with views across to Moreton Island, encompassing pineapple and sugar cane fields.

Consisting of ten volcanic cones, the Glasshouse Mountains were formed 20 million years ago. The craggy volcanic peaks were named by Captain Cook in 1770 because they reminded him of the glass furnaces in his native Yorkshire.

Maryborough ❹

🏛 *21,300.* ✈ 🚃 🚌 🛈 *City Hall, Kent St (07) 4190 5742.* **www**.*visitmaryborough.info*

Situated on the banks of the Mary River, Maryborough has a strong link with Australia's early history. Founded in 1843, the town provided housing for Kanakas' labour *(see p235)* and was the only port apart from Sydney where free settlers could enter. This resulted in a thriving town – the buildings reflecting the wealth of its citizens.

Many of these buildings survive, earning Maryborough the title of "Heritage City". A great many of the town's private residences also date from the 19th century, ranging from simple workers' cottages to beautiful old "Queenslanders". These houses are distinctive to the state, set high off the ground to catch the cool air currents and with graceful verandas on all sides.

Hervey Bay ❺

🏛 *41,000.* ✈ 🚃 🚢 🛈 *401 The Esplanade, Torquay, Hervey Bay (07) 4125 9855.* **www**.*visitherveybay.info*

As recently as the 1970s Hervey Bay was just a string of five fishing villages. However, the safe beaches and mild climate have quickly turned it into a metropolis of over 40,000 people and one of the fastest growing holiday centres in Australia.

Hervey Bay is also the best place for whale-watching. Humpback whales migrate more than 11,000 km (7,000 miles) every year from the Antarctic to northern Australian waters to mate and calve. On their return, between August and October, they rest at Hervey Bay to give the calves time to develop a protective layer of blubber before they begin their final run to Antarctica.

Bundaberg rum

Since whaling was stopped in the 1960s, numbers have quadrupled from 300 to approximately 5,000.

Environs
The sugar city of central Queensland, Bundaberg is 62 km (38 miles) north of Hervey Bay. It is the home of Bundaberg ("Bundy") rum, the biggest selling spirit label in Australia.

Bundaberg is an attractive town with many 19th-century buildings. The city's favourite son, Bert Hinkler (1892–1933), was the first man to fly solo from England to Australia in 1928. His original "Ibis" aircraft is displayed in the **Hinkler Hall of Aviation.**

🏛 **Hinkler Hall of Aviation**
Young St, Botanic Gardens. **Tel** *(07) 4130 4400.* ⬤ *9am–4pm Tue–Fri, 10am–1pm Sat & Sun.* ⬤ *Good Fri, 25 Apr, 25 Dec.* 🦽 📷

Classic Queenslander-style house in Maryborough

Fraser Island ⑥

Situated off the Queensland coast near Maryborough *(see p241)*, Fraser Island World Heritage area is the largest sand island in the world. Measuring 123 km (76 miles) in length and 25 km (16 miles) across, the island is a mix of hills and valleys, rainforest and clear lakes. Ferries to the island operate from Urangan, River Heads and Inskip Point. There is a range of resorts and numerous camp sites on the island. Vehicle (4WD only) and camping permits are required.

VISITORS' CHECKLIST

ℹ️ Fraser Coast–South Burnett Regional Tourism, (07) 4122 3444 🚢 from Urangan, River Heads & Inskip Point. 🚻 🚾 🏊 🍴 🛏️

Indian Head was named by Captain James Cook *(see pp50–51)* as a result of "a number of the natives" he saw assembled here on arrival.

Sandy Cape has treacherous waters; its lighthouse has saved many ships from potential danger.

Lake Allom, fringed by melaleuca trees and sedges, is surrounded by a towering rainforest. Freshwater turtles can be seen in the lake.

Watumba

HERVEY BAY

The Cathedrals
These striking, deep red sand formations stretch 18km (11 miles) along the beach.

Lake McKenzie
The beautiful clear waters here are surrounded by white sands and blackbutt trees.

PACIFIC OCEAN

Seventy-Five Mile Beach is notable as the site of the *Maheno*, the only visible shipwreck on the island.

Kingfisher Bay

Central Station was once the hub of the island's logging industry and is a starting point for beautiful walks.

Eli Creek is large and spectacular, pouring gallons of water each hour into the surf.

Lake Birabeen   Eurong

Lake Boomahjin

0 km	5
0 miles	5

KEY

▬	4WD road
▬	Walking trail
ℹ️	Tourist information
🏞️	Picnic area
⛺	Camp site
🚢	Ferrypoint
🔆	Viewpoint

Hook Point

JAMES AND ELIZABETH FRASER

In 1836, survivors from the shipwreck *Stirling Castle*, including Captain James Fraser and his wife Elizabeth, known as Eliza, landed on Fraser Island and were captured by Aboriginals. Captain Fraser perished, but Eliza was rescued and returned to England, where she told her story widely. The story inspired Patrick White's novel *A Fringe of Leaves (see p35)*.

Survivor Elizabeth Fraser

Loggerhead turtle laying eggs on Mon Repos Beach

Mon Repos Conservation Park **❼**

Tel *(07) 4159 1652, tour bookings (07) 4153 8888.* ⬭ *daily.* 🐢 *Turtle tours.* ♿ ☑ *obligatory Nov–Mar.* www.epa.qld.gov.au

Mon Repos Beach, 15 km (9 miles) from Bundaberg *(see p241)*, is one of the most significant and accessible turtle rookeries on the Australian mainland. Egg-laying of loggerhead and other turtles takes place from November to February. By January, the first young turtles begin to hatch and make their way down the sandy beach to the ocean.

An information centre within the environmental park has videos and other information about these fascinating reptiles. Supervised public viewing ensures that the turtles are not unduly disturbed.

Just behind Mon Repos Beach is an old stone wall built by Kanakas and now preserved as a memorial to these South Sea Island inhabitants *(see p235)*.

Gladstone **❽**

👥 *29,000.* ✈ 🚃 🚌 🚍
ℹ *Gladstone Marina, Bryan Jordan Drive (07) 4972 9000.*

Gladstone is a town dominated by industry. However, industry is in harmony with tourism and the environment. Tours of the area are popular with visitors. The world's largest alumina refinery is located here,
processing bauxite mined in Weipa on the west coast of Cape York Peninsula. Five per cent of the nation's wealth and 20 per cent of Queensland's wealth is generated by Gladstone's industries. Gladstone's port, handling more than 35 million tonnes of cargo a year, is one of the busiest in Australia.

There are, however, more attractive sights in and around the town. The town's main street has an eclectic variety of buildings, including the Grand Hotel, rebuilt to its 1897 form after fire destroyed the original in 1993. Gladstone's Botanic Gardens were first opened in 1988 as a bicentennial project and consist entirely of native Australian plants. South of Gladstone are the tiny coastal villages of Agnes Waters and the quaintly named "1770" in honour of Captain Cook's brief landing here during his journey up the coast *(see p50)*. About 20 km (12 miles) out of town lies the popular holiday location of Boyne Island.

Gladstone is also the access point for Heron Island, considered by many to be one of the most desirable of all the Great Barrier Reef islands, with its wonderful coral and diving opportunities. Other islands in the southern half of the reef can also be accessed from Gladstone by boat or helicopter *(see pp216–17)*.

Pretty coastal village of Agnes Waters, near Gladstone

Rockhampton ⑨

61,000. Capricorn Info. Centre, Gladstone Rd (07) 4927 2055.

Rockhampton is situated 40 km (25 miles) inland, on the banks of the Fitzroy River. Often referred to as the "beef capital" of Australia, the town is also the administrative and commercial heart of central Queensland. A spire marks the fact that, geographically, the Tropic of Capricorn runs through the town.

Rockhampton was founded in 1854 and contains many restored 19th-century buildings. Quay Street flanks the tree-lined river and has been classified in its entirety by the National Trust. Particularly outstanding is the sandstone Customs House. The beautiful **Botanic Gardens** were established in 1869, and have a fine collection of tropical plants. There is also on-site accommodation.

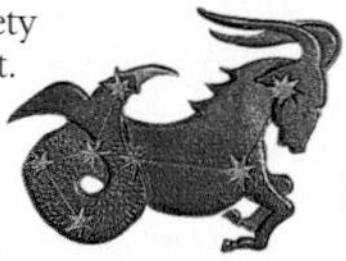

Plaque at base of the Tropic of Capricorn spire

Built on an ancient tribal meeting ground, the **Aboriginal Dreamtime Cultural Centre** is owned and operated by local Aboriginals. Imaginative displays give an insight into their life and culture.

Botanic Gardens
Spencer St. ***Tel*** *(07) 4922 1654.*
6am–6pm daily.

Aboriginal Dreamtime Cultural Centre
Bruce Hwy. ***Tel*** *(07) 4936 1655.*
10am–3:30pm Mon–Fri.
public hols.

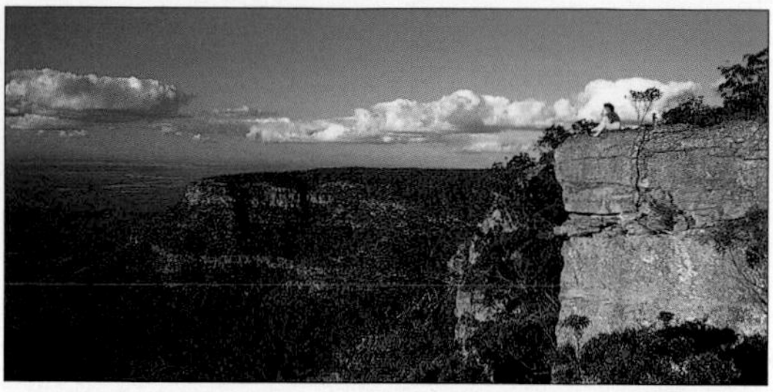

Sandstone cliff looking out over Blackdown Tableland National Park

Environs

The heritage township of Mount Morgan is 38 km (25 miles) southwest of Rockhampton. A 2 sq km (0.5 sq mile) open-cut mine of first gold, then copper, operated here for 100 years and was an important part of the state's economy until the minerals ran out in 1981.

Some 25 km (15 miles) north of Rockhampton is Mount Etna National Park, containing spectacular limestone caves, discovered in the 1880s. These are open to the public via Olsen's Capricorn Caverns and Camoo Caves. A major feature of the caves is "cave coral" – stone-encrusted tree roots that have forced their way through the rock. The endangered ghost bat, Australia's only carnivorous bat, nests in these caves.

The stunning sandy beaches of Yeppoon and Emu Park are only 40 km (25 miles) northeast of the city. Rockhampton is also the access point for Great Keppel Island *(see pp216–17).*

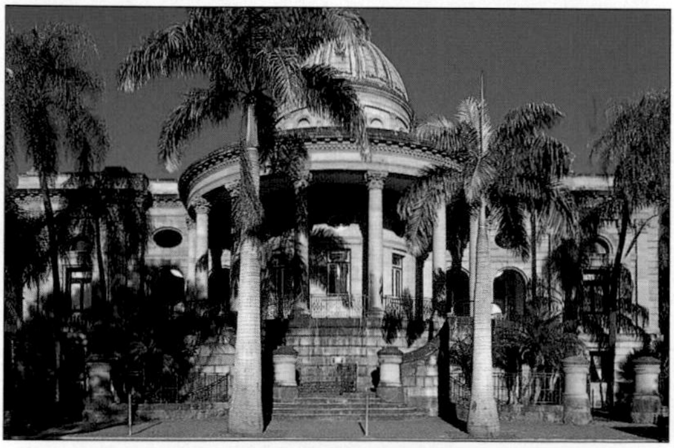

Façade of Customs House on Quay Street, Rockhampton

Blackdown Tableland National Park ⑩

Off Capricorn Hwy, via Dingo. **Park Ranger** ***Tel*** *(07) 4986 1964.*

Between Rockhampton and Emerald, along a 20-km (12-mile) untarmacked detour off the Capricorn Highway, is Blackdown Tableland National Park. A dramatic sandstone plateau which rises 600 m (2,000 ft) above the flat surrounding countryside, the Tableland offers spectacular views, escarpments, open forest and tumbling waterfalls. Wildlife includes gliders, brushtail possums, rock wallabies and the occasional dingo.

Emerald is a coal mining centre and the hub of the central highland region, 75 km (45 miles) west of the park; the town provides a railhead for the surrounding agricultural areas. Its ornate 1900 railway station is one of the few survivors of a series of fires that occurred between 1936 and 1969 that destroyed much of the town's heritage. About 60 km (37 miles) southwest of Emerald is Cullin-la-ringo, where there are headstones marking the mass grave of 19 European settlers killed in 1861 by local Aboriginals. At Comet is a tree carved with the initials of explorer Ludwig Leichhardt during his 1844 expedition to Port Essington *(see p249).*

More in tune with its name, Emerald is also the access point for the largest sapphire fields in the world. The lifestyle of the gem diggers is fascinating, making it a popular tourist area.

Carnarvon National Park ⑪

The main access to Carnarvon National Park lies 250 km (155 miles) south of Emerald, while the park itself covers some 298,000 ha (730,000 acres). There are several sections of the park, but the stunning Carnarvon Gorge is the most accessible area to visitors. A 32-km (20-mile) canyon carved by the waters of Carnarvon Creek, the gorge consists of white cliffs, crags and pillars of stone harbouring plants and animals which have survived through centuries of evolution. The area is also rich in Aboriginal culture, and three cultural sites are open to the public. Comfortable cabin accommodation is available or there are various camp sites, provided you have an advance booking and a camping permit *(see p477).*

VISITORS' CHECKLIST

ℹ️ *Visitors' Centre, Carnarvon Gorge, via Rolleston (07) 4984 4505.* ◯ *8am–5pm daily.* ♿ 🏕️

KEY

═══	Major road
- -	Walking trail
≈	River
ℹ️	Tourist information
🅰️	Camp site
☼	Viewpoint

Wards Canyon is home to the King Fern, a remnant rainforest species.

The Amphitheatre's sheer walls were carved into the rock by water.

Carnarvon Gorge
The gorge is filled with lush eucalypt forests, sandstone cliffs and streams.

Boolimba Bluff has spectacular sunrise views of the park.

Cathedral Cave is a massive rock shelter, more than 30 m (100 ft) high. It is one of the major Aboriginal cultural sites in the park.

The Art Gallery
This important Aboriginal art site features stencil art of boomerangs, stone implements and shell pendants.

0 kilometres 1
0 miles 1

Moss Garden
This lush greenery of ferns, creepers, hornworts and liverworts is sustained by seepage from the spring waters down the rock walls.

Stunning estuary at Whitehaven Beach, the highlight of the Whitsundays

Eungella National Park ⑫

🏠 Mackay. 🚌 Mackay. ℹ️ Mackay (07) 4944 5888. **Park Ranger Tel** (07) 4958 4753 or 1300 130 372.

Eungella National Park is the main wilderness area on the central Queensland coast and encompasses some 50,000 ha (125,000 acres) of the rugged Clarke Ranges. Volcanic rock covered with rainforest and subtropical flora is cut by steep gorges, crystal clear pools and impressive waterfalls tumbling down the mountainside.

Finch Hatton Gorge is the main destination for tourists, where indigenous wildlife includes gliders, ring-tailed possums, bandicoots and pademelons (a kind of wallaby). Broken River is one of the few places in Australia where platypuses can be spotted at dusk and dawn.

The main access point for Eungella is the prosperous sugar town of **Mackay**. Somewhat low-key from a tourist point of view, Mackay boasts a balmy climate by way of the surrounding mountains trapping the warm coastal air even in winter. Thirty beautiful white sand beaches are lined with casuarinas. All around the town sugar cane can be seen blowing in the wind in the many sugar cane fields.

The town centre of Mackay also has a number of historic buildings worth visiting, including the Commonwealth Bank and Customs House, both classified by the National Trust. The second-largest coal-loader in the world is at Hay Point, where trains more than 2 km (1 mile) long haul coal from the western mines for shipping overseas.

Whitsunday Islands ⑬

🏠 Proserpine. 🚌 Airlie Beach. ✈️ Hamilton Island; Proserpine. ⛴️ Shute Harbour. ℹ️ 1300 717 407. **www**.whitsundaytourism.com

The Whitsunday Islands are an archipelago of 74 islands, situated within the Great Barrier Reef Marine Park, approximately 1,140 km (700 miles) north of Brisbane and 640 km (400 miles) south of Cairns. These beautiful islands and sandy atolls are among the most stunning holiday destinations in Australia. Whitehaven Beach on Whitsunday Island is recognized as one of the world's best beaches, with 9 km (6 miles) of pure white silica sand and turquoise sea.

Only a few of the islands offer accommodation, including Hamilton, Daydream, Hayman, South Molle and Lindeman, while some 66 islands remain uninhabited. A wide range of accommodation is available including luxury hotels, hostels, guesthouses and self-catering apartments.

There are many activities on offer include scuba diving, whale watching, seaplane flights and charter sailing. Many companies at Airlie Beach on the mainland offer sailing packages, which include diving or snorkelling and a night or two moored on the Great Barrier Reef.

Ayr ⑭

🏠 8,000. 🚌 🚍 ℹ️ Plantation Park, Bruce Hwy (07) 4786 5988.

The busy town of Ayr, at the heart of the Burdekin River Delta, is the major sugar cane-growing area in Australia.

Within the town itself is the modern Burdekin Cultural Complex, which includes a 530-seat theatre, a library and an art gallery. Among its art

"Living Lagoon" sculpture at the Burdekin Complex, Ayr

collection are the renowned "Living Lagoon" sculptures by the contemporary Australian sculptor Stephen Walker. The Ayr Nature Display consists of an impressive rock wall made from 2,600 pieces of North Queensland rock, intricate pictures made from preserved insects and a display of Australian reptiles, shells, fossils and Aboriginal artifacts. In Plantation Park is the Juru walking trail and Gubulla Munda, a giant snake sculpture 15 m (50 ft) long.

Environs

Approximately 55 km (35 miles) north of Ayr is Alligator Creek, which is the access point for Bowling Green Bay National Park. Here you will find geckos and chirping cicadas living alongside each other in this lush landscape. Within the park are rock pools, perfect for swimming, and plunging waterfalls.

Ornate 19th-century façade of City Hall in Charters Towers

Charters Towers ⑮

🏛 *8,000.* 🚉 🚌 🚐 ℹ *74 Mosman St (07) 4761 5533.*

Charters Towers was once the second-largest town in Queensland with a population of 27,000, following the 1871 discovery of gold in the area by a 10-year-old Aboriginal boy. Gold is still mined in the area, as well as copper, lead and zinc.

The old Charters Towers Stock Exchange is a historic gem set amid a group of other splendid 19th-century buildings in the city centre. This international centre of finance was the only such exchange in Australia outside a capital city and was built during the gold-mining days.

Charters Towers fell into decline when the gold ran out in the 1920s. Its economy now depends on the beef industry and its status as the educational centre for Queensland's Outback and Papua New Guinea – school students make up one-fifth of the population.

Townsville and Magnetic Island ⑯

🏛 *129,000.* ✈ 🚉 🚌 🚐 ⛴ ℹ *303 Flinders Mall (07) 4721 1116.*

Townsville is the second-largest city in Queensland and a major port for the beef, sugar and mining industries. Boasting, on average, 300 sunny days a year, the beachfront is a source of local pride.

The city was founded in the 1860s by Robert Towns, who began the practice of "blackbirding" – kidnapping Kanakas from their homeland and bringing them to Australia as cheap labour *(see p235).*

Among the city's tourist attractions is **Reef HQ**, a "living coral reef aquarium" and the **Museum of Tropical Queensland**, which displays artifacts from the *Pandora.* Townsville is also an access point for the Barrier Reef and a major diving centre, largely because of the nearby wreck of the steamship *Yongala,* which sank in 1911.

Situated 8 km (5 miles) off-shore and officially a suburb of Townsville, Magnetic Island has 2,500 inhabitants and is the only reef island with a significant permanent population. It was named by Captain Cook, who erroneously believed that magnetic fields generated by the huge granite boulders he could see were causing problems with his compass. Today, almost half of the island is a national park.

🤿 **Reef HQ**
Flinders St East. **Tel** *(07) 4750 0800.*
⬜ *daily.* ⬤ *25 Dec.* 🏷 🚻 ⬜

🏛 **Museum of Tropical Qld**
Flinders St East. **Tel** *(07) 4726 0600.*
⬜ *9:30am–5pm daily.* ⬤ *25 Dec, 25 Apr (am), Good Fri.* 🏷

Idyllic blue waters of Rocky Bay on Magnetic Island

NORTHERN AND OUTBACK QUEENSLAND

Euoropean explorers who made epic journeys into the previously impenetrable area of Northern and Outback Queensland in the 1800s found a land rich in minerals and agricultural potential. They also discovered places of extreme natural beauty, such as the Great Barrier Reef and other unique regions now preserved as national parks.

Northern Queensland was first visited by Europeans when Captain Cook was forced to berth his damaged ship, the *Endeavour*, on the coast. The area remained a mystery for almost another 100 years, however, until other intrepid Europeans ventured north. These expeditions were perilous and explorers were faced with harsh conditions and hostile Aboriginal tribes. In 1844, Ludwig Leichhardt and his group set out from Brisbane to Port Essington, but most of the men were wounded or killed by Aboriginals. In 1848, Edmund Kennedy led an expedition from Cairns to the top of Cape York. All but two of this party perished, including Kennedy, who was killed by Aboriginals.

In the late 19th century, Northern Queensland found sudden prosperity when gold was discovered in the region. The population rose and towns grew up to service the mines, but by the beginning of the 20th century much of the gold had dried up. These once thriving "cities" are now little more than one-street towns, lined with 19th-century architecture as a reminder of their glory days. Today, much of the area's wealth stems from its booming tourist trade. Luxury resorts line the stunning coastline, and tourists flock to experience the spectacular natural wonders of the Great Barrier Reef.

Queensland's Outback region has a strong link with Australia's national heritage. The Tree of Knowledge at Barcaldine marks the meeting place of the first Australian Labor Party during the great shearer's strike of 1891. The town of Winton is where "Banjo" Paterson *(see p35)* wrote Australia's national song "Waltzing Matilda" in 1895. Today, the vast Outback area is known for agriculture and a wide range of mining operations.

A rodeo rider and clown perform in Laura near Lakefield National Park in Northern Queensland

◁ The beautiful coral cay of Green Island on the Great Barrier Reef

Exploring Northern Queensland

The area north of Townsville leading up to Cairns is Australia's sugar-producing country, the cane fields backed by the Great Dividing Range. Northern Queensland is sparsely populated: Cairns is the only city, while Port Douglas and Mossman are small towns. The only other villages of note in the region are Daintree and Cooktown. Cape York Peninsula is one of the last untouched wildernesses in the world, covering 200,000 sq km (77,220 sq miles) – roughly the same size as Great Britain. The landscape varies according to the time of year: in the green season (November–March) the rivers are swollen and the country is green; during the dry winter the riverbeds are waterless and the countryside is bare and arid.

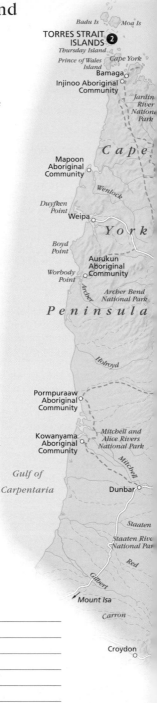

Lush rainforest in Daintree National Park, near Cairns

Pier Marketplace and Marlin Marina in Cairns

GETTING AROUND

Cairns is well served by public transport, with regular air, train and coach connections from southern Queensland and other states. It also benefits from an international airport. North of Cape Tribulation to Cooktown and the Outback requires approved hire cars unless you take an organized tour. The 326-km (202-mile) coast road from Cairns to Cooktown requires a 4WD vehicle after Cape Tribulation, although most car rental companies will insist on a 4WD all the way. During the wet season, Cape York is generally impassable.

KEY

▬▬	Major road
═══	Minor road
‑ ‑	Track
▬▬	Scenic route
═▬═	Main railway
▬▬	Minor railway

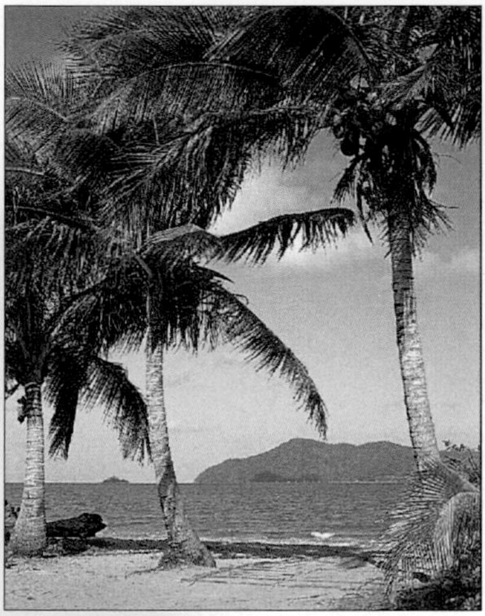

Dunk Island seen from the Queensland coast

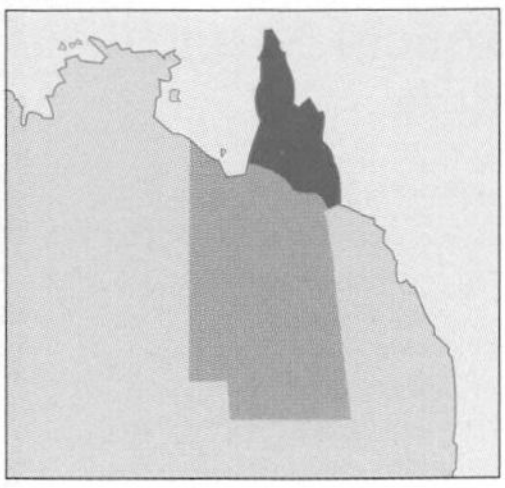

LOCATOR MAP

- *Northern Queensland*
- *Queensland's Outback pp256–7*

SIGHTS AT A GLANCE

Atherton Tableland 8
Babinda and the Boulders 10
Bellenden Ker National Park 9
Cairns p254 7
Cooktown 3
Daintree National Park 4
Dunk Island 11
Green Island 6
Hinchinbrook Island 12
Lakefield National Park 1
Port Douglas 5
Torres Strait Islands 2

Queensland's Outback
See pp256–7
Burketown 14
Longreach 16
Mount Isa 15
Normanton & Gulf Savannah 13

SEE ALSO

• ***Where to Stay*** pp493–4

• ***Where to Eat*** pp538–40

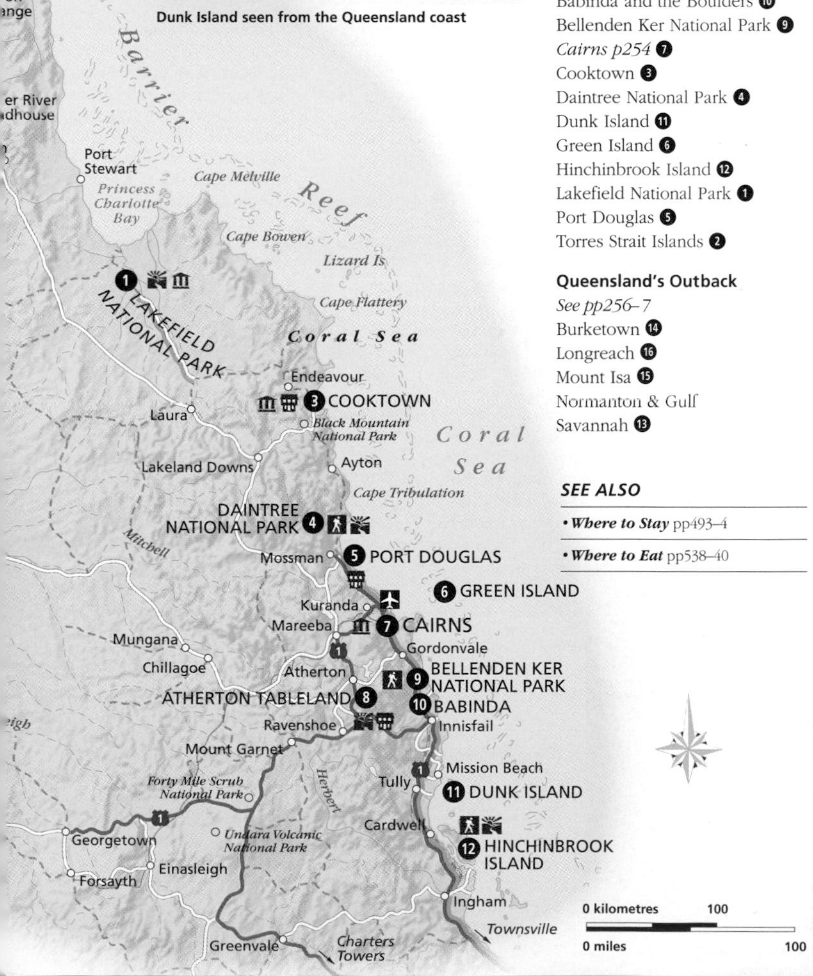

Lakefield National Park ❶

🏠 Cooktown. 🛈 Cooktown (07) 4069 5446. **Park Office** (07) 4060 3271. 🕒 Jun–Nov: Mon–Fri. **www**.epa.qld.gov.au

Covering approximately 540,000 ha (1,300,000 acres), Lakefield National Park is the second-largest national park in Queensland. It encompasses a wide variety of landscapes, including river forests, plains and coastal flats. The centre of the park abounds with birds. Camping is the only accommodation option and a permit must be obtained at the self-registration stations throughout the park. The park is largely inaccessible during the wet season between December and April when the rivers flood the plains.

The nearby town of **Laura**, at the base of the Cape York Peninsula, is a typical Australian Outback town, with a sealed road flanked by a pub, a general store and a few houses. In the late 19th century, Laura was the rail terminus for the Palmer River gold fields and some 20,000 people passed through each year. Today, it is almost forgotten, but the discovery in 1959 of Aboriginal art sites of great antiquity is reviving interest in the area. One of the most notable sites is the "giant horse gallery", which contains huge horse paintings thought to record the first sightings of European explorers.

River forest in Lakefield National Park

Thursday Island, in the Torres Strait island group

Torres Strait Islands ❷

❌ from Cairns. 🚢 from Cairns. 🛈 Cairns (07) 4051 3588.

The Torres Strait divides the northern coastline of Australia from Papua New Guinea and is dotted with numerous islands. Approximately 19 of these islands are inhabited and have been governed by Queensland since 1879.

Thursday Island is the "capital" island and was once the centre of the local pearling industry. Many Japanese pearlers who lost their lives in this occupation are buried in the island's cemetery. In 1891, Green Hill Fort was built to prevent invasion by the Russians. Murray Island was the birthplace of Eddie Mabo, who, in 1992, won his claim to traditional land in the Australian High Court and changed Aboriginal-European relations (see p58).

Chinese gravestone in Cooktown

Cooktown ❸

🚶 1,300. ❌ 🏠 🚌 ⛴ 🛈 Charlotte St (07) 4069 5446.

When the *Endeavour* was damaged by a coral reef in 1770, Captain Cook and his crew spent six weeks in this area while repairs to the ship were made (see pp50–51).

Cooktown's proud boast, therefore, is that it was the site of the first white settlement in Australia.

Like most towns in the area, Cooktown originally serviced the gold fields and its present-day population of less than 2,000 is half the 4,000 inhabitants who once sustained its 50 pubs. However, many of its historic buildings survive, including the Westpac Bank, originally the Old National Bank, with its stone columns supporting an iron-lace veranda. The **James Cook Museum**, which houses the old anchor from the *Endeavour*, started life in the 1880s as a convent. In the cemetery of the town, a memorial and numerous gravestones are testimony to the difficulties faced by the many Chinese who came to the gold fields in the 1870s (see p55).

Between Cooktown and Bloomfield, Black Mountain National Park is named after the geological formation of huge black granite boulders. The boulders were formed around 260 million years ago below the earth's surface and were gradually exposed as surrounding land surfaces eroded away.

🏛 **James Cook Museum**
Cnr Helen & Furneaux sts. **Tel** (07) 4069 5386. 🕒 9:30am–4pm daily. 🎟 ♿ limited.

Daintree National Park [4]

🚌 *from Port Douglas.* ℹ *Port Douglas (07) 4099 5599.* **Park Office** *Mossman (07) 4098 2188.* 🕐 *daily.* **www**.epa.qld.gov.au

Daintree National Park, north of Port Douglas, covers more than 76,000 ha (188,000 acres). The Cape Tribulation section of the park is a place of great beauty, and one of the few places where the rainforest meets the sea. Captain Cook named Cape Tribulation in rueful acknowledgment of the difficulties he was experiencing navigating the Great Barrier Reef. Today, it is a popular spot with backpackers.

The largest section of the park lies inland from Cape Tribulation. It is a mostly inaccessible, mountainous area, but 5 km (3 miles) from Mossman lies the Mossman Gorge, known for its easy and accessible 2.7-km (1-mile) track through the rainforest.

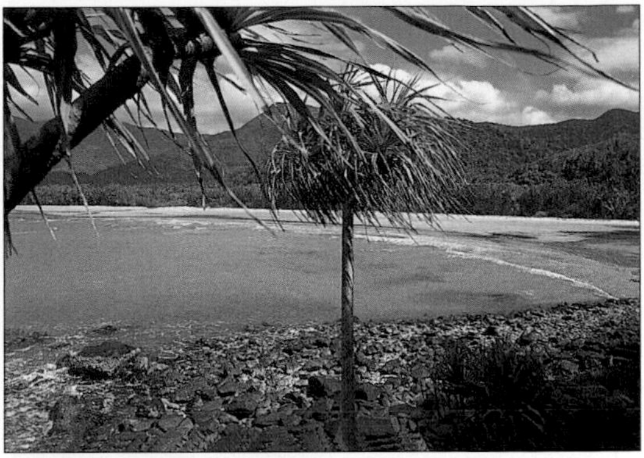

Tropical Myall Beach in Daintree National Park

Port Douglas [5]

👥 *3,500.* 🚌 🚍 ℹ *23 Macrossan St (07) 4099 5599.*

Situated 75 km (47 miles) from Cairns, Port Douglas was once a tiny fishing village. Today it is a tourist centre, but it has managed to preserve some of its village atmosphere.

Macrossan Street is typical of Australian country thoroughfares, and at the end of the street is the beautiful Four-Mile Beach, which is a very popular walking spot. Many 19th-century buildings still line the street, such as the Courthouse Hotel, and the modern shopping centres have been designed to blend with the town's original architecture.

The original port was set up during the gold rush of the 1850s, but it was superseded by Cairns as the main port of the area. A disastrous cyclone in 1911 also forced people to move elsewhere, leaving the population at less than 500. The construction of the luxurious Sheraton Mirage Resort in the early 1980s heralded the beginning of a new boom, and now a range of accommodation and restaurants is on offer *(see p494 and p541)*.

Port Douglas is also the main departure point for Quicksilver, a major Great Barrier Reef tour operator.

Green Island [6]

⛴ *from Cairns.* ℹ *(07) 4051 4070.* ♿ **www**.epa.qld.gov.au

Green Island is one of the few inhabited coral cays of the Great Barrier Reef *(see pp216–17)*. Despite its small size (a brisk walk around the entire island will take no more than 15 minutes), it is home to an exclusive, luxurious five-star resort which opened in 1994.

Green Island's proximity to the mainland tourist areas and the consequent marine traffic and pollution means that the coral is not as spectacular as around islands further afield. But its accessibility by ferry from Cairns makes the island very popular.

Also on Green Island is the Marineland Melanesia complex, where there are crocodile enclosures and an aquarium.

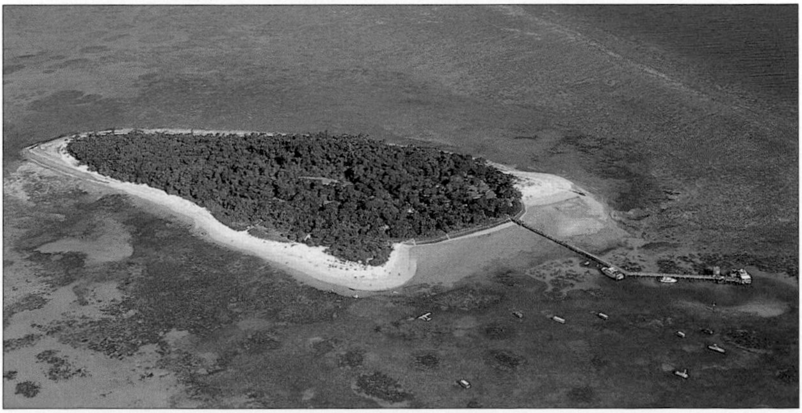

Green Island, a coral cay at the heart of the Great Barrier Reef

Cairns 🟢

Boomerang from Kuranda craft market

Cairns is the main centre of Northern Queensland. Despite its beachfront esplanade, it has a city atmosphere and instead of sandy beaches there are mud-flats, abundant with native birdlife. Its main attraction is as a base for exploring the Great Barrier Reef (*see pp212–17*), the Daintree Rainforest (*p253*) and the Atherton Tableland (*p255*). However, Cairns itself does have several places of interest to visit.

VISITORS' CHECKLIST

🏙 130,000. ✈ 6 km (3.5 miles) N of the city. 🚉 Cairns railway station, Bunda St. 🚌 Lake St Terminus, Lake St; (interstate); Trinity Wharf, Wharf St. ⛴ Reef trips, Pier Point Rd. 🛈 51 The Esplanade (07) 4051 3588. 🎉 The Reef Festival (Oct); Cairns Show (Jul).

🌿 Flecker Botanic Gardens

Collins Ave, Edge Hill. **Tel** (07) 4044 3398. ☐ daily. ♿ 🅿

Dating from 1886, the Flecker Botanic Gardens are known for their collection of more than 100 species of palm trees. They also house many other tropical plants. The gardens include an area of Queensland rainforest with native birdlife. The Centenary Lakes were created in 1976 to commemorate the city's first 100 years.

🏛 Cairns Historical Society Museum

City Place, cnr Lake & Shield sts. **Tel** (07) 4051 5582. ☐ 10am–4pm Mon–Sat. ● Good Fri, 25 Apr, 25 Dec. 🖳 www.cairnsmuseum.org.au

Housed in the 1907 School of Arts building, this museum is a fine

Tropical orchid in the Flecker Botanic Gardens

example of the city's early architecture. Among the exhibits are the contents of an old Chinese joss house.

🚢 Reef Fleet Terminal

Pier Point Rd

This is the departure point for most cruises to the Great Barrier Reef. Some

19th-century façades nearby offer a glimpse of the city's early life.

Cairns is the game-fishing centre of Australia and, from August to December, tourists crowd Marlin Jetty to see the anglers return with their catch. Adjacent Pier Marketplace has boutiques, restaurants, markets and accommodation.

Environs

On the eastern edge of the Atherton Tablelands is the tiny village of **Kuranda**. A hippie hang-out in the 1960s, it has since developed into an arts and crafts centre with markets held here every day. Nearby, at Smithfield, is the Tjapukai Cultural Centre, home to the renowned Aboriginal Tjapukai Dance Theatre.

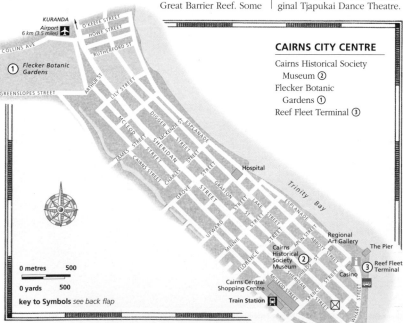

CAIRNS CITY CENTRE

Cairns Historical Society Museum ②
Flecker Botanic Gardens ①
Reef Fleet Terminal ③

0 metres   500
0 yards   500
key to Symbols *see back flap*

Mount Hypipamee Crater's green lake, Atherton Tableland

Atherton Tableland ❽

ℹ️ *Cnr Silo & Main St, Atherton (07) 4091 4222.* ⬜ *9am–5pm daily.* ⬤ *1 Jan, Good Fri, Easter Sun, 25 Dec, 26 Dec.* **www**.trc qld.gov.au

Rising sharply from the coastal plains of Cairns, the northern landscape levels out into the lush Atherton Tableland. At their highest point, the tablelands are 900 m (3,000 ft) above sea level. The cool temperature, heavy rainfall and rich volcanic soil make this one of the richest farming areas in Queensland. For many decades, tobacco was the main crop, but, with the worldwide decline in smoking, farmers have diversified into peanuts, macadamia nuts, sugar cane, bananas and avocados.

The town of **Yungaburra**, with its many historic buildings, is listed by the National Trust. Nearby is the famed "curtain fig tree". Strangler figs attach themselves to a host tree and eventually kill the original tree. In this case, the aerial roots, growing down from the tree tops, form a 15-m (50-ft) screen. Southwest of Yungaburra is the eerie, green crater lake at Mt Hypipamee. Stretching 60 m (200 ft) in diameter.

Millaa Millaa contains the most spectacular waterfalls of the region. A 15-km (9-mile) sealed circuit drive takes in the Zillie and Ellinjaa falls, while not far away are the picturesque Mungalli Falls.

Atherton is the main town of the region, named after its first European settlers, John and Kate Atherton, who established a cattle station here in the mid-19th century. The wealthy agricultural centre of Mareeba now stands on the site of this former ranch.

Bellenden Ker National Park ❾

🚆 *Innisfail.* 🚌 *Innisfail.* ℹ️ *1 Edith St, Innisfail (07) 4063 2655.*

Bellenden Ker National Park contains the state's two highest mountains. Bartle Frere, reaching 1,611 m (5,285 ft) and Bellenden Ker, rising to 1,591 m (5,220 ft), are often swathed in cloud. Cassowaries (large flightless birds, under threat of extinction) can often be spotted on the mountains.

Much of the park is wilderness, although tracks do exist. A popular area to visit is Josephine Falls to the south of the park, about 8 km (5 miles) from the Bruce Highway.

Babinda and the Boulders ❿

🏞️ *1,300.* ℹ️ *Cnr Munro St & Bruce Hwy, Babinda (07) 4067 1008.*

The rural town of Babinda is a quaint survivor of old-world Queensland, lined with veranda-fronted houses and a wooden pub.

The Babinda Boulders, 7 km (4 miles) inland, are water-worn rock shapes and a popular photographic subject.

Dunk Island ⓫

🚆 *Tully.* 🚌 *Mission Beach.* ⛴️ *Mission Beach.* ℹ️ *Mission Beach (07) 4068 7099.*

Dunk Island is one of the best known of the Great Barrier Reef islands *(see p217)*. The rugged terrain is covered with a variety of vegetation. Day trips from the mainland are popular, offering snorkelling, diving and windsurfing.

Dunk Island is perhaps best known as the setting for EJ Banfield's 1906 book, *Confessions of a Beachcomber*. Today it is also known for its resident artists' colony and as a convenient stepping stone to exclusive Bedarra Island, 30 minutes away by launch.

Hinchinbrook Island ⓬

🚆 *Ingham.* 🚌 *Cardwell.* ⛴️ *Lucinda, Cardwell.* ℹ️ *Ingham (07) 4776 5211.*

Hinchinbrook is the largest island national park in Australia, covering 635 sq km (245 sq miles). Dense rainforest, much of which remains unexplored, makes the island popular with bushwalkers. Hinchinbrook's highest point, Mount Bowen, rises 1,121 m (3,678 ft) above sea level and is often capped with cloud. The native wildlife includes wallabies, dugongs and the magnificent blue Ulysses butterfly. The island is separated from the mainland town of Cardwell by a narrow, mangrove-fringed channel.

Water-worn boulders near the town of Babinda

Queensland's Outback

In stark contrast to the lush green of the eastern rainforests, the northwest of Queensland is made up of dry plains, mining areas and Aboriginal settlements. The vast distances and high temperatures often dissuade tourists from venturing into this harsh landscape; yet those willing to make the effort will be rewarded with unique wildlife and an insight into Australia's harsh Outback life.

(Map showing the region with locations including Wellesley Islands, Hells Gate Roadhouse, Karumba, Normanton and Gulf Savannah (13), Burketown (14), Gregory Downs, Gunpowder, Croydon, Iffley, Georgetown, Townsville, Tennant Creek, Cloncurry, Richmond, McKinlay, Hughenden, Mount Isa (15), Corfield, Urandangi, Winton, Lake Galilee, Bladensburg National Park, Aramac, Boulia, Longreach (16), Rockhampton, Bedourie, Isisford, Blackall, Great Artesian Basin, Jundah, Idalia National Park, Birdsville, Windorah, Adavale, Charleville, Warrego Highway, Eromanga, Wyandra, Brisbane, Balonne Hwy, Cunnamulla, Bourke)

0 km   150
0 miles   150

LOCATOR MAP

■ Queensland's Outback
☐ Northern Queensland pp248–55

SIGHTS AT A GLANCE

Burketown ⑭
Longreach ⑯
Mount Isa ⑮
Normanton and Gulf Savannah ⑬

KEY

▬ Major road
▭ Minor road
- - Track
▬ Minor railway
▬ State border

Normanton and Gulf Savannah ⑬

🚉 Normanton. ℹ 29–33 Haig St, Normanton (07) 4745 1065.

Normanton, situated 70 km (45 miles) inland on the Norman River, is the largest town in the region. It began life as a port, handling copper from Cloncurry and then gold from Croydon. The famous Gulflander train still commutes once a week between Normanton and Croydon.

En route from Normanton to the Gulf of Carpentaria, savannah grasses give way to glistening salt pans, barren of all vegetation. Once the rains come in November, however, this area becomes a wetland and a breeding ground for millions of birds, including jabirus, brolgas, herons and cranes, as well as crocodiles,

prawns and barramundi. Karumba, at the mouth of the Norman River, is the access point for the Gulf of Carpentaria and the headquarters of a multi-million-dollar prawn and fishing industry. It remains something of an untamed frontier town, especially when the prawn trawlers are in.

Covering approximately 350,000 sq km (135,000 sq miles), the most northwesterly region of Queensland is the Gulf Savannah. Largely flat and covered in savannah grasses, abundant with bird and animal life, this is the remotest landscape in Australia. The economic base of the area is fishing and cattle. Prawn trawlers go out to the Gulf of Carpentaria for months at a time and cattle stations cover areas of more than 1,000 sq km (400 sq miles). Given the distances, local pastoralists are more likely to travel via light aircraft than on horseback.

Gum trees and termite mounds on the grassland of Gulf Savannah

For hotels and restaurants in this region see pp493–4 and pp538–40

Mount Isa, dominated by Australia's largest mine

Environs
Cloncurry, 120 km (75 miles) east of Mount Isa, was the departure point for the Queensland and Northern Territory Aerial Service's (QANTAS) first flight in 1921. Now Australia's national airline, Qantas is also the oldest airline in the English-speaking world.

Longreach ⓰

🏛 3,000. ✈ 🚋 🚌 ℹ Qantas Park, Eagle St (07) 4658 4150.

Situated in the centre of Queensland, Longreach is the main town of the central west of the state.

From 1922 to 1934, Longreach was the operating base of Qantas and there is a Founders Museum at Longreach Airport. Opened in 1988, the **Australian Stockman's Hall of Fame** is a fascinating tribute to Outback men and women. Aboriginal artifacts, as well as documented tales of the early European explorers are included in the impressive displays.

There are daily flights or a 17-hour coach ride from Brisbane to Longreach. Other access points are Rockhampton and Townsville.

🏛 **Australian Stockman's Hall of Fame**
Landsborough Hwy. **Tel** (07) 4658 2166. ◯ daily. ● 25 Dec. 🅿 👍 📷 📷

Burketown ⓮

🏛 170. ✈ ℹ 19 Musgrave St (07) 4745 5111, City Council, 65 Musgrave St (07) 4745 5177.

In the late 1950s, Burketown found fleeting fame as the setting for Neville Shute's famous novel about life in a small Outback town, *A Town Like Alice*. Situated 30 km (18 miles) from the Gulf of Carpentaria, on the Albert River, Burketown was once a major port servicing the hinterland. The spectacular propagating roll cloud known as a Morning Glory appears here in the early mornings from September to November. Burketown is rich in history and Aboriginal culture. It is also famous for the World Barramundi Fishing Championship.

About 150 km (90 miles) west of Burketown is Hell's Gate, an area so named at the beginning of the 20th century because it was the last outpost where the state's police guaranteed protection.

Mount Isa ⓯

🏛 19,000. ✈ 🚋 🚌 ℹ 19 Marian St (07) 4749 1555.

Mount Isa is the only major city in far western Queensland. Its existence is entirely based around the world's largest silver and lead mine, which dominates the town's industry and landscape. Ore was first discovered at Mount Isa in 1923 by a prospector called John Campbell Miles and the first mine was set up in the 1930s. In those early days, "the Isa" was a shanty town, and Tent House, now owned by the National Trust, is an example of the half-house-half-tents that were home to most early settlers. Also in town is **Outback at Isa**, which incorporates mine tours, the Riversleigh Fossil Centre and Isa Experience Gallery *(see pp26–7)*.

One of the most popular events in town is the Mount Isa Rodeo in August *(see p43)*. With prize money totalling more than A$100,000, riders come from all over the world to perform spectacular displays of horsemanship.

🏛 **Outback at Isa**
19 Marian St. **Tel** (07) 4749 1555. ◯ daily. ● Good Fri, 25 Dec. 📷 👍

THE ROYAL FLYING DOCTOR SERVICE

The Royal Flying Doctor Service was founded by John Flynn, a Presbyterian pastor who was sent as a missionary to the Australian Outback in 1912. The young cleric was disturbed to see that many of his flock died due to the lack of basic medical care and he founded the Australian Inland Mission together with Hudson Fysh (the founder of Qantas), self-made millionaire Hugh Victor McKay, Alfred Traeger (the inventor of the pedal wireless) and Dr Kenyon St Vincent Welch. Today, the Royal Flying Doctor Service deals with some 130,000 patients a year, and most Outback properties have an airstrip on which the Flying Doctor can land. Emergency medical help is rarely more than two hours away and advice is available over a special radio channel.

A Royal Flying Doctor plane flying over Australia's Outback

THE NORTHERN TERRITORY

The Northern Territory at a Glance

That most famous of Australian icons, the red monolith of Uluṟu (Ayers Rock) lies within the Northern Territory, but it is just one of the area's stunning natural features, which also include the tropical splendour of Kakadu National Park. The main centres are Darwin in the lush north and Alice Springs in the arid Red Centre. Much of the Outback land is Aboriginal-owned, enabling their ancient culture to flourish. The Northern Territory has yet to achieve full statehood owing to its low population and relatively small economy, but it has been self-governing since 1978.

Tiwi Islands (see p274) *lie 80 km (50 miles) off the north coast. The islands are inhabited by Tiwi Aboriginals, who have preserved a culture distinct from the mainland which includes unique characteristics such as these burial poles.*

0 kilometres 150

0 miles 150

Darwin (see pp270–73) *is the Northern Territory's capital city with an immigrant population of more than 50 nationalities (see pp264–5). The colonial Government House is one of the few 19th-century survivors in what is now a very modern city.*

THE RED CENTRE
(see pp278–289)

Kakadu National Park (see pp276–7) *is an ancient landscape of tropical rainforest and majestic rock formations. Covering 1.7 million ha (4.3 million acres), it is the largest national park in Australia. The Jim Jim Falls are the most impressive in the park, and the Aboriginal rock art sites are among the most important in the country.*

Uluṟu-Kata Tjuṯa National Park (see pp286–9) *is dominated by the huge sandstone rock rising up out of the flat, arid desert and the nearby Olgas, a series of 36 mysterious rock domes.*

◁ **Desert oaks (*Allocasuarina*) in the heart of the Northern Territory**

Elsey Homestead Replica, *110 km (70 miles) southeast of Katherine (see pp274–5), was the setting for Jeannie Gunn's novel* We of the Never Never, *depicting 19th-century Outback life.*

DARWIN AND THE TOP END
(see pp266–277)

Devil's Marbles (see p285) *are a remarkable collection of granite boulders in the heart of the flat, sandy desert. Caused by millions of years of erosion, they are traditionally believed to be the eggs of the Rainbow Serpent.*

Alice Springs (see pp282–3) *lies at the heart of Australia. Its Old Telegraph Station Historical Reserve was the site of the area's first settlement in 1871.*

Chambers Pillar Historical Reserve (see p284) *is a strange, 50-m (165-ft) sandstone column which served as a landmark for explorers of the area in the 19th century.*

For additional map symbols see back flap

Aboriginal Lands

**Sign for
Aboriginal site**

Aboriginal people are thought to
have lived in the Northern
Territory for between 20,000 and
50,000 years. The comparatively
short 200 years of European
settlement have damaged their
ancient culture immensely, but in the Northern
Territory more traditional Aboriginal communities
have survived intact than in other states – mainly
due to their greater numbers and determination
to preserve their identity. Nearly one-third of
the Northern Territory's people are Aboriginal
and they own almost 50 per cent of the land
via arrangements with the federal government
(see p59). For Aboriginals, the concept of land
ownership is tied to a belief system that
instructs them to care for their ancestral land.

This X-ray image *(see p33) of the
dreaming spirit Namarrgon at Nourlangie Rock is centuries old, but was
continually repainted until the 1900s.*

Nourlangie Rock *in Kakadu
National Park is significant to
Aborigines as home of the Light-
ning Dreaming (see pp276–7).*

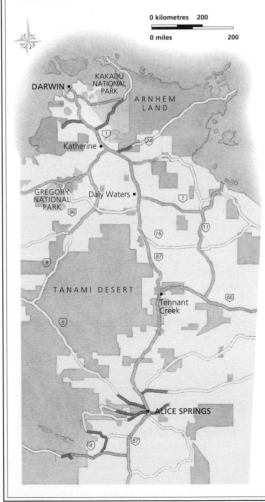

KEY

▨	Aboriginal land
▢	National park
▬	Highway
▬	Major road
═	Unsurfaced road

ACCESS AND PERMITS

Northern Land Council
Tel (08) 8920 5100.
*For access to all Aboriginal land
in the Top End, including
Arnhem Land.* **www**.nlc.org.au

**Parks and Wildlife Service
of the Northern Territory**
*Tel (08) 8999 4555. For permits
to Gurig National Park.
(08) 8979 0244.*
www.nt.gov.au/nreta/parks

Tiwi Land Council
Tel (08) 8981 4898.
*For access to Melville and
Bathurst (Tiwi) islands.*
www.tiwilandcouncil.net.au

Central Land Council
Tel (08) 8951 6211.
*For access to all Central
Australian Aboriginal lands.*
www.clc.org.au

ABORIGINAL TOURISM

Most visitors who come to the Northern Territory are keen to learn more about the region's unique Aboriginal culture. There are now many Aboriginal organizations which take tourists into Aboriginal areas that would otherwise be inaccessible, and explain the Aboriginal view of the land. Excursions available include boat trips in Kakadu National Park *(see pp276–7)* with a Guluyambi guide; bush camping with the Manyallaluk community near Katherine; or a safari camp in Arnhem Land with Umorrduk Safaris. Also well worth visiting are the information and cultural centres, such as those in Kakadu and Uluru-Kata Tjuta national parks, where native owners share their creation stories and culture, adding another layer to visitors' appreciation of these special places.

Ubirr *in Kakadu National Park is one of the finest Aboriginal rock art sites in the Northern Territory. Many paintings in Ubirr's gallery depict the area's wildlife in an x-ray style (see p33), such as this barramundi. They date from 20,000 years ago to the present day.*

Visitors climbing to the lookout at Ubirr

Uluru (see pp286–9) *has many sites sacred to the Anangu people around its base. Almost all of these are closed to the public, but it is possible to walk around the area and learn the associated stories.*

Bush Tucker Dreaming, *painted in 1991 by Gladys Napanangka of the Papunya community of the Central Western Desert, records the Dreaming or creation stories passed down to the artist through hundreds of generations (see pp30–31).*

ABORIGINAL CULTURE AND LAW

Every Aboriginal tribe lives according to a set of laws linking the people with their land and their ancestors. These laws have been handed down through generations and are embedded in Aboriginal creation stories. The stories, which tell how the first spirits and ancestors shaped and named the land, also form a belief system which directs all aspects of Aboriginal life. All Aboriginals are born into two groups: their family clan and a "Dreaming" totem group such as the crocodile – determined by place and time of birth. These decide their links with the land and place in the community and the creation stories they inherit.

Aboriginals in body make-up for a traditional tribal dance

Multicultural Northern Territory

Thai dish

The Northern Territory, with its proximity to Indonesia and the Pacific Islands, has long served as Australia's "front door" to immigrants. Around 500 years ago, Portuguese and Dutch ships charted the waters of the northern coast and from the 1700s traders from the Indonesian archipelago visited the northern shores. From 1874, when Chinese gold prospectors arrived in Darwin, the tropical north has appealed to Southeast Asians and, being closer to Indonesia than to Sydney or Melbourne, the city markets itself as Australia's gateway to Asia. There are now more than 50 ethnic groups living in Darwin, including Greeks and Italians who arrived in the early 20th century, and East Timorese, Indonesians, Thais and Filipinos, together with the town's original mix of Aboriginals and those of Anglo-Celtic stock.

Harry Chan, *elected in 1966, was the first Mayor of Darwin of Chinese descent.*

Mindil Beach market *is one of several Asian-style food markets in the Darwin area. More than 60 food stalls serve Thai, Indonesian, Indian, Chinese, Sri Lankan, Malaysian and Greek cuisine (see p272).*

The Indonesian language Bahasa is taught in many of Darwin's schools due to Indonesia's proximity to the city.

THE CHINESE IN THE TOP END

In 1879, a small carved figure dating from the Ming dynasty (1368–1644) was found in the roots of a tree on a Darwin beach, causing much speculation that a Chinese fleet may have visited this coast in the 15th century. If so, it was the start of an association between China and the Top End which endures today. Chinese came here in search of gold in the 1870s. By 1885, there were 3,500 Chinese in the Top End, and 40 years later Darwin had become a Chinese-run shanty town

Chinese man using buffalo to haul wood in early 19th-century Darwin

with Chinese families managing its market gardens and general stores. Today, many of the area's leading families are of Chinese origin; Darwin has had two Lord Mayors of Chinese descent, and fifth-generation Chinese are spread throughout the city's businesses.

Aboriginal people *are believed to have arrived in the Northern Territory 20,000 to 50,000 years ago, overland from Asia when the sea level was much lower. Here, young male initiates from an Arnhem Land tribe are carried to a ceremony to be "made men".*

With a quarter of its present population born overseas and another quarter Aboriginal, Darwin's racial mix is best seen in the faces of its children.

THE CHILDREN OF DARWIN

The faces of Darwin's children show an incredible ethnic diversity, something many believe will be typical of all Australia in 50 years time. The Northern Territory, and especially Darwin, is renowned for a relaxed, multicultural society and a racial tolerance and identity rarely found in other Australian cities.

Darwin's children, whatever their ethnic origin, are united by their casual Australian clothes and relaxed attitude.

The Filipino community *in Darwin preserves its traditions, as seen by these two girls in national costume at the Festival of Darwin.*

Paspaley Pearls *is Darwin's wealthiest local company. Founded by Greek settlers, it owns pearl farms across northern Australia.*

The East Timorese *community of Darwin performs traditional dancing at a city arts festival. Most of the East Timorese have arrived in the city since 1975, in the wake of Indonesia's invasion of East Timor.*

DARWIN AND THE TOP END

The tropical tip of the Northern Territory is a lush, ancient landscape. For thousands of years it has been home to large numbers of Aboriginals and contains the greatest and oldest collection of rock art in the world. Its capital, Darwin, is small and colourful. The World Heritage-listed Kakadu National Park has a raw beauty combined with the fascinating creation stories of its Aboriginal tribes.

The Port of Darwin was first named in 1839, when British captain John Lort Stokes, commander of HMS *Beagle*, sailed into an azure harbour fringed by palm trees, sandy beaches and mangroves, and named it after his friend Charles Darwin. Although the biologist would not publish his theory of evolution in the *Origin of the Species* for another 20 years, it proved to be a wonderfully apt name for this tropical region, teeming with unique and ancient species of birds, plants, reptiles and mammals. The Aboriginal tribes that have lived for many thousands of years in the northern area known as the Top End are recognized by anthropologists as one of world's oldest races.

Darwin itself is a city that has fought hard to survive. From 1869, when the first settlement was established at Port Darwin, it has endured isolation, bombing attacks by the Japanese in World War II *(see p270)* and devastation by the force of Cyclone Tracy in 1974 *(see p272)*. Despite having been twice rebuilt, it has grown into a multicultural modern city, with a relaxed atmosphere, great beauty and a distinctly Asian feel.

Beyond Darwin is a region of Aboriginal communities and ancient art sites, wide rivers and crocodiles, lotus-lily wetlands and deep gorges. For visitors, Kakadu National Park superbly blends sights of great scenic beauty with a cultural and spiritual insight into the complex Aboriginal culture. Also to be enjoyed are the plunging waterfalls and giant termite mounds of Litchfield National Park, the deep red-rock gorge of Nitmiluk (Katherine Gorge) National Park, and expeditions into the closed Aboriginal communities of Arnhem Land and Melville and Bathurst Islands.

An Aboriginal child gathering water lilies in the lush and tropical Top End

◁ Katherine Gorge cutting an awesome scar across the landscape

Exploring Darwin and the Top End

The Top End is a seductive, tropical region on the remote tip of the massive Northern Territory. On the turquoise coast there are palm trees; inland are winding rivers, grassy wetlands, gorge pools and ochre escarpments. The Territory's capital, Darwin, has many attractions and is a good base for day trips to areas such as Berry Springs and Melville and Bathurst Islands. The climate is hot, but the dry season has low humidity, making it the best time to visit. The wet season, however, compensates for its humidity and tropical downpours with the spectacle of thundering rivers and waterfalls, and lush vegetation.

Pearl lugger-turned-cruise boat in Darwin Harbour

GETTING AROUND

The Top End's reputation as an isolated region is long gone. Darwin is linked by the Stuart Highway to Alice Springs, Adelaide and Melbourne in the south, and along interstate hwys to Mount Isa, Cairns and Brisbane in the east. The centre of Darwin can be explored on foot or using the open trolley Tour Tub which stops at all the main attractions in an hourly circuit. The Top End's major attractions, such as Kakadu National Park and Katherine Gorge, can be visited without driving on a dirt road. Bus connections to the main towns are regular, but a car is vital to make the most of the scenery. Distances are not great for Australia; Kakadu is 210 km (130 miles) from Darwin and Katherine 300 km (186 miles) away on the Stuart Hwy.

Spectacular Jim Jim Falls in Kakadu National Park

Arafura Sea

Cape Stewart
Maningrida
Ramingining

Elcho Island
Galiwinku

Gove Peninsula
Gapuwiyak

Wessel Islands
Marchinbar Island

Nhulunbuy
Cape Arnhem

Camburinga

Arnhem Land

Mann
Wilton
Parsons Range
Mitchell Range
Rose

Isle Woodah

Bulman

Milyakburra
Angurugu

Umbakumba
Groote Eylandt

Numbulwar

Roper Bar
Ngukurr
ROPER HWY
Roper
Towns
Cox

Gulf of Carpentaria

Sir Edward Pellew Group

Limmen Bight

King Ash Bay
Borroloola

CARPENTARIA HWY

McArthur

Barkly

Cape Crawford Roadhouse

Tableland

China Wall

Tarrabool Lake

TABLELANDS HWY

Connells Lagoon Conservation Area

Lake Sylvester

STUART HWY

87

Three Ways Roadhouse

Tennant Creek

BARKLY HIGHWAY

Barkly Homestead

66

↓ Alice Springs

Rankern

Mount Isa

0 kilometres   100

0 miles   100

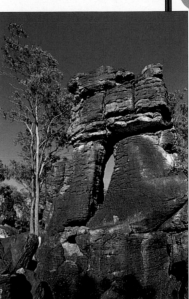

Unusual sandstone formations of the Lost City, Litchfield National Park

SEE ALSO

SIGHTS AT A GLANCE

KEY

— Major road

⋯⋯ Minor road

-- Track

— Scenic route

— State border

Darwin ●

Following European settlement in 1864, for the first century of its life Darwin was an outpost of the British Empire, with vast cattle farms being established around it. In its short, colourful history it has experienced the gold rush of the 1890s, life as an Allied frontline during World War II and almost total destruction in 1974 by the fearful winds of Cyclone Tracy (*see p272*). Darwin has now emerged as a modern but relaxed town where more than 50 ethnic groups mingle, including Asian-born Australians, Aboriginals, Europeans, particularly Greeks, and Chinese.

Old pearl diver's helmet

Shady palm trees in Bicentennial Park, seen from The Esplanade

⚜ Old Town Hall
Smith St. ♿
The limestone ruin of the Old Darwin Town Hall lies at the bottom of Smith Street. The original council chambers, built in 1883, became a naval workshop and store in World War II. Subsequently it was a bank and then a museum, before being destroyed by Cyclone Tracy in 1974. Curved brick paving built against the remaining wall symbolizes the fury of the cyclone's winds.

⚜ Brown's Mart
12 Smith St. *Tel (08) 8981 5522.* ♿
Directly opposite the town hall ruins is Brown's Mart, built in 1885 during the gold boom. It was once a mining exchange and is now home to an intimate theatre.

⚜ Old Police Station and Courthouse
Cnr Smith St & The Esplanade. *Tel (08) 8999 7103.* ♿
The 1884 limestone Old Police Station and Courthouse have both been restored after being damaged by Cyclone Tracy and are now administration offices.
Across the road is Survivors' Lookout, which overlooks the harbour. Here photographs

and written accounts tell of Darwin's wartime ordeal as an Allied frontline. Thousands of US and Australian troops were based in the Top End, which endured 63 bombing raids by Japanese forces (*see p57*).

⚜ Lyons Cottage
Cnr Knuckey St & The Esplanade. *Tel (08) 8981 1750.* ⭘ *10am–3pm daily.* ● *Easter, 25 Dec.* ♿
The old stone building known as Lyons Cottage was built in 1925. It is maintained in a 1920s style and contains an exhibition of photographs detailing life in the Top End during that era.

⬛ Smith Street Mall
Bennett & Knuckey sts. ♿
The heart of Darwin's shopping area is Smith Street Mall, with its glass air-conditioned plazas shaded by tall tropical trees. Always full of buskers, tour operators offering trips, locals and visitors, the mall is a favourite meeting place. Noteworthy buildings include the 1890 Victoria Hotel, a popular landmark and one of the few old structures in the town to survive Cyclone Tracy.

✿ Bicentennial Park
The Esplanade. ♿
This lush, green park, with its pleasant shady walks and panoramic lookouts, is home to many World War II memorials. One commemorates the attack by Japanese bombers which flew over Darwin Harbour on 19 February 1942, sinking 21 of the 46 US and Australian naval vessels in port and killing 243 people. It was the closest Australia came to war on its own soil.

Front entrance of Parliament House

⚜ Parliament House
State Square. *Tel (08) 8946 1434.* ⭘ *8am–6pm daily.* ☀ *May–Aug.* ♿
Dominating the edge of Darwin's sea cliffs is the new Parliament House, which was opened in 1994. With architecture that appears to borrow from both Middle Eastern and Russian styles, this imposing building is home to the Territory's 25 parliamentarians, who administer just 200,000 people. It has a granite and timber interior which is filled with Aboriginal art. Visitors may also get a glimpse of the parliamentarian chambers and use the library – the largest in the territory, with an excellent local reference section.

Darwin's Old Police Station and Courthouse

♛ Government House

The Esplanade. *Tel (08) 8999 7103.* ♿

On a small plateau above the harbour, Government House is Darwin's oldest surviving building, built in 1879. It has withstood the ravages of three cyclones and bombing attacks. It is now home to the Administrator of the Northern Territory, the representative of the Queen and Commonwealth of Australia in the Territory.

♛ Old Admiralty House

Cnr Knuckey St & The Esplanade.

Across the road from Lyons Cottage is Old Admiralty House, once the headquarters of the Australian navy and one of the oldest surviving buildings in Darwin. It was built in the 1930s by the territory's principal architect, Beni Carr Glynn Burnett, in an elevated tropical style using louvres, open eaves and three-quarter-high walls to aid ventilation.

♛ Stokes Hill Wharf

McMinn St. ♿ 🅿 🚻

The long, wooden Stokes Hill Wharf, stretching out into Darwin Harbour, was once the town's main port area. Now a centre for tourist and local life, it has restaurants and shops. Boats leave on tours from the wharf.

At the wharf entrance is the excellent Indo-Pacific Marine exhibit, which has re-created local coral reef ecosystems, with bright tropical fish in its

tanks. In the same building, the Australian Pearling Exhibition describes the history and science of local pearl farming.

Restaurant at the end of Stokes Hill Wharf overlooking the harbour

DARWIN CITY CENTRE

0 metres   250

0 yards   250

Key to Symbols *see back flap*

Greater Darwin

Decorated emu egg

Many of Darwin's best attractions are not in the city centre but located a short drive away. The Tour Tub, an open-sided trolley bus that picks up from major hotels, does an hourly circuit of tourist attractions, allowing visitors to hop on and off at will for a daily charge. Outside Darwin, alongside the mango farms and cattle stations, there are some fine bush and wetland areas which provide excellent opportunities for swimming, fishing and exploring.

Feeding the friendly fish at Aquascene in Doctor's Gully

⚓ Aquascene

Doctor's Gully, cnr of Daly St & The Esplanade. *Tel* (08) 8981 7837. ◯ *daily, with the tide.* ● *25 Dec.* ♿

Ever since the 1950s, the fish of Darwin Harbour have been coming in on the tides for a feed of stale bread in Doctor's Gully. At Aquascene, visitors can feed and play with hundreds of scats, catfish, mullet and milkfish. Feeding times vary from day to day.

Ethnic food stall at Mindil Beach Sunset Markets

🎪 Mindil Beach Sunset Markets

Mindil Beach. *Tel* (08) 8981 3454. ◯ *May–Oct: Thu, Sun.* ♿

Thursday and Sunday nights during the dry season are when Darwinians flock to Mindil Beach at dusk to enjoy some 60 outdoor food stalls, street theatre, live music and over 200 craft stalls.

🌺 George Brown Darwin Botanic Gardens

Gardens Rd, Stuart Park. *Tel* (08) 8981 1958. ◯ *daily.* ♿ *limited.*

Just north of town, the 42-ha (100-acre) Botanic Gardens, established in the 1870s, boast over 1,500 tropical species, including 400 palm varieties and wetland mangroves.

⚔ East Point Military Museum and Fannie Bay Gaol

Alec Fong Lim Drive, East Point. *Tel* (08) 8981 9702. ◯ *9:30am–5pm daily.* ♿

An attraction for all the family, this attractive harbourside reserve contains an artificial lake, ideal for swimming, and the East Point Military Museum. Nearby Fannie Bay Gaol is now an interesting museum.

🏛 Australian Aviation Heritage Centre

557 Stuart Hwy, Winnellie. *Tel* (08) 8947 2145. ⛟ *5, 8.* ◯ *9am–5pm daily.* ● *Good Fri, 25 Dec.* ♿♿

Along the Stuart Highway at Winnellie, 6 km (4 miles) from the city centre, Darwin's Aviation Centre displays a variety of historic and wartime aircraft. Its exhibits are dominated by a B-52 bomber, one of only two in the world on display outside the US.

🦘 Territory Wildlife Park

Cox Peninsula Rd, Berry Springs. *Tel* (08) 8988 7200. ◯ *8:30am–6pm daily.* ● *25 Dec.* ♿♿ 🖥 **www**.territorywildlifepark.com.au

Only 60 km (37 miles) from Darwin is the town of Berry Springs and the Territory Wildlife Park with its hundreds of unique indigenous species, in natural surroundings. Nearby, Berry Springs Nature Reserve has a series of deep pools, fringed with vegetation, that make for great swimming.

🐢 Howard Springs Nature Park

Howard Springs Rd. *Tel* (08) 8983 1001. ◯ *daily.* ♿ *limited.*

This nature park, 35 km (22 miles) south of Darwin, has clear, freshwater spring-fed pools, filled with barramundi and turtles. It's an ideal place to have a barbecue or a picnic in the shade after a hot day of exploring.

CYCLONE TRACY

Late Christmas Eve, 1974, a weather warning was issued that Cyclone Tracy, gathering force off the coast, had turned landward and was heading for Darwin. Torrential rain pelted down and winds reached a record 280 km/h (175 mph) before the measuring machine broke. On Christmas morning, 66 people were dead, thousands injured and 95 per cent of the buildings flattened. More than 30,000 residents were airlifted south in the biggest evacuation in Australia's history. The city ruins were bulldozed and Darwin has been rebuilt, stronger and safer than before.

Cyclone Tracy's devastation

Museum and Art Gallery of the Northern Territory

The Museum and Art Gallery of the Northern Territory has exhibitions on regional Aboriginal art and culture, maritime history, visual arts and natural history.

The museum's collection of Aboriginal art is considered to be the best in the world and has some particularly fine carvings and bark paintings, along with explanations of Aboriginal culture. Other displays include a chilling exhibition on Cyclone Tracy and displays that explain the evolution of some of the Top End's unique and curious wildlife, including the popular stuffed crocodile named "Sweetheart".

VISITORS' CHECKLIST

Conacher St. *Tel* (08) 8999 8264.
4, 5. ◯ 9am–5pm Mon–Fri,
10am–5pm Sat & Sun. ◉ some
public hols. ⊘ ♿ ◻ ◻ ◻
www.magnt.nt.gov.au

KEY

- ◻ Aboriginal Art Gallery
- ◻ Natural Sciences Gallery
- ◻ Cyclone Tracy Gallery
- ◻ Visual Art Gallery
- ◻ Amphitheatre
- ◻ Maritime Galleries
- ◻ Temporary exhibitions
- ◻ Non-exhibition space
- ◻ Monsoon Forest Pathway
- ◻ Fish Pond

★ Aboriginal Art Gallery
In this gallery, exhibits describe both the anthropology and creation stories of local Aboriginal groups as an introduction to the artworks on display that portray their lives and culture.

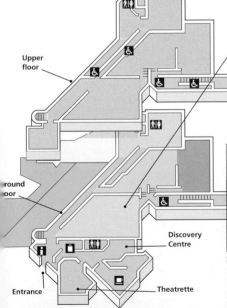

Upper floor

round oor

Discovery Centre

Entrance

Theatrette

Sweetheart
This large male crocodile, measuring 5 m (16 ft) in length, is called Sweetheart. It was caught in 1979 in the Finnis River, which is between Darwin and Kakadu.

Façade of the Museum and Art Gallery
Located 4 km (2 miles) north of Darwin's centre, the museum's stylish low-level building is in a tropical beachside setting overlooking Fannie Bay.

STAR FEATURES

★ Aboriginal Art Gallery

Tiwi islander making handicrafts from local fibres, Bathurst Island

Tiwi Islands [2]

✈ ℹ *Tiwi Tours, Mitchell St, Darwin (08) 8923 6523.*

Just 80 km (50 miles) north of Darwin lie the Tiwi Islands, the collective name given to the small island of Bathurst and its larger neighbour, Melville. The latter is the second-largest island off the Australian coast after Tasmania and is rich in history and Aboriginal culture. The islands' inhabitants, the Tiwi people, had little contact with mainland Aboriginals until the 20th century.

With beautiful waters, sandy beaches and lush forest, the islands are a tropical paradise, but, because of their ownership by the Tiwi, only Bathurst Island is visited on tours from Darwin. Running May to October, day trips offer a glimpse of the unique blend of Aboriginal, Indonesian and Tiwi traditions. Tourists can visit Aboriginal art centres, Tiwi batik printworks and a *pukumani* burial site.

Cobourg Peninsula [3]

ℹ *Venture North Australia, Darwin (08) 8927 5500.*
www.northernaustralia.com

The Cobourg Peninsula is one of the most remote parts of Australia. It is only accessible by vehicle during the dry season and with an access permit *(see p262)*, travelling through the closed Aboriginal Arnhem Land to the wild coastal beaches of Gurig National Park. The number of vehicles allowed to enter the region each week is restricted and there are permit fees, too, so going on a tour is sometimes a convenient option.

Gurig is a large park, with sandy beaches and the calm waters of Port Essington. Two attempts by the British to settle this area in the early 19th century were abandoned, due to inhospitable Aborigines and malaria epidemics. The ruins of Victoria Settlement can be reached by boat from Smith Point. Luxury accommodation is available at Seven Spirit Bay Wilderness Lodge, reached by plane from Darwin.

Kakadu National Park [4]

See pp276–7.

Litchfield National Park [5]

ℹ *Parks and Wildlife Service of the Northern Territory (08) 8980 6000 or 1300 138 886.*
www.nt.gov.au/nreta/parks

The spectacular Litchfield National Park, only 129 km (80 miles) south of Darwin, is very popular with Darwinians. There are waterfalls, gorges and deep, crocodile-free pools for swimming at Florence Falls, Wangi, in the wet season, and Buley Rockhole. The park has some amazing giant magnetic termite mounds. They are so-called because they point north in an effort by the termites to control temperature by having only the mound's thinnest part exposed to the sun. Also popular are the sandstone block formations further south, known as the "Lost City" due to their resemblance to ruins.

Giant magnetic termite mound in Litchfield National Park

Katherine [6]

👥 *11,000.* ✈ 🚆 🚌 ℹ *Cnr Stuart Hwy & Lindsay St (08) 8972 2650.*
www.visitkatherine.com.au

The town of Katherine, situated on the banks of the Katherine River, 320 km (200 miles) south of Darwin, is both a thriving regional centre and a major Top End tourist destination. Home for thousands of years to the Jawoyn Aboriginals, Katherine River has long been a rich source of food for the Aboriginal people. The river was first crossed by white explorers in 1844, and the area was not settled by Europeans until 1872, with the completion of the Overland Telegraph Line. Springvale Homestead was built on the Katherine River in 1879. It is now the oldest building in the Territory and is open to the public.

Only 30 km (20 miles) from town lies the famous **Nitmiluk (Katherine Gorge) National Park**. Its string of 13 separate gorges along 50 km (30 miles) of the Katherine River has been carved out by torrential summer rains cutting through cliffs of red sandstone which are 1,650 million years old. The result is a place of deep pools, silence and grandeur.

The best way to explore the park is by boat or canoe. Canoe trips are self-guided, with nine navigable gorges and overnight camping possible. There are also boat trips operated by the Jawoyn people, who own the park and run it in conjunction with the Parks and Wildlife Service of the Northern Territory. Each gorge can be explored in a separate boat, interspersed with swimming holes and

For hotels and restaurants in this region see pp495–6 and pp540–2

Upper waterfall and pools of Edith Falls, Nitmiluk (Katherine Gorge) National Park near Katherine

short walks. There are also 100 km (60 miles) of marked trails in the park, ranging from the spectacular but easy look-out walk to the five-day 72-km (45-mile) hike to Edith Falls, which can also be reached by car from the Stuart Highway.

Environs

Just 27 km (17 miles) south of Katherine are the Cutta Cutta caves, limestone rock formations 15 m (50 ft) under the earth's surface and formed five million years ago. They are home to both the rare orange horseshoe bat and the brown tree snake.

Further southeast, 110 km (70 miles) from Katherine, lies the small town of Mataranka. This is "Never Never" country, celebrated by female pioneer Jeannie Gunn in her 1908 novel, *We of the Never Never*, about life at nearby Elsey Station at the turn of the century. The area is called Never Never country because those who live here find they never,

Limestone Gorge, Gregory National Park

never want to leave it. About 8 km (5 miles) east of Mataranka is Elsey National Park. Visitors can swim in the hot waters of the Mataranka Thermal Pool which flow from Rainbow Springs to this idyllic spot. Built in 1916 **Mataranka Homestead** is now back-packer accommodation and part of the Mataranka Homestead resort, which includes a motel, cabins and camping.

🏠 **Mataranka Homestead**
Tel (08) 8975 4544. ⬜ *daily.*
🚋 ⏸ 📷

Gregory National Park ➐

ℹ️ *Timber Creek (08) 8975 0888, Bullita (08) 8975 0833.* ⬜ *7am–4pm Mon–Fri.* **www**.nt.gov.au/nreta/parks

This massive national park is in cattle country, 280 km (174 miles) by road southwest of Katherine. Broken into two sections, its eastern part contains a 50-km (31-mile) section of the Victoria River gorge, mostly inaccessible. In the north of the larger western section of the park are some crocodile-infested areas of the Victoria River. Here boat trips combine close-up views of

the crocodiles. In the west of the park, the stunning Limestone Gorge has dolomite blocks, huge cliffs and good fishing opportunities.

Walking trail by a sandstone escarp-ment, Keep River National Park

Keep River National Park ➑

ℹ️ *Victoria Hwy (08) 9167 8827.* ⬜ *Apr–Sep: daily; Oct–Mar: Mon–Fri. Closed when inaccessible.*

Located only 3 km (2 miles) from the Western Australian border, Keep River National Park includes the dramatic Keep River gorge and some of Australia's most ancient rock art sites. The park, once the location of an ancient Aboriginal settlement, today has some superb walking trails for all levels of trekkers.

Kakadu National Park

Aboriginal calendar at the Bowali Visitors' Centre

The vast 19,757 sq km (7,628 sq miles) of Kakadu National Park, with its stunning diversity of stony plateaux, red escarpment cliffs, waterfalls, billabongs, long twisting rivers, flood plains and coastal flats, is one of Australia's most extraordinary places. A UNESCO World Heritage Area *(see pp26–7)*, Kakadu encompasses both scenic wonders and huge galleries of Aboriginal rock art. The park is Aboriginal land leased back to the government *(see p59)* and is managed jointly. The entire catchment area of the South Alligator River lies within the park, and is home to thousands of plant and animal species. Some areas in Kakadu are not accessible during the wet season.

Yellow Water
A cruise on the wetlands of Yellow Water shows Kakadu in all its glory. Lotus lilies, crocodiles, kookaburras, magpie geese, jabirus and other bird species can be seen.

FLORA AND FAUNA IN KAKADU NATIONAL PARK

More than one-third of all bird species recorded in Australia live in Kakadu National Park; as do more than 60 mammal species, 117 reptile species, 1,700 plant species and at least 10,000 insect species. Approximately 10 per cent of the birds are estimated to be unique to Kakadu. Magpie geese are especially abundant; at times there are three million in the park, which is 60 per cent of the world's population.

The stately jabiru, seen near shallow water in the dry season

Map labels:
Wildman River
West Alligator River
South Alligator River
Four Mile Hole
Two Mile Hole
36
Kakadu Holiday Village
DARWIN
Cooinda
Jim Jim (Old Darwin) Road
Black Jungle Spring
PINE CREEK
Mary River Roadhouse

Gunlom Waterhole
The southern and drier end of Kakadu is less visited, but holds some magical places such as the Gunlom plunge pool and waterfall, home to the rainbow serpent, Borlung, in Aboriginal legend.

Guluyambi Cultural Cruises take visitors up the East Alligator River with Aboriginal guides who explain local Aboriginal traditions and culture.

Ubirr

This rock has many Aboriginal rock art galleries, some with paintings more than 20,000 years old (see p33).

Oenpelli is a small Aboriginal town in Arnhem Land outside Kakadu. Some day tours take visitors to this restricted area.

Jabiru is a small town that provides accommodation for visitors to the park.

Ranger Uranium Mine

This mine is rigorously monitored to ensure that the natural and cultural values of the park are not endangered.

Bowali Visitors' Centre

This award-winning centre features excellent displays describing the animals, Aboriginal culture and geology of Kakadu.

Nourlangie Rock

Another fine Aboriginal rock art site, this includes paintings of Namaragan, the Lightning Man (see p262).

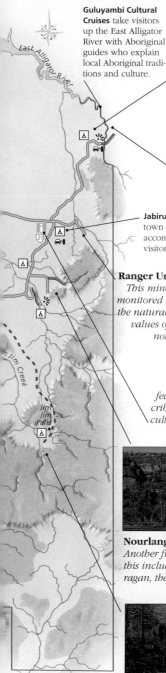

KEY

▬▬	Highway
▬	Major road
- -	4WD only
—	National park boundary
🛢	Petrol station
Ⓐ	Camp site
ℹ	Tourist information
☀	Viewpoint

Twin Falls

This waterfall (accessible by 4WD and boat transfer) flows in the dry season but is dramatic in the wet, when it thunders over a high plateau into deep rock pools.

0 kilometres   20

0 miles   20

THE RED CENTRE

*T*he Red Centre stretches roughly from Tennant Creek to the South Australian border, and is made up almost entirely of huge desert areas. The region occupies the centre of the Australian continent, with its main town, Alice Springs, at the country's geographical heart. Its signature colour is red: red sand, soil, rocks and mountains are all pitched against a typically blue sky.

The Red Centre contains some of the finest natural scenery in the world, much of it dating back about 800 million years. At that time, central Australia was covered by an inland sea; here sediments were laid down which form the basis of some of the region's best-known topographical features today. These include the huge monolith Uluru (formerly Ayers Rock), the domes of Kata Tjuta (also known as the Olgas), the giant boulders of the Devil's Marbles and the majestic MacDonnell Ranges. Between these sights are vast open spaces where remnants of tropical plant species grow beside desert-hardy stock. Verdant plants fed by occasional rains flourish next to animal skeletons.

Aboriginal people have lived in the region for more than 30,000 years, and their ancient tradition of rock painting is one of many tribal rituals still practised. By comparison, the history of white settlement here is recent. Explorers first arrived in the area during the 1860s. Alice Springs, founded in 1888, was a tiny settlement until improved communications after World War II led to the town's growth. It is now a modern, bustling town with much to offer. Tennant Creek, the only other sizeable settlement in the area, lies on the main Stuart Highway that bisects the Red Centre.

Much of the Territory has now been returned to its Aboriginal owners *(see pp262–3)*, and today many Aborigines are actively involved in tourism. Access to Aboriginal lands is restricted but visiting them is a rewarding encounter to add to the unforgettable experience of the Red Centre.

Trekking through the desert landscape on a camel safari near Alice Springs

◁ **The monolith Uluru, sacred to the Aborigines, set against a brilliant blue sky**

Exploring the Red Centre

The Red Centre's biggest draw is its stunning array of natural features. Alice Springs is the main city, with other towns at Yulara (Ayers Rock Resort) and Tennant Creek. The best time to travel is from April to October, thus avoiding the intense summer heat. The MacDonnell Ranges run like a huge spine on either side of Alice Springs; elsewhere the land is largely flat, formed by millions of years of erosion, and covered by spinifex grasslands. The region's gorges have been carved out by rivers, many of which flow only once or twice a year, soaking the surrounding desert plains.

Visually striking Olga Gorge in Uluṟu-Kata Tjuṯa National Park

SEE ALSO

KEY

▬	Major road
═══	Minor road
--	Track
▬	Scenic route
┅	Main railway
▬	State border
△	Summit

SIGHTS AT A GLANCE

Colourful mural painted on a shopping centre in Alice Springs

GETTING AROUND

There is a wide range of transport options available in central Australia. Domestic airports serve Alice Springs and Yulara. Overland, coaches connect the region with all the state capital cities, and the famous Ghan railway *(see p283)* operates between Darwin, Alice Springs and Adelaide. The most popular way to explore the region, however, is by car, and there are many car rental companies in the area. Standard vehicles are adequate for most journeys, but 4WD is advisable for off-road travel. Alternatively, many guided tours are also available. The Stuart Hwy is the main road running through the area, linking Port Augusta in South Australia with Darwin in the north. Alice Springs itself has taxis, bike hire and a town bus service, but the relatively short distances within the city also make walking popular.

0 kilometres 100

0 miles 100

Desert wildflowers in Simpsons Gap, near Alice Springs

Alice Springs ●

Alice Springs is named after the Alice Spring permanent waterhole, near which a staging post for the overland telegraph line was built in the 1870s. The waterhole was named after Alice Todd, wife of the line's construction manager. The town developed nearby in the 1880s, but with no rail link until 1929 and no surfaced road link until the 1940s, it grew slowly. The huge increase in tourism since the 1970s, however, has brought rapid growth and Alice Springs is now a lively city with around 400,000 visitors a year, many of whom use it as a base from which to tour the surrounding spectacular natural sights.

Exploring Alice Springs

Although many of its sights are spread around the city, Alice Springs is small enough to tour on foot. Its compact centre, just five streets across running from Wills Terrace in the north to Stuart Terrace in the south, contains many of the town's hotels and restaurants, as well as the pedestrianized Todd Mall. The city's eastern side is bordered by Todd River, dry and sandy most of the time and scene of the celebrated Henley-on-Todd Regatta *(see p40)*.

Meteorite fragment in the Museum of Central Australia

🐾 Anzac Hill

West Terrace. 🚹
At the northern end of Alice Springs, Anzac Hill overlooks the city and affords fine views of the MacDonnell Ranges *(see p284)*. Named after the 1934 Anzac memorial at the site, the hill is a perfect vantage point for visitors to familiarize themselves with the city's layout, as well as for viewing the area at sunrise or sunset, when it is bathed in a beautiful light.

🏛 Museum of Central Australia

Alice Springs Cultural Precinct, Larapinta Dr. **Tel** *(08) 8951 1121.* ☐ *daily.* ● *Good Fri, two weeks over Christmas.* 📷 🚹
This museum, situated in the Cultural Precinct, focuses on local natural history with displays of fossils, flora and fauna, meteorite pieces and minerals. It also houses fine pieces of Aboriginal art and artifacts.

🏠 Adelaide House

Todd Mall. **Tel** *(08) 89521856.* ☐ *Mar–Nov: Mon–Sat.* ● *Good Fri.* 📷 🚹
Adelaide House, Alice Springs' first hospital, opened in 1926. It was designed by John Flynn, founder of the Royal Flying Doctor Service *(see p257)*, and is preserved as a museum dedicated to his memory.

🏠 Old Courthouse

Cnr Parsons & Hartley sts. **Tel** *(08) 8952 9006.* ☐ *10am–5pm daily.* ● *mid-Dec–1 Feb.* 📷 🚹

Built in 1928 by Emil Martin, who was also responsible for The Residency, the Old Courthouse was in use until 1980, when new law courts were opened nearby.

Old Stuart Town Gaol

🏠 Old Stuart Town Gaol

8 Parsons St. **Tel** *(08) 8952 4516.* ☐ *Wed, Thu & Sat.* ● *mid Dec–1 Feb, public hols.* 📷 🚹
The oldest building in central Alice Springs is the Old Stuart Town Gaol, which operated as a jail between 1909 and 1938 when a new prison was built on Stuart Terrace. The gaol is now open to the public.

🏠 The Residency

29 Parsons St. **Tel** *(08) 8953 6073.* ☐ *10am–2pm Mon–Fri.* ● *Dec–Mar, Good Fri, 25 Dec.* 📷 **Donation.**
The Residency, built in 1927 for the regional administrator of Central Australia, was the home of Alice Springs' senior public servant until 1973. After restoration, it was opened to the public in 1996 and now houses a local history display.

🏛 The Women's Hall of Fame

Old Alice Springs Gaol, 2 Stuart Tce. **Tel** *(08) 8952 9006.* ☐ *10am–5pm daily.* ● *mid-Dec–1 Feb.* 📷 🚹
www.pioneerwomen.com.au
This museum is devoted to the extraordinary lives of ordinary women who made a special contribution to Australia's heritage. Its displays document the achievements of the country's pioneering women.

🏠 Alice Springs Telegraph Station Historical Precinct

Off Stuart Hwy. **Tel** *(08) 8952 3993.* ☐ *8am–5pm daily.* ● *25 Dec.* 📷 🚹
This, the site of the first settlement in Alice Springs, features the original buildings and

View over central Alice Springs from the top of Anzac Hill

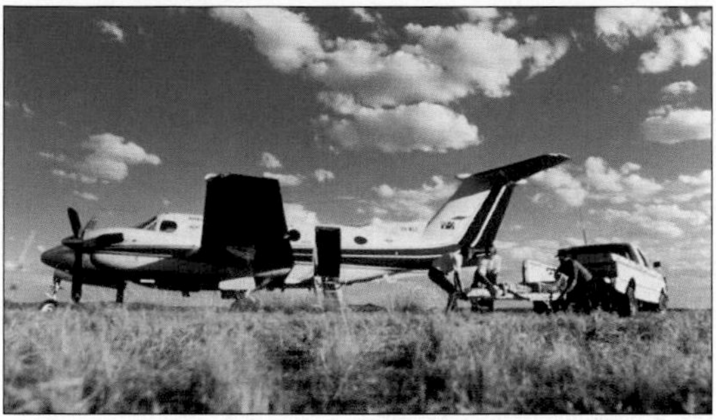

Plane used for the Royal Flying Doctor Service

equipment of the telegraph station built in 1871. A small museum describes the amazing task of setting up the station and operating the overland telegraph.

🦅 Alice Springs Desert Park

Larapinta Drive. ***Tel*** *(08) 8951 8788.*
🕐 *7:30am–6pm daily.* ● *25 Dec.*
♿
An excellent introduction to Central Australia, this park lies on the western edge of the town and features three habitat types: desert river, sand country and woodlands. Visitors may see many of the birds and animals of Central Australia here at close range.

🏛 National Road Transport Hall of Fame

1 Norris Bell Drive. ***Tel*** *(08) 8953 8940.*
🕐 *9am–5pm daily.* ● *25 Dec, 1 Jan.*
www.roadtransporthall.com
This museum pays homage to all the great trucks, buses and vehicles that have crossed the Australian continent. The Ghan Train, which first ran from Adelaide to Alice Springs in 1929, is commemorated with a collection of memorabilia.

VISITORS' CHECKLIST

👥 *27,000.* ✈ *14 km (9 miles) S of town.* 🚌 *George Crescent.* ℹ *Gregory Terrace (08) 8952 5800.* 🎉 *Henley-on-Todd Regatta (Oct); Camel Cup (Jul).*
www.travelnt.com

🏛 Royal Flying Doctor Service Visitor Centre

8–10 Stuart Terrace. ***Tel*** *(08) 8952 1129.* 🕐 *9am–5pm Mon–Sat, 1–5pm Sun & public hols.* ● *25 Dec, 1 Jan.*
obligatory. ☕ 🛍 ♿
www.flyingdoctor.net
The centre can only be visited accompanied by a guide, and visitors are taken on a 45-minute tour of the base that includes the Radio Communications centre, where staff recount the history of the Service and explain the day to day operations. There is also a museum, containing old medical equipment, model aircraft and an original Traeger Pedal Radio. The Visitor Centre opened in the late 1970s but has been extended to include a café and a souvenir shop.

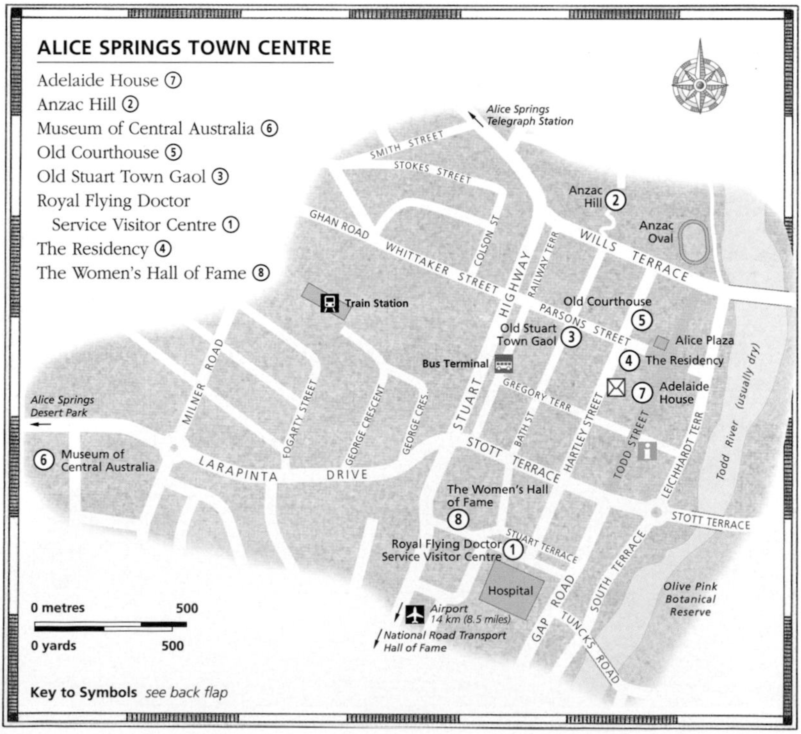
ALICE SPRINGS TOWN CENTRE
Adelaide House 7
Anzac Hill 2
Museum of Central Australia 6
Old Courthouse 5
Old Stuart Town Gaol 3
Royal Flying Doctor Service Visitor Centre 1
The Residency 4
The Women's Hall of Fame 8
Alice Springs Telegraph Station
SMITH STREET
STOKES STREET
Anzac Hill 2
Anzac Oval
GHAN ROAD
COLSON ST
WHITTAKER STREET
WILLS TERRACE
RAILWAY TERR
HIGHWAY
Train Station
Old Courthouse 5
PARSONS STREET
Old Stuart Town Gaol 3
Alice Plaza
4 The Residency
Bus Terminal
7 Adelaide House
GREGORY TERR
Todd River (usually dry)
Alice Springs Desert Park
MILNER ROAD
FOGARTY STREET
GEORGE CRESCENT
GEORGE CRES.
STUART
BATH ST
HARTLEY STREET
TODD STREET
LEICHHARDT TERR
6 Museum of Central Australia
LARAPINTA DRIVE
STOTT TERRACE
The Women's Hall of Fame 8
STOTT TERRACE
STUART TERRACE
Royal Flying Doctor Service Visitor Centre 1
Hospital
GAP ROAD
SOUTH TERRACE
Olive Pink Botanical Reserve
TUNCKS ROAD
Airport 14 km (8.5 miles)
National Road Transport Hall of Fame
0 metres 500
0 yards 500
Key to Symbols see back flap

Chambers Pillar Historical Reserve ❷

Tel (08) 8952 1013 or (08) 8951 8250.
🚂 Alice Springs. 🚌 Alice Springs.
📋 www.nt.gov.au/nreta/parks

Chambers Pillar, a 50-m (165-ft) high sandstone obelisk, was used by explorers as an important navigational landmark during early colonial exploration. The pillar is made of mixed red and yellow sandstone deposited more than 350 million years ago. Many of the explorers, such as John Ross who visited the area in 1870, carved their names and inscriptions into the rock.

Located 160 km (110 miles) south of Alice Springs, with the final section of the journey accessible only by 4WD vehicles, the pillar is also a sacred Aboriginal site.

Henbury Meteorites Conservation Reserve ❸

Tel (08) 8952 1033 or (08) 8951 8250.
🚂 Alice Springs. 🚌 Alice Springs. 📋

This cluster of 12 craters, located 145 km (89 miles) southwest of Alice Springs, was formed by a meteorite which crashed to earth several thousand years ago. It is believed that local Aborigines witnessed the event, as one of the Aboriginal names for the area suggests a fiery rock falling to earth. The largest crater in the group is 180 m (590 ft) across and is 15 m (50 ft) deep. Signs on a trail mark significant features.

Lush Palm Valley in Finke Gorge National Park, MacDonnell Ranges

MacDonnell Ranges ❹

🚂 Alice Springs. 🚌 Alice Springs.
ℹ Alice Springs (08) 8951 8250.
Simpsons Gap ⬭ daily. ♿
Standley Chasm ⬭ daily. 📷 ♿
www.nt.gov.au/nreta/parks

The Macdonnell Ranges are the eroded remnants of an ancient mountain chain which was once as monumental as the Himalayas. Still impressive and filled with striking scenery, the East and West MacDonnells contain gorges, waterholes and walking tracks. Running east and west of Alice Springs and easily accessible, they are popular with day-trippers. Visitors will notice the ranges' thrust-up layers of rock, evidence of geological movements more than 300 million years ago. Culturally, they contain many areas sacred to the Aranda people.

In the West MacDonnells, 7 km (4 miles) from Alice Springs, is John Flynn's Memorial Grave, which honours Presbyterian minister, Rev John Flynn, who founded the Royal Flying Doctor Service (see p257).

A further 10 km (6 miles) from town, **Simpsons Gap** is the first of a series of attractive gorges in the MacDonnells. A pretty spot, it is home to some rare local plant species. Nearby is **Standley Chasm**, a narrow, deep gorge whose sheer rock-faces glow a glorious red, particularly under the midday sun.

The large 18-m (60-ft) deep permanent waterhole within Ellery Gorge at Ellery Creek Big Hole is a good swimming spot. Serpentine Gorge, 20 km (12 miles) further west, is another narrow gorge created by an ancient river. A walking track leading to a lookout gives a fine view of its winding path.

Pushed up out of Ormiston Creek, the 300-m (985-ft) high walls of Ormiston Gorge are an awesome sight. The gorge consists of two layers of quartzite, literally doubled over each other, thus making it twice the height of others in the region.

Along Larapinta Drive is the small Aboriginal settlement of Hermannsburg, site of an 1870s Lutheran Mission which pre-dates Alice Springs. Famous as the home of the Aboriginal painter Albert Namatjira (1902–59), most of the town is contained within the **Hermannsburg Historic Precinct**, which includes a museum devoted to the mission and an art gallery.

Twenty km (12 miles) south of here lies the popular **Finke Gorge National Park**, home to Palm Valley,

Sacred site of Corroboree Rock in the East MacDonnell Ranges near Alice Springs

For hotels and restaurants in this region see pp496–7 and pp542–3

an unusual tropical oasis in the dry heart of the country with rare, ancient palm species.

On the other side of Alice Springs, the East MacDonnell Ranges boast some beautiful sites accessible via the Ross Highway. Close to town is Emily Gap, one of the most significant Aranda sites in Australia. Further east, Corroboree Rock, a strangely shaped outcrop, has a crevice once used to store sacred Aranda objects. Trephina Gorge is the most spectacular of the East MacDonnell sights, with quartzite cliffs and red river gums.

🏛 **Hermannsburg Historic Precinct**
Larapinta Drive. **Tel** (08) 8956 7402. ◯ daily. ⬤ 25 Dec. 🎫 ♿
www.hermannsburg.com.au
🌿 **Finke Gorge National Park**
Tel (08) 8956 7401 or (08) 8951 8250. 🚉 & 🚌 Alice Springs.

Mining building at Battery Hill, Tennant Creek

Tennant Creek ❻

🏯 3,500. ✈ 🚌 ❓ Battery Hill Regional Centre, Peko Rd (08) 8962 3388.

Tennant Creek was chosen as the site of a telegraph station on the Overland Telegraph Line in the late 1800s. The town grew after gold was discovered in the area in 1932. The **Battery Hill Mining Centre** is now a working museum, crushing ore to extract the gold.

Tennant Creek today is the second-largest town in the Red Centre. Nearly 500 km (310 miles) north of Alice Springs, it is also a major stopover along the Stuart Highway, between Darwin and South Australia. Other local attractions include the recreational Mary Ann Dam, 5 km (3 miles) out of town and ideal for boating and swimming. The remote **Tennant Creek Telegraph Station**, 12 km (8 miles) north of the town, built in 1874, is now a museum.

🏛 **Battery Hill Mining Centre**
Battery Hill Regional Centre, Peko Rd. **Tel** (08) 8962 1281. ◯ daily. ⬤ Good Fri, 25 Dec. 🎫 ♿ 🚻
🏛 **Tennant Creek Telegraph Station**
Stuart Highway. **Tel** (08) 8962 4599.

Kings Canyon ❼

🚌 Alice Springs. 🚌 Alice Springs, Yulara. ❓ Alice Springs (08) 8951 8250. www.nt.gov.au/nreta/parks

The spectacular sandstone gorge of Kings Canyon, set within Watarrka National Park, has walls more than 100 m (330 ft) high that have been formed by millions of years of erosion. They contain the fossilized tracks of ancient marine creatures, and even ripplemarks of an ancient sea are visible. Several walking tracks take visitors around the rim of the gorge where there are some stunning views of the valley below. Watarrka National Park has many waterholes and areas of lush vegetation that contain more than 600 plant species. The park also provides a habitat for more than 100 bird species and 60 species of reptiles.

Spherical boulders of the Devil's Marbles

Devil's Marbles Conservation Reserve ❺

Tel (08) 8951 8250, Tennant Creek Office (08) 8962 4599. 🚉 Tennant Creek. 🚌 from Tennant Creek Tourist Information. ♿ 🎫

Approximately 104 km (65 miles) south of Tennant Creek, the Devil's Marbles Conservation Reserve comprises a collection of huge, spherical, red granite boulders, scattered across a shallow valley in the Davenport Ranges. The result of geological activity occurring 1,700 million years ago, the boulders were created when molten lava was compressed to create huge domes just below the earth's surface. Subsequent erosion of the overlying rock exposed the marbles.

Rich vegetation deep in the sandstone gorge of Kings Canyon

Uluṟu-Kata Tjuṯa National Park ⓾

Thorny devil

The most instantly recognizable of all Australian symbols is the huge, red monolith of Uluṟu (Ayers Rock). Rising high above the flat desert landscape, Uluṟu is one of the world's natural wonders, along with the 36 rock domes of Kata Tjuṯa (The Olgas) and their deep valleys and gorges. Both sights are in Uluṟu-Kata Tjuṯa National Park, 463 km (288 miles) southwest of Alice Springs, which was established in 1958 and was named as a World Heritage site in 1987 *(see pp26–7)*. The whole area is sacred to Aboriginal people and, in 1985, the park was handed back to its indigenous owners and its sights reassumed their traditional names. As Aboriginal land, it is leased back to the Australian government and jointly managed with the local Aṉangu people. Within the park is an excellent cultural centre which details the Aboriginal lives and traditions of the area. Yulara, 12 km (7 miles) from Uluṟu, is the park's growing tourist resort *(see p289)*.

The Maruku Gallery
This Aboriginal-owned gallery sells traditional and modern Aboriginal crafts.

Kata Tjuṯa's domes rise in the distance behind Uluṟu.

Kata Tjuṯa (The Olgas)
This magnificent view of Kata Tjuṯa's domes is from the sunset viewing area. The site has drinking water and interpretive panels giving information on local flora and fauna.

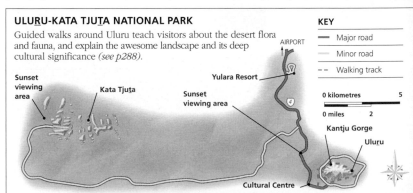

ULUṞU-KATA TJUṮA NATIONAL PARK

Guided walks around Uluṟu teach visitors about the desert flora and fauna, and explain the awesome landscape and its deep cultural significance *(see p288)*.

AIRPORT

Sunset viewing area

Kata Tjuṯa

Yulara Resort

Sunset viewing area

KEY

— Major road

— Minor road

-- Walking track

0 kilometres   5

0 miles   2

Kantju Gorge

Uluṟu

Cultural Centre

Olga Gorge

This scenic gorge runs between two of Kata Tjuta's huge domes. A walking track leads to a cliff face at the end where there is a rock pool and a trickling stream.

Uluru is famous for its colour changes, which range from deep red at sunrise and sunset to shiny black after rain.

Hare Wallaby

This mammal is significant to the Anangu people, who call it Mala. According to tradition, Mala people lived at Uluru and created many of the rock formations that are seen today.

DEHYDRATION IN THE DESERT

Uluru-Kata Tjuta National Park is in the heart of Australia's vast desert region. It can experience summer daytime temperatures of more than 45°C (113°F). To avoid dehydration and heat exhaustion all visitors are advised to wear hats, long-sleeved shirts with collars and sunscreen, and to avoid any strenuous activity between 10am and 4pm. Most importantly, each person should drink one litre of water per hour while walking in hot weather.

Vegetation is sparse on this desert plain except for a few areas of greenery found in sheltered spots where rainwater collects.

Mala Walk

This free, ranger-guided walk leads visitors to places created and used by the ancestral Mala people. It ends at Kantju Gorge, sacred to the Anangu, which contains a waterhole beneath a waterfall.

Exploring Uluṟu-Kata Tjuṯa National Park

Entrance sign to Uluṟu-Kata Tjuṯa National Park

It is impossible to arrive at Uluṟu-Kata Tjuṯa National Park and not be filled with awe. The sheer size of the world's largest monolith, Uluṟu, rising from the flat desert plain, is a moving and impressive sight. Just as magical are the rounded humps of Kata Tjuṯa not far distant. All the rocks change colour from oranges and reds to purple during the day. Getting around the park, understanding some of its deep Aboriginal significance and learning about its geology, flora and fauna should not be rushed. There is much more to this fascinating area than can be seen or experienced in one day, and a two- or three-day stay is recommended.

Tourists enjoying the Mala walk around part of the base of Uluṟu

Blue-tongued lizard basking in the sun

🐾 Uluṟu (Ayers Rock)

Uluṟu, 3.6 km (2.25 miles) long and 2.4 km (1.5 miles) wide, stands 348 m (1,142 ft) above the plains. It is made from a single piece of sandstone which extends 5 km (3 miles) beneath the desert surface. Besides its immense Aboriginal cultural significance, Uluṟu is an outstanding natural phenomenon, best observed by watching its changing colours at dusk and taking a guided walk at the rock's base.

There are a number of walking trails around Uluṟu. The three-hour, 9.5-km (6-mile) tour around the base gives the greatest sense of its size and majesty. Sacred sights en route are fenced off, and entering is an offence. The Mala (hare wallaby) walk takes in several caves, some with rock art. The Liru (snake) walk starts at the cultural centre, with Aboriginal tour guides explaining how they use bush materials in their daily lives. The Kuniya (python) walk visits the Mutijulu waterhole on the southern side of Uluṟu where local Aṉangu people tell creation stories and display art describing various

legends. Details of all walks can be found at the Uluṟu-Kata Tjuṯa Cultural Centre.

🐾 Kata Tjuṯa (The Olgas)

Kata Tjuṯa, meaning "many heads", is a collection of massive rounded rock domes, 42 km (25 miles) to the west of Uluṟu. Beyond lies a vast, remote desert; permits from the Central Land Council

(see p262), 4WDs and full travel survival kits are needed in this inhospitable land.

Kata Tjuṯa is not one large rock; it is a system of gorges and valleys that you can walk around, making it a haunting, quiet and spiritual place. To the Aṉangu people, it is of equal significance to Uluṟu, but fewer stories about it can be told as they are restricted to initiated tribal men. The tallest rock, Mount Olga, is 546 m (1,790 ft) high, nearly 200 m (660 ft) higher than Uluṟu. There are two recommended walking trails. The Valley of the Winds walk takes about three hours and wanders through several deep gorges. This walk is partially closed when the temperature exceeds 36°C (97°F).

CLIMBING ULURU

The climbing of Uluṟu by the chain-rope path that has been in place since the 1960s is a contentious issue. Physically, it is a steep, 1.6-km (1-mile) climb in harsh conditions, and several tourists die each year from heart attacks or falls. Culturally, the route to the top follows the sacred path taken by the ancestral Mala (hare wallaby) men for important ceremonies. The Aṉangu ask that visitors respect their wishes and do not climb the rock; a push to ban all climbing on Uluṟu is now gathering pace.

If you do decide to climb, the ascent takes about two hours. Climbing the rock is banned for the remainder of the day if the temperature at any point of the climb reaches 36°C (97°F). A dawn climb is most popular.

Sign warning tourists of the dangers of climbing Uluṟu

For hotels and restaurants in this region see pp496–7 and pp542–3

THE ANANGU OF ULURU

Archaeological evidence suggests that Aboriginal people have lived at Uluru for at least 22,000 years and that both Uluru and Kata Tjuta have long been places of enormous ceremonial and cultural significance to a number of Aboriginal tribes.

The traditional owners of Uluru and Kata Tjuta are the Anangu people. They believe that both sites were formed during the creation period by ancestral spirits who also gave them the laws and rules of society that they live by today. The Anangu believe they are direct descendants of these ancestral beings and that, as such, they are responsible for the protection and management of these lands.

The Anangu Aborigines performing a traditional dance

The Olga Gorge (Walpa Gorge) walk leads up the pretty Olga Gorge to its dead-end cliff face and a rock pool. Walkers here may spot the small brown spinifex bird or the thorny devil spiked lizard.

🏛 Uluru-Kata Tjuta Cultural Centre
Tel (08) 8956 1128. ◯ 7am–6pm (last entry 5:30pm) daily. 🈸 ♿

Near to the base of Uluru is an award-winning cultural centre, with multilingual displays, videos and exhibitions. It is an excellent introduction to the park and well worth visiting before exploring the rock and its surrounding area. The Nintiringkupai display focuses on the history and management of Uluru–Kata Tjuta National Park and includes up-to-date brochures and information on walking trails, sights and tours. The Tjukurpa display, with its art, sounds and videos, is a good introduction to the complex system of Anangu beliefs and laws. Attached to the cultural centre is the Aboriginal-owned Maruku Arts and Craft shop, where artists are at work and dancers and

musicians give performances for the tourists. The traditional art, on bark and canvas, tells the story of Uluru Tjukurpa legends.

Ayers Rock Resort
Yulara Drive. 🛈 (08) 8957 7377. www.ayersrockresort.com.au

Yulara is an environmentally friendly, modern tourist village well equipped to cater for the 500,000 annual visitors.

Nestling between the desert dunes 20 km (12 miles) north of Uluru and just outside the national park boundary, it serves as a comfortable, green and relaxing base for exploring Uluru–Kata Tjuta. The resort offers all standards of accommodation, from five-star luxury to backpacker accommodation and camping grounds, and is the only option for those who want to stay in the immediate vicinity *(see pp497)*.

The visitors' centre at Yulara has information about the park and its geology, flora and fauna. It also sells souvenirs and helps to arrange tours with the licensed operators in the park. Every day at 7:30am there is a free, early morning guided walk through the wonderful native garden of the Sails in the Desert Hotel *(see p497)*. Each evening at the Amphitheatre there is an hour-long concert of Aboriginal music featuring a variety of indigenous instruments, including the didgeridoo. A Night Sky Show is also available, and this describes both the Anangu and ancient Greek stories of the stars.

Yulara also has a shopping centre, which includes a post office, bank and supermarket, and many different restaurants and outdoor eating options *(see p544)*. Other facilities include a childcare centre for children up to the age of eight.

Aerial view of Yulara Resort, with Uluru in the distance

WESTERN
AUSTRALIA

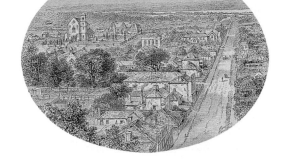

Western Australia at a Glance

The huge state of Western Australia encompasses a land mass of more than 2,500,000 sq km (1,000,000 sq miles). In recent years, the state's popularity as a tourist destination has increased, with large numbers of visitors drawn to its many areas of extreme natural beauty. The landscape ranges from giant karri forests, imposing mountains and meadows of wildflowers to vast expanses of untamed wilderness with ancient gorges and rock formations. The coastline has an abundance of beaches, ideal for surfing, and some stunning offshore reefs. In the east, great deserts stretch to the state border. The capital, Perth, is home to 80 per cent of the state's population, but there are many historic towns scattered around the southwest, such as the gold field settlements of Kalgoorlie and Coolgardie.

Shark Bay World Heritage and Marine Park *is Australia's westernmost point. Visitors flock to this protected area to watch the dolphins swim in the waters close to the shore* (see pp326–7).

Perth *is Australia's most isolated yet most modern state capital. Gleaming skyscrapers, an easy-going atmosphere and its coastal setting make it a popular destination* (see pp302–7).

Fremantle's *heyday as a major port was at the end of the 19th century. Many of its historic buildings remain. Today the town is renowned for its crafts markets* (see pp310–11).

◁ Perth city skyline at night

Karijini National Park *is in the Pilbara region and is a spectacular landscape of gorges, pools and waterfalls. The area is particularly popular with experienced hikers; guided tours are also available for more novice bushwalkers (see p329).*

Purnululu (Bungle Bungle) National Park *is one of Australia's most famous natural sights, with its multi-coloured rock domes. Access is limited, but helicopter flights offer views of the area (see p331).*

NORTH OF PERTH AND THE KIMBERLEY *(see pp320–31)*

Wave Rock *is 15 m (50 ft) high, 110 m (360 ft) long and is so named because its formation resembles a breaking wave. The illusion is further enhanced by years' worth of water stains running down its face (see p318).*

PERTH AND THE SOUTHWEST *(see pp298–319)*

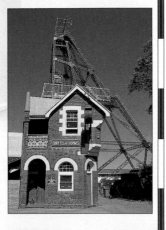

Kalgoorlie *made its name in the 1890s when gold was discovered in the region. Much of its 19th-century architecture has been preserved (see p318).*

0 km   100

0 miles   100

Wildflowers of Western Australia

Western Australia is truly the nation's wildflower state. In the spring, from August to November, more than 11,000 species of flowers burst into brilliantly coloured blooms, carpeting deserts, plains, farmland and forests with blazing reds, yellows, pinks and blues.

A staggering 75 per cent of these flowers are unique to the state, giving it one of the world's richest floras. It is home to such remarkable plants as the kangaroo paw, the cowslip orchid and the carnivorous Albany pitcher plant, as well as giant jarrah and karri forests.

The elegant kangaroo paw looks exactly like its name suggests. The state's floral emblem, it has many different species and mostly grows in coastal heath and dry woodland areas.

WHEN AND WHERE TO SEE THE WILDFLOWERS

Bushwalking or driving among the flower carpets of Western Australia is an experience not to be missed. Most of the wildflowers bloom in spring, but exactly when depends on their location in this vast state. The wildflower season begins in the northern Pilbara in July and culminates in the magnificent flowering around the Stirling Ranges and the south coast in late October and November.

The Albany pitcher plant grows near coastal estuaries around Albany in the southwest. One of the world's largest carnivorous plants, it traps and devours insects in its sticky hairs.

The magnificent royale hakea is one of many hakea species in Western Australia. It is found on the coast near Esperance and in Fitzgerald River National Park.

Much of Western Australia is arid, dusty outback country where the only vegetation is dry bush shrubs and, after rainfall, wildflowers.

Many wild flowers possess an incredible ability to withstand even the driest, hottest ground.

Red flowering gum *trees in the Stirling Ranges burst into bright red flowers every November, attracting honey bees.*

The cowslip orchid is a bright yellow orchid with red streaks and five main petals. It can usually be found in October, in the dramatic Stirling Ranges region.

Leschenaultia biloba *is a brilliant blue, bell-shaped flower found in jarrah forests near Collie, or in drier bush and plain country where it flowers in carpets of blue.*

The boab (baobab) tree *is a specimen related to the African baobab. Growing in the rocky plains of the Kimberley (see pp330–31), it holds a great deal of water in its swollen trunk and can grow many metres in circumference.*

The bright daisy flowers of the everlastings come in a host of creams, pinks, yellows, oranges and reds.

GIANTS OF THE WESTERN AUSTRALIAN FOREST

It is not only the native flowers that are special to Western Australia. So, too, are the trees – especially the towering jarrah and karri eucalypts of the southern forests. A major hardwood timber industry, harvesting the jarrah and karri, remains in the state's southwest near Manjimup and Pemberton *(see p315)* . Today, however, thousands of trees are preserved in national parks such as Shannon and Walpole-Nornalup, which has a walkway high in the trees for visitors.

Giant karri trees *grow to a height of 85 m (280 ft). They live for up to 300 years, reaching their maximum height after 100 years.*

EVERLASTING FLOWERS

Native to Australia, everlastings carpet vast areas in many parts of Western Australia. Especially prolific in the southeast, they can also be seen from the roadside in the north, stretching as far as the eye can see.

Everlastings are so called because the petals stay attached to the flower even after it has died.

The scarlet banksia (see p454), *is one of 41 banksia species found in Western Australia. It is named after Sir Joseph Banks, the botanist who first noted this unusual tree and its flower in 1770.*

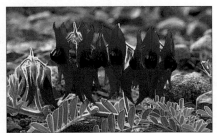

Sturt's desert pea *is actually South Australia's floral emblem, but is also prolific in the dry inland areas of Western Australia. Its bright flowers spring up after rain in the deserts, sometimes after lying dormant for years.*

The Kimberley

One of the last truly remote regions in Australia, the Kimberley in north-western Australia covers 423,000 sq km (164,000 sq miles), yet has a population of less than 35,000. Geologically it is one of the oldest regions on earth. Its rocks formed up to 2,000 million years ago, with little landscape disturbance since. Aboriginal people have lived here for thousands of years, but this unique land has been a tourist attraction only since the 1980s.

Dingo cave painting

KEY

▬▬	Highway
▬▬	Major road
⋯⋯	Unsealed road
----	National park boundary

THE BUNGLE BUNGLES

The tiger-striped beehive mountains that comprise the Bungle Bungle range were only discovered by tourists in the 1980s. These great geological and scenic wonders are now protected in Purnululu National Park *(see p331)*. The large, weathered sandstone domes are most easily viewed by air from Kununurra or Halls Creek, but visitors who make the effort to explore this 4WD-only park will also encounter some stunning narrow gorges and clear pools.

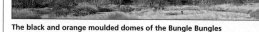

The black and orange moulded domes of the Bungle Bungles

Windjana Gorge National Park is one of the three stunning Devonian Reef national parks *(see p331)*.

The Great Northern Highway is a sealed road that runs from the Northern Territory border to Broome and Perth beyond.

Cape Leveque

King Sound

Charley River

Isdell River

Derby

Meda River

Windjana Gorge National Park

Gibb River Road

Tunnel Creek National Park

Geikie Gorge National Park

0 kilometres   100

0 miles   100

Broome

GREAT SANDY DESERT

Fitzroy River

Fitzroy Crossing

Cable Beach *at Broome attracts many visitors with its vast white beaches and gentle surf. Tourism in the Kimberley is still growing, but already 350,000 tourists enjoy Broome's tropical atmosphere each year.*

The Cockburn Ranges *have deep, inaccessible caves and sandstone cliffs separating the summit from the surrounding plains. The ranges tower above the crocodile-infested Pentecost River on the Gibb River Road. As with many sites in the region, they hold great Aboriginal significance.*

THE ABORIGINES OF THE KIMBERLEY

Legend suggests that the first Aborigines arrived on the continent, near Broome, 200,000 years ago *(see p47)*. While this view has yet to be validated by scientific evidence, the fact that many of the "songlines" *(see p31)* marked by landmarks and ceremonial sites all end or start around the Kimberley certainly suggests that the area has seen a very long period of human habitation.

Two-thirds of the region's population remains Aboriginal, and Aboriginal culture here is one of the most traditional in Australia. Local Aboriginal communities equip their children with a strong identity to help them cope with the demands of living in a mixed-race society.

Aboriginal art in the Kimberley differs from most other parts of Australia. Dot art does not predominate; instead there are the outstanding Wandjina figures of the central Kimberley, and the object paintings of the Purnululu community based near the Bungle Bungles.

The mysterious *Wandjina figures can be seen throughout the Kimberley region.*

Aboriginal rock art *in the Kimberley has now been dated back 125,000 years, 80,000 years earlier than previously thought.*

DRYSDALE RIVER NATIONAL PARK

Drysdale River

Timor Sea

Wyndham

Kununurra

Ord River

Pentecost River

Lake Argyle

256

PURNULULU NATIONAL PARK

Halls Creek

Great Northern Highway

Gibb River Road is a rough highway which is used by locals and adventurous travellers.

Emma Gorge *is one of hundreds of deep, cool waterholes hidden across the Kimberley. Located near El Questro Station, it was made by waterfalls cascading off the red sandstone plateau into gorges and valleys below.*

PERTH AND THE SOUTHWEST

*W*estern Australia's pretty capital, Perth, is the most isolated city in the world, closer to Southeast Asia than it is to any other Australian city. The state's stunning southern region takes in magnificent forests and diverse coastal scenery. To the east, the vast Nullarbor Plain covers more than 250,000 sq km (100,000 sq miles), and rolling wheat fields lead to the arid interior and the gold fields.

Aborigines have lived in the southern region of Western Australia for at least 30,000 years. However, within 20 years of the settlement of the state's first European colony, in 1829, most Aboriginal groups had been either forcibly ejected from the region, imprisoned or stricken by European diseases.

Europeans visited the southern part of the state as early as 1696, but it was not until 1826 that British colonist Captain James Stirling arrived in the Swan River area, declaring the Swan River Colony, later Perth, in 1829. Convicts arrived in 1850 and helped to build public buildings and the colony's infrastructure, until transportation to Western Australia ceased in 1868.

In the 1890s, gold strikes in Coolgardie and Kalgoorlie led to a wave of prosperity in the region. Many ornate late Victorian-style buildings were erected, many of which are still standing.

The beginning of the 20th century saw huge changes: a telegraph cable was laid connecting Perth with South Africa and London, and, in 1917, the railway arrived to join Kalgoorlie with the eastern states. In the 1920s, immigrants and returning World War I servicemen were drafted to the area to clear and develop land under the Group Settlement Scheme. Much of the land, however, was intractable and many people abandoned it.

Today, Perth and the Southwest are fast becoming popular international tourist destinations. Blessed with superb beaches and a glorious climate, the region has everything to offer visitors from climbing the tallest fire-lookout tree in the country to whale-watching along the coast. World-class wineries abound in the Margaret River region and, in springtime, vast tracts of the south are covered with wildflowers.

Dramatic beauty of the Stirling Ranges rising from the plains in the southwest of the state

◁ The glittering night skyline of Western Australia's vibrant state capital, Perth

Exploring Perth and the Southwest

The city of Perth lies on the Swan River, just 20 km (12 miles) from where it flows into the Indian Ocean. The coastal plain on which it stands is bordered to the north and west by the Darling Range, beyond which lie the region's wheat fields. To the south is a diverse landscape: forests with some of the tallest trees on earth, mountains that dramatically change colour during the course of each day and a spectacular coastline. Inland are the gold fields that kept the colony alive in the 1890s; beyond lies the Nullarbor Plain, bordering the raging Southern Ocean.

Beach and raging surf in Leeuwin Naturaliste National Park, near the mouth of the Margaret River

GETTING AROUND

Perth's public transport is fast and reliable, and travel by bus within the city centre is free. TransWa, Greyhound and Skywest (a state-based airline) offer rail, coach and air services to many of the region's towns. Distances are not overwhelming, so travelling by car allows visits to the many national parks in the area. The arterial routes are fast roads often used by gigantic road trains. However, there are many tourist routes which lead to places of interest and great natural beauty. Some national parks have unsealed roads, and a few are accessible only by 4WD.

SIGHTS AT A GLANCE

SEE ALSO

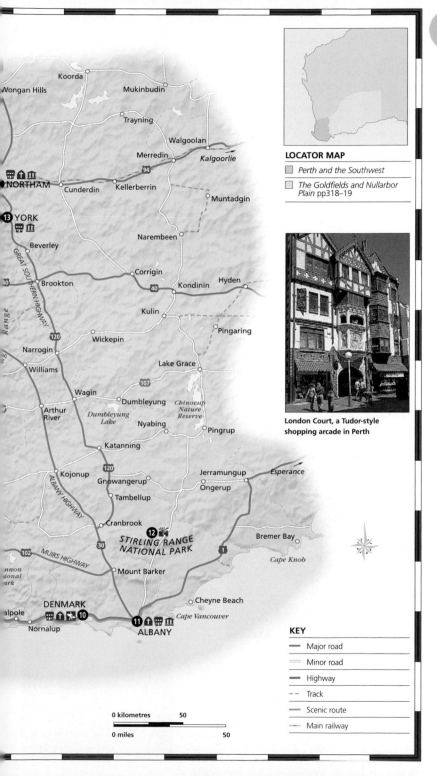

Koorda
Wongan Hills
Mukinbudin
Trayning
Walgoolan
Merredin
Kalgoorlie
94
NORTHAM
Cunderdin
Kellerberrin
Muntadgin
13 YORK
Narembeen
Beverley
GREAT SOUTHERN HIGHWAY
Corrigin
10
Brookton
40
Kondinin
Hyden
Range
Kulin
120
Pingaring
Narrogin
Wickepin
Williams
Lake Grace
Wagin
107
Dumbleyung
Chinocup
Nature
Reserve
Dumbleyung
Lake
Nyabing
Pingrup
Katanning
Kojonup
120
Gnowangerup
Jerramungup
Esperance
ALBANY HIGHWAY
Tambellup
Ongerup
Cranbrook
30
12
STIRLING RANGE
NATIONAL PARK
Bremer Bay
nnon
ional
ark
MUIRS HIGHWAY
102
Mount Barker
1
Cape Knob
DENMARK
Cheyne Beach
alpole
10
Cape Vancouver
Nornalup
11
ALBANY
Arthur
River

LOCATOR MAP

☐ Perth and the Southwest

☐ The Goldfields and Nullarbor
Plain pp318–19

London Court, a Tudor-style
shopping arcade in Perth

KEY

— Major road

≈≈≈ Minor road

— Highway

-- Track

— Scenic route

≈≈≈ Main railway

0 kilometres   50

0 miles   50

Street-by-Street: Perth ●

Fire Brigade badge

The history of Perth has been one of building and rebuilding. The makeshift houses of the first settlers were soon replaced with more permanent buildings, many erected by convicts in the latter half of the 19th century. The gold rush of the 1890s and the mining boom of the 1960s and 1970s brought waves of prosperity, encouraging the citizens to replace their older buildings with more prestigious symbols of the state's wealth. As a result, much of the early city has gone, but a few traces remain, hidden between sky-scrapers or in the city's public parks.

The Bell Tower

Barrack Square

Supreme Court Gardens

★ St George's Anglican Cathedral
This Victorian Gothic Revival-style cathedral, built in the late 19th century, has a fine rose window (see p304).

Government House
Hidden behind walls and trees, the original residence of the state governor was built by convicts between 1859 and 1864. The building's patterned brickwork is typical of the period.

STAR SIGHTS

★ Perth Mint

★ St George's Anglican Cathedral

The Deanery
Built in 1859, the Deanery was originally the residence of the Dean of St George's. It now houses the Cathedral administration.

**Fire Safety Education
and Heritage Centre**
*Constructed at the turn of the
century, this building was once
home to Perth's Fire Brigade. It is
now a museum* (see p305).

**St Mary's Roman
Catholic Cathedral**
*Built in 1865, St Mary's
has undergone an
architecturally stunning
restoration. Opposite
the cathedral is the
beautiful Convent of
Mercy* (see p305).

| 0 metres | 100 |
| 0 yards | 100 |

KEY

– – – Suggested route

Perth
Concert Hall

★ Perth Mint
*Perth Mint is Australia's oldest working
mint. Built in 1899 to utilize the finds
of the gold rush, it is now open to the
public for tours and gold pouring
demonstrations* (see p305).

Central Perth

Bronze plaque in St George's Cathedral

Perth is a relatively small and quiet city compared with those on the east coast. Its main commercial and shopping areas can be easily explored on foot. The city's atmosphere is brisk but not hurried, and traffic is by no means congested. Redevelopment projects in the 1970s brought skyscrapers and more roads, but they also made space for city parks and courtyards lined with cafés and shady trees. The city centre is bordered to the south and east by a wide stretch of the Swan River known as Perth Water, and to the north lies Northbridge, Perth's restaurant and entertainment centre.

The elaborately decorated Brass Monkey Hotel on William Street

Exploring Central Perth

St Georges Terrace is Perth's main commercial street. At its western end stands Parliament House, and in front of this is Barracks Archway. Further east, the Cloisters, built in 1850 as a school, boast some fine decorative brickwork. Nearby is the Old Perth Boys' School, a tiny one-storey building that was Perth's first school for boys.

Perth's shopping centre lies between William and Barrack streets. It is a maze of arcades, plazas and elevated walkways. The main areas are Hay Street Mall and Murray Street Mall. On the corner of William Street and St Georges Terrace lies the Town Hall (1870), close to the site where Perth was founded.

Beyond the railway tracks is Northbridge, the focus of much of Perth's nightlife. James Street is lined with many restaurants, cafés and food halls offering a variety of ethnic cuisines. The ornate façade of the former Brass Monkey Hotel (now a pub), is a perfect example of colonial gold rush architecture.

🏛 Barracks Archway

Cnr St Georges Terrace & Elder St.
Barracks Archway is all that remains of the 1863 barracks that once housed the soldiers who were brought in to police the convict population.

🏛 Perth Cultural Centre

James St. **Tel** (08) 9222 8000.
Art Gallery of Western Australia
Tel (08) 9492 6622. ☐ 10am–5pm Wed–Mon. ● Good Fri, 25 Apr, 25–26 Dec. 🔊 www.artgallery. wa.gov.au
The Perth Cultural Centre is a pedestrianized complex on several levels. The centre is home to the Art Gallery of Western Australia, which has a collection of modern Aboriginal and Australian art, and some international pieces. The Perth Institute of Contemporary Art (PICA), State Library and State Theatre are also here.

🏛 Western Australian Museum – Perth

Perth Cultural Centre, James St. **Tel** (08) 9212 3700. ☐ 9:30am–5pm daily. ● 1 Jan, Good Fri, 25–26 Dec. 🔊 limited. www.museum.wa.gov.au

Within the Perth Cultural Centre stands the Western Australian Museum complex. Among its buildings are the Old Perth Gaol (1856), with exhibitions on life in the original Swan River colony. The exhibition "Western Australia: Land and People" tells the story of Western Australia from indigenous beginnings to the environmental issues now facing the state. International and temporary exhibitions enhance the permanent displays.

🔒 St George's Anglican Cathedral

Cnr Pier St & St Georges Terrace (enter from Cathedral Ave).
Tel (08) 9325 5766. ☐ daily. 🔊
St George's Cathedral, consecrated in 1888, was only the second permanent Anglican place of worship in Perth. Between 1841 and 1845 Perth's first Anglican church was built, in Classical Revival style, close to the site of the existing cathedral, but in 1875 a more prestigious place of worship was required and the old church was demolished after St George's was built, but some artifacts remain, including some of the jarrah pews and the carved eagle lectern. This Gothic Revival building has some notable features including the intricate English alabaster *reredos* at the base of the east window, the modernistic medallions cast for the Stations of the Cross and some original 19th-century Russian icons.

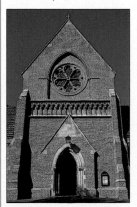

Western façade of St George's Cathedral showing rose window

🏛 Perth Mint

310 Hay St. **Tel** *(08) 9421 7223.*
⭘ *9am–5pm daily.* ⬤ *1 Jan, Good
Fri, 25 Apr, 25–26 Dec.* 📷 ♿
www.perthmint.com.au

Perth Mint was opened in
1899, under British
control, to refine
gold from Western
Australia's gold fields
to make British
sovereigns and
half-sovereigns.

**Perth Fire Station's
original fire bell**

Although it no
longer produces
coins for circulation, the
mint produces proof coins
and specialist pure precious-
metal coins, making it
Australia's oldest operating
mint. The mint has an
interesting exhibition with
coins, precious metal exhibits
and displays on gold mining
and refining. In addition,
every hour a "Gold Pour"
takes place in the Melting
House that has been in
operation for over a century.

🏛 Fire Safety Education and Heritage Centre

Cnr Murray & Irwin sts. **Tel** *(08) 9416
3400.* ⭘ *10am–4pm Tue–Thu.*
⬤ *1 Jan, Good Fri, 25 Apr, 25–26
Dec.* ♿ www.fesa.wa.gov.au

Perth City Fire Brigade
moved from this, its
original home, to a
much larger site in
1979. The old fire
station became a
fascinating museum
charting the history of
the fire service in Perth
and Western Australia, and a
fire safety centre. Exhibits
here include some well-
preserved old fire appliances
and reconstructions of rooms.

🔒 St Mary's Roman Catholic Cathedral

Victoria Sq. **Tel** *(08) 9223 1350.*
⭘ *7am–6pm daily.* ♿
Following an extensive
restoration project, St Mary's
Cathedral is an architectural
delight. The cathedral has

retained its splendid stained-
glass windows and rich
heritage, while also providing
a modern space, seating 1,400
people. St Mary's is renowed
for its superb choir.

🏛 The Bell Tower: Home of the Swan Bells

Barrack Sq. **Tel** *(08) 6210 0444.* ⭘
10am–4pm daily. ⬤ *Good Fri, 25
Dec.* 📷 ♿ www.swanbells.com.au

One of Perth's main attractions, the Bell Tower contains
12 bells from St Martin-in-the-
Fields in London, England.
There are displays and
exhibitions inside the tower,
including a rare collection of
Asian bells, a restored late
Victorian turret clock which is
wound daily for visitors, and
an observation deck. Expert
bell ringers give a brief
history of bell ringing, and
the bells ring daily, except
Wednesday and Friday, when
there is a bell handling
demonstration instead.

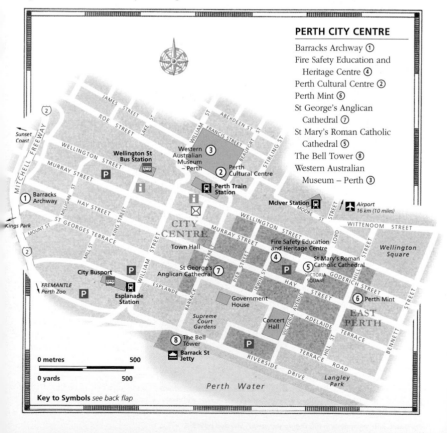

PERTH CITY CENTRE

Exploring Greater Perth

Kings Park memorial

Beyond the city centre, Greater Perth covers the Darling Range in the northeast to the Indian Ocean in the west. It has several large parks, including Kings Park, overlooking the river. On the coast, beaches stretch from Hillarys Boat Harbour in the north to Fremantle in the south *(see pp310–11)*. Perth's suburbs are accessible by train, local bus or car.

Snorkellers and qualified divers can explore the reef at AQWA

SIGHTS AT A GLANCE

AQWA **6**
Hills Forest **3**
Kings Park **1**
Perth Zoo **5**
Sunset Coast **2**
Swan Valley **7**
Whiteman Park **4**

KEY

▨ Central Perth
▨ Greater Perth
━ Highway
▬ Major road
═ Minor road

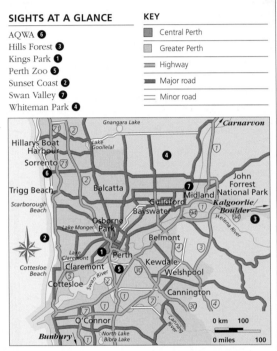

✈ AQWA, Aquarium of Western Australia

Hillarys Boat Harbour, 91 Southside Drive, Hillarys. *Tel* (08) 9447 7500. ⏰ 10am–5pm daily. ● 25 Dec. ▨ ♿ www.aqwa.com.au
At Hillarys Boat Harbour, to the north of Perth's Sunset Coast, this is a magnificent aquarium complex. A transparent submerged tunnel allows visitors to observe native sea creatures, including sharks and stingrays. There is a Touch Pool, where rays and sharks can be stroked. The denizens of the outside seal pool never fail to delight.

🍇 Swan Valley

Swan Valley Visitor Centre, Guildford Courthouse, cnr Meadow & Swan Sts, Guildford. *Tel* (08) 9379 9400. ⏰ daily. www.swanvalley.com
Western Australia's oldest wine-growing region is only a 25-minute drive from Perth. The historic suburb of Guildford is the gateway to a mix of award-winning wineries, breweries and gourmet offerings. Contact the Visitor Centre for details of wine tours and tastings.

🍇 Sunset Coast

Via West Coast Hwy.
Perth's Sunset Coast is lined with 30 km (20 miles) of white sandy beaches, many of them virtually deserted during the week. There are beaches to suit all tastes. Cottesloe Beach, at the southern end, is fringed with grassland and trees, and offers safe swimming and good services, making it popular with families, as is Sorrento Beach in the north.

🌼 Kings Park

Fraser Ave, West Perth.
Tel (08) 9480 3600. ⏰ daily. ♿
www.bgpa.wa.gov.au
Established at the end of the 19th century, Kings Park is 400 ha (1,000 acres) of both wild and cultivated parkland. Situated on Mount Eliza, it offers views of the city and the Swan River. Most of the park is bushland, which can be seen from the DNA Lookout Tower.

A landscaped area on the eastern side includes the Botanic Gardens. Treetops Walkway, a 629-metre (689-yard) long elevated walkway, gives another perspective of the gardens. The War Memorial on Anzac Bluff is dedicated to the Western Australians who died in the two world wars.

The Minmara Gun Gun and Pioneer Women's Memorial are monuments to the women who helped build the Swan River Colony and, later, the state.

Bronze statue of a mother and child in Kings Park Botanic Gardens

For hotels and restaurants in this region see pp497–500 and pp543–6

Scarborough Beach is very popular with surfers, but it is for experienced swimmers only as strong currents can make it dangerous on windy days. Trigg Beach just above Scarborough is also a good surfing spot. Just north of Cottesloe, Swanbourne Beach is a naturist beach.

Many of the city's beaches have no shade whatsoever and Perth residents are constantly reminded that the sun's rays, unshielded due to the hole in the ozone layer, can burn within minutes. Beachgoers are strongly advised to take sunscreen, a hat, T-shirt and sun umbrella *(see p577)*.

Students admiring a magnificent tiger in Perth Zoo

Surfing on Scarborough Beach

✄ Perth Zoo

20 Labouchere Rd. *Tel (08) 9474 0444.* ◯ *9am–5pm daily.* ▨ ₰ ㈙ www.perthzoo.wa.gov.au

In South Perth, a ferry-ride away from the city centre, lies Perth Zoo. Dedicated to conservation, it has all the features of an international-standard zoo. Attractions include a Nocturnal House, a wildlife park, an African savannah exhibit, an Australian walkabout and an Asian rainforest zone.

♣ Hills Forest

Via Great Eastern Hwy.

Only 30 minutes' drive from Central Perth, Hills Forest lies in the Darling Range and offers a wide range of bush-related activities. Conserved since 1919 as the catchment area for the Mundaring Reservoir, which provided water for the southern gold fields in the 19th century *(see p55)*, Hills Forest is now managed as a conservation and recreation area. It is well served with barbecue and picnic areas and camp sites. At Mundaring Weir landscaped gardens are a lovely backdrop for picnics. On the northern edge of the forest is John Forrest National Park, Western Australia's first national park. It consists of woodland and heathland with trails leading to beautiful pools and waterfalls, including Hovea Falls.

♣ Whiteman Park

Lord St, Whiteman. *Tel (08) 9209 6000.* ◯ *8:30am–6pm daily.* ▣ ₰

Northeast of the city centre lies popular Whiteman Park. Visitors can tour the park on a 1920s tram or by train. A craft village displays local craftsmanship and there is also a motor museum with a collection of vehicles from the last 100 years. Within Whiteman Park, Caversham Wildlife Park displays 200 species of native Australian animals from koalas to Tasmanian devils.

A horse-drawn wagon taking visitors on a tour of Whiteman Park

Rottnest Island ❷

Less than 20 km (12 miles) west of Fremantle lies the idyllic island of Rottnest. Settled by Europeans in 1831, it was used as an Aboriginal prison between 1838 and 1902. In 1917, in recognition of its scenic beauty and rich bird life, the island became a protected area and today it is a popular tourist destination. Rottnest's oldest settlement, Thomson Bay, dates from the 1840s. The island's other settlements, all built in the 20th century, are found at Longreach Bay, Geordie Bay and Kingstown. Rottnest's rugged coastline comprises beaches, coves and reefs – ideal for many water-based activities – salt lakes and several visible shipwrecks. Private cars are not allowed on the island, so the only way to get around is by bicycle or bus, or on foot.

Aerial View of Rottnest
Rottnest is 11 km (7 miles) long, 4.5 km (3 miles) wide, and is governed by strict conservation regulations.

City of York Bay was named after Rottnest's most tragic shipwreck. In 1899, a sea captain mistook a lighthouse flare for a pilot's signal and headed towards the rocks.

Wadjemup Lighthouse
The lighthouse on Wadjemup Hill was built in 1895. Wadjemup is the Aboriginal name for the island.

Rocky Bay
Overlooked by the sandy Lady Edeline beach, this popular, picturesque bay also contains the wreck of the barque Mira Flores *which sank in 1886.*

Strickland Bay
was named after Sir Gerald Strickland, governor of Rottnest from 1909 to 1912, and is a prime surfing spot.

0 metres	1000
0 yards	1000

Cape Vlamingh Lookout
Named after Dutch explorer Willem de Vlamingh, Rottnest's most famous early European visitor, this lookout stands at the furthest tip of the island, 10.5 km (6.5 miles) from Thomson Bay. The view is spectacular.

KEY

═══	Minor road
- -	Paths and trails
△	Camp site
⛱	Picnic area
✕	Aerodrome
⛴	Ferry
ℹ	Tourist information
☆	Viewpoint

Hotel Rottnest

With its turrets and crenellations, this was built in 1864 as the state governor's summer residence. Formerly the Quokka Arms, it is now a hotel (see p499).

The Basin is the most popular beach on Rottnest Island, particularly with families with children, as it is easily accessible on foot from Thomson Bay.

Little Parakeet Bay is popular with snorkellers. The bay is also an excellent spot to see the rock parrots after which it is named.

The Rottnest Museum is housed in the old granary, which dates from 1857. Exhibits cover the island's geology, its many ship-wrecks, flora and fauna, and memorabilia of the early settlers and convicts.

Geordie/ Longreach Settlement

Thomson Bay Settlement

Lake Baghdad

Herschell Lake

PERTH

Serpentine Lake

Government House Lake

Kingstown

Henrietta Rocks are a hazardous place for shipping. No less than three ships have been wrecked in the waters off this point.

Mabel Cove

THE QUOKKA

When de Vlamingh first visited Rottnest in 1696, he noted animals somewhat bigger than a cat, with dark fur. Thinking they were a species of rat, he called the island the "rats' nest". In fact the animals were a type of wallaby, called quokkas by the Aborigines. Although there is a small mainland population in Western Australia, this is the best place to see these timid creatures in areas of undergrowth. On Rottnest such habitat is scarce, and they are often visible at dusk. Quokkas are wild and should not be fed.

Oliver Hill

At this lookout stand two 9.2-inch (23.5-cm) guns, brought here for coastal defence purposes in 1937, but obsolete since the end of World War II. A railway to the hill has been renovated by volunteers.

Fremantle ❸

Fremantle is one of Western Australia's most historic cities. A wealth of 19th-century buildings remains, including superb examples from the gold rush period. Founded on the Indian Ocean in 1829, at the mouth of the Swan River, Fremantle was intended to be a port for the new colony, but was only used as such when an artificial harbour was dredged at the end of the 19th century. The town still has thriving harbours and, in 1987, it hosted the America's Cup. Many sites were renovated for the event, and street cafés and restaurants sprang up.

Anchor from the Maritime Museum

Busy fruit and vegetable stall in the Fremantle Markets

Twelve-sided Round House

🎪 The Round House

10 Arthur Head Rd. **Tel** (08) 9336 6897. ◯ 10:30am–3:30pm daily. **Donation**. ♿

Built in 1830, the Round House is Fremantle's oldest building. It was the town's first gaol and, in 1844, site of the colony's first hanging. Beneath is a tunnel, dug in 1837 to allow whalers to transfer cargo from the jetty to the High Street. To the left of the site are clear views across Bathers Bay to Rottnest Island *(see pp308–9)*.

🏛 Western Australian Museum – Shipwreck Galleries

Cliff St. **Tel** (08) 9431 8444. ◯ 9:30am–5pm daily (25 Apr: 1–5pm). ⬤ 1 Jan, Good Fri, 25–26 Dec. **Donation**. ♿ www.museum.wa.gov.au

Housed in the Commissariat building, an 1850s convict-built government storehouse, the Shipwreck Galleries is a renowned centre for maritime archaeology and exploration. The museum's prize possession is a reconstruction of part of the hull of the Dutch East Indiaman *Batavia* from timbers discovered at the wreck off the Abrolhos Islands in 1629 *(see p324)*. The exhibit tells the story of the shipwreck and mutiny of the vessel and gives an insight into life on board.

🎪 Fremantle Markets

Cnr South Terrace & Henderson St. **Tel** (08) 9335 2515. ◯ Fri–Sun, public hols. ⬤ Good Fri, 25 Dec. ♿

In 1897, a competition was announced to design a suitable building to act as Fremantle's market hall. The winning design was built in 1897 and still stands today. It underwent renovation in 1975, and has been used as a market ever since. There are more than 170 stalls offering everything from vegetables to opals. The market is open until 8pm on Fridays.

⛪ St John the Evangelist Anglican Church

Cnr Adelaide & Queen sts. **Tel** (08) 9335 2213. ◯ daily. ♿

This charming church, completed in 1882, replaced a smaller church on the same site. Its Pioneer Window tells the story of a pioneer family across seven generations, from its departure from England in the 18th century, to a new life in Western Australia. The window next to it is from the old church. The ceiling and altars are of local jarrah wood.

🏛 Western Australian Museum – Maritime

Victoria Quay. **Tel** (08) 9431 8444. ◯ 9:30am–5pm daily (25 Apr: 1–5pm). ⬤ 1 Jan, Good Fri, 25–26 Dec. 📷 ♿ www.museum.wa.gov.au

This museum houses the *Australia II*, the racing yacht with the winged keel that won the America's Cup in 1983. Also popular is the submarine HMAS *Ovens*, which can be toured. Visitors can find out what life is like aboard a submarine and immerse themselves in Fremantle's wartime history.

THE AMERICA'S CUP BONANZA

The America's Cup yachting race has been run every four years since 1851. Not until 1983, however, did a country other than the United States win this coveted trophy. This was the year that *Australia II* carried it home. In 1987, the Americans were the challengers, and the races were run in *Australia II*'s home waters, off Fremantle. Investment poured into the town, refurbishing the docks, cafés, bars and hotels for the occasion.

The Americans regained the trophy, but Fremantle remains forever changed by being, for once, under the world's gaze.

The 1983 winner, *Australia II*

🏛 Fremantle Arts Centre

Cnr Ord & Finnerty Sts. *Tel (08)
9432 9555.* ☐ *10am–5pm daily.*
⬤ *Good Fri, 25 Dec.* **Donation.**
♿ *limited.* **www**.fac.gov.au

This beautiful Gothic Revival
mansion with its shady gardens
was first conceived as an
insane asylum. The main wing
was built between 1861 and
1865, and an extension was
added between 1880 and 1902.

The building, which after
its use as an asylum became
the wartime headquarters
for US forces, was slated for
demolition in 1967. But,
principally through the
efforts of Fremantle's mayor,
it was rescued and renovated
to become the Fremantle
Arts Centre.

The centre is one of Western
Australia's most dynamic multi-
arts organisations, offering a
rich cultural program of
exhibitions, residences, art
courses, music and events.
It also showcases local
contemporary artists, with
many of the works for sale.

During the summer months
(October to March), the
centre's Courtyard Music
series takes place on Sunday
afternoons. The outdoor
event is free and features
an extensive line up of
established local acts, touring
artists and young up-and-
coming musicians.

Fremantle Prison's striking façade

⛩ Fremantle Prison

The Terrace, off Hampton Rd. *Tel (08)
9336 9200.* ☐ *10am–5pm daily.* ⬤
Good Fri, 25 Dec. 🎫 📷 ♿ *limited.*
www.fremantleprison.com.au

In the 1850s, when the first
group of convicts arrived in the
Swan River Colony, the need
arose for a large-scale prison.
Fremantle Prison, an imposing
building with a sturdy gate-
house and cold, forbidding
limestone cell blocks, was built
by those first convicts in 1855.
It was not closed until 1991.
Today, visitors tour the
complex, visiting cells,
punishment cells, the chapel
and the chilling gallows room,
last used in 1964. The candlelight tours and tunnel tours
are highly recommended.

FREMANTLE CITY CENTRE

Fremantle Arts Centre ⑥
Fremantle Markets ③
Fremantle Prison ⑦
St John the Evangelist
   Anglican Church ④
The Round House ①
WA Museum – Maritime ⑤
WA Museum – Shipwreck
   Galleries ②

PERTH

Fremantle
Harbour

Western
Australian
Museum –
Maritime ⑤

Swan River

Victoria Quay

Fremantle
Station

Fremantle
Art Gallery

E Shed
Markets

KINGS
SQUARE

Town
Hall

St John the
Evangelist Anglican
Church ④

Fremantle
Prison ⑦

Fremantle
Markets ③

The Round ①
House

Western Australian
Museum – Shipwreck
Galleries ②

Bather's
Bay

Hospital

BUNBURY

Fishing Boat
Harbour

Key to Symbols *see back flap*

| 0 metres | | 500 |
| 0 yards | | 500 |

The Southern Coastline

Western Australia's southwest corner has diverse coastal scenery. Two oceans meet here, the Indian and the Southern, resulting in discernible climate changes: the southern coastline is often windy and cooler than the western coast, and the oceans are much less gentle. Lined by national parks, the coast incorporates limestone, reefs, granite formations, beautiful sand dunes and crags topped by low vegetation. There are also world-class surfing spots in the region.

★ Flinders Bay, Augusta (5)

🌊 🏄 🛟 🚻 ⛺

Augusta was founded in 1830 and is the third oldest settlement in the state. Only 5 km (3 miles) from Cape Leeuwin, the southwestern tip of the continent, today it is a popular holiday resort. The beautiful Flinders Bay is particularly favoured by windsurfers.

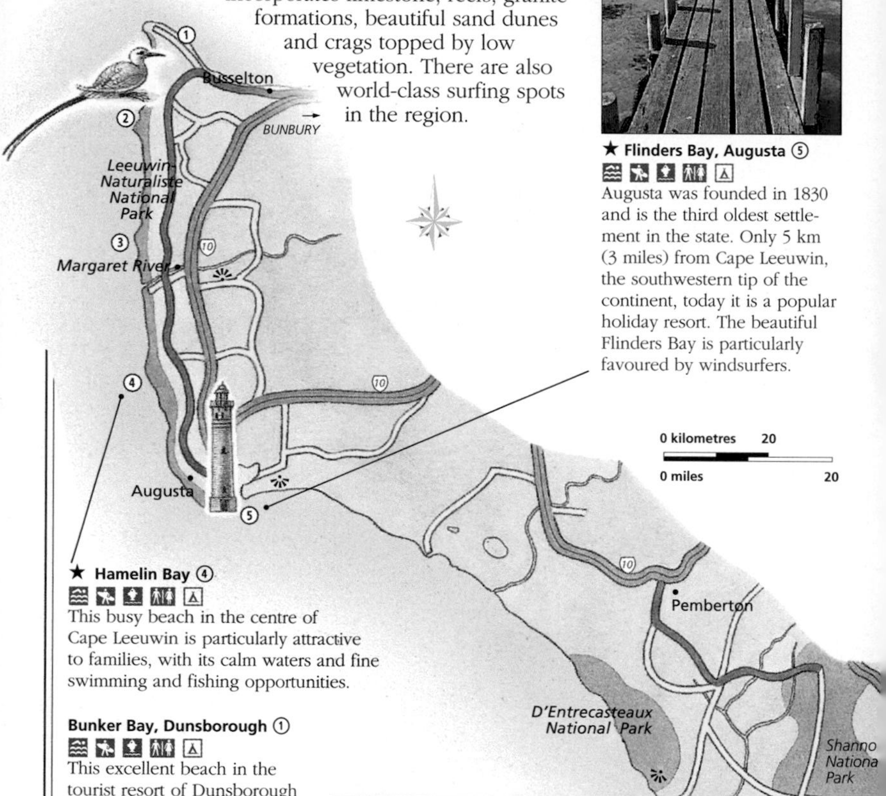

1
Busselton
BUNBURY
2
Leeuwin-Naturaliste National Park
3
Margaret River
10
4
10
Augusta
5
0 kilometres 20
0 miles 20
10
Pemberton
D'Entrecasteaux National Park
Shanno Nationa Park

★ Hamelin Bay (4)

🌊 🏄 🛟 🚻 ⛺

This busy beach in the centre of Cape Leeuwin is particularly attractive to families, with its calm waters and fine swimming and fishing opportunities.

Bunker Bay, Dunsborough (1)

🌊 🏄 🛟 🚻 ⛺

This excellent beach in the tourist resort of Dunsborough benefits from dolphin- and whale-watching in season and fine views of Cape Naturaliste.

Smiths Beach, Yallingup (2)

🌊 🏄 🛟 🚻 ⛺

This popular honeymoon spot (Yallingup is indigenous word for "place of lovers") is also a haven for surfers. Nearby is the spectacular Yallingup Cave.

Boodjidup Beach, Margaret River (3)

🌊 🏄 🛟 🚻 ⛺

The coastline in this holiday town consists of long beaches, sheltered bays and cliff faces looking out on to the surf.

Peaceful Bay (7)

🌊 🏄 🛟 🚻 ⛺

Keen anglers and sailors can often be spotted within this aptly named inlet, which is also a popular picnic spot. Nearby Walpole is the gateway to Walpole-Nornalup National Park, with its impressive karri and eucalypt trees.

Middleton Beach, Albany (10)

🌊 🏄 🛟 🚻 ⛺

The waters of Middleton Beach are regularly filled with windsurfers and bodyboarders (surfing the waves on a short body board). A short drive around the point is Torndirrup National Park, with a multitude of natural coastal formations, including offshore islands and some excellent locations for whale-watching in season.

Key to symbols *see back flap*

Lake Cave, *near Margaret River, is just one of an estimated 200 underground caves along the Leeuwin-Naturaliste Ridge that runs from Busselton to Augusta. It is one of the few caves open to the public and is a fairyland of limestone formations, reflected in dark underground waters.*

LOCATOR MAP

D'Entrecasteaux National Park, *40 km (25 miles) southwest of Pemberton, is a wild and rugged park with spectacular coastal cliffs, pristine beaches and excellent coastal fishing. Much of the park, including some isolated beach camp sites, is only accessible by 4WD. Inland, heathland is home to a range of animal and plant habitats.*

Leeuwin-Naturaliste National Park *is a 15,500-ha (40,000-acre) protected area of scenic coastline, caves, heathlands and woodlands. Its rugged limestone coast with long beaches and sheltered bays faces the Indian Ocean. It has long been popular as a holiday destination and has excellent opportunities for swimming, surfing and fishing.*

★ Ocean Beach, Denmark ⑧

Denmark is a well-known and popular haunt for surfers from many countries. Ocean Beach, in particular, is the setting for international surfing competitions *(see pp34–5)*.

★ Wilson Inlet ⑨

From Denmark's main street it is a relatively short walk through well-kept woodland to Wilson Inlet where there are some spectacular and varied coastal views.

↑ ESPERANCE

Walpole

Walpole
Nornalup
National Park ⑦

Southern Ocean

William Bay
National Park ⑧

West Cape Howe
National Park

Albany ⑩

Torndirrup
National Park

★ Conspicuous Beach ⑥

Impressive cliffs face on to the beautiful white sands of Conspicuous Beach. It is also the access point for the Valley of the Giants, with its massive red tingle trees.

KEY

▬	Highway
▬	Major road
▭	Minor road
⇝	River
⚹	Viewpoint

Wide first-floor veranda and ornate ironwork of the Rose Hotel, Bunbury

Bunbury ❹

🏃 *50,000.* 🔲 🏨 🚌 ⛴
ℹ *Old Railway Station, Carmody Place (08) 9792 7205.*
www.visitbunbury.com.au

The city of Bunbury lies about 180 km (110 miles) south of Perth at the southern end of the Leschenault Inlet. The state's second-largest city, it is the capital of the southwest region. Since the 19th century it has grown into a thriving port and a centre for local industry. It is also a popular holiday destination, with many water sports available.

Historic buildings in Bunbury include the Rose Hotel, built in 1865, with its first-floor veranda and intricate ironwork detail. The Anglican St Boniface Cathedral contains some pretty stained glass. Nearby are the Bunbury Art Galleries, housed in the former Sisters of Mercy convent built in the 1880s. Today they are the centre for community arts events.

On the beachfront stands the **Dolphin Discovery Centre**, which has fascinating audiovisual exhibits and a shallow pool where visitors can interact with dolphins. Wild dolphins regularly appear off the beach in front of the centre, and visitors come to see them and swim with them. The centre also runs cruises and swim with dolphin tours.

The **King Cottage Museum**, is run by the Bunbury Historical Society. It exhibits local artifacts dating from the 1880s to the 1920s and a wealth of photographs.

🐬 **Dolphin Discovery Centre**
447 Koombana Drive. **Tel** (08) 9791 3088. ⭕ *daily.* ● *25 Dec.* 🎫 ♿
🏛 **King Cottage Museum**
77 Forrest Ave. **Tel** (08) 9792 7205. ⭕ *daily.* ● *1 Jan, Good Fri, 25 Apr, 25–26 Dec.* 🎫 ♿

Busselton ❺

🏃 *29,000.* ✈ 🏨 ℹ *38 Peel Terrace (08) 9752 1288.*
www.geographebay.com

Standing on the shores of Geographe Bay, Busselton boasts more than 30 km (19 miles) of beaches and a vast array of water-based activities, including scubadiving, fishing and whalewatching. Busselton Jetty, 2 km (1 mile) long and once the longest in Australia, is a reminder of the town's beginnings as a timber port.

Some of Busselton's oldest

Entrance to Busselton's original courthouse building

surviving buildings are located at the Old Courthouse site, now used as an arts complex. Here, the jail cells, police offices, courthouse and bond store all date from 1856. Local crafts are sold in the old jail cells, and other outbuildings act as studio space for artists.

The 1871 *Ballarat*, the first steam locomotive used in the state, stands in Victoria Park.

Environs
About 10 km (6 miles) north of Busselton is **Wonnerup House**, a lovingly restored house built by pioneer George Layman in 1859 and now owned by the National Trust. Three other buildings share the site, the earliest being the first house Layman erected in the 1830s. Both buildings stand in pretty grounds within farmland and are furnished with Layman family memorabilia and artifacts. In 1874, Layman's son built a school and, in 1885, a teacher's house close by.

About 20 km (12 miles) north of Busselton is the beautiful Ludlow Tuart Forest National Park, probably the largest area of tuart trees left in the world.

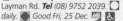
🏚 **Wonnerup House**
Layman Rd. **Tel** (08) 9752 2039. ⭕ *daily.* ● *Good Fri, 25 Dec.* 🎫 ♿

Margaret River ❻

🏃 *100,000.* ✈ 🏨 🚌
ℹ *100 Bussell Hwy (08) 9780 5911.*
www.margaretriver.com

The attractive town of Margaret River, close to the Indian Ocean, was first settled by Europeans in the 1850s. The town became the centre of an agricultural and timber region, but in the past few decades has gained fame for its wineries *(see pp36–7)*, and for its splendid surfing beaches.

Within the town are many galleries, studios and gourmet food and beverage specialists. The **Margaret River Gallery** showcases works by Western Australian artists. Featuring painting, sculpture, jewellery and furniture, the gallery also hosts exhibition openings. Set in 12 ha (30 acres) of bush on the outskirts of town, the **Eagles Heritage Raptor**

Wildlife Centre has a huge collection of birds of prey and gives eagle-flying displays.

🏛 Margaret River Gallery
91 Bussell Hwy. *Tel* (08) 9757 2729.
🕙 10am–5pm daily. ⬤ 1 Jan,
Good Fri, 25 Dec. 📷 🖥 ⬤

✵ Eagles Heritage Raptor Wildlife Centre
Lot 303 Boodjidup Rd. *Tel* (08) 9757 2960. 🕙 daily. ⬤ Good Fri, 25 Dec. 📷 ⬤

Environs

Eight km (5 miles) north of Margaret River stands the region's first homestead, Ellensbrook, built by pioneer Alfred Bussell in the 1850s. The stone cottage is close to a forest trail which leads to the pretty Meekadarribee Falls.

Visiting Margaret River's outlying wineries is very popular. Many, from Vasse-Felix, the oldest, to the large Leeuwin Estates Winery, offer tastings.

Ellensbrook Pioneer Homestead, near the town of Margaret River

Bridgetown ❼

👥 4,000. 🚌 ℹ 154 Hampton St (08) 9761 1740. **www**.bridgetown. com.au

Nestled amid rolling hills on the banks of Blackwood River, Bridgetown began as a single one-room homestead in the 1850s. It was built by settler John Blechynden and can still be seen standing next to the second home he built, Bridgedale House. Both are National Trust properties.

The town's visitors' centre is home to its municipal history museum and the unusual Brierly Jigsaw Gallery, which has hundreds of puzzles.

Hilltop view of picturesque Bridgetown

Sutton's Lookout, off Philips Street, offers panoramic views of the town and surrounding countryside. The Blackwood River and local jarrah and marri forests afford opportunities for walks and drives, and several river-based activities, including canoeing and marron fishing.

Manjimup ❽

👥 5,000. 🚌 ℹ Giblett St (08) 9771 1831.
www.manjimupwa.com

If you are travelling south from Perth, Manjimup acts as the gateway to the great karri forests for which the southwest is so famous. The town was settled in the late 1850s, and has been associated with the timber industry ever since. **Manjimup Timber Park** has a Timber Museum, Historical Hamlet and Bunnings Age of Steam Museum. A sculpture of a woodsman at the entrance commemorates the region's timber industry pioneers.

🏛 Manjimup Timber & Heritage Park
Cnr Rose & Edwards sts. *Tel* (08) 9771 1831 🕙 daily. ⬤ 25 Dec. ⬤

Environs

About 25 km (16 miles) west of Manjimup on Graphite Road lies Glenoran Pool, a pretty swimming hole on the Donnelly River. The adjacent One-

Tree Bridge is the site where early settlers felled a huge karri and used it to carry a bridge across the river. Nearby are the Four Aces, four giant karri trees in a straight line, thought to be up to 300 years old.

Pemberton ❾

👥 1,400. 🚌 ℹ Brockman St (08) 9776 1133.
www.pembertonvisitor.com.au

At the heart of karri country, Pemberton has the look and feel of an old timber town. The Pemberton Tramway, originally built to bring the trees to mills in town, now takes visitors through the forests. The **Pemberton Pioneer Museum** is a fascinating tribute to the pioneers of the area.

🏛 Pemberton Pioneer Museum
Brockman St. *Tel* (08) 9776 1133. 🕙 daily. ⬤ 25–26 Dec. **Donations.** ⬤

Environs

Southeast of the town lies Gloucester National Park, home to the famous giant karri, the Gloucester Tree. At 61 m (200 ft), it is one of the highest fire lookout trees in the world. Southwest of Pemberton is Warren National Park with its beautiful cascades, swimming holes and fishing spots. Attractive Beedelup National Park is northwest of Pemberton.

Sculpture of a woodsman at Manjimup Timber Park

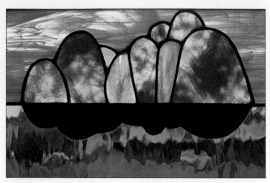

Example of local artist Andy Ducker's stained glass in Denmark

Denmark ⓾

👥 5,000. 🚉 ℹ️ 73 Southcoast Hwy (08) 9848 2055.
www.denmark.com.au

Lying on Western Australia's southern coastline, Denmark was founded as a timber company settlement in 1895, but by the 1920s it was a fully fledged town. The town now attracts a host of visitors, many of whom come seeking the good surf of the Southern Ocean. There is also a large population of artists and artisans, and the atmosphere is distinctly bohemian.

Denmark's oldest building is St Leonard's Anglican Church, built by volunteers in 1899. Its Scandinavian-style pitched roof and interior detail are reminders of the Norwegian timber workers in the town at that time.

Nearby are the Old Butter Factory Galleries and the Wildwood Gallery, just two of Denmark's galleries where visitors can admire and buy paintings and craftwork from the region.

Berridge Park is often the scene for open-air concerts.

Ship's wheel in Jaycee's Whaleworld

Environs
A popular surfing spot is Ocean Beach; more sheltered locations for swimmers include Cosy Corner and Peaceful Bay. The coastline and Wilsons Inlet are popular with boaters and anglers.

Albany ⓫

👥 29,000. ✈️ 🚌 🚆 ℹ️ Old Railway Station, Proudlove Parade (08) 9841 9290. **www**.albanytourist.com.au

Albany was first visited by Captain Vancouver in 1791, but it was not until 1826 that the British settled here. Until Fremantle harbour was constructed (see pp310–11), Albany acted as the colony's main port and the harbour is still the commercial heart of the city. Whale migrations bring them close to the city's shores, which made it a base for whalers in the last century.

The town includes many old buildings. **St John the Evangelist Anglican Church**, built in 1848, was the first Anglican church consecrated in Western Australia and is the epitome of an English country church. Inside, the Lady Chapel contains a piece of an arch from St Paul's Cathedral in London. Much of the stained glass was brought from England at the beginning of the 19th century.

A number of old buildings stand near the western end of Stirling Terrace. The Residency Museum, originally part of the convict hiring depot built in the 1850s, details the history of the town and its surrounding area. The convict hiring depot itself and the Old Gaol now house the collection of the Albany Historical Society.

In Duke Street is Patrick Taylor Cottage, built before 1836 of wattle and daub, and the oldest building in Albany.

On Albany's foreshore is an impressive, fully-fitted replica of the brig *Amity*, which brought the first settlers here from Sydney in 1826.

⛪ **St John the Evangelist Anglican Church**
York St. **Tel** (08) 9841 5015.
🕐 daily. ♿

Environs
The world's largest whaling museum is **Whale World** Tour guides take visitors around the remains of the Cheyne Beach whaling station and explain the process of extracting whale oil. From July to October, incredible breaching displays of migrating whales can sometimes be seen offshore.

🏛 **Whale World**
Frenchman Bay Rd. **Tel** (08) 9844 4021. 🕐 daily. ⬤ 25 Dec. 📷 🖥 ♿

Replica of the brig *Amity*

Stirling Range National Park ⓬

🚗 Albany. ℹ️ Albany (08) 9841 9290. **Park Ranger & information Tel** (08) 9827 9230.

Overlooking the rolling farmland to the north of Albany is the Stirling Range National Park. The mountain peaks, noted for their colour changes from purple to red to blue, rise to more than 1,000 m (3,300 ft) above sea level and stretch for more than 65 km (40 miles). The highest peak is Bluff Knoll, which reaches 1,073 m (3,520 ft). Because of its sudden rise from the

For hotels and restaurants in this region see pp497–500 and pp543–6

View of Stirling Range National Park from Chester Pass Road

surrounding plains, the park has an unpredictable climate which encourages a wide range of unique flora and fauna, including ten species of mountain bell. No less than 60 species of flowering plants are endemic to the park. They are best seen from September to November, when they are likely to be in flower. The park offers visitors a number of graded and signposted walks in the mountains (all are steep) and there are several picturesque barbecue and picnic areas.

York ⑬

🏃 3,200. 🚇 🚌 ℹ️ 81 Avon Terrace (08) 9641 1301. 🎪 Festival of Motoring (Jul), York Jazz Festival (Oct). www.yorkwa.org

The town of York was founded in 1831, in the new colony's drive to establish its self-sufficiency via agriculture. Now registered as a historic town, it retains many mid–19th-century buildings, the majority of which are on Avon Terrace, the main street. The cells of York's Old Gaol, in use from 1865 until 1981, provide a chilling insight into the treatment of 19th-century offenders. Other historic buildings include Settler's House (1860s), now a hotel and restaurant (see p500), and Castle Hotel, built in stages between 1850 and 1932, with

its unusual timber verandas. Nearby stands the **York Motor Museum**, with one of the largest collections of veteran cars and vehicles in Australia. These include the 1886 Benz (the world's first car), the very rare 1946 Holden Sedan Prototype and the extraordinary Bisiluro II Italcorsa racing car.

Also of note is the York Residency Museum, housed in the former home of York magistrate Walkinshaw Cowan, father-in-law to Edith Cowan, the state's first female Member of Parliament (see p56). This extensive collection of artifacts and photographs is justly said to be the finest small museum in the state.

York's 1892 flour mill has now been converted into the Jah-Roc Mill Gallery, which exhibits and sells furniture made from jarra wood.

🏛️ **York Motor Museum**
116 Avon Terrace. **Tel** (08) 9641 1288. ◯ daily. ⬤ Good Fri, 25 Dec. ⬛

Northam ⑭

🏃 7,000. 🚇 🚌 ℹ️ 2 Grey St (08) 9622 2100. www.visitnorthamwa.com.au

At the heart of the Avon Valley and the state's wheat belt, Northam is Western Australia's largest inland town. Settled as an agricultural centre early in the colony's history, the town became a gateway to the gold fields of Kalgoorlie-Boulder for prospectors in the 1890s (see p310). It retains a number of historic buildings, including the Old Girls' School (1877), now the town's Art Centre, and the beautiful St John's Church (1890). The town's jewel is Morby Cottage, built in 1836 and a fine example of the architectural style adopted by the early colonists.

Spanning the Avon River is the longest pedestrian suspension bridge in the country, offering views of the river.

Original 1925 Rolls Royce in the York Motor Museum

The Gold Fields and Nullarbor Plain

Western Australia's southeast is a sparsely populated, flat region of extreme aridity and little fresh water. Vast stretches of its red, dusty landscape are inhabited by small Aboriginal communities and mining companies. The gold rush around Kalgoorlie in the 1890s ensured the state's success, but many places waned and ghost towns now litter the plains. Traversing the Nullarbor Plain, the Eyre Highway runs from Norseman to South Australia, 730 km (455 miles) away, and beyond. To the south is the windswept coast of the Great Australian Bight.

LOCATION MAP

▢ The Gold Fields and Nullarbor Plain

▢ Perth and the Southwest pp298–317

SIGHTS AT A GLANCE

Esperance ⑱
Kalgoorlie-Boulder ⑯
Norseman ⑰
Nullarbor Plain ⑲
Wave Rock ⑮

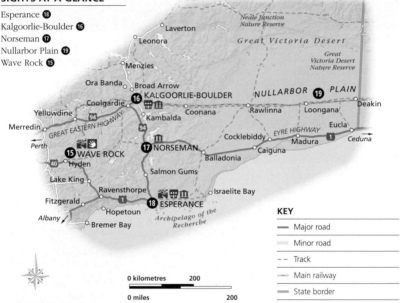

KEY

— Major road
⋯ Minor road
– – Track
Main railway
State border

0 kilometres   200
0 miles   200

Wave Rock, in the shape of a perfect wave about to break

Wave Rock ⑮

🚗 Hyden. **Visitors' Centre Tel** (08) 9880 5182. ⬜ 9am–5pm daily. ♿ 🅿 by arrangement.

In Western Australia's wheat belt, 5 minutes' drive east of the small settlement of Hyden, stands one of the state's most surprising rock formations. A great granite wave has been created from a huge outcrop by thousands of years of chemical erosion, and reaction with rainwater has given it red and grey stripes. Other rock formations nearby include the Breakers and Hippo's Yawn. Facing Wave Rock, Lace Place is the unusual location for the largest collection of lacework in the southern hemisphere.

About 18 km (11 miles) northeast of Hyden lies Mulka's Cave, where several Aboriginal rock paintings can be seen.

Kalgoorlie-Boulder ⑯

🏙 35,000. ✈ 🚉 🚌 🚆 ℹ 250 Hannan St (08) 9021 1966. **www**.kalgoorlietourism.com

Kalgoorlie and the nearby town of Boulder, with which it was amalgamated in 1989, constantly remind visitors of their gold-fever past. Gold was first discovered here by Irishman Paddy Hannan in 1893, and, within weeks, the area was besieged with prospectors. Gold fields in other areas soon dwindled, but this field has yielded rich pickings to this day, bolstered by nickel finds in the 1960s. Today, gold is mined in the world's largest open-cut mine and more than 150,000 visitors a year come to see historic Kalgoorlie.

A variety of heritage trails and tours are available, and details are at the tourist office. The **WA Museum Kalgoorlie–Boulder** has an impressive collection of gold nuggets and jewellery, as well as natural history displays and a history of the gold rush. Visitors can ride in a glass lift for magnificent views of the gold fields, or step back in time at a 1930s miner's cottage.

The ornate buildings hastily erected during the boom years are best seen on Hannan Street, in the York and Exchange hotels, classic examples of gold rush architecture, and Kalgoorlie Town Hall.

Around Kalgoorlie-Boulder are ghost towns, such as Ora Banda and Broad Arrow, deserted by prospectors in search of new mines.

Bronze statue of Paddy Hannan

🏛 WA Museum Kalgoorlie–Boulder
17 Hannan St. *Tel (08) 9021 8533.* ⬤ 10am–4:30pm daily. ⬤ 1 Jan, Good Fri, 25–26 Dec. **Donation.** ⬤

Baxters Cliff, east of Esperance, on the shores of the Southern Ocean

Norseman ⑰

🏚 16,000. ⬤ ℹ 68 Roberts St (08) 9039 1071.

At the start of the Eyre Highway, Norseman is the gateway to the Nullarbor Plain and the eastern states beyond. Like Kalgoorlie-Boulder, the town stands on a gold field, discovered when a horse pawed the ground, uncovering gold deposits. In gratitude, miners named the town after the horse, and its statue was erected in the main street. Many visitors try fossicking, or learn more about the history of gold mining in the area at the **Norseman Historical and Geological Museum** housed in the old School of Mines. Nearby, Beacon Hill offers a panoramic view of the town and surrounding countryside.

🏛 Norseman Historical and Geological Museum
Battery Rd. *Tel (08) 9039 0367.* ⬤ Mon–Sat. ⬤ Good Fri, Easter Mon, 25 Apr, 25 Dec. 📷

Esperance ⑱

🏚 10,000. ✈ ⬤ ℹ Historic Museum Village, Dempster St (08) 9083 1555. **www.**visitesperance.com

Although this area was visited by Europeans as far back as 1627, it was not until 1863 that British colonists established a settlement here. Fronting the Southern Ocean, this part of the coast is said to have some of the most beautiful beaches in Australia. Offshore is the Recherche Archipelago, with its 110 islands, one of which, Woody Island, is a wildlife sanctuary and can be visited.

In Esperance itself, Historic Museum Village includes the town's art gallery, and Esperance Municipal Museum contains local artifacts.

Nullarbor Plain ⑲

🚌 Kalgoorlie. ⬤ Norseman. ℹ Norseman (08) 9039 1071.

The Nullarbor Plain stretches across the southeast of the state and into South Australia *(see p367).* "Nullarbor" derives from the Latin meaning "no trees", and this is indeed a vast treeless plain. Only one road, the Eyre Highway, leads across the plain – one of the great Australian road journeys.

A few tiny settlements consisting only of roadhouses lie along the Eyre Hwy. Cocklebiddy, lying 438 km (270 miles) east of Norseman, has one of the world's longest caves and, at Eucla, 10 km (6 miles) from the state border, a telegraph station's remains can be seen. Nearby Eucla National Park has some fine views of the coastal cliffs.

York Hotel in Hannan Street, Kalgoorlie *(see p498)*

NORTH OF PERTH AND THE KIMBERLEY

estern Australia covers one-third of Australia, and visitors to the area north of Perth start to get a feel for just how big the state really is. The region has many treasures: Ningaloo Reef and the Pinnacles rock formations; the Kimberley gorges; and a host of national parks, including the amazing Bungle Bungles.

The first people to set foot on the Australian land mass, the Aborigines, did so some 60,000 years ago in the north of Western Australia. This area is rich in Aboriginal petroglyphs, and some are thought to be more than 20,000 years old. The north of Western Australia was also the site of the first European landing in 1616 *(see p49)*. In 1688, English explorer William Dampier charted the area around the Dampier Peninsula and, on a later voyage, discovered Shark Bay and the area around Broome.

In the 1840s, the Benedictines set up a mission in New Norcia and, by the 1860s, settlements had sprung up along the coast, most significantly at Cossack, where a pearling industry attracted immigrants from Japan, China and Indonesia. In the 1880s, pastoralists set up cattle and sheep stations in a swathe from Derby to Wyndham. Gold was struck in 1885 at Halls Creek, and the northern part of the state was finally on the map. In the 1960s, mining came to prominence again with the discovery of such minerals as iron ore, nickel and oil, particularly in the Pilbara region.

Today, the region is fast becoming a popular tourist destination, particularly with those visitors interested in ecotourism *(see p568)*. Its climate varies from Mediterranean-style just north of Perth to the tropical wet and dry pattern of the far north. Wildlife includes endangered species such as the dugongs of Shark Bay. Even isolated spots, such as the Kimberley and the resorts of Coral Bay and Broome, are receiving more visitors every year.

Visitors enjoying close contact with the dolphins of Monkey Mia in Shark Bay World Heritage and Marine Park

◁ The strange silica- and lichen-covered domes of the Bungle Bungles in Purnululu National Park

Exploring North of Perth

The north of Western Australia is a vast area of diverse landscapes and stunning scenery. North of Perth lies Nambung National Park, home to the bizarre Pinnacles Desert. Kalbarri National Park is a region of scenic gorges on the Murchison River. The Indian Ocean coastline offers uninhabited islands, coral reefs, breathtaking cliffs and sandy beaches, none more spectacular than in Shark Bay World Heritage and Marine Park. At the tip of the region is the Pilbara, the state's mining area and home to the fascinating national parks of Karijini and Millstream-Chichester.

St Francis Xavier Cathedral, Geraldton

The Pinnacles in Nambung National Park at dusk

SIGHTS AT A GLANCE

0 kilometres   100

0 miles   100

POINT SAMSON
MPIER 10 13 12 COSSACK
ratha 11
ROEBOURNE

Port Hedland
Broome

Millstream-
Chichester
National Park
annawonica

Robe
Fortescue
Hamersley Range
Chichester Range
GREAT NORTHERN HIGHWAY

Wittenoom
Auski
Roadhouse

Tom Price
KARIJINI
NATIONAL
PARK
14

Paraburdoo

95

Newman

Barlee Range
Ashburton
Kenneth Range
Mt Augustus
National Park
Waldburg Range

Collier Range
National Park
Kumarina
Roadhouse

95

Robinson Range
Peak Hill

Murchison
Nicholson Range
Sanford

Meekatharra

Lake
Annean

rchison
adhouse

Tuckanarra
Cue

Lake
Austin

Mount Magnet

Yalgoo
123

95

lorawa
15
rnamah
Wubin

Lake
Moore
Karroun Hill
Nature Reserve

Paynes Find

GREAT NORTHERN HIGHWAY

Watheroo
Kalannie
Wialki

loora
95
Wongan
Hills
Koorda
Mukinbudin

1
NEW NORCIA

Perth

LOCATOR MAP

■ North of Perth

■ The Kimberley and the Deserts
see pp330–31

SEE ALSO

• **Where to Stay** pp500–1

• **Where to Eat** pp546–8

KEY

— Major road

===== Minor road

– – Track

— Scenic route

Flowering mulla mullas in Karijini National Park

GETTING AROUND

Distances in the north of Western Australia are
vast. A 4WD vehicle is desirable if visiting any
national parks by road and essential during the
wet season. The North West Coastal Hwy skirts
the coast as far as Port Hedland, where it joins
the Great Northern Hwy, heading towards the
Northern Territory. Gunbarrel Hwy and Canning
Stock Route across the Gibson Desert are only
for experienced travellers. Greyhound has
regular coach services between major towns *(see
p587)*, and Qantas and Virgin Blue also fly to
Perth *(see pp584–5)*.

New Norcia ❶

🏛 70. 🔲 ℹ *New Norcia Museum and Art Gallery, Great Northern Highway (08) 9654 8056.*

One of Western Australia's most important heritage sites is New Norcia, 130 km (80 miles) northeast of Perth. A mission was established here by Spanish Benedictine monks in 1846, and it is still home to a small monastic community who own and run the historic buildings. There are daily tours of the monastery and visitors can stay at a guesthouse.

The town, known for its Spanish colonial architecture, has a pretty cathedral, built in 1860, at its centre. Also of note are two elegant colleges built early in the 20th century: St Gertrude's Residence for Girls and St Ildephonsus' Residence for Boys. The **New Norcia Museum and Art Gallery** has some fine art treasures and artifacts tracing the town's history.

🏛 **New Norcia Museum and Art Gallery**
Great Northern Hwy. **Tel** (08) 9654 8056. ◯ daily. ⬤ 25 Dec. 🗺 ♿ ground floor only.

Minarets adorning St Ildephonsus' Residence for Boys, New Norcia

Nambung National Park ❷

ℹ *DEC office at Cervantes (08) 9652 7043.* ◯ Mon–Fri.

This unusual national park is composed of beach and sand dunes, with the dunes extending inland from the coast. It is best seen in spring when wildflowers bloom and the heat is not too oppressive. The park is famous for the Pinnacles, a region of curious

The extraordinary Pinnacles, Nambung National Park

limestone pillars, the tallest of which stand 4 m (13 ft) high. Visitors can take either a 3-km (2-mile) driving trail or a shorter walking trail which leads to lookouts with stunning views of the Pinnacles and the coastline.

Most of the park animals are nocturnal, but some, including kangaroos, emus and many reptiles, may be seen in the cool of dawn or dusk.

Geraldton ❸

🏛 37,000. ✈ 🔲 🚌 ℹ *cnr Chapman Rd & Bayly St (08) 9921 3999.* **www**.geraldtontourist.com.au

The city of Geraldton lies on Champion Bay, about 425 km (265 miles) north of Perth. It is known as "Sun City" because of its average eight hours of sunshine per day. The pleasant climate brings hordes of sun-seekers from all over Australia who take advantage of fine swimming and surfing beaches. It can also be very windy at times, a further enticement to windsurfers, for whom Geraldton (particularly Mahomets Beach) is a world centre.

The history of European settlement in the area extends back to the mutiny of the Dutch ship *Batavia*, after it was wrecked on the nearby Houtman Abrolhos in 1629. Two crew members were marooned here

as a punishment. In 1721, the Dutch ship *Zuytdorp* was wrecked, and it is thought that survivors settled here for a brief period. Champion Bay was first mapped in 1849 and a lead mine was established shortly afterwards. Geraldton grew up as a lead shipping point, and today is a port city with a large rock-lobster fleet.

The city retains many of its early historic buildings. The **WA Museum – Geraldton** includes the Shipwrecks Gallery, which contains relics of the area's early shipwrecks. The Old Railway Building has exhibits on local history, wildlife and geology. Geraldton has two fine cathedrals: the modern Cathedral of the Holy Cross, with its beautiful stained glass, and St Francis Xavier Cathedral, built from 1916 to 1938, in Byzantine style.

Point Moore Lighthouse, with its distinctive red and white stripes, was shipped here from Britain and has been in continuous operation since 1878. The 1876 **Lighthouse Keeper's Cottage**, the town's first lighthouse, now houses Geraldton's Historical Society. Also in town, the **Geraldton Art Gallery** is one of the best galleries in the state, exhibiting the work of local artists and pieces from private and public collections.

A number of lookouts such as Separation Point Lookout and Mount Tarcoola Lookout give panoramic views of the city and ocean.

Geraldton's Point Moore Lighthouse

For hotels and restaurants in this region see pp500–1 and pp546–8

🏛 **WA Museum – Geraldton**
1 Museum Place, Batavia Coast
Marina. **Tel** (08) 9921 5080. ◯
9:30am–4pm daily. ● 1 Jan, Good
Fri, 25–26 Dec. **Donation.** &

🏚 **Lighthouse Keeper's Cottage**
355 Chapman Rd. **Tel** (08) 9923
1837. ◯ 10am–3:30pm Tue, Thu,
Fri. ● Good Fri, 25 Dec. 🎫

🏛 **Geraldton Art Gallery**
24 Chapman Rd. **Tel** (08) 9964 7170.
◯ 10am–4pm Tue–Sat, 1–4pm Sun.
● Good Fri, 25 Dec–1 Jan. &

Houtman Abrolhos ❹

🖪 Geraldton. 🛬 from Geraldton.
ℹ Geraldton (08) 9921 3999.

About 60 km (37 miles) off
Geraldton lie more than 100
coral islands called the
Houtman Abrolhos. The
world's southernmost coral
island formation. While it is
not possible to stay on the
islands, tours enable visitors
to fly over them or to fish and
dive among the coral.

Kalbarri National Park ❺

🖪 Kalbarri. ℹ Kalbarri (08) 9937
1140. ◯ sunrise–sunset daily.

The magnificent landscape
of Kalbarri National Park
includes stunning coastal
scenery and beautiful inland
gorges lining the Murchison

River. The park
has a number of
coastal and river
walking trails
which lead to
breathtaking
views and
fascinating rock
formations. The
trails vary in
length, from brief
two-hour strolls to
four-day hikes. Highlights of
the park include Hawks Head,
a picnic area with views of the
gorge; Nature's Window,
where a rock formation frames
a view of the river; and Ross
Graham Lookout, where
visitors can bathe in the river
pools. By the ocean, Pot Alley
provides awesome views of
the rugged coastal cliffs and
Rainbow Valley is made up of
layers of multi-coloured rocks.

The access town for the
park, Kalbarri, is situated on
the coast and provides good
tourist facilities. The park's
roads are accessible to most
vehicles, but are unsuitable for
caravans or trailers. The best
time to visit is from July to
October, when the weather is
dry and the temperatures are
not prohibitive. In summer,
they can soar to 40°C (104°F).

Shark Bay World Heritage and Marine Park ❻

See pp326–7.

Fine arts and crafts centre in Carnarvon

Carnarvon ❼

🏘 7,000. ✈ 🚌 🚍 ℹ Civic Centre,
11 Robinson St (08) 9941 1146.
www.carnarvon.org.au

The town of Carnarvon,
standing at the mouth of the
Gascoyne River, acts as the
commercial and administrative
centre for the surrounding
Gascoyne region, the gateway
to Western Australia's north.
Tropical fruit plantations line
the river here, some offering
tours and selling produce.

In Carnarvon itself, One
Mile Jetty on Babbage Island
is a popular place for fishing,
and Jubilee Hall, built in 1887,
houses a fine arts and crafts
centre. Carnarvon is also
home to a busy prawn and
scallop processing industry.

Environs
About 70 km (43 miles) north
of Carnarvon lie the
Blowholes, a spectacular
coastal rock formation where
air and spray is forced through
holes in the rocks in violent
spurts up to 20 m (66 ft) high.

Stunning gorge views from Hawks Head Lookout, Kalbarri National Park

Shark Bay World Heritage and Marine Park ❻

Historical jetty sign, Monkey Mia

Shark Bay Marine Park was designated a World Heritage Area in 1991 *(see pp26–7)*. The park is home to many endangered species of both plants and animals, and various unusual natural processes have, over the millennia, given rise to some astounding natural features and spectacular coastal scenery. Because this is a World Heritage Area, visitors are asked to abide by conservation rules, particularly when fishing. The only way to travel around the park is by car, and large areas are only accessible by 4WD.

BERNIER ISLAND

DORRE ISLAND

François Peron National Park
At the tip of Peron Peninsula, this national park, now accessible by 4WD, was a vast sheep station until 1990.

Cape Inscription is the place where Dutchman Dirk Hartog became the first known European to set foot in Australia in 1616 *(see p49).*

DIRK HARTOG ISLAND

Denham Sound *FRANÇOIS PERON NATIONAL PARK*

Peron Homestead
Originally the centre of the Peron sheep station, the homestead offers an insight into pastoral life. The station also has two artesian bores which carry hot water (44°C, 111°F) to tubs at the surface in which visitors may bathe.

Denham was originally settled as a pearling community, but is now mainly a fishing and tourist centre.

Useless Loop

Steep Point faces the Indian Ocean and is the westernmost point of mainland Australia. From here it is possible to see the Zuytdorp Cliffs.

Useless Loop Road

Eagle Bluff
The top of this bluff offers fine panoramic views across Freycinet Reach, with a chance of seeing the eagles that nest on the offshore islands and marine creatures in the clear ocean waters.

The Zuytdorp Cliffs are named after the Dutch ship *Zuytdorp*, wrecked in these waters in 1721.

↑EXMOUTH
Gascoyne River

arnarvon

Northwest Coastal Highway

Shark Bay

Wooramel Seagrass Bank

Wooramel River

FAURE ISLAND

HAMELIN POOL MARINE NATURE RESERVE

Hamelin Pool

Denham-Hamelin Road

Henri Freycinet Harbour

Useless Loop Road

GERALDTON ↓

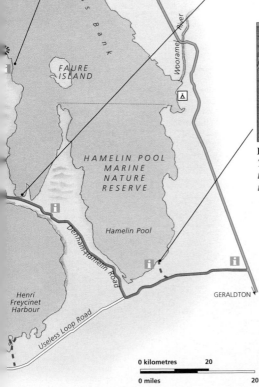

VISITORS' CHECKLIST

Off Northwest Coastal Hwy. 🛈 29 Knight Terrace, Denham (08) 9948 1590; Dolphin Info. Centre, Monkey Mia (08) 9948 1366. 🚌 from Perth. 🚻 to Monkey Mia. 🏕 🛍 🍴 🖵

Monkey Mia

Visitors flock to this small beach to meet the friendly wild dolphins that come to shore to be fed almost every morning. Also available are boat trips that go in search of dugongs, turtles and dolphins.

Shell Beach

This 60-km (40-mile) beach is unique in being comprised of tiny cockle shells, piled on top of each other to a depth of some 10 m (33 ft).

Hamelin Pool Stromatolites

These columns, formed by cyanobacteria, the earliest life on earth, tell scientists much about how life developed.

KEY

══	Highway
──	Major road
══	Minor road
⋯	Unsurfaced road
---	4WD only
▢	Marine park
—	National park border
△	Camp site
🛈	Tourist information
☼	Viewpoint

0 kilometres 20

0 miles 20

Ningaloo Reef Marine Park ❽

🏠 *Exmouth.* ℹ️ *Milyering Visitors' Centre, Yardie Creek Rd, Cape Range National Park (08) 9949 2808.* ⭕ *daily.* ⚫ *25 Dec.*

This marine park runs for 260 km (162 miles) along the west coast of Exmouth Peninsula and around the tip into Exmouth Gulf. The Ningaloo Reef is the largest fringing barrier reef in the state and offers many of the attractions of the east coast's Great Barrier Reef *(see pp212–17)*. In many places, it lies very close to the shore, and its turquoise waters are popular with snorkellers. Apart from numerous types of coral and brightly coloured fish, the marine park also protects a number of species. Several beaches at the northern end of the park are used by sea turtles as mating and breeding areas. Further offshore, it is possible to see the gentle whale shark from late March to May. Capable of growing to up to 18 m (60 ft), this is the largest fish in the world.

The best areas for snorkelling are Turquoise Bay or the still waters of Coral Bay. A number of companies offer organized scuba diving outings. Visitors can camp on the park's coastline at several sites managed by the Department of Environment and Conservation (DEC). Fishing is another popular pursuit here, but catches are very strictly controlled.

Yardie Creek Gorge in Cape Range National Park, near Exmouth

Exmouth ❾

🏠 *3,100.* ✈️ 🚌 ℹ️ *Murat Rd (08) 9949 1176.* **www**.exmouth. wa.com.au

Situated on the eastern side of the Exmouth Peninsula, this small town was originally built in 1967 to service the local airforce base. A military presence is still very much in evidence, but today the town is more important as a tourist destination, used as a base for exploring the Ningaloo Reef Marine Park and the Cape Range National Park. Giant turtles and whale sharks can frequently be seen from the nearby coastline.

Slightly outside of town, at Vlaming Head, lies the wreck of the SS *Mildura*, a cattle transporter which sank in 1907 and is still visible from the shore. Nearby stands the

Vlaming Lighthouse, on a high bluff offering striking, panoramic views across the entire peninsula.

Environs
Cape Range National Park contains a low mountain range with spectacular gorges and rocky outcrops. This area was originally under water and it is possible to discern the fossils of ancient coral in the limestone. Local wildlife includes kangaroos, emus and large lizards. There are two main wilderness walks, but visitors should not attempt these in summer as temperatures can reach as high as 50°C (120°F).

Yardie Creek is on the western side of the park, only 1 km (0.5 miles) from the ocean. A short walk along gorge cliffs leads to the spectacular canyon, where you may catch sight of rock wallabies on the far canyon wall. A cruise through the gorges is also available.

Dampier ❿

🏠 *1,400.* ✈️ 🚌 ℹ️ *4548 Karratha Rd, Karratha (08) 9144 4600.*

Dampier stands on King Bay on the Burrup Peninsula, facing the 40 or so islands of the Dampier Archipelago. It was established and still acts as a service centre and port for mining areas inland; natural gas from the nearby Northwest Shelf Project is processed here for domestic and export markets. The town also has the largest desalination plant in Australia. This can be viewed from the Dampier Solar Evaporated Salt Mine Lookout. Dampier is also a popular base for offshore and beach anglers. Every August, game-fishing enthusiasts converge on the town for the Dampier Classic and Game Fishing Classic.

The Burrup Peninsula is one of the most renowned ancient Aboriginal art sites in Australia, created by the Yapurrara Aborigines.

Environs
The Dampier Archipelago, within 45 km (28 miles) of the town, offers a range of activities

White sands of Turquoise Bay in Ningaloo Reef Marine Park

Honeymoon Cove, one of the most popular beaches in Point Samson

from game fishing to whale-watching. Sport fishing here is particularly good, with reef and game species such as tuna, trevally and queenfish on offer.

Almost half of the islands are nature reserves and are home to rare species, including the Pilbara olive python and the king brown snake. Access to the islands is by boat only.

Simple façade of the Holy Trinity Church in Roebourne

Roebourne ⑪

🏚 2,600. 🚂 🛈 Queen St (08) 9182 1060.

About 14 km (9 miles) inland, Roebourne, established in 1866, is the oldest town in the Pilbara. The town retains several late 19th-century stone buildings, including the Old Gaol which now houses the tourist office and a craft gallery and the Holy Trinity Church (1894). Roebourne also marks the start of the 52-km (32-mile) Emma Withnell Heritage Trail, which takes a scenic route from here to Cossack and Point Samson. Trail guides are available at the tourist office.

Environs
Some 150 km (93 miles) inland lies the 200,000-ha (500,000-acre) Millstream-Chichester National Park with its lush freshwater pools.

Cossack Historical Town ⑫

🚂 🛈 Queen St, Roebourne (08) 9182 1060.

In 1863, the town of Tien Tsin Harbour was established and quickly became the home of a burgeoning pearling industry that attracted people from as far away as Japan and China. The settlement was renamed Cossack in 1872 after a visit by Governor Weld aboard HMS *Cossack*. However, the town's moment soon passed. The pearling industry moved on to Broome (*see p330*) and by 1910 Cossack's harbour had silted up. In the late 1970s, restoration work of this ghost town began and today, under the management of the Shire of Roebourne, it has become a curiosity that continues to fascinate many visitors.

Old courthouse in Cossack Historical Town

Point Samson ⑬

🏚 200. 🛈 Queen St, Roebourne (08) 9182 1060.

This small settlement was founded in 1910 to take on the port duties formerly performed by Cossack. Today, there is a modest fishing industry and two harbours. The town's best beaches are found at Honeymoon Cove and Samson Reef, where visitors can snorkel among the coral or search for rock oysters at low tide.

Karijini National Park ⑭

🛈 Central Rd, Tom Price (08) 9188 1112. ⬤ daily (weather permitting).

Set in the Hamersley Range, in the heart of the Pilbara region, Karijini National Park covers some 600,000 ha (1,500,000 acres). It is the second-largest national park in the state after Purnululu National Park (*see p331*).

The park has three types of landscape: rolling hills and ridges covered in eucalypt forests; arid, low-lying shrubland; and, in the north, spectacular gorges. The best times to visit the park are in winter, when the days are temperate, and in spring, when carpets of wildflowers are in spectacular bloom.

The Kimberley and the Deserts

Australia's last frontier, the Kimberley is a vast, remote upland region of dry, red landscape. Deep rivers cut through mountain ranges, and parts of the coastline have the highest tidal range in the southern hemisphere. Seasonal climatic extremes add to the area's sense of isolation as the harsh heat of the dry season and the torrential rains of the wet hamper access to the hostile terrain. April to September is the best time to visit, offering views of the country's best natural sights such as the Wolfe Creek Meteorite Crater and the Bungle Bungles. To the south lie the huge, inhospitable Great Sandy and Gibson deserts.

Pearler's diving helmet, Broome

LOCATOR MAP

■ The Kimberley and the Deserts

■ North of Perth pp320–29

0 kilometres 200

0 miles 200

SIGHTS AT A GLANCE

Broome ⑮
Derby ⑯
Halls Creek ⑰
Purnululu (Bungle Bungle)
    National Park ⑱
Wyndham ⑲

KEY

— Major road

⋯⋯ Minor road

– – Track

— State border

Broome ⑮

👥 14,500. ✈ 🏢 🚌
ℹ 1 Hamersley St (08) 9195 2200.
www.broomevisitorcentre.com.au

Broome, first settled by Europeans in the 1860s, soon became Western Australia's most profitable pearling region. Pearl divers from Asia swelled the town in the 1880s and helped give it the multicultural flavour that remains today. The tourist industry has now superseded pearling, but the town's past can still be seen in several original stores, as well as the Chinese and Japanese cemeteries that contain the graves of hundreds of pearl divers.

Just outside town is the popular Cable Beach. On Cable Beach Road, **Broome Crocodile Park** has more than 1,000 of these animals.

✕ Broome Crocodile Park
Cable Beach Rd. **Tel** (08) 9192 1489. ◯ daily. 🛇 ♿

Camel trekking along the famous Cable Beach near Broome

A freshwater crocodile basking in the sun, Windjana Gorge, near Derby

Derby ⓰

🏚 *5,000.* ✖ 🚃 ℹ️ *2 Clarendon St (08) 9191 1426, 1800 621 426.*

Derby is the gateway to a region of stunning gorges. Points of interest in the town include the 1920s Wharfingers House, Old Derby Gaol, and the Botanical Gardens.

South of town is the 1,000-year old Prison Boab (baobab) tree, 14 m (45 ft) in circumference. At the end of the 19th century, it was used to house prisoners overnight before their final journey to Derby Gaol.

Environs
Derby stands at the western end of the Gibb River Road, which leads towards the three national parks collectively known as the **Devonian Reef National Parks**. The parks of Windjana Gorge, Tunnel Creek and Geikie Gorge contain spectacular gorge scenery.

🌿 **Devonian Reef National Parks**
🚃 *to Derby.* ℹ️ *Derby (08) 9191 1426.* ⬤ *Mon–Sat.* ⬤ *public hols.*

Halls Creek ⓱

🏚 *1,400.* 🚃 ℹ️ *Great Northern Hwy (08) 9168 6262.*

Halls Creek was the site of Western Australia's first gold rush in 1885, and today is a centre for mineral mining. Close to the original town site is a vertical wall of quartz rock, known as China Wall. About 130 km (80 miles) to the south is the world's second-largest meteorite crater, in **Wolfe Creek Crater National Park**.

🌿 **Wolfe Creek Crater National Park**
🚃 *Halls Creek.* ℹ️ *Halls Creek (08) 9168 6262.* ⬤ *Apr–Sep. daily.* ⬤ *wet weather (roads impassable).*

Purnululu (Bungle Bungle) National Park ⓲

🚃 *Halls Creek.* ℹ️ *Halls Creek (08) 9168 6262.* ⬤ *Apr–Nov: daily.* 🖼️🌿

Covering some 320,000 ha (790,000 acres) of the most isolated landscape in Western Australia, Purnululu National Park was declared in 1987. It is home to the local Kija and

The intriguing domes of the Bungle Bungles, Purnululu National Park

Jaru people, who co-operate with national park authorities to develop cultural tourism.

The most famous part of the park is the Bungle Bungle Range, consisting of unique beehive-shaped domes of rock encased in a skin of silica and cyanobacterium.

Wyndham ⓳

🏚 *900.* ✖ 🚃 ℹ️ *Kimberley Motors, 6 Great Northern Hwy (08) 9161 1281.*

The port of Wyndham lies at the northern tip of the Great Northern Highway, on Cambridge Gulf. The town was established in 1888, partly to service the Halls Creek gold rush and partly as a centre for the local pastoral industry. It also provided supplies, which were carried by Afghan camel-trains, for cattle stations in the northern Kimberley. The town's Afghan cemetery is a reminder of those hardy traders who were essential to the survival of pioneer home-steads in the interior.

The part of the town known as Old Wyndham Port was the original town site and still contains a number of 19th-century buildings, including the old post office, the old courthouse and Anthon's Landing, where the first jetty was erected. The Port Museum displays a vivid photographic history of the port.

The area around Wyndham has a large crocodile popula-tion. Freshwater and saltwater crocodiles can be seen at **Wyndham Crocodile Park** or occasionally in the wild at Blood Drain Crocodile Lookout and Crocodile Hole. To complete the picture, a 4-m (13-ft) high concrete saltwater crocodile greets visitors at the entrance to the town. Saltwater crocodiles have a taste for people, so exercise caution.

About 25 km (15 miles) from Wyndham, Aboriginal petro-glyphs can be seen at the pic-nic spot of Moochalabra Dam.

🐊 **Wyndham Crocodile Farm**
Barytes Rd. **Tel** *(08) 9161 1124.* ⬤ *daily.* ⬤ *25 Dec.* 🖼️ ♿

SOUTH
AUSTRALIA

South Australia at a Glance

South Australia contains a wide range of landscapes. A striking coastline of sandy beaches and steep cliffs gives way to lush valleys, mountains and rolling plains of wheat and barley. Further inland, the terrain changes starkly as the climate becomes hotter and drier. The South Australian Outback encompasses huge areas and includes the Flinders Ranges and Coober Pedy, the opal-mining town with "dugout" homes. Most of the population lives in the capital, Adelaide, and the wine-making towns of the Clare and Barossa valleys.

THE YORKE AND EYRE PENINSULAS AND SOUTH AUSTRALIAN OUTBACK
(see pp358–69)

Coober Pedy *'s golf course is one of the few features above ground in this strange Outback mining town. Many of the town's houses are built underground to escape the area's harsh, dusty climate (see p368).*

Port Augusta (see p365) *is a major road and rail hub that also serves as the gateway to the Far North of the state. It retains several early homesteads among its modern buildings.*

Kangaroo Island (see p354) *is an unspoilt haven for abundant native wildlife. At Kirkpatrick Point in the southwest lie the Remarkable Rocks, sculpted by the wind, rain and sea.*

| 0 kilometres | 100 |
| 0 miles | 100 |

◁ **Profile of the rich red soil in a Coonawarra winery in South Australia**

Quorn (see p369) *was an important railway town at the end of the 19th century and has many reminders of its pioneering days. Today it marks the start of the Pichi Richi Railway, a restored track running vintage trains and locomotives for tourists.*

The Flinders Ranges (see p369) *stretch from north of St Vincent's Gulf far into the Outback. They include some of South Australia's most rugged scenery and offer fine bushwalking.*

The Barossa wine region *encompasses the Barossa Valley and Eden Valley. Both are lush areas of rolling hills and home to dozens of famous wineries dating from the 19th century* (see pp356–7).

Adelaide (see pp344–59) *is an elegant state capital with many well-preserved colonial buildings. Its cosmopolitan atmosphere is enhanced by a lively restaurant, arts and entertainment scene.*

ADELAIDE
AND THE
SOUTHEAST
(see pp340–57)

Mount Gambier (see p354) *lies on the slopes of an extinct volcano of the same name. One of the volcano's crater lakes, Blue Lake, shows its intense hue in the summer months.*

Birds of South Australia

The vast, varied habitats of South Australia are home to some 380 bird species. Gulls, sea eagles and penguins live along the coast, while waders, ducks and cormorants are found in the internal wetlands. Parrots are common in Adelaide's parkland. The mallee scrub, which once covered much of the state, is home to the mallee fowl and an array of honeyeaters. The Flinders Ranges and the South Australian Outback are the domain of birds of prey such as the peregrine falcon and the wedge-tailed eagle. Although much land has been cleared for farming, many habitats are protected in the national parks.

Little penguins *are the smallest penguins found in Australia. The only species to breed on the mainland, they feed on fish and squid skilfully caught underwater.*

THE FLINDERS RANGES AND OUTBACK HABITAT

The rugged mountains and deep gorges of the Flinders Ranges support a wide variety of bird species. Most spectacular are the birds of prey. Wedge-tailed eagles' nests can be found in large gum trees or on rock ledges, and the eagles are commonly seen feeding on dead animals in the arid Outback regions.

MALLEE SCRUB HABITAT

Much of this low-level scrubland has been cleared for agriculture. Remaining areas such as Billiat National Park near Loxton provide an important habitat for several elusive species. Golden whistlers, red and brush wattlebirds and white-eared honeyeaters can be seen here by patient bird-watchers. The best seasons to visit are late winter, spring and early summer.

Wedge-tailed eagles, *with their huge wingspan of up to 2.3 m (7 ft 6 in), typically perch on dead trees and telephone poles.*

Peregrine falcons *do not build nests, but lay their eggs on bare ledges or in tree hollows. Magnificent in flight, they descend on their prey at great speed with wings half or fully closed.*

Mallee fowls, *a wary species, stand 60 cm (24 in) tall and move quietly. They lay their eggs in a ground nest made of decomposing leaves and twigs.*

Western whipbirds *are scarce and extremely secretive, keeping to the undergrowth. They run and fly swiftly, and are usually first noted by their harsh, grating call.*

THE EMU

Emus are huge flightless birds unique to Australia. Second only to the ostrich in height, they stand 1.5–1.9 m (5–6 ft 3 in) tall. They have long powerful legs and can run at speeds of up to 50 km/h (30 mph) over short distances. The females have a distinctive voice like a thudding drum. They lay their eggs on the ground on a thin layer of grass and leaves. The male incubates them for seven weeks, then broods and accompanies the young for up to 18 months. Common all over Australia, emus are found mainly in open, pastoral areas. Moving alone or in flocks, they are highly mobile and have a large home range.

Alert gaze of the Australian emu

Soft, grey-black plumage of the emu

WETLAND HABITAT

Wetlands such as Coorong National Park *(see p351)* are vital feeding and breeding grounds for a wide range of water birds. They provide essential refuge in times of drought for many endangered birds. Migratory birds, such as sharp-tailed sandpipers from Siberia, use these areas to feed and rest before continuing on their annual journeys.

Brolgas *stand up to 1.3 m (4 ft 3 in) tall, with a wingspan of up to 2.3 m (7 ft 6 in). They are renowned for their impressive dancing displays, leaping, bowing and flapping.*

Freckled ducks *are similar to primitive waterfowl, with swan-like characteristics. Dark, with no obvious markings, they are hard to spot. This is one of the world's rarest ducks.*

WOODLAND HABITAT

Habitats in woodland areas such as the Belair National Park near Adelaide support many species such as honeyeaters, rosellas and kookaburras. There is usually an abundance of food in such places and good opportunities to nest and roost. Despite increased human settlement in these areas, the birdlife is still rich. Dawn and dusk are the best times for seeing birds.

Adelaide rosellas *are commonly found in the Mount Lofty Ranges and the parklands of Adelaide. Their plumage is in brilliant shades of red, orange and blue.*

Laughing kookaburras *are the world's largest kingfishers. They are renowned for their loud, manic laughing call, often begun by one bird and quickly taken up by others.*

Wines of South Australia

South Australia produces almost half of Australia's wines, including many of its finest. From its numerous vineyards comes a dazzling diversity of wines – several are made from some of the oldest vines in the world. The state has a long history of wine-making and is home to some very famous producers, such as Hardys, Penfolds, Jacob's Creek and Banrock Station. Virtually all wineries welcome tourists for tastings.

Sevenhill Cellars *is in the heart of the Clare Valley, one of South Australia's prime wine-producing regions.*

Knappstein Winery, *owned by Lionel Nathan, is located in the Enterprise Brewery in Clare Valley and produces Riesling that is European in style.*

Bridgewater Mill *winery is renowned in the area for its excellent restaurant. Daily tastings of its own labels and Petaluma wines are offered at the cellar door.*

Burra

Kadina   Clare

Gawler

ADELAIDE

WINE REGIONS

South Australia has eight designated wine zones and within these zones are many well-known regions. These include the Barossa Valley *(see pp356–7)*, which has been producing wine for 150 years; the Clare Valley, which is noted for its Rieslings, Cabernet Sauvignon and Shiraz; and Coonawarra, which is Australia's best red wine region, due to its soil. McLaren Vale, the Murray Valley, the Adelaide Plains, the Riverland, the Limestone Coast, and the Adelaide Hills are the other major districts.

Cape Jervis

Lake Alexandrina

Cabernet Sauvignon *grapes are very success-ful in the state, with a ripe, fruity flavour.*

The Adelaide Hills *are known for their excellent Pinot Noir, Chardonnay and Riesling grapes.*

Wolf Blass' *Barossa Black Label has a rich, oaky flavour, and is just one of this world-renowned vintner's individual wines. Blass has earned more than 2,000 international medals for his wine.*

KEY

☐ Clare Valley	☐ Riverland
☐ Barossa Valley	☐ Langhorne Creek
☐ Eden Valley	☐ Padthaway
☐ Adelaide Hills	☐ Wrattonbully
☐ McLaren Vale	☐ Coonawarra

KEY FACTS

Location and Climate

The climate of Australia's central state ranges from Mediterranean-style in the Murray Valley to the cool Adelaide Hills and districts in the southeast. Vintage begins in high summer, when grapes are often picked and crushed at night to preserve the maximum flavour.

Grape Varieties

The diverse climate ensures that a wide range of grape varieties is planted. These include the whites of Riesling, Semillon, Sauvignon Blanc, Chardonnay; and the reds of Shiraz, Grenache, Pinot Noir, Cabernet Sauvignon, Merlot.

Good Producers

Penfolds, Bethany, Grant Burge, St Hallett, Henschke, Seppelt, Charles Melton, Turkey Flat, Mountadam, Hardys, Orlando, Wolf Blass, Yalumba, Rockford, Willows, Petaluma, Grosset, Wendoree, Pauletts, Pikes, Wynns, Bowen, Chapel Hill, d'Arenberg, Peter Lehmann, Noons, Bridgewater Mill, Hollicks. (This list represents only a sampling of the state's quality producers.)

Barrel maturation *at the Berri Renmano winery in the Murray Valley is one of the traditional techniques still used in the production of top-quality table wines.*

Wynns Winery *at Coonawarra is known for fine Cabernet Sauvignon and other reds. The winery itself is equally distinctive – an image of its triple gable architecture appears on the wine labels.*

0 km 50

0 miles 50

Yalumba 'Menzies' Vineyard, *founded in 1849, is one of the oldest in the Coonawarra region. The grapes are grown here, but the wine is made at the winery in the Barossa Valley (see page 357). The climate in the Coonawarra area is similar to that of Bordeaux in France.*

ADELAIDE AND THE SOUTHEAST

The Southeast is a region rich with pine forests, wineries and a spectacular coastline. The state capital, Adelaide, is a vibrant city, whose surrounding hills abound with vineyards from the Barossa Valley to McLaren Vale. To the east, the great Murray River meanders from the Victoria border down to the Southern Ocean. Just off the Fleurieu Peninsula lies Kangaroo Island, a haven for wildlife.

Home to Aborigines for more than 10,000 years, this region was settled by Europeans in 1836 when Governor John Hindmarsh proclaimed the area a British colony. William Light, the Surveyor General, chose the site of the city of Adelaide.

The settlement was based on a theory of free colonization funded solely by land sales, and no convicts were transported here. Elegant Adelaide was carefully planned by Colonel Light: its ordered grid pattern, centred on pretty squares and gardens, is surrounded by parkland. Wealth from agriculture and mining paid for many of Adelaide's fine Victorian buildings. In the mid-20th century, the city established a significant manufacturing industry, in particular of motor vehicles and household appliances. Adelaide still has a focus on high technology.

South Australia has always had a tradition of tolerance. Many of the first settlers were non-conformists from Great Britain seeking a more open society. Other early migrants included Lutherans escaping persecution in Germany. They settled in Hahndorf and the Barossa Valley, where they established a wine industry.

With high rainfall and irrigated by the Murray River, the region is the most fertile in the state. The coastline includes the Fleurieu Peninsula and the beautiful Coorong National Park. Offshore, Kangaroo Island has stunning scenery and bountiful native wildlife.

Port and sherry casks at a winery in the Barossa Valley

◁ **The tall twin spires of the neo-Gothic St Peter's Cathedral in Adelaide**

Exploring Adelaide and the Southeast

Adelaide and the Southeast area encompass the most bountiful and productive regions of South Australia. Adelaide, the state's capital city and the most obvious base for exploring the region, lies on a flat plain between the Mount Lofty Ranges and the popular white sandy beaches of Gulf St Vincent, to the east of Cape Jervis. The city itself is green and elegant, with many historic sites to explore. To the northeast, beyond the Adelaide Hills, are quaint 19th-century villages and the many wineries of the Barossa Valley region. To the east and south lie Australia's largest river, the Murray River, and the rolling hills of the Fleurieu Peninsula. Further to the southeast the beauty of the coastal Coorong National Park and the Southern Ocean coastline contrasts with the flat, agricultural area inland. Offshore lies the natural splendour of Kangaroo Island, with its abundance of native wildlife and striking rock formations.

Birds enjoying the wetlands of Bool Lagoon near the Naracoorte Caves National Park

SEE ALSO

- **Where to Stay** pp501–4
- **Where to Eat** pp548–51

St Peter's Anglican Cathedral, seen across Adelaide parkland

SIGHTS AT A GLANCE

Adelaide pp344–9 **1**
Belair National Park **2**
Birdwood **7**
Hahndorf **4**
Kangaroo Island **8**
Mount Gambier **9**
Mount Lofty **6**
Murray River **12**
Naracoorte Caves National Park **11**
Penola **10**
Strathalbyn **5**
Warrawong Wildlife Sanctuary **3**

Tour
Barossa Valley **13**

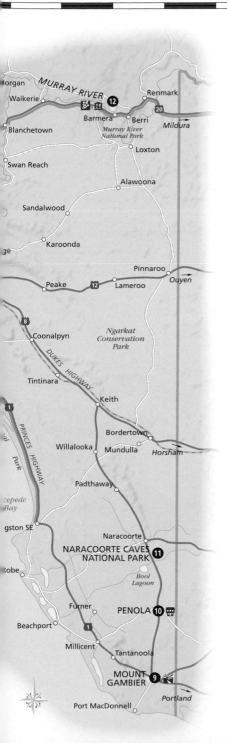

**View of the Murray River, between
Swan Reach and Walker Flat**

GETTING AROUND

The inner city of Adelaide is best explored
on foot; it is compact, well laid out and
flat. There is a public transport system of
mostly buses, and some trains, throughout
the metropolitan area, although services
are often restricted at weekends. However,
for those with a car, the city's roads are
good and the traffic generally light.
Outside Adelaide, public transport is very
limited, although coach tours are available
to most areas. A car provides the most
efficient means of exploring the region,
with a network of high-standard roads and
highways. In addition, a domestic air
service operates between Adelaide and
Mount Gambier. Kangaroo Island is
serviced by air from Adelaide and also by
ferry from Cape Jervis. The predominantly
flat landscape also makes this a popular
area for cyclists and walkers.

KEY

Highway
Major road
Minor road
Scenic route
Main railway
Minor railway
State border

Street-by-Street: Adelaide ❶

Museum figure

Adelaide's cultural centre lies between the grand, tree-lined North Terrace and the River Torrens. Along North Terrace is a succession of imposing 19th-century public buildings, including the state library, museum and art gallery and two university campuses. To the west, on the bank of the river, is the Festival Centre. This multipurpose complex of theatres, including an outdoor amphitheatre, is home to the renowned biennial Adelaide Festival of Arts *(see p41)*. To the east, also by the river, lie the botanic and zoological gardens.

River Torrens
Visitors can hire paddleboats to travel along this gentle river and see Adelaide from water level.

The Migration Museum tells the stories of the thousands of people from more than 100 nations who left everything behind to start a new life in South Australia.

Festival Centre
Completed in 1977, this arts complex enjoys a picturesque riverside setting and is a popular place for a picnic.

VICTORIA

KING WILLIAM ROAD

KINTORE AVENUE

Parliament House
Ten marble Corinthian columns grace the façade of Parliament House, which was completed in 1939, more than 50 years after construction first began.

★ Botanic Garden
Begun in 1855, these peaceful gardens cover an area of 20 ha (50 acres). They include artificial lakes and the beautiful Bicentennial Conservatory in which a tropical rainforest environment has been re-created.

Art Gallery of South Australia
Contemporary works, such as Christopher Healey's Drinking Fountains, *feature here alongside period painting and sculpture.*

0 metres	100
0 yards	100

KEY

− − − Suggested route

STAR SIGHTS

★ Botanic Garden

★ South Australian Museum

The State Library of South Australia houses an extensive collection of reference material and various exhibitions, such as *South Australiana*, a permanent exhibition that explores South Australia's history and culture.

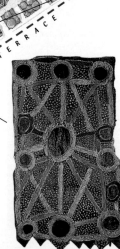

★ South Australian Museum
Chiefly a natural history museum, the South Australian Museum has an excellent reputation for its fine Aboriginal collection, including this painting on bark, Assembling the Totem, *by a Melville Island artist (see p274).*

Exploring Adelaide

South Australian Museum boomerangs

Adelaide, a city of great charm with an unhurried way of life, is easily explored on foot. Well planned on a grid pattern, it is bordered by wide terraces and parkland. Within the city are a number of garden squares and gracious stone buildings. However, while Adelaide values its past, it is very much a modern city. The balmy climate and excellent local food and wine have given rise to an abundance of streetside restaurants and cafés. With its acclaimed arts-based Adelaide Festival *(see p41)*, the city also prides itself on being the artistic capital of Australia.

Detail of the ornate front parapet of Edmund Wright House

🏛 Victoria Square

Flinders & Angas sts.
Victoria Square lies at the geographic heart of the city. In its centre stands a fountain designed by sculptor John Dowie in 1968. Its theme is the three rivers from which Adelaide draws its water: the Torrens, the Murray and the Onkaparinga. Government buildings were erected around much of the square during colonial days and many of these buildings still stand as reminders of a bygone age.

On the north side of Victoria Square stands the General Post Office, an impressive building with an ornate main hall and a clock tower. Opened in 1872, it was hailed by English novelist Anthony Trollope as the "grandest edifice in the town".

On the corner of Wakefield Street, to the east of Victoria Square, stands St Francis Xavier Catholic Cathedral. The original cathedral, dedicated in 1858, was a simpler building and plans for expansion were hampered by the lack of rich Catholics in the state. The cathedral was only completed in 1996, when the spire was finally added.

To the south of the square is Adelaide's legal centre and the Magistrates Court. The Supreme Court, built in the 1860s, has a Palladian façade.

🏛 Adelaide Town Hall

128 King William St. *Tel (08) 8203 7590.* ⬜ Mon–Fri. ⬤ public hols. ♿ www.adelaidetownhall.com.au
When Adelaide Town Hall, designed in Italianate style by Edmund Wright, was built in 1866, it became the most significant structure on King William Street. It was not long before it took over as the city's premier venue for concerts and civic receptions and is still used as such today. Notable features include its grand staircase and decorative ceiling.

🏛 Edmund Wright House

59 King William St. ♿
Edmund Wright House, originally built for the Bank of South Australia in 1878, was set to be demolished in 1971. However, a general outcry led to its public purchase and restoration. The building was renamed after its main architect, Edmund Wright. The skill and workmanship displayed in the finely proportioned and detailed façade is also evident in the beautiful interior. Today the building is the Migrant Resource Centre with limited access to the public.

Further along King William Street, at the corner of North Terrace, stands one of Adelaide's finest statues, the South African War Memorial. It shows a "spirited horse and his stalwart rider" and stands in memory of those who lost their lives in the Boer War.

Apples on display in Adelaide Central Market

🏛 Central Market

Gouger St. *Tel (08) 8203 7494.* ⬜ Tue–Sat (limited stalls on Wed). ⬤ public hols. ♿
Just west of Victoria Square, between Gouger and Grote streets, Adelaide Central Market has provided a profusion of tastes and aromas in the city for more than 125 years. The changing ethnic pattern of Adelaide society is reflected in the diversity of produce available today. Asian shops now sit beside older European-style butchers and delicatessens, and part of the area has become Adelaide's own little Chinatown. Around the market are dozens of restaurants and cafés.

View overlooking Victoria Square in the centre of Adelaide

For hotels and restaurants in this region see pp501–4 and pp548–51

🏛 Tandanya

253 Grenfell St. ***Tel** (08) 8224 3200.*
○ *10am–5pm daily.* ● *Good Fri, 25 Dec, 1 Jan.* 🎟 🛍 ♿
www.tandanya.com.au

Tandanya, the Kaurna Aboriginal people's name for the Adelaide area (it means "Place of the red kangaroo"), is an excellent cultural institute celebrating the Aboriginal and Torres Strait Islander art and cultures. It was established in 1989 and is the first Aboriginal-owned and run arts centre in Australia. The institute features indigenous art galleries, educational workshops and performance areas. It is also possible for visitors to meet indigenous people. A great gift shop sells authentic artifacts, arts and crafts.

🏛 Migration Museum

82 Kintore Ave. ***Tel** (08) 8207 7580.*
○ *10am–5pm Mon–Fri, 1–5pm Sat & Sun.* ● *Good Fri, 25 Dec.* ♿
www.history.sa.gov.au

The Migration Museum is located behind the State Library in what was once Adelaide's Destitute Asylum. It reflects the cultural diversity of South Australian society by telling the stories of people from many parts of the world who came here to start a new life. Exhibits, including re-creations of early settlers' houses, explain the immigrants' reasons for leaving their homeland and their hopes for a new life. The Memorial Wall acknowledges that many people were forced to leave their homelands.

🏛 South Australian Museum

North Terrace. ***Tel** (08) 8207 7500.*
○ *10am–5pm daily.* ● *Good Fri, 25 Dec.* ♿
www.samusuem.sa.gov.au

This museum, whose entrance is framed by huge whale skeletons, has a number of interesting collections including an Egyptian room and natural history exhibits. Its most important collection is its internationally acclaimed collection of Aboriginal artifacts which boasts more than 37,000 individual items and 50,000 photographs, as well as many sound and video recordings.

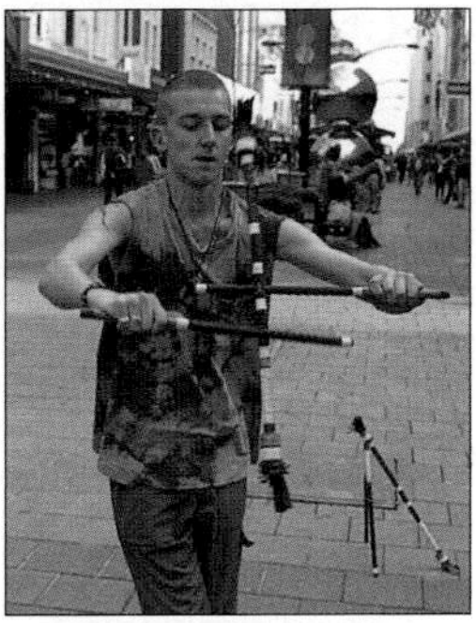

A street performer in Rundle Mall, Adelaide's main shopping precinct

🏪 Rundle Mall

Adelaide Arcade. ***Tel** (08) 8203 7200.* ○ *daily.* ● *public hols.*

Adelaide's main shopping area is centred on Rundle Mall, with its mixture of department stores, boutiques and small shops. Several arcades run off the mall, including Adelaide Arcade. Built in the 1880s, it has Italianate elevations at both ends and a central dome. The interior was modernized in the 1960s, but has since been fully restored to its former glory.

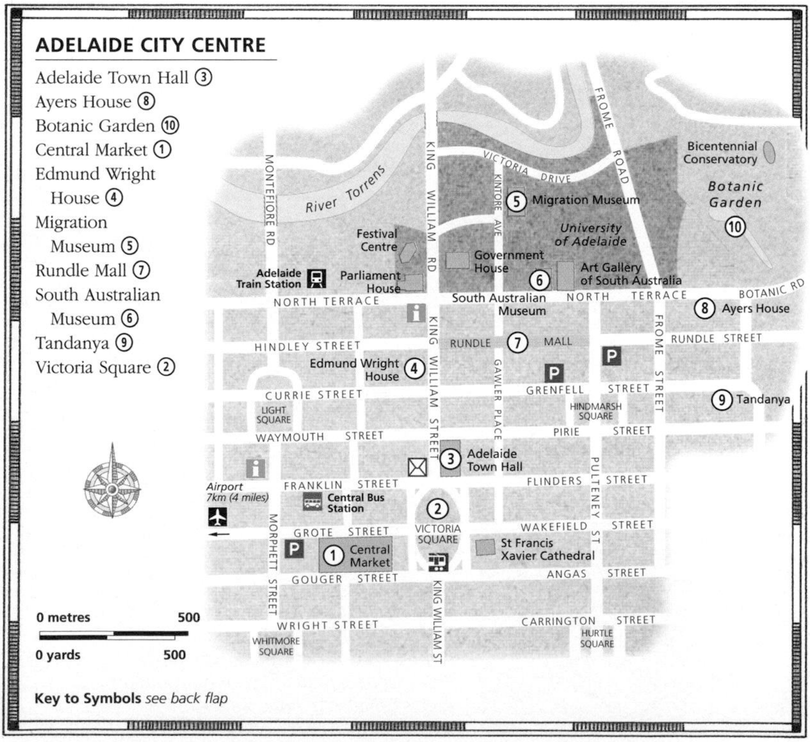
ADELAIDE CITY CENTRE
Adelaide Town Hall 3
Ayers House 8
Botanic Garden 10
Central Market 1
Edmund Wright House 4
Migration Museum 5
Rundle Mall 7
South Australian Museum 6
Tandanya 9
Victoria Square 2
River Torrens
MONTEFIORE RD
KING WILLIAM RD
VICTORIA DRIVE
KINTORE AVE
FROME ROAD
Migration Museum
University of Adelaide
Bicentennial Conservatory
Botanic Garden
Festival Centre
Government House
Art Gallery of South Australia
Adelaide Train Station
Parliament House
South Australian Museum
NORTH TERRACE
BOTANIC RD
Ayers House
HINDLEY STREET
RUNDLE MALL
RUNDLE STREET
FROME STREET
KING WILLIAM STREET
GAWLER PLACE
Edmund Wright House
CURRIE STREET
GRENFELL STREET
Tandanya
LIGHT SQUARE
HINDMARSH SQUARE
WAYMOUTH STREET
PIRIE STREET
Adelaide Town Hall
Airport 7km (4 miles)
FRANKLIN STREET
FLINDERS STREET
PULTENEY ST
Central Bus Station
VICTORIA SQUARE
WAKEFIELD STREET
MORPHETT STREET
GROTE STREET
St Francis Xavier Cathedral
Central Market
ANGAS STREET
GOUGER STREET
KING WILLIAM ST
CARRINGTON STREET
HURTLE SQUARE
WRIGHT STREET
WHITMORE SQUARE
0 metres 500
0 yards 500
Key to Symbols see back flap

Ayers House

Ayers House is one of the best examples of colonial Regency architecture in Australia. From 1855 until his death in 1897, it was the home of Sir Henry Ayers, a former Premier of South Australia and an influential businessman. The original house was quite simple but was expanded over the years with the growing status and wealth of its owner. The final form of this elegant mansion is due largely to the noted colonial architect Sir George Strickland Kingston. The restored house is now run by the National Trust and also incorporates a function centre. The oldest section is open to the public and houses a fine collection of Victorian furniture, furnishings, memorabilia and art.

Front of the house viewed from North Terrace

Slate roof

★ Bedroom
The main bedroom has been carefully restored to its late-Victorian style. Its authentic furnishings reflect the prosperity brought by South Australia's rich mining discoveries in the 1870s.

STAR FEATURES

★ Bedroom

★ State Dining Room

The Library, furnished with a long dining table, can be hired for functions.

Ballroom
This intricately decorated cornice dates from the 1870s. It is likely that it was painted by Charles Gow, an employee of the Scottish firm of Lyon and Cottier, who is believed to have undertaken extensive work at the house.

For hotels and restaurants in this region see pp501–4 and pp548–51

★ State Dining Room
Sir Henry loved to entertain, and lavish dinners were often held here. It boasts a hand-painted ceiling, grained woodwork and the original gasoliers.

VISITORS' CHECKLIST

288 North Terrace, Adelaide.
Tel (08) 8223 1234. 🚌 99c.
⬜ 10am–4pm Tue–Fri; 1–4pm
Sat, Sun & public hols. ⬤ Mon,
Good Fri, 25 Dec. 📷 🎫 🚻 📷
♿ ground floor only.

Local bluestone was used in constructing the house, as with many 19th-century Adelaide houses. The north façade faces onto North Terrace, one of the city's main streets *(see pp344–5).*

The Conservatory is based around the original stables and coachhouse. Now a function centre, the whole area has been flooded with light by the addition of a glass roof.

Front entrance

Veranda's original chequered tile flooring

The family drawing room, along with the adjacent family dining room, had test strips removed from its walls and ceiling to uncover some stunning original decoration. These rooms have now been fully restored.

THE STORY OF SIR HENRY AYERS

Sir Henry Ayers (1821–97) was born in Hampshire, England, the son of a dock worker. He married in 1840 and, a month later, emigrated with his bride to South Australia. After working briefly as a clerk, Ayers made his fortune in the state's new copper mines. Entering politics in 1857, he was appointed South Australia's Premier seven times between 1863 and 1873, and was President of the Legislative Council, 1881–93. Among many

Statesman and business-man, Sir Henry Ayers

causes, he supported exploration of the interior (Ayers Rock, now Uluṟu, was named after him), but is chiefly remembered for his prominent role in the development of South Australia.

Fleurieu Peninsula and Limestone Coast

The coastline south of Adelaide is rich and varied with beautiful beaches, magnificent coastal scenery and abundant birdlife. The southern coastline of the Fleurieu Peninsula is largely exposed to the mighty Southern Ocean. Here there are good surfing beaches, long expanses of sand, sheltered bays and harbours and stark, weathered cliffs. The western side of the peninsula is more sheltered. There are very few commercial developments on the southeast's coastline and it is easy to find quiet, secluded beaches for swimming, surfing, fishing or walking. Just off South Australia's mainland, Kangaroo Island boasts both pristine swimming beaches and ruggedly beautiful windswept cliffs.

★ Cape Jervis ②

🏄 🌊 🛟 🎣 🚻 ⛺ ⛴

Visitors to the tiny hamlet of Cape Jervis can catch the ferry to Kangaroo Island *(see p354)*, 16 km (10 miles) away across Backstairs Passage. The cape has good boating and fishing and is a hang-gliding centre.

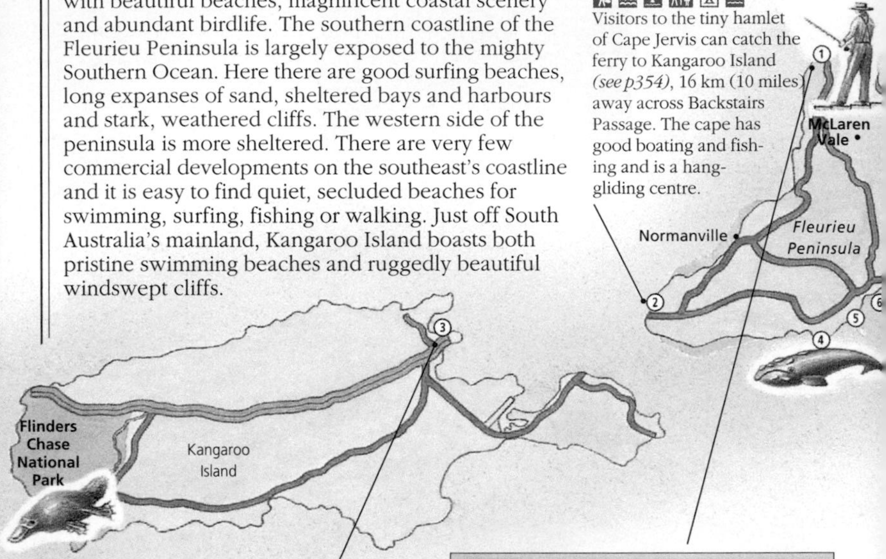
McLaren Vale
Normanville
Fleurieu Peninsula
Flinders Chase National Park
Kangaroo Island

★ Kingscote, Kangaroo Island ③

🏄 🌊 🛟 🎣 ♿ 🚻 ⛺

Kingscote, the island's largest town has a small sandy beach with a tidal pool. There is rich birdlife in swampland south of the town.

★ Port Noarlunga ①

🏄 🌊 🎣 🚻 ⛺

Port Noarlunga boasts a fantastic beach and a protected reef with marine ecosystems that can be explored by snorkellers and scuba divers on a fully marked 800-m (2,600-ft) underwater trail.

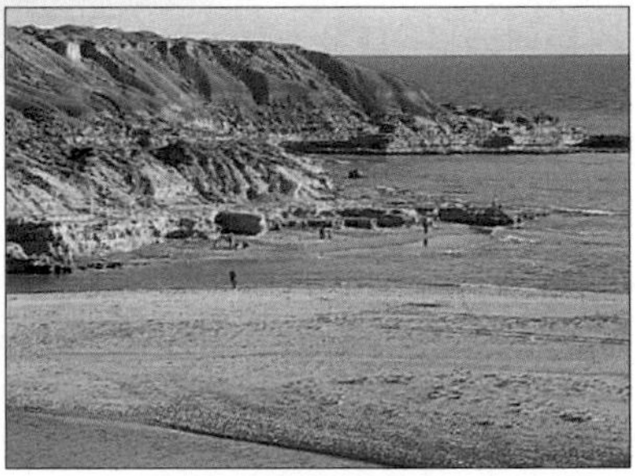

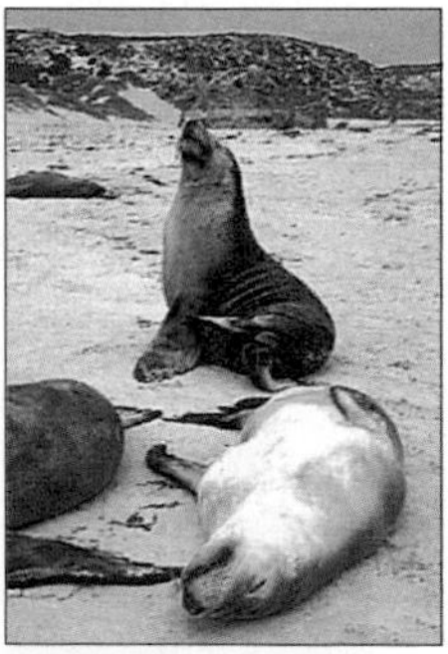

Flinders Chase National Park *covers the western end of Kangaroo Island with undisturbed eucalypt forests and grassland, and seal-inhabited windswept beaches.*

Waitpinga Beach ④

🏄 🎣 🚻 ⛺

Waitpinga Beach, on the southern coast of the Fleurieu Peninsula, is a spectacular surfing beach with waves rolling in off the Southern Ocean. Strong, unpredictable currents make the beach unsafe for swimming and suitable for experienced surfers only. The long stretch of clean white sand is a favourite for beach walkers.

Victor Harbor ⑤

🏄 🌊 🛟 🎣 ♿ 🚻 ⛺

During the early 19th century, Victor Harbor gained notoriety as a whaling station. Today, the southern right whales frolicking offshore from June to October are a popular tourist attraction.

Port Elliot ⑥

🏄 🌊 🎣 🚻 ⛺

Port Elliot, together with nearby Victor Harbor, has long been a favourite place to escape the summer heat of Adelaide. Established in 1854 as a port for the Murray River trade, the town has a safe swimming beach and a fine cliff-top walk.

Hindmarsh Island ⑦

🏄 🌊 🛟 🚻 ⛺

The quiet escapist destination of Hindmarsh Island can be reached by bridge from the town of Goolwa. On the island there are several good vantage points from which visitors can see the mouth of the Murray River.

LOCATOR MAP

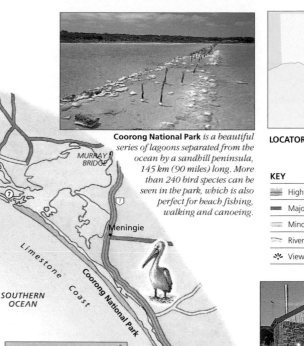

Coorong National Park *is a beautiful series of lagoons separated from the ocean by a sandhill peninsula, 145 km (90 miles) long. More than 240 bird species can be seen in the park, which is also perfect for beach fishing, walking and canoeing.*

LOCATOR MAP

KEY

≋	Highway
▬	Major road
▭	Minor road
⌒	River
✲	Viewpoint

McLaren Vale, *just inland from the coast of the Fleurieu Peninsula, is an important wine-producing region in South Australia (see pp338–9). In addition to 50 wineries, most of which are open for tastings, the vale has many excellent restaurants. On the main road is the Visitors' Centre, which is staffed by volunteers.*

★ Robe ⑧

🥾 🏊 🎣 ♿ 🚻 ⛺

This pretty fishing port and holiday centre has many old buildings, a swimming beach and rugged shoreline. In 1865, more than 16,500 Chinese landed here and walked to Victoria's gold fields to avoid an immigration tax payable by those landing in Victoria *(see p423).*

★ Beachport ⑨

🥾 🏊 🎣 🚻 ⛺

Historic Beachport was first settled as a whaling station in the 1830s. Today it is a quiet, unspoiled haven with swimming, surfing and fishing from its beaches, and a host of other water sports available.

0 kilometres   20

0 miles   20

Old Government House in Belair National Park

Belair National Park ❷

Tel (08) 8278 5477. 🚇 from Adelaide. ⏰ 8am–sunset daily. 🚫 25 Dec. 🅿 for cars only. ♿ limited.

Established in 1891, Belair is the eighth-oldest national park in the world. Only 9 km (5 miles) from Adelaide, it is one of the most popular parks in South Australia. Tennis courts and pavilions are available for hire and there are picnic facilities throughout the park. Visitors can meander through the tall eucalypt forests and cool valleys, and see kangaroos, emus, echidnas and other native wildlife.

In spring, many native plants bloom. The park is closed occasionally in summer on days of extreme fire danger.

Within the park lies **Old Government House**. Built in 1859 as the governor's summer residence, it offers a glimpse of the lifestyle enjoyed by the colonial gentry.

> 🏛 **Old Government House**
> Belair National Park. *Tel* (08) 8278 5477. ⏰ 1–4pm Sun & public hols. 🚫 Good Fri, 25 Dec. 🅿

Warrawong Wildlife Sanctuary ❸

Tel (08) 8370 9197. 🚌 Aldgate. ⏰ 9am–9pm daily. 🚫 25 Dec. 🅿 ♿ 🛈 www.warrawong.com

Warrawong Wildlife Sanctuary attempts to reverse the disastrous trends of recent years which have seen the extinction of 32 mammal species from South Australia.

Only 20 km (13 miles) from Adelaide, via the town of Stirling, the 32 ha (80 acres) of privately owned native bushland is surrounded by a vermin-proof fence. Into this environment Warrawong's owners have introduced some 15 mammal species, many of which are endangered. These include bettongs, potoroos and quolls *(see p455)*. Warrawong Wildlife Sanctuary is also the location of Australia's only successful platypus breeding programme.

The sanctuary offers fun and informative guided walks, including a nocturnal walk that departs at sunset. There's an enjoyable animal show too.

Hahndorf ❹

🏘 1,800. 🚌 from Adelaide. 🛈 41 Main St (08) 8388 1185.

Hahndorf is the oldest surviving German settlement in Australia. The first settlers arrived in 1838 aboard the *Zebra* under the command of Captain Dirk Hahn. Escaping religious persecution in their homeland, they settled in the Adelaide Hills and established Hahndorf (Hahn's Village), a German-style town.

The tree-lined main street has many examples of classic German architecture, such as houses with *fachwerk* timber framing filled in with wattle

Kangaroo roaming through Warrawong Wildlife Sanctuary in the Adelaide Hills

For hotels and restaurants in this region see pp501–4 and pp548–51

Nineteenth-century mill in the historic town of Hahndorf

and daub, or brick. Visitors can take a stroll around the town and enjoy its historic atmosphere.

Just outside Hahndorf is **The Cedars**, the former home of South Australia's best-known landscape artist, the late Sir Hans Heysen *(see p34)*. Both his home and his studio are open to the public. South of the town is Nixon's Mill, a stone mill built in 1842.

The Cedars
Heysen Rd. **Tel** (08) 8388 7277.
10am–4:30pm Tue–Sun.
25 Dec.

Strathalbyn ❺

4,000. ☒ ☒ ℹ️ *Railway Station, South Terrace (08) 8536 3212.*

The designated heritage town of Strathalbyn was originally settled by Scottish immigrants in 1839. Links with its Scottish ancestry can still be seen today in much of the town's architecture, which is reminiscent of small highland towns in Scotland.

Situated on the banks of the Angas River, Strathalbyn is dominated by St Andrew's Church with its sturdy tower. A number of original buildings have been preserved. The police station, built in 1858, and the 1865 courthouse together house the National Trust Museum. The prominent two-storey London House, built as a general store in 1867, has, like a number of buildings in or near the High Street, found a new use as an antiques store. As in many country towns in Australia, the hotels and banks are also architectural reminders of the past.

About 16 km (10 miles) southeast of Strathalbyn, on the banks of the Bremer River, is Langhorne Creek, renowned as one of the earliest wine-growing regions in Australia.

St Andrew's Church, Strathalbyn

Mount Lofty ❻

🚉 *Mount Lofty Summit Rd.*
ℹ️ *Mount Lofty Summit Information Centre (08) 8370 1054.* ☒ ☒ ☒

The hills of the Mount Lofty Ranges form the backdrop to Adelaide. The highest point, Mount Lofty, reaches 727 m

(2,385 ft) and offers a fine view of the city from the modern lookout at the summit, where there is also an interpretive centre. The hills are dotted with grand summer houses to which Adelaide citizens retreat during the summer heat.

Just below the summit is the **Cleland Wildlife Park** where visitors can stroll among the resident kangaroos and emus, have a photograph taken with a koala or walk through the aviary to observe native birds at close quarters.

About 1.5 km (1 mile) south of here, Mount Lofty Botanic Gardens feature temperate-climate plants such as rhododendrons and magnolias.

Cleland Wildlife Park
Mount Lofty Summit Rd. **Tel** (08) 8339 2444. 9:30am–5pm daily.
25 Dec.

Birdwood ❼

600. ℹ️ *FJ Café, Shannon St (08) 8568 5577.*

Nestled in the Adelaide Hills is the quiet little town of Birdwood. In the 1850s, wheat was milled in the town and the old wheat mill now houses Birdwood's most famous asset: the country's largest collection of vintage, veteran and classic motor cars, trucks and motorbikes. The **National Motor Museum** has more than 300 on display and is considered to be one of the best collections of its kind in the world.

National Motor Museum
Shannon St. **Tel** (08) 8568 4000.
10am–5pm daily. 25 Dec.

Hand-feeding kangaroos at Cleland Wildlife Park, Mount Lofty

Kangaroo Island ❽

🚢 Sea Link ferry connection from
Cape Jervis. ℹ️ The Gateway
Information Centre, Howard Drive,
Penneshaw (08) 8553 1185. ♿ ☑
www.tourkangarooisland.com.au

Kangaroo Island, Australia's
third-largest island, is
155 km (96 miles) long and
55 km (34 miles) wide. Located
16 km (10 miles) off the
Fleurieu Peninsula, the island
was the site of South
Australia's first official colonial
settlement, established at
Reeves Point in 1836. The
settlement was short-lived,
and within just four years had
been virtually abandoned. The
island was then settled by
degrees during the remainder
of the 19th century as communications improved with
the new mainland settlements.

There is no public transport
on Kangaroo Island and visitors must travel on a tour or
by car. Though the roads to
the main sights are good,
many roads are unsealed and
extra care should be taken.

Remarkable Rocks at Kirkpatrick Point, Kangaroo Island

Sparsely populated and geographically isolated, the island
has few introduced predators
and is a haven for a wide
variety of animals and birds,
many protected in its 19 conservation and national parks.

At Kingscote and Penneshaw
fairy penguins can often be
seen in the evenings, and the
south coast windswept beach
of Seal Bay is home to a large
colony of Australian sea lions.
In Flinders Chase National

Park, kangaroos will sometimes
approach visitors, but feeding
them is discouraged.

The interior is dry, but does
support tracts of mallee scrub,
and eucalypts. The coastline,
however, is varied. The north
coast has sheltered beaches
ideal for swimming. The south
coast, battered by the Southern
Ocean, has more than 40 shipwrecks. At Kirkpatrick Point to
the southwest stands a group
of large rocks. Aptly named
Remarkable Rocks, they have
been eroded into weird formations by the winds and sea.

Mount Gambier ❾

🚶 23,500. ✈️ 🚉 🚌 ℹ️ Jubilee
Hwy East (08) 8724 9750.

Mount Gambier is a major
regional city midway
between Adelaide and Mel-
bourne, named after the extinct
volcano on the slopes of which
the city lies. Established in
1854, it is now surrounded by
farming country and large pine
plantations. The volcano has
four crater lakes which are
attractive recreation spots, with
walking trails, picnic facilities
and a wildlife park. The Blue
Lake, up to 85 m (280 ft) deep,
is a major draw between
November and March when its
water mysteriously turns an
intense blue. From April to
October, it remains a dull grey.

There are also a number of
caves to explore within the city.
Engelbrecht Cave is popular
with cave divers, and the exposed Umpherston Sinkhole
has fine terraced gardens.

Strange and vividly coloured water of Mount Gambier's Blue Lake

For hotels and restaurants in this region see pp501–4 and pp548–51

Sharam's Cottage, the first house built in Penola

Penola ⑩

🏘 *3,400.* 🚉 ℹ *27 Arthur St (08) 8737 2855.*

One of the oldest towns in the Southeast, Penola is the commercial centre of the Coonawarra wine region *(see pp338–9)*. The region's first winery was built in 1893. There are now some 20 wineries, most of which are open for sales and tastings.

Penola itself is a quiet town which takes great pride in its history. A heritage walk takes visitors past most of its early buildings, including the restored Sharam's Cottage, which was built in 1850 as the first dwelling in Penola.

Environs

Situated 27 km (17 miles) north of Penola, Bool Lagoon (designated a wetland of international significance by UNESCO), is an important refuge for an assortment of native wildlife including more than 150 species of birds. The park provides an opportunity to observe at close quarters many of these local and migratory birds *(see p337)*.

Naracoorte Caves National Park ⑪

Tel (08) 8762 2340. 🚉 *from Adelaide.* 🕐 *9am–5pm daily (last tour 3:30pm).* 🔴 *25 Dec.* 🖼️ 📷 📁 **www.**naracoortecaves.sa.gov.au

Located 12 km (7 miles) south of Naracoorte is the Naracoorte Caves National Park. Within this 600-ha (1,500-acre) park, there are 60 known caves, most notably Victoria Cave, which has been

placed on the World Heritage List as a result of the remarkable fossil deposits discovered here in 1969 *(see pp26–7)*. Guided tours of this and three other caves are available. From November to February thousands of bent wing bats come to breed in the Maternity Cave. They can be seen leaving the cave en masse at dusk to feed. Entrance to this cave is forbidden, but visitors can view the inside via infrared cameras in the park.

Ancient stalactites inside one of the Naracoorte caves

Murray River ⑫

🚉 *from Adelaide.* ℹ *Renmark (08) 8586 6704.* **www.**murrayriver.com.au

Australia's largest river is a vital source of water in this, the driest state in Australia. As well as supplying water for Adelaide it supports a vigorous local agricultural industry that produces 40 per cent of all Australian wine *(see pp338–9)*. It is also a popular destination for houseboating, water-skiing and fishing.

The town of Renmark, close to the Victoria border, lies at the heart of the Murray River irrigation area and is home to the Riverlands' first winery. At the town's wharf is the restored paddlesteamer *Industry*, now a floating museum and a reminder of days gone by.

Just south of Renmark, Berri is the area's commercial centre and site of the largest combined distillery and winery in the southern hemisphere. The Murray River meanders through Berri and on to the small town of Loxton before winding up towards the citrus centre of Waikerie. Surrounded by more than 5,000 ha (12,000 acres) of orchards, Waikerie is a favourite gliding centre and has hosted the world gliding championships.

Another 40 km (25 miles) downstream, the Murray River reaches the town of Morgan, its northernmost point in South Australia, before it turns south towards the ocean. The **Morgan Museum**, located in the old railway station, aims to recapture the river-trading days, telling the story of what was once the second-busiest port in the state. The *Mayflower*, the oldest surviving paddlesteamer in the state, is moored next to the museum.

🏛 **Morgan Museum**
Morgan Railway Station.
Tel (08) 8540 2136. 🕐 *10am–4pm daily.* 🔴 *25 Dec.* 🖼️

An old paddlesteamer cruising along the Murray River

Barossa Valley Tour ⓭

Riesling grapes

The Barossa, which is comprised of the Barossa and Eden valleys, is one of Australia's most famous wine regions and has an international reputation. First settled in 1842 by German Lutheran immigrants, villages were established at Bethany, Langmeil (now Tanunda), Lyndoch and Light's Pass. Signs of German traditions can be seen in the 19th-century buildings, churches and in the region's food, music and festivals. The Barossa Festival takes place in April in every even-numbered year and there is a Music Festival every October.

Seppelt ⑤
Between Tanunda and Greenoch, this winery was established in 1851 by the pioneering German family Seppelt. A historic complex of splendid stone buildings, it is reached via an avenue of palm trees planted in the 1920s.

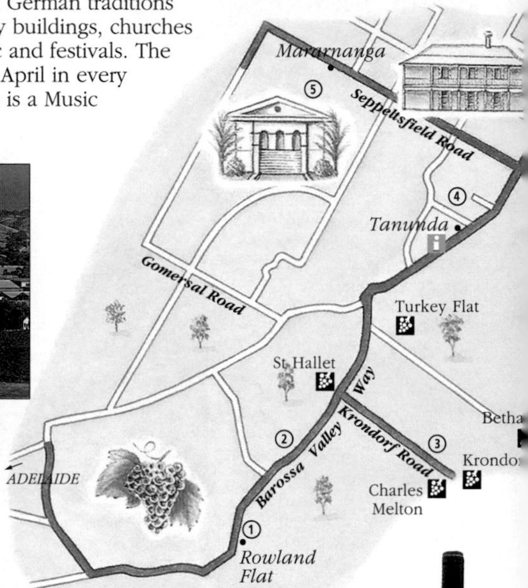

Orlando ①
Established in 1847, this is one of the largest wineries in Australia. Famous for its popular Jacob's Creek range, it is the country's top wine exporter and includes labels such as Wyndham Estate, Poet's Corner and Richmond Grove.

Peter Lehmann ④
A significant producer of quality Barossa wines, this winery was established by Peter Lehmann, a well-known character in the valley. The winery was awarded International Winemaker of the Year in 2004.

Grant Burge ②
Grant and Helen Burge founded this historic winery in 1988 and undertook restoration work on the buildings. The beautifully restored tasting room has custom-made chandeliers and ornamental glass. The winery produces traditional style Barossa wines – the Meshach Shiraz is one of the region's finest.

KEY

Tour route

Other road

Vineyard

0 km 2

0 miles 2

Rockford ③
This winery uses 100-year-old equipment to make its famous traditional hand-crafted wines. In the summer months visitors can see the old equipment working. The winery itself is also more than a century old.

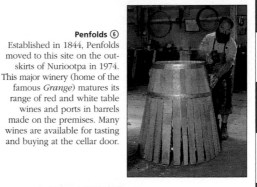

Penfolds ⑥

Established in 1844, Penfolds moved to this site on the outskirts of Nuriootpa in 1974. This major winery (home of the famous *Grange*) matures its range of red and white table wines and ports in barrels made on the premises. Many wines are available for tasting and buying at the cellar door.

Wolf Blass ⑦

One of the younger wineries in the Barossa, established in 1973, Wolf Blass boasts elaborate tasting rooms and a wine heritage museum. It specializes in premium red and white table wines, and sparkling and fortified wines.

Saltram ⑧

Established in 1859, this historic winery is set in beautiful gardens on a Barossa hillside outside Angaston. Popular with red and fortified wine enthusiasts, Saltram also has an excellent restaurant, which is open for lunch daily and dinner Thursday to Saturday.

Collingrove Homestead, Angaston ⑨

Now owned by the National Trust, Collingrove was built in 1856 as a home for a member of the influential pioneering Angas family. It has original furnishings and is set in an English-style garden. Accommodation is available.

Henschke ⑩

This winery is one of the world's greatest producers. Their wines are made from single vineyards, some with 100-year-old vines. After visiting the cellar be sure to walk through the vineyards – with some of the oldest vines in the world.

TIPS FOR DRIVERS

Although a tour of the Barossa Valley can be made in a day from Adelaide, the region is best seen and enjoyed by taking advantage of the excellent local accommodation and restaurants. The roads are generally good, although drivers should take special care on those that are unsealed. Visitors planning to visit a number of wineries and sample the produce may prefer to take one of the many tours or hire a chauffeur-driven vehicle.

THE YORKE AND EYRE PENINSULAS AND SOUTH AUSTRALIAN OUTBACK

From the lush Clare Valley and the dunes of the Simpson Desert, to the saltbush of the Nullarbor Plain, the land to the north and west of Adelaide is an area of vast distances and dramatic changes of scenery. With activities ranging from surfing on the coast to bushwalking in the Flinders Ranges, one is never far from awesome natural beauty.

South Australia was first settled by Europeans in 1836, but suffered early financial problems partly due to economic mismanagement. These were largely remedied by the discovery of copper at Kapunda, north of Adelaide, in 1842, and at Burra, near Clare, in 1845. As these resources were depleted fresh discoveries were made in the north of the Yorke Peninsula, in the area known as Little Cornwall, at the town of Wallaroo in 1859 and at Moonta in 1861. By the 1870s, South Australia was the British Empire's leading copper producer, and copper, silver and uranium mining still boosts the state's economy today.

The Yorke and Eyre peninsulas are major arable areas, producing more than 10 per cent of Australia's wheat and much of its barley. They also have several important fishing ports, most notably Port Lincoln, the tuna-fishing capital of the country. Both peninsulas have stunning coastal scenery. The Yorke Peninsula, only two hours' drive from Adelaide, is a popular holiday destination with excellent fishing, reef diving and surfing opportunities. The much larger Eyre Peninsula is also renowned for fishing and has many superb beaches. Despite extensive arable use, it still retains about half of its land area as parks, reserves and native bushland.

To the west, the vast Nullarbor Plain stretches far into Western Australia *(see p319)*, with the Great Victoria Desert extending above it. Much of this region is protected Aboriginal land and the Woomera prohibited military area.

North of the Yorke Peninsula lies the rugged majesty of the Flinders Ranges. Rich with sights of deep Aboriginal spiritual and cultural significance, the ranges are also home to abundant flora and fauna, and make for superb bushwalking. Further north, the immense, inhospitable but starkly beautiful desert regions of the South Australian Outback provide a challenging but rewarding destination for adventurous travellers.

Oyster beds in Coffin Bay at the southern tip of the Eyre Peninsula

◁ Rock climbing at Moonarie in the spectacular Flinders Ranges National Park

Exploring the Yorke and Eyre Peninsulas

Just north of Adelaide *(see pp344–9)* lie the green
hills of the Clare Valley; then, further inland, as the
rainfall diminishes, the countryside changes dramati-
cally. First comes the grandeur of the Flinders
Ranges with rugged mountains and tranquil gorges.
West of Adelaide are two peninsulas, at the head of
which is the industrial triangle of Port Pirie, Port
Augusta and Whyalla. The Yorke Peninsula is
Australia's richest barley growing district. Eyre
Peninsula is also a wheat and barley producing area.
From here the barren Nullarbor Plain runs beyond
the Western Australian border.

**Fishing boats moored in the
harbour of Port Lincoln**

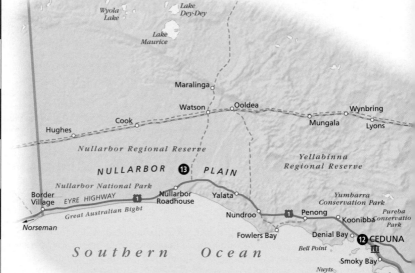

GETTING AROUND

Despite the sparse population,
there is an extensive road network throughout the region. The
Stuart Hwy runs up from
Adelaide to Coober Pedy and
beyond into the Northern
Territory, and the Eyre Hwy
wends its way from Adelaide
along the tops of the Yorke and
Eyre peninsulas, across the
Nullarbor Plain and into Western
Australia. There is no state
railway, but interstate trains running from Sydney to Perth, and
Adelaide to Alice Springs and
Melbourne, stop at major towns
in the region. Scheduled buses
serve most towns, and there are
air services from Adelaide to
regional airports in Port Lincoln,
Ceduna, Coober Pedy, Whyalla,
and Port Augusta.

Raging waters of the Great Australian Bight

SIGHTS AT A GLANCE

Ceduna 12
Clare Valley 6
Coffin Bay National Park 11
Little Cornwall 5
Maitland 4
Minlaton 2
Nullarbor Plain 13
Port Augusta 8
Port Lincoln 10
Port Pirie 7
Port Victoria 3
Whyalla 9
Yorketown 1

South Australian Outback
See pp368–9
Coober Pedy 14
Flinders Ranges 18
Lake Eyre National Park 17
Simpson Desert Conservation Park 16
Witjira National Park 15

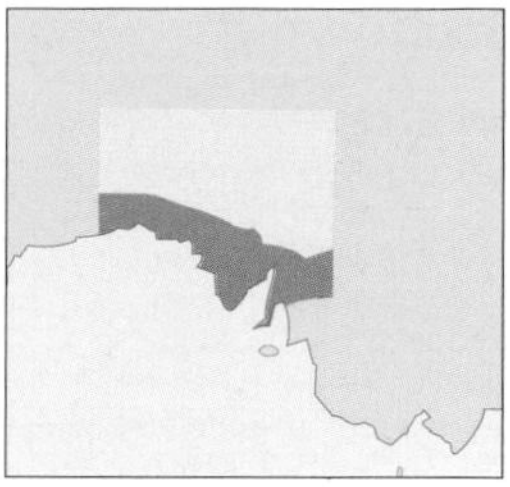

LOCATOR MAP

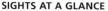

■ *The Yorke and Eyre Peninsulas*

□ *SA Outback* pp368–9

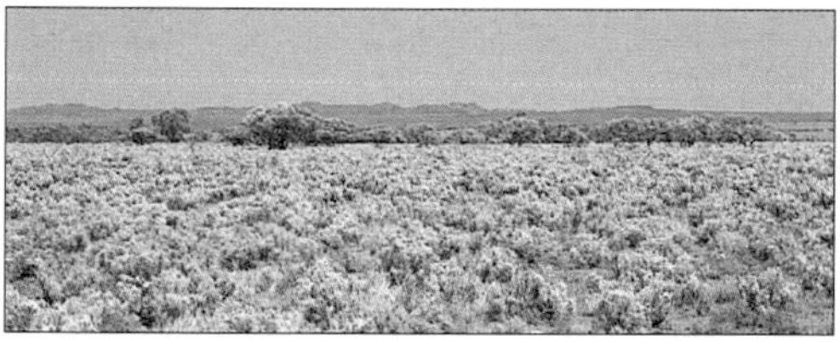

Saltbush landscape of the Eyre Peninsula

KEY

- Major road
- Minor road
- Track
- Scenic route
- Main railway
- Minor railway
- State border
- △ Summit

SEE ALSO

• ***Where to Stay*** pp504–5

• ***Where to Eat*** pp551–2

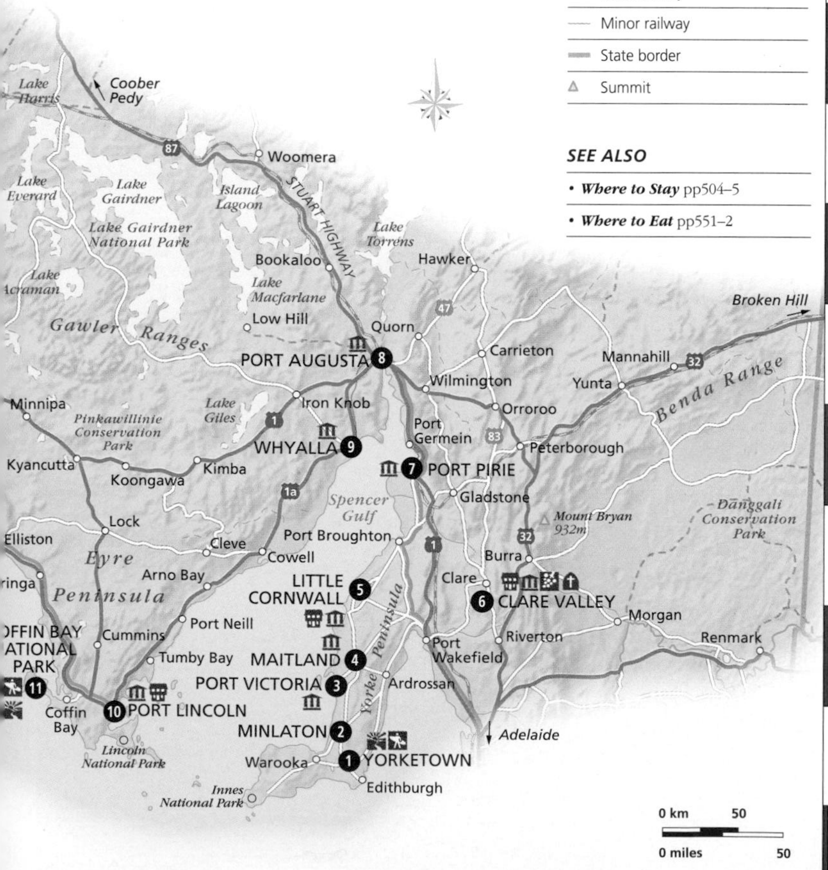

Lake Harris
Coober Pedy
87
Woomera
Lake Everard
Lake Gairdner
Island Lagoon
STUART HIGHWAY
Lake Gairdner National Park
Lake Torrens
Bookaloo
Hawker
Lake Acraman
Lake Macfarlane
47
Broken Hill
Low Hill
Gawler Ranges
Quorn
PORT AUGUSTA 8
Carrieton
Mannahill
32
Wilmington
Yunta
Benda Range
Minnipa
Lake Giles
Iron Knob
Orroroo
Pinkawillinie Conservation Park
1
Port Germein
83
WHYALLA 9
Peterborough
Kyancutta
Kimba
Koongawa
7 PORT PIRIE
1a
Gladstone
Spencer Gulf
Mount Bryan 932m
Danggali Conservation Park
Lock
Port Broughton
32
Elliston
Cleve
1
Eyre Peninsula
Cowell
Burra
Arno Bay
LITTLE CORNWALL 5
Clare
6 CLARE VALLEY
Port Neill
Morgan
COFFIN BAY NATIONAL PARK
Cummins
Yorke Peninsula
Port Wakefield
Riverton
Renmark
Tumby Bay
MAITLAND 4
11
PORT VICTORIA 3
Ardrossan
Coffin Bay
10 PORT LINCOLN
MINLATON 2
Adelaide
Lincoln National Park
Warooka
1 YORKETOWN
Edithburgh
Innes National Park
0 km 50
0 miles 50

Yorketown ①

🏠 685. 🚌 ⓘ *29 Main St, Minlaton (08) 8853 2600 or 1800 202 445.*

Yorketown is the commercial centre of the earliest settled area on the southern Yorke Peninsula. It lies at the heart of a region scattered with nearly 300 salt lakes, many of which mysteriously turn pink at various times of the year, depending on climatic conditions. From the late 1890s until the 1930s, salt harvesting was a major industry in this part of South Australia.

Approximately 70 km (40 miles) southwest of Yorketown, at the tip of the Yorke Peninsula, is the spectacular Innes National Park. The park's geography changes from salt lakes and low mallee scrub inland to sandy beaches and steep, rugged cliffs along the coast. Kangaroos and emus have become accustomed to the presence of humans and are commonly seen, but other native inhabitants, such as the large mallee fowl, are more difficult to spot.

There is good surfing, reef diving and fishing in the park, especially at Browns Beach, the wild Pondalowie Bay, Chinamans Creek and Salmon Hole. Other beaches are considered unsafe for swimming. Also in the park are the rusting remains of the shipwrecked barque *Ethel*, which ran aground in 1904 and now lies with part of its hull protruding through the sand below the limestone cliffs of Ethel Beach.

"Red Devil" fighter plane in Minlaton

Minlaton ②

🏠 770. 🚌 🚆 ⓘ *29 Main St (08) 8853 2600 or 1800 202 445.*

Centrally located, Minlaton is a service town to the surrounding farming community. Minlaton's claim to fame, however, is as the destination of the very first air mail flight across water in the southern hemisphere. Pilot Captain Harry Butler, a World War I fighter ace, set off on this record-breaking mission in August 1919 from Adelaide. Minlaton's Butler Memorial houses his 1916 Bristol fighter plane, "Red Devil", believed to be the only one left in the world, as well as displays detailing Butler's life.

Port Victoria ③

🏠 345. ⓘ *29 Main St, Minlaton (08) 8853 2600 or 1800 202 445.*

Lying on the west coast of the Yorke Peninsula, Port Victoria is today a sleepy holiday destination, popular with anglers, swimmers and divers.

In the early part of the 20th century, however, it was a busy sea port with large clippers and windjammers loading grain bound for the northern hemisphere. The last time a square rigger used the port was in 1949. The story of these ships and their epic voyages is told in the **Maritime Museum**, located adjacent to the jetty.

About 10 km (6 miles) off the coast lies Wardang Island, around which are eight known shipwrecks dating from 1871. Divers can follow the Wardang Island Maritime Heritage Trail to view the wrecks, each of which has an underwater plaque. Boats to the island can be chartered, but permission to land must be obtained from the Community Council in Point Pearce, the nearby Aboriginal settlement which administers the island.

🏛 **Maritime Museum**
Main St, Foreshore. *Tel (08) 8834 2057.* 🕙 *10am–4pm daily.* 🈺 ♿

Maitland ④

🏠 1,050. 🚌 🚆 ⓘ *29 Main St, Minlaton (08) 8853 2600 or 1800 202 445.*

Surrounded by some of the most productive farmland in Australia, Maitland lies in the centre of the Yorke Peninsula, on a ridge

Vast expanse of the salt lakes in the Yorketown region

For hotels and restaurants in this region see pp504–5 and pp551–2

overlooking the Yorke Valley and Spencer Gulf. Originally proclaimed in 1872, it is now the service centre for the surrounding community.

The pretty town, laid out on a classic grid pattern, retains many fine examples of colonial architecture, including the Maitland Hotel, built in 1874, and the 1875 St Bartholomew's Catholic Church.

The **Maitland Museum** has an agricultural and folk collection housed in three buildings and focuses on the region's history and development.

🏛 **Maitland Museum**
Cnr Gardiner & Kilkerran terraces. **Tel** (08) 8832 2220. ◯ Sun, school hols. ⬤ Good Fri, 25 Dec. 📷 ♿

Miners' cottages in Little Cornwall

Little Cornwall ❺

🔲 Kadina. 🚌 Kadina. 🚹 50 Moonta Rd, Kadina (08) 8821 2333.

The three towns of Moonta, Kadina and Wallaroo were established after copper discoveries on Yorke Peninsula in 1859 and 1861. Collectively the towns are known as "The Copper Coast" or "Australia's Little Cornwall". Many miners from Cornwall, England, came here in the 19th century seeking their fortunes. The biennial festival "Kernewek Lowender" *(see p42)* celebrates this Cornish heritage. The wealth created by the mines has left the towns with fine architecture.

Wallaroo, the site of the first copper ore smelting works, was also a shipping port for ore. When mining finished,

Former timber shed now home to the Maritime Museum, Port Victoria

the port was important for agricultural exports. The **Wallaroo Heritage and Nautical Museum** is in the old post office.

Moonta, once home to Australia's richest copper mine, contains a group of sites and buildings in the **Moonta Mines State Heritage Area**. The 1870 Miner's Cottage is a restored wattle and daub cottage. The history museum is in the old Moonta Mines Model School. Also of interest is the Moonta Mines Railway, a restored light-gauge locomotive.

Kadina, where copper was originally found, is the Yorke Peninsula's largest town. The

Farmshed Museum and Tourism Centre has interesting displays on mining and folk history of the area.

🏛 **Wallaroo Heritage and Nautical Museum**
Jetty Rd. **Tel** (08) 8823 3277. ◯ 10am–4pm Mon–Fri, 2–4pm Sat & Sun. ⬤ 25 Dec. 📷 ♿

🏚 **Moonta Mines State Heritage Area**
Moonta Rd. **Tel** (08) 8825 1891. ◯ daily. ⬤ Good Fri, 25 Dec. 📷 ♿

🏛 **Farmshed Museum and Tourism Centre**
50 Moonta Rd. **Tel** (08) 8821 2333. ◯ 9am–5pm Mon–Fri, 10am–3:30pm Sat & Sun. ⬤ 25 Dec. 📷

FISHING AND DIVING ON THE YORKE PENINSULA

There are fantastic opportunities for on- and offshore fishing and diving in the waters off the Yorke Peninsula. Many of the coastal towns have jetties used by keen amateur fishermen, and around Edithburgh anglers may catch tommy ruff, garfish and snook. Divers can enjoy the southern coast's stunning underwater scenery with brightly coloured corals and fish.

Offshore, the wreck of the *Clan Ranald* near Edithburgh is a popular dive and, off Wardang Island, eight wrecks can be explored on a unique diving trail. Angling from boats can be equally fruitful and local charter boats are available for hire.

A large blue grouper close to a diver in waters off the Yorke Peninsula

Restored 19th-century buildings at Burra Mine near the Clare Valley

Clare Valley ❻

🚪 *Clare.* ℹ️ *Town Hall, 229 Main North Rd, Clare 1800 242 131.*

Framed by the rolling hills of the northern Mount Lofty Ranges, the Clare Valley is a picturesque and premium wine-producing region. At the head of the valley lies the town of Clare. This pretty, regional centre has many historic buildings, including the National Trust Museum, housed in the old Police Station, and Wolta Wolta, an early pastoralist's home, built in 1864, which has a fine collection of antiques.

Sevenhill Cellars, 7 km (4 miles) south of Clare, is the oldest vineyard in the valley. It was established by Austrian Jesuits in 1851, originally to produce altar wine for the colony. The adjacent St Aloysius Church was completed in 1875. The winery is still run by Jesuits and now produces both altar and table wines.

East of Sevenhill lies the pleasant heritage town of Mintaro, with many buildings making extensive use of the slate quarried in the area for more than 150 years. Also worth visiting is **Martindale Hall**, an elegant 1879 mansion situated just southeast of town.

Twelve km (7 miles) north of Clare lies **Bungaree Station**. This self-contained Merino sheep-farming complex was established in 1841 and is now maintained as a working 19th-century model. From the historic exhibits visitors can learn about life and work at the station.

About 35 km (22 miles) northeast of Clare is the charming town of Burra. Five years after copper was discovered here in 1845, Burra was home to the largest mine in Australia. As such it was the economic saviour of the fledgling state, rescuing it from impending bankruptcy. Burra is now a State Heritage Area.

The **Burra Mine Open Air Museum**, with its ruins and restored buildings around the huge open cut, is one of Australia's most exciting industrial archaeological sites. An interpretive centre at the Bon Accord Mine allows visitors access to the original mine shaft. The miners' dug-outs, still seen on the banks of Burra Creek, were once home to more than 1,500 mainly Cornish miners. Paxton Square Cottages, built between 1849 and 1852, are unique in Australian mining history as the first decent accommodation provided for miners and their families. Many old buildings, including the police lockup and stables, the Redruth Gaol and the Unicorn Brewery Cellars, have been carefully restored, as have a number of the 19th-century shops and houses. A museum chronicling the local history is located in Burra market square.

🏛️ **Sevenhill Cellars**
College Rd, Sevenhill. *Tel (08) 8843 4222.* ◯ *daily.* ● *1 Jan, Good Fri, 25 Dec.* ♿

🏛️ **Martindale Hall**
Manoora Rd, Mintaro. *Tel (08) 8843 9088.* ◯ *daily.* 📷

🏛️ **Bungaree Station**
Port Augusta Rd, Clare. *Tel (08) 8842 2677.* ◯ *tours only.* 📷 ♿

🏛️ **Burra Mine**
Market St, Burra. *Tel (08) 8892 2154.* ◯ *9am–5pm daily.* ● *25 Dec.* 📷 ♿ *limited.*

Port Pirie ❼

🚶 *13,200.* 🚪 🚌 ℹ️ *Mary Elie St 1800 000 424.*

Port Pirie was the state's first provincial city. An industrial hub, it is the site of the largest lead smelter in the southern hemisphere.

In the town centre, the **National Trust Museum** comprises three well-preserved buildings: the pavilion-style railway station built in 1902, the former Customs House and the Old Police Building. The Regional Tourism and Arts Centre, located in the former 1967 railway station, features artworks on lead, zinc and copper panels interpreting the city's historic wealth.

Every October, Port Pirie hosts the South Australian Festival of Country Music.

🏛️ **National Trust Museum**
Ellen St. *Tel (08) 8632 3435.* ◯ *daily.* ● *25 Dec.* ♿ *limited.*

Victorian grandeur of Port Pirie's old railway station

For hotels and restaurants in this region see pp504–5 and pp551–2

Harbour view of Port Augusta, backed by its power stations

Port Augusta ⑧

🏠 13,000. ✈ 🚇 🚌 🚍 🛈 41 Flinders Terrace 1800 633 060.

Situated at the head of Spencer Gulf, Port Augusta is at the crossroads of Australia; here lies the intersection of the Sydney–Perth and Adelaide–Alice Springs railway lines, as well as the major Sydney–Perth and Adelaide–Darwin highways. Once an important port, its power stations now produce 40 per cent of the state's electricity. The coal-fired Northern Power Station, which dominates the city's skyline, offers free conducted tours.

Port Augusta is also the beginning of South Australia's Outback region. The School of the Air and the Royal Flying Doctor Service offices, both of which provide essential services to inhabitants of remote stations, are open to the public *(see p257).* The **Wadlata Outback Centre** imaginatively tells the story of the Far North from 15 million years ago when rainforests covered the area, through Aboriginal and European history, up to the present day and into the future.

Australia's first **Arid Lands Botanic Garden** was opened nearby in 1996. This 200-ha (500-acre) site is an important research and education facility, as well as a recreational

area. It also commands panoramic views of the Flinders Ranges to the east *(see p369).*

🏛 **Wadlata Outback Centre**
Flinders Terrace. **Tel** (08) 8641 9193. ◯ 9am–5.30pm Mon–Fri, 10am–4pm Sat & Sun. ⬤ 25 Dec.
♿ &

🌿 **Arid Lands Botanic Garden**
Stuart Hwy. **Tel** (08) 8641 1049. ◯ 7am–sunset daily. ▣

Whyalla ⑨

🏠 21,000. ✈ 🚇 🛈 Port Augusta Rd, Lincoln Hwy, 1800 088 589.

At the gateway to the Eyre Peninsula, Whyalla is the state's largest provincial city. Originally a shipping port for iron ore mined at nearby Iron Knob, the city was transformed in 1939 when a blast furnace

was established, a harbour created and a shipyard constructed. The shipyard closed in 1978; however, the first ship built there, the HMAS *Whyalla* (1941), is now a major display of the **Whyalla Maritime Museum**.

Although an industrial centre, Whyalla has a number of fine beaches and good fishing. In recent years, Whyalla's foreshore has been extensively redeveloped. Today, it is home to a bustling marina, lush gardens and cafés.

🏛 **Whyalla Maritime Museum**
Lincoln Hwy. **Tel** (08) 8645 8900. ◯ 10am–4pm daily. ⬤ Good Fri, 25 Dec. ♿
🚢 HMAS Whyalla can be accessed on guided tours only.
& museum only. **www**.whyalla maritimemuseum.com.au

HMAS *Whyalla*, docked beside the Whyalla Maritime Museum

Stunning coastline of Whalers Way at the southern end of the Eyre Peninsula near Port Lincoln

Port Lincoln 🔟

🏘 13,000. ✈ 🚌 ℹ 3 Adelaide Pl, 1300 788 378 or (08) 8683 3544.

At the southern end of the Eyre Peninsula, Port Lincoln sits on the shore of Boston Bay, one of the world's largest natural harbours. A fishing and seafood processing centre, it is home to Australia's largest tuna fleet.

Locals celebrate the start of the tuna season every January with the Tunarama Festival (see p41). This raucous event includes processions, concerts and a tuna-tossing competition.

Fishing and sailing are popular activities. Visitors can take a boat trip to Dangerous Reef, 31 km (20 miles) offshore, to view great white sharks from the relative safety of the boat or submerged cage. In the middle of the bay lies Boston Island, a working

sheep station including an 1842 slab cottage.

The Port Lincoln area has several buildings of note. South of Port Lincoln, **Mikkira Station**, established in 1842, is one of the country's oldest sheep stations. Today it is ideal for picnics or camping, with a restored pioneer cottage and a koala colony. The **Koppio Smithy Museum**, located in the Koppio Hills 40 km (25 miles) north of Port Lincoln, is an agricultural museum with a furnished 1890 log cottage and a 1903 smithy that gives a glimpse into the lives of the pioneers.

Just 20 km (12 miles) south of Port Lincoln is Lincoln National Park with its rocky hills, sheltered coves, sandy beaches and high cliffs. The park is also rich in birdlife. Emus and parrots are common and ospreys and sea eagles frequent the coast. Just west of the park, Whalers

Way has some of Australia's most dramatic coastal scenery. This land is private and entry is via a permit available from the visitors' centre.

🏕 **Mikkira Station**
Fishery Bay Rd. **Tel** 1300 788 378. 📷

🏛 **Koppio Smithy Museum**
Via White Flat Rd. **Tel** 1300 788 378. ⏰ 10am–5pm Tue–Sun. ⬤ 25 Dec. 📷 ♿

The prime surfing spot of Almonta Beach in Coffin Bay National Park

Coffin Bay National Park ⓫

🚌 Port Lincoln. ℹ (08) 8688 3111. ⏰ daily. ⬤ 25 Dec. 📷 per vehicle. ♿ limited.

To the west of the southern tip of the Eyre Peninsula is Coffin Bay Peninsula, which is part of the Coffin Bay National Park. This unspoilt area of

Wedge-tailed eagle

WILDLIFE OF THE EYRE PENINSULA

An enormous variety of wildlife inhabits the Eyre Peninsula. Emus and kangaroos are common, and the hairy-nosed wombat is found in large numbers on the west coast. Wedge-tailed eagles soar over the Gawler Ranges, while sea eagles, ospreys, albatrosses and petrels are all seen over the coast. In the water, dolphins, sea lions and occasional great white sharks feast on an abundance of marine life. The most spectacular sight, however, are the southern right whales which breed at the head of the Great Australian Bight every June to October. They can be seen from the cliffs at the Head of Bight, just east of the Nullarbor National Park.

coastal wilderness has exposed cliffs, sheltered sandy beaches, rich birdlife and fantastic fishing. Wildflowers in the park can be quite spectacular from early spring to early summer.

There are several scenic drives through the park, but some roads are accessible to 4WD vehicles only. A favourite route for conventional vehicles is the Yangie Trail from the small town of Coffin Bay to Yangie and Avoid bays. To the east of Point Avoid is one of Australia's best surfing beaches, Almonta Beach.

Coffin Bay town has long been a popular centre for windsurfing, swimming, sailing and fishing. It now also produces high-quality oysters. The Oyster Walk is a pleasant walking trail along the foreshore through native bushland.

Ceduna 🟰

🏔 2,300. ✈ 🚉 ℹ 58 Poynton St (08) 8625 3343. www.ceduna.net

At the top of the west side of the Eyre Peninsula, sitting on the shores of Murat Bay, Ceduna is the most westerly significant town in South Australia before the start of the Nullarbor Plain. The town's name comes from the Aboriginal word *cheedoona*, meaning "a place to rest".

Today, Ceduna is the commercial centre of the far west. Within the town is the **Old Schoolhouse National Trust Museum** with its collections of restored farm equipment

An Indian-Pacific train crossing the vast Nullarbor Plain

from early pioneer days. It also has an interesting display on the British atomic weapons tests held at nearby Maralinga in the 1950s, and a small selection of Aboriginal artifacts.

In the 1850s, there was a whaling station on St Peter Island, just off the coast of Ceduna, but now the town is a base for whale-watchers. Southern right whales can be seen close to the shore from June to October from the head of the Bight, 300 km (185 miles) from Ceduna.

The oyster farming industry has established itself west and east of Ceduna at Denial and Smoky bays. Between Ceduna and Penong, a tiny hamlet 73 km (45 miles) to the west, there are detours to surfing beaches including the legendary Cactus Beach. Keen surfers are found here all year round trying to catch some of the best waves in Australia, rolling in from the great Southern Ocean.

🏛 Old Schoolhouse National Trust Museum
Park Terrace. **Tel** (08) 8625 2210.
◯ Mon–Sat. ● 25 Dec. 🎫 ♿

Nullarbor Plain 🟰

🚉 Port Augusta. 🚌 Ceduna.
ℹ Ceduna (08) 8625 3343.
◯ 9am–5:30pm Mon–Fri, 10am– 4pm Sat–Sun. ● Good Fri, 25 Dec.

The huge expanse of the Nullarbor Plain stretches from Nundroo, about 150 km (95 miles) west of Ceduna, towards the distant Western Australia border 330 km (200 miles) away, and beyond into Western Australia (*see p319*).

This dry, dusty plain can be crossed by rail on the Trans-Australian Railway or by road on the Eyre Highway. The train travels further inland than the road, its route giving little relief from the flat landscape. The highway lies nearer the coast, passing a few isolated sights of interest on its way west.

Just south of the small town of Nundroo lies Fowlers Bay. Good for fishing, it is popular with anglers seeking solitude. West of here, the road passes through the Yalata Aboriginal Lands and travellers can stop by the roadside to buy souvenirs from the local people. Bordering Yalata to the west is Nullarbor National Park. This runs from the Nullarbor Roadhouse hamlet, 130 km (80 miles) west of Nundroo, to the border with Western Australia 200 km (125 miles) away. The Eyre Highway passes through the park, close to the coastal cliffs. This stretch of the plain has some spectacular views over the Great Australian Bight.

The world's longest cave system runs beneath the plain, and the border area has many underground caves and caverns. These should only be explored by experienced cavers, however, as many are flooded and dangerous.

Watching southern right whales from Head of Bight, near Ceduna

South Australian Outback

South Australia's outback is an enormous area of harsh but often breathtaking scenery. Much of the region is untamed desert, broken in places by steep, ancient mountain ranges, huge salt lakes, gorges and occasional hot springs. Although very hot and dry for most of the year, many places burst into life after heavy winter rains and hundreds of species of wildflowers, animals and birds can be seen. The area's recent history is one of fabled stock routes, now Outback tracks for adventurous travellers. Isolated former mining and railway towns now cater for Outback tourists. Vast areas in the west form extensive Aboriginal lands, accessible by permit only.

LOCATOR MAP

South Australian Outback

The Yorke and Eyre Peninsulas
see pp358–67

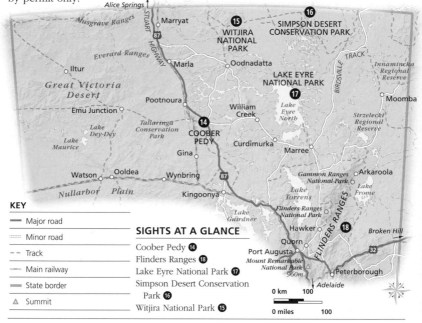

KEY

— Major road

···· Minor road

- - Track

≈ Main railway

— State border

△ Summit

SIGHTS AT A GLANCE

Coober Pedy ⑭

Flinders Ranges ⑱

Lake Eyre National Park ⑰

Simpson Desert Conservation Park ⑯

Witjira National Park ⑮

0 km   100

0 miles   100

Coober Pedy ⑭

🏃 1,400. ✈ 🚌 ℹ 773 Hutchison St, 1800 637 076 or (08) 8672 5298. **www.**opalcapitaloftheworld.com.au

One of Australia's most famous Outback towns, Coober Pedy, 850 km (530 miles) northwest of Adelaide, is an unusual settlement in the heart of an extremely hostile landscape. Frequent duststorms and a colourless desert landscape littered with abandoned mines contribute to the town's desolate appearance, yet the small population has a cultural mix of over 42 nationalities.

Opal was discovered here in 1915, and today Coober Pedy produces 70 per cent of the world's supply. Mining claims, limited to one per person, can measure no more than 100 m by 50 m (320 ft by 160 ft). For this reason opal mining is the preserve of individuals, not large companies, and this adds to the town's "frontier" quality.

Underground "dugout" home in Coober Pedy

Coober Pedy's name comes from the Aboriginal *kupa piti*, meaning white man in a hole, and it is apt indeed. Not only the mines, but also houses, hotels and churches are built underground. This way, the residents escape the extreme temperatures of up to 50°C (122°F) during the day and 0°C (32°F) at night. Several such homes are open to the public.

The **Underground Art Gallery** displays Aboriginal art. It also has displays relating to opal mining, and visitors can dig for their own opals.

🏛 **Underground Art Gallery**
Main St. **Tel** (08) 8672 5985.
⭕ daily. ⬤ 25 Dec. 📷 ♿

Witjira National Park ⓖ

ℹ️ *Pink Roadhouse, Oodnadatta (08) 8670 7822.* ⬭ *daily.* **Park Office** *1800 816 078.* ⬭ *24 hours. Desert Parks pass required.* 🕸️

About 200 km (125 miles) north of Coober Pedy lies the small town of Oodnadatta, where drivers can check the road and weather conditions before heading further north to Witjira National Park.

Witjira has dunes, saltpans, boulder plains and coolibah woodlands, but it is most famous for its hot artesian springs. Dalhousie Springs has more than 60 active springs with warm water rising from the Great Artesian Basin. These springs supply essential water for Aborigines, pastoralists and wildlife, including water snails, unique to the area.

Simpson Desert Conservation Park ⓰

ℹ️ *Pink Roadhouse, Oodnadatta (08) 8670 7822.* ⬭ *daily. Desert Parks pass required.* **Park Office** *1800 816 078.* ⬭ *24 hours.* 🕸️

The Simpson Desert Conservation Park is at the very top of South Australia, adjoining both Queensland and the Northern Territory. It is an almost endless series of sand dunes, lakes, spinifex grassland and gidgee woodland.

The landscape is home to some 180 bird, 92 reptile and 44 native mammal species, some of which have developed nocturnal habits as a response to the aridity of the region.

Dunes stretching to the horizon in Simpson Desert Conservation Park

Lake Eyre National Park ⓱

ℹ️ *Coober Pedy, (08) 8672 5298.* ⬭ *Mon–Fri.* ⬤ *public hols.* **Park Office** *1800 816 078.* ⬭ *24 hours.* 🕸️

Lake Eyre National Park encompasses all of Lake Eyre North and extends eastwards into the Tirari Desert. Lake Eyre is Australia's largest salt lake, 15 m (49 ft) below sea level at its lowest point, with a salt crust said to weigh 400 million tonnes. Vegetation is low, comprising mostly blue bush, samphire and saltbush. On the rare occasions when the lake floods, it alters dramatically: flowers bloom and birds such as pelicans and gulls appear, turning the lake into a breeding ground.

Flinders Ranges ⓲

🚂 *Hawker, Wilpena.* ℹ️ *Wilpena (08) 8648 0048.* ⬭ *daily.* **Park Office** *(08) 8648 0049.* 🕸️

The Flinders Ranges extend for 400 km (250 miles) from Crystal Brook, just north of the Clare Valley, far into South Australia's Outback.

A favourite with bushwalkers, the ranges encompass a great diversity of stunning scenery and wildlife, much of it protected in several national parks.

In the southern part of the Flinders Ranges is Mount Remarkable National Park, renowned for its fine landscape, abundant wildflowers and excellent walking trails.

About 50 km (30 miles) north of here is the town of Quorn, start of the restored Pichi Richi Railway. North of Quorn lie the dramatic Warren, Yarrah Vale and Buckaring gorges.

Much of the central Flinders Ranges are contained within the Flinders Ranges National Park. This beautiful park's best-known feature is Wilpena Pound, an elevated natural basin covering some 90 sq km (35 sq miles) with sheer outer walls 500 m (1,600 ft) high.

To the north is Gammon Ranges National Park, with mountain bushwalking for the experienced only. Just outside the park is **Arkaroola**, a tourist village with a wildlife sanctuary and a state-of-the-art observatory.

🔭 Arkaroola
Via Wilpena or Leigh Creek. **Tel** *1800 676 042.* ⬭ *daily.* 🕸️ *for tours.*

Shimmering expanse of Lake Eyre, the largest salt lake in Australia

VICTORIA

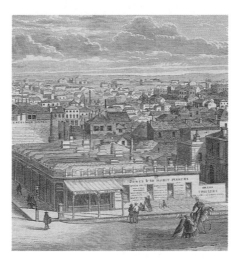

Victoria at a Glance

The state of Victoria can be easily divided into two distinct geographical halves, east and west. Western Victoria is known for its unusual landforms, including the Grampians and the Twelve Apostles. It was also the site of Australia's wealthiest gold rush during the 19th century, the legacy of which can be seen in the ornate buildings in the many surviving gold rush towns *(see pp54–5)*. Eastern Victoria's cooler climate benefits the vineyards that produce world-class wines, while the Alps are Victoria's winter playground. The rugged coastline is known for its lakes, forests and wildlife. Melbourne, the state's capital, is the second most populous city in Australia.

WESTERN VICTORIA
(see pp422–37)

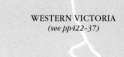

Halls Gap *is the main entrance to the Grampians National Park* (see p427). *This beautiful area is filled with dramatic rock formations, spectacular ridges and wildflowers unique to the region.*

Ballarat's *Arch of Victory on the Avenue of Honour commemorates the soldiers of World War I. It is also the western entrance to this provincial city, which grew up during the 1850s gold rush* (see pp434–5).

The Twelve Apostles *is the evocative name given to these eroded limestone rock formations in Port Campbell National Park, seen from the Great Ocean Road* (see pp428–9). *Sunset is the best time to fully appreciate the view.*

Tahbilk Wines *is one of the best known of all the northeastern Victorian vineyards, not only for its excellent wines but also for the pagoda-style architecture of its winery. Eastern Victoria's cool climate has led to a range of successful wineries (see pp450–51).*

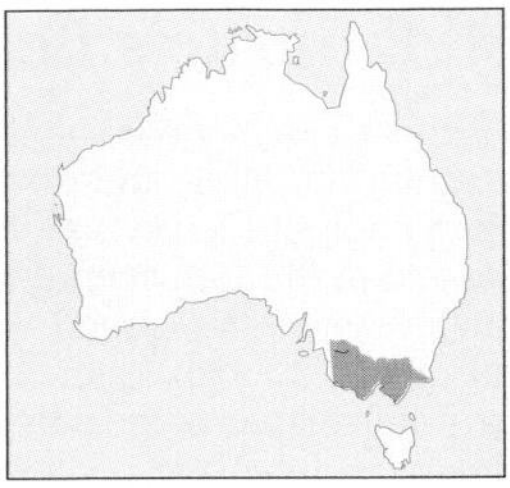

The Victorian Alps *come into their own during the winter months as a premier ski area (see p446).*

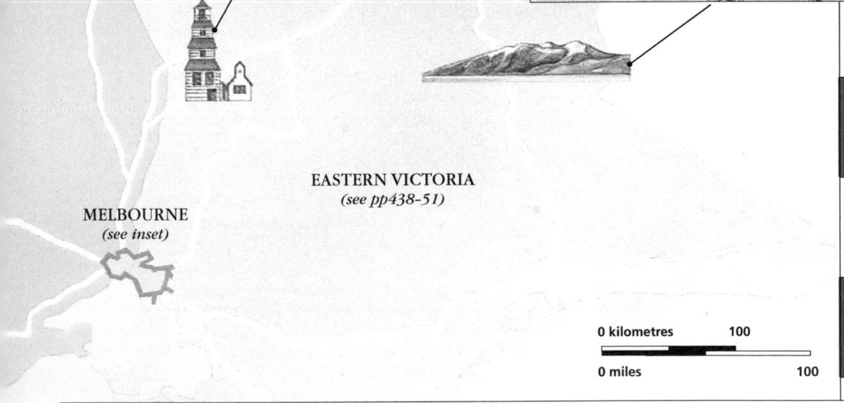

EASTERN VICTORIA
(see pp438–51)

MELBOURNE
(see inset)

0 kilometres 100

0 miles 100

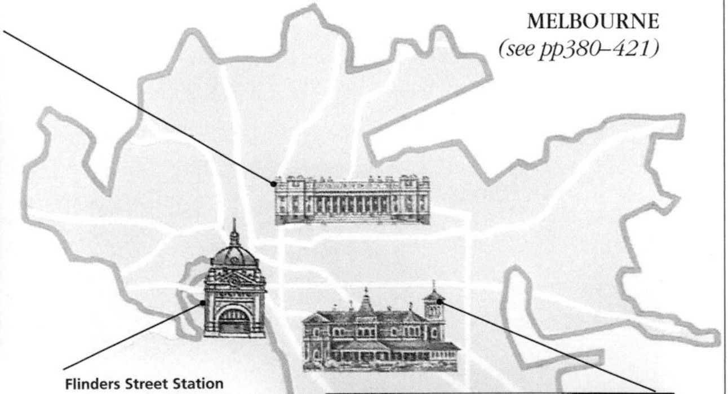

MELBOURNE
(see pp380–421)

Parliament House *in Melbourne, begun in 1856, is one of the city's finest surviving public buildings (see pp392–3).*

Flinders Street Station is the main rail terminus, set in a fine 19th-century edifice *(see p402).*

Rippon Lea's *ornamental garden is an impressive feature of this 19th-century home (see pp404–5).*

0 km 2

0 miles 2

Melbourne's Best: Parks and Gardens

Visitors to Melbourne should not miss the city's magnificent public and private gardens. A large proportion of the city's parks and gardens were created in the 19th century and have a gracious quality which has earned Victoria the nickname of Australia's "Garden State". Central Melbourne is ringed by public gardens, including the outstanding Royal Botanic Gardens, visited by more than 1.6 million people each year. Melbourne also has a network of public parks which offer a mix of native flora and fauna with recreational activities. The annual Open Garden Scheme *(see p40)* allows visitors into some of the best private gardens in Victoria and Australia.

Statue of Queen Victoria in her eponymous gardens

LANDSCAPE GARDENS

Melbourne abounds with carefully planned and formal 19th-century gardens, designed by prominent landscape gardeners.

A variety of trees from all over the world lines the formal avenues of **Carlton Gardens**, designed in 1857 by Edward La Trobe Bateman. The aim of the design was for every path and flowerbed to focus attention on the Exhibition Building, constructed in 1880 *(see p395)*. The main entrance path leads from Victoria Street to the Hochgurtel Fountain, in front of the Exhibition Building, decorated on its upper tier

Statue of Simpson and his donkey in Kings Domain

with stone birds and flowers which are indigenous to the state of Victoria.

The attractive **Fitzroy Gardens** in the heart of the city were also first designed by Bateman in 1856. His original plans were later revised by a Scotsman, James Sinclair, to make them more sympathetic to the area's uneven landscape. The avenues of elms that lead in to the centre of the gardens from the surrounding streets create the shape of the Union Jack flag and are one of the most distinctive features of the gardens *(see pp392–3)*. Fitzroy Gardens' Conservatory is renowned for its five popular annual plant shows.

The **Queen Victoria Gardens** are considered one of the city's most attractive gardens. They were created as a setting for a new statue of the queen, four years after her death, in 1905. Roses now surround the statue. A floral clock near St Kilda Road was given to Melbourne by Swiss watchmakers in 1966. It is embedded with some 7,000 flowering plants.

Kings Domain *(see p398)*, established in 1854, was the dream of a German botanist, Baron von Mueller, who designed this impressive garden. The garden is dominated by elegant statues, including one of Simpson, a stretcher bearer during World War I, with his faithful donkey. The Shrine of Remembrance and Government House are located here.

BOTANIC GARDENS

Begun in 1846, the **Royal Botanic Gardens** now cover 36 ha (90 acres). Botanist Baron von Mueller became the director of the gardens in 1857 and began to plant both indigenous and exotic shrubs on the site, intending the gardens to be a scientific aid to fellow biologists. Von Mueller's successor, William Guilfoyle, made his own mark on the

Conservatory of flowers in Fitzroy Gardens

Ornamental lake in the Royal Botanic Gardens

WHERE TO FIND THE PARKS AND GARDENS

Alexandra Gardens **Map** 3 A2.
Carlton Gardens **Map** 2 D1.
Fawkner Park **Map** 3 C5.
Fitzroy Gardens **Map** 2 E2.
Flagstaff Gardens **Map** 1 A2.
Kings Domain *pp398–9.*
Princes Park, Royal Parade, Carlton.
Queen Victoria Gardens **Map** 2 D4.
Royal Botanic Gardens *pp398–9.*
Treasury Gardens **Map** 2 E3.
Yarra Park **Map** 2 F3.

design, by adding wide paths across the gardens and an ornamental lake.

Today, the gardens are home to more than 10,000 plant species *(see pp398–9).*

RECREATIONAL GARDENS AND PARKS

Melburnians are avid sports participants as well as spectators, and many of the city's gardens offer a range of sporting facilities in attractive surroundings.

Flagstaff Gardens take their name from the site's role as a signalling station from 1840, warning of ships arriving in the Port of Melbourne. In the 1880s, with advances in communication, this role was no longer required and gardens were laid out on the land instead. Today the gardens are used for their recreational facilities, which include tennis courts, a children's playground and a barbecue area.

The **Alexandra Gardens** were designed in 1904 as a riverside walk along the Yarra River. Today, as well as the major thoroughfare of Alexandra Avenue, there is an equestrian path, a cycle path, boat sheds and barbecue facilities.

The **Treasury Gardens** were designed in 1867 and are lined along its avenues with Moreton Bay Figs, which offer very welcome shade in the summer heat. The location in the centre of the city makes these gardens very popular with office workers during their lunch breaks. The gardens also host regular evening concerts and other entertainment gatherings.

Established in 1856, **Yarra Park** is today home to the city's most well-known sports ground, the impressive Melbourne Cricket Ground *(see p397).* The wood and bark of the indigenous river red gums in the park were once used for canoes and shields by local Aborigines and many still bear the scars.

Fawkner Park, named after Melbourne's co-founder, John Pascoe Fawkner *(see pp52–3),* was laid out in 1862 and became a large sports ground in the 1890s. Despite a temporary role as a camp site for the Armed Services during World War II, the 40 ha (100 acres) of the park are still used for cricket, football, hockey and softball games.

Another popular sporting area with Melburnians is **Princes Park**. Two sports pavilions were constructed in 1938, as were two playing fields. The park now contains a football oval and the unique "Fun and Fitness Centre", a jogging track lined with exercise equipment at stages along its 3-km (1.8-mile) route. A gravel running track was also added in 1991.

Cricket match in progress in Fawkner Park

Melbourne's Best: Architecture

In 1835, Melbourne was a village of tents and imper-
manent dwellings. Fed by the wealth of the 1850s'
gold rush and the economic boom of the 1880s, it
rapidly acquired many graceful buildings. Today, the
city's architecture is very eclectic, with a strong
Victorian element. The range of architectural styles is
impressive, from beautiful restorations to outstanding
contemporary novelties. The city's tallest building is
the Eureka Tower, which is 300 m (985 ft) high.

Early colonial Cook's Cottage

EARLY COLONIAL

In colonial days, it was
quite common for small
edifices, such as La Trobe's
Cottage, to be shipped
from England as skilled
builders were in short
supply. Other imported
structures included timber
cottages and corrugated
iron dwellings.

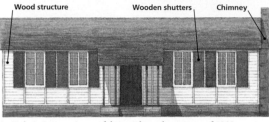

Wood structure   **Wooden shutters**   **Chimney**

La Trobe's Cottage *is a prefabricated wooden cottage of 1839.*

HIGH VICTORIAN

During the 19th century, Melbourne erected several grand state
buildings equal to those in the USA and Europe. State Parliament
House, begun in 1856, included a central dome in its original
design which was omitted due to lack of funds *(see p392)*. South
of the city is the 1934 Shrine of Remembrance, which demonstrates the 20th century's yearning for classical roots *(p398)*.

Detail of Parliament House

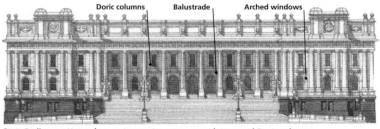

Doric columns   **Balustrade**   **Arched windows**

State Parliament House *has an impressive entrance with its grand Doric columns*

Cast-iron lacework at Tasma Terrace

TERRACE HOUSING

Terrace houses with cast-iron lace balconies
were popular during the Victorian era. Tasma
Terrace (1878) was designed by Charles
Webb and is unusual for its three-storey
houses, double-storey being more typical.

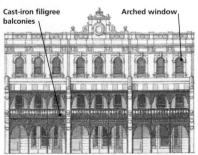

**Cast-iron filigree
balconies**   **Arched window**

Tasma Terrace *is now home to the National Trust.*

MODERNISM AND POST-MODERNISM

The latter half of the 20th century has seen a range of post-modern buildings erected in Melbourne. The National Gallery of Victoria was designed by Sir Roy Grounds *(see p402)* and completed in 1968 (further modified in 2003 by Mario Bellini). It was the first time bluestone, widely used in the 19th century, was used in a modern structure. The stained-glass ceiling of the Great Hall was designed by Leonard French.

Melbourne's unique bluestone used in the walls of the National Gallery of Victoria

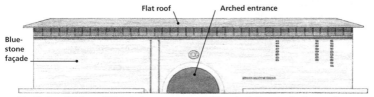

Flat roof   Arched entrance

Blue-stone façade

The National Gallery of Victoria *has a monumental façade, impressive for its smooth simplicity and lack of ornamental details.*

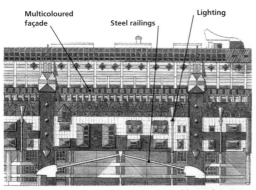

Multicoloured façade   Steel railings   Lighting

Royal Melbourne Institute of Technology's *Building 8 façade is a complex blend of bright colours and diverse shapes.*

CONTEMPORARY

Melbourne is known for its vibrant, experimental architecture scene. Some of the most radical Australian buildings of the 1990s can be found here. The Royal Melbourne Institute of Technology's Building 8 was designed by Peter Corrigan and completed in 1993. The building's interior and façade is both gaudy and Gaudían, with its bold use of primary colours. Whatever your view, it cannot help but attract the attention of every visitor to the northern end of the city.

SPORTS ARCHITECTURE

Melbourne's modern architecture clearly reflects the importance of sport to its citizens. Rod Laver Arena at Melbourne Park, opened in 1988, has a retractable roof, a world first, and seats more than 15,000 people.

Aerial view of Melbourne Park, with Rod Laver Arena on the left

WHERE TO FIND THE BUILDINGS

La Trobe's Cottage
p399.
National Gallery of Victoria
p403.
Rod Laver Arena at Melbourne Park **Map** 2 E4.
Royal Melbourne Institute of Technology's Building 8, Swanston Street.
Map 1 C2.
Shrine of Remembrance
p398.
State Parliament House
p392.
Tasma Terrace,
Parliament Place.
Map 2 E2.

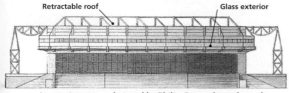

Retractable roof   Glass exterior

Rod Laver Arena *was designed by Philip Cox and now hosts the annual Australian Open tennis championships.*

Wines of Victoria

Victoria has approximately 850 wineries located in 21 distinct wine regions, some easily reached in less than an hour by car from the state capital, Melbourne. The northeast is famous for its unique fortified Muscats and Tokays (often described as liquid toffee), while from the cooler south come silky Chardonnays and subtle Pinot Noirs. There is no better way to enjoy Victorian wine than in one of the many restaurants and bistros in cosmopolitan Melbourne *(see pp552–6).*

Best's *is one of the oldest family-owned wineries in Australia. This producer makes excellent Shiraz, Merlot, Dolcetto and Riesling wines. Self-guided tours of its 130-year-old wooden cellar are free and available every day.*

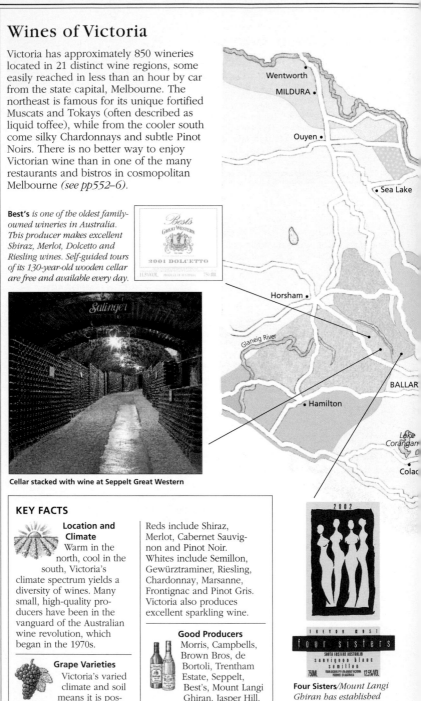

Cellar stacked with wine at Seppelt Great Western

KEY FACTS

Location and Climate
Warm in the north, cool in the south, Victoria's climate spectrum yields a diversity of wines. Many small, high-quality producers have been in the vanguard of the Australian wine revolution, which began in the 1970s.

Reds include Shiraz, Merlot, Cabernet Sauvignon and Pinot Noir. Whites include Semillon, Gewürztraminer, Riesling, Chardonnay, Marsanne, Frontignac and Pinot Gris. Victoria also produces excellent sparkling wine.

Grape Varieties
Victoria's varied climate and soil means it is possible to grow a full range of grape varieties.

Good Producers
Morris, Campbells, Brown Bros, de Bortoli, Trentham Estate, Seppelt, Best's, Mount Langi Ghiran, Jasper Hill, Yarra Yering, Coldstream Hills, Tahbilk Wines, Mitchelton.

Four Sisters/*Mount Langi Ghiran has established itself as a pioneer by winemaker Trevor Mast.*

HOW VICTORIA'S FAMOUS MUSCATS AND TOKAYS ARE MADE

Brown Muscat and Muscadelle grapes are picked late, when they are at their sweetest, to produce fine Muscats and Tokays respectively. Once the grapes have been crushed, the resulting juice is often fermented in traditional open concrete tanks which have been in use for generations. The wine is then fortified with top-quality grape spirit, which will give it an ultimate alcohol strength of around 18.5 per cent. The solera system, in which young vintages are blended with older ones, gives more depth to the wines and also ensures that they retain a consistent quality. Some wineries, such as Morris, use a base wine combined with vintages going back more than a century. The flavour of wine in the oldest barrel is so intense that one teaspoon can add a new dimension to 200 l (45 gal) of base wine.

Mick Morris sampling his famous Muscat from barrels

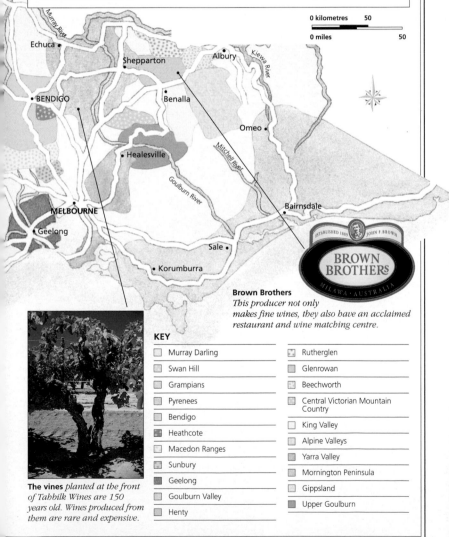

0 kilometres 50

0 miles 50

Brown Brothers
This producer not only makes fine wines, they also have an acclaimed restaurant and wine matching centre.

The vines *planted at the front of Tabbilk Wines are 150 years old. Wines produced from them are rare and expensive.*

KEY

- Murray Darling
- Swan Hill
- Grampians
- Pyrenees
- Bendigo
- Heathcote
- Macedon Ranges
- Sunbury
- Geelong
- Goulburn Valley
- Henty
- Rutherglen
- Glenrowan
- Beechworth
- Central Victorian Mountain Country
- King Valley
- Alpine Valleys
- Yarra Valley
- Mornington Peninsula
- Gippsland
- Upper Goulburn

MELBOURNE

J ohn Batman, the son of a Sydney convict, arrived in what is now known as the Port Phillip district in 1835 and met with Aboriginal tribes of the Kulin, from whom he "purchased" the land. In just over two decades Melbourne grew from a small tent encampment to a sprawling metropolis. Today it is thriving as the second-largest city in Australia.

Melbourne's rapid growth was precipitated in the 1850s by the huge influx of immigrants seeking their fortunes on the rich gold fields of Victoria. This caused a population explosion of unprecedented proportions as prospectors decided to stay in the city. The enormous wealth generated by the gold rush led to the construction of grand public buildings. This development continued throughout the land boom of the 1880s, earning the city the nickname "Marvellous Melbourne". By the end of the 19th century, the city was the industrial and financial capital of Australia. It was also the home of the national parliament until 1927, when it was moved to purpose-built Canberra (see p191).

Fortunate enough to escape much damage in World War II, Melbourne hosted the summer Olympics in 1956. Dubbed the "Friendly Games", the event generated great changes in the city's consciousness. The postwar period also witnessed a new wave of immigrants who sought better lives here. Driven by the will to succeed, they introduced Melburnians to a range of cultures, transforming the British traditions of the city. This transformation continues today with the arrival of immigrants from all parts of Asia.

Melbourne holds many surprises: it has the most elaborate Victorian architecture of all Australian cities; it has a celebrated range of restaurant cuisines and its calendar revolves around hugely popular spectator sports and arts events (see pp40–41). While the climate is renowned for its unpredictability, Melburnians still enjoy an outdoor lifestyle, and the city possesses a unique charm that quietly bewitches many visitors.

Melbourne's café society relaxing along Brunswick Street

◁ Flinders Street Station and St Paul's Cathedral, seen from Queens Bridge

Exploring Melbourne

Melbourne is organized informally into precincts.
Collins Street is a business centre and the site of the
city's smartest stores. To the east is the parliamentary
precinct. Swanston Street contains some fine Victorian architecture. The south bank of the river is arts-
orientated and includes the Victorian Arts Centre. The
city also devotes much land to parks and gardens.

**Eureka Tower and Melbourne
skyline**

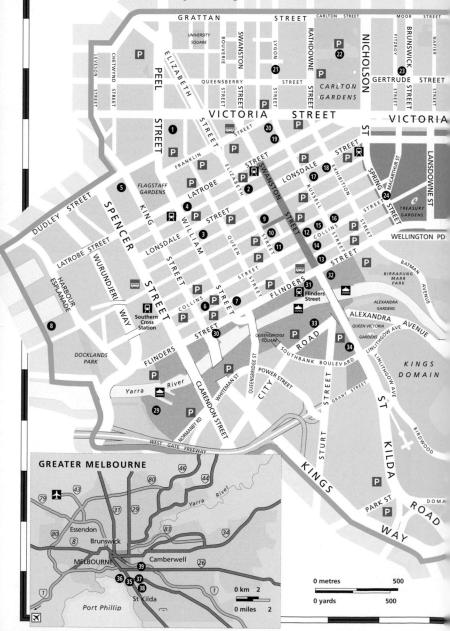

GRATTAN   STREET   CARLTON   STREET   MOOR   STREET

UNIVERSITY
SQUARE

QUEENSBERRY   STREET

VICTORIA   STREET   — VICTORIA

FLAGSTAFF
GARDENS

CARLTON
GARDENS

FRANKLIN   STREET

LATROBE   STREET

LONSDALE   STREET

DUDLEY   STREET

SPENCER   STREET

COLLINS   STREET

FLINDERS   STREET

Southern
Cross
Station

DOCKLANDS
PARK

HARBOUR   ESPLANADE

Yarra   River

WEST GATE FREEWAY

TREASURY
GARDENS

WELLINGTON PD

BATMAN
AVENUE

BIRRARUNG
MARR
PARK

ALEXANDRA
GARDENS

QUEEN VICTORIA
GARDENS

KINGS
DOMAIN

LINLITHGOW   AVENUE

KINGS   KILDA   ROAD   WAY

PARK ST   DOMA

GREATER MELBOURNE

Essendon
Brunswick

MELBOURNE   Camberwell

St Kilda

Port Phillip

Yarra   River

0 km   2

0 miles   2

| 0 metres | | 500 |
| 0 yards | | 500 |

For additional map symbols *see back flap*

GETTING AROUND

Despite the comprehensive Metlink transport system of trams, trains and buses, many Melburnians use cars for commuting *(see pp412–13)*. This has resulted in a network of major roads and highways that lead in all directions from Melbourne's central grid through inner and outer suburbs. CityLink is a tollway linking several of the city's major access routes; drivers must purchase a pass in advance of travelling on CityLink roads. The city's flat landscape is also well suited to bicycles.

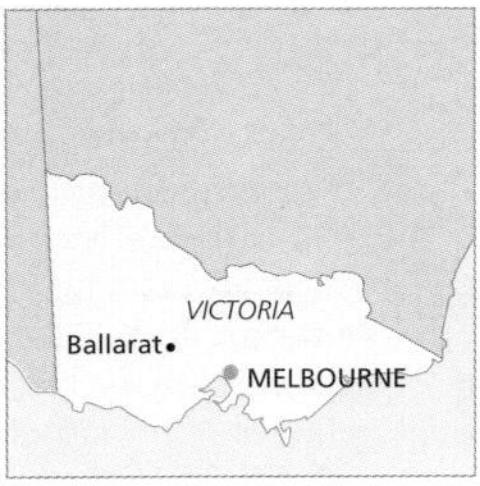

LOCATOR MAP

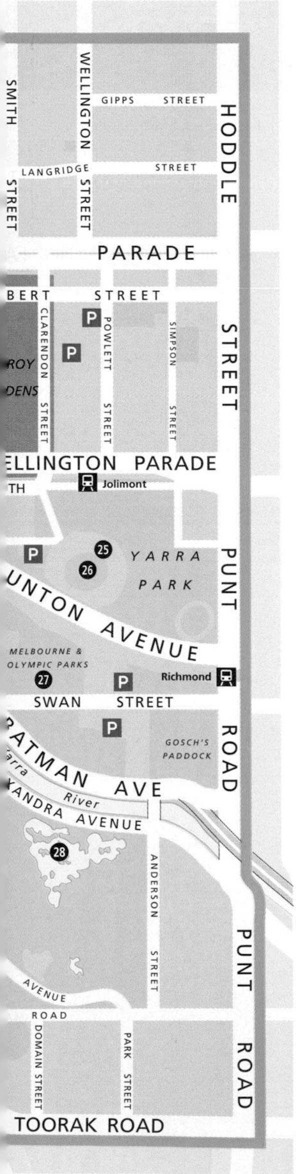

SIGHTS AT A GLANCE

Historic Streets and Buildings

Brunswick Street & Fitzroy 23
Chapel Street 37
Chinatown 17
Como Historic House and Garden 39
Docklands 8
Federation Square 32
Fitzroy & Acland streets 35
Flinders Street Station 31
General Post Office 9
Lygon Street 21
Melbourne Town Hall 12
No. 120 Collins Street 16
Old Magistrate's Court 19
Old Melbourne Gaol 20
Regent Theatre 14
Rippon Lea pp404–5 38
Royal Exhibition Building 22
Royal Mint 4
Supreme Court 3

Shops and Markets

Block Arcade 11
Queen Victoria Market 1
Royal Arcade 10

Churches and Cathedrals

St Francis' Church 2
St James' Old Cathedral 5
St Paul's Cathedral 13
Scots' Church 15

Museums and Galleries

City Museum 24
Immigration Museum 7
Melbourne Aquarium 30
Melbourne Maritime Museum 29
Melbourne Museum 22
Museum of Chinese Australian History 18
National Gallery of Victoria 34
National Sports Museum 25

Parks and Gardens

Royal Botanic Gardens and Kings Domain pp398–9 28

Modern Architecture

Eureka Tower 33
Rialto Towers 6

Sports Grounds

Albert Park 36
Melbourne Cricket Ground 26
Melbourne Park 27

SEE ALSO

• ***Street Finder*** pp416–21
• ***Where to Stay*** pp505–9
• ***Where to Eat*** pp552–6

KEY

Swanston Street Precinct *see pp384–5*
Street-by-Street map *see pp392–3*
The Yarra River *see pp400–1*
Bus station
Train station
[P] Car park
River boat stop
Domestic Airport

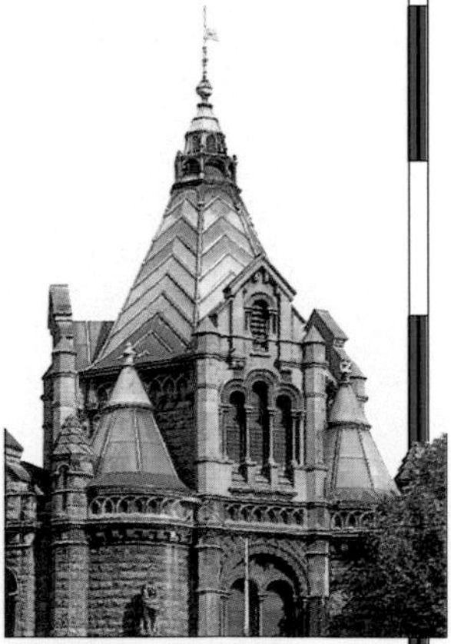

Gothic turrets of the Old Magistrate's Court

Swanston Street Precinct

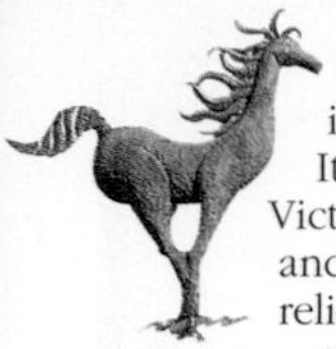

Swanston Street sculpture

Swanston Street, home to Melbourne's town hall and other major civic buildings, has always been a hub of the city. It is an eclectic illustration of the city's Victorian and 20th-century public architecture and exemplary of one of the most interesting relics of Melbourne: an ordered grid of broad, evenly measured and rectilinear streets, lanes and arcades. The area between Flinders Street and La Trobe Street is a pedestrian precinct until 7pm, though pedestrians should still watch out for trams and cyclists.

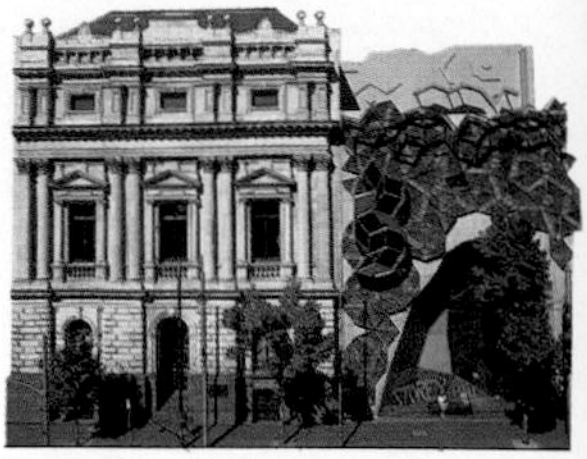

Classically inspired Storey Hall, neighbour of the RMIT Building

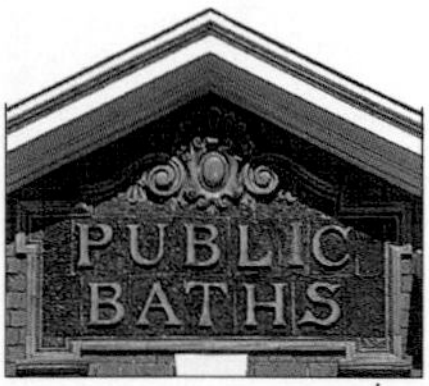
PUBLIC
BATHS

The City Baths are set in a beautiful Edwardian building with twin cupolas as a distinctive feature. They have been carefully restored to their original 1903 condition.

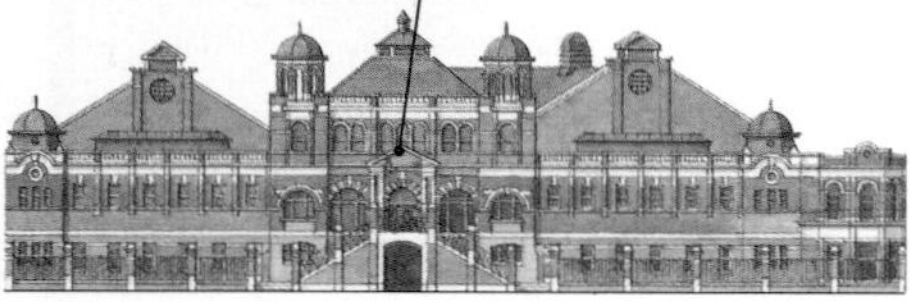

1 **City Baths**

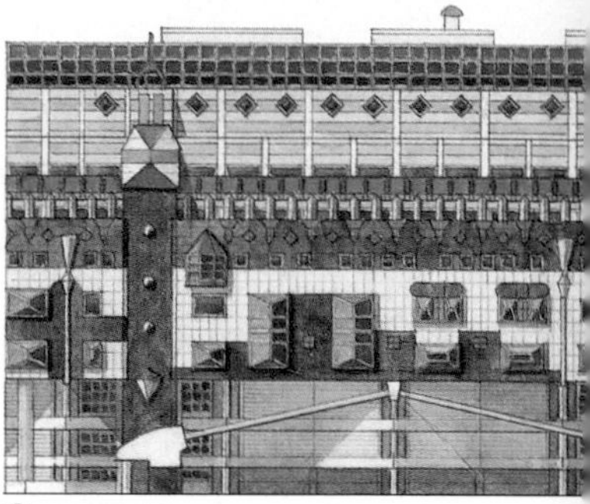

2 **RMIT Building 8**

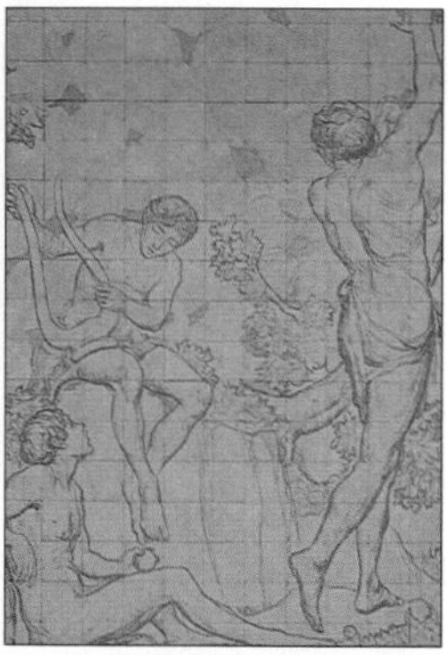

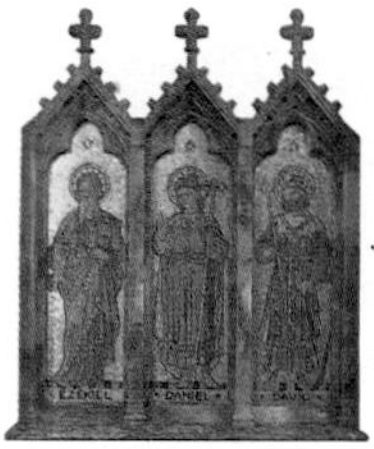

St Paul's Cathedral
Architect William Butterfield designed St Paul's in a Gothic Revival style in the 1880s 13

Melbourne Town Hall
The city's town hall was built in 1867, funded by proceeds of the gold rush (see pp54–5) 12

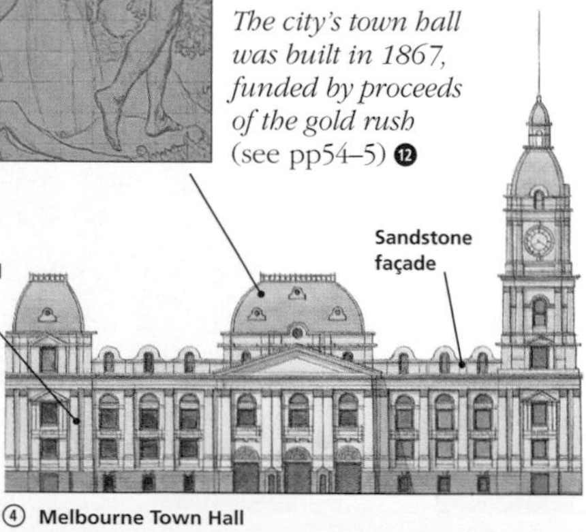
Neo-Classical columns
Sandstone façade

4 **Melbourne Town Hall**

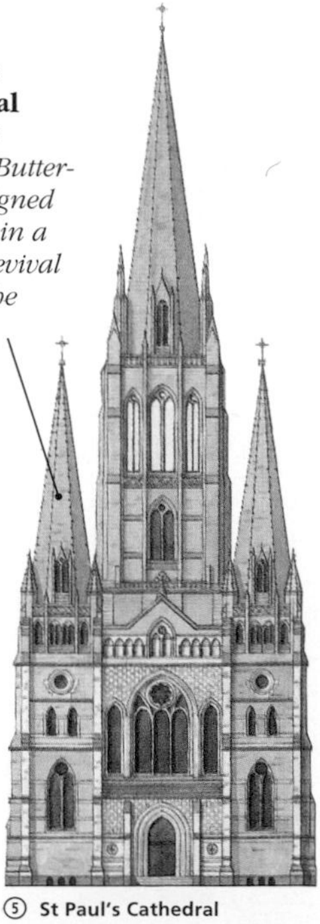

5 **St Paul's Cathedral**

Building 8, RMIT (Royal Melbourne Institute of Technology), is a gaudy, contemporary blend of bold, primary colours utilized within horizontal and vertical lines. It was met with very mixed reviews by Melburnians when it was completed.

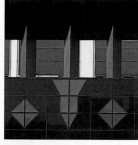

LOCATOR MAP
See Melbourne Street Finder, Map 1

The State Library was the first design by noted architect Joseph Reed in 1854. Inside is an attractive octagonal reading room, covered by the central dome which was added in 1913.

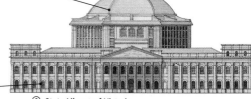

Neo-Classical Corinthian columns line the façade.

③ **State Library of Victoria**

Flinders Street Station
Melbourne's busiest rail terminus is one of the most recognizable sights in the city ㉛

Young and Jackson's, a 19th-century hotel known for its nude portrait *Chloe*, is protected by the National Trust.

The Atrium in Federation Square is a remarkable building made of glass, steel and zinc. The Square itself has become the cultural centre of the city, with its restaurants, various attractions and outdoor events.

Station clock

⑥ **Flinders Street Station**

⑦ **Young and Jackson's**

⑧ **Federation Square**

Fruit stall in Queen Victoria Market

Queen Victoria Market ❶

Elizabeth, Therry, Peel & Victoria sts. **Map** 1 B2. **Tel** (03) 9320 5822. ▣ *Flagstaff & Melbourne Central (Elizabeth St exit).* ▦ *Elizabeth St routes.* ◯ *6am–2pm Tue & Thu; 6am–6pm Fri; 6am–3pm Sat; 9am–4pm Sun.* ◉ *1 Jan, Good Fri, 25 Apr, 1st Tue in Nov, 25–26 Dec.* ♿ ▨

Melbourne's main fresh produce and general goods market has a strange history, occupying the site of the original Melbourne General Cemetery, which was first used in 1837. In 1877, the idea of converting part of the original cemetery into a marketplace for fruit and vegetables was considered a practical one. At the time, it involved the relocation of only three graves. However, the choice created controversy which did not settle down for some time, as the market's popularity made it necessary to acquire further portions of the cemetery. In 1917, an act of Parliament granted the removal of 10,000 remains and the cemetery was razed.

The market began with the construction of the Wholesale Meat Market. In 1884, the Meat Market and Elizabeth Street shop façades were built. Further extensions continued to be built until 1936. Today the complex, occupying 7 ha (17 acres), attracts 130,000 visitors per week. Its decorative high-vaulted ceilings and open sides add to its ornate atmosphere. About 1,000 stalls sell fresh fruit and vegetables,

fish, meat, cheese, organic food and souvenirs and clothing. Every Wednesday from November to February there is a Night Market (5:30–10pm), with theatrical performances.

St Francis' Church ❷

326 Lonsdale St. **Map** 1 C2. **Tel** (03) 9663 2495. ▣ *Melbourne Central.* ▦ *Elizabeth St routes.* ◯ *7am–6:30pm daily.* ♿ ▨ *by arrangement.*

St Francis' Church today is Australia's busiest Roman Catholic church, with 10,000 visitors each week. Built between 1841 and 1845 on the site of an earlier church, it is also Victoria's oldest.

Renowned for its beauty, the church began as a simple Neo-Gothic building and has undergone many alterations. It was the target of a $2.8 million restoration appeal, and major renovations were completed in the early 1990s.

During the ceiling restoration, treasures from the 1860s, such as a painting of angels, stars and a coat of arms, were discovered and beautifully restored. Vandalized statues have since been replaced by faithful copies.

The church holds regular services, and has one of Australia's most celebrated resident choirs.

Roof detail of St Francis' Church

Supreme Court ❸

210 William St. **Map** 1 B3. **Tel** (03) 9603 6111. ▣ *Flagstaff.* ▦ *City Circle & Bourke St routes.* ◯ *9:30am–4pm Mon–Fri (5pm Fri); courts sit 10am–4:15pm.* ♿ ⊘

When the Port Phillip district was still part of the New South Wales colony, criminal and important civil cases were heard in Sydney. To ease the inconvenience, Melbourne's first resident judge arrived in 1841 to set

Domed library in the Supreme Court

up a Supreme Court in the city. Following the Separation Act of 1851, which established the Colony of Victoria, the city set up its own Supreme Court in 1852. The court moved to the present building, with a design inspired by the Four Courts of Dublin in Ireland, in 1884.

The Supreme Court is an imposing building, with street façades on Lonsdale, William and Little Bourke streets. Its style is Classical, with a projecting portico and a double arcade with Doric and Ionic columns. Internally, a labyrinthine plan is centred on a beautiful domed library. The large bronze figure of Justice, defying tradition, is not blindfolded: rumour has it that an early Melbourne judge persuaded the authorities that Justice should be "wide-eyed if not innocently credulous". The Supreme Court Library is now classified by the National Trust.

Royal Mint ❹

280 William St. **Map** 1 B3. **Tel** 13 28 42. 🚇 Flagstaff. 🚋 24, 30. 🚌 Lonsdale & Queen sts routes. ⬤ to the public.

This former Mint, built between 1871 and 1872, contains two courts which were until recently used to cope with the overflow from the Supreme Court.

The building replaced Melbourne's first Exhibition Building, erected in 1854 and subsequently destroyed by fire. When the mint opened in 1872 it processed finds from the Victoria gold fields and was a branch of the Royal Mint of London. The actual coining processes took place in an area now occupied by the car park. After the Commonwealth of Australia was founded in 1901 (see p56), new silver coinage was designed, which the mint produced from 1916 to the mid-1960s. The Melbourne site ceased production in 1967 when the Royal Mint

Royal Mint crest

was relocated to Canberra. Although the Royal Mint building is now closed to the general public, visitors can still take in its imposing structure from the outside.

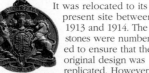

St James' Old Cathedral tower

St James' Old Cathedral ❺

Cnr King & Batman sts. **Map** 1 A2. **Tel** (03) 9329 0903. 🚇 Flagstaff. 🚋 24, 30, 48, 75. 🚌 220, 232. ⬤ 10am–4pm Mon–Fri; 10am service Sun. ⬤ public hols. ♿ 🎥 by appointment.

St James' was the first Anglican cathedral in the city, used until St Paul's opened in 1891 (see p389). It was first built near the corner of Little Collins and William streets to replace a wooden hut, known as the "Pioneers' Church". It was relocated to its present site between 1913 and 1914. The stones were numbered to ensure that the original design was replicated. However, a few changes were made, such as a lower ceiling, a shortening of the sanctuary and a reshaping of the bell tower.

St James' was designed in a colonial Georgian style. The foundations are made of bluestone and the main walls were constructed with local sandstone. The cathedral was opened for worship on 2 October 1842, but was not consecrated until 1853. Charles Perry, the city's first bishop,

was enthroned here in 1848. The cathedral is still used for regular services. A small museum contains photographs, historic documents and cathedral mementos.

Rialto Towers ❻

525 Collins St (between King and William sts). **Map** 1 B4. 🚇 Southern Cross Station. 🚋 Collins St routes. ⬤ 10am–10pm daily. 🎥 ♿ www.melbourne360rialto.com.au

Rialto Towers is a member of the World Federation of Great Towers. It has 58 floors above street level and 8 below. From street level up, it measures 253 m (830 ft).

The structure was built in 1986 by Australian developer Bruno Grollo, who was also responsible for the Eureka Tower (see p403). The former observation deck, on the 55th floor, is now the setting for the Vue de Monde restaurant. This fine establishment is one of the city's most spectacular places to dine, with panoramic views over Melbourne. The bar area is also open to non-diners.

The lift travels from the ground floor to the 55th floor in 38 seconds and is one of the fastest in the world.

The mighty Rialto Towers

General Post Office's magnificent and architecturally eclectic interior

Immigration Museum ❼

400 Flinders St. **Map** 1 B4. **Tel** 13 11 02. 🚉 *Southern Cross Station.* 🚃 *Collins St routes.* ◯ *10am–5pm daily.* ⬤ *Good Fri, 25 Dec.* 🖼 ♿

The Immigration Museum explores the stories – some sad, some funny, but all engaging – of real people from all over the world who have migrated to Victoria. Located in the Old Customs House, it uses moving images, personal and community memories, and memorabilia to recreate the journey and arrival of immigrants and to explore the impact of immigration on indigenous people.

Docklands ❽

Map 1 A4. **Tel** 1300 66 3008. 🚉 *Southern Cross Station.* 🚃 *City Circle 31, 48, 86.* 🚢 *236.* 🖼 *Yarra River Shuttle.* **www**.docklands.com

The spectacular redevelopment of Melbourne Docklands makes it worth visiting for the modern architecture alone.

The total redevelopment area is 200 hectares (490 acres), with 3 km (2 miles) of Yarra River frontage. The final stage of the project is to be completed in 2020. Docklands is also home to the Southern Star ferris wheel.

The area has a beautiful harbour and marina, magnificent public spaces, such as Harbour Esplanade, Grand Plaza and Docklands Park, historic wharves, urban art (by Australian artists such as Bruce Armstrong), shops and restaurants. It hosts events such as the Summer Boat Show and is home to Etihad Stadium where sports events are held.

General Post Office ❾

Cnr Little Bourke St Mall & Elizabeth St. **Map** 1 C3. **Tel** (03) 9663 0066. 🚉 *Flinders St & Melbourne Central.* 🚃 *Bourke & Elizabeth sts routes.* ◯ *10am–6pm Mon–Thu & Sat, 10am–8pm Fri, 11am–5pm Sun.* ⬤ *Good Fri, 25 Dec, 1 Jan.* ♿ *via Little Bourke St.* **www**.melbournesgpo.com

Melbourne's postal service moved to this site in 1841. The present structure was begun in 1859 and completed in 1907. The first and second floors were built between 1859 and 1867, with the third floor and clocktower added between 1885 and 1890. This has resulted in an unusual combination of styles, with Doric columns on the ground floor, Ionic on the second and Corinthian on the top level.

The building had a post-World War I redesign under the direction of architect Walter Burley Griffin *(see p197)*. It closed as a post office in 1993 and is now a shopping complex containing some of the biggest names in international and Australian fashion.

Royal Arcade entrance

Royal Arcade ❿

Elizabeth, Bourke & Little Collins sts. **Map** 1 C3. **Tel** (03) 9670 7777. 🚉 *Flinders St.* 🚃 *Bourke, Elizabeth & Collins sts routes.* ◯ *9am–6pm Mon–Thu, 9am–9pm Fri, 9am–5:30pm Sat, 10am–5pm Sun.*

Royal Arcade is Melbourne's oldest surviving arcade. It is part of a network of lanes and arcades which sprang up to divide the big blocks of the city grid into smaller segments. The network was designed in 1837 by the government surveyor, Robert Hoddle.

The original arcade, built in 1869 and designed by Charles Webb, runs between Bourke Street Mall and Little Collins Street. An annexe, with an entrance on Elizabeth Street, was added in 1902. A statue of Father Time, originally on

Docklands with the Etihad Stadium and the city's CBD in the background

For hotels and restaurants in this region see pp505–9 and pp552–6

the Bourke Street façade, is now located inside the arcade at the northern end.

The arcade's most famous inhabitants are statues of Gog and Magog, mythical representations of the conflict between the ancient Britons and the Trojans. They are modelled on identical figures in the Guildhall in the City of London. Between them is Gaunt's Clock, crafted by an original tenant of the arcade, Thomas Gaunt.

Block Arcade ⓫

282 Collins St. **Map** 1 C3. **Tel** (03) 9654 5244. 🚉 Flinders St. 🚋 Swanston & Collins sts routes. ⏱ 10am–5:30pm Mon–Sat, 11am–5pm Sun (not all shops). ⬤ Good Fri, 25 Dec. ♿ 🎫 Thu only, booking essential.

Built between 1891 and 1893, with period details including a mosaic floor and a central dome, Melbourne's most opulent arcade was named after the promenade taken by fashionable society in the 1890s. Known as "doing the block", the walk involved strolling down Collins Street between Elizabeth and Swanston streets.

The arcade was restored in 1988. It still includes the Hopetoun Tea-rooms, which have been in place since the structure was opened. Guided tours of the arcade are available.

Block Arcade façade

Chapel of Ascension in St Paul's Cathedral

Melbourne Town Hall ⓬

Swanston St. **Map** 1 C3. **Tel** (03) 9658 9658. 🚉 Flinders St. 🚋 Swanston & Collins sts routes. ⏱ 9am–6pm Mon–Fri, 9am–5pm Sat–Sun (ground level foyer only). ⬤ public hols. ♿ 🎫 11am & 1pm daily, obligatory for areas other than ground level foyer.

Melbourne Town Hall was completed in 1870, designed by Joseph Reed's company, Reed & Barnes. The portico was added in 1887. From here there are views of Swanston Street (see pp 384–5) and the Shrine of Remembrance in the Botanic Gardens (see p398).

An adjacent administration block and the council's second chamber were added in 1908. This chamber combines a Renaissance-style interior with uniquely Australian motifs, such as a ceiling plasterwork of gum nuts.

A fire in 1925 destroyed much of the building's interior, including the main hall which had to be rebuilt. The entrance to the building shows four motifs on the young city's coat of arms: a whale, a ship, a bull and a sheep, signifying the main colonial industries. In 1942, the College of Arms ordered an inversion of the motifs according to heraldic convention. This explains the discrepancy between earlier and later coats of arms.

Stained glass in Melbourne Town Hall

St Paul's Cathedral ⓭

Cnr Swanston & Flinders sts. **Map** 2 D3. **Tel** (03) 9653 4333. 🚉 Flinders St. 🚋 Swanston, Flinders & Collins sts routes. ⏱ 8:30am–6pm Sun–Fri, 9am–5pm Sat. ♿ 🎫

St Paul's Cathedral was built in 1866 to replace a far smaller church of the same name on the site.

Construction, however, was plagued by difficulties, with dissension between the English architect, William Butterfield, and the Cathedral Erection Board. Building began in 1880, but Butterfield tendered his resignation in 1884. The final stages of construction were supervised by the architect Joseph Reed, who also designed many of the fittings. The cathedral was eventually consecrated in 1891.

There are many outstanding internal features, including the *reredos* (altar screen) made in Italy from marble and alabaster inset with glass mosaics. The organ, made by TC Lewis & Co. of London, is the best surviving work of this great organ-builder. The cathedral also has a peal of 13 bells – a rarity outside the British Isles.

The cathedral underwent a five-year restoration, completed in 2009, which included the cleaning and upgrading of the spectacular stained-glass windows.

Regent Theatre ⓮

191 Collins St. **Map** 2 D3. **Tel** (03) 9299 9500. 🚉 Flinders St. 🚃 Swanston & Collins sts routes. &. 🏛 outside performance times. 🎭

When the Regent Theatre's auditorium was destroyed by fire in April 1945, the Lord Mayor of Melbourne promised the public that it would be rebuilt, despite the scarcity of building materials due to World War II. Such was the popularity and local importance of the theatre.

Known as "Melbourne's Palace of Dreams", it was first constructed and opened in 1929 and later sold to the Hoyts Theatre Company. Its lavish interiors emulated both the glamour of Hollywood and New York's impressive Capitol Theater.

The building had two main venues. The auditorium up-stairs, for live stage and musical entertainment, was known as the Regent Theatre. Down-stairs, the Plaza Theatre was originally a ballroom, but, following the success of the "talkies", it was converted into a cinema.

Fortunately, the magnificent decor of the Plaza Theatre was not damaged in the fire of 1945 and the renovated auditorium re-opened in 1947.

Assembly hall adjacent to Scots' Church

The advent of television soon resulted in dwindling cinema audiences, and the Regent Theatre closed for almost three decades. The complex was restored in 1996 and is now listed by the National Trust.

Scots' Church ⓯

99 Russell St (cnr Collins St). **Map** 2 D3. **Tel** (03) 9650 9903. 🚉 Flinders St & Parliament. 🚃 Swanston & Collins sts routes. ⊙ Mon–Fri (call to check times). 🏛 1pm, Wed; 11am & 7pm, Sun. &. 🏛 on request.

Scots' Church, completed in 1874, was intended at the time to be "the most beautiful building in Australia". It was designed by Joseph Reed in a "decorated Gothic" style, with bluestone used in the foundations and local Barrabool stone making up the superstructure.

The site also includes an assembly hall which was completed in 1913.

No. 120 Collins Street ⓰

120 Collins St. **Map** 2 D3. 🚉 Flinders St & Parliament. 🚃 Collins St routes. ⊙ 7am–7pm Mon–Fri. &.

Built in 1991, No. 120 Collins Street was designed by Daryl Jackson and Hassell Architects and houses the offices of many blue-chip corporations. In the heart of Melbourne's central business

Grandiose foyer of the Regent Theatre, restored to its original glory

For hotels and restaurants in this region see pp505–9 and pp552–6

district, the office block is now a city landmark. Its communications tower was for many years the highest point in the city, at 265 m (869 ft). Original 1908 Federation-style professional chambers, built on the grounds of the 1867 St Michael's Uniting Church, are incorporated into the building.

Chambers at No. 120 Collins Street

Chinatown ⓱

Little Bourke St. **Map** 2 D2. 🚉 Parliament. 🚃 Swanston & Bourke sts routes.

When Chinese immigrants began arriving in Melbourne to seek gold during the 1850s, many European residents were decidedly hostile. Only recent arrivals in the area themselves, they were still insecure about how strongly their own society had been established. This led to racial tension and violence.

The very first Chinese immigrants landed in Australia as early as 1818, but it was during the late 1840s that larger contingents arrived. These newcomers replaced the pool of cheap labour which had dried up with the winding down of convict settlements in the new colonies. This wave of immigration was harmonious until the vast influx of Chinese visitors who came not for labour, but to seek their fortune in the Victorian gold fields in the 1850s. The large numbers of

immigrants and a decline in gold finds made the Chinese targets of vicious and organized riots.

This attitude was sanctioned by government policy. The Chinese were charged a poll tax in most states of £10 each – a huge sum, particularly as many were peasants. Even harsher was a restriction on the number of passengers that boat-owners could carry. This acted as a disincentive for them to bring Chinese immigrants to Australia. What resulted were "Chinese marathons", as new arrivals dodged the tax by landing in "free" South Australia and walking to the gold fields, covering distances of up to 800 km (500 miles) *(see pp54–5)*.

As an immigrant society in Melbourne, the Chinese were highly organized and self-sufficient. A city base was established during the 1850s, utilizing the cheap rental district of the city centre. As with other Chinatowns around the world, traders could live and work in the same premises and act as a support network for other Chinese immigrants. The community largely avoided prejudice by starting up traditional Asian businesses which included market gardening, laundering, green grocers and furniture-making (but work had to be stamped "Made by Chinese labour").

Stone lion in the Museum of Chinese Australian History

Traditional gateway in Little Bourke Street, Chinatown

Today, Chinatown is known for its restaurants and Chinese produce shops, with the community's calendar culminating in its New Year celebrations in January or February *(see p41)*. Ironically, in view of the early prejudices, this community is now one of Australia's oldest and most successful.

Museum of Chinese Australian History ⓲

22 Cohen Place (off Little Bourke St). **Map** 2 D2. **Tel** (03) 9662 2888. 🚉 Parliament. 🚃 Swanston & Bourke sts routes. ◯ 10am–5pm daily. ● Good Fri, 25 Dec, 1 Jan. 🈲️ ♿ ☑️ www.chinesemuseum.com.au

Opened in 1985 to preserve the heritage of Australians of Chinese descent, this museum is in the heart of Chinatown. The subjects of its displays range from the influx of Chinese gold-seekers in the 1850s to exhibitions of contemporary Chinese art, thus offering a comprehensive history of the Chinese in Victoria and their cultural background. The second floor holds regular touring exhibitions from China and displays of Chinese art. On the third floor is a permanent exhibition covering many aspects of Chinese-Australian history, including elaborate costumes, furniture and temple regalia.

In the basement, another permanent exhibition traces the experiences of Chinese gold miners – visitors step into a booth which creaks and moves like a transport ship, then view dioramas of gold field life, a Chinese temple and a tent theatre used by Chinese performers to entertain miners. A guided heritage walk through Chinatown is also available.

The museum also houses the beautiful Melbourne Chinese dragon, the head of which is the largest of its kind anywhere in the world.

Street-by-Street: Parliament Area

St Patrick's Cathedral icon

The Parliament precinct on Eastern Hill is a gracious area of great historic interest. Early founders of the city noted the favourable aspect of the hill and set it aside for Melbourne's official and ecclesiastical buildings. The streets still retain the elegance of the Victorian era; the buildings, constructed with revenue from the gold rush *(see pp54–5)*, are among the most impressive in the city. The Fitzroy Gardens, on the lower slopes of the hill, date back to the 1850s *(see pp374–5)* and provide a peaceful retreat complete with woodlands, glades, seasonal plantings and magnificent elm tree avenues.

The Hotel Windsor, with its long and ornate façade, was built in 1883 and is the grandest surviving hotel of its era in Australia *(see p508).*

Stanford Fountain
The beautiful centrepiece of the elegant Gordon Reserve was sculpted by the prisoner William Stanford while he was serving his sentence.

MACARTHUR STREET

SPRING STREET

TREASURY PLACE

LANSDOWNE STREET

WELLINGTON PARADE

★ Treasury Building
This Renaissance Revival style building was designed by draughtsman John James Clark in 1857. Built as government offices, with vaults to house the treasury's gold, it is now the City Museum.

Cook's Cottage
This cottage was the English home of the parents of Captain James Cook (see p50). *It was shipped to Australia in 1934 piece by piece and now houses displays about Cook and 18th-century life.*

★ Parliament House
The Legislative Council in this 1850s building sits in a lavish, Corinthian chamber. The crimson colour scheme is based on that of the UK's House of Lords.

LOCATOR MAP
See Melbourne Street Finder, map 2

Tasma Terrace is a superb example of Melbourne's distinctive terrace houses with ornate cast-iron decoration *(see p376)*. It is now the headquarters of the National Trust.

St Patrick's Cathedral
This is one of the best examples of Gothic Revival church architecture in the world. It was constructed between 1858 and 1897, with its impressive spires completed in 1939.

★ Fitzroy Gardens
James Sinclair was head gardener when the superb formal gardens were first laid out, featuring follies, winding paths, a fern gulley and avenues of elms.

STAR SIGHTS

★ Fitzroy Gardens

★ Parliament House

★ Treasury Building

| 0 metres | 100 |
| 0 yards | 100 |

KEY

– – – Suggested route

Old Magistrate's Court ⑲

Cnr La Trobe & Russell sts. **Map** 1 C2. **Tel** (03) 8663 7228. 🚇 *Melbourne Central.* 🚋 *La Trobe & Swanston sts routes.* ⬭ *during school hols and peak periods.* 📷 📹

The Melbourne Magistrate's Court, also called City Court, occupied this building until 1995. The area was formerly known as the police precinct – this is because the court lies opposite the former police headquarters, a very striking Art Deco skyscraper completed in the early 1940s, and next door to the Old Melbourne Gaol.

Built in 1911, the court's façades are made of native Moorabool sandstone. The building's intricate, Romanesque design features gables, turrets and arches. It originally contained three courtrooms. Court One is open to the public during school holidays and peak periods as part of the Old Melbourne Gaol Crime and Justice Experience.

Ornate Romanesque tower of the Old Magistrate's Court

Old Melbourne Gaol ⑳

Russell St. **Map** 1 C2. **Tel** (03) 8663 7228. 🚇 *Melbourne Central.* 🚋 *La Trobe & Swanston sts routes.* ⬭ *9:30am–5pm daily.* ⬤ *Good Fri, 25 Dec.* 📷 📹 ♿ *limited.* **www**.oldmelbournegaol.com.au

Visiting the Old Melbourne Gaol, Victoria's first extensive gaol complex, is a chilling

Corridor of cells in Old Melbourne Gaol

experience, especially on a night tour. Between 1845 and 1929, it was the site of 136 executions. While much of the original complex has been demolished, the imposing Second Cell Block still stands and is home to a fascinating museum.

Ghosts are often reported at the gaol, which is hardly surprising given the tragic and grisly accounts of prisoners' lives and deaths. Conditions, based on London's Pentonville Model Prison, were grim, regulated and silent. When first incarcerated, prisoners were held in solitary confinement and were not permitted to mix with other prisoners until a later date, set according to their sentence. Exhibits showing these conditions include prisoners' chains and a frame used for flogging. But

perhaps the most compelling exhibits are the many accounts of prisoners who were condemned to die at the gaol, accompanied by their death masks. Ned Kelly's death mask is the most famous of those on display. Visitors can also see the original gallows where executions took place.

Included with a ticket to the Old Melbourne Gaol, visitors can now tour the former city Watch House, which served as a central "lock up" for police from 1908 to 1994. With a Charge Sergeant as a guide, visitors are "arrested" and processed through the lock up, experiencing first hand an environment that has not changed since the police and inmates left it. The Watch House has a long and fascinating history, with characters such as the 1920s gangster Squizzy Taylor, last

NED KELLY

The most well-known execution at the Melbourne Gaol was that of Ned Kelly, Australia's most famous bushranger, on 11 November 1880. Edward "Ned" Kelly was the son of Ellen and ex-convict "Red" Kelly. At the time of Ned's final imprisonment and execution, Ellen was serving a sentence in the gaol's Female Ward after hitting a policeman over the head at her house when he came to arrest her son, Dan. She was therefore

Ned Kelly's death mask

able to visit Ned, who had been captured at Glenrowan on 28 June 1880 *(see p451)*. A crowd of 5,000 waited outside the gaol when Kelly was executed, most of them to lend their support to a man perceived to be rightfully rebelling against the English-based law and police authorities. In one instance, the Kelly Gang burned a bank's records of outstanding loans so they no longer had to be repaid. The controversy over whether Kelly was hero or villain continues to this day.

man hanged Ronald Ryan and infamous Chopper Read all having been locked up here. The experience is enhanced by informative multimedia displays that illustrate the stories of former inmates.

Italian restaurant in Lygon Street

Lygon Street ㉑

Lygon St, Carlton. **Map** 1 C1.
🚋 1, 8. 🚌 200, 201, 207.

This Italian-influenced street is one of the main café, restaurant and delicatessen areas in central Melbourne *(see pp552–6)*.

The strong Italian tradition of Lygon Street began at the time of mass post-World War II immigration. With a general exodus to the suburbs in the 1940s, Carlton became unfashionable and new immigrants were able to buy its 19th-century houses and shops cheaply. More importantly, the immigrants were central in protecting these Victorian and Edwardian houses, which were built with post-gold rush wealth, from government plans to fill the area with low-income Housing Commission homes.

A distinctive architectural trait of Lygon Street's two-storey shops is their street verandas, built to protect both customers and merchandise from the sun. In the mid-1960s, the area became fashionable with university students, many of whom moved in to take advantage of its cheap accommodation, then stayed on after graduating to become the base of the suburb's contemporary middle-class and professional community. The

Coffee grinder in a Lygon Street coffee house

street is only one block from the main University of Melbourne campus and can be reached from the city centre by foot, bus or tram. Its wide street resembles a French boulevard and is well suited to the Lygon Street Festa held here every year *(see p40)*.

Melbourne Museum ㉒

Carlton Gardens, Melbourne. **Map** 2 D1. **Tel** (03) 8341 7777. 🚋 86, 96. 🕙 10am–5pm daily. 🔴 25 Dec, Good Fri. 🎫 🖰 🛗 🛒 **www**.
melbourne.museum.vic.gov.au

Having opened in 2000, this museum is one of the newest in the city. Housed in an ultra-modern facility in verdant Carlton Gardens, it has exhibits over six levels, half of which are below ground level. Diverse displays offer insights into science, technology, the environment, the human mind and body, Australian society and indigenous cultures.

One of the highlights is Bunjilaka, the Aboriginal Centre. It combines exhibition galleries with a performance space and meeting rooms. *Wurreka*, the 50-m- (150-ft-) long zinc wall etching at the entrance is by Aboriginal artist Judy Watson. The Two Laws gallery deals with the Indigenous Australians' systems of knowledge, law and property.

The Forest Gallery is a living, breathing exhibit, featuring 8,000 plants from 120 different species. It is also home to around 20 different vertebrate species, including snakes, birds, fish and hundreds of insects. This gallery explores the complex ecosystem of Australia's temperate forests, using plants and animals, art and multimedia installations, soundscapes and other activities.

A dedicated children's museum is in a gallery that resembles a tilted, blue cube. The Blue Box houses multi-sensory displays exploring the theme of growth. There are also Children's Pathways throughout the rest of the museum, providing activities for children in other galleries.

One of the most popular exhibits is in the Australia Gallery. This treats the life of Phar Lap, the champion Australian racehorse of the early 1930s. Exhibits include race memorabilia of the period. Phar Lap himself is seen in an Art-Deco inspired showcase. Other curiosities on show in the museum include the skeleton of a blue whale, a car from Melbourne's first tram, a windmill and the Hertel, the first car to be imported.

Adjacent to the Melbourne Museum is the **Royal Exhibition Building**, offering an interesting 19th-century counterpoint to the Museum's modern architecture. The Exhibition Building was built for the 1880 International Exhibition and is one of the few remaining structures from the 19th-century world fairs. It was designed by Joseph Reed, whose work can be found throughout Melbourne.

Elegant Royal Exhibition Building, near the Melbourne Museum

Leisurely café society in Brunswick Street

National Sports Museum ㉕

Melbourne Cricket Ground, Yarra Park, Jolimont. **Map** 2 F3. **Tel** (03) 9657 8879. ▦ Richmond. ▦ 48, 70, 75. ◯ 10am–5pm daily. ● Good Fri, 25 Dec. ▨ ▤ ▨

Following the redevelopment of the Melbourne Cricket Ground (MCG) for the 2006 Commonwealth Games, the MCG has become the home of the National Sports Museum. The museum honours all things sporting, including Aussie Rules football, cricket and the Olympic Games among others.

Located across two levels of the refurbished Olympic Stand, visitors can view some of the finest sports-related memorabilia using state-of-the-art technology. The Olympic Museum has displays of the history of all summer Olympic meets.

The Australian Cricket Hall of Fame, which opened with ten Australian players as initial members, includes Sir Donald Bradman. Each player is presented through a comprehensive historical display.

After you have wandered through the museum, you can take a tour which includes the Arena, the Great Southern Stand, the Ponsford Stand, the football and cricket change rooms, heritage artworks and the corporate suites. Tours leave from Gate No.3 every half hour between 10am and 3pm, but only on non-event days. Booking is not essential.

Brunswick Street and Fitzroy ㉓

Brunswick St. **Map** 2 E1. ▦ 112.

Next to the university suburb of Carlton, Fitzroy was the natural choice for a post-1960s populace of students and other bohemian characters, who took advantage of the area's cheap postwar Housing Commission properties, unwanted by wealthier Melburnians. Despite becoming gentrified, Fitzroy's main strip, Brunswick Street, maintains an alternative air and a cosmopolitan street life.

Today, Brunswick Street is a mix of cafés, restaurants and trendy shops. A little to the south is Gertrude Street, which has an eclectic mix of record stores, bars and galleries. Nearby Johnston Street is home to Melbourne's Spanish quarter. All the streets in this area are most lively on Saturday nights.

City Museum ㉔

Old Treasury Building, Spring Street (top of Collins Street). **Map** 2 E2. **Tel** (03) 9651 2233. ▦ 109, 112. ◯ 10am–4pm Sun–Fri (other times group bookings only). ● Good Fri, 25 & 26 Dec. ▨ ▤ group tours by request. ▤ ▯
www.citymuseummelbourne.org

The City Museum is housed within Melbourne's beautiful, 19th-century Old Treasury Building (see p392). Designed in 1857 by John James Clark, a nineteen year old architectural prodigy, it provided secure storage for gold that flooded into Melbourne from the wealthy Victorian gold fields. It also served as office accommodation for the Governor of Victoria (a role it still fulfils to this day).

As well as an opportunity to see the building itself, a visit to the museum includes a look at the gold vaults that lie beneath the building. The vaults contain a dynamic multi-media exhibition *Built on Gold*, which tells the story of how Melbourne developed into a city of enormous wealth in a remarkably short period of ten years. In this time it went from a small colonial outpost to a vibrant city with magnificent buildings and grand boulevards, a dynamic theatre culture, a passion for sport and political activism.

Making Melbourne, a permanent exhibition on the ground floor, explores Melbourne's history from the gold rushes of 1852 up until the present day. This more traditional exhibition, which includes a number of famous paintings of Melbourne from the National Gallery of Victoria, provides visitors with an opportunity to explore the economic, cultural and recreational aspects of the city's contemporary life.

Drawn from galleries and museums all over Australia, the temporary exhibition gallery hosts a new exhibition every six weeks. On display are a range of visual arts including sculpture, textiles, photography and architecture.

Olympic Cauldron on display in the Olympic Museum

World-famous Melbourne Cricket Ground backed by the city skyline

Melbourne Cricket Ground ㉖

Yarra Park, Jolimont. **Map** 2 F3. **Tel** (03) 9657 8879. ⊞ Jolimont. ⊞ 48, 70, 75 (special trams run on sports event days). ⬜ for tours or sports events. 🎞 ♿ 🎫 obligatory.

Melbourne Cricket Ground (MCG) is Australia's premier sports stadium and a cultural icon. The land was granted in 1853 to the Melbourne Cricket Club (MCC), itself conceived in 1838.

The MCG predominantly hosts cricket and Australian Rules football, being the site for test matches and the first one-day international match and for the Australian Football League Grand Final, held on the last Saturday of September (see p40). Non-sporting events, such as pop concerts, are also held at the venue.

There have been numerous stands and pavilions over the years, each superseded at different times by reconstructions of the ground. An 1876 stand, now demolished, was reversible, with spectators able to watch cricket on the ground and football in the park in winter. Following massive redevelopment of the ground ahead of the 2006 Commonwealth Games, the MCG can now seat crowds of more than 100,000. Guided tours usually take visitors to the members' pavilion, which includes the Melbourne Cricket Club (MCC) Museum. It traces the history of the MCG with an exhibition of information and artifacts. The Mythical Ashes is a fascinating display of Ashes mementoes.

Melbourne Park ㉗

Batman Ave. **Map** 2 E4. **Tel** (03) 9286 1600. ⊞ Flinders St & Richmond. ⊞ 70. ⬜ for events. ♿ 🎫 of Rod Laver Arena at 11:30am, 1pm, 2:30pm Mon–Fri, 11:30am, 1pm Sat & Sun (call 1300 836 647 to book).

Melbourne Park (formerly the National Tennis Centre) on the northern bank of the Yarra River, is Melbourne's sports and large-scale concerts venue. Events include the Australian Open (see p41), one of the four Grand Slam competitions of tennis, played under Rod Laver Arena's unique retractable roof (see p377). There are also 22 outdoor and seven indoor tennis courts for public use.

Next to Melbourne Park is the Hisense Arena, which is home to Melbourne Vixens netball team. It also hosts a stadium for cycling, dance performances, family shows, concerts and other entertainment. Opposite the park is the Westpac Centre, which was originally built for the 1956 Olympics but has been redeveloped.

Nearby Olympic Park, formerly the location for international and national athletics, is the training ground for Collingwood Football Club.

Australian Open tennis championship in Rod Laver Arena, Melbourne Park

Royal Botanic Gardens and Kings Domain 28

Shrine of Remembrance crypt plaque

These adjoining gardens, established in 1852, form the green heart of Melbourne on what was originally a swamp on the edge of the city. The Botanic Gardens house one of the finest collections of botanic species in the world, as well as being highly regarded for their landscape design. William Guilfoyle, curator of the Gardens between 1873 and 1909, used his knowledge of English garden design to create a horticultural paradise. Kings Domain, once an inner-city wilderness, became instead a gracious parkland. Its civic function grew over the years, with the establishment of its monuments, statues, cultural venues and the hilltop residence of the Governor of Victoria.

Sidney Myer Music Bowl is an architecturally acclaimed music "shell" which can accommodate up to 15,000 people for open-air concerts and ballets. In winter the stage becomes an ice rink.

Pioneer Women's Garden
This sunken, formal garden was built in 1934 to honour the memory of Victoria's founding women. A still, central pool is adorned by a bronze, female statue.

Observatory Gate Precinct

★ Shrine of Remembrance
Based on the description of the Mausoleum of Halicarnassus in Asia Minor, now Turkey, this imposing monument honours Australian soldiers who gave their lives in war.

| 0 metres | | 200 |
| 0 yards | | 200 |

★ Government House
This elaborate Italianate building is a landmark of the gardens. Tours of the state rooms are held each week.

The Perennial Border, based on designer Gertrude Jekyll's traditional colour scheme, is planted with pastels, contrasting with grey and silver foliage.

The Temple of the Winds

Algerian Oak
This magnificent mature oak in the centre of the Oak Lawn is particularly spectacular when it flowers in September.

★Ornamental Lake
William Guilfoyle's lake forms the centrepiece of the Gardens. It reflects his adherence to 18th-century English garden design, which used water as a feature.

Arid Garden
Desert region plants from Australia and around the world thrive in this special garden, watered by a small stream which acts as a natural oasis.

The Ian Potter Foundation Children's Garden

La Trobe's Cottage was shipped from England in 1839 and was home to Victoria's first governor, Charles La Trobe. The building is now preserved by the National Trust.

STAR FEATURES

★ Government House

★ Ornamental Lake

★ Shrine of Remembrance

The Yarra River

The Yarra River winds for 240 km (150 miles) from its source in Baw Baw National Park to the coast. The river has always been vital to the city, not just as its major natural feature, but also in early settlement days as its gateway to the rest of the world. Today, the Yarra is a symbol of the boundary between north and south Melbourne and many citizens live their whole lives on one side or the other. Since the 1980s, the rejuvenation of the central section of the river has given the south bank an important focus. The river is also used for sport: rowers in training are a daily sight and cycle trails run along much of the river.

LOCATOR MAP
See Melbourne Street Finder, maps 1, 2

★ **National Gallery of Victoria**
The Gallery houses one of the largest collections of international art in Australia ㉞

The Victorian Arts Centre
holds regular performances by the Australian Ballet and the Melbourne Theatre Company. The 162-m (531-ft) spire is a Melbourne landmark.

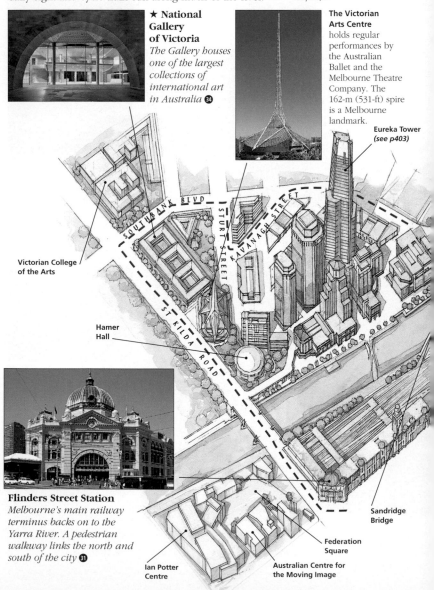

Victorian College of the Arts

Eureka Tower *(see p403)*

SOUTHBANK BLVD

STURT STREET

KAVANAGH STREET

ST KILDA ROAD

Hamer Hall

Flinders Street Station
Melbourne's main railway terminus backs on to the Yarra River. A pedestrian walkway links the north and south of the city ㉛

Ian Potter Centre

Australian Centre for the Moving Image

Federation Square

Sandridge Bridge

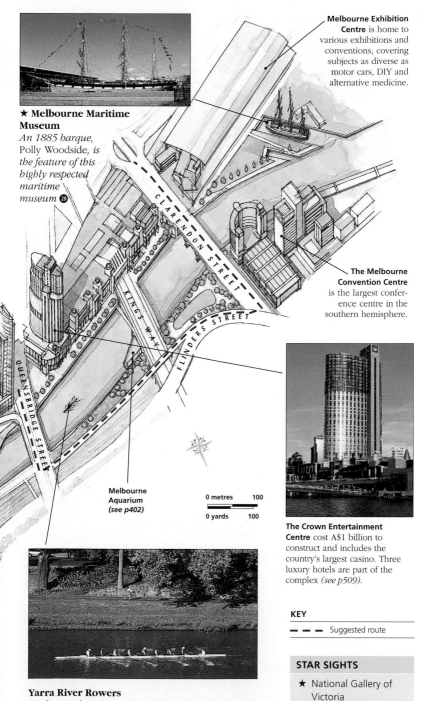

Melbourne Exhibition Centre is home to various exhibitions and conventions, covering subjects as diverse as motor cars, DIY and alternative medicine.

★ **Melbourne Maritime Museum**
An 1885 barque, Polly Woodside, *is the feature of this highly respected maritime museum* ㉙

The Melbourne Convention Centre is the largest conference centre in the southern hemisphere.

CLARENDON STREET

KINGS WAY

FLINDERS STREET

QUEENSBRIDGE STREET

Melbourne Aquarium
(see p402)

| 0 metres | 100 |
| 0 yards | 100 |

The Crown Entertainment Centre cost A$1 billion to construct and includes the country's largest casino. Three luxury hotels are part of the complex *(see p509).*

KEY

— — — Suggested route

STAR SIGHTS

★ National Gallery of Victoria

★ Melbourne Maritime Museum

Yarra River Rowers
Professional and amateur rowing teams are a regular sight on the Yarra River, and regattas are a regular event. Rowing boats can be hired at various points along the riverbanks.

For hotels and restaurants in this region see pp505–9 and pp552–6

Polly Woodside barque moored on the Yarra River

Melbourne Maritime Museum 🕗

Lorimer St East, Southbank. **Map** 1 A5. **Tel** (03) 9656 9800. 🚊 *Southern Cross.* 🚌 *96, 109, 112.* 🚏 *Grimes Street Bridge.* ⏰ *10am–4pm daily.* 🔴 *Good Fri, 25 Dec.* 📷 ♿ *except for ship.* 🎫 *book in advance.* **www.**melbournemaritimemuseum.com.au

The Maritime Museum is also known as the "Home of *Polly Woodside*", an 1885 barque built in Belfast. When she was retired from service in the 1960s, she was the only deep-water commercial ship still afloat in Australia. Even in 1885, she was rare, as only one in four ships were then built with sails. Most of the last 40 years of her working life were spent as a coal hulk. Donated to the National Trust in 1968, she has been restored. The museum has interactive displays that explore life at sea and working on Melbourne's docks.

Maritime museum exhibit

Melbourne Aquarium 🕥

Cnr Flinders & King sts. **Map** 1 B4. **Tel** (03) 9923 5925. 🚊 *Southern Cross, Flinders St.* 🚌 *70.* ⏰ *9:30am–6pm daily (to 9pm in Jan).* 📷 ♿ 🅿 🌐 **www.**melbourneaquarium.com.au

Featuring species from the Australian, southern and tropical oceans, the Melbourne Aquarium puts humans close to some of the exotic inhabitants of the deep. Among the exhibits is the Oceanarium, approached through a viewing cylinder and housing sharks and rays as well as vibrantly coloured fish. Melbourne Aquarium is the only place in Victoria where you can see King and Gentoo penguins.

Flinders Street Station 🕛

Cnr Flinders & Swanston sts. **Map** 1 C4. **Tel** 13 16 38. 🚌 *Swanston St and Flinders St routes.* ♿

Flinders Street Station is the central metropolitan train terminus of Melbourne and one of the city's favourite meeting places. Generations of Melburnians have met each other on the corner steps of the station "under the Clocks". Although the original clocks are now operated by computer rather than by hand, they remain in working order. The Flinders Street site has been part of the public transport network since the city's early days. The first steam train in Australia left Flinders Street Station, then a small wooden building at the end of Elizabeth Street, in 1854. The present station building, completed in 1910, was designed by Fawcett & Ashworth. The bronze domed building with its bright yellow brickwork was fully restored and refurbished in 1984.

Federation Square 🕝

Cnr Flinders & Swanston sts. **Map** 2 D3/4. **Tel** (03) 9655 1900. 🚌 *Swanston St and Flinders St routes.* ♿ **www.**federationsquare.com.au **The Ian Potter Centre – NGV** **Tel** (03) 8662 1555. **ACMI** **Tel** (03) 8663 2200. **Champions** **Tel** 1300 139 407.

One of Melbourne's newest public spaces, Federation Square opened in October 2002 to commemorate the centenary of the federation of the Australian states.

The square hosts up to 2,000 events each year. Its architectural highlight is the geometric design of the Atrium building, a covered public space. There are many outstanding attractions. **The Ian Potter Centre – NGV: Australia**, an offshoot of the National Gallery of Victoria *(see p403)*, is the world's first major gallery dedicated exclusively to the display of Australian art. Nearby, the **Australian Centre for the Moving Image (ACMI)** celebrates images on multimedia and film. Across four floors of the Alfred Deakin Building, the ACMI has two multi-format cinemas and the world's largest screen gallery. Also worth a visit is **Champions – Australian Racing Museum and Hall of Fame**. The square has two information points: the Melbourne Visitor Centre *(see p411)* and the Melbourne Mobility Centre at the bottom of the Federation Square car park.

Modern architecture of the Atrium building at Federation Square

For hotels and restaurants in this region see pp505–9 and pp552–6

View of Albert Park Lake and its wetlands

Eureka Tower ③

7 Riverside Quay. **Map** 1 C4. *Tel* (03) 9693 8888. ◯ *10am–10pm daily.* for Skydeck.

The 300-m (985-ft) Eureka Tower was named after the Eureka Stockade, a rebellion that took place during the Victoria gold rush *(see p434).* The skyscraper's gold crown and gold-plated windows refer back to this era. The Skydeck on the 88th floor has numerous viewfinders and a glass cube called "The Edge", which slides out 3 m (10 ft) from the side of the building with visitors inside.

National Gallery of Victoria ③

180 St Kilda Rd and Federation Square. **Map** 2 D4. *Tel* (03) 8620 2222. ◯ *10am–5pm daily.* Good Fri, 25 Apr, 25 Dec. **NGV Australia** *Mon;* **NGV International** *Tue.* www.ngv.vic.gov.au

The first public art gallery in Australia, the National Gallery of Victoria opened in 1861 and housed the original State Museum. The gallery moved to St Kilda Rd in 1968 and contains the largest and widest-ranging art collection in the country. Its most significant bequest was from Melbourne entrepreneur Alfred Felton in 1904. Its collections of both Old Masters and contemporary Australian art are outstanding.

The international collection is at 180 St Kilda Road *(see p400)*; the Australian collection is at the Ian Potter Centre in Federation Square *(see p402)*.

Fitzroy and Acland Streets ③

St Kilda. **Map** 5 B5. 16, 96. 246, 600, 623, 606. St Kilda Pier.

Situated 6 km (4 miles) south of the city centre, St Kilda has long been the most popular seaside suburb of Melbourne. During the boom-time era of the 1850s *(see pp54–5)*, the suburb was inhabited by many wealthy families. Other well-off Victorians would holiday in St Kilda during the summer. St Kilda Pier, still a magnet for visitors, was erected in 1859.

Today St Kilda is densely populated, with many Art Deco apartment blocks. The neighbourhood's main streets are Fitzroy and Acland. The latter, renowned as a district of Jewish delicatessens and cake shops, is packed with visitors on Sundays. Fitzroy Street is filled with upmarket restaurants and shops. Rejuvenated in the 1980s, the beachside esplanade attracts crowds to its busy arts and crafts market each Sunday.

Melbourne tram running along the St Kilda Beach route No.16

Albert Park ③

Canterbury Rd, Albert St & Lakeside Drive. **Map** 5 B3. 96.

Encompassing the remains of a former natural swampland, Albert Park Lake is the attractive centrepiece of a 225-ha (555-acre) parkland which includes sporting fields, a public golf course and many other recreational facilities. However, it is now predominantly known as the site of the annual Australian Formula One Grand Prix, which covers a 5,260-m (5,754-yd) circuit around the lake *(see p42)*. Apart from the Grand Prix, the park is used for a variety of purposes. The popular Melbourne Sports and Aquatic Centre is located here. Wetlands have also been developed to promote a diverse wildlife. Sailing here is another popular activity, whether by small yacht, rowing boat or model boat.

A large, ancient river red gum tree standing in the centre of the park is also reputed to have been the site of many Aboriginal *corroborees* (festive night dances).

Chapel Street ③

South Yarra, Prahran and Windsor. **Map** 6 E3. South Yarra, Prahan. 6, 8, 72.

Chapel Street, Melbourne's most fashionable street, with price-tags to match, is lined with shops selling local and international fashion designs. A youthful clientele swarms the street at weekends. Up-market restaurants and cafés abound and the nearby Prahran Market sells the best in fresh, delicatessen produce.

Crossing Chapel Street is Toorak Road, whose "village" is patronized by Melbourne's wealthiest community. More akin to the bohemian area of Brunswick Street *(see p396)* is Greville Street to the west, with its cafés, bars and chic second-hand shops.

A food and fashion festival is sometimes held on the last Sunday before the Melbourne Cup *(see p41)*.

Rippon Lea ⑱

Rippon Lea Mansion, designed by Joseph Reed and built in 1868, is now part of the National Trust's portfolio. The house is a much loved fixture of the city's heritage. The first family of Rippon Lea were the Sargoods, who held many balls and parties during the 1880s and 1890s. The next owner, Premier Sir Thomas Bent, sold off parts of the estate in the early 1900s. The Nathans bought Rippon Lea in 1910 and restored its reputation as a family home. Benjamin Nathan's daughter Louisa added a ballroom and swimming pool to the house, which were the venue for parties in the 1930s and 1940s. The formal gardens are a highlight.

Façade of the elegant mansion, Rippon Lea

Arched windows are a recurring decorative theme throughout the house, bordered by polychrome bricks.

Victorian Bathroom
The decor of the bathroom remains in its original Victorian style as installed by the Sargoods. The earth closets were ingeniously processed into liquid manure and recycled for use in the garden.

The conservatory housed ferns and orchids, beloved flowers of both Frederick Sargood and Benjamin Nathan. Horticultural experts were regularly invited to Rippon Lea.

Main entrance

STAR FEATURES

★ Dining Room

★ Sitting Room

The main staircase is oak and mahogany like much of the rest of the house. Mirrors, another recurring theme in the house, are fitted into an archway at the foot of the stairs, courtesy of Louisa Jones.

For hotels and restaurants in this region see pp505–9 and pp552–6

★ Dining Room
American walnut blends with an Italian Renaissance style for the dining furniture of Louisa Jones.

Como House and its driveway

The Tower was an unusual feature in the design of a domestic house. In this case, it may have been inspired by Sargood, who wanted his home to have the ornateness of a church.

The brickwork was inspired by a trip by Joseph Reed to Lombardy in Italy, where he came across this polychrome design.

Swimming pool and ballroom

★ Sitting Room
Louisa Jones looked to the grand mansions of Hollywood film stars in the 1930s for much of her interior design, including the plush sitting room.

Como Historic House and Garden ㊴

Cnr Williams Rd & Lechlade Ave, South Yarra. **Map** 4 F4. *Tel* (03) 9827 2500. 🚉 South Yarra. 🚌 8. ⏱ 10am–5pm daily (to 4pm Sep–May). ⬤ Good Fri, 25 Dec. ♿ ♿ ground floor and grounds only. ✍ obligatory. **www**.comohouse.com.au

Begun in 1847 by Edward Eyre Williams, Como House was occupied by the Armytage family for almost a century (1865–1959).

One of Como's highlights is its vast collection of original furnishings. These include pieces collected by the Armytage matriarch, Caroline, whilst on a Grand Tour of Europe during the 1870s, and include marble and bronze statues. The tour was undertaken as an educational experience for her nine children after the death of her husband, Charles Henry. It was important to this prominent Melbourne family to be seen as well educated. On their return, they held a series of sophisticated parties here.

Set in the picturesque remnants of its once extensive gardens, the house overlooks Como Park and the Yarra River. The original facets of the magnificent grounds, designed by William Sangster (who also had an input at Rippon Lea), remain: the fountain terrace, croquet lawn and hard standing area at the front of the house.

Como was managed by the Armytage women from 1876 until it was purchased by the National Trust in 1959. The house has undergone major restoration work over the years since then.

SHOPPING IN MELBOURNE

The Central Business District (CBD) is a magnet for the city's shoppers. Major department stores are supplemented by a network of boutiques and specialist shops, many of which are tucked away in arcades and lanes. There is also a network of inner-city and suburban shopping streets: fashionable clothing and retail stores abound in urban areas, while large one-stop shopping towns are a feature of Greater Melbourne. There are areas known for particular products, such as High Street, which runs through Armadale and Malvern, with its antiques stores. The city's multicultural society is also reflected in its shopping districts: Victoria Street, Richmond, has a stretch of Vietnamese stores; Sydney Road, Brunswick, is renowned for its shops selling Middle Eastern goods; and Carlisle Street, St Kilda, has many Jewish delicatessens.

Dinosaur Designs, South Yarra

Ornate and elegant Royal Arcade, which was built in 1869

SHOPPING HOURS

In Victoria, most traders are open every day. Some small businesses close on Sundays but, increasingly, many stay open, competing with the long hours of chain stores and supermarkets (some of which are open 24 hours a day). Standard hours are 9am to 5:30pm (10am to 6pm in the CBD), although some retailers have extended hours on Thursdays or Fridays. Hours can vary at weekends. Most shops close on Christmas Day and Good Friday.

DEPARTMENT STORES

There are two major department stores in central Melbourne: **Myer** and **David Jones**, both are open for business seven days a week.

Australia's largest department store, Myer, encompasses a full two blocks of the city centre, with seven floors in Lonsdale Street and six in Bourke Street. Its main entrance is in Bourke Street Mall. Myer have nine other stores throughout Melbourne. David Jones, known to locals as DJs, has more up-market stock and high-quality service. The store has three sites within the city, with a main entrance adjacent to Myer in Bourke Street Mall; opposite is its menswear department. A third section is accessed in Little Bourke Street, again adjacent to Myer.

Two other popular stores are **Target** and K-mart. Both offer discounted prices on a range of goods. There are many branches of K-mart but they are located outside the CBD.

ARCADES, MALLS AND SHOPPING CENTRES

Melbourne's best arcades and malls are located in the heart of the CBD. Chief among these are Bourke Street Mall, with shopfronts for the Myer and David Jones department stores. Occupied mostly by speciality stores and boutiques, other arcades and malls include the **Galleria Shopping Plaza**, with an emphasis on Australiana and Australian-owned stores. The ABC Shop sells merchandise associated with the national television and radio network, such as books, videos and DVDs. Australian Geographic is an excellent shop for information on Australian landscape and geology.

Located on Collins Street, renowned for its upmarket shops, clothing and shoes, are **Australia on Collins**, Block Arcade (see p389) and 234 Collins Street. Australia on Collins comprises 60 shops on five levels, with fashion, homeware and other retail stores. The Sportsgirl Centre, at 234 Collins Street, is known for its designer fashion shops, which are located on three levels. Both complexes have food halls. Block Arcade, itself of historic interest, sells more classic clothing amid a beautifully

Upmarket window display in Melbourne Central shopping centre

Locally grown fruit on sale at Queen Victoria Market

restored 1890s interior; there is an entrance on Elizabeth Street. Also on Elizabeth Street is the GPO (see p388), which has been transformed into a beautiful and vibrant shopping complex.

Further up on Collins Street, past Russell Street, there are stores located in Collins Place, and in the Royal Arcade (see p388) nearby, which is also of historic and architectural interest. Running between Bourke Street Mall and Little Collins Street, further east, you will find **The Walk Arcade**, containing a small selection of smart and exclusive boutiques.

Little Bourke Street, above Elizabeth Street, and the intersecting Hardware Lane, are well known for a range of stores specializing in travel and adventure products.

Melbourne Central and **QV** are two outstanding shopping centres located on Lonsdale and Swanston streets. Between them, there are literally hundreds of shops to visit. Away from the city centre, the **Southgate Complex**, with its 40 shops on three levels, should not be missed by the avid shopper. Products include upmarket fashion and shoes, music, furniture, jewellery and ethnic products.

MARKETS

Melbourne has a number of fresh food markets. The most notable is the Queen Victoria Market (see p386).

Other kinds of market are also popular. There is a huge range of second-hand goods for sale each Sunday at the

Camberwell Market. For arts and crafts, **The Esplanade Market** is held on Sundays on Upper Esplanade. Other Sunday markets include the food market in **Prahran** and the arts and crafts market at the Victorian Arts Centre (see p411). One of the oldest markets is the **South Melbourne Market**, which has has been in continuous operation since 1867. It is open every Friday to Sunday, and also Wednesday.

Brunswick Street has vintage clothing stores and retro boutiques

SHOPPING STRIPS

Village-style shopping centres abound in the many suburbs of Melbourne. Popular spots include High Street in Armadale; Sydney Road in Brunswick; Brunswick and Gertrude streets in Fitzroy; Bridge Road in Richmond; Chapel Street in South Yarra; and Maling Road in Canterbury.

Another major shopping centre in South Yarra is the **Como Centre**, which has stores selling furniture, homewares and fashion.

Specialist Shops and Souvenirs

Melbourne is Australia's most fashion-conscious capital and hosts major fashion weeks. The Melbourne Fashion Festival in March sees young designers launch their autumn/winter collections, while established labels showcase their spring/summer collections during Spring Fashion Week in September. New boutiques have opened in the Flinders Lane and Little Collins Streets precincts, either side of Swanston Street, and in the Central Business District's (CBD) revitalized arcades and laneways. This area rivals Fitzroy's Brunswick Street for funky shopping. Melbourne is also a great place to buy outdoor gear, with several retailers located around Hardware Lane and Little Bourke Street. The city has a reputation for excellent bookshops and record stores, most of which are found in the city centre and inner suburbs of Carlton, Fitzroy, St Kilda and South Yarra.

MEN'S CLOTHING

The **Marcs** range is characterized by lightweight and colourful sweaters, shirts, t-shirts and trousers. Myer department store (see pp406–7) stocks a limited range of Marcs items, often on sale. For sharp designer suits, head for **Calibre**, who also stock imported designer accessories. Little Collins Street east of Swanston Street has a selection of menswear stores, including **Déclic**, which specialises in business shirts and designer ties with names such as Duchamp, Vivienne Westwood and Zegna. Down the hill, **Ben Sherman** in the beautiful shopping complex at the General Post Office or GPO (see p388) has a good range of smart casual gear. **Out of the Closet**, opposite Flinders Street Station, stocks groovy vintage wear. They also have a store in Brunswick Street, Fitzroy. Nearby, **Route 66** stocks worn-in 501s, cowboy boots, bowling shirts and vintage western gear. Brunswick Street is a good place to browse for vintage clothing, and Chapel Street, South Yarra is great for jeanswear.

WOMEN'S CLOTHING

The CBD is the centre for haute couture in Melbourne. **Alannah Hill**'s and **Bettina Liano**'s fashions are feminine and sophisticated, the latter with a glam edge. **Scanlon & Theodore** have made a name for themselves with elegant outfits, earthy tones and breezy designs. **Issey Miyake** is one of several international design houses represented in Melbourne. The appointment-only **Le Louvre**, in South Yarra, has been Melbourne society's couturier for decades. Young design outfit **Fat** has shops in Fitzroy, Prahran and at the GPO shopping complex. **Genki** has a range of funky tops and t-shirts designed for women that are also very popular with the kids, while **Kinki Gerlinki** stocks a appealing range of retro clothing. Ben Sherman and Marcs stock a good range of casual gear for women. **Peter Alexander** has several branches throughout the city centre and is well regarded for a range of sleepwear, while **Smitten Kitten** offers imported lingerie, jewellery and exotic accessories. Bridge Road, Richmond has numerous discount fashion outlets.

CHILDREN'S CLOTHING

Brunswick Street, Fitzroy is a good starting point for hunting down kids' clothes. Check out **Pumpkin Patch** for a comprehensive range of quality kidswear. **World Wide Wear**, which started life in Fitzroy, has relocated to an outer-suburban shopping centre, but it is worth the trip to lay your hands on groovy kids' t-shirts, jackets, jeans and outdoor gear. **Genki** sells a cute range of t-shirts for babies and young children.

JEWELLERY

Kozminsky's on Bourke Street has been a Melbourne institution for decades. It specialises in fine art and antique jewellery. Collins Street has a profusion of jewellery stores and international fashion labels, including **Bulgari**. **Maker's Mark** showcases exquisite designer jewellery and glassware. Their flagship store is opposite the Rialto Building on Collins Street. **Dinosaur Designs** fashion distinctive and contemporary jewellery, and homewares from lustrous resins. They have several stores, including one in Chapel Street. **Studio Ingot** sells contemporary pieces made by over 60 artisans.

SHOES AND BAGS

The Westin hotel building in Collins Street is home to **Miss Louise**, a favourite with Melbourne's well-heeled women. The GPO has several retailers selling groovy casual shoes for men and women, stylish boots and classy bags. Melbourne's **Catherine Manuell** designs colourful handbags, daypacks, kids' bags and travel gear. **Crumpler** bags are the brainchild of a former bicycle courier who saw a market for comfortable, durable and funky shoulder bags. They come in a variety of styles and types to suit everything from laptops, to videos to homework: a Melbourne design icon.

OUTDOOR GEAR

To stock up on ski equipment and apparel, rock-climbing gear, tents, sleeping bags, maps and designer outdoor clothing, head for the Hardware Lane and Little Bourke Street precinct. There are numerous shops with good quality gear. Both **Paddy Pallin**, an established name in outdoor equipment, and **Snowgum**, which has shops across Melbourne, are recommended outlets. Smith Street, Collingwood has several factory shops for outdoor retailers selling discount clothing.

BOOKS AND MUSIC

Collins Booksellers, an Australian chain, has several outlets including the **Hill of Content Bookshop**, which has an interesting range of local and overseas books. **Readings** is another homegrown favourite, which regularly hosts literary events. Its flagship store is in Carlton and it has a branch in Acland Street, St Kilda. The **Brunswick Street Bookstore** is a quiet and relaxed venue for browsing quality books and magazines. **Discurio**, in a quiet corner of the CBD, is the place for Bach, Coltrane and alternative grooves. **Blue Moon Records** stocks a range of world music.

DIRECTORY

MEN'S CLOTHING

Ben Sherman
Shop G10, GPO,
Melbourne 3000.
Map 1 C3.
Tel (03) 9663 7911.
www.bensherman.com.au

Calibre
483 Chapel St, Sth Yarra
3141. **Map** 6 E1.
Tel (03) 9826 4394.
www.calibre.com.au

Déclic
186 Little Collins St,
Melbourne 3000. **Map** 1
C3. **Tel** (03) 9650 2202.
www.declic.com.au

Marcs
576-584 Chapel St, Sth
Yarra 3141. **Map** 6 E1.
Tel (03) 9826 4906.
www.marcs.com.au

Out of the Closet
238B Flinders St,
Melbourne 3000.
Map 1 C3.
Tel (03) 9639 0980.

Route 66
Shop 7, Cathedral Arcade,
37 Swanston St,
Melbourne 3000.
Map 1 C3.
Tel (03) 9639 5669
www.route66.com.au

WOMEN'S CLOTHING

Alannah Hill
533 Chapel St, Sth Yarra
3141. **Map** 4 E5.
Tel (03) 9826 2755.
www.alannahhill.com.au

Bettina Liano
269 Little Collins St,
Melbourne 3000.
Map 1 C3. **Tel** (03) 9654
1912. www.bettinaliano.
com.au

Fat
272 Chapel St, Sth Yarra
3141. **Map** 6 E2.
Tel (03) 9510 2311.
www.fat4.com

Genki
Shop 5, Cathedral Arcade,
37 Swanston St, Melbourne
3000. **Map** 1 C3.
Tel (03) 9650 6366.
www.genki.com.au

Issey Miyake
Shop 2, 177 Toorak Rd,
Sth Yarra 3141. **Map** 4 E5.
Tel (03) 9826 4900.
www.isseymiyake.com

Kinki Gerlinki
22 Centre Place, Melbourne
3000. **Map** 1 C3.
Tel (03) 9650 0465.

Le Louvre
2 Daly St, Sth Yarra 3141.
Map 4 E5. **Tel** (03) 9823
5300. www.lelouvre.
com.au

Peter Alexander
Level 2, Shop 228
Melbourne Central, 300
Lonsdale St, Melbourne
3000. **Map** 1 C2. **Tel** (03)
9639 1299. www.
peteralexander.com.au

Scanlon & Theodore
566 Chapel St, Sth Yarra
3141. **Map** 4 E5. **Tel** (03)
9824 1800. www.scan
lonandtheodore.com.au

Smitten Kitten
Shop 6, Degraves St,
Melbourne 3000. **Map** 1
C3. **Tel** (03) 9654 2073.
www.smittenkitten.com.au

CHILDREN'S CLOTHING

Pumpkin Patch
Centrepoint Mall, 283–297
Bounce St Mall. **Map** 1 C3.
Tel (03) 9650 1503.

World Wide Wear
Shop B10-B11, Chadstone
Shopping Centre,
1341 Dandenong Rd,
3148. **Tel** (03) 9530 9864.

JEWELLERY

Bulgari
119 Collins St, Melbourne
3000. **Map** 2 D3.
Tel (03) 9663 8100.
www.bvlgari.com.au

Dinosaur Designs
562 Chapel St,
Sth Yarra 3141.
Map 4 E5. **Tel** (03) 9827
2600. www.
dinosaurdesigns.com.au

Kozminsky
421 Bourke St,
Melbourne 3000.
Map 1 C3.
Tel (03) 9670 1277.
www.kozminsky.com.au

Maker's Mark
464 Collins St,
Melbourne 3000.
Map 1 B4.
Tel (03) 9621 2488.
www.makersmark.com.au

Studio Ingot
Shop 2, 234 Brunswick St,
Fitzroy 3065.
Tel (03) 9415 6000.
www.studioingot.com.au

SHOES AND BAGS

Catherine Manuell
273 Little Lonsdale St,
Melbourne 3000. **Map** 1
C2. **Tel** (03) 9499 9844.
www.catherinemanuell
design.com

Crumpler
355 Little Bourke St,
Melbourne 3000. **Map** 1
C3. **Tel** (03) 9600 3799.
www.crumpler.com.au

Miss Louise
The Westin, 205 Collins
St, Melbourne 3000.
Map 2 D3.
Tel (03) 9654 7730.

OUTDOOR GEAR

Paddy Pallin
360 Little Bourke St,
Melbourne 3000. **Map** 1
C3. **Tel** (03) 9670 4845.
www.paddypallin.com.au

Snowgum
370 Little Bourke St,
Melbourne 3000.
Map 1 C3
Tel (03) 9642 4340.
www.snowgum.com.au

BOOKS AND MUSIC

Blue Moon Records
54 Johnston St,
Fitzroy 3065.
Tel (03) 9415 1157.

**Brunswick Street
Bookstore**
305 Brunswick Street,
Fitzroy 3065. **Tel** (03) 9416
1030. www.brunswick
streetbookstore.com

Discurio
113 Hardware St,
Melbourne 3000. **Map** 1
B3. **Tel** (03) 9600 1488.
www.discurio.com.au

**Hill of Content
Bookshop**
86 Bourke St, Melbourne
3000. **Map** 2 D2.
Tel (03) 9662 9472.

Readings
309 Lygon St, Carlton
3053. **Tel** (03) 9347 6633.
112 Acland St, St Kilda,
3182. **Tel** (03) 9525 3852.
www.readings.com.au

ENTERTAINMENT IN MELBOURNE

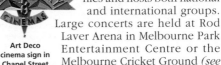

Art Deco cinema sign in Chapel Street

Melbourne could be defined as Australia's city of the arts. All year round there is a wealth of cultural events and entertainment on offer. The city's major festivals include the Melbourne Food and Wine Festival and Moomba *(see pp41–3)*. There are also fringe festivals and many other independent events. The Victorian Arts Centre, which includes Hamer Hall *(see p400)*, stages productions by the state's theatrical companies and hosts both national and international groups. Large concerts are held at Rod Laver Arena in Melbourne Park Entertainment Centre or the Melbourne Cricket Ground *(see p397)*. Cinema chains are supplemented by smaller, arthouse cinemas.

Evening concert at the Sidney Myer Music Bowl *(see p398)*

INFORMATION

The best guide to the range of events in Melbourne is the entertainment guide in the *Age*, published each Friday. This has comprehensive listings, along with more information on all the upcoming highlights. The tabloid newspaper *Herald Sun* and both newspapers' Saturday editions are also good sources of information and reviews. There is an array of free publications covering arts, entertainment and the nightclub scene. Visitors can obtain these from retailers and cafés in main inner-city precincts such as Fitzroy *(see p403)* and St Kilda. The

Melbourne Visitor Information Centre has a range of publications listing events.

There are also a number of websites that provide good events coverage, as well as other information helpful to visitors: www.melbourne. citysearch.com.au, www. visitvictoria.com and www. thatsmelbourne.com.au are worth a look. The **Victorian Arts Centre** *(see p400)* has a bi-monthly diary which it mails out free of charge worldwide, covering all up-to-date events at the complex. Most ticket agencies and some venues also provide information of events taking place in the city.

TICKET BOOKING AGENCIES

Buying tickets in Melbourne is reasonably straightforward. There are two major ticket booking agencies in Victoria, **Ticketmaster** (with more than 50 outlets) and **Ticketek** (with more than 30 outlets). Both agencies offer ticketing for all major sporting events, concerts, theatre performances and festivals, as well

Grand 1930s foyer of the Regent Theatre *(see p390)*

as for theme parks and other attractions. There are some venues which handle their own bookings independently, but these are rare and tickets for most major events are more easily purchased at these agencies.

Bookings can either be made in person at the various outlets, or with a credit card by phone, fax or post. Alternatively, bookings can be made online. The agencies also accept bookings from overseas. If not bought directly over the counter, tickets can be mailed out to customers for a small handling fee. If the event is impending, tickets can usually be picked up at the venue half-an-hour before the booked performance starts.

The hours for outlets vary according to their location, but almost all are open Monday through to Saturday, and some are open on Sundays. Neither Ticketmaster nor Ticketek offer refunds or exchanges, unless a show is

Façade of the Princess Theatre, opposite the Parliamentary Precinct *(see p392)*

Street entertainers, a regular sight throughout Melbourne

DIRECTORY

INFORMATION CENTRE

Melbourne Visitor Information Centre
Federation Square, cnr Swanston & Flinders sts. **Map** 2 D3.
Tel (03) 9658 9658.
www.visitvictoria.com

MAJOR VENUES

Athenaeum Theatre
188 Collins St. **Map** 2 D3.
Tel (03) 9650 1500.

Comedy Theatre
240 Exhibition St. **Map** 2 D2.
Tel (03) 9299 4950.

CUB Malthouse
113 Sturt St. **Map** 2 D4.
Tel (03) 9685 5111.
www.malthousetheatre.com.au

Forum Theatre
154 Flinders St. **Map** 2 D3.
Tel (03) 9299 9700.

Her Majesty's
219 Exhibition St. **Map** 2 D2.
Tel (03) 8643 3300.
www.hermajestystheatre.com.au

Melbourne Town Hall
Cnr Swanston & Little Collins sts.
Map 1 C3. **Tel** (03) 9658 9658.
www.melbournetownhall.com.au

Palais Theatre
3182 Lower Esplanade, St Kilda.
Map 5 B5. **Tel** (03) 9525 3240.

Princess Theatre
163 Spring St. **Map** 2 D2.
Tel (03) 9299 9800.

Regent Theatre
191 Collins St. **Map** 2 D3.
Tel (03) 9299 9500.

Victorian Arts Centre
100 St Kilda Rd. **Map** 2 D4.
Tel 1300 182 183.
www.theartscentre.net.au

TICKET AGENCIES

Half Tix
Melbourne Town Hall, cnr
Swanston and Little Collins sts.
Map 1 C3. **Tel** (03) 9650 9420.
www.halftixmelbourne.com

Ticketek
Tel 132 849.
www.ticketek.com

Ticketmaster
Tel 136 100.
www.ticketmaster.com.au

cancelled. Remember that a nominal booking fee will be added to all ticket prices bought via a ticket agency.

TICKET DEALS

Some major companies, particularly those playing at the Victorian Arts Centre, offer special "rush hour" ticket deals. These are available for tickets purchased in person after 6pm. The **Half Tix** booth at the Melbourne Town Hall on Swanston Street offers half-price deals for many events. Tickets must be bought in person and paid for in cash. They are also generally available only on the day of performance. Shows with tickets available are displayed at the booth.

Half Tix ticket booth sign on Swanston Street

SECURING THE BEST SEATS

If booking in person, you can usually consult a floor-plan showing the location of available seats. Over the telephone, both Ticketmaster and Ticketek have a "best available" system, with remaining seats arranged in a best-to-last order by individual venues. It is also possible to request particular seats and the booking agency will check their availability. Some seats are retained for sale at the venue itself and this can be a way of getting good seats at the last minute.

DISABLED VISITORS

The vast majority of venues have access and facilities for disabled visitors. Booking agencies will take this into account. You should also enquire at individual venues and the Mobility Centre, Federation Square (www.melbourne.vic.gov.au).

OUTDOOR AND STREET ENTERTAINMENT

Melbourne has a strong tradition of outdoor and street entertainment. Every summer there is a broad programme of theatre and music for adults and children in most major parks and gardens. During February, the Melbourne Symphony Orchestra (MSO) presents a series of free concerts at the Sydney Myer music bowl.
Street buskers, many travelling on an international circuit, also frequent a number of areas, the most popular being Fitzroy (see p403) and St Kilda, and appear at festivals. The main spot for regular street performances is the Bourke Street Mall, outside Myer and David Jones department stores and at the Southgate Complex (see p406). The Victorian Arts Centre also has regular programmes featuring free weekend street entertainment.

MELBOURNE PRACTICAL INFORMATION

Melbourne is well served by public transport and is easy to negotiate, given the grid structure of the city centre and the flat layout of its suburbs. Many of the public facilities have been upgraded, with the aim of attracting both business and tourists. Driving in the city is also easy and taxis are plentiful. Bureaux de change and automatic cash dispensers are located throughout the city. Melbourne is safe compared with many major cities, but common sense will also keep you out of trouble.

Road sign

DRIVING AND CYCLING

Driving in Melbourne is straightforward. However, at particular intersections in the CBD marked by "Safety Zone" signs, a "hook turn" is required; cars must queue on the left to turn right in order to accommodate or give way to trams. Cars left in No Standing zones will be towed away. The city has a tollway system known as **CityLink**, which uses electronic tolling:

drivers must purchase a pass before travelling. Melbourne's flat landscape is well suited to cyclists and there are many cycle tracks. Helmets are compulsory. Information on bicycle hire and good cycle routes can be found at **Bicycle Victoria**.

TRAVELLING BY PUBLIC TRANSPORT

Melbourne has a comprehensive system of trains, buses and trams, known as **Metlink**. This system also provides access to country and interstate travel, operated by the **V/Line** network.

The main railway station for suburban services is Flinders Street Station (*see p402*). Southern Cross Station is the main terminus for country and interstate trains.

The free City Circle Tram circuits the city every 15 minutes, while the City Explorer hop-on hop-off tourist bus departs at half-hour

TRAM ROUTES

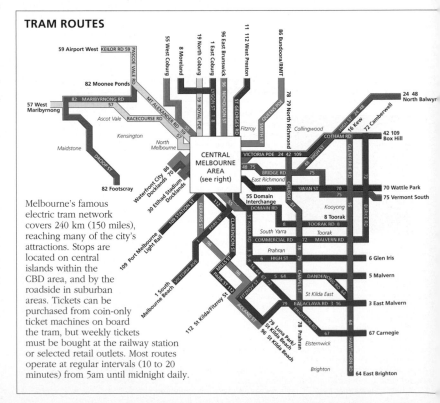

Melbourne's famous electric tram network covers 240 km (150 miles), reaching many of the city's attractions. Stops are located on central islands within the CBD area, and by the roadside in suburban areas. Tickets can be purchased from coin-only ticket machines on board the tram, but weekly tickets must be bought at the railway station or selected retail outlets. Most routes operate at regular intervals (10 to 20 minutes) from 5am until midnight daily.

Flinders Street Station, the city's main suburban rail terminus

intervals. Details are available from the **Melbourne Visitor Information Centre**. Another way to get around the city is via water taxis and cruises along the Yarra River.

TICKETS

Metropolitan tickets can be bought from railway stations, on board trams or from newsagencies. Ask at railway stations for discounts, including city-only travel and travel before 7am. Melbourne Visitor Information Centre sells

Smartvisit cards which allow entry to over 50 attractions and include use of public transport.

TOURIST INFORMATION

The main Tourist Information stop is the Melbourne Visitor Information Centre, which has free maps and guides to all attractions and activities. They also provide information on accommodation and arrange bookings.

There is a range of free travel publications available from information centres, covering attractions in Melbourne and Victoria.

DISABLED TRAVELLERS

The useful "CBD Mobility Map" is available from the Melbourne Visitor Information Centre and shows the smoothest path of travel along the city's streets. The majority of public facilities in the city have disabled access and toilets. Parking zones are allocated in the city and suburbs for disabled drivers; disabled driver permits are available from Melbourne Town Hall (see p389).

Central Melbourne area

KEY

- Swanston Street
- Elizabeth Street
- William Street
- Latrobe Street
- Bourke Street
- Collins Street
- Flinders Street
- Batman Avenue
- City Circle
- Suburban trams

River cruise boats providing a leisurely way to see the city

DIRECTORY

DRIVING AND CYCLING

Bicycle Victoria
Tel (03) 8636 8888.
www.bv.com.au

CityLink
Tel 13 26 29.
www.citylink.com.au

Royal Automobile Club of Victoria
Tel 13 11 11.
www.racv.com.au

Transport Information Line
Tel 13 16 38.

PUBLIC TRANSPORT

Metlink
Tel 13 16 38.
www.metlinkmelbourne.com.au

Skybus Information Service
Tel (03) 9335 3066.
www.skybus.com.au

Southern Cross Coach Terminal
Spencer St. *Tel 13 61 96.*
www.vline.com.au

V/Line
Spencer Street Station.
Tel 13 61 96. www.vline.com.au

RIVER CRUISES

Melbourne Water Taxis
No 4 Southgate (outside Langham Hotel).
Tel 0416 068 655.
www.melbournewatertaxis.com.au

Williamstown Ferries: Bay and River Cruises
No. 1 Southgate.
Exhibition Centre, St Kilda Pier.
*Tel (03) 9517 9444 (info),
(03) 9682 9555 (booking).*
www.williamstownferries.com.au

TOURIST INFORMATION

Melbourne Visitor Information Centre
Federation Sq, Cnr Swanston & Flinders sts. *Tel 13 28 42.*

Smartvisit Card
Tel 1300 661 711.
www.seemelbournecard.com

Victorian Tourism Information Service
Tel 13 28 42.
www.visitvictoria.com

MELBOURNE STREET FINDER

The key map below shows the areas of Melbourne covered in the *Street Finder*. All places of interest in these areas are marked on the maps in addition to useful information, such as railway stations, bus termini and emergency services. The map references given for sights described in the Melbourne chapter refer to the

Bourke Street sculpture

maps on the following pages. Map references are also given for the city's shops and markets *(see pp406–9)*, entertainment venues *(see pp410–11)*, as well as hotels *(see pp505–9)* and restaurants *(see pp552–6)*. The different symbols used for catalogue sights and other major features on the *Street Finder* maps are listed in the key below.

KEY TO STREET FINDER

■	Major sight
■	Place of interest
□	Other building
▣	CityRail station
🚌	Bus station
🚍	Coach station
⛴	Ferry boarding point
🚕	Taxi rank
P	Car Park
ℹ	Tourist information
✚	Hospital with casualty unit
🚔	Police station
✝	Church
✡	Synagogue
☪	Mosque
⊠	Post office
⛳	Golf course
═	Highway
═	Railway line
▬	Pedestrian street

0 metres	250
0 yards	250

0 kilometres	1
0 miles	1

Deborah Halpern sculpture at the city's Southgate complex *(see pp400–1)*

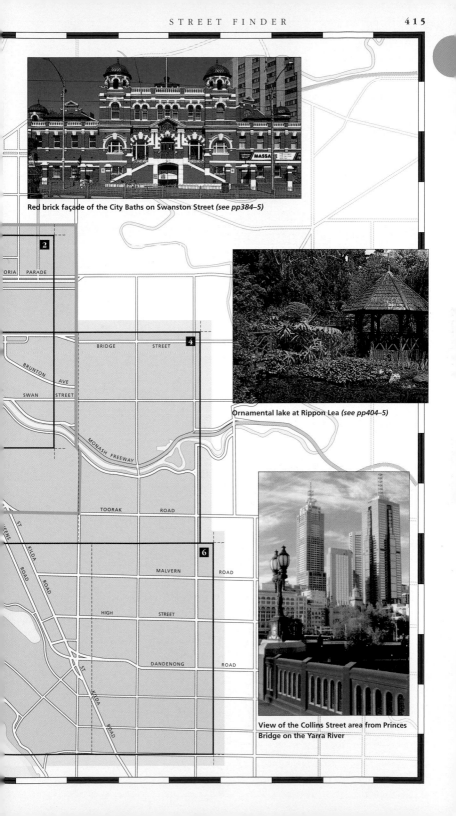

Red brick façade of the City Baths on Swanston Street *(see pp384–5)*

Ornamental lake at Rippon Lea *(see pp404–5)*

View of the Collins Street area from Princes Bridge on the Yarra River

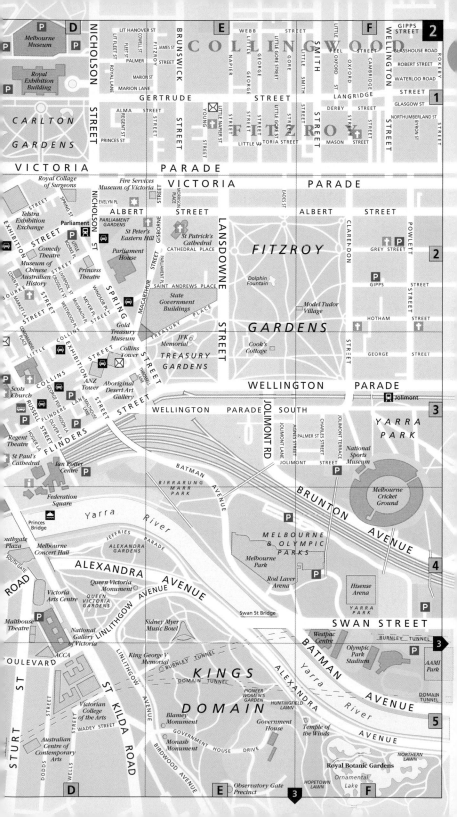

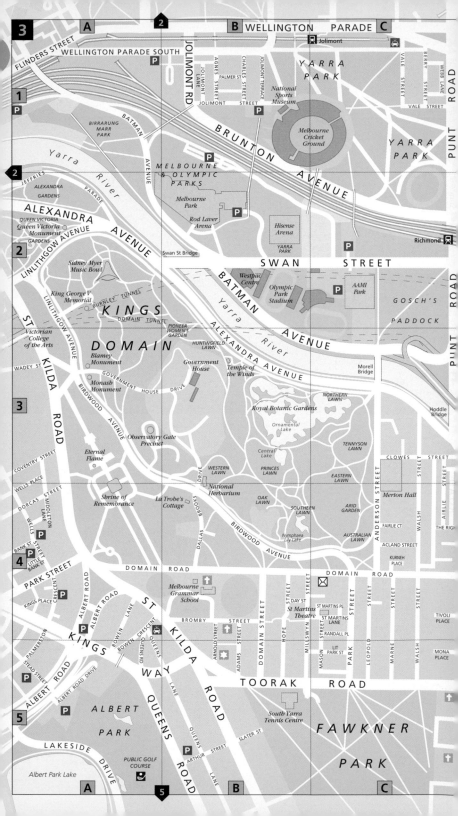

WESTERN VICTORIA

The theme of Western Victoria is diversity. For nature lovers, there is the bare beauty of the mallee deserts of the north or the forested hills and coastal scenery of the south. For a sense of the region's history, 19th-century gold-mining towns lie in the centre, surrounded by beautiful spa towns which have attracted visitors for more than a century. The area's sights are all within easy reach of one another.

Just as the Aboriginal tribes of Western Victoria had their lives and culture shaped by the region's diverse landscape, so the lives of the early European settlers were inevitably determined by the region's geographical features and immense natural resources.

The discovery of gold was the single most important event in Victoria's economic history, drawing prospectors from all over the world and providing the state with unprecedented wealth. Part of the legacy of this period is seen in the grand 19th-century buildings still standing in a number of central western towns. Also of interest are the spa towns clustered nearby, which draw their therapeutic waters from the same mineral-rich earth.

To the northwest, Victoria's major agricultural region, the Murray River, supports several large townships. The area is blessed with a Mediterranean-type climate, resulting in wineries and fruit-growing areas. In the south, the spectacular Grampian mountain ranges have long been of significance to the Aborigines. Fortunately, the steep cliffs and heavily forested slopes offered little prospect for development by early settlers and this beautiful area is today preserved as a wilderness. Wheat and sheep farmers have settled in parts of the Mallee region in the north of Western Victoria but, as in the Grampians, other settlers have been discouraged by its semi-arid conditions, and large areas of this stunning desert vegetation and its native wildlife have been left intact.

The southwestern coast was the site of the first settlement in Victoria. Its towns were developed as ports for the rich farmland beyond and as whaling stations for the now outlawed industry. Besides its history, this coastline is known for its extraordinary natural scenery of sandstone monoliths, sweeping beaches, forests and rugged cliffs.

Pioneer Settlement Museum, a re-created 19th-century port town on the Murray River at Swan Hill

◁ The spectacular coastal rock formations of the Twelve Apostles in Port Campbell National Park

Exploring Western Victoria

Western Victoria abounds with holiday possibilities. The spa towns close to Melbourne make perfect weekend retreats, with excellent facilities set amid gentle rural scenery. By contrast, the large number of historic sites and architectural splendours of the Goldfields region requires an investigative spirit and sightseeing stamina. The Grampians National Park contains trekking opportunities and rugged views, while the Mallee region offers wide open spaces and undulating sandhills. The Murray River towns have their fair share of historic sites, as well as many recreational facilities, restaurants and accommodation. The Great Ocean Road is a popular touring destination – set aside several days to explore the historic towns and scenic beauty of the coastline.

Rupertswood mansion in the Macedon Ranges

GETTING AROUND

The roads in Western Victoria are well signed and offer good roadside facilities. The Western Hwy is the route to Ballarat, the Grampians and the Mallee region. The Calder Hwy leads to the spa country and beyond to Bendigo, where it connects with highways to Mildura, Swan Hill and Echuca. Take the Princes Hwy to reach Geelong and the Great Ocean Road. All these places can also be reached by rail or a combination of rail and connecting coaches. However, in remoter areas, public transport may be a problem. A good solution is to take one of the tours from Melbourne offered by Metlink or V/Line *(see p413).*

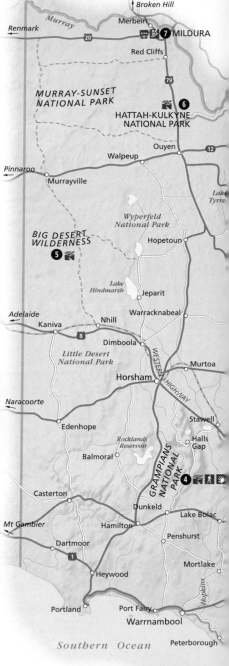

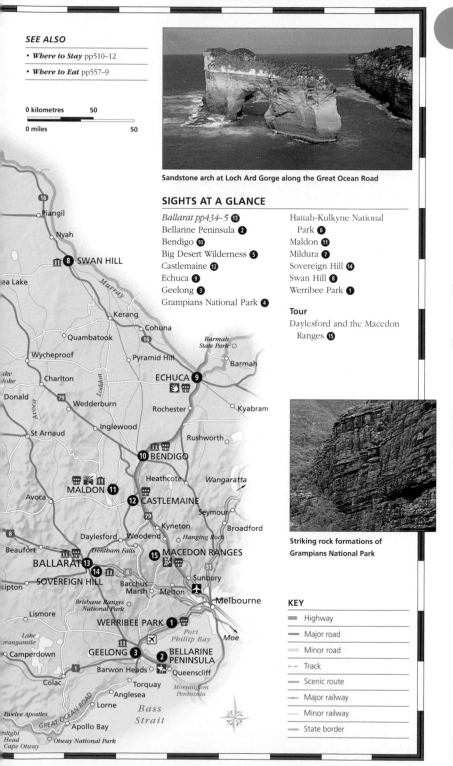

SEE ALSO

- ***Where to Stay*** pp510–12
- ***Where to Eat*** pp557–9

0 kilometres 50

0 miles 50

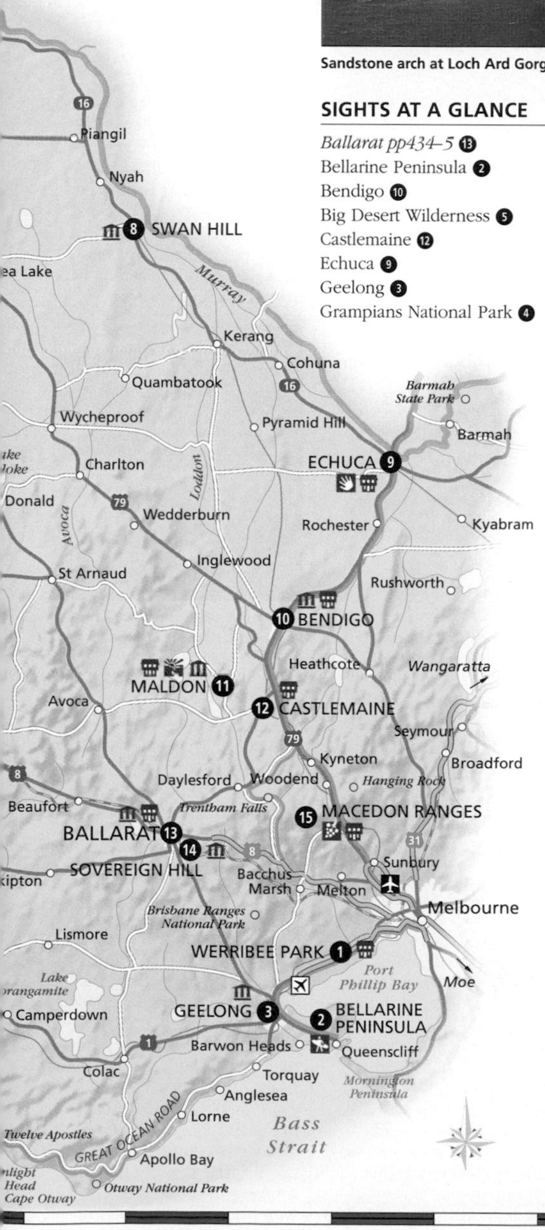

Sandstone arch at Loch Ard Gorge along the Great Ocean Road

SIGHTS AT A GLANCE

Ballarat pp434–5 13
Bellarine Peninsula 2
Bendigo 10
Big Desert Wilderness 5
Castlemaine 12
Echuca 9
Geelong 3
Grampians National Park 4
Hattah-Kulkyne National Park 6
Maldon 11
Mildura 7
Sovereign Hill 14
Swan Hill 8
Werribee Park 1

Tour

Daylesford and the Macedon Ranges 15

Striking rock formations of Grampians National Park

KEY

- Highway
- Major road
- Minor road
- Track
- Scenic route
- Major railway
- Minor railway
- State border

Flamboyant Italianate façade of Werribee Park Mansion

Werribee Park ❶

K Rd, Werribee. **Tel** *(03) 8734 5100.*
🚉 *Werribee.* ⬜ *daily.* 🏛️ ♿ ✔️
📧 🍴 www.werribeepark.com.au

From 1860 until 1890, the
wool boom made millionaires
of Australia's sheep farmers,
with the Chirnside family of
Werribee Park and later of
Victoria's Western District
among the richest and most
powerful. Their former
mansion is a striking Italianate house, built between 1873
and 1878. It has now been
restored to reflect the lifestyle
of wealthy pastoral families.
Visitors can stroll through the
sandstone mansion and see
the room where renowned
opera singer Dame Nellie
Melba once slept. A wing
added in the 1930s has been
converted into a luxury hotel.

Next to Werribee Park Mansion and its formal gardens
with popular picnic areas is
the Victoria State Rose Garden,
laid out in a symbolic Tudor
Rose-shaped design. It contains more than 5,000 beautiful rose bushes of different
varieties and colours that
are in flower from
November to
April. Also
attached to
Werribee Park
is **Werribee
Open Range Zoo**,
containing a range
of exotic animals, including
giraffes and hippopotami. The
National Equestrian Centre is
also part of the estate. This is
home to some of Australia's
premier show-jumping and
polo events. For bird-watchers,

**Chaise longue in
Werribee Park**

the nearby Werribee sewage
farm and Point Cook Coastal
Park provide magnificent views
of some rare species from
specially designated hides.
Migratory birds such as the
eastern curlew and tiny red-
necked stint spend the whole
summer in these protected
wetlands before flying north
to Japan and Siberia.

**🦌 Werribee Open
Range Zoo**
Werribee Park Mansion. **Tel** *(03)*
9731 9600. ⬜ *9am–5pm daily.*
🏛️ ♿ ✔️ www.zoo.org.au

Bellarine Peninsula ❷

🚉 *Geelong.* 🚌 *Ocean Grove,
Point Lonsdale, Portarlington,
Queenscliff.* ⛴️ *Queenscliff.*
ℹ️ *Queenscliff (03) 5258 4843.*

The Bellarine Peninsula, at
the western entrance to Port
Phillip *(see p430)*, is
one of Melbourne's many
summer resorts. The white
sand beaches of Barwon
Heads, Point
Lonsdale
and Ocean
Grove mark
the start of the
Great Ocean
Road and its
famous surf
beaches *(see
pp428–9)*.

The little village of **Point
Lonsdale** lies at the entrance
to the treacherous Heads –
the most dangerous entry to
any bay in the world due to
its churning seas and whirl-
pools. It is only 3 km (2 miles)

from Point Lonsdale, across
the swirling water (known as
the Rip) with its hidden rocks,
to Point Nepean on the Mornington Peninsula in Eastern
Victoria *(see p442)*.

The graceful old town of
Queenscliff faces Port
Phillip Bay so its beaches are
calm. Its fort was the largest
British defence post in the
southern hemisphere during
the 1880s, when a Russian
invasion was feared. At the
time Queenscliff was also a
fashionable resort for
Melburnians – its elegant
hotels, such as the Vue Grand,
are reminders of that opulent
era *(see p512)*. St Leonards
and Portarlington are also
popular holiday villages.

The peninsula has around 20
wineries, most offering cellar
door sales and tastings.

**Graceful wrought-iron detail on a
Queenscliff façade**

Geelong ❸

🏛️ *180,000.* ✈️ 🚉 🚌 🚌 ℹ️
26–32 Moorabool St (03) 5222 2900.

Geelong is the second largest
city in the state and has
a rural and industrial past.
Positioned on the north-facing
and sheltered Corio Bay, the
city has started to look once
again on its port as a recreational front door, so popular
in the first years of the 20th
century. The wooden 1930s
bathing complex at Eastern
Beach, with its lawns, sandy
beach and shady trees, was
restored to its former Art Deco
glory in 1994. Steampacket
Place and Pier were part of
an extensive redevelopment
project that saw the gradual
renovation of the old
warehouses into a thriving

waterfront quarter filled with excellent seafood restaurants, cafés, shops and hotels.

Opposite Steampacket Place are the historic wool stores. Wool was auctioned, sold and stored here prior to its being shipped around the globe from the 1880s until the 1970s. This generated Geelong's wealth. These buildings have been transformed; the largest houses the award-winning **National Wool Museum**, tracing Australia's wool heritage from the shearing shed to the fashion catwalks.

A short drive from Geelong is the Brisbane Ranges National Park, near Anakie, with lovely walks and native wildflowers, such as grevilleas, wattles and wild orchids, in bloom between August and November. Nearby is Steiglitz, a ghost town from the 1850s gold rush. Few buildings remain of this once thriving town, among them the elegant 1870s courthouse, which is closed to the public.

🏛 **National Wool Museum**
26–32 Moorabool St. **Tel** (03) 5227 4701. ⬜ daily. ● Good Fri, 25 Dec.
🖼 & ⬜ www.nwm.vic.gov.au

Grampians National Park ❹

🚉 Stawell. 🚌 Halls Gap.
ℹ Stawell (03) 5358 2314; Brambuk National Park and Cultural Centre (03) 5361 4000. ⬜ daily.

The mountains, cliffs and sheer rock faces of the Grampians rise like a series of

---

FLORA AND FAUNA OF THE GRAMPIANS

The Grampians are a haven for a wide range of birds, animals, native wildflowers and plants. The park is home to almost one-third of all Victorian plant species, with many, such as the Grampians guinea flower and boronia, found only within its rocky walls. Koalas grunt at night around Halls Gap and the kangaroos at Zumsteins are unusually tame and friendly. The air, trees and scrub teem with beautiful blue wrens, rainbow lorikeets, gang gang cockatoos, scarlet robins and emus. In spring, various wildflowers, orchids and pink heath burst from every crevasse and valley floor, and the creeks and rivers are full of rare brown-tree frogs. Just south of the Grampians in the town of Hamilton, a few surviving eastern barred bandicoots, once thought to be extinct, were discovered on the town rubbish tip. They were quickly rescued and have now become part of an active breeding and protection programme.

Rainbow lorikeet

---

waves above the flat western plains. Within this awesome national park, the third largest in Victoria, is a diversity of natural features and wildlife.

There are craggy slopes, cascading waterfalls and sandstone mountain tops, all formed 400 million years ago by an upthrust of the earth's crust. It has been known as *gariwerd* for thousands of years to local Aboriginal tribes, for whom it is a sacred place, and 80 per cent of Victoria's indigenous rock art is here. The Brambuk National Park and Cultural Centre is partly run by local Aboriginal communities who conduct tours to the many sites.

The Grampians offer many different experiences for tourists. Day trips take in the spectacular MacKenzie Falls and the Balconies rock formation. Longer stays offer bush camping, wildflower studies, exploration of the Victoria Valley over the mountains from Halls Gap and overnight hiking trips in the south of the park. Experienced rock climbers come from around the world to tackle the challenging rock forms in the park and also at the nearby Mount Arapiles.

Excellent maps of the area and guides to the best walks are all available from the park's visitors' centre.

Panoramic view from the rugged crags of the Grampians

The Great Ocean Road Coastline

The Great Ocean Road is one of the world's great scenic drives. Close to Melbourne, pretty holiday towns are linked by curving roads with striking views at every turn. Inland, the road cuts through the Otways, a forested landscape, ecologically rich and visually splendid. Between Port Campbell and Port Fairy is a landscape of rugged cliffs and swirling seas. The giant eroded monoliths, the Twelve Apostles, in Port Campbell National Park, are an awesome spectacle. To the far west, old whaling ports provide an insight into one of Australia's early industries; at Warrnambool, Southern Right Whales can still be seen.

Portland, *a deep-water port at the end of the Princes Highway, was the site of the first European settlement in Victoria in 1834. Stunning scenery of craggy cliffs, blowholes and rough waters can be found near the town at Cape Bridgewater.*

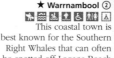

MOUNT GAMBIER Portland

Tower Hill Game Reserve

CAMPERDOWN

Lady Julia Percy Island

SOUTHERN OCEAN

★ Port Fairy ①

The tiny cottages of Port Fairy are reminders of the days when the town thrived as a centre for whaling in the 1830s and 1840s. Although the whaling industry has come to an end, the town is now a popular tourist destination.

★ Warrnambool ②

This coastal town is best known for the Southern Right Whales that can often be spotted off Logans Beach between May and October. The town itself has many fine art galleries, museums and old churches.

0 kilometres   25

0 miles   25

KEY

≋	Highway
▬	Major road
▭	Minor road
〜	River
☆	View point

Tower Hill Game Reserve, *13 km (8 miles) west of Warrnambool, is set in an extinct volcano crater. Dusk is the best time to visit and spot emus, koalas and kangaroos roaming the forests.*

Otway National Park *provides an introduction to some of the species of the southern temperate rainforest, including a famed 400-year-old myrtle beech tree.*

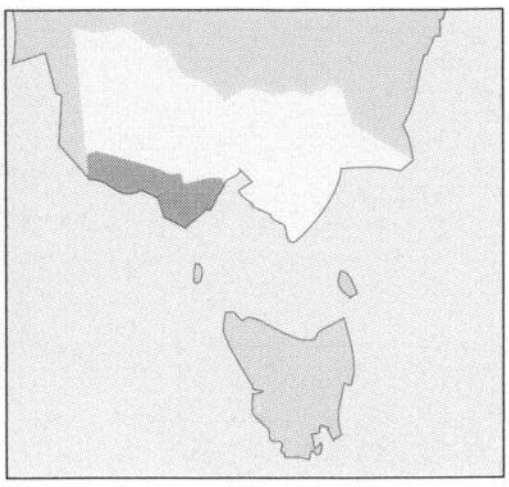

LOCATOR MAP

★ Loch Ard Gorge 5
♿
This treacherous area claimed the clipper *Loch Ard* in 1878. Local walks focus on the shipwreck, geology and Aboriginal history of the site.

★ Johanna Beach 7
🏄 🏊 🛟 🚻 ⛺
Another of Victoria's renowned surf beaches is backed by rolling green hills. The area is quite remote, but popular with campers in summer.

★ Lorne 9
🏄 🏊 ⛵ 🛟 ♿ 🚻 ⛺
Very popular in summer, this charming seaside village boasts excellent cafés, restaurants and accommodation. Nearby forests provide a paradise for walkers.

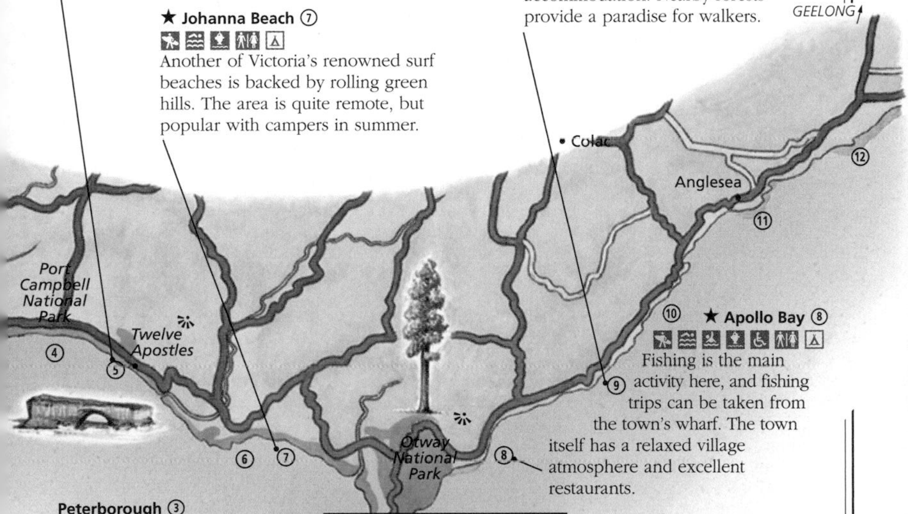
GEELONG
Colac
Anglesea
Port Campbell National Park
Twelve Apostles
Otway National Park

★ Apollo Bay 8
🏄 🏊 ⛵ 🛟 ♿ 🚻 ⛺
Fishing is the main activity here, and fishing trips can be taken from the town's wharf. The town itself has a relaxed village atmosphere and excellent restaurants.

Peterborough 3
🏄 🏊 🛟 🚻 ⛺
Victoria's dairy industry is based on this stretch of coastline. A popular rock pool beneath the cliff is known as the Grotto.

Port Campbell 4
🏄 🏊 🛟 ♿ 🚻 ⛺
Port Campbell beach is a sandy bay, safe for swimming. The town, set on a hill, has great views of the ocean.

Moonlight Head 6
🛟
Massive cliffs give way to rock platforms here in the heart of Otway National Park. Embedded anchors are reminders of the many ships lost along this perilous coastline.

Aireys Inlet 10
🏄 🏊 ⛵ 🛟 ♿ 🚻 ⛺
The red and white lighthouse is a landmark of this tiny coastal town with its beautiful ocean views.

Point Addis 11
🏄 🛟
The Great Ocean Road leads right to the headland with spectacular views from the car park of waves beating the rocks. There are also steps leading down the cliff for a more exhilarating experience of the rolling surf.

Bells Beach 12
🏄 🛟 🚻
An underwater rock platform is one of the natural features which contribute to the excellent surfing conditions at Bells. An international surfing competition is held here at Easter, bringing thousands of tourists to the area *(see p42)*.

Murrayville track in the Big Desert Wilderness Park

Kulkyne Park make for fine fishing, picnics, camping and bird-watching. Murray-Sunset National Park is also home to Victoria's largest flower, the Murray lily.

Mildura ❼

🏘 25,000. ✈ 🚌 🚆 ℹ 180–190 Deakin Ave (03) 5018 8380.

In 1887, Mildura was little more than a village on the banks of the Murray River, situated in the middle of a red sandy desert. That year, two Canadian brothers, William and George Chaffey, came to town direct from their successful irrigation project in California and began Australia's first large-scale irrigation scheme. Since then, the red soil, fed by the Murray and Darling rivers, has become a vast plain of farms stretching for nearly 100 km (60 miles).

Today, Mildura is a modern city with a thriving tourist trade. The former home of William Chaffey, the magnificent **Rio Vista** is worth a visit. Built in 1890, it has now been restored with its colourful furnishings. Grapes, olives, avocados and citrus fruit are grown successfully in the

Big Desert Wilderness ❺

🚍 Hopetoun. 🚌 Hopetoun. ℹ 75 Lascelles St, Hopetoun (03) 5083 3001; Parks Victoria Information Line 131963. **www**.parkweb.vic.gov.au

Victoria is so often seen as the state of mountains, green hills, river valleys and beaches that many visitors don't realize that a large part of the west of the state consists of arid desert and mallee scrubland.

These are areas of beauty and solitude, with sand hills, dwarf she-oaks, lizards, snakes and dry creek systems. Big Desert Wilderness Park and Murray-Sunset National Park are true deserts, with hot days and freezing nights. Murray-Sunset National Park is also home to Australia's rarest bird, the black-eared miner.

To the south, Wyperfeld and Little Desert national parks are not true deserts, as they contain lake systems that support diverse flora and fauna, including a wide range of reptiles.

Hattah-Kulkyne National Park ❻

🚍 Mildura. 🚌 Mildura. ℹ Mildura (03) 5018 8380; Parks Victoria Information Line 13 19 63.

Unlike its drier Mallee region counterparts, Hattah-Kulkyne National Park is a haven of creeks and lakes that are linked to the mighty Murray River through a complex

billabong (natural waterhole) overflow system.

Its perimeters are typical dry Mallee country of low scrub, mallee trees and native pine woodland, but the large lakes, including Lake Hattah, Mournpoul and Lockie, are alive with bird and animal life. Ringed by massive red gums, the surrounding habitat is home to an abundance of emus, goanna lizards and kangaroos. The freshwater lakes teem with fish, while pelicans, ibis, black swans and other water birds flock on the surface.

The lakes are ideal for canoeing, and the twisting wetlands and billabongs along the Murray and in Murray-

---

THE MURRAY RIVER PADDLESTEAMERS

Old paddlesteamer on the Murray River

Between the 1860s and 1880s, Australia's economy "rode on the sheep's back" – from the Western District of Victoria to the Diamantina Plains in central Queensland, wool was king. But the only way to transport it from the remote sheep stations to coastal ports and then on to its thriving English market was by river. There were no roads other than a few dirt tracks, so the paddlesteamers that plied the Murray, Murrumbidgee and Darling river systems were the long-distance lorries of the day. Towing barges loaded with wool, they reached the Port of Echuca after sailing for days from inland Australia. Then, stocked up with supplies for the sheep stations and distant river settlements, they returned upriver. However, by the 1890s railway lines had crept into the interior and the era of the paddlesteamer was gone. Now the Port of Echuca is once again home to beautifully restored, working paddlesteamers, such as the PS *Emmylou*, PS *Pride of the Murray* and PS *Canberra*.

Rio Vista, the elaborate home of irrigation expert William Chaffey, in Mildura

region and the area is rapidly expanding its vineyards and wineries *(see pp378–9).* The stark desert of Mungo National Park is only 100 km (60 miles) to the northeast of town.

🏛 Rio Vista

199 Cureton Ave. *Tel (03) 5018 8330.* ◯ *11am–4pm Wed–Mon.* ◉ *Good Fri, 25 Dec.* 🎟 🚻

Swan Hill ⑧

🏚 *10,000.* 🚍 🚉 ⛴ ❑ *306 Campbell St (03) 5032 3033.*

Black Swans are noisy birds, as the early explorer Major Thomas Mitchell discovered in 1836 when his sleep was disturbed by their early morning calls on the banks of the Murray River. That's how the vibrant river town of Swan Hill got its name, and the black swans are still a prominent feature.

One of the most popular attractions of Swan Hill is the **Pioneer Settlement Museum**, a 3-ha (7-acre) living and working re-creation of a river town in the Murray-Mallee area during the period from 1830 to 1930. The settlement buzzes with the sound of printing presses, the black-smith's hammer, the smell of the bakery and general daily life. "Residents" dress in period clothes and produce old-fashioned goods to sell

to tourists. Some of the log buildings are made of Murray pine, a hardwood tree impen-etrable to termites. The sound and light show at night (book-ings essential) is particularly evocative, providing a 45-minute journey through the town with accompanying sound effects, such as pounding hooves and a thundering steam locomotive.

🏛 Pioneer Settlement Museum

Monash Drive, Swan Hill. *Tel (03) 5036 2410.* ◯ *9:30am–4pm daily.* ◉ *25–26 Dec.* 🎟 🖥 🚻 **www**.pioneersettlement.com.au

Echuca ⑨

🏚 *11,000.* 🚍 🚉 ⛴ ❑ *2 Hey-garth St (03) 5480 7555.*

Ex-convict and entrepre-neur Henry Hopwood travelled to the Murray River region in 1853, at the end of his prison sentence. He seized upon the need for a river punt at the Echuca crossing by setting up a ferry service, as well as the Bridge Hotel. However, Echuca really came into its own in 1864 when the railway from Melbourne reached the port. Suddenly the town, with its paddle-steamers on the Murray River, became the largest inland port in Australia.

Today the port area features horse-drawn carriages, work-ing steam engines and old-fashioned timber mills. Tours of the area are available, along with regular river trips on a paddlesteamer. Visit the Star Hotel and discover the secret tunnel that let patrons leave after hours. There is also a paddlesteamer display opposite the hotel.

Approximately 30 km (19 miles) upstream from Echuca is Barmah Forest, the largest red gum forest in the world. A drive in the forest, with its 300-year-old river red gums and important Aboriginal sites, is highly recommended, as is the wetlands ecocruise that operates out of Barmah.

Gum trees on the road to Barmah Forest, outside Echuca

Bendigo ⑩

🏠 85,000. ✕ 🚗 🚉 🚌
ℹ️ 51–67 Pall Mall (03) 5434 6060.
○ daily. www.bendigotourism.com

Bendigo celebrated the gold rush like no other city, and with good reason – the finds here were legendary. In 1851, the first year of gold mining, 23 kg (50 lbs) of gold were extracted from only one bucketful of dirt. When the surface gold began to disappear, the discovery of a gold-rich quartz reef in the 1870s reignited the boom.

Reflecting the city's wealth, Bendigo's buildings are vast and extravagant, often combining several architectural styles within one construction. Government architect GW Watson completed two buildings, the Law Courts and Post Office, in the French and Italian Renaissance styles. The tree-lined boulevard Pall Mall is reminiscent of a French provincial city. The elegant Shamrock Hotel opened to great fanfare in 1897 and is still in operation (see p510). The European-style building is given a distinctly Australian feel with its front veranda. Self-guided heritage walk brochures are available from Bendigo's information centre, and the Vintage Talking Tram provides an excellent commentary on the town's history.

A major part of Bendigo's gold rush history was made by its Chinese population. The **Joss House**, dating from the 1860s, is a restored Chinese

Entrance to the Chinese Joss House in Bendigo

temple. It is a reminder of the important role played by the Chinese in the history of Bendigo. The **Golden Dragon Museum** also has displays that chart the history of the Chinese in the city. A ceremonial archway links the museum with the **Garden of Joy**, built in 1996. Based on a traditional Asian design, the garden resembles the Chinese landscape in miniature, with valleys, mountains, trees and streams.

The **Bendigo Art Gallery** has a splendid collection of Australian painting, including works depicting life on the gold fields. Nearby are shops selling pieces from Australia's oldest working pottery, Bendigo Pottery, established in 1858.

Bendigo's local pottery

The **Central Deborah Goldmine** offers visitors tours 86 m (260 ft) down to the last deep reef mine in town.

🏯 **Joss House**
Emu Point, Finn St, North Bendigo.
Tel (03) 5442w 1685. ○ 11am–4pm Wed, Sat & Sun. ● 25 Dec. 🏛

🏛 **Golden Dragon Museum and Garden of Joy**
1–11 Bridge St. **Tel** (03) 5441 5044.
○ 9:30am–5pm daily. ● 25 Dec.
🏛 ♿ 11

🏛 **Bendigo Art Gallery**
42 View St. **Tel** (03) 5434 6088.
○ 10am–5pm daily. ● 25 Dec.
🏛 ♿ by arrangement.

🏯 **Central Deborah Goldmine**
76 Violet St. **Tel** (03) 5443 8322.
○ 9:30am–5pm daily. ● 25 Dec.
🏛 ♿

Typical 19th-century building in Maldon

Maldon ⑪

🏠 1,200. 🚗 🚌 ℹ️ 93 High St (03) 5475 2569.

The perfectly preserved town of Maldon offers an outstanding experience of an early gold-mining settlement. This tiny town is set within one of the loveliest landscapes of the region. The hills, forests and exotic trees are an attractive setting for the narrow streets and 19th-century buildings. Maldon was declared Australia's "First Notable Town" by the National Trust in 1966. Cafés, galleries and museums cater to the town's stream of tourists.

Other attractions include Carmen's Tunnel, an old gold mine, and a 70-minute round-trip ride aboard a steam train to Muckleford. Visit at Easter to see the glorious golden leaves of the plane, oak and elm trees. There is also an Easter Fair, including an Easter parade and a street carnival (see p42).

Castlemaine ⑫

🏠 7,000. 🚗 🚗 🚌 ℹ️ Market Building, 44 Mostyn St (03) 5471 1795.

Castlemaine's elegance reflects the fact that gold finds here were brief but extremely prosperous. The finest attraction is the Market Hall, built in 1862. Architect William Benyon Downe designed this building in the Palladian style, with a portico and a large arched entrance leading into the building's restrained interior. The building is now the Visitors' Information Centre. **Buda Historic Home and Garden** was occupied from 1863 to 1981 by two generations of Hungarian silversmith, Ernest Leviny and his family. The house displays an extensive collection of arts and crafts works. The property is also noted for its largely intact 19th-century garden, a unique survivor of its period.

Castlemaine is also home to many writers and artists from Melbourne and has a lively collection of museums, cafés and restaurants.

🏛 Buda Historic Home and Garden
42 Hunter St. *Tel* (03) 5472 1032. ⭘ *Wed–Sun.* ⬤ *Good Fri, 25 Dec.* 🎫 ♿ *teahouse and upper garden area.*

Ballarat ⑬

See pp434–5.

Sovereign Hill ⑭

Bradshaw St, Ballarat. *Tel* (03) 5337 1100. ⭘ *10am–5pm daily.* ⬤ *25 Dec.* 🎫 🚗 ♿ **www**.sovereignhill.com.au

Sovereign Hill is the gold fields' living museum. Located on the outskirts of Ballarat *(see pp434–5)*, it

THE CHINESE ON THE GOLD FIELDS

The first Chinese gold-seekers landed in Melbourne in 1853. Their numbers peaked at around 40,000 in 1859. They worked hard in large groups to recover the tiniest particles of gold, but the Europeans became hostile, claiming that the new arrivals were draining the colony's wealth. In 1857, several Chinese were murdered. The state government tried to quell hostility by introducing an entry tax on Chinese who arrived by boat – the Chinese then landed in neighbouring states and walked overland to Victoria. At the end of the gold rush many stayed on to work as gardeners, cooks and factory hands. There is still a large Chinese community in the state.

Chinese working on the gold fields

offers visitors the chance to explore a unique period of Australia's history. Blacksmiths, hoteliers, bakers and grocers in full period dress ply their trades on the main streets, amid the diggers' huts, tents, old meeting places and the Chinese Village. Among the most absorbing displays are those that reproduce gold mining methods. The town's fields produced an estimated 640,000 kg (630 tonnes) of gold before being exhausted in the 1920s.

The nearby Gold Museum is part of the Sovereign Hill complex. Its changing exhibits focus on the uses of gold throughout history.

Sovereign Hill opens in the evenings for an impressive sound and light show, which re-enacts the events of the Eureka Stockade *(see p434)*.

Actors in period costume walking along the main street in Sovereign Hill

Ballarat ⑬

Ballarat gold nugget

In 1851, the cry of "Gold!" shattered the tranquillity of this pleasant, pastoral district. Within months, tent cities covered the hills and thousands of people were pouring in from around the world, eager to make their fortune. While there were spectacular finds, the sustainable prosperity was accrued to traders, farmers and other modest industries, and Ballarat grew in proportion to their growing wealth. The gold rush petered out in the late 1870s. However, the two decades of wealth can still be seen in the lavish buildings, broad streets, ornate statuary and grand gardens. Today, Ballarat is Victoria's largest inland city.

Ornate façade of Her Majesty's Theatre on Lydiard Street

🏛 Lydiard Street

The wealth of the gold fields attracted a range of people, among them the educated and well travelled. Lydiard Street reflects their influence as a well-proportioned streetscape, boasting buildings of exemplary quality and design.

At the northern end lies the railway station. Built in 1862, it features an arched train entrance and Tuscan pilasters. A neat row of four banks was designed by prominent architect Leonard Terry, whose concern for a balanced streetscape is clearly expressed in their elegant façades. Her Majesty's Theatre is an elaborate 19th-century structure and Australia's oldest surviving purpose-built theatre.

Opposite the theatre is Craig's Royal Hotel, begun in 1852. The hotel was extensively renovated in 1867 for a visit by Prince Alfred, Duke of Edinburgh, including the construction of a special Prince's Room and a further

22 bedrooms. In 1881, royal lanterns were constructed outside to honour a visit by the Duke of Clarence and the Duke of York (later King George V). This historic hotel is still in operation *(see p510)*.

🏛 Art Gallery of Ballarat

40 Lydiard St North. *Tel (03) 5320 5858.* ⬤ 9am–5pm daily. ⬤ Good Fri, 25 Dec. 📷 ♿ www.bagal.com

Ballarat has always enjoyed the spirit of benefaction. Huge fortunes were made overnight and much of these found their way into the town's institutions. The Art Gallery of Ballarat has been a major recipient of such goodwill, enabling it to establish an impressive reputation as Australia's largest and arguably best provincial art institution.

More than 6,000 works chart the course of Australian art from colonial to contemporary times. Gold field artists include Eugene von Guerard, whose work *Old Ballarat as it was in the summer of 1853–54* is an extraordinary evocation of the town's early tent cities. The gallery's star exhibit is the original Eureka Flag, which has since come to symbolize the basic democratic ideals which are so much a part of modern Australian society.

🏛 Eureka Centre

Cnr Eureka and Rodier streets. *Tel (03) 5333 1854.* ⬤ for redevelopment until mid-2012. 📷 ♿ www.eurekaballarat.com

The Eureka Centre is located in East Ballarat at what was the site of the Eureka Stockade. The $4 million centre, opened in 1998, commemorates the sacrifices of those who took part in a rebellion that came

---

THE EUREKA STOCKADE

An insurrection at Eureka in 1854, which arose as a result of gold diggers' dissatisfaction with high licensing fees on the gold fields, heralded the move towards egalitarianism in Australia. When hotel-owner Peter Bentley was acquitted of murdering a young digger, James Scobie, after a row about his entry into the Eureka Hotel, it incited anger among the miners. Led by the charismatic Peter Lalor, the diggers built a stockade, burned their licences and raised the blue flag of the Southern Cross, which became known as the Eureka Flag. On Sunday, 3 December 1854, 282 soldiers and police made a surprise attack on the stockade, killing around 30 diggers. After a public outcry over the brutality, however, the diggers were acquitted of treason and the licence system was abolished.

Rebel leader Peter Lalor

Lily pond in Ballarat's beautiful Ballarat Botanical Gardens

to signify "a fair go for all" and even, some would argue, the birthplace of Australian democracy. The five exhibition galleries bring the story of the Eureka Stockade to life using clever background sounds, back projection and life-sized displays. After visiting the centre, take a stroll in the centre's gardens, which are a place for contemplation and reflection.

🌷 Ballarat Botanical Gardens

Wendouree Drive. **Tel** (03) 5320 5135. 🔾 daily. ⬤ 25 Dec. 🚻 📷
These gardens, in the northwest of the city, are a telling symbol of Ballarat's desire for Victorian gentility. The rough and ready atmosphere of the gold fields could be easily overlooked here among the statues, lush green lawns and exotic plants. The focus of the gardens has

always been aesthetic rather than botanical, although four different displays are exhibited each year in the Robert Clark Conservatory. The most famous of these is the lovely begonia display, part of the Begonia Festival held here each March (see p42).

There is a Statuary Pavilion featuring female biblical figures in provocative poses, as well as a splendid centrepiece, *Flight from Pompeii*. The Avenue of Prime Ministers is a double row of staggered busts of every Australian prime minister to date, stretching off into the distance. The gardens run along the shores of the expansive Lake Wendouree.

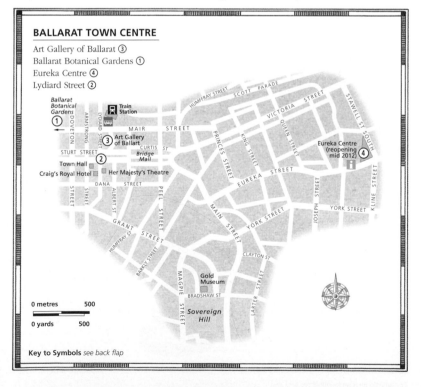

BALLARAT TOWN CENTRE

Art Gallery of Ballarat ③
Ballarat Botanical Gardens ①
Eureka Centre ④
Lydiard Street ②

0 metres 500
0 yards 500

Key to Symbols *see back flap*

Tour of Daylesford and the Macedon Ranges ⑮

Daylesford and the Macedon Ranges lie to the northwest of Melbourne. The landscape is dotted with vineyards, small townships, craft markets and bed-and-breakfasts *(see pp510–12).* The tour follows the Calder Highway, once taken by gold prospectors to the alluvial fields of Castlemaine and Bendigo *(see pp432–3)* before heading west into the spa country around Daylesford. The region's wealthy past is reflected in the 19th-century bluestone buildings, including wool stores and stately homes.

Malmsbury ⑧
During the gold rush, this peaceful hamlet was a busy stop for prospectors on their way to the gold fields.

BENDIGO

Malmsbury Reservoir

Lauriston Reservoir

Upper Coliban Reservoir

Hepburn Springs ⑨
The Mineral Springs Reserve is a large area of native bushland. It is an idyllic place for walkers and those who want to "take the waters" from the old-fashioned pumps.

Daylesford

WOMBAT STATE FOREST

Trentham Falls ⑩
Victoria's largest single-drop falls, 33 m (108 ft) high, are a few minutes' walk from Falls Road.

RUPERTSWOOD AND THE ASHES

During the Christmas of 1882, eight members of the touring English cricket team were house guests of Sir William John Clarke at Rupertswood. The English won a social game between them and their hosts. Lady Clarke burnt a bail, placed the ashes in an urn and presented them to the English captain, Ivo Bligh. The urn was later presented to Marylebone Cricket Club by Bligh's widow, and thus the cricketing tradition of contesting for The Ashes began.

The original 1882 Ashes urn

0 kilometres   5

0 miles   5

KEY

▬ Tour route

═ Other roads

✸ Viewpoint

Kyneton [7]
Historic Kyneton was once a supply town for diggers during the gold rush. It still has part of its 19th-century streetscape intact. The town has some good cafés and antique shops.

Hanging Rock [5]
This rock was formed 6 million years ago when lava rose up from the earth's surface and solidified. Erosion has caused the fissures through which you can now walk. Scene of the film *Picnic at Hanging Rock*, the area is steeped in Aboriginal history.

Woodend [6]
Named for its location at the edge of the Black Forest, Woodend has long been a haven for travellers. It has many restaurants, hotels and speciality shops.

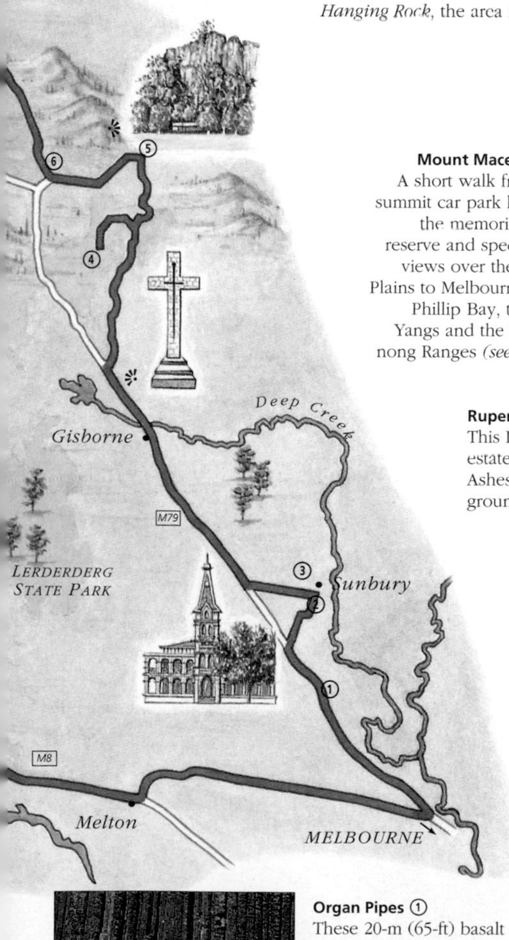
6
5
4
Deep Creek
Gisborne
M79
3
2
Sunbury
1
LERDERDERG STATE PARK
M8
Melton
MELBOURNE

Mount Macedon [4]
A short walk from the summit car park leads to the memorial cross reserve and spectacular views over the Keilor Plains to Melbourne, Port Phillip Bay, the You Yangs and the Dandenong Ranges *(see p443)*.

Rupertswood [3]
This Italianate mansion was built in 1874. The estate includes the cricket field on which The Ashes were created. The once magnificent grounds are now used by a boys' school.

Goona Warra [2]
The original vineyards of this 1863 bluestone winery were replanted during the 1980s. They now produce highly respected wines, available for tasting and sales daily from the cellar door.

Organ Pipes [1]
These 20-m (65-ft) basalt columns were formed by lava flows a million years ago. The Pipes can be seen from a viewing area near the car park or via a trail down to the creek bed.

TIPS FOR DRIVERS

Tour length: *215 km (133 miles).*
Stopping off points: *There are numerous places to stay and eat along the route, particularly at Woodend and Daylesford. Daylesford is also ideal for a romantic dinner or weekend lunch* (see p558).

EASTERN VICTORIA

Eastern Victoria is a region of immense natural beauty with snow-topped mountains, eucalyptus forests, fertile inland valleys, wild national parks and long sandy beaches. Some of the state's finest wine-growing areas are here, set around historic towns of golden sandstone. Fast rivers popular with rafters flow through the region and ski resorts resembling Swiss villages are found in the Victoria Alps.

Eastern Victoria has a range of attractions for the visitor. The fertile plains of the northeast, crossed by the Goulburn, Ovens, King and Murray rivers, offer a feast for the tastebuds: Rutherglen red wines; Milawa mustards; local cheeses; and luscious peaches, pears and apricots from Shepparton. Historic 19th-century towns such as Beechworth and Chiltern are beautifully preserved from their gold-mining days. Glenrowan is the site where Australia's most famous bushranger, Ned Kelly, was captured. An old-fashioned paddlesteamer rides regularly on the broad Murray River near Wodonga.

But towards the Victorian Alps and the towns of Bright and Mansfield another landscape emerges. This one is wild and very beautiful. In winter, there is exciting downhill skiing among the snow gums and peaks at village resorts such as Mount Buller and Falls Creek *(see pp 448–9)*. In summer, walk among the wildflowers in Alpine National Park, hike to the summit of Mount Feathertop, or try a rafting expedition down rivers such as the mighty Snowy.

To the east of Melbourne are the magnificent beaches of the Gippsland region. Favourite attractions here include Phillip Island with its fairy penguins, and Wilsons Promontory National Park with its wildlife, granite outcrops and pristine waters. Near the regional centres of Sale and Bairnsdale lie the Gippsland Lakes, Australia's largest inland waterway and an angler's paradise. Beyond, stretching to the New South Wales border, is Croajingolong National Park and 200 km (125 miles) of deserted coastline.

Canoeing down the Kiewa River near Beechworth in Eastern Victoria

◁ Mount Buller Alpine Village ski resort high in the Victorian Alps

Exploring Eastern Victoria

Excellent highways give access to the most popular
tourist attractions and towns of Eastern Victoria. The
Dandenong Ranges, Yarra Valley and Phillip Island
are within an easy day trip from Melbourne; the
region's coastline, which includes Gippsland Lakes,
around Lakes Entrance, Wilsons Promontory and
Croajingolong National Park, is
further to the south and east.
The mountains, ski resorts
and inland farm valleys are
better accessed from the
northeast of the state.
While most of the
major sights can be
reached by road,
some areas of the
Gippsland forests
and the Victorian Alps
must be explored in
4WD vehicles.

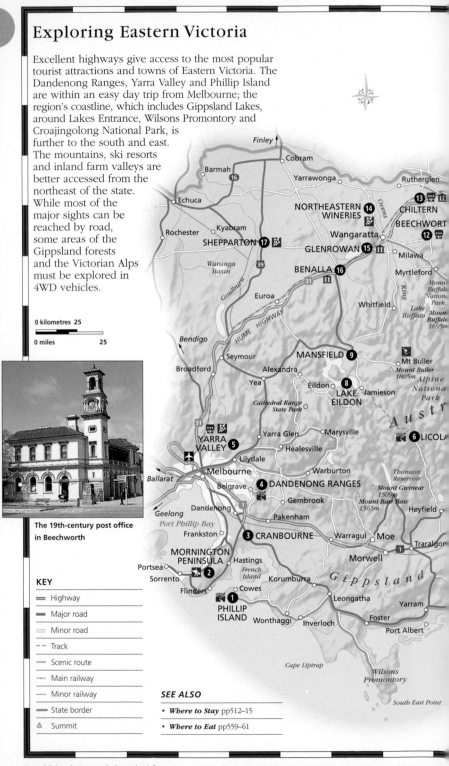

The 19th-century post office
in Beechworth

KEY

▬▬	Highway
▬▬	Major road
═══	Minor road
‑ ‑	Track
▬▬	Scenic route
▬▬	Main railway
▬▬	Minor railway
▬▬	State border
△	Summit

SEE ALSO

SIGHTS AT A GLANCE

Beechworth 12
Benalla 16
Bright 11
Buchan Caves 7
Chiltern 13
Dandenong Ranges 4
Glenrowan 15
Lake Eildon 8
Licola 6
Mansfield 9
Mornington Peninsula 2
Mount Beauty 10
Northeastern Wineries 14
Phillip Island 1
Royal Botanical Gardens, Cranbourne 3
Shepparton 17
Yarra Valley 5

Upper Murray Valley in the heart of northeastern Victoria

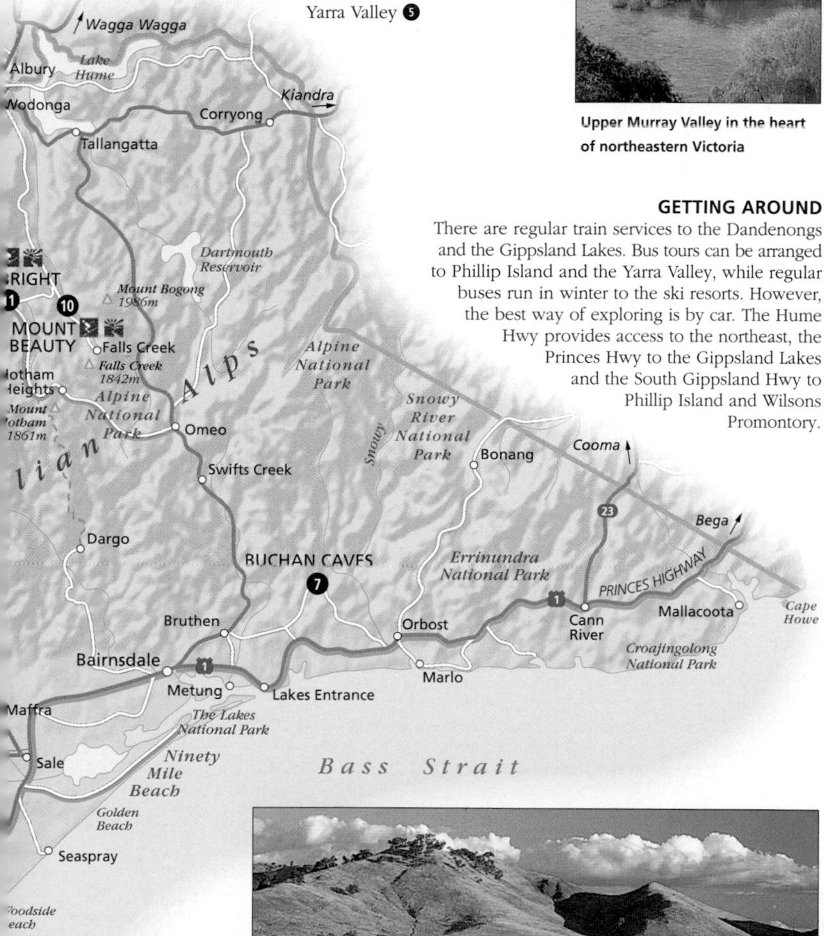

GETTING AROUND

There are regular train services to the Dandenongs and the Gippsland Lakes. Bus tours can be arranged to Phillip Island and the Yarra Valley, while regular buses run in winter to the ski resorts. However, the best way of exploring is by car. The Hume Hwy provides access to the northeast, the Princes Hwy to the Gippsland Lakes and the South Gippsland Hwy to Phillip Island and Wilsons Promontory.

Lake Eildon at the gateway to the Victorian Alps

Phillip Island ❶

🏛 *Cowes.* 🚢 *Cowes.* ℹ️ *Newhaven (03) 5956 7447.* ⏰ *9am–5pm daily; summer hols: 9am–6pm daily.* **www**.visitphillipisland.com

The penguin parade on Phillip Island is an extraordinary natural spectacle. Every evening at sunset at all times of the year, hundreds of little penguins come ashore at Summerland Beach and waddle across the sand to their burrows in the spinifex tussocks (spiky clumps of grass), just as their ancestors have been doing for generations. Once ashore, the small penguins spend their time in the dunes preening themselves and, in summer, feeding their hungry chicks.

At Seal Rocks, off the rugged cliffs at the western end of the island, is Australia's largest colony of fur seals. Approximately 16,000 of these seals can be seen playing in the surf, resting in the sun or feeding their pups on the rocks. Tourists can watch them from the cliff top or on an organized boat trip. There is also a large koala colony on Phillip Island.

Cape Woolamai, with its red cliffs and wild ocean seas, has good walking trails, excellent bird-watching opportunities and some great surfing. The peaceful town of Cowes is ideal for swimming, relaxing and dining.

The island gets very crowded during car and motorcycle race events so you need to reserve accommodation at these times.

Fairy penguins making their way up the sand dunes of Phillip Island

Rock pools at Sorrento on the Mornington Peninsula

Mornington Peninsula ❷

🚆 *Frankston.* 🚌 *to most peninsula towns.* 🚢 *Stony Point, Sorrento.* ℹ️ *Dromana (03) 5987 3078.*

Only an hour's drive from Melbourne, on the east side of Port Phillip Bay, the Mornington Peninsula is the city's summer and weekend getaway. From Frankston down to Portsea near its tip, the area is ideal for relaxing beach holidays. The sandy beaches facing the bay are sheltered and calm, perfect for windsurfing, sailing or paddling, while the rugged coast fronting the Bass Strait has rocky reefs, rock pools and surf beaches.

Arthur's Seat, a high, bush ridge offers views of the peninsula. The surrounding Red Hill wineries are fast gaining a reputation for their fine Chardonnays and Pinot Noirs. Sip a glass of one of these wines in the historic village of Sorrento or take a ferry trip across the narrow and treacherous Rip to the beautiful 19th-century town of Queenscliff *(see p426).*

Running the length of the peninsula, the Mornington Peninsula National Park has lovely walking tracks. Point Nepean, formerly a quarantine station and defence post, is now part of the national park. The beach at the tip of The Heads and Cheviot Beach, where Prime Minister Harold Holt disappeared while surfing in 1967, are both beautiful spots.

Environs
The village of Flinders is a peaceful, chic seaside resort, while Portsea is the summer playground of Melbourne's rich and famous. The atmosphere at the remote French Island, a short ferry trip from Crib Point, is unique, with no electricity or telephones. The island also teems with wildlife, including rare potoroo.

Royal Botanic Gardens, Cranbourne ❸

Off South Gippsland Hwy, 1000 Ballarto Rd. **Tel** *(03) 5990 2200.* 🚆 *Cranbourne.* 🚌 *Cranbourne.* ⏰ *9am–5pm daily.* ⚫ *25 Dec, days of total fire ban.* ♿ 🚻

The Royal Botanic Gardens in Melbourne are the city's pride and joy *(see pp398–9),* but they have not concentrated exclusively on native flora. The Cranbourne Botanic Gardens fill that niche. Amid the lakes, hills and dunes of this bushland park, banksias, wattles, grevilleas, casuarinas, eucalypts and pink heath bloom, while wrens, honeyeaters, galahs, rosellas, cockatoos and parrots nestle among the gardens' trees.

Dandenong Ranges ❹

🚉 Ferntree Gully & Belgrave. 🚌 to most towns. 🛈 Upper Ferntree Gully (03) 9758 7522. 🕐 9am–5pm daily.

Since the mid-19th century, the Dandenong Ranges, to the east of Melbourne, have been a popular weekend retreat for city residents. The cool of the mountain ash forests, lush fern gullies and bubbling creeks provide a welcome relief from the bayside heat.

The great gardens of the Dandenongs, many of which once belonged to the mansions of wealthy families, are magnificent for walks and picnics. Particularly popular is the Alfred Nicholas Memorial Garden at Sherbrooke with its oaks, elms, silver birches and Japanese maples around a boating lake. Flowers are the obvious attraction of the National Rhododendron Gardens at Olinda and Tesselaar's Tulip Farm at Silvan. A steam train, Puffing Billy, runs several times daily from Belgrave through 24 km (15 miles) of gullies and forests to Emerald Lake and on to Gembrook.

The superb lyrebird makes its home in the Dandenongs, particularly in Sherbrooke Forest. The 7-km (4-mile) Eastern Sherbrooke Lyrebird Circuit Walk through mountain ash offers a chance to glimpse these beautiful but shy birds. Another tranquil

Domaine Chandon vineyard in the Yarra Valley

walk is the 11-km (6-mile) path from Sassafras to Emerald.

Healesville Sanctuary, with its 30 ha (75 acres) of natural bushland, remains the best place to see indigenous Australian animals in relatively relaxed captivity. Highlights of any visit are the sightings of rare species such as platypuses, marsupials and birds of prey. This is a popular place to bring children who want to learn about Australian wildlife.

Further east are the Steavenson Falls and also nearby are the mountains of the Cathedral Ranges and the snow fields and trails of Lake Mountain (see pp448–9).

Sparkling wine of the Yarra Valley

🍴 **Healesville Sanctuary**
Badger Creek Rd, Healesville.
Tel (03) 5957 2800. 🕐 9am–5pm daily. 📷 ♿ www.zoo.org.au

Yarra Valley ❺

🚉 Lilydale. 🚌 Healesville service. 🛈 Healesville (03) 5962 2600.

The beautiful Yarra Valley, at the foot of the Dandenong Ranges, is home to some of Australia's best cool-climate wineries (see pp378–9). They are known for their Méthode Champenoise sparkling wines, Chardonnays and Pinot Noirs. Most of the wineries are open daily for wine tastings. Several also have restaurants, serving food to accompany their fine wines.

Just past the bush town of Yarra Glen with its old hotel, the Yarra Glen Grand (see p515), is the historic Gulf Station. Owned by the National Trust, it provides an authentic glimpse of farming life at the end of the 19th century.

Famous Puffing Billy steam train, making its way through the Dandenong Ranges

The Gippsland Coastline

The beautiful coastline of Gippsland is equal to any natural wonder of the world. Approximately 400 km (250 miles) of deserted beaches, inlets and coves are largely protected by national park status. There is the largest inland lake system in Australia, Gippsland Lakes, the pristine sands of Ninety Mile Beach and rare natural features such as the Mitchell River silt jetties. Birds, fish, seals and penguins abound in the area. With little commercial development, the coastline is a popular location with anglers, sailors, divers, swimmers and campers.

★ Lakes Entrance (9)

⛱ 🌊 🏊 🛟 ♿ 🚻

Lakes Entrance is the only entrance from the Gippsland Lakes to the sea, through the treacherous Bar. This major fishing port is also well equipped with motels, museums and theme parks for children.

1856
GENERAL STORE
The Sun

Port Albert, *the oldest port in Gippsland, was used by thousands of gold diggers heading for the Omeo and Walhalla gold fields in the 1850s. Quaint buildings with shady verandas line its streets, and it is home to the oldest pub in the state.*

★ Letts Beach (90 Mile Beach) (5)

⛱ 🌊 🛟 🚻

This sandy beach benefits from the ocean on one side and beautiful lakes on the other. Part of the Lakes National Park, the beach is home to the endangered fairy tern.

Corner Inlet (2)

🌊 🚻

This small inlet protects some of the world's most southerly mangroves and seagrass beds, as well as rare birds such as the red-necked stint.

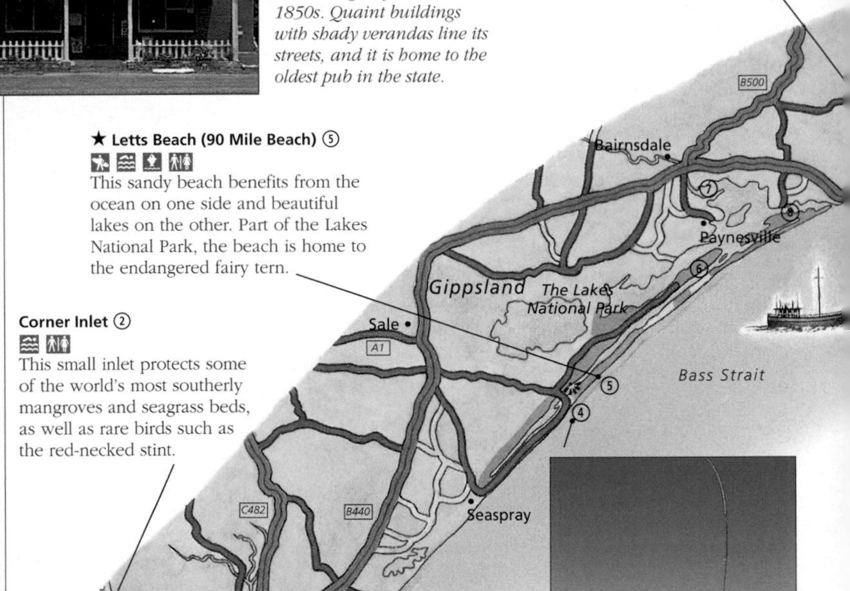
B500
Bairnsdale
Paynesville
Gippsland
The Lakes National Park
Sale
A1
Bass Strait
Seaspray
C482
B440
Yarram
MELBOURNE
B440
Port Albert
Wilsons Promontory National Park
Tidal River

★ Squeaky Beach, Wilsons Promontory National Park (1)

⛱ 🌊 🛟 ♿ 🚻

The white sand beach of this former land bridge to Tasmania is framed by granite boulders, spectacular mountain views, fern gullies and open heathlands which are a sanctuary for plants and wildlife.

★ Golden Beach (90 Mile Beach) (4)

⛱ 🌊 🛟 🚻

The calm waters of this stretch of ocean make it a popular destination for water sports enthusiasts. Fishing and sailing are two of the regular activities available in the area.

Bairnsdale *is one of the major towns of the Gippsland region, together with its neighbour, Sale. St Mary's Church, in the centre of the town, has distinctive Italianate-style painted walls and ceilings, as well as beautiful carved statuary set in its exterior walls.*

★ **Gipsy Point, Mallacoota Inlet** ⑫

This idyllic spot within a pleasant holiday region is ideal for summer picnics. Bird-watching and bushwalking are popular local activities.

LOCATOR MAP

BEGA

⑫

⑪

Croajingolong National Park

Orbost

⑩

⑨ **Lakes Entrance**

Woodside Beach ③

This easily accessible white sandy beach is popular with families, sunbathers and surfers. The area behind the beach benefits from many well-signposted bushwalks.

Gippsland Lakes ⑥

The lagoons, backwaters, islands and lakes of this region make up Australia's biggest inland waterway. Lakeside settlements are home to large sailing and fishing fleets.

Eagle Point ⑦

Silt banks from the Mitchell River stretch 8 km (5 miles) out into Lake King from Eagle Point. The silt banks are second only in length to those of the Mississippi River.

Metung ⑧

This pretty boating and holiday region, popular with campers, benefits from hot mineral pools.

Marlo ⑩

Located at the mouth of the great Snowy River, Marlo is a popular holiday destination, particularly with avid local anglers. Nearby is the large town of Orbost, the centre of East Gippsland's extensive timber industry.

Mallacoota ⑪

This remote fishing village is extremely popular with both Victorian and overseas tourists. It is set on an inland estuary of the Bass Strait, ideal for canoeing, fishing and sailing.

Croajingolong National Park *is a magnificent stretch of rugged and coastal wilderness, classified as a World Biosphere Reserve. Captain Cook caught his first sight of Australia in 1770 at Point Hicks.*

| 0 kilometres | 25 |
| 0 miles | 25 |

KEY

▨	Freeway
▬	Major road
▭	Minor road
▱	River
☀	Viewpoint

Licola ⑥

🏠 20. 🚉 Heyfield. ℹ️ Licola Wilderness Village, Jamieson Rd (03) 5148 8791. **www**.licola.org.au

Licola is a tiny village perched on the edge of Victoria's mountain wilderness. North of Heyfield and Glenmaggie, follow the Macalister River Valley north to Licola. The 147-km (90-mile) journey from Licola to Jamieson, along unsealed roads, takes in the magnificent scenery of Victoria's highest peaks. Only 20 km (12 miles) from Licola is Mount Tamboritha and the start of the popular Lake Tarli Karng bushwalk in the Alpine National Park, also a good base for those keen to explore the surrounding country. The village store has information.

Licola is entirely owned by the Lions Club of Victoria (the only privately owned town in the state). The club has developed the Lions Wilderness Village, which provides camp sites and a range of activities for young people.

Farmland near the tiny mountain village of Licola

Buchan Caves ⑦

Buchan Caves Reserve, Buchan. **Tel** (03) 5155 9264 or 13 19 63. ○ daily except 25 Dec. 🎫 daily (payable). **www**.parkweb.vic.gov.au

Some of the most spectacular limestone formations in Australia can be found at Buchan Caves. Two of the finest are Fairy Cave and Royal Cave, within Buchan Caves Reserve. Both caves are lit and have walkways; guided tours are conducted through-out the day, alternating between the two caves.

Dating back 300–400 million years, the caves and their awe-inspiring stalactites and stalag-mites were made by ancient rivers coursing and seeping through the limestone rock. Royal Cave also has colourful calcite-rimmed pools.

Entry to the reserve, where there are picnic facilities and a spring-fed pool suitable for swimming, is free. There are also camp sites and walking trails, while the nearby township of Buchan offers other accommodation. The reserve is a wildlife refuge to native animals such as kangaroos, possums, bellbirds and lyrebirds.

Limestone formations at Buchan Caves

Lake Eildon ⑧

🚉 Eildon. ℹ️ Eildon Visitors' Infor-mation Centre, Main St, Eildon (03) 5774 2909. **www**.lakeeildon.com

Lake Eildon, the catchment for five major rivers, including the Goulburn River, is a vast irrigation reserve that turns into a recreational haven in summer. Surrounded by the Great Dividing Range and Fraser and Eildon national parks, the lake is a good loca-tion for water-skiing, house-boat holidays, horse-riding, fishing and hiking. Kangaroos, koalas and rosellas abound around the lake, and trout and Murray cod are common in the Upper Goulburn River and in the lake. Canoeing on the Goulburn River is also a popular activity.

A variety of accommodation is available, from rustic cabins and camp sites in Fraser National Park to luxurious five-star lodges and guest-houses (see pp512–15).

Mansfield ⑨

🏠 2,500. 🚉 ℹ️ Visitors' Informa-tion Centre, 175 High St, Mansfield (03) 5775 7000.

Mansfield, a country town surrounded by mountains, is the southwest entry point to Victoria's alpine country. A memorial in the main street of Mansfield, just near to the 1920s cinema, commemorates the death of three troopers shot by the infamous Ned Kelly and his gang at nearby Stringybark Creek in 1878 – the crime for which he was

Blue waters of Lake Eildon, backed by the Howqua Mountain Ranges

Classic 19th-century architecture in the rural town of Mansfield

hung in Melbourne in 1880 (*see p394*).

The scenery of Mansfield became well known as the location for the 1981 film *The Man from Snowy River*, which was based on the poet "Banjo" Paterson's legendary ballad of the same name (*see p35*). Many local horsemen rode in the film and they still compete in the annual Cattleman's Cup, a horse race that is part of a weekend of celebration to mark the skills of the mountain cattlemen. Activities include woodchopping, whipcracking, haystacking and bushcraft, as well as displays of the cattlemens' horse-riding abilities.

Environs

The excellent downhill slopes of the Mount Buller ski resort (*see pp448–9*) is less than one hour's drive from Mansfield. Mount Stirling (*see pp448–9*) offers year-round activities, such as mountain bike riding (*see p566*).

Mount Beauty ⓾

🏠 2,300. 🚉 ℹ *31 Bogong High Plains Rd, Mt Beauty (03) 5755 0596.*

The town of Mount Beauty was first built to house workers on the Kiewa hydro-electricity scheme in the 1940s. It has since developed into a good base for exploring the beauty of the Kiewa Valley, with its tumbling river and dairy farms. Also nearby is the wilderness of the Bogong High Plains and the Alpine National Park (*see pp448–9*), with their walks, wildflowers and snow gums.

Within the national park, Mount Bogong, Victoria's

highest mountain, rises an impressive 1,986 m (6,516 ft) above the town. The sealed mountain road to Falls Creek (*see pp448-9*) is one of the main access routes to the region's ski slopes in winter. In summer, Rocky Valley Dam near Falls Creek is a popular rowing and high-altitude athletics training camp. There are beautiful bush walks, and at the top of the High Plains, there are opportunities for fishing, mountain biking, horse-riding and hang-gliding.

Bright ⓫

🏠 2,500. 🚉 ℹ *76a Gavan St (03) 5755 2275.*

Bright is a picturesque mountain town near the head of the Ovens River Valley, with the towering rocky cliffs of

Mount Buffalo (*see pp448–9*) to the west and the peak of the state's second highest mountain, Mount Feathertop, to its south. The trees along Bright's main street flame into spectacular colours of red, gold, copper and brown for its Autumn Festival in April and May (*see p42*). In winter, the town turns into a gateway to the snow fields, with the resorts of Mount Hotham and Falls Creek in the Victorian Alps close by (*see pp448–9*). In summer, swimming and fly-fishing for trout in the Ovens River are popular activities.

The spectacular **Mount Buffalo National Park** is also popular all year round; visitors can camp amid the snow gums by Lake Catani and walk its flower-flecked mountain pastures and peaks, fish for trout, hang-glide off the granite tors over the Ovens Valley or rock-climb the imposing sheer cliffs. During the winter, Mount Buffalo is a great place for cross-country skiing and snow play. A range of walking trails are available with wonderful views of Buckland Valley. Other activities on offer include canoeing, caving, horse-riding and paragliding.

🌸 **Mount Buffalo National Park**
Mount Buffalo Rd. **Tel** 13 19 63.
📷 ♿ *some areas.*

Buffalo River meandering through Mount Buffalo National Park

Skiing in the Victorian Alps

Child skiing

Australia offers fantastic skiing opportunities that rival the best in the world. Most of the resorts fall within Alpine National Park (see pp440-41), and are open for business from June to late September. Given that the season is so short, conditions can be variable. Mount Buller, Falls Creek and Mount Hotham are the main resort villages, and the whole region is very fashionable. There are chic lounge bars, top-end lodges and fine dining prepared by some of Melbourne's best chefs. Pistes are not as long as those in Europe and the USA, but the views of the High Plains are an unmissable experience.

Mount Buffalo 🎿 🎿
These less-crowded slopes are popular with beginners, intermediates and cross-country skiers.

Mount Buller 🎿 🎿 🎿
This is the most accessible of the major resorts, and hence the busiest and trendiest. Slopes suit beginners through to advanced skiers, with 80 km (48 miles) of groomed trails and a 405-m (1,300 ft)-vertical drop. The entrance car park at Mirimbah is 16 km (10 miles) from the village; there is a free shuttle bus for daytrippers.

Mount Stirling Entry to Mount Buller includes free cross-country skiing on Mount Stirling's groomed trails.

Lake Mountain This resort is ideal for cross-country skiing. Most runs are for beginners to intermediates. There is no on-mountain accommodation. Nearby Mount Donna Buang is fine for snowmen and toboggan runs.

Mount Baw Baw 🎿 🎿
The closest downhill ski resort to Melbourne is an excellent option for beginners, families and skiers on a budget. Nearby Mount St Gwinear offers superb cross-country skiing but no on-mountain accommodation.

Australian Alps Walking Track The 655-km (393-mile) Australian Alps Walking Track runs from historic Walhalla north-east to the Brindabella Ranges outside Canberra.

Map labels

Mount Buffalo (5558ft/1695m)
Lake Buffalo
Mour Buffa Chale
MT BUFFALO NATIONAL PARK
Mansfield
Lake Eildon
Mount Stirling Alpine Resort
Mount Buller Alpine Village
Mount Buller (5922 ft/1805m)
Eildon
Jamieson
ALPINE NATIONAL PARK
AUSTRALIAN
Lake Mountain
Licola
YARRA RANGES NATIONAL PARK
Mount Baw Baw (5134ft/1565m)
Mount St Gwinear (4915ft/1509m)
Thomson Resevoir
Mount Baw Baw Alpine Village
Walhalla

Falls Creek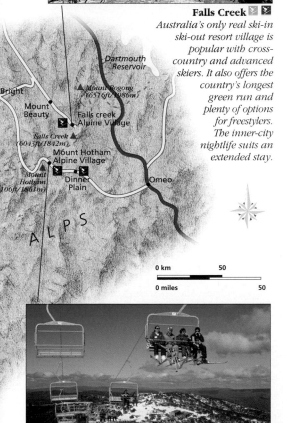

Australia's only real ski-in ski-out resort village is popular with cross-country and advanced skiers. It also offers the country's longest green run and plenty of options for freestylers. The inner-city nightlife suits an extended stay.

ADVICE FOR SKIERS

Costs
Entry fees are about A$30 per car per day. Lifts cost about A$100 per day per adult.

Transport and Equipment Hire
Roads are sealed to all resorts except Dinner Plain, Mount Baw Baw and Mount Stirling. By law, vehicles must carry chains. Equipment can be hired from the resorts listed here. Coaches run from Melbourne to every resort except Mount Baw Baw. Aircraft and helicopters from Melbourne and Sydney fly to Mount Hotham and Mount Buller. A helicopter shuttle flies between Mount Hotham and Falls Creek.

Ski Resorts
Dinner Plain
www.dinnerplain.com
Tel *(03) 5159 6451 or 1800 670 019 (toll free).*
Falls Creek
www.fallscreek.com.au
Tel *(03) 5758 1202.*
Lake Mountain
www.lakemountainresort.com.au
Tel *(03) 5957 7222.*
Mount Baw Baw
www.mountbawbaw.com.au
Tel *(03) 5165 1136.*
Mount Buller
www.mtbuller.com.au
Tel *(03) 5777 6077.*
Mount Hotham
www.mthotham.com.au
Tel *(03) 5759 4444.*
Mount Stirling
www.mtstirling.com.au
Tel *(03) 5777 6441 or (03) 5777 6077.*

For hotels in the area, see pp512–15.

Mount Hotham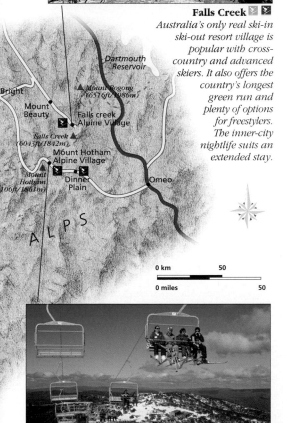

Featuring mostly challenging terrain, this area best suits intermediate to more advanced skiers. The resort has definitely gone more up-market in recent years. There is an airstrip 20 km (12 miles) from the village. Nearby Dinner Plain is popular with cross-country skiers.

KEY

▲	Peak
	Resorts
▬	Major road
═	Minor road
- -	Walking track
	Beginner
	Intermediate
	Advanced

Typical 19th-century honey granite building in Beechworth

Beechworth ⓬

🏠 3,500. 🚉 ℹ️ Shire Hall, Ford St (03) 5728 8065.
www.beechworth.com

Beautifully sited in the foothills of the Victorian Alps, Beechworth was the centre of the great Ovens gold fields during the 1850s and 1860s (see pp54–5). At the height of its boom, the town had a population of 42,000 and 61 hotels.

Today, visiting Beechworth is like stepping back in time. One of the state's best-preserved gold rush towns, it contains more than 30 19th-century buildings now classified by the National Trust. Its tree-lined streets feature granite banks and a courthouse, hotels with wide verandas and dignified brick buildings on either side. The majority of these are still in daily use, modern life continuing within edifices of a bygone era. Many of the old buildings are now restaurants, and bed-and-breakfasts. Dine in the stately old bank which is now the Bank Restaurant (see p560), stand in the dock of the courthouse where Ned Kelly was finally committed for his trial in Melbourne (see p394) and marvel at the old channel blasted through the granite to create a flow of water in which miners panned for gold.

The evocative Chinese cemetery is also worth a visit as a poignant reminder of the hundreds of Chinese who worked and died on the gold fields (see pp54–5).

Chiltern ⓭

🏠 1,500. 🚉 ℹ️ 30 Main St (03) 5726 1611.

This sleepy village was once a booming gold mining town with 14 suburbs. Only 1 km (half a mile) off the Hume Highway, halfway between the major towns of Wangaratta and Wodonga, today its colonial architecture and quiet atmosphere, as yet unspoiled by large numbers of tourists, make a visit to this pleasant town a worthwhile experience.

Chiltern has three National Trust properties: Dow's Pharmacy; the Federal Standard newspaper office; and Lakeview House. The last is the former home of Henry Handel Richardson, the pen name of Ethel Richardson, who wrote The Getting of Wisdom (see p35). Chiltern was her childhood home. The house, on Lake Alexander, has been restored with period furniture, and gives an insight into the life of the wealthy at the turn of the 20th century.

An unusual sight is the **Grapevine** museum. This shows the oldest and largest grapevine in the southern hemisphere – it once covered Chiltern's Star Hotel in its entirety.

For opening hours and other information on these attractions, check with the tourist information office in the town.

Lakeview House in Chiltern

Northeastern Wineries ⓮

🚉 Wangaratta & Rutherglen.
🚉 Wangaratta & Rutherglen.
ℹ️ Rutherglen (02) 6033 6300; Wangaratta (03) 5721 5711. **Campbells Winery Tel** (03) 6033 6000.
◻️ 9am–5pm Mon–Sat, 10am–5pm Sun. ⬤ Good Fri, 25 Dec.
Chambers Rosewood Winery Tel (02) 6032 8641. ◻️ 9am–5pm Mon–Sat, 10am–5pm Sun & public hols. ⬤ Good Fri, 25 Dec. **Brown Bros Tel** (03) 5720 5500. ◻️ 9am–5pm daily. ⬤ Good Fri, 25 Dec.
www.brownbrothers.com.au

The Northeastern area of Victoria is famous throughout the world for its vineyards and wineries (see pp378–9). In a region that now spreads south to encompass the King and Ovens valleys around Glenrowan, Milawa, Everton, Rutherglen and Whitfield, the wines produced can vary in style enormously, depending on the elevation and microclimate of each vineyard.

Rutherglen is best known for its full-bodied "Rutherglen Reds", such as Cabernet

Rows of grapevines in one of northeastern Victoria's many vineyards

Elegant Benalla Art Gallery on the shores of Lake Benalla

Sauvignons from 100-year-old wineries including Campbells and Chambers. The Muscats, Tokays and ports from both Rutherglen and Glenrowan are even more internationally renowned, with Bullers, Morris and Bailey's among the best. Rutherglen itself is a graceful town lined with antiques shops, and a selection of hotels and restaurants.

The grapes grown in the cool-climate region around Whitfield and Milawa make for crisp whites and lighter, softer reds. One of the more popular wineries in Northeastern Victoria is Brown Brothers at Milawa. The winery is open daily for both wine tasting and sales at the cellar door, and its excellent restaurant specializes in local delicacies from the region, including particularly good trout, cheese, honey and lamb. While at Milawa, visits to the Milawa Cheese Factory and Milawa Mustards are recommended.

Iron effigy of Ned Kelly

Street near the town's railway station, Kelly was finally captured after more than two years on the run. During this time he had earned almost hero status among Victoria's bush poor, particularly its many Irish Catholic farming families, as a Robin Hood-type character. Kelly knew the country around Glenrowan, especially the lovely Warby Ranges, in great detail and often used Mount Glenrowan, west of town, as a lookout. He was later hanged at Melbourne Gaol.

Today Glenrowan thrives on its Kelly history as a tourist attraction. A giant iron effigy of the bush-ranger greets visitors at the entrance to the town and there are various displays, museums and re-enactments depicting the full Kelly story, including his last defeat.

Glenrowan ⑮

🏃 1,000. 🚌 🚉 Wangaratta
ℹ️ Kate's Cottage, Gladstone St (03) 5766 2448.

Glenrowan was the site of the last stand by Australia's most notorious bushranger, Ned Kelly, and his gang *(see p394)*. In a shoot-out with police in 1880, on Siege

Benalla ⑯

🏃 8,500. ✕ 🚌 🚉 ℹ️ *The Creators' Gallery, 14 Mair St (03) 5762 1749.*

The rural town of Benalla is where Ned Kelly grew up and first appeared in court at the age of 15. Today it is most famous for its art gallery, built over Lake Benalla, which contains a fine collection of contemporary and Australian art. A Rose Festival is held in its magnificent rose gardens each November.

The town is also known as the Australian "capital" of gliding, with excellent air thermals rising from both the hot plains and nearby mountains.

Shepparton ⑰

🏃 30,000. ✕ 🚌 🚉 🚐 ℹ️ *534 Wyndham St (03) 5831 4400, 1800 808 839.*

The modern city of Shepparton, at the heart of the fertile Goulburn River Valley, is often called the "fruit bowl of Australia". The vast irrigation plains around the town support Victoria's most productive pear, peach, apricot, apple, plum, cherry and kiwi fruit farms. A summer visit of the town's biggest fruit cannery, SPC, when fruit is being harvested, reveals a hive of activity.

The area's sunny climate is also ideal for grapes. The two well-known wineries of Mitchelton and Tahbilk Wines, 50 km (30 miles) south of town, are both open for tours and tastings *(see pp378–9)*.

Harvesting fruit in Shepparton's orchards

TASMANIA

Tasmania's Wildlife and Wilderness

Tasmanian blue gum

Tasmania's landscape varies dramatically within its small area. Parts of Tasmania are often compared to the green pastures of England; however, the west of the state is wild and untamed. Inland there are glacial mountains and wild rivers, the habitat of flora and fauna unique to the island. More than 20 per cent of the island is now designated as a World Heritage Area (see pp26–7).

Russell Falls at Mount Field National Park

MOUNTAIN WILDERNESS

Inland southwest Tasmania is dominated by its glacial mountain landscape, including the beautiful Cradle Mountain – the natural symbol of the state. To the east of Cradle Mountain is the Walls of Jerusalem National Park, an isolated area of five rocky mountains. To the south is Mount Field National Park, a beautiful alpine area of glacial tarns and eucalypt forests, popular with skiers in the winter months.

Deciduous beech (Nothofagus gunnii) *is the only such native beech in Australia. The spectacular golden colours of its leaves fill the mountain areas during the autumn.*

The Bennett's wallaby (Macropus rufogriseus) *is native to Tasmania's mountain regions. A shy animal, it is most likely to be spotted at either dawn or dusk.*

Cradle Mountain, looking down over a glacial lake

COASTAL WILDERNESS

Tasmania's eastern coastline is often balmy in climate and sustains a strong fishing industry. The western coast, however, bears the full brunt of the Roaring Forties winds, whipped up across the vast expanses of ocean between the island state and the nearest land in South America. As a result, the landscape is lined with rocky beaches and raging waters, the scene of many shipwrecks during Tasmania's history.

The Tasmanian devil (Sarcophilus harrisii) *is noisy, potentially vicious and one of only three marsupial carnivores that inhabit the island.*

Banksia *comes in many varieties in Tasmania, including* Banksia serrata *and* Banksia marginata. *It is distinctive for its seed pods.*

Rugged coastline of the Tasman Peninsula

◁ **Autumn in Pine Valley, Cradle Mountain Lake St Clair National Park**

Calm area of Franklin Lower Gordon Wild River

RIVER WILDERNESS

The southwest of Tasmania is well known for its wild rivers, particularly among avid whitewater rafters. The greatest wild river is the 120-km (75-mile) Franklin River, protected within Franklin-Gordon Wild Rivers National Park by its World Heritage status. This is the only undammed wild river left in Australia, and despite its sometimes calm moments it often rages fiercely through gorges, rainforests and heathland.

Huon pine (Lagarostrobus franklinii) *is found in the southwest and in the south along the Franklin-Gordon River. It is prized for its ability to withstand rot. Some examples are more than 2,000 years old.*

Brown trout (Salmo trutta), *an introduced species, is abundant in the wild rivers and lakes of Tasmania, and a popular catch with fly-fishers.*

The eastern quoll (Dasyurus viverrinus) *thrives in Tasmania, where there are no predatory foxes and forests are in abundance.*

PRESERVING TASMANIA'S WILDERNESS

An inhospitable climate, rugged landforms and the impenetrable scrub are among the factors that have preserved such a large proportion of Tasmania as wilderness. Although there is a long history of human habitation in what is now the World Heritage Area (Aboriginal sites date back 35,000 years), the population has always been small. The first real human threat occurred in the late 1960s when the Tasmanian government's hydro-electricity programme drowned Lake Pedder despite conservationists' protests. A proposal two decades later to dam a section of the Franklin River was defeated when the federal government intervened. The latest threat to the landscape is tourism. While many places of beauty are able to withstand visitors, others are not and people are discouraged from visiting these areas.

Protest badges

Dam protests *were common occurrences in Tasmania during the 1980s, when conservationists protested against the damming of the Franklin River. The No Dams sticker became a national symbol of protest.*

TASMANIA

uman habitation of Tasmania dates back 35,000 years, when Aborigines first reached the area. At this time it was linked to continental Australia, but waters rose to form the Bass Strait at the end of the Ice Age, 12,000 years ago. Dutch explorer Abel Tasman set foot on the island in 1642 and inspired its modern name. He originally called it Van Diemen's Land, after the governor of the Dutch East Indies.

Belying its small size, Tasmania has a remarkably diverse landscape that contains glacial mountains, dense forests and rolling green hills. Its wilderness is one of only three large temperate forests in the southern hemisphere; it is also home to many plants and animals unique to the island, including a ferocious marsupial, the Tasmanian devil. Tasmanians are fiercely proud of their landscape and the island saw the rise of the world's first Green political party, the "Tasmanian Greens". One-fifth of Tasmania is protected as a World Heritage Area (see pp26–7).

The Tasmanian Aboriginal population was almost wiped out with the arrival of Europeans in the 19th century, however more than 4,000 people claim Aboriginality in Tasmania today. Evidence of their link with the landscape has survived in numerous cave paintings. Many Aboriginal sites remain sacred and closed to visitors, but a few, such as the cliffs around Woolnorth, display this indigenous art for all to see.

The island's early European history has also been well preserved in its many 19th-century buildings. The first real settlement was at the waterfront site of Hobart in 1804, now Tasmania's capital and Australia's second-oldest city. From here, European settlement spread throughout the state, with the development of farms and villages, built and worked by convict labour.

Today, Tasmania is a haven for wildlife lovers, hikers and fly-fishermen, who come to experience the island's many national parks and forests. The towns scattered throughout the state, such as Richmond and Launceston, with their rich colonial histories, are well worth a visit, and make excellent bases from which to explore the surrounding wilderness.

The historic port area of Battery Point in Hobart

◁ Breathtaking natural scenery in the Walls of Jerusalem National Park

Exploring Tasmania

Part, and yet not a part, of Australia, Tasmania's distinctive landscape, climate and culture are largely due to its 300-km (185-mile) distance from the mainland. The isolation has left a legacy of unique flora and fauna, fresh air, an abundance of water and a relaxed lifestyle. More than 27 per cent of Tasmania's land surface is given over to agriculture, with the emphasis on wine and fine foods. The state also benefits from vast expanses of open space, since approximately 40 per cent of Tasmanians live in the capital, Hobart. Tasmania, therefore, offers the perfect opportunity for a relaxing holiday in tranquil surroundings.

Nelson Falls in Franklin-Gordon Wild Rivers National Park

Yachts in Constitution Dock, Hobart

Three Hummock Island

Hunter Island

17 WOOLNORTH

15 STANLEY

Smithton

Marrawah   Trowutta   Wynyard

Arthur   BURNIE **14**   Penguin

Temma   **10**   DEVONPORT **13**

Gunns Plains

Sandy Cape   Waratah   Sheffield

Savage River   Cradle Valley   Liena

Corinna   **18**

Pieman River State Reserve   Rosebery   CRADLE MOUNTAIN
          Walls of Jerusalem National Park

Zeehan   **10**   LAKE ST CLAIR NATIONAL PARK

Southern Ocean   Queenstown   *Lake St Clair*

Strahan   Derwent Bridge

MACQUARIE HARBOUR **19**   **20**

          FRANKLIN-GORDON WILD RIVERS NATIONAL PARK
          Derwe...

Strathgordon   *Lake Gord...*

Lake Pedder   *South West National Park*

KING ISLAND

Cape Wickham

0 km   15

0 miles   15

Egg Lagoon

Yambacoona

16

KING ISLAND   *KING ISLAND*

Naracoopa

Currie   *TASMANIA*

Grassy

Stokes Point

0 km   25

0 miles   25

KEY

— Major road

═══ Minor road

— Scenic route

GETTING AROUND

Within this small, compact island, traffic is rarely a problem, and any visitor can journey across the diverse landscape with little difficulty. While all major cities and towns are linked by fast highways and major roads, some of the most splendid mountain, lake, coastal and rural scenery lies off the key routes, along the many alternative and easily accessible country roads.

A car is recommended, but coach services run between most towns and to some of the state's natural attractions.

SIGHTS AT A GLANCE

Ben Lomond National Park **9**
Bicheno **7**
Bothwell **4**
Bruny Island **22**
Burnie **14**
Cradle Mountain Lake St Clair National Park **18**
Devonport **13**
Flinders Island **11**
Franklin-Gordon Wild Rivers National Park **20**
Freycinet National Park **6**
Hadspen **12**
Hobart pp460–61 **1**
King Island **16**
Launceston **10**
Macquarie Harbour **19**
Mount Field National Park **21**
New Norfolk **3**
Oatlands **5**
Port Arthur pp470–71 **23**
Richmond **2**
Ross **8**
Stanley **15**
Woolnorth **17**

SEE ALSO

Wineglass Bay in Freycinet National Park

Hobart ●

Drunken Admiral

Spread over seven hills between the banks of the Derwent River and the summit of Mount Wellington, Australia's second oldest city has an incredible waterfront location, similar to that of her "big sister", Sydney. Hobart began life on the waterfront and the maritime atmosphere is still an important aspect of the city. From Old Wharf, where the first arrivals settled, round to the fishing village of Battery Point, the area known as Sullivans Cove is still the hub of this cosmopolitan city. Like the rest of the state, the capital city makes the most of its natural surroundings.

General view of Hobart and its docks on the Derwent River

🏛 Narryna Heritage Museum
103 Hampden Rd, Battery Point. **Tel** (03) 6234 2791. ◯ 10:30am–5pm Mon–Fri, 12:30–5pm Sat & Sun. ● July, Good Fri, 25 Apr, 25 Dec.
Located in an elegant 1836 Georgian house called Narryna, in Battery Point, this is the oldest folk museum in Australia. Beautiful grounds make a fine backdrop for an impressive collection of early Tasmanian pioneering relics.

🏛 Battery Point
✎ (03) 6230 8233 to book.
This maritime village grew up on the hilly promontory adjacent to the early settlement and wharves. The site was originally home to a gun battery, positioned to ward off potential enemy invasions. The old guardhouse, built in 1818, now lies within a leafy park, just a few minutes' walk from Hampden Road with its antiques shops, art galleries, tea-rooms and restaurants.
Battery Point retains a strong sense of history, with its narrow gas-lit streets lined with tiny fishermen's and workers' houses, cottage gardens and

colonial mansions and pubs. Hobart Historic Walks depart daily at 10am from the Visitors Centre located on Davey and Elizabeth streets.

🏛 Salamanca Place
Once the site of early colonial industries, from jam-making to metal foundry and flour milling, this graceful row of sandstone warehouses at Salamanca Place is now the heart of Hobart's lively atmosphere and creative spirit.
Mount Wellington towers above the buildings lining the waterfront, which have been

converted into art galleries, antique stores and antiquarian book shops. The Salamanca Arts Centre houses artists' studios, theatres and galleries. The area also has some of the city's best pubs, cafés and restaurants *(see pp562)*. The Salamanca Market is held every Saturday morning.

🏛 Castray Esplanade
Castray Esplanade was originally planned in the 19th century as a riverside walking track and it still provides the most pleasurable short stroll within the city. En route are the old colonial Commissariat Stores. These have been beautifully renovated for inner-city living, architects' offices and art galleries, focussing on Tasmanian arts and crafts.

🏛 Parliament House
Salamanca Place. **Tel** (03) 6233 2200. ◯ Mon–Fri. ● public hols. ✎ ✎ 10am & 2pm non-sitting days.
One of the oldest civic buildings in Hobart, designed by John Lee Archer and built by convicts between 1835 and 1841. Partly open to the public.

🏛 Maritime Museum of Tasmania
Cnr Davey & Argyle sts. **Tel** (03) 6234 1427. ◯ 9am–5pm daily. ● Good Fri, 25 Dec. ✎ ✎
Steeped in seafaring history, the museum is housed in the Carnegie Building, the former Hobart Public Library. It contains a fascinating collection of old relics, manuscripts, and voyage documents, as well as an important photographic collection which records Tasmania's maritime history.

Bustling Saturday market in Salamanca Place

Constitution Dock

Davey St.

The main anchorage for fishing boats and yachts also serves as the finish line of the annual Sydney to Hobart Yacht Race. This famous race attracts an international field of competitors *(see p41)*.

Constitution Dock borders the city and the old slum district of Wapping, which has now been redeveloped. Many of the old warehouses have been restored to include restaurants and cafés. One houses the idiosyncratic restaurant, the Drunken Admiral.

Tasmanian Museum and Art Gallery

40 Macquarie St. ***Tel*** *(03) 6211 4177.* 🕒 *10am–5pm daily.* ● *Good Fri, 25 April, 25 Dec.* ♿ 👥 ☕ **www**.tmag.tas.gov.au

This 1863 building, designed by the city's best-known colonial architect, Henry Hunter, is now home to a fine collection of prints and paintings of Tasmania, Aboriginal artifacts, and botanical displays.

Hunter Street

Once joined to Hobart Town by a sandbar and known as Hunter Island, this historic harbour-side locale is an art and culture precinct. It is lined with colonial warehouses and was once the site of the Jones & Co. IXL jam factory. The heart of this redevelopment is the award-winning Henry Jones Art Hotel *(see p516)*. Hunter Street is around the corner from the Federation Concert Hall.

Theatre Royal

29 Campbell St. ***Tel*** *(03) 6233 2299.* **Auditorium** 🕒 *Mon–Sat.* ● *public hols.* 📷 *for shows only.* ♿

Built in 1837, this is the oldest theatre in Australia. Almost gutted by fire in the 1960s, the ornate decor has since been meticulously restored. One of the most charming theatres in the world.

Criminal Courts and Penitentiary Chapel

6 Brisbane St. ***Tel*** *(03) 6231 0911.* 🕒 *10am–2pm daily.* ● *Good Fri, 25 Dec.* 📷 👥 *obligatory, by appt 10am, 11:30am, 1pm, 2:30pm.*

VISITORS' CHECKLIST

Hobart. 👥 *195,000.* ✈ *20 km (12 miles) NE of the city.* 🚌 *Red Line Coaches, Transit Centre, 199 Collins St.* ℹ *20 Davey St (03) 6230 8233.* 🎉 *Sydney–Hobart Yacht Race (26–29 Dec).* **www**.discovertasmania.com.au

In colonial days, courts and prison chapels were often next to each other, making the dispensing of swift judgment convenient. The complex also exhibits solitary confinement cells and an execution yard.

Museum of Old and New Art (MONA)

655 Main Rd, Berriedale. ***Tel*** *(03) 6277 9900.* 🕒 *10am–6pm daily.* ♿ ☕ 🛍 **www**.mona.net.au

MONA offers one of the country's most unique museum experiences. Carved out of a sandstone cliff, the museum houses an eclectic collection that ranges from ancient Egyptian mummies to some of the world's most unusual contemporary art.

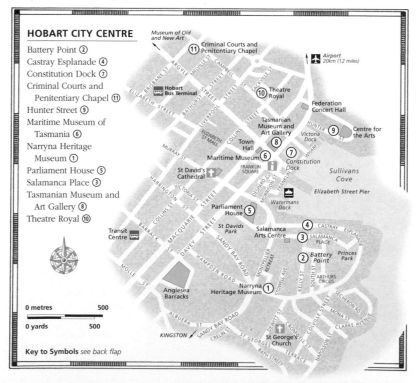

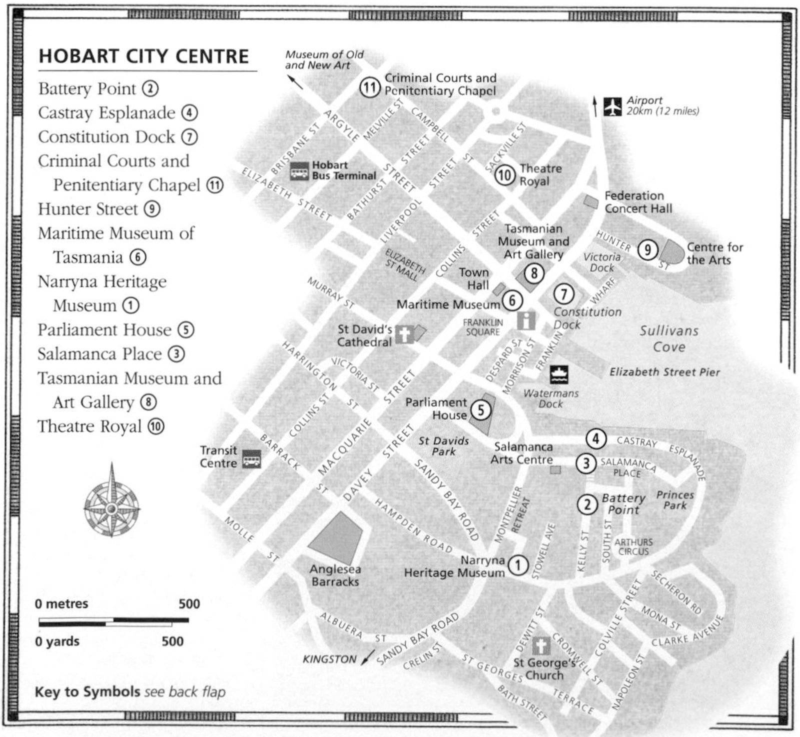
HOBART CITY CENTRE
Battery Point 2
Castray Esplanade 4
Constitution Dock 7
Criminal Courts and Penitentiary Chapel 11
Hunter Street 9
Maritime Museum of Tasmania 6
Narryna Heritage Museum 1
Parliament House 5
Salamanca Place 3
Tasmanian Museum and Art Gallery 8
Theatre Royal 10
Museum of Old and New Art
Criminal Courts and Penitentiary Chapel
Airport 20km (12 miles)
Hobart Bus Terminal
Theatre Royal
Federation Concert Hall
Tasmanian Museum and Art Gallery
Centre for the Arts
Victoria Dock
Town Hall
Maritime Museum
Constitution Dock
Sullivans Cove
Franklin Square
St David's Cathedral
Elizabeth Street Pier
Watermans Dock
Parliament House
St Davids Park
Salamanca Arts Centre
Transit Centre
Castray Esplanade
Salamanca Place
Battery Point
Princes Park
Arthurs Circus
Anglesea Barracks
Narryna Heritage Museum
St George's Church
Kingston
0 metres 500
0 yards 500
Key to Symbols see back flap

Hop farm on the Derwent River in New Norfolk

Richmond ❷

🏠 880. 🚌 ℹ️ Old Hobart Town, Bridge St (03) 6260 2502. **www**.richmondvillage.com.au

In the heart of the countryside, 26 km (16 miles) from Hobart, lies the quaint village of Richmond. This was the first area granted to free settlers from England for farming, and at its centre they established a township reminiscent of their homeland. Richmond now includes some of Australia's oldest colonial architecture. Most of the buildings were constructed by convicts, including the sandstone bridge built in 1823, the gaol of 1825 and the Roman Catholic Church of 1834.

Today, Richmond is a lively centre for rural artists and artisans. On the main street, between the old general store and post office, they occupy many of the historic homes.

New Norfolk ❸

🏠 5,200. 🚌 ℹ️ Circle St (03) 6261 3700. **www**.newnorfolk.org

From Hobart, the Derwent River heads north, then veers west through the Derwent River Valley. The hop farms and oast houses along the willow-lined river are testimony to the area's history of brewing.

At the centre of the valley, 38 km (24 miles) from Hobart, is the town of New Norfolk. Many of the first settlers in the region abandoned the colonial settlement of Norfolk Island to come here, hence the name. One of Tasmania's classified historic towns, it contains many interesting buildings, such as the Bush Inn of 1815, which claims to be one of Australia's oldest licensed pubs.

Typical 19th-century building in Bothwell

Bothwell ❹

🏠 400. 🚌 ℹ️ Australasian Golf Museum, Market Place (03) 6259 4033.

Nestled in the Clyde River Valley, Bothwell's wide streets are set along a river of the same name, formerly known as the "Fat Doe" river after a town in Scotland. The area's names were assigned by early Scottish settlers, who arrived from Hobart Town in 1817 with their families and 18-l (5-gal) kegs of rum loaded on bullock wagons.

The town's heritage is now preserved with some 50 National Trust buildings dating

Richmond Bridge, constructed with local sandstone

from the 1820s, including the Castle Hotel, the Masonic Hall (now an art gallery), Bothwell Grange Guest House and the Old Schoolhouse, now home to the Australasian Golf Museum. The stone heads above the door of the Presbyterian St Luke's Church depict a Celtic god and goddess. Even the town's golf course has a claim on history as the oldest in Australia, as it was laid out in the 1820s.

The town lies at the centre of the historic sheep-farming district of Bothwell, stretching along Lakes Hwy from the southern midlands to the famous trout fishing area of the Great Lakes. It is also the gateway to the ruggedly beautiful Central Plateau Conservation Area – a tableland which rises abruptly from the surrounding flat countryside to an average height of 600 m (nearly 2,000 ft).

Oatlands ❺

🏛 550. 🚉 🛈 *Heritage Highway Visitor Centre, 1 Mill Lane (03) 6254 1212.*

Oatlands was one of a string of military stations established in 1813 during the construction of the old Midlands Hwy by convict chain gangs. Colonial Governor Lachlan Macquarie ordered the building of the road in 1811, to connect the southern settlement of Hobart *(see pp460–61)* with the northern settlement of Launceston *(see p464).* During a later trip, he chose locations for the townships en route, naming them after places in the British Isles. The road ran through the area of Tasmania corresponding in name and geography to that of the British Midlands region, giving it its original name, but since the 1990s it has been dubbed the Heritage Hwy.

Oatlands soon became one of the colonial coaching stops for early travellers. Today, it has the richest endowment of Georgian buildings in the country, mostly made of local sandstone, including the 1829 courthouse and St Peter's Church (1838). As a result,

Coles Bay, backed by the Hazards Mountains, Freycinet Peninsula

the township is classified by the National Trust. Its most distinctive building, the Oatlands Flour Mill, was in operation until 1890.

Distinctive façade of the Oatlands Flour Mill

Freycinet National Park ❻

🚉 *from Bicheno.* 🛈 *Visitors' Centre (03) 6256 7000.* 🕐 *Nov–Apr: 8am–5pm daily; May–Oct: 9am–4pm daily.* ⬤ *25 Dec.* www.parks.tas.gov.au

The Freycinet Peninsula on the east coast of Tasmania is a long, narrow neck of land jutting south, dominated by the granite peaks of the Hazards Mountain Range. Named after an early French maritime explorer, the peninsula consists of ocean beaches on its eastern rim and secluded coves and inlets to the west. The fishing village of Coles Bay lies in the largest cove, backed by the Hazards.

Freycinet National Park on the tip of the peninsula is criss-crossed with walking tracks along beaches, over

mountains, around headlands and across lagoons. The most popular walk is Wineglass Bay – a short, steep trip up and over the saddle of the mountains. The blue waters of the bay are cupped against a crescent of golden sand, which inspired the name.

The drive up the east coast is a highlight of Tasmania. There are superb ocean views and marshlands inhabited by black swans. Small towns such as Orford and Swansea are good for overnight stays.

Bicheno ❼

🏛 640. 🚉 🛈 *41B Foster St (03) 6375 1500.*

Together with Coles Bay, Bicheno is the holiday centre of Tasmania's east coast. In summer, the bay is very popular due to its sheltered location, which means temperatures are always a few degrees warmer than elsewhere in the state.

The area also includes Tasmania's smallest national park, the 16,080 ha (39,700 acre) Douglas Apsley National Park. It contains the state's largest dry sclerophyll forest, patches of rainforest, river gorges, waterfalls and spectacular views along the coast. This varied landscape can be taken in along a three-day north to south walking track through the park. The north of the park is only accessible by 4WD. Other attractions in the area include the Apsley Gorge Winery and a 3-km long penguin breeding colony.

Man-O-Ross Hotel at the Four Corners of Ross crossroads

Ross ❽

🏃 275. ⊟ ℹ️ *Tasmanian Wool Centre, Church St (03) 6381 5466.*

Set on the banks of the Macquarie River, Ross, like Oatlands *(see p463)*, was once a military station and coaching stop along the Midlands Hwy. It lies at the heart of the richest sheep farming district in Tasmania, internationally recognized for its fine merino wool. Some of the large rural homesteads in the area have remained within the same families since the 1820s when the village was settled.

The town's most famous sight is Ross Bridge, built by convict labour and opened in 1836. It features 186 unique carvings by convict sculptor Daniel Herbert, who was given a Queen's Pardon for his intricate work. The town centres on its historic crossroads, the Four Corners of Ross: "Temptation,

Man O'Ross hotel sign

Damnation, Salvation and Recreation". These are represented respectively on each corner by the Man-O-Ross Hotel, the jail, the church and the town hall.

Ben Lomond National Park ❾

🖼️ *when ski slopes are open.* ℹ️ *National Parks & Wildlife Service, 167 Westbury Rd Prospect, Launceston (03) 6336 5312.* 🖼️

In the hinterlands between the Midlands and the east coast, 50 km (30 miles) southeast of Launceston, Ben Lomond is the highest mountain in northern Tasmania and home to one of the state's two main ski slopes. The 16,000-ha (40,000-acre) national park surrounding the mountain covers an alpine plateau of barren and dramatic scenery, with views stretching over the northeast of the

state. The vegetation includes alpine daisies and carnivorous sundew plants. The park is also home to wallabies, wombats and possums. From Conara Junction on the Heritage Hwy, take the Esk Main Road east before turning off towards Ben Lomond National Park.

The mountain's foothills have been devastated by decades of mining and forestry, and many of the townships, such as Rossarden and Avoca, have since suffered an economic decline. The road through the South Esk Valley along the Esk River loops back to the valley's main centre of Fingal. From here, you can continue through the small township of St Marys before joining the Tasman Hwy and travelling up the east coast.

Launceston ❿

🏃 71,400. ✈️ 🚌 *Georgetown 🛥️ to Devonport, then bus (summer only).* ℹ️ *Travel & Information Centre (inside Cornwall Square Transit Centre), cnr St John & Cimitiere sts 1800 651 827.*

In colonial days, the coach ride between Tasmania's capital, Hobart, and the township of Launceston took a full day, but today the 200-km (125-mile) route is flat and direct. Nestling in the Tamar River Valley, Launceston was settled in 1804 and is Australia's third-oldest city. It has a charming ambience of old buildings, parks, gardens, riverside walks, craft galleries

Alpine plateau in Ben Lomond National Park, backed by Ben Lomond Mountain

For hotels and restaurants in this region see pp515–17 and pp561–3

Riverside view of Penny Royal World in Launceston

and hilly streets lined with weatherboard houses. The **Queen Victoria Museum and Art Gallery** has the country's largest provincial display of colonial art, along with an impressive modern collection. It also shows Aboriginal and convict relics, and has displays on minerals, flora and fauna of the region.

Penny Royal World in Paterson Street is a complex of historic windmills, corn mills and gunpowder mills, which were carefully dismantled and moved from their original locations stone by stone. The working replica of a 19th-century gunpowder mill has 14 barges that take visitors underground so that they can observe the production process.

Cataract Gorge Reserve is alive with birds, wallabies, pademelons, potoroos and bandicoots, only a 15-minute walk from the city centre. A chairlift, believed to have the longest central span in the world, provides a striking aerial overview.

🏰 **Penny Royal World**
147 Paterson St, Launceston. **Tel** (03) 6334 3975. ◐ for renovations – phone for details. 🎫 ♿ limited.

🏰 **Queen Victoria Museum and Art Gallery**
Museum 2 Wellington St, Royal Pk, Launceston; **Gallery** 2 Invermay Rd, Inveresk. **Tel** (03) 6323 3777. ◯ 10am–5pm daily. ◐ Good Fri, 25 Dec. ♿ www.qvmag.tas.gov.au

Environs
In the 1830s, the Norfolk Plains was a farmland district owned mainly by wealthy settlers who had been enticed to the area by land grants. The small town of **Longford**, with its historic inns and churches, is still the centre of a rich agricultural district. It also has the greatest concentration of colonial mansions in the state. Many, such as Woolmers and Brickendon, are open for public tours.

Cape Barren geese in the Patriarch Sanctuary on Cape Barren Island

Flinders Island ⓫

✈ from Launceston, Melbourne. 🚢 from Bridport. ℹ Travel & Information Centre (inside Cornwall Square Transit Centre), cnr St John & Cimitiere sts, Launceston 1800 651 827.

On the northeastern tip of Tasmania, in the waters of the Bass Strait, Flinders Island is the largest within the Furneaux Island Group. These 50 or so dots in the ocean are all that remains of the land bridge which once spanned the strait to the continental mainland *(see pp22–3)*.

Flinders Island was also the destination for the last surviving 133 Tasmanian Aborigines. With the consent of the British administration, the Reverend George Augustus Robinson brought all 133 of them here in the 1830s. His aim was to "save" them from extinction by civilizing them according to European traditions and converting them to Christianity. In 1847, however, greatly diminished by disease and despair, the 47 survivors were transferred to Oyster Cove, a sacred Aboriginal site south of Hobart, and the plan was deemed a failure. Within a few years, all full-blooded Tasmanian Aborigines had died.

Much of Flinders is now preserved as a natural reserve, including Strezelecki National Park, which is particularly popular with hikers. Off the island's south coast is Cape Barren Island, home to the Patriarch Sanctuary, a protected geese reserve.

Flinders Island is reached by air from Launceston and Melbourne. There is also a leisurely ferry trip aboard the *Matthew Flinders* from Launceston and the small coastal town of Bridport.

Entally House in Hadspen

Hadspen ⓬

🏠 *1,900.* 🚉 **i** *Travel & Information Centre, cnr St John & Cimitiere sts, Launceston 1800 651 827.*

Heading west along the Bass Highway, a string of historic towns pepper the countryside from Longford through to Deloraine, surrounded by the Great Western Tiers Mountains. The tiny town of Hadspen is a picturesque strip of Georgian cottages and buildings which include an old 1845 coaching house.

The town is also home to one of Tasmania's most famous historic homes open to the public. Built in 1819 on the bank of the South Esk River, the beautiful **Entally House**, with its gracious veranda, has its own chapel, stables, horse-drawn carriages and lavish 19th-century furnishings.

Period furniture in Entally House

🏛 Entally House
Meander Valley Rd, via Hadspen. **Tel** *(03) 6393 6201.* ◯ *10am–4pm daily.* ⬤ *Good Fri, 25 Dec.* 🎦 🕭

Devonport ⓭

🏠 *22,500.* ✈ 🚉 🚌 ⛴
i *Devonport Visitor Centre, 92 Formby Rd (03) 6424 4466.*

Named after the county of Devon in England, the state's third-largest city is strategically sited as a river and sea port. It lies at the junction of the Mersey River and the Bass Strait, on the north coast. The dramatic

rocky headland of Mersey Bluff is 1 km (half a mile) from the city centre, linked by a coastal reserve and parklands. Here, Aboriginal rock paintings mark the entrance of **Tiagarra Aboriginal Culture Centre and Museum**, with its collection of more than 2,000 ancient artifacts.

From Devonport, the overnight car and passenger ferry *Spirit of Tasmania* sails to the Port of Melbourne on the mainland several times each week. With a local airport, Devonport is also an excellent starting point for touring northern Tasmania. Heading northwest, the old coast road offers unsurpassed views of the Bass Strait.

🏛 Tiagarra
Mersey Bluff, Devonport. **Tel** *(03) 6424 8250.* ◯ *9am–5pm daily.* ⬤ *Good Fri, Jun, 25 Dec.* 🎦 🕭

Burnie ⓮

🏠 *16,000.* ✈ 🚉 🚌 **i** *2 Bass Highway (03) 6430 5831.*

Further along the northern coast from Devonport is Tasmania's fourth-largest city, founded in 1829. Along its main streets are many attractive 19th-century buildings decorated with wrought ironwork. Previously, Burnie's prosperity centred on a thriving wood-pulping industry. One of the state's main enterprises, Associated Pulp and Paper Mills, established in 1938, was sited here. The city has shed its industrial character

in recent years, although some industry survives, notably the Lactos company, which has won many awards for its French- and Swiss-style cheeses. The sampling room has tastings and a café. Burnie also has a number of gardens, including Fern Glade, where platypuses are often seen feeding at dusk and dawn. Situated on Emu Bay, the area's natural attractions include forest reserves, fossil cliffs, waterfalls and canyons and panoramic ocean views from nearby Round Hill.

"The Nut" chairlift in Stanley

Stanley ⓯

🏠 *470.* 🚉 **i** *Stanley Visitors Centre, 45 Main Rd (03) 6458 1330.*

The rocky promontory of Circular Head, known locally as "the Nut", rises 152 m (500 ft) above sea level and looms over the fishing village of Stanley. A chairlift up the rock face offers striking views of the area.

Stanley's quiet main street runs towards the wharf, lined with fishermen's cottages and many bluestone buildings dating from the 1840s. Stanley also contains numerous top-quality bed-and-breakfasts and cafés serving fresh, local seafood (see p517).

Nearby, **Highfield House** was the original headquarters of the Van Diemen's Land

Company, a London-based agricultural holding set up in 1825. The home and grounds of its colonial overseer are now open for public tours.

🚪 **Highfield House**
Green Hills Rd, via Stanley. *Tel (03) 6458 1100.* ⬤ *Sep–May: 10am–4pm daily.* ⬤ *Jun–Aug: weekends.* 📷

King Island ⑯

✉ ⓘ *Tasmanian Travel and Information Centre, cnr Davey & Elizabeth sts, Hobart (03) 6230 8233.*

Lying off the northwestern coast of Tasmania in the Bass Strait, King Island is a popular location for wildlife lovers. Muttonbirds and elephant seals are among the unusual attractions.

Divers also frequent the island, fascinated by the shipwrecks that lie nearby. The island is also noted for its cheese, beef and seafood.

Woolnorth ⑰

Via Smithton. ⓘ *Woolnorth Rd (03) 6452 1493.* 🔒 *obligatory.*

The huge sheep, cattle and dairy farming property on the outskirts of Smithton is the only remaining land holding of the Van Diemen's Land Company. The last four Tasmanian tigers held in captivity were caught in the bush backing on to Wool-

Elephant seal bull on King Island – males can weigh up to 3 tonnes

north in 1908. Day-long tours of the property, booked in advance, include a lunch of local beef fillet and a trip to Cape Grim, known for the cleanest air in the world.

Cradle Mountain Lake St Clair National Park ⑱

🏕 *Cradle Mountain, Lake St Clair.* ⓘ *Cradle Mountain (03) 6492 1110 (shuttle from gate is every 20mins in summer, infrequent at other times). Lake St Clair (03) 6289 1172.* 📷 ♿

The distinctive jagged peaks of Cradle Mountain are now recognized as an international symbol of the state's natural environment. The second-highest mountain in Tasmania reaches 1,560 m (5,100 ft) at the northern end of the 161,000-ha (400,000-acre) this national park. The park then stretches 80 km (50 miles) south to the shores of Lake St Clair, the deepest freshwater lake in Australia.

In 1922, the area became a national park, founded by Austrian nature enthusiast Gustav Weindorfer. His memory lives on in his forest home Waldheim Chalet, now a heritage lodge in Weindorfer's Forest. Nearby at Ronny Creek is the registration point for the celebrated Overland Track, which traverses the park through scenery ranging from rainforest, alpine moors, buttongrass plains and water-fall valleys. Walking the track takes an average of six days, stopping overnight in tents or huts. At the halfway mark is Mount Ossa, the state's highest peak at 1,617 m (5,300 ft). In May, the park is ablaze with the autumn colours of Tasmania's deciduous beech *Nothofagus gunnii*, commonly known as "Fagus" *(see p454)*.

Dove Lake backed by the jagged peaks of Cradle Mountain

Boats sailing on the deceptively calm waters of Macquarie Harbour

Macquarie Harbour ⑲

🚌 Strahan. 🛈 The Esplanade, Strahan 1800 352 200.

Off the wild, western coast of Tasmania there is nothing but vast stretches of ocean until the southern tip of Argentina, on the other side of the globe. The region bears the full brunt of the "Roaring Forties" – the name given to the tremendous winds that whip southwesterly off the Southern Ocean.

In this hostile environment, Tasmania's Aborigines survived for thousands of years before European convicts were sent here in the 1820s and took over the land. Their harsh and isolated settlement was a penal station on Sarah Island, situated in the middle of Macquarie Harbour.

The name of the harbour's mouth, "Hell's Gates", reflects conditions endured by both seamen and convicts – shipwrecks, drownings, suicides and murders all occurred here. Abandoned in 1833 for the "model prison" of Port Arthur (see pp458–9), Sarah Island and its penal settlement ruins can be viewed on a guided boat tour available from the fishing port of Strahan.

Strahan grew up around an early timber industry supported by convict labour. It became well-known in the early 1980s when protesters from across Australia came to Strahan to fight government plans to flood the wild and beautiful Franklin River for a hydroelectric scheme. A fascinating exhibition at the visitor centre in Strahan charts the drama of Australia's most famous environmental protest.

Strahan today is one of Tasmania's loveliest towns, with its old timber buildings, scenic port and natural backdrop of fretted mountains and dense bushland. The town's newest attraction is a restored 1896 railway, which travels 35 km (22 miles) across rivers and mountains to the old mining settlement at Queenstown.

Franklin-Gordon Wild Rivers National Park ⑳

🚌 Strahan. 🛈 The Esplanade, Strahan (03) 6472 6020.
www.parks.tas.gov.au

One of Australia's great wild river systems flows through southwest Tasmania. This spectacular region consists of high ranges and deep gorges. The Franklin-Gordon Wild Rivers National Park extends southeast from Macquarie Harbour and is one of four national parks in the western part of Tasmania that make up the Tasmanian Wilderness World Heritage Area (see pp26–7). The park takes its name from the Franklin and Gordon rivers, both of which were saved by conservationists in 1983.

Within the park's 442,000 ha (1,090,000 acres) are vast tracts of cool temperate rainforest, as well as waterfalls and dolerite- and quartzite-capped mountains. The flora within the park is as varied as the landscape, with impenetrable horizontal scrub, lichen-coated trees, pandani plants and the endemic conifers, King William, celery top and Huon pines. The easiest way into this largely trackless wilderness is via a boat cruise from Strahan. Visitors can disembark and take a short walk to see a 2,000-year-old Huon pine. The park also

Imposing Frenchmans Cap looming over the Franklin-Gordon Wild Rivers National Park

For hotels and restaurants in this region see pp515–17 and pp561–3

Idyllic, deserted beach on the rugged Bruny Island

contains the rugged peak of Frenchmans Cap, accessible to experienced bushwalkers. The Franklin River is also renowned for its rapids.

The Wild Way, linking Hobart with the west coast, runs through the park. Sections of the river and forest can be reached from the main road along short tracks. Longer walks into the heart of the park require a higher level of survival skills and equipment.

Russell Falls in Mount Field National Park

Mount Field National Park ㉑

ℹ️ *Lake Dobson Rd, at entrance to the Park, (03) 6288 1149.* 🅿️

Little more than 70 km (45 miles) from Hobart along the Maydena Road, Mount Field National Park's proximity and beauty make it a popular location with nature-loving tourists. As a day trip from

Hobart, it offers easy access to a diversity of Tasmanian vegetation and wildlife along well-maintained walking tracks.

The most popular walk is also the shortest: the 10-minute trail to Russell Falls starts out from just within the park's entrance through a temperate rainforest environment. Lake Dobson car park is 15 km (9 miles) from the park's entrance up a steep gravel path. This is the beginning of several other walks.

The 10-km (6-mile) walk to Tarn Shelf is a bushwalker's paradise, especially in autumn, when the glacial lakes, mountains and valleys are spectacularly highlighted by the red-orange hues of the deciduous beech trees. Longer trails lead up to the higher peaks of Mount Field West and Mount Mawson, southern Tasmania's premier ski slope.

Bruny Island ㉒

Travel by car only – no public transport or taxis on Bruny Island. ℹ️ *Bruny D'Entrecasteaux Visitors' Centre, ferry terminal, Kettering (03) 6267 4494.*

On Hobart's back doorstep, yet a world away in landscape and atmosphere, the Huon Valley and D'Entrecasteaux Channel can be

enjoyed over several hours or days. In total, the trip south from Hobart, through the town of Huonville, the Hartz Mountains and Southport, the southernmost town in the country, is only 100 km (60 miles). On the other side of the channel are the orchards, craft outlets and vineyards around Cygnet.

The attractive marina of Kettering, just 40 minutes' drive from Hobart, is the departure point for a regular ferry service to Bruny Island.

Truganini, the Bruny Island Aborigine

The name Bruny Island actually applies to two islands joined by a narrow neck. The south island townships of Adventure Bay and Alonnah are only a half-hour drive from the ferry terminal in the north. Once home to a thriving colonial whaling industry, Bruny Island is now a haven for bird-watchers, boaters, swimmers and camel riders along its sheltered bays, beaches and lagoons.

Unfortunately, Bruny Island also has a sadder side to its history. Truganini, of the Wuenonne people of Bruny Island, is said to have been one of Tasmania's last full-blooded Aborigines. It was also from the aptly named Missionary Bay on the island that Reverend Robinson began his ill-fated campaign to round up the indigenous inhabitants of Tasmania for incarceration (*see p465*).

Port Arthur ㉓

Handcuffs from Port Arthur museum

Port Arthur was established in 1830 as a timber station and a prison settlement for repeat offenders. While transportation to the island colony from the mainland ceased in 1853, the prison remained in operation until 1877, by which time some 12,000 men had passed through what was commonly regarded as the harshest institution of its kind in the British Empire. Punishments included incarceration in the Separate Prison, a building set apart from the main penitentiary, where inmates were subjected to sensory deprivation and extreme isolation in the belief that such methods promoted "moral reform". Between 1979 and 1986, a conservation project was undertaken to restore the prison ruins. The 40-ha (100-acre) site is now Tasmania's most popular tourist attraction.

Commandant's House
One of the first houses at Port Arthur, this cottage has now been restored and furnished in early 19th-century style.

The Semaphore was a series of flat, mounted planks that could be arranged in different configurations, in order to send messages to Hobart and across the peninsula.

MASON COVE

The Guard Tower was constructed in 1835 in order to prevent escapes from the settlement and pilfering from the Commissariat Store, which the tower overlooked.

To Jetty, Dock Yard and Isle of the Dead cemetery

JETTY ROAD

0 metres 50
0 yards 50

★ Penitentiary
This building was thought to be the largest in Australia at the time of its construction in 1844. Originally a flour mill, it was converted into a penitentiary in the 1850s and housed almost 500 prisoners in dormitories and cells.

STAR FEATURES

★ The Separate Prison

★ Penitentiary

Hospital
This sandstone building was completed in 1842 with four wards of 18 beds each. The basement housed the kitchen with its own oven, and a morgue, known as the "dead room".

The Paupers' Mess was the dining area for poor ex-convicts.

Museum and café

Asylum
By 1872, Port Arthur's asylum housed more than 100 mentally ill or senile convicts. When the settlement closed, it became the town hall, but now serves as a museum and café.

★ **The Separate Prison** was influenced by Pentonville Prison in London. Completed in 1854, the prison was thought to provide "humane" punishment. Convicts lived in 50 separate cells in silence and anonymity, referred to by number not by name.

CHAMP STREET

TARLETON STREET

Trentham Cottage was owned by the Trenham family who lived in Port Arthur after the site closed. The refurbished interior is decorated with early 20th-century furnishings.

CHURCH STREET

Church
Completed in 1836, Port Arthur's church was never consecrated because it was used by all denominations. The building was gutted by fire in 1884, but the ruins are now fully preserved.

Government Cottage was built in 1853 and was used by visiting dignitaries and government officials.

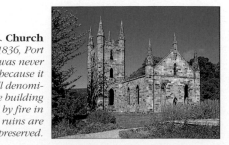

TRAVELLERS'
NEEDS

WHERE TO STAY

The wide range of places to stay in Australia is a reflection of the country's size, diversity and emergence as a major tourist destination. There are tropical island resorts, luxury and "boutique" city hotels, ski lodges, converted shearers' quarters on vast sheep stations, colonial cottage bed-and-breakfasts, self-catering

Sydney hotel doorman

apartments, youth hostels, house-boats and, of course, all the usual international chain hotels. Whether you simply want a bed for the night or an all-inclusive holiday resort, the appropriate accommodation can always be found. The listings on pages 478–517 give full descriptions of places to stay to suit all budgets throughout the country.

Art Deco façade of the Criterion Hotel in Perth *(see p499)*

GRADINGS AND FACILITIES

Australia has no formal national grading system. Terms such as four- and five-star are often used, but have no official imprimatur. State motoring organizations and some state and regional tourism bodies do, however, produce their own rankings and they are a useful indicator of standards and facilities.

In hotels and motels, air-conditioning in summer and heating in winter are almost always provided. Other standard features generally include coffee- and tea-making facilities, televisions, radios and refrigerators. En suite bathrooms are the norm, but specify if you want a bathtub: shower cubicles are more common. For double rooms, you will need to stipulate whether you require a double bed or twin beds. Luxury accommodation often features on-site swimming pools, exercise facilities and a hotel bar or restaurant.

PRICES

Prices for accommodation vary according to location and the facilities on offer. At the top end of the scale, the presidential, or similar, suite in a luxury hotel may have a four-figure daily rate, while a bed in a backpacker hotel will generally cost less than A$20. Budget motels and the majority of bed-and-breakfasts operate within the A$80–A$100 range. Prices may be increased slightly during peak

seasons, but equally many hotels offer discount rates during the low season.

BOOKINGS

Pressure on room availability is increasing, especially in the capital cities and the Queensland coastal destinations. This becomes particularly acute during school holidays and any major cultural and sporting events *(see pp40–41)*. It is therefore advisable to book far in advance and to specify if you have any special requests.

State tourist offices can help with or make bookings. Major airlines serving Australia also often have discounted packages on offer to cater to all price ranges *(see pp582–5)*.

CHILDREN

Travelling with children is relatively easy throughout Australia. Almost all accommodation will provide a small bed or cot in family rooms, often at no extra charge – enquire about any special rates in advance. Many major

Hyatt Hotel near the Parliamentary Triangle in Canberra *(see p487)*

◁ Surfers waiting for the next big wave at Bronte Beach, Sydney

Ornate Victorian architecture of the Vue Grand Hotel in Queenscliff *(see p512)*

hotels also offer baby-sitting services, while smaller establishments will be happy to check on a sleeping child while the parents are dining.

However, some of the country house hotels are strictly child-free zones.

Conrad Treasury luxury hotel in Brisbane *(see p488)*

DISABLED TRAVELLERS

Australian building codes now stipulate that any new buildings or renovations must provide facilities for the disabled. It is always advisable, however, to check on the facilities in advance.

LUXURY HOTELS AND RESORTS

The capital cities of each state are well endowed with luxury hotels. Well-known, international names such as **Hyatt, Hilton, Sheraton, Inter-Continental, Westin** and **Four**

Seasons stand side by side with such local institutions as The Hotel Windsor in Melbourne *(see p508)*.

Major tourist destinations abound with both luxury and budget beach resorts.

CHAIN HOTELS

There are various chain hotels and motels throughout Australia, which offer reliable and comfortable, if occasionally bland and indistinctive, accommodation. They vary in style and price, but the more reasonable end of the market includes reliable and well-known chains such as **Choice Hotels,** and motels such as **Metro Inns, Best Western, Country Comfort** and **Travelodge**. These hotels are popular with business travellers and often have facilities such as fax and internet connection available.

Stained glass at Simpsons in Sydney *(see p480)*

COUNTRY HOUSE HOTELS

Country house hotels, ranging from elegant mansions to simple bed-and-breakfast cottages, now exist throughout Australia. These offer personalized accommodation and an insight into the Australian way of life, in contrast to chain hotels. Many of these hotels have only one or two rooms so that stays are extremely peaceful, with many of the comforts of home.

Among the best country houses are those found in the wine regions *(see pp36–7)*, around the old gold fields *(see pp54–5)* and in Tasmania *(see pp452–71)*. **Tourism Australia** and state tourist offices will be able to supply full, up-to-date listings of bed-and-breakfast accommodation available in each area of the country.

Indoor pool at the Observatory Hotel in Sydney *(see p481)*

"The Grand" ballroom in the Hotel Windsor, Melbourne *(see p508)*

BOUTIQUE HOTELS

Many of the "boutique" hotels in Australia offer high-quality accommodation, often with luxury facilities, within an intimate atmosphere and few rooms.

Most boutique hotels do not advertise in glossy brochures, but operate through recommendations. However, tourist offices can provide information and many can be found on the internet. Some of the best are also listed on the following pages.

Australian bed and breakfasts (B&Bs), many in heritage-listed premises, also tend to be of a high standard. They range from farmstays to glamorous country house hotels.

Backpackers' resort sign

BACKPACKER HOTELS AND YOUTH HOSTELS

One of the fastest growing areas of Australia's accommodation industry is hotels for the increasing number of young backpackers. Despite their budget prices and basic facilities, the majority are clean and comfortable, although standards can vary widely in different areas. The internationally renowned **Youth Hostel Association** also has its own chain of hostels across the country, in all the major cities, ski resorts and many of the national parks. These offer clean and comfortable accommodation, particularly for those travellers on a tight budget.

While it is necessary to book in advance at some hostels, others do not take bookings and beds are on a first come, first served basis. Apartments, rooms and dormitories are all available, but dormitories may be mixed sex, so check, if necessary, before arriving.

The backpacker scene changes quickly, so it is often worth asking other travellers for the latest developments and for their recommendations, as well as gathering up-to-date information from the state tourist offices.

It is also worth remembering that, despite its name, the Youth Hostel Association also caters for senior citizens.

PUB ACCOMMODATION

Australian pubs are generally also referred to as hotels because historically they accommodated travellers. Many pubs still offer bed-and-breakfast accommodation. The quality can vary, but they are usually good value for money.

SELF-CATERING APARTMENTS

Self-Catering apartments are the latest accommodation trend in Australia. Full kitchen and laundry facilities are usually provided. Within cities, some apartments also cater for business travellers. Prices are generally on a par with the major chain motels.

Ornate Victorian Lenna of Hobart Hotel in Tasmania's capital *(see p516)*

Classic Australian pub accommodation at the Bellbird Hotel in the Hunter Valley *(see p482)*

FARM STAYS AND HOUSEBOATS

Many sheep and cattle stations welcome visitors for farm stays, offering a unique insight into rural Australian life. Many are near major cities, while others are in the vast Outback *(see pp28–9)*. Accommodation may be in traditional shearers' or cattle herders' quarters, or within the homestead itself. A stay usually includes the opportunity to be involved in the working life of the station. Ask State tourist offices for details. Another interesting and very relaxing holiday can be had on a houseboat along the vast Murray River which crosses from New South Wales and Victoria to South Australia. An international driving licence is the only requirement to be your own riverboat captain.

CAMPING AND CARAVAN PARKS

Camp and caravan sites are found throughout the country, the majority dotted along the vast coastline and in the inland national parks. They offer a cheap and idyllic way of enjoying the natural beauty and wildlife of Australia.

Many camp sites allow "walk in" camping without the need for booking, provided space is available. However, some areas may require a camping permit. The majority of caravan parks have on-site vans for rent at relatively low prices. Facilities usually include laundry and shower blocks and a small general store for provisions.

DIRECTORY

TOURIST OFFICES

Queensland Travel Centre
The Mall, Brisbane, QLD 4001. *Tel 138 833.*
www.sunloverholidays.com.au

South Australian Travel Centre
18 King William St, Adelaide, SA 5000.
Tel 1300 655 276.
www.southaustralia.com

Tourism ACT
333 Northbourne Ave, ACT 2602. *Tel 1300 554 114.* **www**.visitcanberra.com.au

Tourism Australia UK
Australia House, 6th Floor, The Strand, London WC28 4LG. *Tel (020) 7438 4601.*

Tourism NSW
55 Harrington St, Sydney, NSW 2000. *Tel 13 20 77.*
www.visitnsw.com

Tourism Tasmania
22 Elizabeth St, Hobart, Tasmania 7000.
Tel 1300 655 145.
www.discover tasmania.com

Tourism Top End
38 Mitchell St, Darwin NT 0801.
Tel 136 768.
www.ntholidays.com.au

Tourism Victoria
55 Collins St, Melbourne, VIC 3000.
Tel 132 842. **www**.visit victoria.com

United States
6100 Center Drive, Los Angeles, CA 90045.
Tel (310) 695 3200.

Western Australia Tourist Centre
469 Wellington St, Perth, WA 6000.
Tel 1300 361 351.
www.western australia.com

LUXURY HOTELS

Four Seasons
Tel 1800 222 200.
www.fourseasons.com/sydney

Hilton
Tel 1800 024 766.
www.hilton.com

Hyatt
Tel 131 234.
www.hyatt.com

InterContinental
Tel 138 388.
www.ichotelsgroup.com

Sheraton
Tel 1800 073 535.
www.sheraton.com

Westin
Tel 1800 656 535.
www.westin.com.au

CHAIN HOTELS

Accor Hotels
Tel 1300 656 565. **www**.accorhotels.com.au

Best Western
Tel 131 779.
www.bestwestern.com.au

Country Comfort
Tel 1300 272 132.
www.constellationhotels.com

Choice Hotels
Tel 132 400.
www.choicehotels.com

Metro Inns
Tel 1800 004 321.
www.metrohotels.com.au

Travelodge
Tel 1300 886 886.
www.travelodge.com.au

BACKPACKER HOTELS AND YOUTH HOSTELS

YHA Australia
422 Kent St, Sydney, NSW 2000. *Tel (02) 9261 1111.*
www.yha.com.au

Choosing a Hotel

The hotels in this guide have been selected for their good value, excellent facilities and location. The chart lists the hotels by region, starting with Sydney, in the same order as the rest of the guide. Within each region, entries are listed alphabetically within each price category, from the least to the most expensive.

PRICE CATEGORIES
For a standard double room per night inclusive of breakfast, service charges and additional taxes:

$ under A$100
$$ A$100–$150
$$$ A$150–$200
$$$$ A$200–$250
$$$$$ over A$250

SYDNEY

BONDI BEACH Ravesi's $$$$

Cnr Campbell Parade and Hall Street, NSW 2026 **Tel** *(02) 9365 4422* **Fax** *(02) 9365 1481* **Rooms** *12*

This lovely boutique hotel epitomizes the relaxed style of beach life at Bondi. Split-level suites cost more but are gorgeous, opening onto private terraces with ocean views. There is also a restaurant downstairs and a popular, award-winning bar *(see p524)*. **www.ravesis.com.au**

BONDI BEACH Swiss Grand Resort and Spa $$$$$

Cnr Campbell Parade and Beach Road, NSW 2026 **Tel** *(02) 9365 5666* **Fax** *(02) 9365 5330* **Rooms** *203*

This all-suite hotel is a kitsch take on the style of the French Riviera. Its exterior of terraces and balustrades looks a little like a giant wedding cake. Inside, marble adorns the lobby's every surface. Unbeatable location right on the beachfront, full resort and facilities, a rooftop pool, and two bars and restaurants. **www.swissgrand.com.au**

BONDI JUNCTION Meriton, Bondi Junction $$$$

95–97 Grafton Street, Bondi Junction, NSW 2022 **Tel** *(02) 8305 7600* **Fax** *(02) 9388 0391* **Rooms** *140*

Built above the Bondi Junction bus and train interchange, these two-bedroom apartments have views of Sydney Harbour or the ocean. Great features include full-sized kitchens and laundries, pools, tennis courts and virtual golf. **www.meritonapartments.com.au**

BOTANIC GARDENS AND THE DOMAIN Sir Stamford at Circular Quay $$$$$

93 Macquarie Street, Sydney, NSW 2000 **Tel** *(02) 9252 4600* **Fax** *(02) 9252 4286* **Rooms** *105*   **Map** *1 C3*

The decor is built around the hotel's collection of 18th-century antiques and fine art. Paying a little extra per night allows guests access to the Executive Lounge, and with it a host of benefits including complimentary breakfast, snacks, drinks, garment pressing and faxes. Fitness facilities and parking also available. **www.stamford.com.au/sscq**

BOTANIC GARDENS AND THE DOMAIN Sydney Inter-Continental $$$$$

117 Macquarie Street, Sydney, NSW 2000 **Tel** *(02) 9253 9000* **Fax** *(02) 9240 1240* **Rooms** *509*   **Map** *1 C3*

The foyer and lower stories of this luxurious hotel are made up of part of the 1851 Treasury Building. Well-equipped rooms have window seats, chaise longues and views of the city or harbour and Botanic Gardens. High tea is served in the lobby for guests and visitors. **www.sydney.intercontinental.com**

CITY CENTRE Railway Square YHA $$

8–10 Lee Street, Sydney, NSW 2000 **Tel** *(02) 9281 9666* **Fax** *(02) 9281 9688* **Rooms** *64*   **Map** *4 E5*

Located in a historic 1904 building, this YHA hostel adjoins Central Station's "Platform Zero". Some rooms are inside converted railway carriages, while others are in the main building. There's an Internet café, over-sized spa pool, tour desk and 24-hour access. They do not accept Diners or American Express. **www.yha.com.au**

CITY CENTRE Sydney Central YHA $$

11 Rawson Place, Sydney, NSW 2000 **Tel** *(02) 9218 9000* **Fax** *(02) 9218 9099* **Rooms** *110*   **Map** *3 E5*

Located opposite the city's main train and bus terminal, this hostel puts the city on your doorstep for a fraction of the price of the upmarket hotels. Housed in a heritage-listed building, it comes with a heated, indoor pool, spa and rooftop terrace offering panoramic views. **www.yha.com.au**

CITY CENTRE Y Hotel Hyde Park $$

5–11 Wentworth Avenue, Sydney, NSW 2000 **Tel** *(02) 9264 2451* **Fax** *(02) 9285 6288* **Rooms** *121*   **Map** *4 F3*

This budget hotel caters for everyone with a range of refurbished rooms, including backpacker dorms and modern, stylish private rooms with en-suite bathrooms. Coffee, tea and breakfast are included in the price and guests have access to a kitchen, laundry and Internet facilities. **www.yhotel.com.au**

CITY CENTRE Castlereagh Boutique Hotel $$$$

169–171 Castlereagh Street, Sydney, NSW 2000 **Tel** *(02) 9284 1000, 1800 801 576* **Rooms** *82*   **Map** *1 B5*

Full of character, this hotel is great value. Don't miss the plush old-fashioned dining room, decorated with chandeliers and elaborate paint and plasterwork. The rooms, furnished with period pieces and patterned upholstery, offer essentials such as televisions, bars, fridges, and tea and coffee facilities. **www.thecastlereagh.net.au**

Key to Symbols *see back cover flap*

CITY CENTRE Establishment Hotel 🖥️🍴🎵📺🗄️ $$$$$

*5 Bridge Lane, Sydney, NSW 2000 Tel (02) 9240 3100 Fax (02) 9240 3101 **Rooms** 31* **Map** *1 B3*

One of the most fashionable places in town. Two penthouses and 29 rooms offer a choice of lively or tranquil colour schemes, marble or stone bathrooms with separate baths and showers. Although there are eight bars, two restaurants and a nightclub in the building, sound-proofing ensures a peaceful stay. **www.establishmenthotel.com**

CITY CENTRE Hilton Sydney 🖥️🍴♿🎿⛄♿📺🗄️ $$$$$

*488 George Street, Sydney, NSW 2000 Tel (02) 9266 2000 **Rooms** 577* **Map** *1 B5*

An enormous renovation was carried out on this hotel, with the aim of setting new standards in luxury. The slick design is immediately apparent and upgraded features include stylish interior design, quality furniture, LCD televisions and avant-garde Internet phones. There's even a pillow menu. **www.hiltonsydney.com.au**

CITY CENTRE Hotel Mercure Sydney 🖥️🍴♿🎿📺🗄️ $$$$$

*818–820 George Street, NSW 2000 Tel (02) 9217 6666 Fax (02) 9217 6616 **Rooms** 517* **Map** *4 D5*

Close to trains and buses which depart from Central Station and Railway Square, this hotel is also a comfortable walking distance from Darling Harbour and Chinatown. It is a popular choice for families because two children are able to stay for free in their parents' room. **www.mecuresydney.com**

CITY CENTRE Meriton World Tower ♿♿🎿📺🗄️ $$$$$

*91 Liverpool Street, Sydney, NSW 2000 Tel (02) 9287 2890 Fax (02) 9261 5722 **Rooms** 114* **Map** *4 E3*

Some serviced apartments are available short term in this vertical village, the tallest residential building in Sydney. There are no one-bedroom options; spacious two-bedroom apartments can sleep up to five. Everything guests might need is just a short stroll away. **www.meritonapartments.com.au**

CITY CENTRE Sheraton on the Park 🖥️🍴♿🎿♿📺🗄️ $$$$$

*161 Elizabeth Street, Sydney, NSW 2000 Tel (02) 9286 6000 Fax (02) 9286 6686 **Rooms** 557* **Map** *1 B5*

Arriving at this hotel's very grand entrance, it's clear that no expense has been spared. Amenities include marble bathrooms, stylish furnishings, 24-hour room service, helpful concierges and lounges. Many rooms have views over Hyde Park. **www.sheraton.com**

CITY CENTRE Sofitel Wentworth 🖥️🍴♿🎿📺🗄️ $$$$$

*61–101 Phillip Street, Sydney, NSW 2000 Tel (02) 9230 0700 Fax (02) 9228 9133 **Rooms** 436* **Map** *1 B4*

Located in the heart of Sydney's Central Business District (CBD), this hotel is only minutes away from the Sydney Opera House, The Rocks, the Harbour Bridge and the Royal Botanic Gardens. It provides a luxury experience, successfully blending 21st-century design with the hotel's heritage-listed features. **www.sofitelsydney.com.au**

CITY CENTRE Waldorf Apartment Hotel ♿🎿📺🗄️ $$$$$

*57 Liverpool Street, NSW 2000 Tel (02) 9261 5355 Fax (02) 9261 3753 **Rooms** 48* **Map** *4 E3*

From this handy hotel, it's a short stroll to the city shopping centres and cinemas and a slightly longer one to Darling Harbour's attractions. The apartments are spacious, with balconies overlooking the city. Facilities include a rooftop pool, complimentary in-house movies and parking. **www.waldorf.com.au**

CITY CENTRE The York by Swiss-Belhotel 🖥️🍴♿🎿📺🗄️ $$$$$

*5 York Street, Sydney, NSW 2000 Tel (02) 9210 5000 Fax (02) 9290 1487 **Rooms** 130* **Map** *1 A3*

There is an understated elegance throughout this centrally located hotel. Each of its apartments is individually designed and has a balcony, fully equipped modern kitchen and large bathroom. Apartments vary in size from studios to executive two-bedroom penthouses. **www.theyorkapartments.com.au**

COOGEE Dive Hotel 🎿📺 $$$

*234 Arden Street, Coogee, NSW 2034 Tel (02) 9665 5538 Fax (02) 9665 4347 **Rooms** 16*

A stylish hotel, its rooms have polished floorboards, high ceilings and designer bathrooms. This is a great sanctuary from the backpacker madness of Coogee Beach. The two front rooms have spectacular views. Continental breakfast is included in the price. **www.divehotel.com.au**

DARLING HARBOUR Citigate Central Sydney 🖥️🍴♿♿🎿📺 $$$$

*169–179 Thomas Street, Haymarket, NSW 2000 Tel (02) 9281 6888 Fax (02) 9281 4237 **Rooms** 251 **Map** *4 D5*

Located near Paddy's Market in Chinatown, this reasonable hotel is close to many city attractions. All rooms and suites are large. Guest facilities include a rooftop pool, barbecue area and garden. The hotel specializes in arranging theatre tickets and usually offers several packages. **www.mirvachotels.com**

DARLING HARBOUR Four Points By Sheraton 🖥️🍴♿🎿♿📺🗄️ $$$$$

*161 Sussex Street, Sydney, NSW 2000 Tel (02) 9290 4000 Fax (02) 9290 4040 **Rooms** 630* **Map** *4 D2*

With 630 rooms, this is Australia's largest hotel. Located on the CBD side of Darling Harbour, it is close to restaurant and entertainment areas, including King Street and Cockle Bay wharfs. The hotel is also an easy walk from the Queen Victoria Building and Town Hall station. There is a great fitness centre. **www.fourpoints.com**

DARLING HARBOUR Holiday Inn Darling Harbour 🖥️🍴♿🎿📺🗄️ $$$$$

*68 Harbour Street, Darling Harbour, NSW 2000 Tel (02) 9291 0200 Fax (02) 9281 1212 **Rooms** 304* **Map** *4 D3*

Perfectly located in the dynamic heart of Darling Harbour. The restaurant offers à la carte and casual dining plus a breakfast buffet, and guests can cook their own lunches on the stonegrill in the hotel's pub.
www.holidayinndarlingharbour.com.au

DARLING HARBOUR Novotel Sydney on Darling Harbour $$$$$

100 Murray Street, Pyrmont, NSW 2009 ***Tel*** *(02) 9934 0000* ***Fax*** *(02) 9934 0099* ***Rooms*** *525* ***Map*** *3 C2*

This modern superstructure towers above the Harbourside centre at Darling Harbour, close to the Powerhouse and Maritime museums. The rooms are four and a half-star quality and have views across the city. In cooler weather, guests can visit the Imax Theatre or play tennis instead. **www.novoteldarlingharbour.com.au**

DOUBLE BAY The Savoy Hotel Double Bay $$

41–45 Knox Street, Double Bay, NSW 2028 ***Tel*** *(02) 9326 1411* ***Fax*** *(02) 9327 8464* ***Rooms*** *39* ***Map*** *6 F1*

This small, well-established hotel offers personal service in a tranquil environment. The Savoy is close to Double Bay's many cafés, restaurants and late-night bookshops. Nearby is a bus and ferry service to the city centre. Price does not include breakfast. **www.savoyhotel.com.au**

KINGS CROSS AND DARLINGHURST Morgan's Boutique Hotel $$

304 Victoria Street, Darlinghurst, NSW 2010 ***Tel*** *(02) 8354 3444* ***Fax*** *(02) 9360 9217* ***Rooms*** *26* ***Map*** *2 E5*

This boutique Art Deco hotel is set in a leafy location in the café district and has a rooftop area with views and daybeds. It also has an upmarket restaurant serving breakfast, lunch and dinner. Rooms have cable and kitchens, and can accommodate a third person for a small extra charge. **www.morganshotel.com.au**

KINGS CROSS AND DARLINGHURST Devere Hotel Sydney $$$

44–46 Macleay Street, Potts Points, NSW 2011 ***Tel*** *(02) 9358 1211* ***Fax*** *(02) 9358 4685* ***Rooms*** *117* ***Map*** *5 C1*

A boutique bed and breakfast-style hotel with an on-site Indian restaurant. The rooms are clean and comfortable and some have views over nearby Elizabeth Bay. Within walking distance from vibrant Oxford Street with its trendy restaurants, cafés and nightspots. **www.devere.com.au**

KINGS CROSS AND DARLINGHURST Hotel Altamont $$$

207 Darlinghurst Road, Sydney, NSW 2010 ***Tel*** *(02) 9360 6000,1800 991 110* ***Rooms*** *14* ***Map*** *5 A2*

At this fun budget hotel, formerly a Georgian mansion, all standard rooms have king- or queen-sized beds and solid, comfy wooden furniture. There are discount weekly rates and a few good quality backpacker rooms: they fill up quickly so book early. Every room has cable television. **www.altamont.com.au**

KINGS CROSS AND DARLINGHURST L'otel $$$

114 Darlinghurst Road, NSW 2010 ***Tel*** *(02) 9360 6868* ***Fax*** *(02) 9331 4536* ***Rooms*** *16* ***Map*** *5 A2*

A large terrace house has been converted into a designer hotel with small but lovely rooms decorated in white on white French Provincial style with painted furniture and art pieces. There's a hip bar and restaurant downstairs, and the hotel is close to Oxford Street's cafés and bars. **www.lotel.com.au**

KINGS CROSS AND DARLINGHURST Regents Court $$$

18 Springfield Avenue, Potts Point, NSW 2011 ***Tel*** *(02) 9356 6902* ***Fax*** *(02) 9358 1833* ***Rooms*** *30* ***Map*** *2 E5*

An innovative team transformed this Art Deco gentlemen's chambers into a stylish boutique hotel, favoured by artists, actors and writers. Each spacious and well-equipped studio sleeps two adults, in either twin or queen beds. A rooftop garden has great views over the city, particularly at sunset. **www.regentscourtsydney.com.au**

KINGS CROSS AND DARLINGHURST Simpsons of Potts Point $$$$

8 Challis Avenue, Potts Point, 2011 ***Tel*** *(02) 9356 2199* ***Fax*** *(02) 9356 4476* ***Rooms*** *12* ***Map*** *2 E4*

A charming B&B at the "Paris" end of Potts Point, where the complimentary breakfast is served in a glass-roofed conservatory. Built in 1892 as a family residence, the hotel has been exquisitely restored and boasts elegantly designed rooms. Guests staying in the romantic Cloud Suite enjoy a private spa bath. **www.simpsonshotel.com**

KINGS CROSS AND DARLINGHURST Blue Sydney $$$$$

6 Cowper Wharf Road, Woolloomooloo, NSW 2011 ***Tel*** *(02) 9331 9000* ***Fax*** *(02) 9331 9031* ***Rooms*** *100* ***Map*** *2 D5*

This hotel's glamour and reputation as the coolest in Sydney makes up for the far from spacious rooms. There is a fabulous cocktail bar and a row of great restaurants below on the fingerwharf. All rooms, including 36 loft rooms, are equipped with cutting-edge business technology and 27-inch television screens. **www.tajhotels.com**

KINGS CROSS AND DARLINGHURST Medusa $$$$$

267 Darlinghurst Road, Darlinghurst, NSW 2010 ***Tel*** *(02) 9331 1000* ***Fax*** *(02) 9380 6901* ***Rooms*** *18* ***Map*** *5 B1*

Medusa makes its own rules as only a boutique hotel can. This old Victorian house has been transformed into a brightly coloured miracle of modernism, with inspiration from Caravaggio's *Medusa*. Lindt chocolates and Aveda toiletries are complimentary, as is use of a neighbouring gym. **www.medusa.com.au**

MANLY Periwinkle Manly Cove Guest House $$$

18–19 East Esplanade, Manly, NSW 2095 ***Tel*** *(02) 9977 4668* ***Fax*** *(02) 9977 6308* ***Rooms*** *18*

A striking Federation-era mansion has been converted into a B&B with antique furniture and tasteful colour schemes. Rooms with a view attract only a small premium. High ceilings, wrought-iron verandas and a leafy courtyard are features. There are private outdoor areas. Parking available. **www.periwinkle.citysearch.com.au**

MANLY Manly Pacific $$$$$

55 North Steyne, Manly, NSW 2095 ***Tel*** *(02) 9977 7666* ***Fax*** *(02) 9977 7822* ***Rooms*** *218*

Manly's ocean beach is one of Sydney's most famous, host to ironman competitions and triathlons, herds of surfers and plenty of people (tourists and locals) just after a sun tan. Situated right on the beach, this hotel has unbeatable views of sand and surf. All rooms are light and spacious with balconies. **www.accorhotels.com**

Key to Price Guide *see p478* **Key to Symbols** *see back cover flap*

NEWTOWN Rydges Camperdown · $$$$

9 Missenden Road, Camperdown, NSW 2050 **Tel** *(02) 9516 1522* **Fax** *(02) 9519 4020* **Rooms** *144*

One of the few hotels in the gay and lesbian enclaves of Newtown and Camperdown. The hotel is also near Parramatta Road where buses leave for the city and Leichhardt. Relax in the pool, sauna or games room. The bar has a daily happy hour between 5:30 and 6:30pm. Parking available. **www.rydges.com/camperdown**

PADDINGTON Arts Hotel · $$$

21 Oxford Street, Paddington, NSW 2021 **Tel** *(02) 9361 0211* **Fax** *(02) 9360 3735* **Rooms** *64* **Map** *5 B3*

Standard rooms at this family owned hotel face the bustle of Oxford Street. It's worth paying a tiny bit more for a garden room which overlooks the courtyard and has free wireless Internet access. The breakfast room, with its large windows looking out onto Oxford Street, is a great place to people watch. **www.artshotel.com.au**

PADDINGTON Hughenden Boutique Hotel · $$$$

14 Queen Street, Woollahra, NSW 2025 **Tel** *(02) 9363 4863* **Fax** *(02) 9362 0398* **Rooms** *35* **Map** *6 E4*

This rambling old building, once a 19th-century family home, has been restored to its original grandeur. Rooms are comfortably furnished and the restaurant is very good. Writers' groups meet and artists exhibit their work, providing a connection to the surrounding arty community. **www.hughendenhotel.com.au**

SURRY HILLS Adina on Crown · $$$$$

359 Crown Street, Surry Hills, NSW 2010 **Tel** *(02) 8302 1000* **Fax** *(02) 9361 5965* **Rooms** *85* **Map** *5 A1*

Close to the groovy Crown Street shops and restaurants, Sydney Cricket Ground and the Entertainment Quarter at Fox Studios, this hotel is a favourite with visiting rock bands. It is also right above the legendary restaurants, Bills, Marque and Billy Kwong. Apartments are spacious and have full kitchens. **www.adinahotels.com.au**

THE ROCKS AND CIRCULAR QUAY Sydney Harbour YHA · $

110 Cumberland Street, The Rocks, NSW 2000 **Tel** *(02) 8272 0900* **Fax** *(02) 8272 0950* **Rooms** *106* **Map** *1 B2*

Enjoy luxury views for a budget price at the only place in the Rocks offering backpacker accommodation. Rooms are basic but clean and comfortable and all have bathrooms. Relax on the rooftop terrace with its uninterrupted views of the Opera House and Harbour Bridge. **www.yha.com.au**

THE ROCKS AND CIRCULAR QUAY Lord Nelson Brewery Hotel · $$$

19 Kent Street, The Rocks, NSW 2000 **Tel** *(02) 9251 4044* **Fax** *(02) 9251 1532* **Rooms** *9* **Map** *1 A2*

The top floor of the celebrated pub, famous for its home brews, offers cosy bedrooms with stone walls and rustic furnishings. There are two basic rooms with shared bathrooms; for those not on a tight budget en suite rooms are available. It's an easy walk to Circular Quay. **www.lordnelsonbrewery.com**

THE ROCKS AND CIRCULAR QUAY The Observatory Hotel · $$$$$

89–113 Kent Street, Sydney, NSW 2000 **Tel** *(02) 9256 2222* **Fax** *(02) 9256 2233* **Rooms** *99* **Map** *1 A2*

This luxury hotel is one of Sydney's most expensive, but there are often great Internet deals. It is tastefully furnished, with original antiques and fine artwork. There is a choice of two restaurants, and afternoon tea is available. There are also excellent facilities for the business traveller. **www.observatoryhotel.com.au**

THE ROCKS AND CIRCULAR QUAY Old Sydney Holiday Inn · $$$$$

55 George Street, The Rocks, NSW 2000 **Tel** *(02) 9252 0524* **Fax** *(02) 9251 2093* **Rooms** *175* **Map** *1 B2*

Big enough to offer all the facilities of a grand establishment, this hotel is also small enough to provide personal attention. Great location within the historic Rocks area and close to Circular Quay and the Sydney Opera House. The view from the sparkling blue rooftop pool is spectacular. **www.holidayinn.com.au**

THE ROCKS AND CIRCULAR QUAY Park Hyatt Sydney · $$$$$

7 Hickson Road, The Rocks, NSW 2000 **Tel** *(02) 9241 1234* **Fax** *(02) 9256 1555* **Rooms** *158* **Map** *1 B1*

Many rooms in this five-star hotel have views of the Opera House, as does the rooftop swimming pool. Walking up the road for a few minutes takes you to the small park beneath the Harbour Bridge, a few minutes in the other direction to Circular Quay. Well equipped for business travellers. **http://sydney.park.hyatt.com**

THE ROCKS AND CIRCULAR QUAY Rendezvous Stafford · $$$$$

75 Harrington Street, The Rocks, NSW 2000 **Tel** *(02) 9251 6711* **Fax** *(02) 9251 3458* **Rooms** *61* **Map** *1 B2*

There really is something for everyone at this unusual boutique hotel. Most rooms are studio and one-bedroom apartments with good kitchen facilities. There are also more suites available in seven 1870 terrace houses nearby. There are excellent business services, a spa, pool and sauna. **www.rendezvoushotels.com**

THE ROCKS AND CIRCULAR QUAY The Sebel Pier One Sydney · $$$$$

11 Hickson Road, Walsh Bay, NSW 2000 **Tel** *(02) 8298 9999* **Fax** *(02) 8298 9777* **Rooms** *161* **Map** *1 A2*

This is Sydney's first over-the-water hotel, built on a 1912 fingerwharf in the Walsh Bay World Heritage precinct, beside the Harbour Bridge. The hotel's luxurious rooms combine original features with contemporary design. Look right into the water through the lobby's glass floor. **www.sebelpierone.com.au**

THE ROCKS AND CIRCULAR QUAY Shangri-La · $$$$$

176 Cumberland Street, The Rocks, NSW 2000 **Tel** *(02) 9250 6000* **Fax** *(02) 9250 6250* **Rooms** *563* **Map** *1 A3*

This hotel has just spent A$40 million on a complete refurbishment and it shows. The spacious rooms are now decorated in neutral tones with rich gold brocade highlights. On the top floor, Altitude restaurant and the Blu Horizon bar are popular dining and night spots. **www.shangri-la.com**

THE BLUE MOUNTAINS AND BEYOND

ARMIDALE Abbotsleigh Motor Inn

76 Barney Street, Armidale, NSW 2350 **Tel** *(02) 6772 9488* **Fax** *(02) 6772 7066* **Rooms** *33*

In the gorge country of Oxley Wild Rivers National Park and surrounded by native wilderness, this motor inn has a licensed restaurant, cosy fireplaces and free wireless internet access. The staff at Abbotsleigh's tour desk can provide you with plenty of information, plus they offer guided tours. **www.armidaleabbotsleighmotorinn.com.au**

BALLINA Ballina Heritage Inn

229 River Street, Ballina, NSW 2478 **Tel** *(02) 6686 0505* **Fax** *(02) 6686 0788* **Rooms** *27*

Ballina got its name from an Aboriginal word meaning "place where oysters are plentiful", and this still rings true in this seafood-rich region. Close to seafood restaurants, this comfortable motel prides itself on service, offering babysitting facilities so parents can relax and enjoy the local offerings. **www.ballinaheritageinn.com.au**

BARRINGTON TOPS Barringtons Country Retreat

1941 Chichester Dam Rd, Brandon Grove via Dungog, NSW 2420 **Tel** *(02) 4995 9269* **Fax** *(02) 4995 9279* **Rooms** *31*

There is an abundance of Australian birds and wildlife at this tranquil retreat set on the edge of the Barrington Tops wilderness. The country cabins and lodges are built to complement the natural environment and are only 3 hours from Sydney and 20 minutes from the town of Dungog with its cafés and galleries. **www.thebarringtons.com.au**

BLACKHEATH High Mountains Motor Inn

193 Great Western Highway, Blackheath, NSW 2785 **Tel** *(02) 4787 8216* **Fax** *(02) 4787 7802* **Rooms** *21*

The 21 ground-floor rooms are comfortable and affordable. But for guests preferring something larger, there are also two inter-connected cottages – ideal for a family or large group. The motel is conveniently located near the local village centre and also provides a home-made room service breakfast. **www.highmountainsmotel.com**

BLUE MOUNTAINS Lilianfels

Lilianfels Avenue, Echo Point, Katoomba, NSW 2780 **Tel** *(02) 4780 1200* **Fax** *(02) 4780 1300* **Rooms** *85*

Following a multi-million dollar refurbishment, this historic country house, set amidst two acres of English-style gardens, continues to offer idyllic escapes for romantics, as well as for lovers of great food and stunning scenery. Both the house and its restaurant, Darley's, have won many prestigious awards. **www.lilianfels.com.au**

BYRON BAY The Oasis Resort

24 Scott Street, Byron Bay, NSW 2481 **Tel** *(02) 66857390* **Fax** *(02) 6685 8290* **Rooms** *24*

A venue that allows guests to select their style of accommodation between spacious Mediterranean-style apartments and secluded tree-top vacation houses with private decks and outdoor spas. If stairs are a problem, try the cottage next door featuring modern Asian interior and design. **www.byronbayoasis.com.au**

COFFS HARBOUR Breakfree Aanuka Beach

11 Firman Drive, Coffs Harbour, NSW 2450 **Tel** *(02) 6652 7555* **Fax** *(02) 6652 7053* **Rooms** *70*

Enjoying a superb beach front location, this low-rise resort is a tranquil and relaxing place to stay. The accommodation comprises villas as well as traditional hotel rooms and the on-site restaurant offers outdoor dining with ocean views. A short drive to Coffs Harbour city and jetty precincts. **www.breakfreeaanukabeachresort.com.au**

DUBBO Quality Inn Dubbo International

165 Whylandra Street, Dubbo, NSW 2830 **Tel** *(02) 6882 4777* **Fax** *(02) 6881 8370* **Rooms** *60*

The comfortable accommodation includes king size beds in all rooms, tennis courts, a pool and two restaurants. The hotel overlooks a golf course and is close to many historic landmarks and visitor attractions such as Old Dubbo Gaol, Taronga Zoo *(see p126)* and Dubbo Observatory. **www.qualityinn.com**

FAULCONBRIDGE Rose Lindsay Cottage

113 Chapman Parade, Faulconbridge, NSW 2776 **Tel** *(02) 4751 4273* **Fax** *(02) 4751 9497* **Rooms** *2*

Rambling wildflowers surround this beautifully private sandstone cottage – designed by Rose, the wife of famed Australian artist Norman Lindsay. Take a seat amongst the fragrant, secluded garden, home to native birdlife and fauna. They do not accept American Express or Diners cards. **www.roselindsay.com.au**

HUNTER VALLEY The Bellbird Hotel

388 Wollombi Road, Bellbird, NSW 2325 **Tel** *(02) 4990 1094* **Fax** *(02) 4991 5475* **Rooms** *15*

Within minutes of the valley's famous wineries *(see p174)* and golf courses, this historic pub built in 1914 offers bed and breakfast. A typical turn-of-the-century Australian country hotel it has a large beer garden and a reliable bistro. They have live music every Sunday afternoon.

JUNEE Loftus on Humphreys

6 Humphreys Street, Junee, NSW 2263 **Tel** *(02) 6924 1511* **Fax** *(02) 6924 1511* **Rooms** *23*

This bed and breakfast accommodation features 23 clean and comfortable rooms catering to singles and families in a converted pub built in 1896. A huge verandah wraps around the building, providing views over the town. There is also a restaurant on the ground floor and secure parking. **www.juneemotorinn.com.au**

Key to Price Guide *see p478* **Key to Symbols** *see back cover flap*

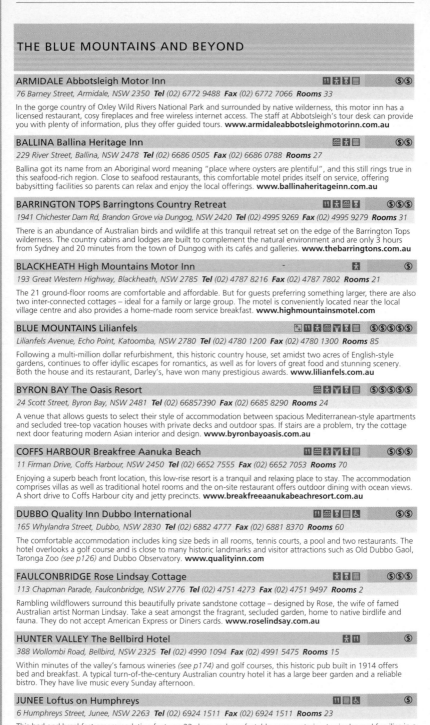

KATOOMBA Mountain Heritage Hotel & Spa Retreat

Cnr Apex and Lovel sts, Katoomba, NSW 2780 **Tel** *(02) 4782 2155* **Fax** *(02) 4782 5323* **Rooms** *41*

Commanding spectacular views of the Blue Mountains wilderness, this property blends the romance and charm of the past with modern-day comforts. Its quiet location is just a few minutes' stroll from Katoomba's town centre. Relax in the gardens, swimming pool or by open log fires in the cosy lounge. **www.mountainheritage.com.au**

LITHGOW Eagle View Escape

271 Sandalls Drive, Rydal via Lake Lyell, NSW 2790 **Tel/Fax** *(02) 6355 6311* **Rooms** *24*

Catering exclusively for couples, Eagle View provides all the ingredients for a truly romantic getaway. Three room styles are offered – wilderness spa cabins, studio spa suites or executive spa suites. There's no restaurant, but all kinds of meals can be arranged. They do not accept American Express or Diners cards. **www.eagleview.com.au**

MUDGEE Cobb & Co Court Boutique Hotel

97 Market Street, Mudgee, NSW 2850 **Tel** *(02) 6372 7245* **Fax** *(02) 6372 7525* **Rooms** *13*

Crisp, white linen sheets await guests at this delightful boutique hotel, close to the region's many wineries. Each room is stylishly decorated and features a spa, individually controlled air conditioning and much more. The hotel's Wineglass Restaurant serves loads of tasty local produce. **www.cobbandcocourt.com.au**

NEWCASTLE Crowne Plaza

Cnr Merewether Street and Wharf Rd, Newcastle, NSW 2300 **Tel** *(02) 4907 5000* **Fax** *(02) 4907 5055* **Rooms** *175*

This award-winning venue provides all you could ask for in a hotel. Situated in front of the foreshore promenade leading past the historic Nobby's Lighthouse and five kilometres of picturesque walking path, the Crowne Plaza features a 25-metre pool and gym. **www.crowneplaza.com.au**

NULKABA Hunter Valley YHA

100 Wine Country Drive, Nulkaba, NSW 2325 **Tel** *(02) 4991 32 78* **Fax** *(02) 4991 3278* **Rooms** *13*

In the heart of wine country, this hostel joined the YHA family in late 2005 and is well located at the gateway to the region's attractions. The lodge runs daily wine tours, and bikes are available for free. The outdoor eating area has a woodfired pizza oven for guests to use. **www.yha.com.au**

POKOLBIN Tower Lodge

Halls Road, Pokolbin, NSW 2320 **Tel** *(02) 4998 7022* **Fax** *(02) 4998 7164* **Rooms** *12*

This stunning retreat offers a luxurious getaway for the most discerning of guests. Each of its 12 rooms has been individually styled, and one even features an outdoor plunge tub. The dining room serves breakfasts only. Tower Lodge was named World Luxury Hotel Award Winner in 2010. **www.towerestate.com**

PORT STEPHENS Peppers Anchorage

Corlette Point Road, Corlette, Port Stephens, NSW 2315 **Tel** *(02) 4984 2555* **Fax** *(02) 4984 0300* **Rooms** *80*

Making the most of its water frontage, all rooms at Peppers have balconies which overlook the waters beneath the Anchorage Marina. Whether you opt for the cosy Loft Suite or supremely decadent Master Suite, you will experience absolute luxury. Be sure not to miss out on a meal at Merrett's restaurant. **www.peppers.com.au**

TAMWORTH Plumes on the Green

25 The Ringers Road, Tamworth, NSW 2340 **Tel** *(02) 6762 1140* **Fax** *(02) 6762 1165* **Rooms** *5*

Tamworth is more than just the nation's country music capital. Golfers in particular will love this boutique guesthouse, which sits alongside the picturesque Longyard Golf Course, designed by Greg Norman. Plumes also offers stunning bird-watching packages. Limited wheelchair access. **www.plumesonthegreen.com.au**

TERRIGAL Terrigal Pacific Motel

224 Terrigal Drive, Terrigal, NSW 2260 **Tel** *(02) 4385 1555* **Fax** *(02) 4385 1476* **Rooms** *35*

Just an hour's drive north of Sydney, beautiful Terrigal is home to some of the central coast's most stunning beaches and lagoons. Within walking distance of the water and close to local eateries, these spacious apartments have sleek polished floorboards and offer views of lush tropical gardens. **www.terrigalaccommodation.com**

TOUKLEY Beachcomber

200 Main Road, Toukley, NSW 2263 **Tel** *(02) 4397 1300* **Fax** *(02) 4396 1128* **Rooms** *61*

There's something for everyone at this resort, which prides itself on entertainment for all ages. Relax by the pool or take in the regular live acts and DJs. Have a cocktail at the bar or milkshake at Beachie Bites Café. As they say at The Beachie: it's not a hotel, it's an experience! **www.beachcomber.net.au**

WAGGA WAGGA Country Comfort

Cnr Morgan and Tarcutta streets, Wagga Wagga, NSW 2650 **Tel** *(02) 6921 6444* **Fax** *(02) 6921 2922* **Rooms** *85*

Wagga Wagga sits on the highway between Sydney and Melbourne, and this hotel offers overnight respite for travellers as well as longer stays for guests enjoying the Riverina region. It boasts good conference facilities, with Capers Restaurant serving breakfast and dinner daily, and two swimming pools. **www.countrycomforthotels.com.au**

WINDSOR Windsor Terrace Motel

47 George Street, Windsor, NSW 2756 **Tel** *(02) 4577 5999* **Fax** *(02) 4577 2708* **Rooms** *24*

Situated at the edge of the historic part of Windsor, this motel has beautiful views of the Blue Mountains and the Hawkenbury River from its rooms. Guests can make the most of the large verandas, taking breakfast there. Rooms are basic, but clean and roomy, with typical motel-style decor. Parking available. **www.windsorterracemotel.com**

THE SOUTH COAST AND SNOWY MOUNTAINS

ADAMINABY Reynella Rides and Country Farmstay
699 Kingston Road, NSW 2629 **Tel** *(02) 6454 2386, 1800 029 909* **Fax** *(02) 6454 2530* **Rooms** *20*

Set in the foothills of the Snowy Mountains, this 2429-hectare (6000-acre) sheep and cattle farm offers lodge accommodation with spectacular views. From October to May there are horse treks and bush camping through the nearby ranges of the Kosciuszko National Park. Horse treks not included in price. **www.reynellarides.com.au**

BATEMANS BAY Best Western Reef Motor Inn
27 Clyde Street, NSW 2536 **Tel** *(02) 4472 6000* **Fax** *(02) 4472 6059* **Rooms** *34*

Located beside the broad Clyde River, this motel is popular with flathead anglers. It is 4 hours south of Sydney and less than 2 hours from Canberra. It is close to the highway, shops, restaurants and the oceanfront. It offers car parking and good access for wheelchairs. **www.reefmotorinnbestwestern.com.au**

BATEMANS BAY Comfort Inn Lincoln Downs
Princes Highway, NSW 2536 **Tel** *(02) 4478 9200* **Fax** *(02) 4478 9299* **Rooms** *33*

This luxury country resort, which is set amidst pretty English country-style gardens with ornamental lake, is a peaceful retreat by the sea. Enjoy a hit of tennis or relax in the billiard room with a cocktail before enjoying a memorable evening of fine food and wine at the Briars Restaurant. **www.lincolndowns.com.au**

BERMAGUI Beachview Motel
12 Lamont Street, NSW 2546 **Tel** *(02) 6493 4155* **Fax** *(02) 6493 4879* **Rooms** *8*

This environmentally friendly motel faces the ocean beach. Some rooms have a balcony overlooking the ocean: perfect for whale watching in autumn and spring. Mimosa Rocks National Park is 15 minutes by car, and shops and restaurants are within walking distance. **www.beachview.thebegavalley.com**

BERRY Bunyip Inn Guesthouse
122 Queen Street, NSW 2535 **Tel** *(02) 4464 2064* **Fax** *(02) 4464 2324* **Rooms** *13*

Housed in a heritage-listed 1885 Victorian-era bank building, this cosy guesthouse is a perfect base from which to explore Shoalhaven. The guesthouse is a smart and comfortable accommodation option, close to shops, restaurants and Shoal-haven. There is car parking and good wheelchair access, and lots of cafés nearby for breakfast. **www.berryinn.com.au**

BOWRAL Craigieburn Resort and Conference Centre
Centennial Avenue, NSW 2576 **Tel** *(02) 4682 8000* **Fax** *(02) 4862 1690* **Rooms** *71*

Craigieburn is a large garden estate, boasting its own nine-hole golf course, two tennis courts, fly fishing lake, gym, snooker room and jogging track. Its old world charm has been refurbished with modern amenities. **www.pepperscraigieburn.com.au**

BOWRAL Milton Park Country House Hotel
Horderns Road, NSW 2576 **Tel** *(02) 4861 1522* **Fax** *(02) 4861 7962* **Rooms** *47*

This early 20th-century mansion is located in tranquil parkland just east of Bowral, with nearby golf courses, horse-riding, bush picnics and tennis courts. The mansion is a fine example of the Federation Arts and Crafts architectural style. There is also a day spa, good wheelchair access, room service and views. **www.milton-park.com.au**

BUNDANOON Treetops Guesthouse Bundanoon
101 Railway Avenue, NSW 2578 **Tel** *(02) 4883 6372* **Fax** *(02) 4883 6176* **Rooms** *22*

Enjoy the gardens of this quiet, Edwardian guesthouse furnished with four-poster beds, Persian rugs, artworks and roaring log fires. The tariff includes an old-fashioned country breakfast. Four of the rooms offer spa baths. They do not accept American Express or Diners cards. **www.treetopsguesthouse.com.au**

CHARLOTTE PASS Kosciuszko Chalet
Kosciuszko Road, NSW 2624 **Tel** *(02) 6457 5254 1800 026 369* **Fax** *1800 802 687* **Rooms** *35*

This chalet was built in the 1930s Austrian style. At 1,760 metres (5,770 ft) above sea level, it is Australia's highest resort. It is snow bound for much of the ski season, so its position metres from the ski lift is a bonus. It offers spectacular views and peace and quiet. Breakfast and dinner included. Only open in winter. **www.charlottepass.com.au**

COOMA Kinross Inn
15 Sharp Street, NSW 2630 **Tel** *(02) 6452 3577, 1800 223 229* **Fax** *(02) 6452 4410* **Rooms** *16*

Historic Cooma's only four-star motel is tucked away, just back from the town's shops and restaurants. It is one hour from the Snowy Mountains and the southern ski slopes. It has five spa baths, BBQ facilities, undercover parking adjacent to every room, and free pay TV in every room. **www.kinrossinn.com.au**

EDEN Wonboyn Lake Resort
204 Daunceys Road, NSW 2551 **Tel** *(02) 6496 9162* **Fax** *(02) 6496 9100* **Rooms** *15*

This resort is in an isolated location off the highway and surrounded by national park with abundant wildlife and birdlife. The self-contained cottages are ideal for a family beach and fishing holiday. Bream, flathead and salmon are commonly caught. Canoes and hire boats are available. **www.wonboynlakeresort.com.au**

Key to Price Guide *see p478* **Key to Symbols** *see back cover flap*

EROWAL BAY Sea Shacks

6 Caulfield Parade, NSW 2540 **Tel** *(02) 4443 8912* **Fax** *(02) 4443 7422* **Rooms** *4*

These two two-bedroom shacks are set in landscaped gardens, planted with indigenous species, overlooking a saltwater lake. The shacks are a stylish take on the Australian beach shack vernacular and offer polished wooden floors, balconies overlooking the water and hand-crafted hardwood furniture.

GOULBURN Pelican Sheep Station

Braidwood Road, NSW 2580 **Tel** *(02) 4821 4668* **Fax** *(02) 4822 1179* **Rooms** *23*

This family-owned sheep station is to the south of Goulburn. It offers bunkhouse accommodation with a shared common room, four self-contained cabins, a five-bedroom house and a three-bedroom cottage. They do not accept American Express or Diners cards. **www.pelicansheepstation.com.au**

JERVIS BAY Bay of Plenty Lodges

Ellmoos Road (via Booderee National Park), NSW 2540 **Tel** *(02) 4441 2018* **Fax** *(02) 4441 0021* **Rooms** *16*

Beach front, eco-friendly accommodation in the form of cabins, cottages and units on the Sussex inlet at Jervis Bay. The lodges are reached via a beautiful, 13-km (8-mile) drive through the rainforests of Booderee National Park. Explore the bay on complimentary kayaks or delight in the kangaroos hopping around the grounds. **www.bayofplentylodges.com.au**

KIAMA Kiama Cove Boutique Motel

10 Bong Bong Street, NSW 2533 **Tel** *(02) 4232 3000* **Fax** *(02) 4232 3911* **Rooms** *31*

This stylishly refurbished hotel offers all the mod cons as well as a pleasant garden, great views and good wheelchair access. It is located in central Kiama, close to shops and restaurants, overlooking the surfbeach and within walking distance of the harbour, blowhole, lighthouse and Pilot's Cottage Museum. **www.kiamacove.com.au**

MERIMBULA Albacore Apartments

Market Street, NSW 2548 **Tel** *(02) 6495 3187* **Fax** *(02) 6495 3439* **Rooms** *20*

Luxury accommodation offering self-contained one- and two-bedroom apartments with ocean views from private balconies. The apartments are located opposite Merimbula Lake and close to shops, restaurants and some of the Sapphire Coast's best surf beaches. The apartments have disabled facilities. **www.albacore.com.au**

NAROOMA Mystery Bay Cottages

121 Mystery Bay Road, NSW 2546 **Tel** *(02) 4473 7431* **Fax** *(02) 4473 7431* **Rooms** *12*

The six two-bedroom self-contained cottages at this peaceful location are light, airy and modern with cosy log fires. They are surrounded by countryside and are only a minute's walk from the beach. All of the cottages enjoy beautiful views. They do not accept American Express or Diners cards. **www.mysterybaycottages.com.au**

NORTH WOLLONGONG Novotel Northbeach Wollongong

2–14 Cliff Road, NSW 2500 **Tel** *(02) 4224 3111* **Fax** *(02) 4229 1705* **Rooms** *204*

An hour's drive south of Sydney and only minutes from the centre of Wollongong, this hotel is nestled between the spectacular Illawarra Escarpment and the sea. Some rooms have a balcony with great views overlooking the ocean. There are peaceful walking and cycle tracks nearby, a sauna and tennis courts. **www.novotelnorthbeach.com.au**

NOWRA Shoalhaven Lodge

480 Longreach Road, NSW 2541 **Tel** *(02) 4422 6686* **Fax** *(02) 4423 2638* **Rooms** *11 (4 lodges)*

The self-contained lodges, cottage and studio apartment enjoy peaceful surroundings and views over nearby mountains and the beautiful Shoalhaven River. The property is a beef cattle farm with 2 km (1 mile) of prime river frontage only 10 minutes from Nowra. Disabled guests welcome. **www.shoalhavenlodge.com.au**

TATHRA Tathra Beach House Apartments

57 Andy Poole Drive, NSW 2550 **Tel** *(02) 6499 9900* **Fax** *(02) 6499 9950* **Rooms** *26*

Opposite the surf beach, these one-, two- and three-bedroom apartments are set in landscaped surrounds and feature private decks with spa. The apartments are walking distance from shops and the historic 150-year-old wharf, but are available only for weekly hire during the peak Christmas period. **www.tathrabeachhouse.com.au**

THREDBO Thredbo Alpine Hotel

Friday Drive, NSW 2625 **Tel** *(02) 6459 4200* **Fax** *(02) 6459 4201* **Rooms** *65*

This large complex in Thredbo Village is a favourite with skiers in the winter months as it is only a minute's walk from the ski lifts. It is far cheaper, and quieter, in the summer months. Facilities include a sauna, spa and masseuse. There is plenty of chalet character, great views and room service. **www.rydges.com.au**

THREDBO Novotel Lake Crackenback Resort

Lake Crackenback, 1650 Alpine Way via Jindabyne, NSW 2627 **Tel** *(02) 6451 3000* **Rooms** *48 apartments*

The self-contained apartments at this luxury resort are ideally located for skiers, with a courtesy bus running to and from the Skitube Alpine Rail Way. The resort is only 14 km (8 miles) from Kosciuszko National Park at Thredbo. One- and two-day guided tours of the park are available during the summer. **www.novotellakecrackenback.com.au**

TILBA TILBA The Two-Story Bed & Breakfast

Bate Street, Central Tilba, NSW 2546 **Tel/Fax** *(02) 4473 7290 , 1800 355 850* **Rooms** *3*

Located in the National Trust village of Central Tilba, this 1894 building was once the post office. Close to the beach, open gardens, craft shops, bushwalks in the lush coastal hinterland and peaceful fishing spots. There is car parking and the lounge room features an open fire. Perfect for winter guests. **www.tilbatwostory.com**

CANBERRA AND ACT

BRINDABELLA Brindabella Station

Brindabella Valley, 2611 **Tel** *(02) 6236 2121* **Fax** *(02) 6236 2128* **Rooms** *4 (2 cabins)*

Bushwalking, bird-watching and trout fishing are on offer at this scenic and historic working farm. Miles Franklin, one of Australia's most famous authors, lived here as a child. The farm is bounded on three sides by national parks. Guests must provide their own food and payment is by cash only. **www.brindabellastation.com.au**

BUNGENDORE Carrington Inn

21 Malbon Street, NSW 2621 **Tel** *(02) 6238 1044* **Fax** *(02) 6238 1036* **Rooms** *26*

Originally built in 1885 as a Cobb & Co inn, this lavishly restored Victorian house is a luxurious country retreat. The elegant restaurant with five dining rooms, the 200-year-old carved mahogany and etched glass bar, and the large gardens are highlights. **www.thecarringtoninn.com.au**

CANBERRA Kingston Hotel

73 Canberra Avenue, Griffith, NSW 2603 **Tel** *(02) 6295 0123* **Fax** *(02) 6295 7871* **Rooms** *36*

Low prices ensure that this lively country-style pub is popular with backpackers. Rooms and bathrooms are shared. Cooking facilities are available and the pub itself serves good-value counter meals. The heritage-listed building is a short walk from the city centre and close to shops and restaurants. Car parking is available. Payment is by cash only.

CANBERRA Victor Lodge

29 Dawes Street, Kingston, ACT 2604 **Tel** *(02) 6295 7777* **Fax** *(02) 6295 2466* **Rooms** *30*

A family run guesthouse within walking distance of the CBD and Manuka and Kingston pubs and restaurants. There is a free pick-up and drop-off service from Jolimont coach terminal during business hours. There is also mountain bike hire, parking, a barbecue area and garden, TV room and Internet. Payment is by cash only. **www.victorlodge.com.au**

CANBERRA Blue and White Lodges

524 & 528 Northbourne Avenue, Downer, ACT 2602 **Tel** *(02) 6248 0498* **Fax** *(02) 6248 8277* **Rooms** *19*

This establishment in Canberra's inner north is a friendly and comfortable bed-and-breakfast (reputedly Canberra's first B&B). It provides several budget and family accommodation options, and one room has a spa. It is 5-minutes' drive from the city centre and close to shops and several Asian and Italian restaurants. **www.blueandwhitelodge.com.au**

CANBERRA Last Stop Ambledown Brook

198 Brooklands Road, via Hall, ACT 2618 **Tel** *(02) 6230 2280* **Rooms** *6*

Sleep in a converted 1929 Melbourne tram or a 1935 Sydney train carriage at this rustic guesthouse, just 20 minutes from Canberra. Enjoy views of the nearby Brindabella Ranges, or hop in the car and visit nearby restaurants and cool climate vineyards. BBQ facilities and tennis courts are available. Payment is by cash only. **www.laststop.com.au**

CANBERRA Miranda & Parkview Lodges

526 & 534 Northbourne Avenue, Downer, ACT 2602 **Tel** *(02) 6249 8038* **Fax** *(02) 6247 6166* **Rooms** *22*

These two lodges, only metres apart, are managed by the same owners. They are pleasant guesthouses in renovated two-storey duplexes, 4 km (2 miles) north of the GPO and within walking distance of the Yowani Country Club, Kamberra Winery, the Racecourse and 30 cafés and restaurants in nearby Dixon. **www.mirandalodge.com.au**

CANBERRA University House

Cnr Balmain & Liversidge sts, ACT 2601 **Tel** *(02) 6125 5276* **Fax** *(02) 6125 5252* **Rooms** *105*

This hotel is situated in the peaceful gardens of the Australian National University. It offers conference facilities, Internet access and two restaurants and bars. As well as spacious standard rooms and suites, there are several one- and two-bedroom apartments and a suite for disabled guests. **www.anu.edu.au/unihouse**

CANBERRA Brassey Hotel

Belmore Gardens, Barton, ACT 2600 **Tel** *(02) 6273 3766, 1800 659 191* **Fax** *(02) 6273 2791* **Rooms** *81*

This 1927 heritage-listed building is set amid fine gardens. It enjoys a quiet location close to both Parliament House buildings, Lake Burley Griffin, the Press Club, the High Court of Australia and the National Gallery of Australia. It offers conference and Internet facilities, and heritage and standard rooms. **www.brassey.net.au**

CANBERRA Canberra Rex Hotel

150 Northbourne Avenue, Braddon, ACT 2601 **Tel** *(02) 6248 5311, 1800 026 103* **Rooms** *157*

This friendly upmarket hotel, near the university and only 1 km (half a mile) north of the city centre, is a good option for disabled and corporate travellers. It offers free off-street parking, conference rooms, boardrooms, a games room, a sauna, a gym and room service. Some rooms have balconies with great views. **www.canberrarexhotel.com.au**

CANBERRA Hotel Kurrajong

8 National Circuit, Barton, ACT 2604 **Tel** *(02) 6234 4444* **Fax** *(02) 6234 4466* **Rooms** *26*

JS Murdoch, the architect who designed Canberra's first Parliament House, designed this 1926 Art Deco, pavilion-style hotel. Over the years it has welcomed several Australian prime ministers, and was home to Prime Minister Ben Chifley from 1940 to 1951. It offers conference and wheelchair access. **www.hotelkurrajong.com.au**

Key to Price Guide *see p478* **Key to Symbols** *see back cover flap*

CANBERRA Rydges Lakeside Hotel Canberra $$$$

London Circuit, Canberra City, ACT 2600 **Tel** *(02) 6247 6244, 1800 026 169* **Rooms** *201*

Wonderful views over Lake Burley Griffin and the city distinguish this modern hotel, especially those from the 15th-floor restaurant. The hotel is only ten minutes' walk from the city centre and 20 minutes' walk from the National Gallery of Australia. Car parking, wheelchair access and room service are available. **www.rydges.com**

CANBERRA Belconnen Premier Inn $$$$$

110 Benjamin Way, Belconnen, ACT 2617 **Tel** *(02) 6253 3633, 1800 672 076* **Fax** *(02) 6253 3688* **Rooms** *74*

This stylish hotel offers the business traveller excellent convention facilities and a business centre. Rooms range from standard rooms (sleep two) to de luxe rooms to self-contained one- and two-bedroom apartments, some with spa. There is a gym, cocktail bar and three rooms with wheelchair access. **www.belconnenpremierinn.com**

CANBERRA Capital Tower $$$$

2 Marcus Clarke Street, ACT 2601 **Tel** *(02) 6276 3444* **Fax** *(02) 6247 0759* **Rooms** *40*

One-, two- and three-bedroom apartments and a quiet location make this an ideal option for travellers with children. The apartments enjoy views over Lake Burley Griffin, the mountains or the city. The lake is 1-minutes' walk, and the city is an easy 10-minute walk. **www.breakfree.com.au**

CANBERRA Crowne Plaza Canberra  $$$$$

1 Binara Street, ACT 2601 **Tel** *(02) 6247 8999, 1800 007 697* **Fax** *(02) 6247 3706* **Rooms** *295*

This modern four-and-a-half star hotel right in the heart of the city offers a range of facilities, including sauna, internet access and secretarial services. It is particularly popular with visiting business people. It is close to shops and restaurants, the Australian War Memorial and the National Gallery of Australia. **www.crowneplaza.com.au**

CANBERRA Hyatt Hotel $$$$$

Commonwealth Avenue, Yarralumla, ACT 2600 **Tel** *(02) 6270 1234* **Fax** *(02) 6281 5998* **Rooms** *249*

This centrally located heritage-listed hotel, surrounded by manicured lawns and gardens, is Canberra's five-star showpiece. Its decor oozes 1920s sophistication, and the morning and afternoon teas in The Tea Lounge are a Canberra institution. It also offers first-class fitness and disabled facilities. **www.canberra.park.hyatt.com**

CANBERRA Olims Canberra Hotel $$$$$

Cnr Ainslie & Limestone aves, Braddon, ACT 2612 **Tel** *(02) 6243 0000, 1800 475 337* **Rooms** *125*

This four-star 1927 Art Deco hotel, close to the War Memorial, the National Gallery of Australia and the city centre, is classified by the National Trust. It offers peaceful formal gardens, a cocktail bar, wheelchair access and a mixture of room styles and prices to suit most budgets, including heritage and de luxe rooms. **www.olimshotel.com**

CANBERRA Pavilion on Northbourne $$$$$

242 Northbourne Avenue, Dickson, ACT 2602 **Tel** *(02) 6247 6888* **Fax** *(02) 6248 7866* **Rooms** *156*

This refurbished hotel and serviced apartments, popular with business travellers, has gone upmarket. It has excellent conference and Internet facilities. There are several spa suites and there is an indoor tropical atrium. It is close to shops and restaurants and only 2 km (1 mile) from the city centre. **www.pavilioncanberra.com**

MACGREGOR Ginninderry Homestead B&B $$$

468 Parkwood Road, ACT 2615 **Tel** *(02) 6254 6464* **Fax** *(02) 6254 1945* **Rooms** *4*

This elegant guesthouse on a working farm offers pastoral views framed by the distant snow-capped Brindabella Ranges. The homestead has gracious formal gardens, verandas, a Victorian gazebo, a sunny courtyard, spa and BBQ area. Inside you'll find formal dining and lounge rooms and a charming billiards room. **www.ginninderry.com.au**

BRISBANE

CITY CENTRE Base Brisbane Backpackers $

Cnr Edward & Ann Streets, QLD 4000 **Tel** *(07) 3211 2433* **Fax** *(07) 3211 2466* **Rooms** *32*

Conveniently located backpacker hotel, the Base offers dormitory rooms, single rooms and double rooms. Built in an historic hotel with laced wrought-iron balconies, renovated for modern travellers, this is a budget stay with historical value in a part of Brisbane's past. **www.stayatbase.com**

CITY CENTRE Eton Bed & Breakfast $$

436 Upper Roma Street, QLD 4000 **Tel** *(07) 3236 0115* **Fax** *(07) 3102 6120* **Rooms** *6*

This fully renovated, heritage-listed guesthouse is situated in a colonial Queenslander, built in 1877. Conveniently located on the edge of Brisbane's CBD, it is a 15-minute walk from the heart of the city and Brisbane's Exhibition and Convention Centre. A relaxed place, it is close to Caxton Street's nightlife and eateries. **www.babs.com.au/eton**

CITY CENTRE Explorers Inn Hotel $$

63 Turbot Street (cnr George Street), QLD 4000 **Tel** *(07) 3211 3488* **Fax** *(07) 3211 3499* **Rooms** *58*

Under its banner as Brisbane's cheapest three-star hotel, this comfortable inn offers accommodation for the budget conscious traveller. Testimonals boast "a friendly stay, clean rooms, well-prepared food, and a convenient location". Rooms include an en-suite bathroom, designer decor, security and a colour TV. **www.explorers.com.au**

CITY CENTRE Central Summit Apartments

32 Leichhardt Street, Spring Hill, QLD 4000 **Tel** *(07) 3839 7000* **Fax** *(07) 3832 2821* **Rooms** *48*

Overlooking Roma Street parkland, Central Summit offers studios and one- and two-bedroom apartments with modern interiors. Perfect for families or business travellers with train and bus connections just moments from the door. The CBD is within walking distance. **www.centralapartmenthotels.com.au**

CITY CENTRE Clarion Rendezvous Hotel Brisbane

255 Ann Street, QLD 4000 **Tel** *(07) 3001 9888* **Fax** *(07) 3001 9700* **Rooms** *137*

Only a minute from the Queen Street Mall, this hotel offers private rooms and one- and two-bedroom self-contained apartments. The apartments have the added attraction of a separate bedroom, living/dining room and kitchen facilities. Bistro and wine bar open every evening. **www.rendezvoushotels.com**

CITY CENTRE Conrad Treasury Brisbane

130 William Street, QLD 4000 **Tel** *(07) 3306 8888* **Fax** *(07) 3306 8823* **Rooms** *130*

Lit softly at night, this historic sandstone heritage building has a romantic ambience. The hotel offers two-service a day rooms, valet, laundry, easy access for wheelchairs and limousine services. The casino is open 24 hours and has a range of dining options. **www.conrad.com.au**

CITY CENTRE Holiday Inn

Roma Street, QLD 4000 **Tel** *(07) 3238 2222* **Fax** *(07) 32382288* **Rooms** *192*

Located next to the Brisbane Transit Centre and a short walk from the CBD and Queen Street Mall, this hotel is convenient for a City holiday and onward travel. It offers a comfortable stay with a great range of extra services. Staff speak English, Hindi, Spanish and Tagalog. The restaurant has a kids-eat-free deal. **www.holidayinn.com**

CITY CENTRE Hotel George Williams

317 George Street, QLD 4000 **Tel** *1800 064 858* **Fax** *(07) 3308 0703* **Rooms** *81*

Hotel George Williams is located a short stroll from the city centre. It hosts one of the largest gyms in Australia – free for hotel guests. Other features include outdoor terrace rooms and free undercover parking. Alfresco dining is offered at Cerello's bar and restaurant. Located close to the Transit Centre. **www.hgw.com.au**

CITY CENTRE Hotel Ibis

27 Turbot Street, QLD 4000 **Tel** *(07) 3237 2333* **Fax** *(07) 3237 2444* **Rooms** *218*

Situated close to the banks of the busy Brisbane River, the Ibis Hotel offers spacious rooms with modern decor at a reasonable price. Child-minding is available at an extra cost. It is linked to its sister hotel, the Mecure Hotel Brisbane, situated next door and guests can enjoy the Mercure's bars and restaurants. **www.accorhotels.com.au**

CITY CENTRE Mercure Hotel

85 North Quay, QLD 4000 **Tel** *(07) 3237 2300* **Fax** *(07) 3236 1035* **Rooms** *194*

Check the prices daily for this luxury hotel as it offers dynamic pricing from A$120 in low season. The hotel is situated on the banks of the Brisbane River and offers panoramic views over the Southbank Parklands, Victoria Bridge and the Cultural Centre. Parking is limited and can be arranged at an extra cost. **www.mercurebrisbane.com.au**

CITY CENTRE Brisbane Hilton

190 Elizabeth Street, QLD 4000 **Tel** *(07) 3234 2000* **Fax** *3231 3199* **Rooms** *321*

The Brisbane Hilton is a modern hotel with a dramatic atrium soaring 20 floors above the lobby. The hotel was built in 1986 and has been renovated to include an Events floor and Atrium lounge. Features include a car park, wheel-chair access, room service, and a safety deposit box in all rooms. Excellent city views. **www.brisbane.hilton.com**

CITY CENTRE Brisbane Marriot Hotel

515 Queen Street, QLD 4000 **Tel** *(07) 3303 8000* **Fax** *(07) 3303 8088* **Rooms** *267*

With panoramic views of the city skyline and the river, the Marriot Hotel is well situated for business travellers and tourists. It features elegantly appointed rooms, exquisite timber veneers, marble bathrooms, a luxury spa, swimming pool, gym facilties and sauna. Alfresco dining is available. **www.marriot.com/bnedt**

CITY CENTRE Chifley at Lennons

66 Queen Street, QLD 4000 **Tel** *1300 272 132* **Fax** *(07) 3221 9389* **Rooms** *154*

The Chifley at Lennons is located on the Queen Street Mall and close to shopping and the CBD. It is a short stroll away from the Botanical Gardens, Southbank Parklands and the Art Gallery. It has a variety of accommodation, including de luxe spa rooms. **www.chifleyhotels.com**

CITY CENTRE Citigate King George Square

Cnr Ann & Roma Street, QLD 4000 **Tel** *(07) 3229 9111* **Fax** *(07) 3229 9618* **Rooms** *438*

This elegantly appointed hotel offers two kinds of accommodation in two towers. The Sebel Tower offers de luxe rooms and suites; the Citigate Tower has standard guest rooms. Special hotel features include a rooftop heated swimming pool, business centre, gym and sauna, and a selection of dining options. **www.mirvachotels.com**

CITY CENTRE Quality Hotel The Inchcolm

73 Wickham Terrace, QLD 4000 **Tel** *(07) 3226 8888* **Fax** *(07) 3226 8899* **Rooms** *35*

This elegantly appointed, heritage hotel features handcrafted timber fittings and custom-built furniture. A cityscape pool provides stunning views. Tasteful refurbishing has retained the old caged lift and silky oak panelling. Downstairs is Armstrongs, an award-winning restaurant. **www.inchcolmhotel.com.au**

Key to Price Guide *see p478* **Key to Symbols** *see back cover flap*

CITY CENTRE Urban Brisbane

345 Wickham Terrace, QLD 4000 **Tel** *(07) 3831 6177* **Fax** *(07) 3831 6363* **Rooms** *179*

A short stroll from Brisbane's CBD, shopping mall, nightlife and casino, Urban Brisbane is well located overlooking two of Brisbane's parklands and offers a view to the Western mountains. This hotel provides guests with sophisticated dining at the hotel's Gazebo restaurant. **www.hotelurban.com.au**

FORTITUDE VALLEY Balhouse Apartments

30 Costin Street, QLD 4006 **Tel** *(07) 3216 0444* **Fax** *(07) 3252 1810* **Rooms** *12*

These modern self-contained apartments are within an easy walk of Chinatown and the heart of the Valley. Clean and quiet, they are good value and offer a great alternative to the run-of-the-mill backpacker and budget accommodation on offer elsewhere. **www.balhouse.com**

FORTITUDE VALLEY Brisbane Manor Hotel

55 Gregory Terrace, QLD 4006 **Tel** *(07) 32524171* **Fax** *(07) 3252 2704* **Rooms** *46*

This country-style hotel with veranda and sundeck bar is situated in a quiet location, yet close to the Valley nightclubs, restaurants and shopping. It is budget priced, offering clean, comfortable rooms or dormitory stays. A communal kitchen and lounge make this a great spot to meet fellow travellers. **www.brisbanemanor.com.au**

KANGAROO POINT The Point Brisbane

21 Lambert Street, QLD 4169 **Tel** *(07) 3240 0888* **Fax** *(07) 3392 1155* **Rooms** *104*

This hotel is situated at Kangaroo Point and has stunning views over the Story Bridge and Botanical Gardens and an impressive night skyline. A modern hotel, The Point hosts a courtesy shuttle bus to the CBD, a fully licensed bar and café, exercise and pool facilities and a 24-hour room service menu. **www.thepointbrisbane.com.au**

MILTON Cosmo on the Park Road

60 Park Road, QLD 4064 **Tel** *(07) 3858 5999* **Fax** *(07) 3858 5988* **Rooms** *75*

A boutique hotel in the alfresco dining, riverside precinct of Park Road, Cosmo on the Park Road is surrounded by trendy cafés, restaurants and is only a five-minute drive from the city. This is the ideal luxury stay for a weekend break, or a select stay for the business traveller. **www.centralgroup.com.au**

NEW FARM Cream Gables

70 Kent Street, QLD 4005 **Tel** *(07) 3358 2727* **Fax** *(07) 3358 2727* **Rooms** *3*

A stone's throw from New Farm's clubs, pubs, galleries, restaurants and shops, this guesthouse offers well-appointed guest rooms with their own courtyard, en suite and television. The king/twin room is disabled friendly. It is an easy walk to the city. **www.webminders.com.au/creamgables**

PADDINGTON Fern Cottage B&B

89 Fernberg Road, QLD 4064 **Tel** *(07) 3511 6685* **Fax** *(07) 3511 6685* **Rooms** *3*

This is a charming, refurbished 1930s Queenslander home in the upbeat Paddington/Rosalie area. Situated about 2 km (1 mile) from downtown Brisbane, this location is alive with small art galleries, boutiques, bistros, clothes shops, alfresco restaurants and cafes. Rooms are air conditioned with en suites. **www.ferncottage.net**

PADDINGTON The Collingwood

32 Collingwood Street, QLD 4064 **Tel** *(07) 3511 7430* **Rooms** *5*

This superb urban retreat offers bed and breakfast accommodation in a refurbished, colonial property. The elegant, immaculately dressed rooms have free Wi-Fi and bathrobes. The markets, restaurants, cafés and art galleries of Paddington are just a short walk away. **www.thecollingwood.com.au**

SPRING HILL Metro Hotel Tower Mill

239 Wickham Terrace, QLD 4000 **Tel** *(07) 3832 1421* **Fax** *(07) 3832 1421* **Rooms** *77*

This three-and-a-half star hotel is located opposite one of Brisbane's landmarks – the "Mill". The windmill is Brisbane's oldest building and is a relic from the penal settlement of 1824–42. The hotel overlooks Wickham Park and is conveniently close to the CBD and shopping areas. **www.MetroHospitalityGroup.com**

SPRING HILL The Soho Motel

333 Wickham Terrace, QLD 4000 **Tel** *(07) 3831 7722* **Fax** *(07) 3831 8050* **Rooms** *50*

Located opposite the Roma Street parkland and just a short stroll from the city, this popular mid-range hotel offers a range of facilities. Every room opens onto its own private balcony. An extensive à la carte breakfast menu is available until 10am daily. **www.sohobrisbane.com.au**

SPRING HILL Hotel Grand Chancellor

Cnr Leichhardt Street & Wickham Terrace, QLD 4000 **Tel** *(07) 3831 4055* **Fax** *(07) 3831 5031* **Rooms** *180*

Located on the highest point of the CBD, this hotel is situated on the main route to the airport and is a leisurely walk to the CBD down tree-lined stone steps and paths. The hotel features Frescos Restaurant, cocktail bar, garden courtyard, rooftop pool, conference facilities and undercover parking. **www.ghihotels.com**

SPRING HILL Hotel Watermark

555 Wickham Terrace, QLD 4000 **Tel** *(07) 3058 9333* **Fax** *(07) 3058 9350* **Rooms** *95*

The Albert Park Hotel is a boutique hotel overlooking the Roma Street Parklands. The decor is modern. Rooms are well lit and spacious. Added features include 24-hour reception, secure undercover parking, wireless Internet connection, hotel safe and an award-winning restaurant. **www.hotelwatermark.com.au**

WEST END Somewhere to Stay

Cnr Brighton & Franklin streets, QLD 4101 **Tel** *1800 812398* **Fax** *(07) 3846 4584* **Rooms** *32*

For backpacker accommodation in Brisbane, this is an excellent choice. Single dorm rooms are priced from A$19 a night. A free shuttle-bus runs every day from 8am to 7:30pm to collect guests from Roma Street Transit Centre. It leaves every hour on the hour. A saltwater swimming pool makes this a fun stay. **www.somewheretostay.com.au**

WEST END Eskdale B&B

141 Vulture Street, QLD 4101 **Tel** *(07) 3255 2519* **Rooms** *4*

With only four guest bedrooms, there is an opportunity to meet other guests while relaxing in the lounge to read, talk or watch TV. The bathrooms are modern and airy. A stay in this authethic Queenslander (built in 1907) is reasonably priced and convenient for the Southbank. **www.eskdale.homestead.com**

SOUTH OF TOWNSVILLE

AGNES WATER Mango Tree Motel

7 Agnes Street, QLD 4677 **Tel** *(07) 4974 9132* **Fax** *(07) 4974 9132* **Rooms** *13*

Adjacent to the main surf beach in Agnes Water on the Discovery Coast, this budget motel is in one of Queensland's prettiest beach towns on southern end of the Great Barrier Reef. It is a short walk to shops, cafés and beach tracks. The popular beachside bar and restaurant adjoins the motel and is licensed. **www.mangotreemotel.com**

AIRLIE BEACH Club Crocodile Resort Airlie Beach

Shute Harbour Road, Airlie Beach, QLD 4802 **Tel** *(07) 4946 7155* **Fax** *(07) 4946 6007* **Rooms** *160*

This multi-award winning tropicial resort overlooks the magnificent Whitsunday Islands. The resort features free-form pools and waterfalls. Tourists can go sailing, snorkelling, horse riding or fishing or yachting in the aquamarine waters surrounding the islands. The "Hard Croc Café" offers a delicious menu. **www.clubcroc.com.au**

AIRLIE BEACH Coral Sea Resort

25 Oceanview Avenue, QLD 4802 **Tel** *(07) 4946 1300* **Fax** *(07) 4946 6516* **Rooms** *78*

This resort has four styles of holiday suites, two-bedroom apartments, family apartments and one-, two- and three-bedroom penthouses. Decor is nautically themed with bright aqua and turquoise colours, deckside ornamentation, historic boat prints and yachting memorabilia. **www.coralsearesort.com**

BUDERIM Buderim White House Grand Manor

54 Quorn Close, QLD 4556 **Tel** *(07) 5445 1961* **Fax** *(07) 5445 1994* **Rooms** *4*

This five-star boutique B&B is located on the beautiful Buderim Mountain and set amid lush rainforest, complete with trails and abundant birdlife. Minutes from the beaches of Mooloolaba and Noosa, the B&B has four suites, each with a private entrance, kingsize four-poster bed, open fireplace and double spa bath. **www.buderimwhitehouse.com.au**

CARNARVON GORGE Carnarvon Gorge Wilderness Lodge

PMB 1009 Rolleston, QLD 4702 **Tel** *(07) 4984 4503* **Fax** *(07) 4984 4500* **Rooms** *30*

This National Park has some of the best walking tracks in Australia. The lodge features a reference library, access to magnificent views, bird-watching, guided walks and the aboriginal rock art gallery. There is an abundance of flora and fauna to see. Safari cabins are inviting and airy. **www.carnarvon-gorge.com**

CURRUMBIN VALLEY Cottages on the Creek

1464 Currumbin Creek Road, Currumbin Valley, QLD 4223 **Tel** *(07) 5533 0449* **Fax** *(07) 5533 0449* **Rooms** *2*

Cottages on the Creek have been designed with minimal environmental impact. This is a eco-friendly stay in a wildlife haven. Black cockatoos, whipbirds and honey-eaters provide company for breakfast. It is a two-minute drive from the Currumbin rockpools and 15 minutes from the Coolangatta Airport. **www.cottagesonthecreek.com.au**

EUMUNDI Eumundi Country Cottage

47 Memorial Drive, QLD 4562 **Tel** *(07) 5442 7220* **Fax** *(07) 5442 7320* **Rooms** *3*

A luxury guesthouse in a tastefully restored historic Queensland house (built in 1911) with a guest cottage. Each room has its own en suite and private veranda, and is furnished with antiques and period china. This is Queensland hospitality at its best, close to the Eumundi markets and 15 minutes from Noosa.

FRASER ISLAND Eurong Beach Resort

Fraser Island, QLD 4655 **Tel** *(07) 4127 9122* **Fax** *(07) 4127 9178* **Rooms** *114*

This resort offers rooms for families and groups, units and apartments. Situated on the beachfront at Fraser Island's 123-km (76-mile) beach it is ideally suited to access the world heritage wilderness, including rainforest walks, freshwater lakes and creeks, coloured sands and the Maheno shipwreck. **www.eurong.com**

FRASER ISLAND Kingfisher Bay Resort

PMB 1 Urangan Hervey Bay, QLD 4655 **Tel** *(07) 4120 3333* **Fax** *(07) 4120 3326* **Rooms** *261*

A luxury resort on the edge of Fraser's wilderness, offering four-wheel drive eco tours and walks, canoeing and fishing. It has four return catamaran services each day from Hervey Bay. A vehicle barge runs three times a day from River Heads. Transfers are available from the airport and coach terminal. **www.kingfisherbay.com**

Key to Price Guide *see p478* **Key to Symbols** *see back cover flap*

GLADSTONE Auckland Hill B&B · $$$

15 Yarroon Street, QLD 4680 **Tel** *(07) 49724907* **Fax** *(07) 49727300* **Rooms** *6*

A refurbished guesthouse built in 1874, with de luxe rooms with balconies overlooking the harbour and marina. It has a guest lounge with a fireplace, choice of a luxury suite with spa bath and a large open deck for relaxing on while enjoying the sea air. **www.ahbb.com.au**

GOLD COAST Conrad Jupiters · $$$$$

Broadbeach Island, QLD 4218 **Tel** *(07) 5592 8100* **Fax** *(07) 5592 8219* **Rooms** *594*

An ideal location in the heart of the Gold Coast, this luxury hotel and casino offers sweeping views across the Pacific to the east, and across the hinterland and mountains to the west. There are four rooms with special facilities for disabled guests. The Coolongatta airport is a 20-minute drive away. **www.conrad.com.au**

GOLD COAST Palazzo Versace · $$$$$

Seaworld Drive, Main Beach, QLD 4217 **Tel** *(07) 5509 8000* **Fax** *(07) 5509 8888* **Rooms** *205*

With a reputation for elegance, style and discerning taste, the Versace label has been translated to this stunningly designed hotel on the Gold Coast's broadwater. Rooms are decorous with warm timber tones and rich fabric colours. This is a stay for the senses. Try out the spa. **www.palazzoversace.com**

GOLD COAST Sheraton Mirage Resort & Spa · $$$$$

Seaworld Drive, Main Beach, QLD 4217 **Tel** *(07) 5591 1488* **Fax** *(07) 5591 2299* **Rooms** *293*

Sheraton Mirage Resort & Spa is located 35 km (22 miles) from the Gold Coast Airport and 80 km (50 miles) from Brisbane Airport. Situated on the Broadwater Peninsula, the resort has an oceanfront position and views over the Gold Coast's broadwater. **www.sheraton.com/goldcoast**

GOLD COAST HINTERLAND Binna Burra Mountain Lodge · $$$

Lamington National Park, 4211 **Tel** *(07) 5533 3622* **Fax** *(07) 5533 3658* **Rooms** *40*

Binna Burra Lodge is an ecotourism retreat offering the peace and quiet of a natural rainforest setting with an educational adventure. Its rustic timber cabins are built from hand-cut tallow wood slabs. This is a modern stay, but the tranquillity is not interrupted by phones, clocks, radios or television. **www.binnaburralodge.com.au**

GOLD COAST HINTERLAND O'Reilly's Rainforest Retreat · $$$$$

Lamington National Park, QLD 4275 **Tel** *(07) 5544 0644* **Fax** *(07) 5544 0638* **Rooms** *72*

O'Reilly's is situated in the lush rainforest covered mountains of the Lamington National Park, 119 km (74 miles) southwest of Brisbane – the largest world heritage listed sub-tropical rainforest in Australia. Modern rooms offer magnificent views of surrounding landscape, but have no phone, television or radios. **www.oreillys.com.au**

HAMILTON ISLAND Ala Moana · $$$$$

Whitsunday Islands **Tel** *(03) 9387 9712* **Rooms** *5*

Overlooking the eastern Whitsundays, the lavish Ala Moana has upped the ante in luxury on Hamilton Island. The purely private haven offers five opulent guest rooms, each with king-size bed and huge bathrooms. A wrap around deck, personal butler and private 48-foot yacht make a stay here unforgettable. **www.alamoana.com.au**

HERVEY BAY Mango Tourist Hostel · $

110 Torquay Road, Scarness, QLD 4655 **Tel** *(07) 4124 2832* **Rooms** *3*

This friendly hostel caters for budget travellers and backpackers. Housed in a tastefully renovated Queenslander, it is situated a short distance from Hervey Bay's beach, esplanade and shops. Homestyle atmosphere and good advice on Fraser Island's trails and Western beaches is offered. Payment by cash only. **www.mangohostel.com**

HERVEY BAY The Bay B&B · $$

180 Cypress Street, QLD 4655 **Tel** *(07) 4125 6919* **Fax** *(07) 4125 3658* **Rooms** *5*

Set in an idyllic tropical garden, this guesthouse is just one street from the esplanade, beach and shopping. Shady terraces, a saltwater pool and a sumptious breakfast make this stay a great stay. You can take a whale-watching tour or a catamaran to Fraser Island, fish, swim, hike or go for a bicycle ride. **www.baybedandbreakfast.com.au**

HERVEY BAY Susan River Homestead · $$

PO Box 516 Maryborough – off Hervey Bay Road, QLD 4650 **Tel** *(07) 4121 6846* **Fax** *(07) 4122 2675* **Rooms** *16*

Looking for an outback adventure not too far from the Coast, this friendly homestay farm is modern, well situated and offers horse riding, paragliding, waterskiing, absailing, a tennis court and swimming pool. This is the Queensland holiday of a lifetime. Backpackers and children are welcome. **www.susanriver.com**

HERVEY BAY Mantra Hervey Bay · $$$$

Buccaneer Drive, Urangan, QLD 4655 **Tel** *(07) 4197 8202 , 1800 044 422* **Fax** *(07) 4197 8222* **Rooms** *158*

Mantra Hervey Bay is situated right on the Urangan marina. Small boats, idyllic weather, gentle water and relaxed shopping and restaurants make this one of Queensland's favourite holiday destinations. This is a choice spot whether you come to whale watch, trek through Fraser Island's wilderness or just lie on the beach. **www.mantraherveybay.com.au**

HIGHFIELDS Oakleigh Country Cottage B&B · $$$

Lot 10 Bowtell Drive, QLD 4352 **Tel** *(07) 4696 7021* **Fax** *(07) 4696 7284* **Rooms** *3*

Highfields is a 10-minute drive north of Toowoomba and a two-hour drive west of Brisbane. This comfortable guesthouse offers a hearty country breakfast and a cosy wood fire. The cottage and house is surrounded by extensive rose gardens.

MACKAY Cape Hillsborough Nature Resort

MS 895 Mackay, QLD 4740 **Tel** *(07) 4959 0152* **Fax** *(07) 4959 0500* **Rooms** *28*

Providing budget to mid-range accommodation, this unique nature stay offers a choice of motel rooms, huts, cabins or villas. The resort overlooks Causarina Beach and has nature reserve on three sides, creating a secluded environment for relaxing, fishing and hiking. **www.capehillsboroughresort.com.au**

MAGNETIC ISLAND Sails on Horseshoe

13–15 Pacific Drive, Horseshoe Bay, QLD 4819 **Tel** *(07) 4778 5117* **Fax** *(07) 4778 5104* **Rooms** *14*

Horseshoe Bay is the largest of Magnetic Island's 23 bays. "Sails on Horseshoe" features modern fully self-contained townhouse apartments and offers a relaxing island stay in the aquamarine waters of the Coral Coast. All townhouses have two bedrooms and will comfortably sleep a family of six. **www.sailsonhorseshoe.com.au**

NOOSA Sheraton Noosa Resort & Spa

14–16 Hastings Street, QLD 4567 **Tel** *(07) 5449 4888* **Fax** *(07) 5449 2230* **Rooms** *175*

Located in Noosa's famous Hastings Street, this resort offers spacious rooms, each with a private balcony and spa. There are eight poolside villas which feature private courtyards. A comprehensive health club offers a full range of exercise options. **www.sheraton.com/noosa**

ROCKHAMPTON Sundowner Rockhampton

112 Gladstone Road, QLD 4700 **Tel** *(07) 4927 8866* **Fax** *(07) 4927 9711* **Rooms** *32*

Its central location, gleaming pool and laid back bar make this comfortable hotel a good mid-range option in Rockhampton. Room options include a spa suite, family and standard rooms. The coast 40 km (25 miles) away boasts some of the best fishing in Queensland. **www.sundownermotorinns.com.au**

ROCKHAMPTON Myella Farm Stay

Myella Baralaba, QLD 4702 **Tel** *(07) 4998 1290* **Fax** *(07) 4998 1104* **Rooms** *18*

This farm runs 400 head of cattle and offers a range of activity-filled packages including learning to ride a motorbike and horse riding. This is an authentic Queensland holiday experience. Overseas guests love the kangaroos and wallabies. Payment is by cash only. **www.myella.com**

STANToRPE Moonrise Estate

47 Clarke Lane, QLD 4380 **Tel** *(07) 4683 6203* **Fax** *(07) 4683 6203* **Rooms** *3*

This tastefully restored classic country homestead is in the heart of Queensland's wine country. Featuring stunning views of the countryside and Granite Belt, this winery stay is an 8-minute drive from Stanthorpe and offers wine sales and tasting at the cellar door. Accommodation available on weekends only. **www.moonriseestate.com.au**

STRADBROKE ISLAND Straddie Views B&B

26 Cumming Parade, Point Lookout, QLD 4183 **Tel/Fax** *(07) 3409 8875* **Rooms** *2*

Overlooking the Pacific Ocean on one of Queensland's favourite islands, Straddie Views is a modern B&B, with an airy, seaside feel. Guests are welcomed with home-made biscuits and a decanter of port. Ideal for swimming, surfing, fishing, bird-watching, tennis and boating, close to Brisbane and Moreton Bay. **www.northstradbrokeisland.com**

SUNSHINE COAST Whale Watch Ocean Beach Resort

Samarinda Drive, Point Lookout, QLD 4183 **Tel** *(07) 34098555* **Fax** *(07) 3409 8666* **Rooms** *40*

With breathtaking views of Stradbroke Island's beaches, this resort is the ideal spot to watch whales, dolphins, turtles and manta rays off Point Lookout. Located a short walk from Captain Cook's Lookout, the famous North Gorge Headlands walk and the Blowhole, it is also close to the Surf Club and cafés. **www.whalewatchresort.com.au**

SURFERS PARADISE Gold Coast International Backpackers Resort

28 Hamilton Avenue, QLD 4217 **Tel** *(07) 5592 5888* **Fax** *(07) 5538 9310* **Rooms** *25*

Formerly known as Mardi Gras Backpackers, this budget accommodation is in the heart of Surfers Paradise. This is a great spot to stay during the Indy car races or for any action-packed holiday. There is a large self-contained kitchen, a games and recreation area, and a barbecue. **www.goldcoastbackpackers.com.au**

TOOWOOMBA Vacy Hall Bed & Breakfast

67 Margaret Street, QLD 4350 **Tel** *(07) 4632 4053* **Fax** *(07) 4639 5526* **Rooms** *3*

Heritage luxury in the heart of Toowoomba, this fabulous guesthouse is minutes from restaurants, galleries, parks and CBD. Built in 1920, this California bungalow reflects the charm of the region. It has an elegant guest lounge with a fireplace in winter, modern en suite facilities with spas, and gourmet breakfasts. **www.vacyhall.com.au**

TOWNSVILLE Jupiters Townsville

Sir Leslie Thiess Drive, QLD 4810 **Tel** *(07) 4722 2333* **Fax** *(07) 4772 4741* **Rooms** *194*

Jupiters Townsville Hotel and Casino is situated on Queensland's tropical north coast. It overlooks Magnetic Island and provides access to the Great Barrier Reef for snorkelling, fishing and boating adventures. The hotel offers exceptional dining, bars, a swimming pool, sauna, spas, tennis courts and a gym. **www.jupiterstownsville.com.au**

TOWNSVILLE Seagulls Resort

74 The Esplanade, QLD 4810 **Tel** *(07) 4721 3111* **Fax** *(07) 4721 3133* **Rooms** *70*

This resort is set in tropical landscaped gardens, and offers a choice of hotel rooms and self-contained apartments. Extras include rooms with wheelchair access. The resort has a BBQ, tennis courts, playground and swimming pools and is located on the seafront, a 5-minute drive from the airport. **www.seagulls.com.au**

Key to Price Guide *see p478* **Key to Symbols** *see back cover flap*

NORTHERN QUEENSLAND AND THE OUTBACK

ALEXANDER BAY Daintree Wilderness Lodge
$$$$
83 Cape Tribulation Road, QLD 4873 **Tel** *(07) 4098 9105* **Fax** *(07) 4098 9258* **Rooms** *5*

This small lodge in the pristine wilderness of the Daintree National Park has won awards for ecotourism and donates A$1 of every stay to the local Cassowary Care Group. This is a unique holiday experience for nature lovers, bird lovers and travellers wanting to enjoy the lush rainforest of the Daintree. **www.daintreewildernesslodge.com.au**

ATHERTON TABLELAND: MALANDA The Canopy Rainforest Treehouses
$$$$
247 Hogan Road, QLD 4885 **Tel** *(07) 4096 5364* **Fax** *(07) 4096 5380* **Rooms** *5*

Set in an ancient rainforest, perched on a riverbank, the Tree Houses provide the perfect balance of wilderness and luxury. There are fabulous views all round and this lush haven abounds with wildlife – platypuses can be spotted in the river. There is a restaurant nearby. **www.canopytreehouses.com.au**

BURKETOWN Savannah Lodge
$$
Cnr Beames & Bowen streets, QLD 4830 **Tel** *(07) 4745 5177* **Fax** *(07) 47455211* **Rooms** *7*

This unique stay on the edge of the Gulf of Carpentaria offers roomy cabins and friendly service. This lodge is located in Burketown, close to facilities and the airport. Burketown sits on the Albert River between the Gulf wetlands and the savannah. Roads can become inaccessible in the monsoon season. **www.savannah-lodge.com**

CAIRNS Cairns Reef & Rainforest B&B
$$$
112 Mansfield Street, Earlville, QLD 4870 **Tel** *(07) 4033 5597* **Fax** *(07) 4033 5597* **Rooms** *3*

This guesthouse offers a tropical breakfast on the balcony overlooking the crystal clear rockpool and waterfall, a saltwater swimming pool, and a comprehensive tour desk which offers friendly advice and help to plan your ongoing trip. Situated in a pristine rainforest environment. **www.cairnsreefbnb.com.au**

CAIRNS Mercure Hotel Harbourside
$$$
209–217 The Esplanade, QLD 4870 **Tel** *(07) 4051 8999* **Fax** *(07) 4051 0317* **Rooms** *173*

A tropical theme runs through the decor of this upmarket stay. Each room has a private balcony with spectacular views to Trinity Bay. Teshi's Restaurant is open from 6:30am until 10:30pm, offering a fusion of Eastern and Western cuisine and featuring local tropical produce and fresh seafood. **www.mercure-harbourside.com.au**

CAIRNS Novotel Cairns Oasis Resort
$$$$$
122 Lake Street, QLD 4870 **Tel** *(07) 4080 1888* **Fax** *(07) 4080 1889* **Rooms** *314*

Stunning views of the Coral Coast and the Cairns hinterland make this an ideal vacation choice. Set in landscaped tropical gardens, this resort has every modern facility plus a few extras. It has several rooms for disabled guests, a fully-equipped gym, a lagoon, valet parking, laundry services and babysitting. **www.novotelcairnsresort.com.au**

CAIRNS Pullman Reef Hotel Casino
$$$$$
35–41 Wharf Street, QLD 4870 **Tel** *(07) 4030 8888* **Fax** *(07) 4030 8777* **Rooms** *128*

A stylish hotel experience, offering elegance and fun. The Reef Hotel Casino is incorporated into the uniquely designed building, with the Cairns Rainforest Dome situated on top. There are Jacuzzi-style baths in every room, a selection of dining options and a rooftop pool. **www.reefcasino.com.au**

CAIRNS Shangri-La Hotel
$$$$$
Pierpoint Road, QLD 4870 **Tel** *(07) 4031 1411* **Fax** *(07) 4031 3226* **Rooms** *255*

The location of this hotel is breathtaking, situated on the marina at the pier. The marina serves as a gateway to the Great Barrier Reef. Enjoy the fishing, the view of Trinity Bay, rainforest gardens, or a safe swim in the hotel pool. Cairns lagoon is a short stroll away. **www.shangri-la.com**

CAPE TRIBULATION Cape Tribulation Resort
$$$$$
Lot 10, Cape Tribulation Road, QLD 4873 **Tel** *1800 987 077* **Fax** *(07) 4098 0047* **Rooms** *66*

A luxury stay on the edge of the lush rainforest of the Daintree. This resort offers a tropical holiday in a pristine natural setting with every modern convenience, including babysitting. Close to the Great Barrier Reef, this is an ideal stay for snorkelling, kayaking and 4WD trips. **www.capetribulationresort.com.au**

COOKTOWN Pam's Place Motel Hostel
$
Cnr Boundary & Charlotte streets, QLD 4895 **Tel** *(07) 4069 5166* **Fax** *(07) 4069 5964* **Rooms** *32*

Cooktown is an exotic, relaxed coastal town with a rich history including its Aboriginal cultural heritage. It is located only five nautical miles from the Great Barrier Reef and offers scenic flights and day trip charters to Lizard Island. The hostel has single and double rooms and dorms. **www.cooktownhostel.com**

CUNNAMULLA Nardoo Station Tourist Retreat
$
"Nardoo", Cunnamulla, QLD 4490 **Tel** *(07) 4655 4833* **Fax** *(07) 4655 4835* **Rooms** *13*

This is the genuine Australian outback adventure. Lie back in the hot artesian spas or feed-up on good Australian cooking. Stays are catered to suit the individual traveller and whether you prefer to view the abundant wildlife or feed the farm animals, or go yabbying or fishing, this stay is friendly and unique. **www.nardoo.com.au**

DAINTREE Red Mill House

$$$

Red Mill House, Daintree Village, QLD 4873 **Tel** *(07) 4098 6233* **Fax** *(07) 4098 6233* **Rooms** *6*

This spacious, old home renovated in a tasteful modern design is situated in the Daintree and offers amazing bird-watching – seven of Australia's kingfishers have been spotted in the Red Mill House garden. Full breakfast with fresh seasonal fruit is included. **www.redmillhouse.com.au**

LONGREACH Aussie Betta Cabins

$

63 Sir Hudson Fysh Drive, QLD 4730 **Tel** *(07) 4658 3811* **Fax** *(07) 4658 3812* **Rooms** *22*

Longreach, in the heart of Queensland's outback, offers the tourist a chance to visit a famous Australian landmark – the Stockman's Hall of Fame. The cabins are conveniently located in walking distance of both these attractions. Extras include an outdoor pool and barbecue area. **www.queenslandholidays.com.au/outback**

LONGREACH Longreach Motor Inn

$$

Sir Hudson Fysh Drive, QLD 4730 **Tel** *(07) 4658 2322* **Fax** *(07) 4658 1825* **Rooms** *56*

The Longreach Motor Inn has extensive landscaped surrounds exhibiting local trees and shrubs; and is home to local wildlife. There is a resort-style swimming pool, Oasis restaurant and bar, and a playground for children. Longreach is a good base from to explore the local area's attraction. **www.destinationlongreach.com.au**

MOSSMAN Silky Oaks Lodge & Healing Waters Spa

$$$$$

Mossman River Gorge, QLD 4873 **Tel** *1300 134 044* **Fax** *(07) 9299 2103* **Rooms** *50*

On the edge of Mossman Gorge, this luxury retreat has spectacular views of the Daintree. Buildings are designed to blend into the treetops and draw the visitor deep into the rainforest magic. Take a walk through the Mossman Gorge National Park or a trip to the Great Barrier Reef. **www.silkyoakslodge.com.au**

MOUNT ISA Travellers Haven Backpackers

$

75–77 Spence Street, QLD 4825 **Tel** *(07) 4743 0313* **Fax** *(07) 4743 4007* **Rooms** *21*

This backpackers' place offers a free pick up and drop off from the bus or train, and has a relaxed atmosphere. If you want to explore the region take the underground tour of the Mount Isa mine or visit the Riversleigh Fossil Centre. The Mount Isa Rodeo is between late July and early August. **www.travellershaven.com.au**

MOUNT ISA Burke & Wills Motel

$$$$

Cnr Grace & Camooweal Drive, QLD 4825 **Tel** *(07) 4743 8000* **Fax** *(07) 4743 8424* **Rooms** *56*

This Quality Inn branch offers comfortable, air-conditioned rooms to cater for Mount Isa's climate. It is centrally located a short walk from the CBD, shops and cinemas. This hotel has some uniquely designed rooms which feature popular old-time frontshop façades. It also has off-street parking. **www.burkeandwillsmotel.com.au**

NORMANTON The Gulfland Motel

$

PO Box 30, Normanton, QLD 4890 **Tel** *(07) 4745 1290* **Fax** *(07) 4745 1138* **Rooms** *28*

A motel with all the conveniences that a traveller to the Gulf expects, including a shaded garden setting and licensed restaurant. Each room has a television, coffee- and tea-making facilities and ironing facilities. Pre-dinner drinks are available in the licensed restaurant. **www.gulflandmotel.com.au**

PALM COVE Sea Temple Resort & Spa

$$$$$

5 Triton Street, QLD 4879 **Tel** *(07) 4059 9600* **Fax** *(07) 4059 9699* **Rooms** *126*

This luxury resort is beautifully located on a palm-studded beach less than an hour's drive north of Cairns airport. It offers a serene environment and a range of rooms, a spacious restaurant, indulgent spa and a bar built around the lagoon pool – opulent and fun. **www.mirvachotels.com**

PORT DOUGLAS Mantra Portsea

$$$$

76 Davidson Street, QLD 4877 **Tel** *(07) 4087 2000* **Fax** *(07) 4087 2001* **Rooms** *145*

A Mediterranean-style resort in the tropics, with lagoon pools and waterways, shady palms and open verandas. Classically furnished air-conditioned apartments with balconies overlooking the pools and gardens, this resort offers privacy and fun. Tone up in the gym or take a short stroll into Port Douglas. **www.mantra.com.au**

TORRES STRAIT ISLANDS: HORN ISLAND Gateway Torres Strait Resort

$$

24 Outie Street, QLD 4875 **Tel** *(07) 4069 2222* **Fax** *(07) 4069 2211* **Rooms** *22*

Only a 2-minute walk from the wharf on Horn Island, this resort offers a saltwater pool, an outdoor entertainment area and is home to the largest collection of Torres Strait history. It houses the Torres Strait Heritage Museum. The licensed restaurant boasts its differently themed nights and a "well-stocked bar". **www.torresstrait.com.au**

TORRES STRAIT ISLANDS: PORUMA ISLAND Poruma Island Resort

$$$$$

Poruma Island, Torres Strait, QLD 4875 **Tel** *(07) 4090 0170* **Fax** *(07) 4090 0190* **Rooms** *2*

On a small coral island in the Torres Strait, Poruma is about as far removed from civilization as you can get. Overlooking a pristine white beach, the resort consists of two luxuriously fitted-out thatched-roofed lodges with plunge pool and elevated king size bed. Try snorkelling and fishing and enjoy the best of Poruma culture. **www.poruma.com**

WEIPA Heritage Resort

$$$

Commercial Avenue, QLD 4874 **Tel** *(07) 4069 8000* **Fax** *(07) 4069 8011* **Rooms** *30*

Located in the town centre adjacent to the Heritage Shopping Village, this resort features a licensed à la carte restaurant and bar and a landscaped tropical pool and barbecue area. Rooms are clean and comfortable with a homestyle touch. This is a great spot for fishing. **www.heritageresort.com.au**

Key to Price Guide *see p478* **Key to Symbols** *see back cover flap*

DARWIN AND THE TOP END

DARWIN Frogshollow Backpackers

27 Lindsay Street, NT 0800 **Tel** *(08) 8941 2600* **Fax** *(08) 8941 0758* **Rooms** *25*

Located opposite historic Frog's Hollow Park, this is one of Darwin's most popular backpacker hostels. It features an open-air saltwater plunge pool and two spas. As a licensed travel agent the hostelry offers the extra service of helping travellers with plans and bookings. **www.frogs-hollow.com.au**

DARWIN Crowne Plaza

32 Mitchell Street, NT 0800 **Tel** *(08) 89820000* **Fax** *(08) 89811765* **Rooms** *233*

Located in the heart of Darwin's CBD, Darwin's Crowne Plaza is a 15-minute drive from Darwin's International Airport. The hotel has an exciting cosmopolitan atmosphere and looks out over the Timor Sea, and is just a stroll from major shopping spots, cafés and Darwin's nightlife. **www.crowneplaza.com.au**

DARWIN Mantra on the Esplanade

88 The Esplanade, NT 0800 **Tel** *(08) 8943 4333* **Fax** *(08) 8943 4388* **Rooms** *204*

Overlooking Darwin's harbour with views to the Arafura Sea, this Australian luxury stay offers a licensed restaurant, bar, swimming pool and spa. Apartments have large private balconies, 24-hour room service and laundry facilities. Features include spacious rooms, lounge and dining areas. **www.mantraresorts.com.au**

DARWIN Skycity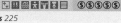

Gilruth Avenue The Gardens, NT 0800 **Tel** *(08) 8943 8888* **Fax** *(08) 8946 8999* **Rooms** *117*

This multi-award winning hotel is uniquely designed to blend into the landscape of the golf links. This hotel and casino offers world-class dining facilities and 24-hour entertainment and gambling. Close to the Mindil Beach markets, the grounds are home to goannas, colourful birds and green tree-frogs. **www.skycitydarwin.com.au**

DARWIN Travelodge Mirambeena Resort

64 Cavenaugh Street, NT 0800 **Tel** *(08) 8946 0111* **Fax** *(08) 8981 5116* **Rooms** *225*

Mirambeena means "welcome" and this tourist resort offers two swimming pools, two spas, a licensed restaurant, games room and fitness room. This hotel is conveniently located for the golf course and the Port of Darwin. The choice of accommodation includes town houses, de luxe or standard rooms. **www.mirambeena.com.au**

DARWIN LUDMILLA Bremer B&B

27 Bremer Street, Ludmilla, NT 820 **Tel** *(08) 8981 3900* **Rooms** *2*

This guesthouse offers the visitor to Darwin quality accommodation at a budget price. Situated in a quiet, leafy street with a park across the road, it is located just a 10-minute walk from the Ludmilla Saturday markets and a short bus ride to the Thursday night markets.

HOWARD SPRINGS Howard Springs Holiday Park

170 Whitewood Road, NT 0835 **Tel** *(08) 8983 1169* **Fax** *(08) 8983 2487* **Rooms** *46 (units)*

Set amid lush tropical surroundings, this holiday park offers a range of budget accommodation, including backpacker dorms, cabins, cottages and even camping, just 20 minutes from Darwin city centre. Activities include squash courts and water aerobics classes. Alternatively, relax by or in one of the three pools. **www.big4howardsprings.com.au**

HUMPTY DOO Mango Meadows Homestay

2759 Bridgemary Crescent, NT 0836 **Tel** *(08) 8988 4417* **Fax** *(08) 8988 2883* **Rooms** *4*

This is an oasis in the bush, a stylish, relaxing guesthouse with wide verandas and attractive gardens. Mango Meadows is situated 45 km (28 miles) from Darwin CBD, 17 km (10 miles) from Palmerston City and 7 km (4 miles) from Humpty Doo Village. Tariff includes a full continental breakfast. Payment by cash only. **www.mangomeadows.com**

HUMPTY DOO Zanadu Rural Retreat

Arnhem Highway, NT 2232 **Tel** *(08) 8988 5869* **Rooms** *6*

Located on the outskirts of Humpty Doo, 2 km (1 mile) off the Arnhem Highway, this rural retreat offers spacious, simply furnished units. Each unit has ceiling fans, tiled floors and lovely verandahs. Kitchenettes make this accommodation a good self-catering option. **www.zanadururalretreat.com.au**

KAKADU NATIONAL PARK Gagudju Lodge Cooinda

Kakadu National Park, Kakadu Highway, Jim Jim, NT 0886 **Tel** *(08) 8979 0145* **Fax** *(08) 8979 0148* **Rooms** *48*

Picturesque and awe inspiring, this lodge is situated on Yellow Water Billabong in Kakadu National Park. Kakadu is home to one third of Australia's birdlife. Gagudju Lodge features two restaurants, a swimming pool, general store, airport and tour desk. **www.gagudjulodgecooinda.com.au**

KATHERINE Palmcourt Kookaburra Backpackers

Cnr Third & Lindsay streets, NT 0850 **Tel** *(08) 8972 2722* **Fax** *(08) 8971 1443* **Rooms** *26*

This unique backpackers offers free transfers to and from the Ghan train. Free breakfast, tea and coffee and 20 minutes of Internet access are part of the deal. There is a large garden with swimming pool and barbecue. Offering four- and eight-bedroom dormitories and single or double rooms. **www.travelnorth.com.au**

KATHERINE Knotts Crossing Resort 🍴🏊🅿❄ $$

NT 0850 ***Tel*** *(08) 8972 2511* ***Fax*** *(08) 8972 2628* ***Rooms*** *56*

This five times winner of the Brolga Award for accommodation offers family suites for up to six guests; executive suites with mini-bar and fax; and de luxe and standard rooms with tea- and coffee-making facilities. Each private cabin has its own outside en suite. **www.knottscrossing.com.au**

MARY RIVER The Bark Hut Tourism Centre 🍴🏊❄ $$

Arnhem Highway, Annaburroo, NT 0850 ***Tel*** *(08) 8978 8988* ***Fax*** *(08) 8978 8932* ***Rooms*** *32*

The Bark Hut Tourism Centre is a historic icon in the Northern Territory. It was built in the era of crocodile and buffalo hunting, and is a hub of activity for visitors in Mary River and Kakadu National Park. The property features powered caravan sites, grassed camp sites and air-conditioned rooms.

THE RED CENTRE

ALICE SPRINGS Alice Motor Inn 🏊👪❄ $

27 Undoolya Road, NT 870 ***Tel*** *(08) 8952 2322* ***Fax*** *(08) 8953 2309* ***Rooms*** *20*

A friendly and inexpensive motel, only a short distance from the centre of town in the quiet eastside of Alice Springs. A clean, comfortable, family-orientated environment with a lovely barbecue area by the outdoor swimming pool. Breakfast upon request and transport to and from the airport is also available. **www.alicemotorinn.com.au**

ALICE SPRINGS Desert Rose Inn 🏊👪❄ $

15 Railway Terrace, NT 870 ***Tel*** *(08) 8952 1411* ***Fax*** *(08) 8952 3232* ***Rooms*** *35*

This inexpensive hotel has rooms overlooking the MacDonnell Ranges. Rooms are ideally suited to the budget traveller looking for a quiet location that is close to just about everything. The rooms are what you'd expect for the price. All have standard facilities, some have a private balcony as well. **www.desertroseinn.com.au**

ALICE SPRINGS Alice in the Territory 🍴🏊👪🍸🅿❄ $$

46 Stephens Road, NT 870 ***Tel*** *(08) 8952 6100* ***Fax*** *(08) 8952 1988* ***Rooms*** *138*

This resort-style complex is adjacent to the convention centre and golf course, it also has outstanding views of the nearby MacDonnell Ranges. It's an ideal base for travellers taking day trips to Ayers Rock, Stanley Chasm, Ormiston Gorge and the Alice Springs Desert Park. **www.alicent.com.au**

ALICE SPRINGS Desert Palms Resort 🏊👪❄ $$

74 Barrett Drive, NT 870 ***Tel*** *(08) 8952 5977* ***Fax*** *(08) 8953 4176* ***Rooms*** *80*

This resort offers air-conditioned villa accommodation with private verandas set in a tropical paradise. Check out the stunning pool with its own island, footbridge and waterfall. A short distance from Lasseter's casino and close to the town centre. An ideal family destination. **www.desertpalms.com.au**

ALICE SPRINGS Diplomat Motel 🍴🏊👪❄ $$

Cnr Gregory Terrace and Hartley Street, NT 870 ***Tel*** *(08) 8952 8977* ***Fax*** *(08) 8953 0225* ***Rooms*** *81*

The All Seasons Diplomat is located in the city centre. The hotel features two restaurants and bars, barbecue and a swimming pool. It's a handy base from which to explore Flynn's memorial, the Old Ghan train, Desert Park and the Botanical Gardens, and it's close to several art galleries and museums. **www.diplomatmotel.com.au**

ALICE SPRINGS Heavitree Gap Outback Lodge 🍴🏊👪🅿❄ $$

1 Palm Circuit, NT 870 ***Tel*** *(08) 8950 4444* ***Fax*** *(08) 8952 9394* ***Rooms*** *78*

This lodge nestles amongst eucalypts at the base of the spectacular MacDonnell Ranges. Every night, wild black-footed rock wallabies come down from the mountains, and guests are able to feed them specially prepared food. The rooms have all the standard amenities and there is also a swimming pool. **www.auroraresorts.com.au**

ALICE SPRINGS MacDonnell Range Holiday Park 🏊👪🅿❄ $$

Palm Circuit, NT 870 ***Tel*** *(08) 8952 6111* ***Fax*** *(08) 8952 5236* ***Rooms*** *48*

This multi-award-winning holiday park in the picturesque surroundings of the MacDonnell Ranges has a lot to offer the keen traveller. There are nightly talks on stars, bush tucker and 4WD preparation. There is music a couple of times a week. There's also a BMX track and two pools. Pets are not allowed. **www.macrange.com.au**

ALICE SPRINGS All Seasons Oasis 🍴🏊👪🅿❄ $$$

10 Gap Road, NT 870 ***Tel*** *(08) 8952 1444* ***Fax*** *(08) 8952 3776* ***Rooms*** *102*

Set amongst lush green gardens, this affordable hotel is a handy place to base yourself while you explore the variety of activities on offer, including Aboriginal Dreamtime tours, camel rides, hot-air balloon trips, bush restaurants, 4WD safaris, a desert golf course and a visit to Central Australia's only winery. **www.allseasons.com.au**

ALICE SPRINGS Chifley Hotel Alice Springs Resort 🍴🏊👪🅿❄ $$$

34 Stott Terrace, NT 870 ***Tel*** *(08) 8951 4545* ***Fax*** *(08) 8953 0995* ***Rooms*** *139*

Situated on the banks of the Todd River with its magnificent river red gums, this award-winning resort combines efficient and friendly Outback service with modern, comfortable facilities. Low-rise architecture and lush green lawns contribute to the relaxed atmosphere, and the bustling city centre is only five minutes away. **www.chifleyhotels.com.au**

Key to Price Guide *see p478* **Key to Symbols** *see back cover flap*

ALICE SPRINGS Quest Apartments Alice Springs $$$

9–10 South Terrace, NT 870 **Tel** *(08) 8959 0000* **Fax** *(08) 8959 0099* **Rooms** *68*

Overlooking the Todd River and with views of the MacDonnell Ranges, these superb serviced apartments are affordable and convenient. There's on-site parking, conference facilities and a fantastic alfresco barbecue area and swimming pool. **www.questapartments.com.au**

ALICE SPRINGS Aurora Alice Springs $$$$

11 Leichhardt Terrace, NT 870 **Tel** *(08) 8950 6666* **Fax** *(08) 8952 7829* **Rooms** *108*

Aurora Alice Springs is the only hotel situated on the bustling Todd Mall – the town's main shopping, restaurant and entertainment precinct. It's also home to the famous Red Ochre Grill Café Restaurant, on whose walls hang one of the finest collections of Central Australian panoramic photography in the world. **www.auroraresorts.com.au**

ALICE SPRINGS Crowne Plaza Hotel $$$$$

89 Barrett Drive, NT 870 **Tel** *(08) 8950 8000* **Fax** *(08) 8952 3822* **Rooms** *235*

Renovated to add a more contemporary feel, this hotel offers a wide range of services for the leisure and business traveller in a relaxed and stylish environment. Alice Springs Golf Course lies immediately behind it, and it's close to most of the town's main attractions. Breakfast is not included in the standard fare. **www.crowneplaza.com**

ERLDUNDA Desert Oaks Resort $$

Cnr Stuart Highway and Lasseters Highway, NT 872 **Tel** *(08) 8956 0984* **Fax** *(08) 8956 0942* **Rooms** *48*

Located 200 km (124 miles) from Alice Springs, this is a fine affordable place to stay, especially if you are planning on visiting Uluru or Kata Tjuta. Suited to families, there is a swimming pool and tennis court available for use. There's also a restaurant and tavern on site. Enjoy the old-fashioned country hospitality. **www.desertoaksresort.com**

TENNANT CREEK Eldorado Motor Inn $$

195 Paterson Street, NT 860 **Tel** *(08) 8962 2402* **Fax** *(08) 8962 3034* **Rooms** *78*

This friendly motel is situated at the northern end of town. Wander around the grounds and marvel at the intricate work in the large termite hills, the fine detail of the swallow nests or just sit back and view the most stunning sunsets across unspoilt native lands and on to the MacDonnell Ranges. **www.eldoradomotorinn.com.au**

WATARRKA NATIONAL PARK Voyages Kings Canyon Resort $$$$

Luritja Road, NT 872 **Tel** *(08) 8956 7442* **Fax** *(08) 8956 7410* **Rooms** *128*

This sensitively designed resort is just 7 km (4 miles) from Watarrka National Park, the home of the magical sandstone formation of Kings Canyon. For those keen to enjoy a romantic evening, try the Sounds of Firelight four-course dinner for two, served under a canopy of stars. **www.kingscanyonresort.com.au**

YULARA Outback Pioneer Hotel $$$$

Yulara Drive, NT 870 **Tel** *(08) 8957 7605* **Fax** *(08) 8957 7615* **Rooms** *167*

There's a good friendly atmosphere around this place, with its huge cook-your-own communal barbecue area and nightly live entertainment. It's a good hotel to meet other travellers who like a beer and a fun time. There are plenty of budget rooms available, although in some cases this means sharing bathroom facilities. **www.voyages.com.au**

YULARA Desert Gardens Hotel $$$$$

Yulara Drive, NT 872 **Tel** *(08) 8957 7888* **Fax** *(08) 8957 7716* **Rooms** *218*

This luxury hotel caters well for those who like to travel in style. A short walk to one of its many lookouts and you can view what is arguably one of Australia's greatest sunsets with a spectacular display of colours stretching across the face of Uluru and the surrounding desert. **www.voyages.com.au**

YULARA The Lost Camel Hotel $$$$$

Yulara Drive, NT 872 **Tel** *(08) 8957 7650* **Fax** *(08) 8957 7657* **Rooms** *99*

This boutique hotel has apartment-style studios furnished in vibrant colours, mixing urban chic with traditional Aboriginal artifacts. The studio rooms are located around a sparkling pool and garden courtyard. It's one for those who would like a funky, contemporary feel to their Outback experience. **www.voyages.com.au**

YULARA Sails in the Desert Hotel $$$$$

Yulara Drive, NT 872 **Tel** *(08) 8957 7888* **Fax** *(08) 8957 7474* **Rooms** *224*

Named after the soaring white sails that crown its roof, this is Ayers Rock Resort's premier five-star hotel. Exquisitely furnished and designed, the interior decor focuses on Aboriginal heritage and culture, with a gallery in the lobby and significant artworks featured throughout the public areas and in the private rooms. **www.voyages.com.au**

PERTH AND THE SOUTHWEST

ALBANY Ace Motor Inn $$

314 Albany Highway, Albany, WA 6330 **Tel** *(08) 9841 2911* **Fax** *(08) 9841 4443* **Rooms** *56*

Good, clean affordable lodging. All rooms have ground floor access and include satellite TV, free movies, electric blankets, hairdryer, tea and coffee facilities, iron and ironing board. Family rooms and spa suites are also available. Nestled in a peaceful garden a short distance from the town's main thoroughfare. **www.acemotorinn.com.au**

BRIDGETOWN Nelson's of Bridgetown

38 Hampton Street, Bridgetown, WA 6255 **Tel** *(08) 9761 1641/1800 635 565* **Fax** *(08) 9761 2372* **Rooms** *35*

Self-described as "olde worlde" lodging, this triple Tourism Award winner has extras like a large hot tub spa. A pretty courtyard is nestled beside the 1898 hotel building. In keeping with tradition, the rooms have antique decor and Baltic federation furniture. **www.nelsonsofbridgetown.net.au**

BUNBURY The Rose Hotel

Victoria Street, Bunbury, WA 6230 **Tel** *(08) 9721 4533* **Fax** *(08) 9721 8285* **Rooms** *25*

One of the best-preserved historic buildings in the city centre, this Victorian hotel retains the opulence and extravagant details of the glory days of the 19th century. The architectural highlights are the intricate ironwork and the ornate first-floor veranda. Some of the ground-floor units are accessible for wheelchair-users. **www.rosehotel.com.au**

BUSSELTON Mandalay Holiday Resort

652 Geographe Bay Road, Busselton, WA 6280 **Tel** *(08) 9752 1328, 1800 248 231* **Rooms** *54*

Accommodation options at this budget resort complex include villas, chalets, cabins, cottages and onsite caravans. Standard en suite cabins include fully-equipped kitchens. Resort facilities include barbecues, games rooms, adventure playgrounds, bicycle hire and a communal TV lounge. **www.mandalayresort.com.au**

DENMARK Sensational Heights Bed and Breakfast

159 Suttons Road, Denmark, WA 6333 **Tel** *(08) 9840 9000* **Fax** *(08) 9840 9800* **Rooms** *4*

Perched above 100 acres of karri forest, these luxury suites offer sensational views of the coast and mountains. Accommodation options include two deluxe suites with spas and king-sized beds and a two-bedroom family unit. Relax in the lounge, reading room or courtyard or take a walking trail through the forest. **www.sensationalheightsbandb.com.au**

ESPERANCE Best Western Hospitality Inn

The Esplanade, Esperance, WA 6450 **Tel** *(08) 9071 1999* **Fax** *(08) 9071 3915* **Rooms** *50*

All standard rooms are light and roomy with quality, queen-size beds, TV, mini bar and tea- and coffee-making facilities. Set on the shores of the Great Southern Ocean in Esperance Bay, the hotel is only a two-minute walk to the heart of the township. Caters for the disabled. **http://hinnesperance.bestwestern.com.au**

FREMANTLE Backpackers Inn

11 Pakenham Street, Fremantle, WA 6160 **Tel** *(08) 9431 7065* **Fax** *(08) 9336 7106* **Rooms** *40*

This well-managed youth hostel comes with an excellent reputation for comfortable, budget accommodation. Set in the heart of Fremantle, it has a lounge area, open fireplace, reading room and table tennis. Internet bookings are recommended ahead of time. Reception open from 8am to 8pm. **www.backpackersinnfreo.com.au**

FREMANTLE Old Firestation Backpackers

18 Phillimore Street, Fremantle, WA 6160 **Tel** *(08) 9430 5454* **Rooms** *6*

Budget-style accommodation in this heritage-listed building close to the railway station. Dormitory style sleeping arrangements plus six double rooms. Facilities include free parking, sun lounge and barbecue area, 24-hour Internet access, TV and fridge, playstation, DVDs and games room. **www.old-firestation.net**

FREMANTLE Esplanade Hotel Fremantle

Cnr Marine Terrace & Essex Street, Fremantle, WA 6160 **Tel** *(08) 9432 4000* **Fax** *(08) 9430 4539* **Rooms** *300*

A famous building in the heart of Fremantle, this grand hotel has homely rooms, most with private balconies. Standard rooms include mini bar, hairdryer, voice mail messaging, radio alarm and satellite TV. Facilities include sauna, three outdoor spas and bicycle hire. **www.esplanadehotelfremantle.com.au**

FREMANTLE Harbour Village Quest Apartments

43 Mews Road, Fremantle, WA 6160 **Tel** *(08) 9430 3888* **Fax** *(08) 9430 3800* **Rooms** *56*

This modern apartment hotel on the quay in Challenger Harbour offers a spa, barbecue area, in-house movies, Internet access and laundry. The smart, functional rooms have fully-equipped kitchens and excellent views. **www.questharbourvillage.com.au**

HYDEN Wave Rock Motel

2 Lynch Street, Hyden, WA 6359 **Tel** *(08) 9880 5052* **Fax** *(08) 9880 5041* **Rooms** *54*

Surrounded by Australian bushland, this Outback motel has excellent facilities, including three restaurants. It's a good base for visitors to nearby Wave Rock *(see p318)*, the bizarre granite rock formation. The hotel rooms are basic but they are clean and comfortable enough. **www.waverock.com.au/motel.htm**

KALGOORLIE York Hotel

259 Hannan Street, Kalgoorlie, WA 6430 **Tel** *(08) 9021 2337* **Fax** *(08) 9021 2337* **Rooms** *20*

A air of grace and elegance to this magnificently preserved Kalgoorlie iconic building. It was built during the gold rush in 1896 and the Victorian architecture features an ornate façade and domed roof *(see p319)*. Rooms are simple and snug, and some have balconies. It is ideally situated in the centre of town.

MARGARET RIVER Surfpoint Resort

12 Riedle Drive, Margaret River, WA 6285 **Tel** *(08) 9757 1777* **Fax** *(08) 9757 1077* **Rooms** *16*

This budget beachside lodging won the WA Tourism Award in 2003. The 16 double rooms and nine dorms are clean and comfortable. There is also a lounge, dining area, kitchen, barbecue, laundry and Internet access. Guests can hire boogie boards, surf boards and mountain bikes from the hotel. Fully wheelchair accessible. **www.surfpoint.com.au**

Key to Price Guide *see p478* **Key to Symbols** *see back cover flap*

MARGARET RIVER Grange on Farrelly 🏨🏊🎿🛗 $$$$$

18 Farrelly Street, Margaret River, WA 6285 **Tel** *1800 650 100* **Fax** *(08) 9757 3076* **Rooms** *29*

A tranquil location close to the centre of town. Rooms are cosy and offer a choice of four-poster beds or canopy beds, and have ground-floor access. Outside are native gardens, a barbecue area and half-court tennis court. A spa and free in-house movies are also available. **www.grangeonfarrelly.com.au**

NORTHAM Shamrock Hotel 🏨🛗 $$

112 Fitzgerald Street, Northam, WA 6401 **Tel** *(08) 9622 1092* **Fax** *(08) 9622 5707* **Rooms** *14*

This historic colonial building dates back to 1866. It has been restored and contains memorabilia documenting the history of the town. The beautiful bedrooms all come with king-size bed, en suite, TV, fridge and hot-drink facilities while de luxe suites have personal spas. **www.shamrockhotelnortham.com.au**

PEMBERTON Karri Valley Resort 🏨🎿🛶 $$$$

Vasse Highway, Pemberton, WA 6260 **Tel** *(08) 9776 2020/1800 245 757* **Fax** *(08) 9776 2012* **Rooms** *62*

Nestled in the heart of the Karri Valley overlooking Lake Beedelup, these cosy chalets are fully equipped for self-catering visitors. Many chalets have lake views and a private balcony and the resort feaures mini golf and two tennis courts. A general store on site for basic food and souvenirs. **www.karrivalleyresort.com.au**

PERTH Criterion Hotel 🛗🏨🛗 $$

560 Hay Street, Perth, WA 6000 **Tel** *(08) 9325 5155 or 1800 245 155* **Fax** *(08) 9325 4176* **Rooms** *69*

This dependable, good-value hotel has an impressive Art Deco façade. It is well positioned in the centre of Perth, within walking distance of most of the city's notable sights. The rooms are spacious, have en suite bathrooms and are well appointed with all the usual modern facilities. **www.criterion-hotel-perth.com.au**

PERTH Scarborough Indian Ocean Hotel 🛗🏨🏊🎿🛗 $$

23 Hastings Street, Scarborough, WA 6019 **Tel** *(08) 9341 1122* **Fax** *(08) 9341 1899* **Rooms** *59*

This good value accommodation is very popular in summer, so be sure to book ahead. The basic, neat and tidy rooms come as economy, de luxe or poolside. There is a games room, internet access and free in-house movies. The hotel also offers babysitting and an airport shuttle service. **www.ioh.com.au**

PERTH All Seasons 🛗🏨🛶🛗 $$$

15 Robinson Avenue, Northbridge, WA 6003 **Tel** *(08) 9328 0000* **Fax** *(08) 9328 0100* **Rooms** *96*

Bright, modern rooms feature mini bar, satellite TV, long bathtub and hairdryer. Excellent location in the nightlife and restaurant zone. Other features include 24-hour reception, free undercover parking and room access for the disabled. Various package deals also available. **www.all-seasons-hotels.com**

PERTH Miss Maud Swedish Hotel 🛗🏨🎿🛗 $$$

97 Murray Street, Perth, WA 6000 **Tel** *(08) 9325 3900* **Fax** *(08) 9221 3225* **Rooms** *52*

Self-dubbed "our little bit of Sweden in the heart of the city". Awarded Best Mid-range Accommodation in Australia for two years running. Uniquely designed Nordic and Scandinavian rooms. Some rooms have Internet access. Smorgasbord breakfasts available in the downstairs restaurant. **www.missmaud.com.au**

PERTH Intercontinental Burswood Resort 🛗🏨🏊🎿🛶🛗🛗 $$$$$

Cnr Bolton Ave & Great Eastern Hwy, Burswood, WA 6100 **Tel** *(08) 9362 8888* **Fax** *(08) 9362 8866* **Rooms** *413*

A large stylish resort with nine restaurants, six bars, a nightclub, a 24-hour casino, gift stores, tennis courts and a golf course. It's only a five-minute drive to the city centre and 15 minutes from the airport, and the modern rooms come with bathtub, satellite TV and Internet access. **www.intercontinental.com**

PERTH Pan Pacific Perth 🛗🏨🏊🎿🛶🛗🛗 $$$$$

207 Adelaide Terrace, Perth, WA 6000 **Tel** *(08) 9224 7777* **Fax** *(08) 9224 7788* **Rooms** *390*

Everything you expect from a genuine five-star luxury hotel. Located in Perth's Central Business District and a few minutes' walk from the main shopping and dining district. Most rooms have panoramic views of the Swan River, 24-hour room service, safety deposit boxes and Internet access. **www.panpacific.com/perth**

PERTH Rendezvous Observation City Hotel 🛗🏨🏊🎿🛶🛗🛗 $$$$$

The Esplanade, Scarborough, WA 6019 **Tel** *(08) 9245 1000* **Fax** *(08) 9245 1345* **Rooms** *333*

This high-rise luxury hotel is a landmark in Perth. Smartly furnished rooms include big-screen TV and in-house movies. Many rooms have a spa and superb ocean views. The heated pool, sun lounge, children's wading pool and spa occupy the tenth floor. The poolside bar features a tropical garden. **www.rendezvoushotels.com**

ROTTNEST ISLAND Hotel Rottnest 🏨🎿 $$$$

Bedford Avenue, Rottnest Island, WA 6161 **Tel** *(08) 9292 5011* **Fax** *(08) 9292 5188* **Rooms** *18*

Built in 1864, this was originally the summer residence of the governors of Western Australia. Its hotel rooms include mini bars, en suite bathrooms and satellite TV with complimentary movie channels. Choose between bayside or garden courtyard rooms and enjoy superb ocean views from the beer garden. **www.hotelrottnest.com.au**

ROTTNEST ISLAND Rottnest Lodge 🏨🏊🎿🛶 $$$$$

Kitson St, Rottnest Island, WA 6161 **Tel** *(08) 9292 5161* **Fax** *(08) 9292 5158* **Rooms** *80*

Popular with families, this hotel has five styles of accommodation from budget rooms to premium suites. Standard rooms have plain decor, ceiling fans, private bathroom, fridge, satellite TV with pay-to-view movies and shared veranda. An idyllic setting by the water's edge. **www.rottnestlodge.com.au**

WALPOLE Comfort Inn Tree Top Walk

501 Nockolds Street, Walpole, WA 6398 **Tel** (08) 9840 1444 **Fax** (08) 9840 1555 **Rooms** 35

A top location in the Walpole wilderness area. Close to Conspicuous Beach and the impressive Valley of the Giants *(see p313)* to the east of Walpole, where a treetop walk takes visitors through the high canopy of massive tingle trees. The hotel has en suite standard rooms and two two-bedroom family units. **www.treetopwalkmotel.com.au**

YORK Settlers House

125 Avon Terrace, York, WA 6302 **Tel** (08) 9641 1096 **Fax** (08) 9641 1093 **Rooms** 18

Situated in York's main street, this historic local landmark was built in 1845 and is classified by the National Trust. Now refurbished, the classic furniture and colonial decor match the hotel's yesteryear style. Log fires, lace table clothes, lamp-lit passages, cobbled courtyards and country hospitality. **www.settlershouse.com.au**

NORTH OF PERTH AND THE KIMBERLEY

BROOME Courthouse B&B

10 Stewart Street, Broome, WA 6725 **Tel** (08) 9192 2733 **Fax** (08) 9192 2956 **Rooms** 3

A huge two-storey family home which has three luxurious rooms: the pearling masters room; the Broome room; and the Oriental room. Cooked, tropical breakfasts can be enjoyed beside the pool or on the balcony. Centrally located across from Broome's Saturday markets and a three-minute walk from Chinatown. **www.thecourthouse.com.au**

BROOME Cable Beach Club Resort

Cable Beach Road, Broome, WA 6725 **Tel** (08) 9192 0400/1800 199 099 **Fax** (08) 9192 2249 **Rooms** 280

A prominent resort hotel on the edge of famous Cable Beach *(see p296)*. Western-Oriental fusion of architectural styles includes eastern artifacts and a Buddha sanctuary. Beautifully landscaped gardens and ocean views. Studio rooms have polished timber floors and private veranda. **www.cablebeachclub.com**

CARNARVON Gateway Motel

379 Robinson Street, Carnarvon, WA 6701 **Tel** (08) 9941 6900 **Fax** (08) 9941 2606 **Rooms** 66

Located five minutes' drive out of town, this basic motel offers a range of accommodation, including standard and de luxe rooms as well as self-contained apartments. Breakfasts are served in the restaurant, which is also open for buffet dinners. The grounds contain a swimming pool and a children's playground. **www.carnarvonmotel.com.au**

CAVERSHAM Perth Vineyards Holiday Park

91 Benara Road, Caversham, WA 6055 **Tel** (08) 9279 6700/1800 679 992 **Fax** (08) 9377 4599

Tucked away in the heart of the Swan Valley wine region, yet only 14 km (9 miles) from Perth, this holiday park offers cabins, chalets, camping and caravan facilities in beautiful gardens surrounded by vineyards. There are plenty of activities to choose from, including river cruises, horse riding, walking trails and golf. **www.aspenparks.com.au**

CORAL BAY Ningaloo Reef Resort

1 Robinson Street, Coral Bay, WA 6701 **Tel** (08) 9942 5934/1800 795 522 **Fax** (08) 9942 5953 **Rooms** 36

Superbly located accommodation beside the shores of stunning Coral Bay and the outer reef, the perfect spot for snorkelling trips in crystal turquoise sea. Standard rooms are en suite with pool and ocean views. The resort also has self-contained apartments has a bar, games room and barbecue in the garden. **www.ningalooreefresort.com.au**

DAMPIER Dampier Mermaid Hotel & Motel

The Esplanade, Dampier, WA 6713 **Tel** (08) 9183 1222 **Fax** (08) 9183 1028 **Rooms** 63

This hotel overlooking King Bay has tropical gardens, a spa and an outdoor barbecue, where guests can make the most of the balmy evenings. There is also a cocktail bar, pool table and billiards tables. All rooms are en suite and have satellite TV. The hotel caters for families and cots provided upon request. **www.dampiermermaid.com.au**

DENHAM Bay Lodge

113 Knight Terrace, Denham, WA 6537 **Tel** (08) 9948 1278/1800 812 780 **Fax** (08) 9948 1031 **Rooms** 17

Cheap accommodation in a great spot for reaching some of the loveliest attractions of Shark Bay, one of the highlights of the West Coast, such as the bright white Shell Beach, the dolphins of Monkey Mia and the bizarre Stromatolites *(see pp326–7)*. The lodge has a swimming pool. **www.baylodge.info**

DENHAM Heritage Resort Shark Bay

73 Knight Terrace, Denham, WA 6537 **Tel** (08) 9948 1133 **Fax** (08) 9948 1134 **Rooms** 27

First-class service in this oceanside lodging in Denham's main street. Contemporary, spacious rooms each with king-size bed, en suite, fridge, TV and in-room movies. The hotel has a cocktail lounge, saloon bar, liquor store and fresh local seafood menu. **www.heritageresortsharkbay.com.au**

DERBY King Sound Resort Hotel

Loch Street, Derby, WA 6728 **Tel** (08) 9193 1044 **Fax** (08) 9191 1649 **Rooms** 75

This established resort hotel is a good base for arranging trips to the magnificent Kimberley *(see p296–7)*. The hotel has a cocktail bar and an outdoor barbecue, and rooms are cosy, modern and fully equipped with queen-size beds, en suite bathrooms and free in-house films. **www.kingsoundresort.com.au**

Key to Price Guide *see p478* **Key to Symbols** *see back cover flap*

EXMOUTH Exmouth Cape Holiday Park
$$

Cnr Murat Road & Truscott Crescent, Exmouth, WA 6707 **Tel** *(08) 9949 1101* **Fax** *(08) 9949 1402* **Rooms** *12*

Budget accommodation popular with backpackers. Exmouth is a great place for learning to dive. The nearest beach is a four-minute drive away and idyllic Turquoise Bay, where the Ningaloo Reef comes right into the shore, is also not far off. The resort runs a free beach bus and rents out mountain bikes. **www.aspenparks.com.au**

HALLS CREEK Kimberley Hotel
$$$

Roberta Avenue, Halls Creek, WA 6770 **Tel** *(08) 9168 6101* **Fax** *(08) 9168 6071* **Rooms** *63*

Halls Creek is in the heart of the Kimberley and close to the remarkable Bungle Bungles. The hotel contains 42 well-appointed units built in the design of small station homesteads. Standard rooms are self-contained with high roofs and wide verandas. There is a spa and airport shuttle service. **www.kimberleyhotel.com.au**

KALBARRI Kalbarri Palm Resort
$$

8 Porter Street, Kalbarri, WA 6536 **Tel** *(08) 9937 2333/1800 819 029* **Fax** *(08) 9937 1324* **Rooms** *78*

A popular, family-style lodging in beautiful Kalbarri. The spectacular estuary is the perfect place for swimming or horse riding at sunset. The resort accommodates its active guests by offering indoor cricket, lawn bowls and tennis courts. There is also a heated outdoor spa for those who just want to relax. **www.kalbarripalmresort.com.au**

KARRATHA The All Seasons
$$$$$

Searipple Road, Karratha, WA 6714 **Tel** *(08) 9159 1000* **Fax** *(08) 9185 4325* **Rooms** *60*

All standard rooms in this centrally located hotel are en suite. Business suites and family rooms are also available. There is a 24-hour reception, spa, Internet access, three bars, dry-cleaning and laundry service. Outside the hotel are barbecue facilities in a tropical courtyard. **www.all-seasons-hotels.com**

KUNUNURRA Country Club Resort
$$$

47 Coolibah Drive, Kununurra, WA 6743 **Tel** *(08) 9168 1024* **Fax** *(08) 9168 1189* **Rooms** *88*

Lovely tropical gardens surround this pleasant lodging. Choose from 40 ground-floor units and 48 rooms in eight sets of two-storey buildings. Standard rooms include en suite bathroom, satellite TV and in-room movies. The hotel has a bar-side pool, cocktail bar, guest laundry and shared veranda. **www.kununurracountryclub.com.au**

MONKEY MIA Monkey Mia Dolphin Resort
$$$$

Monkey Mia, Denham, WA 6537 **Tel** *(08) 9948 1320/1800 653 611* **Fax** *(08) 9948 1034* **Rooms** *90*

Superb seaside spot with beach front, garden and limestone villas, which are very popular. People come in droves to see the dolphins *(see p 327)*. There are also hot tubs, three eateries, two bars and a tennis court at the resort. Standard beachside units have king-size beds and are en suite. **www.monkeymia.com.au**

NEW NORCIA New Norcia Hotel
$

Great Northern Highway, New Norcia, WA 6509 **Tel** *(08) 9654 8034* **Fax** *(08) 9654 8011* **Rooms** *16*

This hotel located beside a monastery offers plain, simple, tidy rooms run by friendly management. Rooms have overhead fans, fridge, plus shared bathroom and toilet. Also available is one en suite room with a queen-size bed and two bunks. The bar is open until midnight Friday to Saturday. **http://newnorcia.wa.edu.au**

ADELAIDE AND THE SOUTHEAST

ADELAIDE Plaza Hotel
$$

85 Hindley Street, SA 5000 **Tel** *(08) 8231 6371* **Fax** *(08) 8231 2055* **Rooms** *20*

This very central hotel is situated on one of Adelaide's busiest and most famous streets. It shares a colonial estate building with a hairdressers, coffee/café bar, trendy clothes shop and art studio. There is a magnificent palm tree garden in the centre of the hotel, featuring one of the oldest palm trees in Adelaide. **www.plazahotel.com.au**

ADELAIDE Mercure Grosvenor

$$$$

125 North Terrace, SA 5000 **Tel** *(08) 8407 8888* **Fax** *(08) 8407 8866* **Rooms** *243*

This hotel has a reputation for friendly, unobtrusive and attentive service. Opposite Adelaide Casino, Adelaide Convention Centre and the Festival Theatre, it's an ideal base for exploring Adelaide's plethora of cultural offerings. **www.mercuregrosvenorhotel.com.au**

ADELAIDE Adelaide on Hindley

$$$$$

65 Hindley Street, SA 5000 **Tel** *(08) 8231 5552* **Fax** *(08) 8237 3800* **Rooms** *181*

This well run and modern hotel is conveniently located right in the middle of Adelaide's main nightlife strip. The stylish rooms have superb city views and modern facilities. There are several rooms that cater for people with disabilities. The staff are wonderful. **www.ghihotels.com**

ADELAIDE Chifley on South Terrace
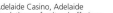
$$$$$

226 South Terrace, SA 5000 **Tel** *(08) 8223 4355* **Fax** *(08) 8232 5997* **Rooms** *93*

Homely decor, earthy red colours, couches and a fireplace in the foyer make this hotel seem all the more welcoming. The rooms overlook the South Parklands and the hotel itself is close to the city and the airport. It also has convenient public transport – the nearby tram will take you all the way to Glenelg. **www.chifleyhotels.com.au**

ADELAIDE Hilton Adelaide  $$$$$
233 Victoria Square, SA 5000 **Tel** *(08) 8217 2000* **Fax** *(08) 8217 2001* **Rooms** *380*

It has everything you would expect from a Hilton hotel and is located near to Adelaide's famous bustling Central Markets and around the corner from one of the city's best restaurant strips, Gouger Street. The views across the city are spectacular and Adelaide's main shopping precinct is only a few minutes' walk away. **www.hilton.com**

ADELAIDE Hotel Grand Chancellor Adelaide $$$$$
18 Currie Street, SA 5000 **Tel** *1800 801 849* **Fax** *(08) 8112 8899* **Rooms** *60*

Ideally positioned in the Central Business District, this hotel is within walking distance of the major cultural attractions, shopping precincts and entertainment centres. The interior is extremely pleasing to the eye, with Art Nouveau-style decor and rich vibrant colours throughout. Breakfast is included in the standard room price. **www.ghihotels.com**

ADELAIDE Hotel Richmond $$$$$
128 Rundle Mall, SA 5000 **Tel** *(08) 8215 4444* **Fax** *(08) 8232 2290* **Rooms** *30*

Located in the heart of Adelaide's Rundle Mall, this hotel has an ultra modern feel about it. The decor is classy and contemporary. The rooms are stunningly presented, some with flatscreen TVs and marble en suite bathrooms with separate bath and shower. The staff are friendly and professional. **www.hotelrichmond.com.au**

ADELAIDE Intercontinental Adelaide $$$$$
North Terrace, SA 5000 **Tel** *(08) 8238 2400* **Fax** *(08) 8231 1120* **Rooms** *367*

Next to the Adelaide Casino, this hotel is typical of the Hyatt hotel chain. Most of the rooms have spectacular views of the city. The service and facilities are top class. The Adelaide Convention Centre is next door, the Festival Theatre is a minute's walk away and the hustle and bustle of Hindley Street is one block over. **www.ichotelsgroup.com**

ADELAIDE Majestic Roof Garden Hotel $$$$$
55 Frome Street, SA 5000 **Tel** *(08) 8100 4400* **Fax** *(08) 8100 4488* **Rooms** *120*

This unique hotel has a landscaped garden on the roof that will make your jaw drop. Designed by award-winning architect David Baptiste and with views of the Adelaide Hills and CBD, it makes for an inspiring haven. The rest of the place is modern and welcoming and the staff are attentive and friendly. **www.majestichotels.com.au**

ADELAIDE Rockford Adelaide $$$$$
164 Hindley Street, SA 5000 **Tel** *(08) 8211 8255* **Fax** *(08) 8231 1179* **Rooms** *68*

The modern rooms are extremely satisfying in this quality hotel. Situated right in the heart of Adelaide's hip West End, on the corner of Hindley Street and Morphett Street the Rockford Adelaide is merely minutes from most of the city's attractions. **www.rockfordhotels.com.au**

ADELAIDE Rydges South Park Hotel $$$$$
1 South Terrace, SA 5000 **Tel** *(08) 8212 1277* **Fax** *(08) 8212 3040* **Rooms** *97*

The Rydges at South Park has impressive views of Adelaide's parklands and the Adelaide Hills. It's very reasonably priced for its location and is the closest hotel to the Adelaide Showgrounds. All rooms come with full amenities and are spacious, attractive and comfortable. **www.rydges.com/southpark**

ANGASTON Collingrove Homestead $$$
Eden Valley Road, SA 5353 **Tel** *(08) 8564 2061* **Fax** *(08) 8564 3600* **Rooms** *6*

This stunning heritage-listed 1800s homestead is one of the most beautiful buildings in South Australia. Its seven uncluttered, luxurious, private rooms have all the modern facilities you would expect. Breakfasts are an absolute highlight, including home-made jams, muffins and croissants. **www.collingrovehomestead.com.au**

COONAWARRA Chardonnay Lodge Coonawarra Wine Resort $$$
Riddoch Highway, SA 5263 **Tel** *(08) 8736 3309* **Fax** *(08) 8736 3383* **Rooms** *38*

Located in the heart of the Coonawarra Vineyards on beautifully landscaped grounds, this lodge is perfect for travellers who appreciate some fine wine – it has its own wine label. Light breakfasts are provided free of charge but there is a small extra fee for those requiring a cooked meal. **www.chardonnaylodge.com.au**

CRAFERS Grand Mercure Mount Lofty House $$$$$
74 Mount Lofty Summit Road, SA 5152 **Tel** *(08) 8339 6777* **Fax** *(08) 8339 5656* **Rooms** *29*

This historic country house has been made into an award-winning boutique hotel. Most of the comfortable, well-equipped guestrooms have fantastic views of the Adelaide Hills. It has a relaxed atmosphere but there's plenty to do if you feel like it, with tennis, volleyball and swimming facilities all available. **www.mtloftyhouse.com.au**

GLENELG Norfolk Motor Inn $$
71 Broadway, SA 5045 **Tel** *(08) 8295 6354* **Fax** *(08) 8295 6866* **Rooms** *20*

This small peaceful motel is in one of the nicest old suburbs of Adelaide. It's only 5-minutes' walk from the beach and two minutes from the hustle and bustle of Glenelg's trendy Jetty Road. It's very affordable, the rooms are small but comfortable and a continental breakfast is available upon request. **www.norfolkmotorinn.com.au**

GLENELG Oaks Plaza Pier $$$$$
16 Holdfast Promenade, SA 5045 **Tel** *(08) 8350 6688* **Fax** *(08) 8350 6699* **Rooms** *180*

This award-winning, five-star hotel is right on the beachfront in Glenelg, close to Jetty Road and only 10 minutes' drive from the city. It has outstanding facilities, including a lap pool, spa, plunge pool and sauna. There is also a couple of on-site bars that have stunning ocean views. All rooms have private balconies. **www.oakshotelsresorts.com**

Key to Price Guide *see p478* **Key to Symbols** *see back cover flap*

GLENELG Stamford Grand Hotel

Moseley Square, SA 5045 Tel (08) 8376 1222 Fax (08) 8376 1111 Rooms 241

Plum in the middle of the most vibrant area of Glenelg, the Stamford Grand is a luxury hotel boasting magnificent views of the ocean, the city and the Adelaide Hills. The rooms are ultra modern and have top-class facilities. Expensive ocean-view rooms and suites. The hotel is just minutes from the airport. **www.stamford.com.au**

HAHNDORF The Hahndorf Old Mill

98 Main Street, SA 5245 Tel (08) 8388 7888 Fax (08) 8388 7242 Rooms 22

Part of an 1854 flour mill has been incorporated into this complex in Australia's oldest German town. Located in the heart of Hahndorf's bustling main street, it offers a range of accommodation from motel rooms to spa chalets. The service is friendly and there are art galleries and craft shops nearby. **www.hahndorfoldmill.com**

KANGAROO ISLAND Wisteria Lodge Motel

7 Cygnet Road, Kingscote, SA 5223 Tel (08) 8553 2707 Fax (08) 8553 2200 Rooms 20

All of the units in this quiet seafront lodge have lovely panoramic views of the ocean. They are perfect for those who want to escape the rat race for a little while and maybe just watch a yacht race instead. Modern facilities throughout and a few extras such as private spa baths in the de luxe suites. **www.wisterialodge.com.au**

KANGAROO ISLAND Aurora Ozone Hotel

The Foreshore, Kingscote, SA 5223 Tel (08) 8553 2011 Fax (08) 8553 2249 Rooms 37

First opened in 1907 and situated on the shores of Nepean Bay, this affordable family retreat blends country style charm with modern facilities. There is an outdoor solar-heated pool, Internet access, extensive conference facilities and plenty more. It's also only a two-minute walk to the beach. **www.auroraresorts.com.au**

KANGAROO ISLAND Wanderers Rest

Bayview Road, American River, SA 5221 Tel (08) 8553 7140 Fax (08) 8553 7282 Rooms 9

Set high on the island hillside, this intimate classy guesthouse has marvellous views across the ocean to the far-off mainland. It's surrounded by native bush and wildlife, including wallabies and a myriad of bird species. The emphasis on intimacy and peacefulness means it is unsuitable for children. **www.wanderersrest.com.au**

LYNDOCH Lyndoch Hill Retreat

Barossa Valley Highway, SA 5351 Tel (08) 8524 4268 Fax (08) 8524 4725 Rooms 34

This motel, set in a stunning garden of 30,000 roses, is situated at the gateway to the Barossa Valley. There are daily tours of the nearby chateau which houses one of the world's great collections of Meissen porcelain, antique furniture, tapestries and paintings. **www.lhretreat.com**

MOUNT GAMBIER Lakes Resort

17 Lakes Terrace West, SA 5290 Tel (08) 8725 5755 Fax (08) 8723 2710 Rooms 40

This four-star resort suits people who are after somewhere quiet to stay, as it is the only one that isn't built along the highway. Also, it's the only resort with views over the town of Mount Gambier. Built on the slopes of an extinct volcano it offers a variety of options from budget accommodation to executive suites. **www.lakesresort.com.au**

NORTH ADELAIDE Regal Park Motor Inn

44 Barton Terrace East, SA 5006 Tel (08) 8267 3222 Fax (08) 8239 0485 Rooms 35

Within walking distance of Adelaide and numerous local restaurants and cafés, this friendly inn is affordable and comfortable. The peaceful location affords magnificent views of the adjacent parkland. There is a pool, barbecue area and off-street parking. Tours available. **www.regalpark.com.au**

PADTHAWAY Padthaway Caravan Park

Beeamma Road, SA 5271 Tel (08) 8765 5212

Overlooking historic Padthaway Homestead, this well-maintained caravan park offers a range of accommodation options comprising cabins, backpacker rooms, caravans and camping. Modern amenities include a fully-equipped laundry, clean kitchen and free gas BBQ. Pets welcome. **www.padthawaycaravanpark.com.au**

PARKSIDE Tiffins on the Park

176 Greenhill Road, SA 5063 Tel (08) 8271 0444 Fax (08) 8272 8675 Rooms 54

Adjacent to the city, nestled in tranquil parklands, this spacious and elegant boutique style hotel is only a short distance from two major shopping precincts. The enthusiastic and attentive staff are bound to make an impression and the poolside bar/restaurant is a winner. **www.tiffinsonthepark.com.au**

ROBE Robe House

Hagen Street, SA 5276 Tel (08) 8768 2770 Fax (08) 8768 2770 Rooms 4

Built in 1847 from locally quarried sandstone, this charming building is only a short walk from fine art galleries and restaurants. The four self-contained guesthouse units feature local artworks and Australian furnishings. It's a handy place to stay if you are travelling along the Great Ocean Road. Payment by cash only. **www.robehouse.com.au**

STIRLING Thorngrove Manor Hotel

2 Glenside Lane, SA 5152 Tel (08) 8339 6748 Fax (08) 8370 9950 Rooms 5

This is an extraordinary hotel with an international reputation for its luxury, striking originality and attention to aesthetic detail – the pinnacle of hotel experiences. Privacy is absolute and you may never even see the other guests. The dining and comfort levels surpass all five-star ratings. **www.thorngrove.com.au**

TANUNDA Barossa Weintal Resort
    $$$

Murray Street, SA 5352 **Tel** *(08) 8563 2303* **Fax** *(08) 8563 2279* **Rooms** *40*

Centrally located at Tanunda, the largest of the Barossa Valley towns, this resort is a great place from which to access all the local wineries. The rooms are clean and comfortable. Tea/coffee facilities, hair dryers and direct-dial telephone and Internet access are complimentary with all accommodation suites. **www.barossaweintal.com.au**

VICTOR HARBOR Whaler's Inn Resort
    $$$$

121 Franklin Parade, The Bluff, SA 5211 **Tel** *(08) 8552 4400* **Fax** *(08) 8552 4240* **Rooms** *47*

Nestled at the base of the Bluff, the Whalers Inn Resort is one of South Australia's best-kept secrets. Most rooms have views across Encounter Bay and of nearby Granite Island. There is a swimming pool, tennis court and barbecue facilities and you can also get access to mountain bikes, games and videos. **www.whalersinnresort.com.au**

THE YORKE AND EYRE PENINSULAS

ARDROSSAN Ardrossan Hotel/Motel
 $

36 First Street, SA 5571 **Tel** *(08) 8837 3008* **Fax** *(08) 8837 3468* **Rooms** *11*

This family run hotel is within walking distance of shops, a museum, walking trails, a playground and, of course, the beach – a great place for fishing or catching the renowned Blue Swimmer crabs. Each room has its own en suite bathroom, air conditioning and TV. There is also a family room available. **www.ardrossanhotelmotel.com.au**

ARKAROOLA Arkaroola Wilderness Sanctuary
    $$$

North Flinders Ranges, SA 5732 **Tel** *(08) 8648 4848* **Fax** *(08) 8648 4846* **Rooms** *50*

The largest resort in the Flinders Ranges offers a range of accommodation. The rooms are comfortable and functional. Scenic flights and 4WD tours are available. The resort itself is widely recognized as being one of Australia's premier eco-tourist destinations. **www.arkaroola.com.au**

ARNO BAY Hotel Arno
    $

Government Road, SA 5603 **Tel** *(08) 8628 0001* **Fax** *(08) 8628 0150* **Rooms** *75*

Across the road from the beach and a caravan park, Hotel Arno is a friendly place to stay. Rooms are cheap and fairly simple, but they are air conditioned and children are welcome. Arno Bay itself is a sleepy little village. It is an ideal place for people who really do want to get away from it all.

AUBURN Rising Sun Hotel
   $$

Main North Road, SA 5451 **Tel** *(08) 8849 2015* **Fax** *(08) 8849 2266* **Rooms** *10*

This classic 1850s building was actually the very first business in Auburn. Considerably renovated since those days, it now houses ten comfy spacious rooms, all with en suites. A continental breakfast is included in the standard room price and dinner can be enjoyed in the adjacent restaurant.

BLINMAN Blinman Hotel
   $$

Main Street, SA 5730 **Tel** *(08) 8648 4867* **Fax** *(08) 8648 4621* **Rooms** *17*

It's the centre of the Flinders Ranges, so it's an easy drive to all the attractions. Just at the end of Main Street is a miner's cottage that dates back to 1862, or, if you feel like a longer journey, the stunning Chambers Gorge is 80 km (50 miles) away. The hotel itself is pretty standard. Breakfast is not included in price. **www.blinmanhotel.com.au**

BURRA Burra Heritage Cottages
    $$$

Tivers Row, 8–18 Truro Street, SA 5417 **Tel** *(08) 8892 2461* **Fax** *(08) 8892 2948* **Rooms** *6 (cottages)*

These spacious bluestone cottages date back to 1856. Generous breakfast provisions are included in the tariff so that you can cook a country-style breakfast and enjoy it in the privacy of your cottage garden. Open fires add a special touch indoors. It's a real journey to the past, travelling first class. **www.burraheritagecottages.com.au**

CLARE Thorn Park Country House
   $$$$

College Road, Sevenhill, SA 5453 **Tel** *(08) 8843 4304* **Fax** *(08) 8843 4296* **Rooms** *6*

Situated close to wineries and the famous Riesling Trail, this gourmet retreat has earned a reputation for being the best place to stay in South Australia. In 1997 it was inducted into the South Australian Tourism hall of fame. Rooms are marvellously decorated with quality art and antiques. **www.thornpark.com.au**

COOBER PEDY The Underground Motel
    $$

Catacomb Road, SA 5723 **Tel** *(08) 8672 5324* **Fax** *(08) 8672 5911* **Rooms** *8*

The world's first underground guesthouse has a spectacular view of the desert sunsets from its veranda. All guest rooms are underground and equipped with en suites and fans, and are perfect for escaping the fierce summer heat. There's a children's play area and pets are welcome. **www.theundergroundmotel.com.au**

COOBER PEDY Desert Cave Hotel
   $$$$

Hutchison Street, SA 5723 **Tel** *(08) 8672 5688* **Fax** *(08) 8672 5198* **Rooms** *50*

This award-winning hotel provides underground shops, bar and opal display areas – all within sandstone surrounds in the heart of Coober Pedy. You can stay either above ground or underground, and there are excellent dining and convention facilities. It's the world's only truly international underground hotel. **www.desertcave.com.au**

Key to Price Guide *see p478* **Key to Symbols** *see back cover flap*

EDITHBURGH The Anchorage Motel $$

25 O'Halloran Parade, SA 5583 **Tel** *(08) 8852 6262* **Fax** *(08) 8852 6147* **Rooms** *9*

Located on the foreshore near the jetty, these hotel units offer all the amenities needed for self-contained relaxation. Fish-cleaning tables, a freezer for bait and boat-washing facilities are all on hand. For a small extra charge, guests can enjoy a home-cooked breakfast delivered to their rooms. **www.anchorage-edithburgh.net**

EDITHBURGH Edithburgh House $$

7 Edith Street, SA 5583 **Tel** *(08) 8852 6373* **Fax** *(08) 8852 6373* **Rooms** *6*

This delightful building has been used as a guesthouse since the 1890s. Just a minute's walk from the seashore and across the road from the local museum, and is an ideal base from which to explore Edithburgh, a town steeped in maritime history. All the rooms are en suite. **www.edithburghhouse.com.au**

MINTARO Martindale Hall $$$$

Manoora Road, SA 5145 **Tel** *(08) 8843 9088* **Fax** *(08) 8843 9082* **Rooms** *9*

This authentic luxurious 19th-century Georgian mansion was featured in the famous Australian film *Picnic at Hanging Rock*. You can enjoy a formal dinner served by a butler and maid, browse through the extensive private library or simply have a lazy game of pool on the 125-year-old billiard table. **www.martindalehall.com**

PORT LINCOLN Blue Seas Motel $$

7 Gloucester Terrace, SA 5606 **Tel** *(08) 8682 3022* **Fax** *(08) 8682 6932* **Rooms** *15*

This family owned and operated motel overlooks the beautiful Boston Bay, one of the largest protected natural harbours in the world. All rooms have queen-size beds, electric blankets, TVs and air conditioning. The motel is literally across the road from the beach and a short walk from the Port Lincoln CBD. **www.blueseasmotel.com**

PORT LINCOLN Lincoln Cove Villas $$

42 Parnkalla Avenue, SA 5606 **Tel** *(08) 8683 0657* **Fax** *(08) 8683 3165* **Rooms** *3 (villas)*

These four-star villas are located at the marina. They are also right on the breathtakingly scenic Parnkalla walking trail. The yards have childproof fencing and the bedrooms are all decorated in a marine sea theme. Cook your own breakfast in the fully-equipped kitchens. **www.lincolncovevillas.com**

RAWNSLEY PARK Rawnsley Park Station $$$

Hawker-Wilpena Road, SA 5434 **Tel** *(08) 8648 0030* **Fax** *(08) 8648 0013* **Rooms** *28 (cabins)*

Rawnsley Park Station won the Hall of Fame Award for standard accommodation at the South Australian Tourism Awards in 2004. The de luxe cabins are self-contained and serviced every second day. The staff can help travellers with a range of activities such as horse riding, cycling and sheep-shearing. **www.rawnsleypark.com.au**

WHYALLA Alexander Motel $$

99 Playford Avenue, SA 5600 **Tel** *(08) 8645 9488* **Fax** *(08) 8645 2211* **Rooms** *40*

This comfortable motel has single and two-bedroom suites available. Children are most welcome. There is a nice walking path through the adjacent wetlands. The inn has good facilities but breakfast is not included in the standard room price. **www.alexandermotel.com.au**

WILPENA Wilpena Pound Resort $$$

Hawker-Wilpena Road, SA 5434 **Tel** *(08) 8648 0004* **Fax** *(08) 8648 0028* **Rooms** *60*

The sheer range of available accommodation makes this resort suitable for families, couples, groups and backpackers alike. The staff at the Visitor Information Centre can help you organize 4WD tours and scenic flights, or assist you with planning a walk through the vast landscapes of the Flinders Ranges. **www.wilpenapound.com.au**

WUDINNA Gawler Ranges Motel $$

72 Eyre Highway, SA 5652 **Tel** *(08) 8680 2090* **Fax** *(08) 8680 2184* **Rooms** *23*

Less than an hour's drive from the Gawler Ranges, this motel offers pleasant accommodation for the whole family. There's an indoor heated pool and spa, an onsite conference room and all basic amenities are supplied. Breakfast is available for a small extra fee. **www.gawlerrangesmotel.com**

MELBOURNE

ALBERT PARK Citigate Albert Park & The Sebel Albert Park  $$$

65 Queens Road, VIC 3004 **Tel** *(03) 9529 4300* **Fax** *(03) 9521 3111* **Rooms** *379*   **Map** *3 B5*

This popular option for business travellers offers generous rooms, some with views of Albert Park Lake and golf course. The hotel is convenient for city transport, the Botanic Gardens and Shrine of Remembrance, South Yarra's shops and restaurants, St Kilda and the Sports and Aquatic Centre. **www.mirvachotels.com**

CARLTON Carlton Terrace  $$$

196 Drummond Street, VIC 3053 **Tel** *(03) 9662 2735* **Fax** *(03) 9662 2735* **Rooms** *3*   **Map** *1 C1*

This elegant, boutique-style hotel is located on a quiet, tree-lined street and occupies a restored 19th-century house that once belonged to a French count. Rooms have modern furnishings and are well equipped and there is a peaceful courtyard. The hotel is close to Lygon Street and its many cafés, restaurants and shops. **www.carltonterrace.com.au**

CARLTON Downtowner on Lygon

66 Lygon Street, VIC 3053 **Tel** *(03) 9663 5555* **Fax** *(03) 9662 3308* **Rooms** *98*   **Map** *1 C1*

This quality motel accommodation is conveniently located at the CBD end of the bustling Lygon Street restaurant strip and just up the road from the historic Trades Hall building. It offers a range of rooms, some with kitchens and spas. It is suitable for disabled travellers and offers room service. **www.downtowner.com.au**

CARLTON Rydges on Swanston

701 Swanston Street, VIC 3053 **Tel** *(03) 9347 7811, 1300 857 922* **Fax** *(03) 9347 8225* **Rooms** *107*

Within a stone's throw of Melbourne University and only two blocks from Lygon Street, this hotel is a good option for visiting academics. It is also popular with country and business travellers. Fitness facilities include a spa and sauna and there is also the Prime wine bar and grill (sea food and steak focus). **www.rydges.com**

CITY CENTRE King Street Backpackers

197–199 King Street, VIC 3000 **Tel** *(03) 9670 1111* **Fax** *(03) 9670 9911* **Rooms** *40*   **Map** *1 A3*

Previously known as The Friendly Backpacker, this hostel is close to Southern Cross Station and is popular with international travellers. The rooms and facilities are clean and airy, the self-catering kitchen is excellent, one room is wheelchair accessible, and it is a great place to chill out. **www.kingstreetbackpackers.com.au**

CITY CENTRE The Greenhouse

228 Flinders Lane, VIC 3000 **Tel** *(03) 9639 6400, 1800 249 207* **Fax** *(03) 9639 6900* **Rooms** *63*   **Map** *1 C3*

This is an excellent central choice for those on a budget. Rooms are pleasant, there is a games room, self-contained kitchen, TV room and free pancake brunches on Sundays. The relaxing rooftop terrace is upstairs, and downstairs is the slick Nectar Lounge bar and Internet café, sometimes featuring live music. **www.greenhousebackpacker.com.au**

CITY CENTRE Atlantis Hotel

300 Spencer Street, VIC 3000 **Tel** *(03) 9600 2900* **Fax** *(03) 9600 2700* **Rooms** *232*   **Map** *1 A3*

This hotel is well positioned for visitors arriving via train or bus at Southern Cross Station. It offers comfortable and spacious rooms, some overlooking the Etihad Stadium and the emerging Docklands precinct. It is within walking distance of the Casino, Melbourne Convention Centre and Southbank. **www.atlantishotel.com.au**

CITY CENTRE Hotel Enterprize Melbourne

44 Spencer Street, VIC 3000 **Tel** *(03) 9629 6991* **Fax** *(03) 9614 7963* **Rooms** *280*   **Map** *1 B4*

Another well-located option for budget travellers, especially if arriving at Southern Cross Station by train or bus. There is an Asian restaurant and pizza café, and rooms range from budget options to luxury suites. It is also close to Etihad Stadium, but can get noisy when the "footy" crowds descend. **www.hotelenterprize.com.au**

CITY CENTRE The Crossley Hotel managed by Mercure

51 Little Bourke Street, VIC 3000 **Tel** *(03) 9639 1639* **Fax** *(03) 9639 0566* **Rooms** *88*   **Map** *2 D2*

Located at the top end of Chinatown and the theatre district, this comfortable hotel is also close to some of Melbourne's finest eateries, including Grossi Florentino, Becco and Madam Fang. It offers exceptional service and the rooms are large. **www.crossleyhotel.com.au**

CITY CENTRE Jasper Hotel

489 Elizabeth Street, VIC 3000 **Tel** *(03) 8327 2777, 1800 468 359* **Fax** *(03) 9329 1469* **Rooms** *65*   **Map** *1 B2*

The old Hotel Y has never looked so good. Within a bagel's throw of the Queen Victoria Market, this refurbished option offers light and pleasant boutique-style rooms. It also provides a helpful tour desk, off-site parking, café, 24-hour reception, a business centre and access to local gym and swimming facilities. **www.jasperhotel.com.au**

CITY CENTRE Crowne Plaza Hotel Melbourne

Cnr Flinders & Spencer Sts, VIC 3005 **Tel** *(03) 9648 2777* **Fax** *(03) 9629 5631* **Rooms** *383*   **Map** *1 B4*

On the bank of the Yarra River opposite the Melbourne Exhibition Centre and the Polly Woodside Maritime Museum, this modern hotel is close to Docklands, the Etihad Stadium, the Melbourne Aquarium, Southbank, the Casino and the Arts Centre. Rooms offer views of Port Phillip Bay and the CBD. **www.crowneplaza.com.au**

CITY CENTRE Nova Stargate

118 Franklin Street, VIC 3000 **Tel** *(03) 9321 0300* **Fax** *(03) 9321 0301* **Rooms** *60*   **Map** *1 B2*

This hotel at the northern end of the CBD is close by Queen Victoria Market, Melbourne Central and the Royal Melbourne Institute of Technology (RMIT). It offers several one- and two-bedroom apartment options. The fitness facilities include a gym and sauna. **www.novastargate.com.au**

CITY CENTRE Victoria Hotel

215 Little Collins Street, VIC 3000 **Tel** *(03) 9669 0000* **Fax** *(03) 9669 0001* **Rooms** *130*   **Map** *1 C3*

Built in 1880, this centrally located hotel is close to theatres, department stores, restaurants and boutiques. For years it has been the hotel of choice for country guests who enjoy its no fuss hospitality and reasonable tariffs. It now boasts an indoor pool, gym, sauna, spa, Internet café and conference facilities. **www.victoriahotel.com.au**

CITY CENTRE Adelphi Hotel and Spa

187 Flinders Lane, VIC 3000 **Tel** *(03) 9650 7555* **Fax** *(03) 8080 8800* **Rooms** *34*   **Map** *2 D3*

This small and groovy luxury hotel is known for both its innovative architecture (especially the glass-bottomed rooftop swimming pool, which partially overhangs the street below) and its classy restaurant in the hotel basement. It is right in the middle of the CBD, just around the corner from Federation Square. **www.adelphi.com.au**

Key to Price Guide *see p478* **Key to Symbols** *see back cover flap*

CITY CENTRE The Grand Hotel Melbourne

33 Spencer Street, VIC 3000 **Tel** *(03) 9611 4567* **Fax** *(03) 9611 4655* **Rooms** *95*   **Map** *1 B4*

This luxury all-suite boutique hotel occupies a heritage-listed former railways building at the western end of the CBD. Facilities include spa, sauna, gym and courtyard pool (which features a retractable roof, not unlike the nearby Etihad Stadium). All suites have a fully-equipped kitchenette and Victorian features. **www.grandhotelmelbourne.com.au**

CITY CENTRE Grand Hyatt

123 Collins Street, VIC 3000 **Tel** *(03) 9657 1234* **Fax** *(03) 9650 3491* **Rooms** *548*   **Map** *2 D3*

A member of the Hyatt hotel chain, this five-star hotel is within walking distance of some of Melbourne's best boutiques, galleries, theatres, restaurants and bars. Its own cocktail bar has an enviable reputation, and views from the upper floors include sweeping views of the CBD. **www.melbourne.grand.hyatt.com**

CITY CENTRE Hotel Causeway

275 Little Collins Street, VIC 3000 **Tel** *9660 8888, 1800 660 188* **Fax** *(03) 9660 8877* **Rooms** *45*   **Map** *1 C3*

Tucked away in Little Collins Street, this boutique hotel occupies a 1920s building in the heart of the city. It is perfectly located for those who want to savour Melbourne's bars, laneways and arcades. It has a rooftop terrace, excellent fitness facilities (including a steam room) and stylish, contemporary decor. **www.causeway.com.au**

CITY CENTRE Hotel Lindrum

26 Flinders Street, VIC 3000 **Tel** *(03) 9668 1111* **Fax** *(03) 9668 1199* **Rooms** *59*   **Map** *2 D3*

This chic boutique hotel occupies a heritage-listed building at the eastern edge of the CBD. It overlooks the historic Jolimont Railyards, the Yarra River and Botanic Gardens. The rooms are contemporary, with minimalist decor and are very comfortable. It is within walking distance of Federation Square and Birrarung Marr. **www.hotellindrum.com.au**

CITY CENTRE Mantra on the Park

333 Exhibition Street, VIC 3000 **Tel** *(03) 9668 2500* **Fax** *(03) 9668 2599* **Rooms** *144*   **Map** *2 D2*

One- and two-bedroom suites are available in this modern hotel close to the theatre district and Chinatown. All apartments feature full-size kitchens, lounge, bathrooms and balconies. Perfect for families and in a great location on the free City Circle tram route and within walking distance of Carlton Gardens. **www.mantra.com.au**

CITY CENTRE Melbourne Marriott Hotel

Cnr Exhibition & Lonsdale sts, VIC 3000 **Tel** *(03) 9662 3900* **Fax** *(03) 9663 4297* **Rooms** *185*   **Map** *2 D2*

A favourite of Melbourne's theatre crowd, with elegant rooms and grand suites, this hotel is adjacent to Chinatown and the theatre district and within walking distance of the Melbourne Museum and historic Exhibition Buildings. Fitness facilities include spa, sauna and gym, and the business facilities are first rate. **www.marriott.com.au**

CITY CENTRE Novotel Melbourne on Collins

270 Collins Street, VIC 3000 **Tel** *(03) 9667 5800* **Fax** *(03) 9667 5805* **Rooms** *380*   **Map** *1 C3*

Melbourne's most central hotel overlooks Collins Street and the Australia on Collins shopping centre. Rooms are spacious and comfortable. It caters to mainly corporate clients, and offers conference rooms, a business centre, car parking, room service and fitness facilities, including spa, sauna, pool and gym. **www.novotelmelbourne.com.au**

CITY CENTRE Oaks on Market

60 Market Street, VIC 3000 **Tel** *(03) 8631 1111* **Fax** *(03) 9629 9686* **Rooms** *280*   **Map** *1 B4*

This 28-storey hotel provides serviced apartment accommodation combined with fitness and business facilities. All rooms feature modern decor and a well-equipped kitchenette, and overlook either the Yarra River, Botanic Gardens and Southbank or the CBD. **www.theoaksgroup.com.au**

CITY CENTRE Rendezvous Hotel

328 Flinders Street, VIC 3000 **Tel** *(03) 9250 1888* **Fax** *(03) 9250 1877* **Rooms** *340*   **Map** *1 C4*

Originally built in 1913 as the Commercial Travellers Club, this renovated heritage-listed building at the southern end of the CBD blends historic detailing with contemporary decor. It offers valet parking, attentive room service and business facilities. The Club Lounge and Bar overlook the grand foyer. **www.rendezvoushotels.com.au**

CITY CENTRE Rydges Melbourne

186 Exhibition Street, VIC 3000 **Tel** *(03) 9662 0511* **Fax** *(03) 9663 6988* **Rooms** *363*   **Map** *2 D2*

This stylish hotel is located in the heart of the theatre district, just uphill from Chinatown and just downhill from the 19th-century Parliament House and Treasury buildings. It offers luxury suites and the overall decor is contemporary. The hotel's Events Centre is well suited to business travellers. **www.rydges.com/melbourne**

CITY CENTRE Sofitel Melbourne

25 Collins Street, VIC 3000 **Tel** *(03) 9653 0000* **Fax** *(03) 9650 4261* **Rooms** *363*   **Map** *2 D3*

The hotel occupies the top floors of an old building at the "Paris End" of Collins Street. There are several room types, but all feature floor-to-ceiling windows and panoramic views over the CBD, the Bay or Yarra River. The fitness facilities are excellent and the service is first class. **www.sofitelmelbourne.com.au**

CITY CENTRE Somerset Gordon Place

24 Little Bourke Street, VIC 3000 **Tel** *(03) 9663 2888, 1800 766 377* **Fax** *(03) 9639 1537* **Rooms** *64*   **Map** *2 D2*

These self-contained serviced apartments occupy a National Trust listed former doss house, built in 1884 at the top end of Chinatown. The apartments are set around an attractive courtyard, and all feature well-equipped kitchens and stylish decor. It is a good option for families or those planning an extended stay. **www.the-ascott.com**

CITY CENTRE Stamford Plaza Melbourne $$$$$

111 Little Collins Street, VIC 3000 ***Tel*** *(03) 9659 1000* ***Fax*** *(03) 9659 0999* ***Rooms*** *283* ***Map*** *2 D3*

At the "Paris End" of Collins Street, the Stamford is Melbourne's only five-star all-suite hotel. Its stylish one-, two- and three-bedroom suites have fully-equipped kitchens and lounges. There is a business centre, private offices, conference rooms and a gym, spa, sauna and pleasant rooftop pool. **www.stamford.com.au**

CITY CENTRE The Hotel Windsor $$$$$

103 Spring Street, VIC 3000 ***Tel*** *(03) 9633 6002* ***Fax*** *(03) 9633 6005* ***Rooms*** *180* ***Map*** *2 D2*

This grand Victorian hotel, built in 1883, is a stunning reminder of Marvellous Melbourne's gold rush era. Rooms provide five-star luxury and charm, and many enjoy views of Parliament House and Treasury buildings. Don't miss Afternoon Tea downstairs – a Melbourne institution in an Merchant Ivory setting. **www.thehotelwindsor.com.au**

CITY CENTRE The Westin Melbourne $$$$$

205 Collins Street, VIC 3000 ***Tel*** *(03) 9635 2222* ***Fax*** *(03) 9635 2333* ***Rooms*** *262* ***Map*** *1 C3*

This hotel is Number One for travellers with children. It is a stylish and award-winning hotel, opposite the Town Hall and down the road from Federation Square. It also offers a wellness centre, business facilities and elegant rooms overlooking the City Square, some with balconies. **www.westin.com/melbourne**

EAST MELBOURNE Georgian Court Bed & Breakfast $$

21–25 George Street, VIC 3002 ***Tel*** *(03) 9419 6353* ***Fax*** *(03) 9416 0895* ***Rooms*** *30* ***Map*** *2 F3*

This traditional guesthouse in a large Georgian house in historic East Melbourne enjoys a peaceful location. However, it is only a short stroll through the Fitzroy Gardens before you find yourself at the eastern edge of the city centre. It is within walking distance of the MCG. **www.georgiancourt.com.au**

EAST MELBOURNE Magnolia Court Boutique Hotel $$$

101 Powlett Street, VIC 3002 ***Tel*** *(03) 9419 4222* ***Fax*** *(03) 9416 0841* ***Rooms*** *26* ***Map*** *2 F2*

This family owned boutique hotel, established in the 1880s and only one block back from the Fitzroy Gardens, occupies a charming Victorian terrace house. Several rooms have their own balconies and there are luxury suites and single units. The downstairs terrace café has outdoor seating. **www.magnolia-court.com.au**

FITZROY The Nunnery $

116 Nicholson Street, VIC 3065 ***Tel*** *(03) 9419 8637, 1800 032 635* ***Fax*** *(03) 9417 7736* ***Rooms*** *35*

There are two accommodation options here with prices to match: Guesthouse and Budget. The clean, comfortable budget option, opposite Melbourne Museum, is the former residence of the Daughters of Charity. It features a grand staircase, stained-glass windows and 1880s Georgian decor. **www.nunnery.com.au**

FITZROY Quest Royal Gardens Apartments $$$$

8 Royal Lane, VIC 3065 ***Tel*** *(03) 9419 9888, 1800 334 033* ***Fax*** *(03) 9416 0451* ***Rooms*** *70* ***Map*** *2 D1*

Tucked away in a back alley off Gertrude Street, these spacious self-contained one-, two- and three-bedroom apartments are within a stone's throw of the Carlton Gardens, Royal Exhibition Buildings and Melbourne Museum, and within easy walking distance of the CBD and Brunswick Street. **www.questroyalgardens.com.au**

FITZROY Metropole Hotel Apartments $$$$$

44 Brunswick Street, VIC 3065 ***Tel*** *(03) 9411 8100, 1800 061 441* ***Fax*** *(03) 9411 8200* ***Rooms*** *60* ***Map*** *2 E1*

At the southern end of Brunswick Street and opposite a historic row of terrace houses, these modern hotel rooms and apartments are perfectly situated for those who enjoy restaurants, bars and nightlife. Trams run past the front door into town every few minutes, although the city centre is an easy 10-minute walk. **www.metropole.org**

NORTH MELBOURNE Melbourne Metro YHA $

78 Howard Street, VIC 3051 ***Tel*** *(03) 9329 8599* ***Fax*** *(03) 9326 8427* ***Rooms*** *281* ***Map*** *1 A1*

A five-minute walk to Queen Victoria Market and just down the road from Errol Street, North Melbourne's pubs and cafés, this is an excellent budget option. The rooftop terrace offers 360° views of the CBD, there are bicycles for hire, self-catering kitchen facilities and clean, comfortable rooms. **www.yha.com.au**

RICHMOND Richmond Hill Hotel $$

353 Church Street, VIC 3121 ***Tel*** *(03) 9428 6501* ***Fax*** *(03) 9427 0128* ***Rooms*** *60* ***Map*** *4 E2*

A little farther out, but only minutes from town by tram, this boutique hotel and guesthouse in a heritage-listed Victorian terrace offers pleasant rooms and relaxing courtyards and gardens. There is a guest lounge, bar, off-street parking, family rooms and apartments. **www.richmondhillhotel.com.au**

RICHMOND Amora Hotel Riverwalk $$$

649 Bridge Road, VIC 3121 ***Tel*** *(03) 9246 1200* ***Fax*** *(03) 9246 1222* ***Rooms*** *111*

With self-contained apartments and clean, modern hotel rooms offering views over the Yarra River, this is a pleasant option for those wanting something quieter than the city centre. A lovely walking and cycle path meanders beside the Yarra, and Bridge Road's restaurants and shops are within easy walking distance. **www.amorahotels.com**

SOUTH YARRA The Albany $$$

Cnr Toorak Road and Millswyn Street, VIC 3141 ***Tel*** *(03) 9866 4485* ***Fax*** *(03) 9820 9419* ***Rooms*** *70* ***Map*** *3 B5*

Tastefully renovated in the style of the 1960s, this attractive Victorian mansion has large rooms which are suitable for families or those planning a long stay. Added extras include parking, laundry service and alfresco breakfasts. Great value accommodation. **www.bloomfieldgroup.com.au**

Key to Price Guide *see p478* **Key to Symbols** *see back cover flap*

SOUTH YARRA The Como Melbourne
630 Chapel Street, VIC 3141 **Tel** *(03) 9825 2222, 1800 033 400* **Fax** *(03) 9824 1263* **Rooms** *107* **Map** *4 E5*

Just down from the intersection of Chapel Street's stylish café and fashion strip and trendy Toorak Road, this hotel is a favourite with entertainers and sports people. Expect valet parking, 24-hour room service, first-class business facilities, contemporary decor and a free daily limousine service to the city centre. **www.mirvachotels.com.au**

SOUTHBANK Crown Promenade Hotel
8 Whiteman Street, VIC 3006 **Tel** *(03) 9292 6688* **Fax** *(03) 9292 6677* **Rooms** *465* **Map** *1 C5*

Stylish contemporary luxury on 23 levels, just behind the Crown Casino, with views of the CBD and Port Phillip Bay. If you really need to unwind, the leisure facilities here are first class, including male and female sauna and steam rooms, gym, two outdoor decks, heated spas and an infinity lap pool. **www.crownpromenade.com.au**

SOUTHBANK Langham Hotel
1 Southgate Avenue, VIC 3006 **Tel** *(03) 8696 8888, 1800 858 662* **Fax** *(03) 9690 5889* **Rooms** *387* **Map** *1 C4*

Overlooking the Yarra River and CBD, and close to Federation Square, the Casino and the Arts precinct, this luxury hotel lays it on thick with chandeliers, sweeping staircases and marble bathrooms. The business centre is well equipped and the pool, spa and fitness facilities are perfect for gym junkies. **www.langhamhotels.com**

ST KILDA Base Backpackers
17 Carlisle Street, VIC 3182 **Tel** *(03) 8598 6200* **Fax** *(03) 8598 6222* **Rooms** *43* **Map** *5 C5*

Gone are the days of grungy accommodation for budget travellers. This modern establishment in a central St Kilda location rightly assumes that even those travelling on a budget appreciate a little bit of style now and again. There is a girls-only "Sanctuary" level, a bar and speedy Internet facilities. **www.basebackpackers.com.au**

ST KILDA Boutique Hotel Tolarno
42 Fitzroy Street, VIC 3182 **Tel** *(03) 9537 0200* **Fax** *(03) 9534 7800* **Rooms** *34* **Map** *5 B4*

In the heart of St Kilda's café scene, this modernized hotel features contemporary artworks by local artists and original works by noted Melbourne artist Mirka Mora, which adorn the restaurant walls. Rooms are comfortable with mod cons such as a flat screen TV. Some rooms have views over Fitzroy Street. **www.hoteltolarno.com.au**

ST KILDA Jackson's Manor
53 Jackson Street, VIC 3182 **Tel** *(03) 9534 1877* **Rooms** *30* **Map** *5 B4*

This renovated former homestead is located in a quiet back street just behind hectic Fitzroy Street, a two-minute walk to Acland Street and a five-minute walk to St Kilda Beach. It is a pleasant budget option offering cable TV, a barbecue area, car parking, Internet access, laundry and kitchen facilities.

ST KILDA Fountain Terrace
28 Mary Street, West St Kilda, VIC 3182 **Tel** *(03) 9593 8123* **Fax** *(03) 9593 8696* **Rooms** *7* **Map** *5 B4*

A well-located guesthouse in a charmingly restored and refurbished 1880s Victorian terrace residence, close to Fitzroy Street's bustling cafés and restaurants, yet surprisingly quiet. All rooms are individually styled and beautifully furnished. There is also a shady courtyard, a guest dining and sitting room. **www.fountainterrace.com.au**

ST KILDA The Prince
2 Acland Street, VIC 3182 **Tel** *(03) 9536 1111* **Fax** *(03) 9536 1100* **Rooms** *40* **Map** *5 B5*

In the 1980s and 1990s, The Prince was one of St Kilda's grungiest pubs. Now, nothing could be further from the truth. Slick, minimalist interior design and understated luxury is the order of the day at this boutique hotel. Call into the day spa and retreat for a little pampering, before enjoying dinner at Circa, The Prince. **www.theprince.com.au**

ST KILDA PRECINCT Albert Park Manor Hotel
405 St Kilda Road, VIC 3004 **Tel** *(03) 9821 4486* **Fax** *(03) 9821 4496* **Rooms** *20* **Map** *3 B5*

Situated opposite the Royal Botanic Gardens and within easy reach of the city centre, this century-old, family-run Victorian hotel has Old World style. Trams pass by the front door every three minutes during normal business hours. Family rooms, spa rooms and budget rooms with shared bathrooms are available. **www.albertparkmanor.com.au**

ST KILDA PRECINCT Royce Hotel
379 St Kilda Road, VIC 3004 **Tel** *(03) 9677 9900, 1800 820 909* **Fax** *(03) 9677 9922* **Rooms** *100* **Map** *3 B4*

This boutique option on leafy St Kilda Road occupies a National Trust listed 1920s former Rolls Royce showroom. The rooms feature contemporary styling and the hotel is within easy walking distance of the Royal Botanic Gardens, Albert Park Lake and upmarket Toorak Road, South Yarra. **www.roycehotels.com.au**

ST KILDA PRECINCT St Kilda Road Parkview Hotel
562 St Kilda Road, VIC 3004 **Tel** *(03) 9529 8888* **Fax** *(03) 9525 1242* **Rooms** *206* **Map** *2 D5*

St Kilda Road is a grand, tree-lined boulevard linking the city with the beach. Parkview's rooms are spacious and comfortable, and some have city or park views. Hotel facilities include an indoor, rooftop spa and sauna and 24-hour room service. The hotel is a short tram ride from the city and most attractions. **www.viewhotels.com.au**

ST KILDA PRECINCT The Hotel Charsfield
478 St Kilda Road, VIC 3004 **Tel** *(03) 9866 5511, 1300 301 830* **Fax** *(03) 9867 2277* **Rooms** *41* **Map** *5 B1*

A private dining room, reading room and billiards room; massage, reflexology and beauty treatment; dinners served on the lawn in summer; easy access to the St Kilda Road Arts precinct – these are just some of the treats on offer at this boutique hotel, occupying an 1889 heritage-listed mansion on a tree-lined boulevard. **www.charsfield.com**

WESTERN VICTORIA

AIREY'S INLET Airey's Overboard Seaside Cottage

1 Barton Court, VIC 3231 **Tel** *(03) 5289 7424* **Fax** *(03) 5289 7424* **Rooms** *2*

This environmentally friendly cottage, clad with radial-sawn timber, is nestled amongst native trees on the beach side of the Great Ocean Road. The decor is nautical and the cottage is within walking distance of the lighthouse and several beaches. The outdoor shower is perfect after a day at the beach. **www.aireysoverboard.com.au**

APOLLO BAY Chris's Beacon Point Restaurant & Villas

270 Skenes Road, VIC 3233 **Tel** *(03) 5237 6411* **Fax** *(03) 5237 6930* **Rooms** *9*

Panoramic ocean views are the main selling point for these self-contained mountaintop villas. It is only a ten-minute drive down the hill to Apollo Bay, however, most guests see no need to leave as the adjoining Greek restaurant enjoys a reputation as one of the coast's best. **www.chriss.com.au**

APOLLO BAY Claerwen Retreat

480 Tuxian Road, VIC 3233 **Tel** *(03) 5237 7064* **Fax** *(03) 5237 7054* **Rooms** *8*

Every room at this hilltop retreat offers views over the ocean and Otway Ranges. There is modern, architect-designed guesthouse accommodation, two self-contained cottages and two studios, as well as an outdoor saltwater pool, tennis court and horses. Bushwalking in the Otway Ranges is just as popular as days spent on the beach. **www.claerwen.com.au**

APOLLO BAY Whitecrest Holiday Retreat

5230 Great Ocean Road, VIC 3221 **Tel** *(03) 5237 0228* **Fax** *(03) 5237 0245* **Rooms** *14*

Each of these modern one-, two- and three-bedroom self-contained split-level apartments offers an en suite spa bath and a private balcony with stunning ocean views. Single rooms also available. As well as the swimming pool, there is a tennis court, billiards room, table tennis and barbecue facilities. **www.whitecrestonline.com.au**

BALLARAT Quest Ansonia Ballarat

32 Lydiard Street South, VIC 3350 **Tel** *(03) 5332 4678* **Fax** *(03) 5332 4698* **Rooms** *19*

This restored 1870s building is centrally located in one of Australia's best-preserved 19th-century streets. It offers comfortable, modern rooms that look out onto the central atrium with its potted ferns and rattan seating. There is a guest library and lounge room, and the sunny courtyard restaurant is popular. **www.theansonianlydiard.com.au**

BALLARAT Ballarat Heritage Homestay

185 Victoria St, Ballarat, VIC 3350 **Tel** *(03) 5332 8296* **Fax** *(03) 5331 3358* **Rooms** *7*

This accommodation service offers six self-contained Victorian and Federation cottages and one B&B. All feature modern amenities, pleasant cottage gardens and convenient central locations in Ballarat and Creswick. They are suitable for travellers with children and some are suitable for disabled travellers. **www.heritagehomestay.com**

BALLARAT Craig's Royal Hotel

10 Lydiard Street South, VIC 3350 **Tel** *(03) 5331 1377* **Fax** *(03) 5331 7103* **Rooms** *41*

This classic old hotel in the historic heart of this gold-rush era city has undergone a major renovation. It now offers some of Ballarat's grandest accommodation. All suites have en suite spa baths, and there is a magnificent downstairs public bar, banquet rooms and a private dining cellar. **www.craigsroyal.com**

BENDIGO Hotel Shamrock

Cnr Pall Mall & Williamson Street, VIC 3550 **Tel** *(03) 5443 0333* **Fax** *(03) 5442 4494* **Rooms** *28*

This ornate 1855 Victorian hotel with upper floor verandas is perfectly located opposite Roslyn Park and Law Courts precinct and just down the hill from Bendigo's impressive art gallery. Some rooms have access to the veranda, which is the perfect spot to enjoy a cold beer on a hot afternoon. **www.hotelshamrock.com.au**

BENDIGO Byronsvale Vineyard Bed and Breakfast

51 Andrews Road, Maiden Gully, VIC 3551 **Tel** *(03) 5447 2790* **Fax** *(03) 5447 3094* **Rooms** *3*

The Byronsvale is set in beautifully restored 19th-century sandstone stables and is surrounded by 160 acres of vineyards and forest. The accommodation comprises three apartments with pretty verandahs and the surrounding area has an abundance of birdlife and kangaroos. A lovely place to retreat to after exploring Bendigo. **www.byronsvale.net.au**

CASTLEMAINE The Empyre Boutique Hotel

68 Mostyn Street, VIC 3450 **Tel** *(03) 5472 5166* **Fax** *(03) 5472 2304* **Rooms** *6*

This boutique hotel delivers contemporary but understated luxury. Two rooms have balcony access overlooking one of Castlemaine's historic main streets. Two suites open onto the walled private garden at the rear. The restaurant serves Mod Oz cuisine and the lounge area is a pleasant place to unwind before dinner. **www.empyre.com.au**

DAYLESFORD Central Springs Inn

Cnr Camp & Howe sts, VIC 3350 **Tel** *(03) 5348 3134* **Fax** *(03) 5348 3967* **Rooms** *26*

The inn has three buildings located just back from Daylesford's lively Vincent Street, and only a ten-minute walk from the scenic lake or botanic gardens. One of the buildings, built in 1875, is listed by the National Trust. It comprises 16 suites, with period decor, mezzanine sleeping lofts and open fireplaces. **www.centralspringsinn.com.au**

Key to Price Guide *see p478* **Key to Symbols** *see back cover flap*

DAYLESFORD Lake House

3 King Street, VIC 3460 **Tel** *(03) 5348 3329* **Fax** *(03) 5348 3995* **Rooms** *33*

This boutique hotel surrounded by 3 hectares (7 acres) of manicured gardens complements the award-winning restaurant, cellar and day spa (offering mineral spas and treatments) and delivers a memorable package. There are several room options, most overlooking the picturesque lake, including waterfront rooms. **www.lakehouse.com.au**

DUNKELD Southern Grampians Cottages

33–35 Victoria Valley Road, VIC 3294 **Tel** *(03) 5577 2457* **Fax** *(03) 5577 2489* **Rooms** *9*

Tucked beneath Mount Sturgeon and offering spectacular views of the Grampians, these log cabins combine modern amenities with rustic features such as log fires and open verandas. Some cabins also have spas. It is a great option for travellers with children. **www.grampianscottages.com.au**

ECHUCA Cock n' Bull Boutique Hotel

17–21 Warren Street, VIC 3564 **Tel** *(03) 5480 6988* **Fax** *(03) 5482 5995* **Rooms** *6*

This hotel has a delightful swimming pool surrounded by beautiful gardens and courtyards. The original building dates to 1876 and has been sympathetically modernized. Enjoy a drink in the bar (which features local wines) while taking in the views of the Campaspe River. **www.cocknbullapartments.com**

GEELONG Four Points by Sheraton Geelong

10–14 Eastern Beach Road, VIC 3220 **Tel** *(03) 5223 1377* **Fax** *(03) 5223 3417* **Rooms** *109*

On the waterfront overlooking the marina and Corio Bay, but only a few minutes' walk from Geelong's main shopping area, this resort-style hotel offers a bar, café, steam room, fitness centre, indoor heated pool, conference centre, undercover parking, good disability access and 24-hour reception. **www.fourpoints.com/geelong**

HALLS GAP YHA Eco-Hostel

Cnr Buckler Street and Grampians Road, VIC 3381 **Tel** *(03) 5356 4544* **Fax** *(03) 5536 4543* **Rooms** *20*

This environmentally friendly YHA hostel offers dorm, single, double and family rooms. They also offer free bike use and organize abseiling, rock climbing, horse riding, canoeing, cycling and wine-tasting tours. There is a self-contained kitchen and a coach service to and from Melbourne daily. **www.yha.com.au**

LORNE Great Ocean Road Cottages

10 Erskine Avenue, VIC 3232 **Tel** *(03) 5289 1070* **Fax** *(03) 5289 2508* **Rooms** *8*

These charming timber cottages are set in bushland beside the Erskine River. Each cottage is self contained with a private verandah; all have views over the hills and to the beach and can comfortably accommodate up to five guests. A short walk from Lorne with its many shops and restaurants. **www.greatoceanroadcottages.com**

LORNE Cumberland Lorne Resort

150–178 Mountjoy Parade, VIC 3232 **Tel** *(03) 5289 4444, 1800 037 010* **Fax** *(03) 5289 2256* **Rooms** *99*

Overlooking (some would say overshadowing) this upmarket township is a resort-style complex with a range of modern and refurbished apartments, most with ocean views. There is a Kid's Club, toddler pool and games area, and also free use of surfboards, tennis racquets and mountain bikes. **www.cumberland.com.au**

MALDON Heritage Cottages of Maldon

43 Main Street, VIC 3463 **Tel** *(03) 5475 1094* **Fax** *(03) 5475 1800* **Rooms** *8*

Each of these eight self-contained properties has a pleasant garden and is within a few minutes of Australia's first "Notable Township". Some of the properties are Victorian homes, some are renovated miner's cottages, and one is an octagonal stone house with a resident magpie that guards the stairwell. **www.heritagecottages.com.au**

MILDURA Quality Hotel Mildura Grand

Cnr Deakin Avenue & Seventh Street, VIC 3502 **Tel** *(03) 5023 0511* **Fax** *(03) 5002 1801* **Rooms** *120*

A former bellboy and his extended Italian family has transformed this 1891 coffee palace into a luxury hotel offering a range of modern rooms and guest facilities, including two cafés, bars, grill room, boutique brewery, wine room, ballrooms and Victoria's only three-hat restaurant outside Melbourne. **www.qualityhotelmilduragrand.com.au**

NHILL Little Desert Nature Lodge

Nhill-Harrow Road, VIC 3418 **Tel** *(03) 5391 5232* **Fax** *(03) 5391 5217* **Rooms** *40*

There are 23 rooms with en suite facilities, 16 bunk rooms which share amenities, and powered and unpowered camp sites on this 117-hectare (288-acre) natural bushland property outside Nhill and adjacent to the Little Desert National Park. The lodge organizes wildlife tours. **www.littledesertlodge.com.au**

OCEAN GROVE Ti-Tree Village

34 Orton Street, VIC 3226 **Tel** *(03) 5255 4433* **Fax** *(03) 5225 5700* **Rooms** *19*

These 19 self-contained one- and two-bedroom log cabins, which feature modern interiors and amenities, are only five minutes' walk from town and two minutes' walk from the beach. Some offer spas and open fireplaces. The grounds are pleasant and have barbecue areas. **www.ti-treevillage.com.au**

PORT FAIRY Oscars Waterfront Boutique Hotel

41B Gipps Street, VIC 3284 **Tel** *(03) 5568 3022* **Fax** *(03) 5568 3042* **Rooms** *5*

Some might say there is no better place to enjoy breakfast in Port Fairy than on the veranda of this "French Provincial" hotel overlooking the Moyne River marina. Or no better place for a stylish dinner than in its grand dining room. All suites have views of the water or the garden. Children are not permitted. **www.oscarswaterfront.com**

PORTLAND Victoria House $$$
5–7 Tyers Street, VIC 3305 **Tel** *(03) 5521 7577* **Fax** *(03) 5523 6300* **Rooms** *9*

This Georgian-style, 1850s double-storey bluestone mansion first operated as a hotel in 1856. It enjoys a central location close to the beach, shops, restaurants and harbour. The rooms are large and tastefully decorated with en suite facilities. There is a guest lounge, dining room and sitting room with open fire. **www.babs.com.au/vichouse**

QUEENSCLIFF Queenscliff Hotel 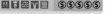 $$$$$
16 Gellibrand Street, VIC 3225 **Tel** *(03) 5258 1066* **Fax** *(03) 5258 1899* **Rooms** *18*

One of the world's grand 19th-century seaside hotels, this elegant 1887 Victorian mansion, across the road from the beach and jetty, is furnished with period decor throughout. All rooms have en suites, but in keeping with the historic atmosphere and emphasis on relaxation, no rooms have a TV, telephone or radio. **www.queenscliffhotel.com.au**

QUEENSCLIFF Vue Grand $$$$$
46 Hesse Street, VIC 3225 **Tel** *(03) 5258 1544* **Fax** *(03) 5258 3471* **Rooms** *32*

Rooms at this opulent, restored 19th-century hotel are designed to pamper with Old-World style and creature comforts. There is also a grand dining room, spa, club lounge, billiards room, indoor heated pool, gymnasium, conservatory and courtyard. It has spectacular views across Port Phillip Bay. **www.vuegrand.com.au**

SWAN HILL All Seasons Swan Hill Resort $$$
405–415 Campbell Street, VIC 3585 **Tel** *(03) 5032 2726, 1800 034 220* **Fax** *(03) 5032 9109* **Rooms** *62*

You have the choice of an indoor heated pool or an outdoor saltwater swimming pool with spa at this tropical-themed motel-style resort. Also a tennis court, games room, mini golf, squash court and bicycle hire. It's a 10-minute walk to the Murray River and a 5-minute walk to town. **www.swanhillresort.com.au**

TYLDEN Barondem Park Country House $$$
6 Trentham Road, VIC 3444 **Tel** *(03) 542 8191* **Rooms** *3*

Indulge your senses and return to yesteryear at this 1850s colonial country house which provides a true immersion in the area's historic architecture. Lovingly restored, with every attention to detail and comfort, the suites have antique fittings. Chauffeur-driven tours of the Macedon Ranges area also on offer. **www.barondempark.com.au**

WARRNAMBOOL Manor Gums $$
Shady's Lane, Mailors Flat, VIC 3275 **Tel** *(03) 5565 4410* **Fax** *(03) 5565 4409* **Rooms** *4*

This modern, architect-designed retreat offers four private self-contained suites set in native bushland a ten-minute walk from the beach. Each suite offers something different in terms of style and amenities, but all deliver relaxing views and numerous encounters with the abundant local birdlife. **www.travel.to/manorgums**

WOODEND Campaspe Country House Hotel & Restaurant $$$$$
29 Goldies Lane, VIC 3442 **Tel** *(03) 5427 2273* **Fax** *(03) 5429 1049* **Rooms** *20*

This property is set within 13 hectares (32 acres) of historic Edna Walling gardens and native bushland. It offers 16 courtyard rooms, a two-bedroom cottage, and two manor rooms in the main residence. There is also a purpose-built conference facility, croquet lawns and an award-winning restaurant. **www.campaspehouse.com.au**

EASTERN VICTORIA

BAIRNSDALE Comfort Inn Riversleigh $$$$$
1 Nicholson Street, VIC 3875 **Tel** *(03) 5152 6966* **Fax** *(03) 5152 4413* **Rooms** *20*

Sit back and enjoy relaxing views of the Mitchell River, mountains and farmland from the balconies of these grand, 1886, National Trust-listed Victorian terraces. All rooms are en suite and there is a ground-floor suite for disabled guests in one terrace. The restaurant is open for breakfast, lunch and dinner. **www.riversleigh.info**

BEECHWORTH Finches of Beechworth $$$
3 Finch Street, VIC 3747 **Tel** *(03) 5728 2655* **Fax** *(03) 5728 2656* **Rooms** *6*

This restored Victorian residence in a peaceful location two blocks from the main street features antique furniture and period fittings, a delightful wisteria-clad veranda and English-style gardens. The six rooms all have their own bathroom, and there is a guest sitting room. **www.beechworth.com/finches**

BRIGHT Ashwood House Cottage $$
22A Ashwood Avenue, VIC 3741 **Tel** *(03) 5755 1081* **Fax** *(03) 5755 1115* **Rooms** *3*

For absolute peace and quiet, and complete privacy, these three architect-designed and self-contained one-bedroom cottages are perfect. They share native bushland with abundant wildlife beside the Ovens River. It is an easy and pleasant 20-minute riverside walk into the centre of Bright. **www.ashwoodcottages.com.au**

DANDENONG RANGES Cottages of Mount Dandenong $$$$$
17 Sunset Ave, Olinda, VIC 3788 **Tel** *(03) 9751 2447* **Fax** *(03) 9751 2391* **Rooms** *3*

Nestled into the forest is a charming two-bedroom 100-year-old cottage. If you have spent a long day bushwalking through the National Park, there are 20 restaurants within 2 km (1 mile) of the cottage, close to Rickett's Sanctuary, to choose from.

Key to Price Guide *see p478* **Key to Symbols** *see back cover flap*

DINNER PLAIN Rundell's Alpine Lodge

Big Muster Drive, VIC 3898 **Tel** *(03) 5159 6422* **Fax** *(03) 5159 6500* **Rooms** *15*

Open year round, this resort offers spas, saunas and tennis courts, and can organize horse and
They also provide ski equipment and free transfers to Mount Hotham. Rooms accommodate six p
restaurant serves breakfast, lunch and dinner, and the bar presents live bands. **www.rundells.com**

EILDON Robyn's Nest Country Cottage

35 Wappan Crt, Bonnie Doon, VIC 3720 **Tel** *(03) 5779 1064* **Fax** *(03) 5779 1064* **Rooms** *4*

This self-contained cottage is perched high on a ridge and is surrounded by 6 hectares (15 acres) of well est
trees and natural wildlife. The cottage can accommodate up to ten guests and has a wood fire for winter stays
outdoor campfire area. Lovely views over Lake Eildon and the High Country Mountains. **www.robyns-nest.co**

FALLS CREEK The Falls Creek Hotel

23 Falls Creek Road, VIC 3699 **Tel** *(03) 5758 3282* **Fax** *(03) 5758 3296* **Rooms** *24*

The main attraction at this chalet-style hotel is the "Ski In, Ski Out" facility. There are three lifts to choose from within
a ski boot's throw of the front door. All rooms have views of the slopes and can accommodate up to five guests.
There is an excellent Kid's Club and the tariff is per person and inclusive of dinner. **www.fallscreekhotel.com.au**

GIPPSLAND LAKES The Moorings at Metung

44 Metung Road, VIC 3904 **Tel** *(03) 5156 2750* **Fax** *(03) 5156 2755* **Rooms** *39*

These one-, two- and three-bedroom apartments (and penthouse) enjoy waterfront views over Bancroft Bay. Located
in the centre of Metung village, this complex offers water frontage and private boat berthing. There is a tennis court,
barbecue area, boat and kayak hire. The friendly local pub is a two-minute walk. **www.themoorings.com.au**

GIPPSLAND LAKES Wattle Point Waterfront Retreat

200 Wattle Point Road, Wattle Point, VIC 3875 **Tel** *(03) 5157 7517* **Fax** *(03) 5157 7677* **Rooms** *16*

This peaceful retreat 15 km (9 miles) from Bairnsdale offers private self-contained one- to four-bedroom cedar lodges
nestled within 8 hectares (20 acres) of native bushland on the edge of Lake Victoria. There is an indoor pool, mineral
spa, tennis court, sauna, fishing jetty and canoe and mountain bike hire. **www.wattlepointholiday.com.au**

KING VALLEY Casa Luna Gourmet Accommodation

1569 Boggy Creek Road, Myrrhee, VIC 3732 **Tel** *(03) 5729 7650* **Rooms** *2*

Close to some of Victoria's best wineries and gourmet cheese producers, the rooms at this stylish retreat overlook a
peaceful valley and vineyards. The restaurant specializes in regional Italian cuisine and can provide guests with
breakfast and dinner hampers. There is a petanque court and private dining room. **www.casaluna.com.au**

LAKES ENTRANCE Comfort Inn & Suites Emmanuel

151 Esplanade, VIC 3909 **Tel** *(03) 5155 1444* **Fax** *(03) 5155 2401* **Rooms** *32*

A good option for travellers with children, these modern self-contained two-bedroom suites, which sleep up to
seven, have access to adult and toddler pools, spa, landscaped gardens, barbecue areas and playground. Some
rooms are suitable for disabled travellers. **www.comfortinnemmanuel.com.au**

MALLACOOTA Melaleuca Grove Holiday Units

178 Mirrabooka Road, VIC 3892 **Tel** *(03) 5158 0407* **Fax** *(03) 5158 0407* **Rooms** *10*

Five modern and self-contained two-bedroom units with private courtyards are set within 1 hectares (2.5 acres) of
bushland and surrounded by a National Park. There is a playground and barbecue facilities, and pets are welcome.
The shops, beach and lake are a five-minute drive, and boat and bicycle hire is available.

MANSFIELD Mansfield Valley Motor Inn

Cnr Elvins Street & Maroondah Highway, VIC 3722 **Tel** *(03) 5775 1300* **Fax** *(03) 5775 1693* **Rooms** *23*

This motel offers a straightforward range of two-bedroom and motel-style units at the edge of town, a 40-minute
drive from Mount Buller. The motel has big gardens, barbecue facilities and views of Mount Buller. All rooms are en
suite and look out onto the gardens, bushland or horse paddocks **www.mansfieldvalley.com.au**

MANSFIELD The Riverhouse at Howqua Dale

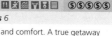

85 Howqua River Road, VIC 3722 **Tel** *(03) 5777 3503* **Fax** *(03) 5777 3896* **Rooms** *6*

Set among beautiful riverside gardens, this country house provides absolute privacy and comfort. A true getaway
from the city, it offers self-catering or bed and breakfast packages, as well as horse riding and fly fishing. **www.
theinspiredtraveller.com.au/howqua_dale**

MORNINGTON PENINSULA Bayplay Adventure Lodge

46 Canterbury Jetty Road, Blairgowrie, VIC 3942 **Tel** *(03) 5984 0888* **Fax** *(03) 5984 0111* **Rooms** *8*

This inexpensive lodge, a short walk from the beach, provides accommodation ranging from bunkrooms to family
rooms. There is a licensed café and communal kitchen, bus transfers to and from Melbourne, and free bicycle hire.
Also organizes swimming with dolphins, kayaking, scuba diving, surfing and horse riding. **www.bayplay.com.au**

MORNINGTON PENINSULA Carmel of Sorrento

142 Ocean Beach Road, Sorrento, VIC 3943 **Tel** *(03) 5984 3512* **Fax** *(03) 5984 0094* **Rooms** *10*

There are several options here, including traditional guesthouse accommodation in an original Federation
guesthouse, self-contained units and a heritage beach cottage that sleeps six. The property is halfway between the
front beach and the back beach of Sorrento. **www.carmelofsorrento.com.au**

...elly's Lodge
*Tel (03) 5165 1129 **Fax** (03) 5165 1159 **Rooms** 4*

...nis lodge is its central location within the Baw Baw Alpine Resort. The toboggan run is just ...or and it is only metres to the ski lift, and for those whose equipment needs upgrading or who ...ne latest in ski wear, there is an excellent ski shop right next door. **www.kellyslodge.com.au**

...UTY Harrietville Hotel/Motel
*...pine Road, Harrietville, VIC 3698 **Tel** (03) 5759 2525 **Fax** (03) 5759 2766 **Rooms** 24*

...el-style family rooms in a quiet township below Mount Hotham offer ski and chain hire, and drying rooms. ...also a licensed restaurant, bar and beer garden. And an outdoor pool and mountain bike hire for those ...who enjoy the area's summer attractions. **www.harrietvillehotelmotel.com**

...OUNT BULLER Grand Mercure Chalet
*.Mount Buller Village, VIC 3723 **Tel** (03) 5777 6566 **Fax** (03) 5777 6455 **Rooms** 65*

This luxurious hotel, only metres from the ski lift, offers single and twin rooms (all en suite) and first-class fitness facilities, including an indoor heated pool, sauna, gym and squash court. There is also a library for the less frenetic, and the chalet is child friendly. **www.mtbullerchalet.com.au**

MOUNT HOTHAM Snowbird Inn
*Great Alpine Road, VIC 3741 **Tel** (03) 5759 3503, 1800 659 009 **Fax** (03) 8325 0094 **Rooms** 24*

Ski in, Ski out. This central, no-frills lodge opposite the ski lift offers backpacker-style accommodation with 24 bunkrooms sleeping from four to eight guests. There is a guest lounge with open fire, a bistro, a bar, a ski-wear boutique and equipment hire and good balcony views. Closed during summer. **www.snowbirdinn.com.au**

NARBETHONG Woodlands Rainforest Retreat
*137 Manby Road, VIC 3778 **Tel** (03) 5963 7150 **Rooms** 4*

For couples only and built using local timbers, each cottage is secluded, with a private view of lake and gullies. The multi award-winning retreat is set at the gateway to the skifields and surrounding national parks, including the Black Spur Drive, famous for its spectacular scenery and mountain ash trees. **www.woodlandscottages.com.au**

PHILLIP ISLAND The Island Spa
*Cnr Justice & Ventnor Road, Cowes, VIC 3922 **Tel** (03) 5952 6466 **Fax** (03) 5952 6467 **Rooms** 4*

Surrounded by large coastal gardens, these environmentally sustainable, self-contained cottages deserve their four-star AAA tourist rating. The two one-bedroom cottages (Banksia and Melaleuca) feature spas and wood heaters. The third cottage (Acacia) has two bedrooms. The spa offers massage and hydrotherapy. **www.theislandspa.com.au**

PHILLIP ISLAND Glen Isla House
*230–232 Church Street, Cowes, VIC 3923 **Tel** (03) 5952 1882 **Fax** (03) 5952 5028 **Rooms** 6*

This award-winning luxury hotel is set in the grounds of an historic homestead. There are rooms plus two separate cottages available and guest numbers are kept small to ensure peace and privacy. The hotel boasts a heritage garden with 100-year-old oak trees and is close to a sandy white beach and the centre of Cowes. **www.glenisla.com**

POREPUNKAH Buffalo Motel & Country Retreat
*6774 Great Alpine Road, VIC 3740 **Tel** (03) 5756 2242 **Fax** (03) 5756 2242 **Rooms** 20*

The famous "Rail Trail" bike track is just a stone's throw from this relaxed family retreat with comfortable, warm cabins. It's a modest, no-frills option for a summer or winter vacation, set at the foot of Mount Buffalo and free from the tourist traffic of nearby Bright township. **www.buffalomotelretreat.com.au**

RUTHERGLEN Mount Ophir Estate
*Stillards Lane, VIC 3685 **Tel** (03) 6032 8920 **Fax** (03) 6032 9911 **Rooms** 15*

The 1891 French Provincial tower set in a vineyard and organic olive farm seems incongruous, but this accommodation complex does not disappoint. Options include a 1902 homestead guesthouse, a self-contained farmhouse, and three floors of four-star luxury in the tower. Children are welcome. **www.marketplaceconnections.com/ophir**

SOUTH GIPPSLAND Waratah Park Country House
*Thomson Road, Waratah Bay, VIC 3959 **Tel** (03) 5683 2575 **Fax** (03) 5683 2275 **Rooms** 6*

This four-star accommodation is located in a bushland setting overlooking Wilson's Promontory and Bass Strait. The views are spectacular and the restaurant enjoys a well-deserved reputation. It is only a short drive to nearby beaches and a 20-minute drive to Wilson's Promontory. **www.wpe.com.au**

WALHALLA Windsor House B&B
*Lot 66 Right hand Branch Road, VIC 3825 **Tel** (03) 5165 6237 **Rooms** 5*

This guesthouse's website boasts it hasn't seen a ghost in weeks. The two-storey, fully restored 1878 Georgian guesthouse is Walhalla's original accommodation. There are six rooms – one is reserved for those who snore, and one is named after a well-known local poacher. **www.windsorhouse.com.au**

WILSONS PROMONTORY Tidal River Cottages
*National Parks Service, Tidal River, VIC 3690 **Tel** (03) 5680 9555/131963 **Fax** (03) 5680 9516 **Rooms** 42*

A favourite destination for Melburnians, so book well ahead. It is the only accommodation service in the National Park, but it offers everything from unpowered camp sites to eco-friendly units and luxury safari-style tents. There is only a general store, post office and takeaway food in Tidal River, so bring provisions. **www.parkweb.vic.gov.au**

Key to Price Guide *see p478* **Key to Symbols** *see back cover flap*

YARRA VALLEY Yarra Valley Sanctuary House Resort Motel $$

326 Badger Creek Road, Healesville, VIC 3777 **Tel** *(03) 5962 5148* **Fax** *(03) 5962 5392* **Rooms** *24*

On the same road as the Healesville Sanctuary and surrounded by native bush and gardens, this resort-style motel offers several room types and units (including spa rooms), barbecue areas, a guest lounge, pool, sauna, spa, adventure playground, restaurant and beer garden. **www.sanctuaryhouse.com.au**

YARRA VALLEY The Yarra Valley Grand Hotel $$$$$

19 Bell Street, Yarra Glen, VIC 3775 **Tel** *(03) 9730 1230* **Fax** *(03) 9730 2434* **Rooms** *10 (4 suites)*

This 1888 National Trust classified hotel in the centre of the Yarra Valley comes with all the trimmings: four-poster beds, lashings of antique furniture, à la carte dining in three venues, winery tours and hot-air balloon flights with champagne breakfast packages. Price includes dinner and breakfast though B&B is also possible. **www.yarravalleygrand.com.au**

TASMANIA

BICHENO Bicheno Gaol Cottages $$

Cnr James & Burgess sts, TAS 7215 **Tel** *(03) 6375 1430* **Rooms** *3*

The National Trust listed gaol house is the oldest building in this seaside holiday town and has been converted into a charming and comfortable guesthouse. Also on the site is the Old School House, providing self-contained accommodation ideal for families. **www.bichenogaolcottages.com**

BINALONG BAY Bay of Fires Character Cottages $$$$

64–74 Main Road, Binalong Bay, TAS 7216 **Tel** *(03) 6376 8262* **Fax** *(03) 6376 8261* **Rooms** *8*

Overlooking the breathtaking Binalong Bay and the Bay of Fires, these cottages are a short distance from the beach and nestled in the seaside village. Dine in the onsite restaurant or make the most of the self-contained kitchen (breakfast not included). **www.bayoffirescottages.com.au**

BRIDPORT Platypus Park Country Retreat $$$

20 Ada Street, Bridport, TAS 7262 **Tel** *(03) 6356 1873* **Rooms** *7*

Country hospitality by the seaside can be found at Platypus Park. Located in the holiday town of Bridport in the state's northeast, the retreat is just a short drive from the spectacular Barnbougle Dunes golf links course, a lavender farm and a number of wineries. **www.platypuspark.com.au**

BRUNY ISLAND Morella Island Retreats $$$$$

46 Adventure Bay Road, Adventure Bay, TAS 7150 **Tel** *(03) 6293 1131* **Fax** *(03) 6293 1137* **Rooms** *5*

The hosts of Morella Island Retreats invite you to escape from the real world in one of their five themed cottages. Boasting incredible views over the "neck", an onsite art gallery, café, landscaped gardens, the retreat is suitable for families or those seeking a private island retreat. Breakfast not included. **www.morella-island.com.au**

BURINE The Duck House $$

26 Queen Street, TAS 7320 **Tel** *(03) 6431 1712* **Fax** *(03) 6431 1712* **Rooms** *3*

Early last century the Duck family called this Federation cottage home. Now it is a comfortable, centrally located guesthouse with a pleasant veranda, antique furniture and modern amenities. Rooms come with provisions for a self-catered full English breakfast. There are concessions for children and longer stays. **www.ozpal.com/duck**

COLES BAY Iluka Holiday Centre $$

Esplanade, Coles Bay, TAS 7215 **Tel** *(03) 6257 0115* **Fax** *(03) 6257 0384* **Rooms** *15*

The Iluka Holiday Centre is in the centre of Coles Bay village, across the road from Muirs Beach. The self-contained two-bedroom cabins come with television, covered deck and carport. The centre also incorporates a YHA Backpackers lodge, powered caravan sites and camping ground. **www.ilukaholidaycentre.com.au**

COLES BAY Edge of the Bay Resort $$$$$

2308 Coles Bay Road, Coles Bay, TAS 7215 **Tel** *(03) 6257 0102* **Fax** *(03) 6257 0437* **Rooms** *22*

This private resort retreat is positioned on the edge of Great Oyster Bay with stunning views to the Hazards Mountain Range and Freycinet National Park. Offering waterfront suites and self-contained cottages, there is a restaurant on site and no shortage of activities. Breakfast baskets are available. **www.edgeofthebay.com.au**

COLES BAY Freycinet Lodge $$$$$

Freycinet National Park, TAS 7215 **Tel** *(03) 6257 0101* **Fax** *(03) 6225 3909* **Rooms** *60*

Award-winning, ecologically friendly lodge overlooking Great Oyster Bay backed by the Hazards Mountains. The ideal base for exploring the World Heritage listed Wineglass Bay and the glorious coast of the Tasmanian east coast. Wooden cabins and boardwalks complement the lodge's setting. **www.puretasmania.com.au**

CRADLE MOUNTAIN Cradle Mountain Lodge  $$$$$

Cradle Mountain Road, National Park, TAS 7306 **Tel** *(03) 6492 1303* **Fax** *(03) 6492 1309* **Rooms** *86*

This rustic alpine retreat is located on the edge of the World Heritage listed Cradle Mountain/Lake St Clair National Park. Featuring cosy log cabins (some with spas), guided tours, lodge-style restaurant and guest lounge with stone fireplace. The Waldheim Spa onsite offers spa treatment. **www.cradlemountainlodge.com.au**

516   T R A V E L L E R S '　N E E D S

DEVONPORT Birchmore of Davenport

8–10 Oldaker Street, TAS 7310 **Tel** *(03) 6423 1336* **Fax** *(03) 6423 1338* **Rooms** *7*

Birchmore offers guests outstanding accommodation and personal service in the heart of Devonport. Only a minute from the city centre, Birchmore is ideally located for restaurants, shopping and business. Rooms are designed with the business guest in mind. Hearty breakfast included.

HOBART Battery Point Manor

13–15 Cromwell Street, TAS 7004 **Tel** *(03) 6224 0888* **Fax** *(03) 6224 2254* **Rooms** *8*

This grand Georgian home was built in 1834 and is now a European-style guesthouse, with commanding views across the River Derwent. Choose from the seven en suite rooms, or the privacy of the two-bedroom self-contained cottage. Take advantage of the historic village's restaurants, cafés and shops. **www.batterypointmanor.com.au**

HOBART Motel 429

429 Sandy Bay Road, Sandy Bay, TAS 7005 **Tel** *(03) 6225 2511* **Fax** *(03) 6225 4354* **Rooms** *33*

Conveniently located in Sandy Bay with views of the River Derwent, close to Wrest Point Casino and the Sandy Bay shopping village. The motel is well served by public transport direct to the city centre. Some rooms have been renovated and have air conditioning. The motel has a spa and sauna. **www.motel429.com.au**

HOBART Henry Jones Art Hotel

25 Hunter Street, Hobart, TAS 7000 **Tel** *(03) 6210 7700* **Fax** *(03) 6210 7755* **Rooms** *50*

Winner of the Australian Hotel Association Best Overall Hotel in 2005, this is a stylish, first-class hotel with a strong focus on Tasmanian art and design. Formerly the site of the Jones & Co. IXL jam factory, it is part of a sympathetic redevelopment of this historic area of Hobart into an art and cultural centre. **www.thehenryjones.com**

HOBART Lenna of Hobart

20 Runnymede Street, Battery Point, TAS 7004 **Tel** *(03) 6232 3900* **Fax** *(03) 6224 0112* **Rooms** *50*

The heritage-listed Lenna – formerly the residence of Scottish merchant Alexander McGregor – is now a gracious boutique hotel just around the corner from Salamanca Place. It offers spacious en-suite rooms adjoining the original mansion, well-equipped function venues and the award-winning Alexander's restaurant. **www.lenna.com.au**

HOBART Hotel Grand Chancellor

1 Davey Street, Hobart, TAS 7000 **Tel** *(03) 6235 4535* **Fax** *(03) 6223 8175* **Rooms** *240*

Located right on the waterfront, adjacent to the Federation Concert Hall, the Hotel Grand Chancellor offers rooms with waterfront, city and mountain aspects. There is a range of facilities and services including a fully-equipped gym, indoor swimming pool, restaurant and comprehensive business and conference facilities. **www.hgchobart.com**

HOBART Islington Hotel

321 Davey Street, Hobart, TAS 7000 **Tel** *(03) 6220 2123* **Fax** *(03) 6220 2124* **Rooms** *11*

This ultra luxe boutique hotel is set in an old Regency House and fuses old-world charm with contemporary style. There are five rooms in the original house and six modern garden rooms; all are sumptuously furnished with an eclectic mix of antiques and art. Sweeping views of Mount Wellington and private dinners on request. **www.islingtonhotel.com**

LAUNCESTON Ashton Gate

32 High Street, Launceston, TAS 7250 **Tel** *(03) 6331 6180* **Fax** *(03) 6334 2232* **Rooms** *8*

Ashton Gate (c.1880) was built by Mr AW Birchall, the owner of Australia's oldest bookshop. The home became a guesthouse after World War II and today the accommodation includes de luxe suites and a self-contained apartment. Breakfast is included and can be enjoyed on the outdoor deck. **www.ashtongate.com.au**

LAUNCESTON Colonial Launceston

31 Elizabeth Street, Launceston, TAS 7250 **Tel** *1800 060 955* **Fax** *(03) 6334 2765* **Rooms** *66*

Part of the Quality Hotel chain, the Colonial Launceston is housed in an 1847 National Trust building that was once a school. Guest accommodation ranges from classic doubles to family rooms and executive suites, all with private balconies and great views of Launceston. **www.colonialinn.com.au**

LAUNCESTON Peppers Seaport Hotel

28 Seaport Boulevard, TAS 7250 **Tel** *(03) 6345 3333* **Fax** *(03) 6345 3300* **Rooms** *60*

Peppers Seaport Hotel is the centre of Launceston's newest lifestyle precinct on the North Esk River. This sleek and very modern hotel comprises en-suite rooms and fully self-contained apartments. There are several restaurants and bars on site, a marina, boardwalk and the city's first-class sports stadium is just a short walk away. **www.peppers.com.au**

NEW NORFOLK Tynwald Willow Bend Estate

Hobart Road, New Norfolk, TAS 7140 **Tel** *(03) 6261 2667* **Fax** *(03) 6261 2040* **Rooms** *7*

This gracious 1830s mansion overlooking the River Derwent was once a part of an old flour mill. Set in 16 hectares (39 acres) featuring garden walks, a solar-heated outdoor swimming pool and tennis court. There are six rooms within the mansion and a self-contained stone cottage known as "The Granary". **www.tynwaldtasmania.com**

RICHMOND Hatchers Richmond Manor

73 Prossers Road, Richmond, TAS 7025 **Tel** *(03) 6260 2622* **Fax** *(03) 6260 2744* **Rooms** *8*

A luxury rural getaway for couples and families, set among gardens, orchards and a private lake. Start the day with a full country breakfast before exploring the quaint historic township of Richmond. Rooms are very well equipped, including Internet access. **www.hatchersmanor.com.au**

Key to Price Guide *see p478* **Key to Symbols** *see back cover flap*

ROSS Man-O-Ross Hotel $$

35 Church Street, TAS 7209 **Tel** *(03) 6381 5445* **Fax** *(03) 6381 5440* **Rooms** *7*

This attractive sandstone building, situated on the highway coming into Ross, was constructed in 1835 and has been carefully refurbished. The traditional elegance of the interior is complemented by the friendly, homey decor of the rooms. **www.manoross.com.au**

ROSS Colonial Cottages and Ross Bed & Breakfast $$

12 Church Street, TAS 7209 **Tel** *(03) 6381 5354* **Fax** *(03) 6331 1895* **Rooms** *7*

These charming cottages in the historic town of Ross date from the 1840s and are situated in the town centre. Each cottage has been affectionately restored and features antiques, thick sandstone walls and wooden four-poster beds. Free Wi-Fi is available. **www.rossaccommodation.com.au**

SHEFFIELD Wild Gowrie Park $

1447 Claude Road, Gowrie, TAS 7306 **Tel** *(03) 6491 1385* **Fax** *(03) 6491 1848* **Rooms** *4*

Tucked away within ancient forests, beneath the rugged Mount Roland, these cosy well-equipped cabins provide the perfect base for exploring the magnificent wilderness of the Walls of Jerusalem and Cradle Mountain-Lake St Clair National Parks. Self-cater or take advantage of the on-site restaurant. Payment in cash only.

STANLEY Beachside Retreat West Inlet $$$$

253 Stanley Highway, TAS 7331 **Tel** *(03) 6458 1350* **Fax** *(03) 6458 1350* **Rooms** *6*

Waterfront nature retreat and haven for wildlife and cattle, across from a secluded beach and close to the historic township of Stanley. Offering three types of contemporary self-contained accommodation: a spacious spa lodge, contemporary ecocabins and a luxury nature cabin. **www.beachsideretreat.com**

STRAHAN Aldermere Estate $$$$$

27 Harvey Street, Strahan, TAS 7468 **Tel** *(03) 6471 7418* **Fax** *3 6471 7418* **Rooms** *8*

Aldermere Estate is a modern establishment designed with an eye to Tasmania's colonial past. The fully self-contained two-storey apartments have been tastefully decorated in period style with all the modern conveniences and continental breakfast provisions. **www.aldermere.com.au**

STRAHAN Franklin Manor $$$$$

The Esplanade, Strahan, TAS 7468 **Tel** *(03) 6471 7311* **Fax** *(03) 6471 7267* **Rooms** *18*

Overlooking the vast Macquarie Harbour at the gateway to the rugged west coast, Franklin Manor is steeped in history and charm. The grand old home is now a haven for those seeking to experience the pristine wilderness and savour the delicious food and wine in Franklin Manor's first-class restaurant. **www.franklinmanor.com.au**

SWANSEA Swansea Holiday Park at Jubilee Beach $$

2 Bride Street, Swansea, TAS 7190 **Tel** *(03) 6257 8148* **Fax** *(03) 6257 8511* **Rooms** *14*

One of the two locations of the Swansea Holiday Park, situated at Jubilee Beach, within the heritage township of Swansea. There are a range of self-contained cabins plus powered sites for caravans. There is an outdoor swimming pool and games room, as well as a barbecue. **www.swansea-holiday.com.au**

SWANSEA Schouten House $$$

1 Waterloo Road, TAS 7190 **Tel** *(03) 6257 8564* **Fax** *(03) 6257 8564* **Rooms** *6*

This is a beautifully restored Georgian house (c.1846) on Tasmania's stunning east coast. It provides bed-and-breakfast accommodation and each room features antique heritage furniture, mini bar and en suite bathroom. Adding to the welcome is a log fire. **www.schoutenhouse.com.au**

SWANSEA Avalon Coastal Retreat $$$$$

11922 Tasman Hwy, TAS 7004 **Tel** *1300 361136* **Rooms** *3*

At Avalon a world of marine blue opens up before you via the floor-to-ceiling windows that double as the exterior walls of this award-winning, Craig Rosevears-designed house. Its secluded location overlooking Oyster Bay makes this modernistic retreat popular with honeymooners. **www.avaloncoastalretreat.com.au**

SWANSEA Kabuki By the Sea $$$$$

Rocky Hills, Tasman Highway, Swansea, TAS 7190 **Tel** *(03) 6257 8588* **Fax** *(03) 6257 8588* **Rooms** *7*

These Japanese-inspired cottages are perched on a clifftop and boast spectacular views of the Freycinet Peninsula. There are five one-bedroom cottages, each with bathroom, sitting/dining room and kitchen facilities. The on-site restaurant uses the local produce to create exquisite Japanese and oriental cuisine. **www.kabukibythesea.com.au**

TASMAN PENINSULA Norfolk Bay Convict Station $$$

5862 Arthur Highway, Taranna, TAS 7180 **Tel** *(03) 6250 3487* **Fax** *(03) 6250 3701* **Rooms** *5*

Built with convict labour in 1838, this was once the site of Australia's first railway station, linking Hobart with the penal settlement of Port Arthur. Today the commissariat store has been transformed into a haven of comfort with log fires and bay views, and five themed suites. **www.convictstation.com**

WOODBRIDGE Old Woodbridge Rectory $$

15 Woodbridge Hill Road, Woodbridge, TAS 7162 **Tel** *(03) 6267 4742* **Fax** *(03) 6267 4746* **Rooms** *2*

Just a 30-minute drive from Hobart along the scenic Channel Highway, this boutique bed and breakfast is perfectly positioned for those wanting to explore the Huon Valley, Bruny Island and local wineries. The Old Rectory has been tastefully restored and comprises two en suite rooms. **www.oldwoodbridgerectory.com.au**

WHERE TO EAT

A ustralia has developed its own culinary identity in the past 20 years or so and modern Australian food, often with a Mediterranean or Asian twist, is now widely available. Reflecting the country's multicultural population, there is also a wealth of ethnic restaurants. Every cuisine, from Algerian to Zambian, is on a menu somewhere in Australia, particularly in the major cities. Australian restaurants

Fresh seafood, Chinese style

make good use of the variety of homegrown produce, especially seafood and beef. No Australian meal is complete without a glass of one of the many local wines or beers *(see pp522–3)*.

For a cheaper eating-out option, try one of the many BYO (Bring Your Own) unlicensed restaurants, where customers take their own wine, but may be charged a minimal corkage fee.

Marco Polo Restaurant at the Conrad in Brisbane *(see p535)*

TYPES OF RESTAURANTS

All major Australian cities offer a wide choice of restaurants. Formal dining establishments, bistros, stylish cafés and pubs are all readily available to suit any budget. Food on offer ranges from haute cuisine to informal snacks. Outside the main cities, some of the best restaurants can be found in the many wine regions and often in the wineries themselves *(see pp36–7)*.

Prices, however, vary widely. They tend to be highest in Sydney, Melbourne and other major tourist resorts, although prices are usually lower than in comparable places in Europe and the United States. As a general guideline, the bill at a showcase Melbourne or Sydney restaurant featuring a celebrity chef will be at least A$150 per head, including a shared bottle of

wine. At a Bring Your Own (BYO) or an unpretentious Asian or Italian restaurant it may only be A$30–40 per head. A counter meal at a pub, café or at a snack bar should generally cost around A$15–20 per head, if you include the cost of a drink.

A welcome trend in Australia is the increasing emphasis on courtyard, garden, boulevard and other outdoor eating facilities, making the most of the country's benevolent climate.

EATING HOURS AND RESERVATIONS

Most restaurants serve lunch between 12:30pm and 3pm; dinner is served from 6:30 to 10:30pm. Many establishments, however, particularly the big city bistros and cafés, have become more flexible, opening for breakfast and closing late. Most budget and ethnic restaurants often close a little

earlier, at around 9:30pm, depending on the demand. Most establishments are also open six days a week, while hotel dining rooms open daily. However, it is advisable to check in advance with individual restaurants, particularly those outside the capital cities. To avoid disappointment, advance telephone bookings are generally recommended.

PAYING AND TIPPING

Major credit cards are accepted in the majority of Australian restaurants, although it is a good idea to confirm this in advance or on arrival. A Goods and Services Tax (GST) is included in restaurant bills in Australia. Tipping is not compulsory, but in recognition of outstanding service or a particularly fine meal, a small gratuity is always appreciated. How much to leave is the prerogative of the customer,

Skillogalee Winery and Restaurant in the Clare Valley *(see p552)*

Doyle's On the Beach in Watsons Bay, Sydney *(see p528)*

but 10 per cent of the total bill would generally be appropriate in a restaurant. This can be left either as a cash tip on the table when you are ready to leave or by adding it to the total if paying your bill by cheque or credit card.

Ravesi's, one of the many eateries at Bondi Beach, Sydney *(see p524)*

CHILDREN

Few restaurateurs will refuse admission to children as long as they are well behaved. Many restaurants also provide high chairs and a children's menu. The best family budget options are local sports club bistros, pub bistros, hamburger chains or Italian or Asian eateries.

WHEELCHAIR ACCESS

Spurred by legislation in the various states, most restaurants now provide special wheelchair access and toilet facilities for the disabled.

However, it is still advisable to check in advance on the facilities available.

VEGETARIANS

It is rare for a restaurant not to feature at least one dish for vegetarians, and a variety of choices is the norm, particularly in regions where there is an abundance of homegrown produce. There are also specialist vegetarian restaurants and cafés in the major cities. If you have special dietary requirements, it is sensible to call the restaurant in advance, especially in more rural areas.

ALCOHOL AND OTHER DRINKS

If a restaurant is described as licensed, it refers to its licence to sell alcohol. Australian wine lists are outstanding and generally highlight the wines of the particular state

or district *(see pp32–3)*. Wine is sold by the bottle, carafe or glass. There is usually a good choice of beers, ales, ciders and spirits as well.

BYO restaurants, which are not licensed to sell alcohol, are extremely popular in Australia and offer diners the opportunity to bring the wines they wish to drink with their meal, although beer is not usually permitted. For non-alcohol drinkers, tap water is entirely safe, but many people prefer to drink bottled still or sparkling water. Fresh fruit juices are also very popular *(see pp522–3)*.

DRESS

Dress codes are virtually non-existent in Australian restaurants, although a handful of the more up-market establishments may ask men to wear a tie in the evenings. Most establishments, however, including beachside cafés, frown on scant beachwear.

For most situations, the phrase "smart casual" sums up the Australian approach to eating out.

SMOKING

Smoking is banned inside restaurants and cafés, though smoking is permitted in designated outside areas. Fines may be levied if these regulations are disregarded. Smoking restrictions are also strictly applied in traditional pubs. There is no smoking indoors or near food.

Café Provincial in the heart of Fitzroy in Melbourne *(see p555)*

The Flavours of Australia

Modern Australian cuisine has been evolving from traditional British since World War II. An influx of people from Italy, Greece, Turkey, Lebanon, Thailand, China, Malaysia, Indonesia and Vietnam (to name but a few) have contributed influences to what is now known as Mod-Oz cuisine. However, a lot of Aussies will still sit down to a Sunday roast and swelter over turkey on a midsummer Christmas day. Dramatically varying climates over such a large country mean an abundance and diversity of local produce, so it's no surprise that some of the world's best chefs hail from this rich and exciting culinary playground.

Wattleseed, pepperberry and lemon myrtle

Chef filleting snapper, one of Australia's finest fish

NATIVE INGREDIENTS

There are many native foods in Australia that have been used by aborigines for thousands of years, and which are now becoming widely popular. Quandong, munthari, bush tomato, wild limes and rosellas are native fruits with distinctive colours, flavours and textures, while warrigal greens are a spinach-like herb. All of them are still primarily wild-harvested by aboriginal communities. Although native Australians never used seasonings in their campfire cooking, modern Australians have discovered the exciting flavours of such indigenous herbs and spices as lemon myrtle, wattleseed, mountain pepperleaf, pepperberry, forest berry and akudjura. Native meats such as kangaroo and emu are also being used more frequently, although don't expect to see witchity grubs on many menus. These native meats sit alongside a vast and impressive array of beef, lamb and, of course, seafood. Fish native to Australia include barramundi, trevally and blue-eye trevalla. The popular native shellfish, yabbies and Moreton Bay bugs, are similar to, but smaller than, lobster. Also worth a mention is the lovely fragrant honey produced out of native Australian forests.

Samphire · Snapper · Lobster · Red mullet · Oysters · Scallops

Selection of seafood to be found in the oceans around Australia

AUSTRALIAN DISHES AND SPECIALITIES

Australians love a barbecue, as a social and culinary hub, and you will find a wide variety of meats and cuisines on the grill. Major cities offer a huge choice of foods, from high end French-style fare to fish and chips or cheap and cheerful noodle bars. Melbourne, in particular, has a strong Greek and Italian influence and prides itself on a vibrant café culture, serving unbeatable coffee. Meat pies are a staple in the Aussie diet with the annual Meat Pie Competition

Anzac biscuits

attracting great interest, and you will see pies inspired by different cuisines such as Thai, Indian and Moroccan.

For those with a sweet tooth, pumpkin scones are a traditional Australian favourite, alongside passionfruit tart, Lamingtons, Pavlova, and oat and coconut Anzac biscuits.

Kangaroo pizza *This Italian classic is given a modern Australian spin with the addition of seared lean fillet.*

Vegetable stall at Queen Victoria Market, Melbourne *(see p386)*

THE WORLD ON A PLATE

Having one of the most eclectic populations on earth means great things for food (or "tucker"). Australians are as happy exporting their wealth of homegrown produce as they are embracing international cuisine.

Farming plays a very important role in Australia, the world's largest producer of beef. The lush pastures on the coast are particularly good for farming, and the milk-fed lamb from New South Wales is as wonderful as the brie produced in South Australia. King Island, between Victoria and Tasmania in Bass Strait, is dedicated to dairy produce; farmers sell their amazing cheese and creams all around the country. Alongside the rapidly

growing wine industry is olive oil and balsamic vinegar production, examples of which are found at the cellar door of many vineyards.

Australia has one of the most diverse marine faunas in the world, due to its range of

Wooden crate of sweet, juicy apples from Tasmania

habitats, from the warm tropical northern waters to the sub-Antarctic Tasman sea, as well as its geographical isolation. A total of 600 marine and freshwater species are caught in Australian waters, providing chefs with plenty of inspiration.

Every kind of fruit and vegetable is produced in Australia. Pineapples and mangoes are widely grown in Queensland, apples in Victoria, strawberries in New South Wales and rambutans in the Northern Territory. Exotic and notoriously hard to farm, truffles have been cultivated in several states, highlighting just how versatile Australia's land is.

FOOD ON THE RUN

Sushi Major cities are dotted with tiny counters offering fresh sushi to grab on the go.

Juice bars This booming industry is found on most city streets, serving delicious, cool blends of fruit.

Milk bars As well as milkshakes, ice creams and salads, these sell a wide range of deep-fried foods.

Coffee & cake Little cafés everywhere also sell Italian-style cakes and pastries.

Pubs Most pubs serve a decent steak sandwich.

Pies An Aussie institution, pies are readily available. Look out for gourmet versions.

Grilled barramundi *Served on ginger and bok choy risotto, this is a great mix of local seafood and Asian flavours.*

Prawn Laksa *This spicy coconut noodle soup can be found all over the country in noodle bars, cafés and pubs.*

Lamingtons *These little Victoria sponge cakes are coated in chocolate icing and shredded coconut.*

What to Drink in Australia

Semillon Chardonnay

Australia has one of the world's finest cuisines and part of its enjoyment is the marriage of the country's wine with great food. Australians have a very relaxed attitude to food and wine mixes, so red wine with fish and a cold, dry Riesling as an aperitif can easily be the order of the day. Also, many of the restuarants in the wine regions offer exclusive brands, or offer rare wines so these are worth seeking out. Australians also enjoy some of the best good-value wine in the world (see pp36–7). It is estimated that there are 10,000 different Australian wines on the market at any one time. Australians do love their beer, and it remains a popular drink, with a wide range of choices available. While the health-conscious can choose from a variety of bottled waters and select-your-own, freshly-squeezed fruit juices. Imported wines, beers and spirits are also readily available.

SPARKLING WINE

Domaine Chandon in the Yarra Valley (see p433) in Eastern Victoria

Australia is justly famous for its sparkling wines, from Yalumba's Angas Brut to Seppelts Salinger. Most recently, Tasmania has showed considerable promise in producing some high quality sparkling wines, particularly Pirie from Pipers Brook. However, the real hidden gems are the sparkling red wines – the best are made using the French *Méthode Champenois*, matured over a number of years and helped by a small drop of vintage port. The best producers of red sparkling wines are Rockford and Seppelts. These sparkling wines are available throughout the country from "bottle shops".

Angus Brut premium

WHITE WINE

Rhine Riesling   **Botrytis Semillon**

The revolution in wine making in the 1970s firmly established dry wines made from international grape varieties on the Australian table. Chardonnay, Sauvignon Blanc, and more recently Viognier and Pinot Gris are all popular. However, in recent years there has also been a renaissance and growing appreciation for Riesling, Marsanne and Semillon, which age very gracefully. Australia's other great wines are their fortified and desert wines. Australian winemakers use *botrytis cinera*, or noble rot, to make luscious dessert wines such as De Bortoli's "Noble One".

Some of the vines in Australia are the oldest in the world

GRAPE TYPE	STATE	BEST REGIONS	BEST PRODUCERS
Chardonnay	VIC	Geelong, Beechworth	Bannockburn, Giaconda, Stoniers
	NSW	Hunter Valley	Lakes Folly, Rosemount, Tyrrell's
	WA	Margaret River	Leeuwin Estate, Pierro, Cullen
	SA	Barossa Valley, Eden Valley	Penfolds, Mountadam
Semillon	NSW	Hunter Valley	Brokenwood, McWilliams, Tyrrell
	SA	Barossa Valley	Peter Lehmann, Willows, Penfolds
	WA	Margaret River	Moss Wood, Voyager, Evans & Tate
Riesling	SA	Clare Valley and Adelaide Hills	Grosset, Pikes, Petaluma, Mitchells
	SA	Barossa Valley	Richmond Grove, Leo Buring, Yalumba
	TAS	Tasmania	Piper's Brook
Marsanne	VIC	Goulburn Valley	Chateau Tahbilk, Mitchelton

Vineyards of Leeuwin
Estate, Margaret River

RED WINE

Australia's benchmark red is Penfold's Grange, the creation of the late vintner Max Schubert in the 1950s and 1960s. Due to his work, Shiraz has established itself as Australia's premium red variety. However, there is also plenty of diversity with the acknowledged quality of Cabernet Sauvignon produced in the Coonawarra. Recently, there has also been a re-appraisal of traditional "old vine" Grenache and Mourvedre varieties in the Barossa Valley and McLaren Vale.

Shiraz   Pinot Noir

GRAPE TYPE	BEST REGIONS	BEST PRODUCERS
Shiraz	Hunter Valley (NSW)	Brokenwood, Lindmans, Tyrrells
	Great Western, Sunbury (VIC)	Bests, Seppelts, Craiglee
	Barossa Valley (SA)	Henschke, Penfolds, Rockford, Torbreck
	McLaren Vale (SA)	Hardys, Coriole, Chapel Hill
	Margaret River, Great Southern (WA)	Cape Mentelle, Plantagenet
Cabernet Sauvignon	Margaret River (WA)	Cape Mentelle, Cullen, Moss Wood
	Coonawarra (SA)	Wynns, Lindemans, Bowen Estate
	Barossa, Adelaide Hills (SA)	Penfolds, Henschke, Petaluma
	Yarra Valley, Great Western (VIC)	Yarra Yering, Yerinberg, Bests
Merlot	Yarra Valley, Great Western (VIC)	Bests, Yara Yering
	Adelaide Hills, Clare Valley (SA)	Petaluma, Pikes
Pinot Noir	Yarra Valley (VIC)	Coldstream Hills, Tarrarawra
	Gippsland, Geelong (VIC)	Bass Philip, Bannockburn, Shadowfax

BEER

Most Australian beer is vat fermented real ale or lager, both consumed chilled. Full-strength beer has an alcohol content of around 4.8 per cent, mid-strength beers have around 3.5 per cent, while "light" beers have less than 3 per cent. Traditionally heat sterilized, cold filtration is now becoming increasingly popular. Among the hundreds of fine lagers and stouts are James Boag and Cascade from Tasmania, Castlemaine XXXX from Queensland, Fosters and Melbourne Bitter from Victoria, Toohey's New from New South Wales and Cooper's Sparkling Ale from South Australia. Aficionados of real ale should seek out a pub brewery. Beer is ordered by glass size: a schooner is a 426 ml (15 fl oz) glass and a middy is 284 ml (10 fl oz) in NSW, though glass sizes can vary.

Tooheys   Cascade
Red Bitter Premium Lager

SPIRITS

Australian distillers produce fine dark and white rums from Queensland's sugar cane plantations *(see p246)*. Notable labels include Bundaberg, from the town of that name, and Beenleigh. Australia's grape vintage is also the basis of good-value domestic brandies. Popular labels are St Agnes and McWilliams.

Bundaberg
rum

OTHER DRINKS

With a climate ranging from tropical to alpine, Australia has year-round fresh fruit for juicing. Its apples are also used to make cider. Scores of still and sparkling mineral and other bottled waters now supply an annual market of nearly 200 million litres. Hepburn Spa, Deep Spring and Mount Franklin have national distribution. Coffee, prepared in a wide variety of ways, is another immensely popular drink with Australians.

White coffee

Pear and
kiwi frappé

Banana
smoothie

Strawberry
juice

Caffe latte

Choosing a Restaurant

The restaurants in this guide have been selected for their exceptional food, good value and interesting location. They are listed by region, starting with Sydney, in the same order as the rest of the guide. Within each region, entries are listed alphabetically by price category, from the least to the most expensive.

SYDNEY

BONDI BEACH Bondi Trattoria $$$
34 Campbell Parade, Bondi Beach, NSW 2026 **Tel** *(02) 9365 4303*

With spectacular views of the beach from every table, both inside and outside, join the Bondi locals at the refurbished Bondi Trattoria. A café by day and a restaurant at night, the food served here is a fusion of traditional Italian and modern Australian.

BONDI BEACH Ravesi's on Bondi Beach $$$
118 Campbell Parade, Bondi Beach, NSW 2026 **Tel** *(02) 9365 4422*

Dine inside and enjoy the relaxed and stylish atmosphere, or sit out on the terrace and take in the buzz of the beach. Under the direction of acclaimed chef Darren Elmes, Ravesi's serves an innovative menu and blends an exciting mix of flavours from the Pacific, with influences from Asia, Latin America and the Mediterranean.

BONDI BEACH Sean's Panorama $$$$
270 Campbell Parade, Bondi Beach, NSW 2026 **Tel** *(02) 9365 4924*

Like an oversized family dining room, Sean's is intimate and friendly. Serving a small range of seasonal dishes, with a few constants such as pasta with shredded arugula, lemon, chilli and Parmesan, and the famous white chocolate, fig and rosemary nougat. Booking essential.

BONDI BEACH Icebergs Dining Room $$$$$
1 Notts Avenue, Bondi Beach, NSW 2026 **Tel** *(02) 9365 9000*

The first really swish restaurant to hit the surf at Bondi is this dining room above the famous swimming pool. The decor gives a glamorous beach feel with a palette of ocean blues, giant rustic chandeliers and a scattering of silk cushions. Food is simple, modern Italian.

BOTANIC GARDENS AND THE DOMAIN The Art Gallery Restaurant $$$$
The Art Gallery of New South Wales, Art Gallery Road, The Domain, NSW 2000 **Tel** *(02) 9225 1819*   **Map** *2 D4*

Open for lunch daily and also for brunch on weekends, this restaurant provides a sophisticated place to discuss the latest exhibition. The menu is small but should please most. There's also a more casual café on the lower level, which is great for kids, offering cardboard boxes with sandwiches, a drink and a chocolate.

BOTANIC GARDENS AND THE DOMAIN Botanic Gardens Restaurant $$$$
Royal Botanic Gardens, Mrs Macquaries Road, NSW 2000 **Tel** *(02) 9241 2419*   **Map** *2 D4*

Set among the lush greenery this excellent value lunch venue opens on to a terrace, letting in the sounds of the gardens, even the squawks of the famous bats. Serious gourmets might try the grilled beef tenderloin with potato fondant and beetroot. Weekend brunch is lovely too and there's a café below.

BOTANIC GARDENS AND THE DOMAIN Pavilion $$$$
1 Art Gallery Road, The Domain, NSW 2000 **Tel** *(02) 9232 1322*   **Map** *2 D4*

Close to the city centre, yet serene and enchanting, the Pavilion is the ideal location to escape to and enjoy a leisurely meal. With a menu to match your mood, enjoy a decadent breakfast, an extravagant lunch or one of the light treats available. The adjacent café offers a tempting selection of salads and great coffees.

CITY CENTRE Mother Chu's Vegetarian Kitchen $
367 Pitt Street, Sydney, NSW 2000 **Tel** *(02) 9283 2828*   **Map** *4 E3*

A cheap and cheerful restaurant that offers large portions of hearty food, blending the flavours of Taiwan, China and Japan. Often full of students and arty types, enjoying the warm Buddhist hospitality, and delicious stir-fries and curries you can trust are truly vegetarian. Don't be put off by the canteen decor.

CITY CENTRE Bodhi Restaurant Bar $$
Cook & Phillip Park, 2-4 College Street, Sydney, NSW 2000 **Tel** *(02) 9360 2523*   **Map** *1 C5*

This is a wonderful place to come for lunch on a sunny day, or for dinner on a summer's night, when you can take an outside table under the trees. You'll be amazed by the realistic vegan versions of fish and chicken. The not-pork sang choy bau is excellent, as is the signature dish, a skin-and-all vegan Peking duck. A good wine list.

Key to Symbols *see back cover flap*

CITY CENTRE Diethnes
$$

336 Pitt Street, Sydney, NSW 2000 **Tel** *(02) 9267 8956* **Map** *1 B5*

A Sydney institution, Diethnes has been in the same basement spot for 35 years, and you can tell. But get past the kitsch decor, and you'll find healthy portions of hearty meals. With dozens of meaty dishes, pasta, rice, salads and traditional Greek dishes like *tzaziki* and *spanakopita*, there's something for everyone.

CITY CENTRE Industrie, South of France
$$$$

107 Pitt Street, Sydney, NSW 2000 **Tel** *(02) 9221 8001* **Map** *1 B4*

It's a café, bar, restaurant, club – anything you want it to be really, from breakfast through to dinner, drinks and dancing; all infused with the flavour and spirit of the French Riviera. There are live jazz/soul bands plus cocktail offers on Thursday nights, a resident DJ on Fridays and club events on Saturdays.

CITY CENTRE Spice Temple
$$$$

10 Bligh Street, Sydney, NSW 2000 **Tel** *(02) 8078 1888* **Map** *1 B4*

The menu at this modern Chinese restaurant draws inspiration from provinces throughout China. Chillies feature in many forms – dried, fresh, salted, pickled, brined and fermented. The food is cooked to excite and designed to be shared. Chinese lanterns offer soft lighting in the romantic basement setting.

CITY CENTRE Bilson's
$$$$$

27 O'Connell St, Sydney, NSW 2000 **Tel** *(02) 8214 0496* **Map** *4 E1*

The "godfather of Sydney cuisine", Tony Bilson has been a leading Australian chef for more than four decades. His contemporary French cuisine is offered à la carte or on tasting menus with matching wines from Bilson's impressive list. The chef's own art collection adorns the walls of this smart hotel restaurant. Closed on Mondays.

CITY CENTRE est.
$$$$$

Level 1, 252 George Street, Sydney, NSW 2000 **Tel** *(02) 9240 3010* **Map** *1 B3*

est. is a fine dining restaurant with elegant furnishings and luxurious fittings. Head chef Peter Doyle is widely regarded as a founding father of modern Australian cuisine. Lunch and dinner tasting menus offer diners a chance to try several key dishes, all matched with wines.

CITY CENTRE Tetsuya's
$$$$$

529 Kent Street, Sydney, NSW 2000 **Tel** *(02) 9267 2900* **Map** *4 E3*

Internationally revered and widely considered Australia's best restaurant, Tetsuya's serene space puts the emphasis on the food and wine. The dégustation (only) menus fuse Japanese flavours with French technique. Wines can be matched to each course and vegetarian dégustations are available on request. Book well in advance.

DARLING HARBOUR Pasteur
$

709 George Street, Haymarket, NSW 2000 **Tel** *(02) 9212 5622* **Map** *4 E4*

Finish your A\$9-bowl of beef and rice noodle soup and you may not need dinner. *Pho* is a Vietnamese speciality, which may come with chicken or beef. These float in fragrant broth, served with a pile of mint and basil leaves, chilli and fish sauce. Fresh spring rolls are another delicious snack, filled with pork and prawns.

DARLING HARBOUR Zibar
$$

49a Druitt Street, Sydney, NSW 2000 **Tel** *(02) 9268 0222* **Map** *4 E2*

A small restaurant/café conveniently situated between the city centre and Darling Harbour. The food is consistently good and the coffee is arguably the best to be found in the whole area. A busy and friendly place often filled with hotel guests from next door and local business types.

DARLING HARBOUR Chinta Ria... The Temple of Love
$$$

The Roof Terrace, Cockle Bay Wharf, 201 Sussex Street, Darling Harbour, NSW 2000 **Tel** *(02) 9264 3211* **Map** *4 D2*

Feelings of happiness are brought into this restaurant by the giant Buddha that takes centre stage. Its reasonable prices and fun atmosphere make it popular with a young crowd. The fresh and spicy Malaysian food is great for sharing. No bookings are taken for dinner, so be prepared to have a drink while you wait for a table.

DARLING HARBOUR Golden Century
$$$

393–399 Sussex Street, Sydney, NSW 2000 **Tel** *(02) 9212 3901* **Map** *4 E4*

The menu is huge, the staff are friendly and the selection of live seafood, including crab, abalone, lobster, parrot fish, barramundi and coral trout, is enormous. But what's truly amazing about this restaurant, in a city that catches plenty of sleep, is that its kitchen stays open until 3:30am. It's not unusual to find other chefs relaxing here after work.

DARLING HARBOUR Marigold
$$$

683 George Street, Sydney, NSW 2000 **Tel** *(02) 9261 8988* **Map** *4 E3*

Away from the bustle of Dixon and Hay Streets, the Regal is decked out with glittering chandeliers and private rooms. Waiters pushing dim sum-laden trolleys make it reminiscent of the yum cha places of Hong Kong. Cantonese seafood is popular, as well as plenty of hearty roast suckling pig and steamed fish chosen from the tank.

DARLING HARBOUR Zaaffran
$$$

Level 2, 345 Harbourside Shopping Centre, Darling Harbour, NSW 2000 **Tel** *(02) 9211 8900* **Map** *3 C2*

The pick of Darling Harbour's eateries, this Indian restaurant is heaven for vegetarians. The food goes beyond the standards, to offer spicy mixed vegetable in a tomato and coconut sauce. Carnivores will be satisfied by an aromatic lamb shank stew or chicken biryani. The best tables are outside and there are good value set menus.

DARLING HARBOUR Coast 🧒♿▦ $$$$

The Roof Terrace, Cockle Bay Wharf, 201 Sussex Street, Sydney, NSW 2000 ***Tel*** *(02) 9267 6700* ***Map*** *4 D2*

Eating fresh local seafood by the water is a quintessential Sydney experience. Chef Jonathan Barthelmess is at the helm, producing a unique and celebrated style of Italian cuisine. The dining room and views are spectacular, and there is also a beautiful outdoor terrace as well as a private dining room.

DARLING HARBOUR Jordon's Seafood Restaurant 🧒♿🎵▦ $$$$

197 Harbourside, Darling Harbour, NSW 2000 ***Tel*** *(02) 9281 3711* ***Map*** *3 C2*

This restaurant overlooks Darling Harbour and offers quality fresh seafood. Sushi, sashimi, char-grilled baby octopus, salmon, deep-fried snapper and calamari are available. Splashing out on a de luxe platter for two, will see you served a hot and cold selection of the market's best, including lobster.

KINGS CROSS AND DARLINGHURST Bill and Toni's 🧒♿🌿⛱☰▦ $

74 Stanley Street, East Sydney, NSW 2010 ***Tel*** *(02) 9360 4702* ***Map*** *5 A1*

A Sydney stalwart, loved for its strong coffee, old-fashioned feel with their famous red tablecloths. Upstairs you'll find basic but delicious home-style Italian, like spaghetti bolognese and veal schnitzel, and fast, friendly service. Afterwards, head downstairs for *macchiato* and *gelato*. Good place to bring kids, with its pinball machines.

KINGS CROSS AND DARLINGHURST Govinda's 🧒☰▦ $

112 Darlinghurst Road, Darlinghurst, NSW 2010 ***Tel*** *(02) 9380 5155* ***Map*** *5 B1*

Since the 1980s Sydneysiders have been dining at this vegetarian Hindu restaurant, piling up a plate of delicious curries, breads and salads from the all-you-can-eat buffet. Many of the dishes are Indian, but pastas and casseroles are often available too. For a little extra you can see a film in the upstairs movie room.

KINGS CROSS AND DARLINGHURST Fu Manchu 🧒⛱☰ $$

249 Victoria Street, Darlinghurst, NSW 2010 ***Tel*** *(02) 9360 9424* ***Map*** *5 B2*

A small, hip Chinese noodle bar, serving Northern Chinese and Southeast Asian hawker-style and home-cooked dishes. This is a fun place for a quick dinner at a communal table. The menu offers fresh and tasty dumplings, soups and stir-fries and good vegetarian choices. Open for dinner. Booking essential.

KINGS CROSS AND DARLINGHURST Mahjong Room 🧒⛱▦☰ $$

312 Crown Street, Surry Hills, NSW 2010 ***Tel*** *(02) 9361 3985* ***Map*** *5 A2*

This modern Chinese restaurant, packed with a young crowd, is very different from the big Chinatown diners. Instead, dishes such as bang bang chicken with century eggs and stir-fried prawns and snow peas are served at mahjong tables in a series of small rooms.

KINGS CROSS AND DARLINGHURST Fish Face 🧒⛱▦ $$$

132 Darlinghurst Road, Darlinghurst, NSW 2010 ***Tel*** *(02) 9332 4803* ***Map*** *5 B2*

In a tiny space which seats just 26, this restaurant may look humble, but it offers the best value, superb fish in town. The beer-battered fish and handcut chips are famous, and there's also a sushi bar and a menu full of appealing choices including the signature dish of blue-eye cod topped with thin rounds of potato shaped into scales.

KINGS CROSS AND DARLINGHURST Yellow Bistro & Food Store ♿🧒▦☰ $$$

57 Macleay Street, Potts Point, NSW 2011 ***Tel*** *(02) 9357 3400* ***Map*** *2 E4*

Van Gogh yellow walls make this, one of the most famous buildings in the Cross, stand out. In the 1970s it was an artists' commune which housed Brett Whiteley. Today creative genius is obvious in the food. The brunch menu is lovely but nothing beats the celebrated date tart created by pastry chef Lorraine Godsmark when it is on the menu.

KINGS CROSS AND DARLINGHURST Lotus ♿☰▦ $$$$

22 Challis Avenue, Potts Point, NSW 2010 ***Tel*** *(02) 9326 9000* ***Map*** *2 E4*

A bistro full of clean lines, blond wood and designer wallpaper – a favourite haunt of the Potts Point glamour set. Chef Lauren Murdoch produces contemporary Australian cuisine with fresh Mediterranean flavours. The intimate cocktail bar is a perfect place to relax.

KINGS CROSS AND DARLINGHURST Tilbury Hotel ♿▦ $$$$

12–18 Nicholson Street, Woolloomooloo, NSW 2010 ***Tel*** *(02) 9368 1955* ***Map*** *2 D5*

The Tilbury Hotel was refurbished, resulting in its transformation into one of the sexiest pubs in Sydney. The restaurant offers excellent, hearty Italian fare, and the daily menu might include gnocchi with chicken, sausage, borlotti beans and fennel. There's also a café serving wraps, melts and coffees.

KINGS CROSS AND DARLINGHURST Otto 🧒☰♿▦ $$$$$

Area 8, The Wharf, 6 Cowper Wharf Road, Woolloomooloo, NSW 2011 ***Tel*** *(02) 9368 7488* ***Map*** *2 D4*

It's a piece of Melbourne brought to Sydney's waterfront and so appreciated that it often draws celebrities to its handsome surrounds, from Kylie Minogue to footballers. Italian fare is jazzed up with great local ingredients, such as the braised shank of milk-fed veal with Taleggio polenta, broccolini, roasted garlic, olives and rosemary.

MANLY The Manly Wharf Hotel ♿🧒☰▦ $$

Manly Wharf East Esplanade, Manly, NSW 2095 ***Tel*** *(02) 9977 1266*

Not much beats sharing a seafood platter packed with oysters, prawns, salt-and-pepper squid, octopus, scallops and fish, while looking out over Sydney Harbour. Even better, this is a pub you can bring your kids to, keeping them happy with one of the well-priced offerings from the kids' menu.

Key to Price Guide *see p524* **Key to Symbols** *see back cover flap*

MANLY Alhambra

1/54 West Esplanade, Manly, Sydney, NSW 2095 **Tel** *(02) 9976 2975*

Hugely popular on Friday and Saturday nights, when flamenco dancers add to the din, this casual restaurant has views of the Manly wharf. The Moroccan chef cooks Moorish and Spanish food. A meal might begin with tapas, followed by a Moroccan *tagine* of chicken and preserved lemon.

PADDINGTON Paddington Inn

338 Oxford Street, Paddington, NSW 2010 **Tel** *(02) 9380 5913* **Map** *6 D4*

This popular pub in the heart of the Paddington strip is especially busy on weekend afternoons, when hip locals meet over beers and tapas-style plates. Pub classics like bangers and mash and fish and chips are given a restaurant touch. There are also plenty of lighter meals, such as salads and seafood. No bookings.

PADDINGTON Buzo
3 Jersey Road, Woollahra, NSW 2025 **Tel** *(02) 9328 1600* **Map** *6 D4*

Buzo is another piece of evidence showing that bistro food is booming in Sydney. Bookings are essential at this restaurant, just off Oxford Street. A great meaty menu, offering roast lamb, char-grilled steak and even various offal dishes. You'll need to order some side dishes to accompany your main, preventing meals here from being great value.

PADDINGTON Buon Ricordo
108 Boundary Street, Paddington, NSW 2021 **Tel** *(02) 9360 6729* **Map** *5 C2*

Ask a Sydney chef where he goes on nights off and the answer is likely to be this small restaurant, which has been refurbished in a blend of modern and traditional styles. The menu emphasizes Roman and Neapolitan dishes, with a signature dish of fettuccine with parmesan, cream and truffled egg tossed at table. Bookings essential.

PADDINGTON Claude's
10 Oxford Street, Woollahra, NSW 2025 **Tel** *(02) 9331 2325* **Map** *6 D4*

A Sydney icon for over 30 years, this special, intimate restaurant in a converted terrace house seats just 45 people. In season, the set-price menu features fresh Tasmanian truffles. Dishes sound simple on paper but are actually as close to works of art as food can get. Bookings are essential. Ring the doorbell when you arrive.

PADDINGTON Lucio's Italian Restaurant

47 Windsor Street, Paddington, NSW 2021 **Tel** *(02) 9380 5996* **Map** *6 D3*

Lucio's is right in the middle of the area of Sydney densest with art galleries and the walls of the restaurant display a large collection of contemporary Australian artists, such as John Olsen, John Coburn, Gary Shead and Tim Storrier. There's art on the plate, too; the expertly cooked Italian food varies according to what's in season. Vegetarian options.

ROSE BAY Catalina
1 Sutherland Avenue, Rose Bay, NSW 2029 **Tel** *(02) 9371 0555*

A long-established restaurant where the executive chef Paul McMahon concentrates on Italian and Spanish flavours in a contemporary Oz fashion. With floor-to-ceiling glass sliding doors the full length of the building, every table in the minimalist interior has views across Rose Bay.

ROSE BAY Pier
594 New South Head Road, Rose Bay, NSW 2029 **Tel** *(02) 9327 6561*

This restaurant is one long, light room which runs the length of a small pier and juts out into the harbour. Yachts moored in the marina float all around and make you feel like you are on one. Wonderful quality fish is treated with care and cooked to perfection in dishes such as carpaccio of John Dory and roasted barramundi.

SURRY HILLS Café Mint
579 Crown Street, Surry Hills, NSW 2010 **Tel** *(02) 9319 0848*

Mint's precursor, Fez, was a top breakfast venue, often with long queues. This café is tiny and can seem equally crammed. The coffee is excellent and food is fabulous value, particularly at lunch. For a rainbow of dips and pickles, try the large *meze* plate. The Lebanese *fattoush* salad with garlicky, crunchy pitta is great too.

THE ROCKS AND CIRCULAR QUAY Vintage Café on the Rocks

Shop R2, Nurses Walk, The Rocks, NSW 2000 **Tel** *(02) 9252 2055* **Map** *1 B2*

Tucked away in a little cobble-stoned courtyard, in this earliest-settled part of Sydney, this sweet diner is a great place for a quick lunch or afternoon pit stop. Pierce Brosnan and Princess Anne were both spotted here when in town, though it's unknown whether they were dining on sandwiches or Devonshire tea. Excellent, big all-day breakfasts.

THE ROCKS AND CIRCULAR QUAY Heritage Belgium Beer Café
135 Harrington Street, The Rocks, NSW 2000 **Tel** *(02) 9241 1775* **Map** *1 A3*

There are other options listed on the menu but for anyone in the know, mussels provide the only authentic Belgian experience, cooked one of eight ways and served in a pot. Use the shell of the first mussel you eat as a pincher to draw out the rest. Of course, there are Belgian beers on tap and an amazing range of artisan brews.

THE ROCKS AND CIRCULAR QUAY MCA Café
Museum of Contemporary Art, 140 George Street, The Rocks, NSW 2000 **Tel** *(02) 9241 4253* **Map** *1 B2*

A menu full of Sydney favourites like pan-fried kingfish, risotto and twice-baked cheese soufflé, and its fabulous location on the Circular Quay side of the MCA building make this restaurant a good pick. After satisfying sweet teeth with a fabulous dessert, diners head upstairs to absorb the art.

THE ROCKS AND CIRCULAR QUAY harbourkitchen&bar 🧒 ▤ ♿ $$$$

Park Hyatt Sydney, 7 Hickson Road, The Rocks, NSW 2000 ***Tel** (02) 9256 1661* ***Map** 1 B1*

Especially lovely by day, when the bustle of Circular Quay can be fully appreciated and ferries pass close by the wall of windows. Good value lunch and pre-theatre deals are available. Modern high tea is served in the more casual little kitchen, which is a better choice for children.

THE ROCKS AND CIRCULAR QUAY Sailors' Thai ▤ ⛱ $$$$

106 George Street, The Rocks, NSW 2000 ***Tel** (02) 9251 2466* ***Map** 1 B3*

While chef and Thai food expert David Thompson is now earning acclaim at his London restaurant, he continues to oversee the menu at this restaurant in the historic Sailors' Home. The food is far removed from the neighbourhood Thai you'll find in every Sydney suburb. The cheaper canteen, upstairs, is open for lunch and dinner too.

THE ROCKS AND CIRCULAR QUAY The Wharf Restaurant 🧒 ♿ ⛱ $$$$

Sydney Theatre Company, harbour end of Pier 4, Hickson Road, Walsh Bay, NSW 2000 ***Tel** (02) 9250 1761* ***Map** 1 A1*

A wonderful setting in a restored fingerwharf also offers an unusual view of the Harbour Bridge. In the winter truffle season, special dishes such as truffle-infused Brie are added to the menu. Plan to dine after 8pm to avoid the theatre crowd. Disabled access should be arranged in advance.

THE ROCKS AND CIRCULAR QUAY Café Sydney 🧒 ▤ ♿ ♫ ⛱ $$$$$

Level 5, Customs House, 31 Alfred Street, Circular Quay, NSW 2000 ***Tel** (02) 9251 8683* ***Map** 1 B3*

This buzzy restaurant, on the top floor of historic Customs House, has dress circle views. Sitting on the terrace is wonderful, in winter gas heaters keep diners warm and special resin lamps make each table glow. The kitchen's tandoor oven, wood-fired grill, wok and rotisserie turn out a great variety of food. Live jazz on Sunday afternoons.

THE ROCKS AND CIRCULAR QUAY Guillaume at Bennelong ▤ $$$$$

Sydney Opera House, Bennelong Point, NSW 2000 ***Tel** (02) 9241 1999* ***Map** 1 C2*

You can't beat the excitement of dining in the Opera House, especially in such a romantic, elegant space. An emphasis on seafood produces dishes like the signature basil-infused tuna with mustard seed and soy vinaigrette. A cheaper way to taste chef Guillaume Brahimi's marvellous food is by ordering tapas-style dishes from the cocktail bar.

THE ROCKS AND CIRCULAR QUAY Quay ▤ ♿ ⛱ $$$$$

Upper Level, Overseas Passenger Terminal, The Rocks, NSW 2000 ***Tel** (02) 9251 5600* ***Map** 1 B2*

Another spectacular view, and food to match, with star chef Peter Gilmore making magic out of the best and freshest produce and combining ingredients in suprising ways. Try the crisp pressed duck, white turnips, sea scallops, radish and mustard greens and the famous five-textured chocolate cake made from the finest couverture.

THE ROCKS AND CIRCULAR QUAY Rockpool 🧒 ♿ $$$$$

107 George Street, The Rocks, NSW 2000 ***Tel** (02) 9252 1888* ***Map** 1 B3*

Neil Perry opened his Sydney fine-dining institution in 1989 and invented Modern Australian cuisine with his fusion of European and Asian techniques and flavours. Choose between eight-course tasting menus and a set four-course menu with choices such as Muscoby dubk pastrami or Burrawong chicken.

THE ROCKS AND CIRCULAR QUAY Yoshii $$$$$

115 Harrington Street, The Rocks, NSW 2000 ***Tel** (02) 9247 2566* ***Map** 1 A3*

Ryuichi Yoshii is one of Sydney's top sushi chefs and the author of a sushi cookbook. His restaurant serves dinner in the *kaiseki* style, a series of unique small dishes that gradually warm the stomach like a small stone (a Japanese precursor to the hot water bottle). Though pricey, this is excellent value. Lunchtime bento boxes are cheaper.

WATSON'S BAY Doyles on the Beach 🧒 ♿ ⛱ $$$$

11 Marine Parade, Watson's Bay ***Tel** (02) 9337 2007* ***Map** 1 C2*

Five generations on, the Doyles are still serving great fish and chips. Eat at a table outside and admire the stunning view of the CBD across the harbour. The menu offers an array of fish and seafood dishes, including wild barramundi fillets and live lobster mornay. Open daily. There are two more casual eateries at Watson's Bay wharf and Fish Markets.

THE BLUE MOUNTAINS AND BEYOND

BYRON BAY Byron Beach Café ⛱ $$$

Clarke's Beach, Lawson St, Byron Bay NSW 2481 ***Tel** (02) 6685 8400*

For the ultimate relaxed dining experience, grab a table for breakfast, lunch or dinner on the deck of this stylishly renovated beach-front café. Quality café fare in a bright and breezy setting with ocean and mountain views.
If you want to eat on the beach, takeaway options are also available from the kiosk.

COFFS HARBOUR Maria's Italian Restaurant 🧒 ♿ ⬈ ▤ ⛱ $$

368 Harbour Drive, Coffs Harbour, NSW 2450 ***Tel** (02) 6651 3000*

It has been around for a decade and is quite a local icon, but there's something new to discover each time you dine at Maria's. The chefs are flexible and will prepare almost anything, with particular attention paid to food allergies. This is basic, quality Italian food, and the pizzas are the best in town.

Key to Price Guide *see p524* **Key to Symbols** *see back cover flap*

COFFS HARBOUR Shearwater 🚼♿🌳🍸 [$][$][$]

321 Harbour Drive, Coffs Harbour, NSW 2450 ***Tel*** *(02) 6651 6053*

Enjoy fresh local seafood in the relaxed atmosphere of this great restaurant in the heart of Coffs Harbour looking out over Coffs Creek. The Shearwater is open for breakfast, lunch and dinner, seven days a week, and is suitable for a quick working lunch or a leisurely dinner.

EAST GOSFORD Caroline Bay Brasserie 🌳▤♿🍸 [$][$]

36 Webb Street, Gosford East, NSW 2250 ***Tel*** *(02) 4324 8099*

Tasty, fuss-free food is the order of the day at Caroline Bay Brasserie. Open for breakfast, lunch and morning and afternoon teas, it's the place to go to indulge in a classic Devonshire tea. Lunches include a range of salads, burgers, melts and more, and the picturesque grounds are simply stunning.

GOSFORD Upper Deck ▤🌳 [$][$][$]

61 Masons Parade, Gosford, NSW 2250 ***Tel*** *(02) 4324 6705*

Perfectly positioned with breathtaking views over the water, Upper Deck has been serving the locals of Gosford for many years now. Specializing in oysters and steak cooked to perfection, the restaurant offers great value set menus and a private dining room for special intimate gatherings.

JUNEE Loftus on Humphreys 🚼♿🍸▤ [$][$][$]

6 Humphreys Street, Junee, NSW 2663 ***Tel*** *(02) 6929 2555*

Enjoy views of the town and the railway from this café located in an historic 1896 building. Antique furniture and crisp white linen enhance the traditional feel. Hearty dishes include chicken stuffed with brie or smoked salmon and baby spinach with a pesto cream sauce.

KATOOMBA Swiss Cottage ☒🌳▤♿🍸 [$][$][$]

132 Lurline Street, Katoomba, NSW 2780 ***Tel*** *(02) 4782 2281*

Remember to visit the bank before dining at the Swiss Cottage as they only accept cash, but don't let that keep you away from this culinary gem! Housed in a cottage built in 1898, the Swiss Cottage serves what some call the best fondue in Australia as well as a sumptuous Lindt hot chocolate in a mug.

KATOOMBA The Rooster 🌳♿🍸 [$][$][$][$]

48 Meriwa Street, Katoomba, NSW 2780 ***Tel*** *(02) 4782 1206*

Sit near the fireplace in this gorgeous federation-style building and experience utterly delicious French cuisine. The view from the clifftops overlooking the Jamison Valley is stunning, but it's near impossible to see anything at night, so outside dining is offered only during the day.

KATOOMBA Darley's ♿▤🍸 [$][$][$][$][$]

Lilianfels, Lilianfels Avenue, Katoomba, NSW 2780 ***Tel*** *(02) 4780 1200*

The building housing this beautiful restaurant is over a century old. Well known for serving local venison, Darley's also boasts an enviable wine list. Dine on the balcony with magnificent views or sit indoors to experience the ambience of open fireplaces.

KINGSCLIFF Fins 🚼▤♿🍸 [$][$][$][$]

5–6 Bells Blvd, Salt Village, South Kingscliff, NSW 2487 ***Tel*** *(02) 6674 4833*

Fins is a unique place where only the freshest produce is used – often from the chef's own garden – and the fish is line-caught where possible, sometimes only hours before eating. Fins also has one of the most extensive wine lists to be found, including local varieties and overseas gems.

LAKE MACQUARIE Milano's On The Lake 🚼♿▤🍸 [$][$][$][$]

89 Soldier's Road, Pelican, NSW 2281 ***Tel*** *(02) 4972 0550*

The chef at this innovative lakeside restaurant is happy to adapt dishes to suit vegetarian diners. Located in a boutique marina with a veranda that sits out over the water, it is a great place to relax and watch the sun setting over the lake.

LENNOX HEAD Mi Thai Restaurant 🌳♿🍸 [$][$]

76 Ballina Street, Lennox Head, NSW 2478 ***Tel*** *(02) 6687 5820*

Serving a mixture of modern and classic Asian cuisine in an area known to many as the "Surf Capital of the Far North Coast", this intimate restaurant is a favourite with locals after a quick, satisfying meal. And they return again and again for the changing daily specials and mouthwatering Choo Chee Curry.

LEURA Silks Brasserie 🚼▤♿ [$][$][$][$]

128 "The Mall", Leura, NSW 2780 ***Tel*** *(02) 4784 2534*

It's refreshing to find a fine dining restaurant that welcomes children – Silk's even provides coloured pencils for kids to use on the table-top butcher's paper. Adults, meanwhile, will enjoy the delicious dishes and comprehensive wine list. Do not leave the region without experiencing this Leura legend.

MCGRATH'S HILL Valentino's Italian Restaurant 🚼♿▤♿ [$][$][$]

11 Groves Avenue McGrath's Hill NSW 2756 ***Tel*** *(02) 4577 9797*

Valentino's serves Italy up on a plate. The menu at this excellent restaurant is a combination of traditional Italian food with contemporary flair using nothing but the freshest seasonal produce, which is sourced locally where possible. There are plenty of pasta and meat choices on offer, but it is the seafood that is a standout. Closed Sundays and Mondays.

MEGALONG VALLEY Megalong Valley Tea Rooms

Megalong Road, Megalong Valley, NSW 2785 **Tel** *(02) 4787 9181*

Those looking for a place where the food is home-made need go no further than the Megalong Valley Tea Rooms. There's no need to rush here – linger over a classic morning tea with scones or stop for one of their hearty pies for lunch and enjoy the idyllic beauty of the surrounding Megalong Valley.

NELSON BAY Zest Restaurant

16 Stockton Street, Nelson Bay, NSW 2315 **Tel** *(02) 4984 2211*

In an area renowned for quality seafood restaurants, the award-winning Zest goes far beyond the rest. The walls feature a stunning display of local artworks, while the menu offers an equally stunning selection of European-inspired dishes with local seafood, meat and game on offer.

NEWCASTLE Sesame's A Taste Of Asia

52 Glebe Road, The Junction, Newcastle, NSW 2291 **Tel** *(02) 4969 2033*

Dining at this gem is a culinary journey through southeast Asia. Cambodian, Thai, Vietnamese and Malaysian cuisine grace the menu at Sesame's, and there is a separate vegan/vegetarian menu too. Don't miss their signature twice-cooked duck.

NEWCASTLE Customs House Hotel

1 Bond Street, Newcastle, NSW 2300 **Tel** *(02) 4925 2585*

Want to know where to find great food accompanied by pub-priced drinks? Right here. From scallops in French brandy and butter sauce to a hearty grain-fed beef fillet with potato mash and red wine jus, there's a dish to suit your appetite and budget.

NEWCASTLE Scratchley's On The Wharf

200 Wharf Road, Newcastle, NSW 2300 **Tel** *(02) 4929 1111*

Scratchley's On The Wharf proudly boasts eco-friendly architecture and utilizes environmentally-friendly practices wherever possible. This is a terrific place to eat before attending the nearby cinema, as the friendly, helpful staff will ensure you're in and out before the previews begin.

NEWCASTLE Nor' East

150 Wharf Road, Newcastle, NSW 2300 **Tel** *(02) 4929 6444*

This award-winning restaurant has a light-filled, open-plan dining room overlooking Newcastle Harbour. The brasserie-style menu features seafood, organic meat and handmade pasta; the use of fresh, seasonal produce means that the menu changes every few days. Closed for dinner on Sundays.

POKOLBIN San Martino Restaurant

Hunter Resort, Hermitage Road, Pokolbin NSW 2320 **Tel** *(02) 4998 7777*

San Martino, or Saint Martin, is the patron saint of churchgoers, wine-makers and the protector of all drinkers. And considering that this restaurant sits alongside the brewery and winery at the Hunter Resort, that's a good thing! A must for fans of innovative modern Australian cuisine.

POKOLBIN Esca Bimbadgen

Bimbadgen Estate, 790 McDonald's Road, Pokolbin, NSW 2320 **Tel** *(02) 4998 4666*

A part of the respected Bimbadgen Estate Winery, Esca Bimbadgen is positioned overlooking the superb views of the Estate's vineyards. The dessert-tasting plate, served with a glass of botrytis semillon, is great value. Be sure to book at this popular eatery to avoid disappointment.

POKOLBIN Muse Restaurant And Café Hungerford Hill

1 Broke Road Pokolbin NSW 2320 **Tel** *(02) 4998 6777*

Winner of the 2010 Best Contemporary Australian Restaurant award, this classy venue has undergone renovations, producing an entrance and outside dining area on the eastern terrace. Catering for all tastes, Muse has separate children's and vegetarian menus, as well as a tempting tasting menu.

POKOLBIN Restaurant Sanctuary

Peppers Guesthouse, Hunter Valley, Ekerts Road, Pokolbin, NSW 2320 **Tel** *(02) 4993 8999*

A favourite of gourmets and critics alike, the Sanctuary blends fine dining with local produce – indeed, the herbs are grown in the guesthouse's garden! Staff advise which wines best suit your meal, and considering the award-winning wine list, you're in for a treat. Bookings essential.

POKOLBIN Robert's Restaurant

Halls Road Pokolbin, NSW 2325 **Tel** *(02) 4998 7330*

Set in an early settler's slab cottage, Robert's at Pepper Tree doesn't just serve fine food, it delivers a complete gastronomical experience. The delicious French-inspired dishes from the talented owner/chef are carefully matched with complementary wines, ensuring that at Robert's, you won't be disappointed.

PORT STEPHENS Merretts at Peppers Anchorage

Corlette Point Road, Corlette, NSW 2315 **Tel** *(02) 4984 2555*

This renowned restaurant continues to serve up top quality meals boasting French, Mediterranean and Asian influences. Dining here is an utterly decadent experience, and desserts like the ravioli of crème brûlée, frangelico ice cream and jelly with granita – are to die for.

SINGLETON Fusions

Mid City Motor Inn, 180 John Street, Singleton, NSW 2330 **Tel** *(02) 6572 2011*

Comfortable, bright purple chairs complement the decor at this intimate restaurant which is part of the Best Western hotel. Singleton, known largely for its army base, is also home to several vineyards, and the produce of many is offered here. As well as serving daily meals, Fusions will also arrange packed lunches for patrons to take with them.

SOLDIERS POINT The Point Restaurant

Sunset Blvd, Soldiers Point, NSW 2317 **Tel** *(02) 4984 7111*

This waterfront restaurant offers specials that vary according to the freshest catch and might include dishes like wok-tossed squid and scallops with a Vietnamese soy glaze. Even if you're out on a boat, you needn't miss out. The Point will prepare a delicious platter for you to enjoy aboard your vessel.

WAGGA WAGGA Indian Tavern Tandoori Restaurant

81 Peter Street, Wagga Wagga, NSW 2650 **Tel** *(02) 6921 3121*

The owners boast that patrons can "visit India in an hour" with their menu, and they're right. The restaurant's cuisine originates from all regions of India, and ranges in spiciness from super-hot to mild. The butter chicken flavoured with cashew nut butter remains a favourite with locals. Fully licensed and BYOB.

THE SOUTH COAST AND SNOWY MOUNTAINS

BATEMANS BAY Starfish Deli

Shop 1 Promenade Plaza, Clyde Street, NSW 2536 **Tel** *(02) 4472 4880*

This upmarket bistro and function centre, next to a boatshed and overlooking the Clyde River, offers a fine Mod Oz menu. It also serves up excellent wood-fired pizzas, local seafood and Clyde River oysters. It is open for breakfast, lunch and dinner and if you're lucky enough to secure an outside table, you might spy a dolphin cruising past.

BATEMANS BAY On the Pier

Old Punt Road, NSW 2536 **Tel** *(02) 4472 6405*

If you fancy seafood with a waterside view for lunch or dinner, and who could resist after a few hours in Bateman's Bay, then On the Pier is a prize catch. They offer dishes such as char-grilled tuna with spiced lentil and roast pepper salad and minted yoghurt.

BERMAGUI Salt Water at Bermagui

59 Lamont Street, NSW 2546 **Tel** *(02) 6493 4328*

You can enjoy fresh seafood straight off the trawlers in the pleasant and comfortable restaurant on the wharf, or simply grab takeaway fish and chips and enjoy them on the waterfront of Bermagui Harbour, now famous as the setting for the Billy Connelly and Judy Davis movie, *The Man Who Sued God*.

BERRIMA Eschalot

24 Old Pacific Highway, NSW 2546 **Tel** *(02) 4877 1977*

Located in the centre of historic Berrima village, Eschalot occupies an 1840s heritage sandstone building. The fine contemporary cuisine with European influences includes signature dishes such as soufflé, duck and crème brûlée. Dine on the covered terrace overlooking the garden in summer and enjoy pre-dinner drinks by the open fire in winter.

BOWRAL Briar's Inn

653 Moss Vale Road, NSW 1734 **Tel** *(02) 4868 3566*

This Georgian, wisteria-draped inn has been sustaining travellers since 1845, although nowadays it also offers boutique beers on tap and a generous wine list. You can cook your own steak, chicken or fish on the barbecue. Or tuck into something hearty like lamb shanks with tomato and onion. There is also a kid's menu and playground.

EDEN Wheelhouse Restaurant

Main Wharf, NSW 2551 **Tel** *(02) 6496 3392*

Seafood is all the rage at this award-winning restaurant on the wharf overlooking Eden Harbour. It's popular with the locals as much for the fact that it is reasonably priced as for its generous servings of fresh local seafood. The wine list is quite acceptable and it's a pleasant venue with friendly service.

GOULBURN The Fireside Inn Restaurant

23 Market Street, NSW 2580 **Tel** *(02) 4821 2727*

Generous portions of contemporary Australian fare are served up at this cosy restaurant overlooking Belmore Park in the centre of Goulburn. The Fireside occupies a 1930s Tudor-style building and the interior is decorated in classic, old English style. A large, open fire welcomes guests during the winter months. Closed on Mondays.

KIAMA Waves at the Beach

87 Manning Street, NSW 2533 **Tel** *(02) 4232 2777*

Any closer to the beach and you would be eating lunch or dinner on the sand. Waves at the Beach won the 2007 Illawarra Best Catering and Restaurant award. Its delicious variety of menu selections includes seafood, chicken, beef and vegetarian fare, while the floor-to-ceiling glass makes the most of the beach location.

MITTAGONG Esco Pazzo
84 Main St, NSW 2575 **Tel** *(02) 4872 2400*

A taste of Italy in the Southern Highlands. Italian-born and trained chef Emilio Picchio serves up stone-fired pizzas, freshly made pastas and seafood and meat dishes cooked in authentic Roman style. Dine in the courtyard in summer or ask for a table by the large windows overlooking the gardens. Closed on Mondays.

MOLLYMOOK Rick Stein at Bannister's
191 Michell Parade, NSW 2539 **Tel** *(02) 4455 3044*

A classy and award-winning resort restaurant with sweeping ocean views from every table. The Mod Oz menu changes with the seasons but can always be relied on to offer mouthwatering dishes, and delicious desserts are prepared by a French chocolatier chef – all overseen by the owner, English celebrity seafood chef Rick Stein.

NAROOMA Quarterdeck Café
Riverside Drive, NSW 2546 **Tel** *(02) 4476 2723*

Well known as a child-friendly local café overlooking Wagonga Inlet, the Quarterdeck serves up quick, cheap seafood favourites such as fish and chips, salt and chilli squid, bouillabaisse and local Narooma oysters. They are open for breakfast, lunch and dinner.

SNOWY MOUNTAINS The Knickerbocker Restaurant
Riverside Cabins, Thredbo Alpine Village, NSW 2625 **Tel** *(02) 6457 6844*

Hearty cuisine, an extensive, award-winning wine list, a large cocktail bar, a relaxed atmosphere and views over the Thredbo River and snow-capped mountains make for a fine night's dining. The Knickerbocker prides itself on serving up European mountain food for active adventure seekers.

SNOWY MOUNTAINS Cuisine on Lake Crackenback
Lake Crackenback, Alpine Way via Jindabyne, NSW 2627 **Tel** *(02) 6451 3000, 1800 024 524*

The fine cuisine at this resort restaurant comes with amazing views over the lake and nearby hills. There is a kid's menu, but for adults the options are seasonal with an emphasis on local produce such as smoked mountain trout and poached rabbit. It is also open for a buffet breakfast, and picnic and bushwalking hampers can be arranged.

SOUTHERN HIGHLANDS Blue Cockerel Café/Restaurant
95 Hume Highway, Mittagong, NSW 2575 **Tel** *(02) 4872 1677*

This establishment specializes in locally sourced produce. Lunches are casual, but for dinner the Mod Oz cuisine is served in a cosy but more formal atmosphere, with white linen table settings, wood fire and attentive professional service. Open for breakfast, lunch and dinner, except Monday and Tuesday.

SOUTHERN HIGHLANDS Eling Forest Winery Stones Restaurant
Hume Highway, Sutton Forest, NSW 2577 **Tel** *(02) 4878 9499*

This restaurant, just south of Berrima, has already won a regional award for its Italian-influenced menu, with an occasional Asian twist. The wine list features their own vintage as well as other Southern Highlands cool climate wines. There is a sunny courtyard and reasonably priced kid's menu.

SOUTHERN HIGHLANDS Horderns
Hordern's Road, Bowral, NSW 2576 **Tel** *(02) 4861 1522*

Modern Australian food with European and Asian influences is served in this elegant country hotel with two dining rooms, high-backed chairs and sumptuous fabrics. Bookings are advised and accommodation is also available. The restaurant offers an extensive wine list and views out over the lovely garden.

ULLADULLA Carmelo Italian Restaurant
Shop 2, 10 Watson Street, NSW 2539 **Tel** *(02) 4454 1443*

Settle down at an outside table at this casual restaurant-cum-café near the harbour and enjoy the water views and straightforward Italian seafood cuisine, including lobsters, seafood platters and pastas. Takeaway food is also an option if you want to sit by the waterfront, and it is child friendly. Closed Tuesdays.

WOLLONGONG Caveau
122–124 Keira Street, NSW 2500 **Tel** *(02) 4226 4855*

This modern French restaurant in a heritage building across the road from Lorenzo's offers seasonal produce and formal dining. The co-owner and chef, Peter Sheppard, hails from one of Sydney's finest restaurants, Banc. Rated the fourth best regional restaurant in NSW by *Gourmet Traveller*.

WOLLONGONG Lorenzo's Diner
119 Keira Street, NSW 2500 **Tel** *(02) 4229 5633*

This award-winning and well-priced restaurant (regarded by many as one of the best on the south coast) incorporates Asian produce into modern Italian cuisine. The warm confit of duck with steamed *gai laan* (chinese broccoli) and baby beetroot is worth trying. The setting is smart-casual with friendly waiters.

WOMBARRA Black Duck Restaurant
578 Lawrence Hargrave Drive, NSW 2515 **Tel** *(02) 4267 2139*

A hidden gem, this restaurant has revitalized the lounge of the local bowling club, which enjoys spectacular views over the ocean. The friendly service has made it popular with locals, who can duck into the bar next door to replenish their glass. Great bistro food in a retro atmosphere.

Key to Price Guide *see p524* **Key to Symbols** *see back cover flap*

CANBERRA AND ACT

CANBERRA Café Barocca $$

Shop 6, 60 Marcus Clarke St, ACT 2601 **Tel** *(02) 6248 0253*

This spacious venue tucked away down a quiet side road is a great central dining option. By day the Barocca languishes as a casual café but at night it transforms into a smart restaurant and bar. Mediterranean and modern Australian fare feature on the extensive menu and wooden booths make for a cosy dining experience. Closed on Sundays.

CANBERRA The Republic $$

20 Allara Street, Canberra City, ACT 2600 **Tel** *(02) 6247 1717*

The atmosphere here is noisy and the decor colourful and inviting. The Modern Australian menu is light, elegant and interesting, often with an emphasis on fresh seafood. It is open for breakfast and lunch only, and the wine list is consistently praised. A well-deserving Canberra favourite. It is closed on weekends.

CANBERRA Ruby Chinese Restaurant $$

Ground Floor, 18-20 Wooley Street, Dickson, ACT 2602 **Tel** *(02) 6249 8849*

Ruby's has a fascinating reputation as being the place where spies of all nationalities rendezvous while enjoying honey prawns and classic Australian Chinese restaurant decor. It is also a favourite with visiting celebrities. Specializing in live seafood, it is in the heart of Canberra's only "Chinatown" street.

CANBERRA Timmy's Kitchen $$

Manuka Village Centre, Furneaux Street, Manuka, ACT 2603 **Tel** *(02) 6295 6537*

This Chinese and Malaysian restaurant and takeaway has moved into these large premises in Manuka. It is a true Canberra experience and popular with the locals, who love its good cheap Southeast Asian food and speedy service. The Malaysian menu items are particularly recommended, including the curry laksas.

CANBERRA Artespresso $$$

31 Giles Street, Kingston, ACT 2600 **Tel** *(02) 6295 8055*

Critics were enthusiastic when they heard that former members of Canberra's Atlantic and Sydney's Arena restaurants were setting up shop in Kingston, and they have not been disappointed. The menu and atmosphere is easygoing brasserie style, with bare floorboards and temporary artworks adorning the walls.

CANBERRA Benchmark Wine Bar $$$

65 Northbourne Avenue, ACT 2600 **Tel** *(02) 6262 6522*

If you love your wine, don't miss Benchmark, which has more than 100 wines by the glass and another 600 bottles lurking in the cellar. This lively venue, where the service is friendly without being intrusive, is perfect for business meetings and quiet civilized conversations. It offers a stylish atmosphere and a European bistro menu.

CANBERRA The Chairman and Yip $$$

108 Bunda Street, Canberra City, ACT 2601 **Tel** *(02) 6248 7109*

This Asian restaurant has all the local food critics raving. Not to mention international scribes from the likes of *Gourmet Traveller*. Its wine list is recommended, the service is friendly and professional, and the menu is light and inventive. How does char-grilled mushroom with coriander and cashew pesto sound?

CANBERRA The High Court Café $$$

High Court of Australia, Parkes Place, Parkes, ACT 2600 **Tel** *(02) 6270 6828*

Situated in the imposing glass edifice of the High Court of Australia (the highest court in the land), this restaurant serves up elegant breakfasts and light lunches, such as foccacias and salads, not to mention panoramic views of Lake Burley Griffin. Canberra's regional wines feature in the wine list. It is closed on weekends.

CANBERRA Hill Station Restaurant $$$

51 Sheppard Street, Hume, ACT 2620 **Tel** *(02) 6260 1393*

This once isolated 1909 homestead and sheep farm has been converted into a charming restaurant and function centre with pleasant formal gardens and period decor and furnishings. It serves sophisticated and award-winning country cuisine. Book ahead as it is only open Friday and Saturday night.

CANBERRA The Lobby Restaurant $$$

King George Terrace, Parkes, ACT 2600 **Tel** *(02) 6273 1563*

Set within the National Rose Gardens opposite old Parliament House, The Lobby has long been a favourite with politicians, journalists and diplomats. The cuisine is seasonal Mod Oz and the setting smart modern with discreet seating and wraparound windows. Choose from a quality set menu or dine à la carte.

CANBERRA Tosolini's $$$

Baileys Corner, Cnr London Circuit and East Row, Canberra City, ACT 2600 **Tel** *(02) 6247 4317*

Open for breakfast, lunch and dinner, this cosy licensed Canberra institution is well known as a place to be seen. The food is inexpensive, and some say the coffee is the best in town, but the service gets mixed reviews, although they have been known to provide blankets for those mad enough to dine alfresco in winter.

CANBERRA Water's Edge $$$

40 Parkes Place, Parkes, ACT 2600 **Tel** *(02) 6273 5066*

Subdued lighting and a stylish setting, sweeping views across Lake Burley Griffin, and an established reputation for excellent cuisine and professional service are your guarantee of a fine dining experience. The menu (ambitious modern European) is complemented by the wine list's quality French, Italian and Australian options.

CANBERRA Axis Restaurant $$$$

National Museum of Australia, Acton Peninsula, Acton, ACT 2601 **Tel** *(02) 6208 5176*

Open for breakfast, lunch and dinner, this award-winning and upmarket restaurant is one of three cafés and restaurants located in the National Museum. It has spectacular views over Lake Burley Griffin, a seasonal Mediterranean and Asian-inspired menu and grill, and a terrific boutique wine list. Book ahead.

CANBERRA The Boat House by the Lake $$$$

Grevillea Park, Menindee Drive, Barton, ACT 2600 **Tel** *(02) 6273 5500*

Situated on the northern edge of Lake Burley Griffin, this restaurant is prized for its views of Canberra's main attractions. Aim for lunch and be sure to book an outside table if the weather is fine. The menu is Mod Oz with limited (but quality) options, such as cider-glazed pork loin, with apple and Szechuan pepper relish.

TORRENS Pistachio Dining at Torrens $$$

3A Torrens Place, Torrens, ACT 2607 **Tel** *(02) 6286 2966*

The menu at this restaurant in Woden Valley, Torrens, is a delightful ode to freshness and simplicity, and dishes such as lamb rump with kipfler potatoes, pea purée, glazed carrots and rosemary sauce are packed full of flavour. On Tuesday evenings there's a great value "all-you-can-eat" family buffet.

BRISBANE

ALBION Breakfast Creek Hotel $$

2 Kingsford Smith Drive, QLD 4010 **Tel** *(07) 3262 5988*

This famous Brisbane icon is noted for its steaks. Part of the experience is to choose your own steak before it is cooked. A Queensland favourite since its construction in 1889, it is situated a short drive from the city, en route to the airport. The menu also offers chicken and fish dishes.

BULIMBA Riverbend Books & Teahouse $$

193 Oxford Street, QLD 4171 **Tel** *(07) 3399 6788*

This is a small bookshop restaurant with outdoor dining, perfect for a warm Brisbane night or a sunny day. Now featuring a full sushi menu and offering meals for vegetarians, this eating place is in the trendy Oxford Street district of Bulimba. It is a ten-minute walk past shops, cinemas and galleries to the CityCat.

BULIMBA Oxford 152 $$$

152 Oxford Street, 4171 **Tel** *(07) 3899 2026*

The uniqueness of this dining experience comes from the microbrewery. Experiment with Bee-Sting seasonal honey beer or an aromatic lager. The Oxford Brewing Co. was the most awarded small brewery at the Australian International Beer Awards. The Oxford Premium Battered Barramundi is featured on the modern menu.

CAMP HILL Restaurant Rapide $$$

Shop 1/4 Martha Street, QLD 4152 **Tel** *(07) 3843 5755*

This small suburban restaurant is hidden away in a sidewalk of Camphill but worth the ten-minute drive out of the city. This bistro run by chef Paul McGivern and his wife Prue boasts modern Australian food and inspirational variations to Italian favourites, including grilled whitefish with sweet corn and crab pancake.

CITY CENTRE Gilhooley's Irish Pub and Restaurant $$

Cnr Albert & Charlotte Streets, QLD 4000 **Tel** *(07) 3229 0672*

This is Brisbane's original Irish restaurant, a great spot in the city for food and entertainment. The menu offers succulent steaks, traditional beef and Guiness, or braised steak served with salad and chips and a range of other Australian and Irish meals. A friendly place to sit with a drink while the Irish musicians rehearse.

CITY CENTRE Vespa $$

Shop 2, 148 Merthya Road, New Farm, QLD 4005 **Tel** *(07) 3358 4100*

This hip pizzeria serves mouthwatering wood-fired pizzas that are crisp and light and drip with mozzarella. There are also plenty of vegetarian and gluten-free options for those with special dietary requirements. Don't forget to leave room for dessert. Takeaway available.

CITY CENTRE Custom's House $$$

399 Queen Street, QLD 4001 **Tel** *(07) 3365 8921*

Custom's House, a heritage icon in Brisbane situated close to the CBD operates a fully licensed restaurant. Alfresco dining is also available, overlooking the river and the Story Bridge. Excellent innovative international cuisine, fantastic river views and friendly professional service. The wine list has quality wines at competitive prices.

Key to Price Guide *see p524* **Key to Symbols** *see back cover flap*

CITY CENTRE Fix Bar and Restaurant

*40 Edward Street, Port Office, QLD 4000 **Tel** (07) 3210 6016*

Located in an old post office building, Fix offers world-class dining in a sophisticated 19th-century setting. The contemporary Australian menu emphasises seafood and steak. Try the Cape Grim ribeye fillet served with potato and onion rosti, asparagus and a Bordelaise sauce or sample wines at the bar along with a range of tapas and pizzas. Closed on Sundays.

CITY CENTRE Il Centro Restaurant and Bar

*Eagle Street Pier, QLD 4000 **Tel** (07) 3221 6090*

Located at the Eagle Street Pier in the city, this restaurant has photographic views of the Brisbane River and Story Bridge. The menu is modern Italian but the flavours are unique to Queensland – fresh seafood, prime cuts of meat, tropical fruit, seasonal vegetables and delicate garden herbs. Try the sandcrab lasagne and the vanilla pannacotta.

CITY CENTRE Moda

*12 Edward Street, QLD 4000 **Tel** (07) 3221 7655*

Modern elegance and fine cuisine is what's on offer at this restaurant located in the heart of Brisbane. To begin try the avocado and crab *rillette*. For a main meal, the suckling piglet or Darling Downs Wagyu beef sirloin. To finish experience the chocolate and vanilla bean ice cream.

CITY CENTRE Cha Cha Char

*Shop 5 Eagle Street Pier Eagle Street, QLD 4000 **Tel** (07) 3211 9944*

Specializing in Wagyu grain- and grass-fed beef, this restaurant is in a stunning location with sweeping views of the Brisbane River. It features a separate bar and cocktail area. Try the roasted duck, the fish of the day or the extensive vegetarian menu, while for dessert, chocolate tart.

CITY CENTRE E'cco Bistro

*100 Boundary Street (cnr Adelaide Street), QLD 4000 **Tel** (07) 3831 8344*

This award-winning bistro is simple and welcoming. Run by chef Phillip Johnson, it boasts a menu based on fresh seasonal food "that hasn't been fussed over". Main courses include porcini-dusted lamb loin with potato gnocchi or Sichuan spiced duck breast with Asian greens. Give in to the poached gooseberry and almond biscotti for dessert.

CITY CENTRE Marco Polo

*Level 2 Treasury Casino Queen Street, QLD 4000 **Tel** (07) 3306 8744*

This heritage restaurant in the elegantly appointed riverscape dining room of the Conrad Treasury has an opulent and sophisticated atmosphere. Themed around Marco Polo's journey, the decor and menu reflects his travels. Choose from lamb, duck, chicken or seafood dishes on a sumptious menu. What about pistachio ice cream to finish?

CITY CENTRE Restaurant Two

*2 Edward Street, QLD 4000 **Tel** (07) 3210 0600*

With a lovely location overlooking the Botanic Gardens in the heritage-listed Old Mineral House, this long-serving restaurant is known for its elegant and fine-flavoured menu. Specialities include seared scallops with green tea noodles, and rich wagyu beef with pumpkin and ginger mash. The bar is stocked with fine wines.

CITY CENTRE Urbane

*181 Mary Street, QLD 4000 **Tel** (07) 3229 2271*

Already renowned as a fine restaurant, Urbane's reputation has been elevated to a critic's favourite under head chef Kym Machin. The innovative concept behind Urbane's menu is aimed at allowing diners to experience more flavours by having several smaller dishes. For instance, the first two courses are half the size of a regular entrée.

COOPAROO The Curry Hut

*Cnr Cavendish Road & Holdsworth Street, QLD 4151 **Tel** (07) 3397 5545*

A long established favourite in Coorparoo, this authentic Indian restaurant offers superb butter chicken and an excellent beef vindaloo. It is a 12-minute drive from the city to find this gem, hidden behind the main shopping complex, but it is worth it. The atmosphere is inviting and subdued with soft candle lighting.

COOPAROO Belesis

*198 Old Cleveland Road, QLD 4158 **Tel** (07) 3324 2446*

This fabulous Mediterranean café in Cooparoo is worth the short drive out of the city. The meals are crafted with fresh ingredients and include seafood pastas, roasted vegetables, ravioli and a rack of lamb with rosemary worthy of the wait. Desserts include a range of Greek cakes and pastries. Great coffee and an intimate atmosphere for a liqueur.

EAST BRISBANE Green Papaya Vietnamese Restaurant

*898 Stanley Street, QLD 4169 **Tel** (07) 3217 3599*

A short drive out of the city, this authentic North Vietnamese restaurant is run by Lien Yeomans. The emphasis in Lien's cooking is on the perfect balance of flavours. Dishes include turmeric fish, grilled lemon myrtle prawns and curried duck Vietnamese style. For a side dish try a lotus salad and to finish, the black rice pudding or a sorbet.

FORTITUDE VALLEY Asian Fusion

*149 Wickham Street, QLD 4006 **Tel** (07) 3852 1144*

Specializing in Vietnamese and Chinese dishes, Asian Fusion cooks great Asian meals with fresh local ingredients while you wait, or sit down and enjoy. The menu includes such favourites as chicken and cashew or barbecue pork noodle dishes. Vietnamese rice paper rolls are made in the kitchen.

MILTON La Dolce Vita
20 Park Road Savoir Faire, QLD 4064 **Tel** *(07) 3368 1191*

Sit out in the morning sun or under the Brisbane stars on a warm night and smell the Italian food of La Dolce Vita. Feel the buzzy atmosphere of busy Park Road while you relax for breakfast, lunch or dinner and enjoy authentic pastas, coffee, pastries, fresh salads, cakes and ice creams.

MILTON Drift Café
330 Coronation Drive, QLD 4064 **Tel** *(07) 3368 1866*

Located on the riverbank, this dining experience is unique. Eating at Drift gives the sensation of dining on a cruise ship. An à la carte menu offers steamed Moreton Bay bugs and rosemary-scented prawns, or stay with the set menu for a choice of steak, seafood, chicken or veal. For dessert try the citrus and passionfruit torte.

MOUNT COOT-THA Kuta Café
Sir Samuel Griffith Drive, QLD 4066 **Tel** *(07) 3369 9922*

Situated adjacent to Mount Coot-tha Lookout, Kuta Café offers a varied menu as well as an array of self-select food complemented by a wide choice of coffees and alcoholic beverages. This small café is open from 7am to 11pm with indoor and outdoor dining with excellent views of Brisbane and the surrounding countryside.

NEW FARM The Purple Olive
79 James Street, QLD 4005 **Tel** *(07) 3254 0097*

This Mediterranean-style restaurant is situated in trendy James Street, close to shops, galleries and cinemas. Having all the charms of the classic alfresco cafés of Europe, this popular BYO captures the modern gourmet dining experience. The menu offers the authentic flavours of southern Europe, while catering to modern Australian tastes.

PADDINGTON Kookaburra Café
280 Given Terrace, QLD 4064 **Tel** *(07) 3369 2400*

This is a popular Brisbane spot to meet friends. It is famous for its pizzas, which include the spicy chicken or chicken satay, the gorgonzola special, and the Aussie with sizzling bacon, egg and onion. A favourite pasta dish is the Ravioli Alaskan – ricotta-filled ravioli with a delicious wine sauce and smoked salmon.

RED HILL Olivetto's
5 Enoggera Terrace, QLD 4059 **Tel** *(07) 3369 0610*

Internationally acclaimed chef Paul Newsham runs the kitchen at this Red Hill favourite and presents a unique menu. For a main meal with a difference, try the Bo-Kapp, a South-African chicken and prawn curry. Desserts include baked apple tart with gingerbread ice cream.

SOUTH BRISBANE Dell' Ugo Southbank
Shop 6a, 182 Grey Street, Southbank, QLD 4101 **Tel** *(07) 3844 0500*

The younger sibling of the New Farm favourite of the same name, Dell' Ugo Southbank offers sophisticated dining along with sensational park views. The authentic Italian menu is dominated by seafood dishes teamed with fresh pasta made on site by the chef.

TENERIFFE Beccofino
10 Vernon Terrace, QLD 4005 **Tel** *(07) 3666 0207*

In the mood for a wood-fired pizza with a glass of wine while you wait for a table? The short wait is worth it, as the menu is tantalizing. Try the *calamari fritti con rucola e balsamico* (baby calamari) for an entrée or a Scotch fillet of steak for a main course; or perhaps a shellfish and fish stew on a cool night.

TOOWONG Boatshed at Regatta
543 Coronation Drive, Toowong, QLD 4064 **Tel** *(07) 3871 9533*

This is just for starters – oysters, Moreton Bay bugs, fresh ocean king prawns, smoked salmon on fried caper potato salad, or barramundi spring rolls. This hotel restaurant has been a local favourite for decades. It is situated close to the river, university and train station at Toowong.

TOOWONG Brent's, The Dining Experience
85 Miskin Street, QLD 4066 **Tel** *(07) 3371 4558*

An excellent restaurant that offers a perfect romantic dinner menu for two. Alternatively, try the speciality menu of chef Brent Farrell. All the dishes on this menu are created using only fresh local produce and are changed daily. This restaurant has developed and maintains a reputation for fine dining.

WEST END Bombay Dhaba
5/220 Melbourne Street, QLD 4101 **Tel** *(07) 3846 6662*

For lamb, beef, chicken, seafood or vegetarian curries, it is difficult to beat the Bombay Dhaba. This authentic Indian restaurant in Brisbane's ethnic West End offers great food and a warm atmosphere. Try the Kashmiri naan or the *aloo paratha* (bread stuffed with potatoes). There is an adequate car park underneath the restaurant.

WEST END The Gunshop Café
53 Mollison Street, QLD 4101 **Tel** *(07) 3844 2241*

A hit with locals, the menu includes spiced crusted salmon, fantastic seafood or linguine with a range of vegetable dishes, such as sweet potato curls, wild mushrooms or Asian greens. This little café is all about taste sensation – ginger and lime, chilli and garlic, hot greens with garlic butter.

Key to Price Guide *see p524* **Key to Symbols** *see back cover flap*

WEST END Mondo Organics

166 Hardgrave Road, West End, QLD 4101 **Tel** *(07) 3844 1132*

Offering vegetarian and organic dishes, this venue in Brisbane's bohemian centre is a favourite with the locals. An antipasti of roast pepper *harissa*, *baccala*, and almond verjuice pesto is indicative of the menu. Entrées include grilled almond-encrusted scallops with accompaniments. Try the braised duck with caramelized radicchio.

SOUTH OF TOWNSVILLE

AIRLIE BEACH Mangrove Jack's Café Bar

Cnr The Esplanade & Coconut Grove, QLD 4802 **Tel** *(07) 4964 1888*

Combining an alfresco café with an exciting entertainment venue, Mangrove Jack's, in the Airlie Beach Hotel, offers dinner, music and a wine bar, which sells over 35 wines and champagnes by the glass. This hotel is located on the busy Shute Harbour Road and has a reputation for wood-fired pizzas and a superb bistro menu.

BROADBEACH Moomoo the Wine Bar & Grill

Shop 2, Broadbeach on the Park, 2685 Gold Coast Highway, QLD 4218 **Tel** *(07) 5539 9952*

This funky and fun restaurant with fabulously flamboyant retro appeal has turned the traditional steakhouse on its head. The menu focuses on beef and their signature dish – spiced rubbed wagyu rump roast – is a crowd pleaser. For non-beef eaters there's also lamb, poultry and a few vegetarian options.

BUDDINA The Curry Bowl

7/115 Point Cartwright Drive, QLD 4575 **Tel** *(07) 5478 0800*

This Indian restaurant is situated on the Sunshine Coast close to Caloundra. It has a reputation with the locals for friendly service and tasty Indian meals made with fresh ingredients. The menu includes all the favourites, including samosas, curry puffs and great naan breads. Try the Madras curry or the superb chicken curry.

BUNDABERG Pier One Bistro (Across the Waves)

1 Miller Street, QLD 4670 **Tel** *(07) 4152 1531*

Offering a range of Australian club-style meals including seafood, steak, Chinese, Irish and Italian meals, this restaurant situated in the Sports Club has a great reputation with the locals. Waves buffet operates weekly. If you wait more than 30 minutes after you place your order – your meal is free!

CALOUNDRA Café by the Beach

Seaview Terrace, Moffat Beach, QLD 4551 **Tel** *(07) 5491 9505*

This small, busy café is popular with the locals for an evening meal or for lunch or snacks. The menu offers pancakes, burgers with chips and salad, succulent steaks, pizzas with a range of fresh toppings, pastas, fresh fish and all-day breakfast. Specials are offered every night and there is a children's meal.

GLADSTONE Chattin Cafe

Shop 5/100 Goondoon Street, QLD 4680 **Tel** *(07) 4972 4912*

This café-restaurant, a short walk from the marina, is open for breakfast and lunch every day, and dinner on Thursday, Friday and Saturday nights. The evening menu offers modern Australian meals with an Asian influence using fresh produce and seafood. Try the pan-fried Atlantic salmon.

GOLD COAST The Burleigh Bluff Café

The Old Burleigh Theatre Arcade, QLD 4220 **Tel** *(07) 5576 6333*

This café is a favourite with locals. Situated opposite the beach in Burleigh with tables in the sun, or sit inside. It is a lively spot for breakfast – open every morning. It offers reasonably priced food with friendly service. Try the apple pancakes with cream or a burger and chips. A beautiful spot in the evening.

GOLD COAST Conrad Jupiters Charters Towers

Broadbeach Island, Broadbeach, QLD 4218 **Tel** *(07) 5592 8100*

Mouthwatering entrée suggestions on this menu include Moorish spiced veal or Tas salmon sashimi. It is difficult to ignore the Black Angus tenderloin, or try the terrine of poached chicken and grilled quail. An excellent wine list includes a fine Margaret River white wine by the glass. A buffet is also available.

GOLD COAST Shogun Japanese Karaoke Restaurant

90 Bundall Road, Surfers Paradise, QLD 4217 **Tel** *(07) 5538 2872*

Offering Japanese and à la carte menus, this karaoke restaurant is a popular spot for tourists and visitors to Surfers Paradise and features an authentic Japanese water garden. Vegetarian food is also available. Dress is smart-casual – no bare arms. This restaurant is licensed and does not allow BYO. Children require strict parental supervision.

GOLD COAST Point Break Bar and Grill

43 Goodwin Terrace, Burleigh Beach Pavillion, Burleigh Heads, QLD 4220 **Tel** *(07) 5535 0822*

Overlooking the sea at Burleigh Heads, Point Break promises fabulous ocean views and a serene dining experience. The contemporary Australian menu focuses on steak and seasonal seafood. The impressive wine list offers a superb selection including some excellent Barossa drops.

GOLD COAST Palazzo Versace Vanitas Restaurant $$$$

94 Seaworld Drive, Surfers Paradise, QLD 4217 **Tel** *(07) 5509 8000*

This sensational venue, overlooking the lagoon, attracts tourists and dining enthusiasts alike. The atmosphere and decor are indicative of Versace, elegant and tasteful with original art and fine quality furnishings. The food is equally superb. Try the Moreton Bay bugs and don't miss the fabulous wine list.

MOUNT MEE Birches $$$

1350 Mount Mee Road, QLD 4521 **Tel** *(07) 5498 2244*

Situated near the Glass House Mountains in the Caboolture Shire, this modern restaurant offers a range of dishes including special meals for coeliacs and vegetarians. The superb country atmosphere is welcoming to the traveller and the timber decor is enhanced by a fireplace in the winter.

NOOSA Jasper $$$

The Emerald Hastings Street, QLD 4567 **Tel** *(07) 5474 9600*

Would you like to be seen dining out on Noosa's famous Hastings Street? Here is the opportunity to do so and have good food in a relaxed garden atmosphere at the same time. Enjoy local seafood and a fine wine selection. Dinner is served by candlelight and the bar provides a trendy, relaxed spot to sit and watch the passing people.

NOOSAVILLE Magic of India $$

Islander Resort Thomas Street, QLD 4566 **Tel** *(07) 5449 7788*

Customers travel from Brisbane to eat at this delightful Indian restaurant in Noosaville. The pride of the kitchen is the boneless butter chicken. Situated a short distance from the river, this is a relaxed place to eat an evening meal. It has a friendly atmosphere and is highly recommended by the locals.

ROCKHAMPTON Hog's Breath Café $$

1 Aquatic Place North Rockhampton, QLD 4702 **Tel** *(07) 4926 3646*

This franchise is well known in Rockhampton for offering inventive entrées, such as fried chicken tenders, or crumbed calamari. Mains include the favourite prime rib, a New York grill or fish of the day. For snacks, try the burgers or salads.

SAMFORD Samford Valley Hotel $$

Main Street, QLD 4520 **Tel** *(07) 3289 1212*

For entrée the home-made fishcakes are delicious. The oysters are Queensland favourites and the Moreton Bay prawns are succulent. This hotel, a 30-minute drive from Brisbane city, has been an icon for decades for locals, tourists and those en route to Mount Glorious. Try the rosemary-infused lamb rump or the grilled Atlantic salmon.

SOUTH TOWNSVILLE Scirocco Café Bar & Grill $$$

Palmer Street, QLD 4810 **Tel** *(07) 4724 4508*

Offering an interesting combination of Italian and Thai foods, this Townsville restaurant is popular with the locals. The restaurant caters for 100 people inside and has a small garden section with sails and umbrellas, which seats 40 people outside. It attracts mature diners interested in the tasty menu and relaxed atmosphere.

TOOWOOMBA Weis Restaurant $$$

2 Margaret Street, QLD 4350 **Tel** *(07) 4632 7666*

This homestyle restaurant offers both steak and seafood smorgasbord, an array of delicious hot dishes, fresh garden salads and home-baked desserts. Loved by locals and travellers for many years, it is situated in the historic family home "Alameda" built in 1925. It offers a unique setting and pleasant ambience.

TOWNSVILLE Seagulls Resort on the Seafront $$$

74 The Esplanade, QLD 4810 **Tel** *(07) 4721 3111*

Seagulls offers à la carte dining in either air-conditioned comfort or on the deck overlooking the swimming pool and gardens. This beautiful venue provides a superb menu, friendly service and attention to detail. Choose from one of the delicious seafood dishes or juicy steaks.

NORTHERN QUEENSLAND AND THE OUTBACK

BARCALDINE Lee's Garden Motel and Chinese Restaurant $$

1 Box Street, QLD 4725 **Tel** *(07) 4651 1488*

This 20-room motel in Barcaldine has its own licensed Chinese restaurant, which offers excellent meals for the Outback traveller. Barcaldine is located 1,080 km (670 miles) northwest of Brisbane and is a sleepy town of 1,700 people with plenty of pubs and a wealth of historic buildings. It has an interesting political history.

BLACKALL Acacia Motor Inn $$

Cnr Short Street & Shamrock Street, QLD 4472 **Tel** *(07) 4657 6022*

This is a modern restaurant noted for its homestyle cooking. It is spacious with friendly service. Blackall is famous for its woolscour – the last remaining steam-driven wool-washing plant in Australia. It is also home of the original Black Stump which is the exact centre of a meridian square used by surveyors to align the borders of Queensland in 1887.

Key to Price Guide *see p524* **Key to Symbols** *see back cover flap*

BURKETOWN Savannah Lodge $$

Cnr Beames & Bowen Streets, QLD 4830 **Tel** *(07) 4745 5177*

This lodge provides friendly service and meals and is situated in Burketown on the Gulf of Carpentaria. It offers sunset drinks on the salt flats, bird-watching and fishing expeditions, or the lodge can arrange a small flight over the Gulf country. Travel to Lawn Hill Gorge to see the saltwater crocodile and skink.

CAIRNS Barnacle Bill's Seafood Inn $$

103 The Esplanade, QLD 4870 **Tel** *(07) 4051 2241*

Situated on the esplanade in Cairns, this popular seafood restaurant has been a favourite for over two decades. It offers fresh dishes of oysters, calamari, mussels, scallops, prawns, bugs and fish of the day. The house favourites include the seafood jambalaya – prawns, fish and scallops served in a hot, spicy tomato-based sauce.

CAIRNS Café China Seafood Restaurant $$

Pullman Reef Casino, 35–41 Wharf St, QLD 4870 **Tel** *(07) 4041 2828*

This large and busy restaurant offers Oriental delicacies served by friendly and professional staff. The mouthwatering coral trout fillet with snow peas and ginger is superb for a main course. For dessert, try the black sesame pudding with Kahlua-flavoured strawberries. The wine list is extensive and will please any wine enthusiast.

CAIRNS Red Ochre Restaurant $$$

43 Shields Street, QLD 4870 **Tel** *(07) 4051 0100*

This unique menu is based on Australian native foods. Dishes such as lemon aspen cured ocean trout, twice-cooked Mareeba pork shoulder and blackened yellow-fin tuna fillet entice the tastebuds; or try the Australian game platter for two. For dessert the wattle-seed pavlova is a treat; or experiment with the Quandong brûlée.

CAIRNS Kanis Seafood & Steak Restaurant $$$

59 The Esplanade, QLD 4870 **Tel** *(07) 4051 1550*

Enjoy the water views at this large, wonderful restaurant with its nautical decor. The vast menu has dishes that will please just about every taste, with its seafood, steak, vegetarian and international selections. Kanis is open every day for dinner and has two levels as well as outdoor tables.

CHARLEVILLE Cattle Camp Hotel $$

149 Alfred Street, QLD 4470 **Tel** *(07) 4654 3473*

This popular pub offers meals for guests and travellers. While in town visit the historic house located in Alfred Street. The Queensland National Parks and Wildlife Service office on Park Street has a bird aviary. To the south of town is the Steiger Gun, one of ten, used by meteorologist Professor Clement Wragge to break the 1902 drought.

CHARLEVILLE Hotel Corones $$

Wills Street, QLD 4470 **Tel** *(07) 4654 1022*

Marvel at the grandeur of this historic hotel while enjoying an evening meal. Charleville is situated in the heart of Queensland's mulga country. It is the largest town in the southwest Outback of Queensland and has a direct rail link to Brisbane. The Charleville heritage trail guides visitors through the historic sights.

CLONCURRY The Gidgee Grill $$

Matilda Highway, QLD 4824 **Tel** *(07) 4742 1599*

This à la carte restaurant offers a choice of specially created meals. The menu features top quality fish from the gulf and beef from the surrounding area. Seafood meals include mouthwatering choices of oysters, prawns or barramundi. The char-grilled grain and grass-fed steaks are succulent.

CUNNAMULLA Club Hotel $$

15 Louise Street, QLD 4490 **Tel** *(07) 4655 1209*

A relaxing atmosphere, sparely furnished and simple decor, with artwork brought back from Thailand giving the dining room an attractive, Oriental feel. The specialities of the house are Chinese dishes and pizzas. A good value, reliable restaurant if you're looking for a quick meal.

CUNNAMULLA The Woolshed Restaurant $$

9 Louise Street, QLD 4490 **Tel** *(07) 4655 1737*

The Woolshed Restaurant at the Warrego Hotel provides the traveller with an excellent choice of fine pub meals. In particular, try the roast lamb or chicken with vegetables accompanied with a bottle of Australian wine, perhaps a nice Jacob's Creek.

DAINTREE Crossroads Café Bar & Grill $$

Daintree Road, Lower Daintree, QLD 4873 **Tel** *(07) 4098 7658*

Enjoy a burger or a sit-down dinner and friendly conversation at the Daintree Crossroads Cafe Bar & Grill. Glazed grilled chicken breast supreme filled with fresh mango and crushed macadamia nuts is tempting, or try the fresh local seafood platter of crumbed prawns, reef fish, oysters, scallops and calamari. The Queenslander eye fillet is superb.

DAINTREE Mangroves $$

2054 Mossman Daintree Road, QLD 4873 **Tel** *(07) 4098 7272*

Beer-battered local fish, a rump steak with chips or a chicken curry – whatever you choose from this menu is prepared with care and fresh local ingredients. Try the Kuranda home-made ice cream or fresh fruit salad. For vegetarians, the ricotta and spinach pasta is tasty.

DAINTREE Julaymba $$$
20 Daintree Road, QLD 4873 **Tel** *(07) 4098 6100*

Internationally trained chefs prepare Australian gourmet tropical cuisine in this tantalizing environment. The menu has been designed to balance the multicultural tastes of modern Australia, combining many exotic Queensland fruits, tropical reef fish and local produce with native and indigenous nuts, berries, flowers, leaves and seeds.

LONGREACH Oasis Restaurant & Coolibah Bar $$
Cnr Landsborough Highway & Stork Road, QLD 4730 **Tel** *(07) 4658 2411*

Magnificent setting and excellent cuisine in this Outback town of Longreach makes the Oasis Restaurant an ideal dining location after a long drive. Sit by the campfire and enjoy a conversation. The poolside bar is an ideal setting to share a wine on a starry night. Dine inside or out. Enjoy the country-style menu, local produce and friendly service.

PORT DOUGLAS Cactus Bar & Grill $$
38 Macrossan Street, QLD 4877 **Tel** *(07) 4099 6666*

This is an Internet café and restaurant right in the centre of Port Douglas. The traveller can sip a margarita and munch on potato wedges, have a game of pool, meet with friends or dine alfresco in this popular little street café and bar. Try one of the great lunches or stay for dinner and enjoy fresh seafood, including oysters, bugs and scallops.

PORT DOUGLAS The Funky Cow $$
123 Davidson Street, QLD 4877 **Tel** *(07) 4099 6585*

This place lives up to its name – funky by name, definitely funky by nature, with loads of colours, cushions and a great eclectic mix of music. A restaurant with a fun atmosphere. The menu boasts steaks of all types, including camel, as well as all kinds of seafood.

PORT DOUGLAS On the Inlet $$$
3 Inlet Street, 4871QLD **Tel** *(07) 4099 5255*

Located on the waterfront of Dickson Inlet, this stylish restaurant offers views across the Coral Sea to Mossman and the Daintree. For starters try the oysters with some house-baked bread, then the Coral trout or the whole char-grilled baby barramundi with a sauvignon blanc from the Adelaide Hills.

PORT DOUGLAS Nautilus $$$$
17 Murphy Street, QLD 4871 **Tel** *(07) 4099 5330*

First opening in 1954, Nautilus is as well established in Port Douglas as the natural rainforest in which its beautiful dining area sits. The restaurant is very lively at night and is well worth the expense, so book ahead. The modern Australian dishes are as divine as their surroundings: try the whole coral trout.

TAMBO Fanny Mae's Roadhouse $
15 Arthur Street, QLD 4478 **Tel** *(07) 4654 6137*

Fanny Mae's Roadhouse is in the lovely Matilda Highway town of Tambo. Sit out on the peaceful deck and enjoy the home-cooked meals. They offer roadhouse fare of fish or steak with salad and chips, or try one of the great burgers, which are generous in size and made with fresh salad and served with chips.

THURSDAY ISLAND Pearl Lugger Restaurant $$
Cnr Victoria Parade & Jardine Street, QLD 4875 **Tel** *(07) 4069 1569*

The chef's speciality is local seafood, featuring mudcrab and tropical crayfish. This is a historic hotel built about 1901. It offers popular counter meals in the beer garden from 12pm to 2pm and 6pm to 7:30pm daily, or for a more sophisticated menu indulge in the seafood at the Pearl Lugger. The garlic prawns are succulent and fresh.

WINTON North Gregory Hotel $$
67 Elderslie Street, QLD 4735 **Tel** *(07) 4657 1375*

Situated in the heart of the Outback the North Gregory Hotel lays claim to hosting the first live performance of "Waltzing Matilda" in 1895. While you're in town, be sure to visit the Waltzing Matilda Centre opened in 1998. The North Gregory offers a good range of pub fare.

DARWIN AND THE TOP END

CULLEN BAY Bella Amore $$$
Unit 2/52 Marina Boulevard, NT 0820 **Tel** *(08) 8981 4988*

The decor's fresh autumn colours and simple furnishings create a pleasant, relaxed atmosphere. The menu is not exclusively Italian and includes steak, seafood, game and even live red claw in the dry season. Try the popular cowboy shooter cheesecake speciality.

CULLEN BAY Buzz Café $$$
The Slipway Larrakeyah, NT 0801 **Tel** *(08) 8941 1141*

This unique café provides a beautiful outlook over the marina and waters of Cullen Bay. The pleasant atmosphere is enhanced by the interesting Javanese decor with handmade Indonesian furnishings. It is only a five-minute drive from Darwin's CBD. The menu has a reputation for tasty food. Try the wild barramundi or the salt-and-pepper chilli squid.

Key to Price Guide *see p524* **Key to Symbols** *see back cover flap*

DARWIN Café Kashmir ⓢ
2 Pavonia Place, Nightcliffe, NT 0810 **Tel** *(08) 8948 0688*

This restaurant offers a mouthwatering menu of authentic Indian Mughlai and Punjabi dishes. The rice dishes include biryani served with raita and pappadum. The alu baigan is a wonderful vegetarian dish with eggplant and potato. Try a lamb or chicken vindaloo or a prawn masala in a creamy sauce. Exotic and sensational. Great service.

DARWIN Cafe Olio @ The Cavenagh ⓢⓢ
12 Cavenagh Street, NT 800 **Tel** *(08) 8981 2600*

Offering pizzas, pastas, fish and chips and grills, this café has a courtyard, a bar, indoor eating and outdoor tables on the pavement. It is open 5:30pm until late seven days a week. On Sunday from 4pm until 8pm there is live music on the deck. There are large timber tables for families or more intimate settings for couples.

DARWIN Ducks Nuts ⓢⓢ
76 Mitchell Street, NT 0800 **Tel** *(08) 8942 2122*

Stylish setting, good service and a relaxed atmosphere are offered by this popular Darwin venue. The bar and grill alfresco restaurant serves hearty breakfasts until 11am, tasty lunches from 12pm until 3pm, and dinner until 10pm, Monday to Sunday. Cocktails served on Sundays.

DARWIN Hanuman ⓢⓢ
Shop 1, Mitchell Plaza, NT 0800 **Tel** *(08) 8941 3500*

This long-established Darwin favourite offers Asian food, predominantly Thai. The menu has authentic tandoori, Thai and Nonya dishes prepared with wonderful exotic spices. The fish dishes are prepared with fresh local seafood and the vegetable dishes also use tropical ingredients. The chef Jimmy Shu is passionate about Asian influences.

DARWIN Moorish Cafe ⓢⓢ
37 Knuckey Street, NT 0800 **Tel** *(08) 8981 0010*

This is a Moroccan meets Spanish-style café with comfy corner lounges and candles. The tapas are tasty and the paella is a favourite; or try the warm chick pea and chiroza salad. Meals are cooked with authentic North African and Spanish seasonings and are delicious and flavoursome.

DARWIN Rooftop Restaurant ⓢⓢ
7th Floor, Quality Hotel Frontier Darwin, 3 Buffalo Court, NT 0800 **Tel** *(08) 8981 5333*

Situated in the Quality Hotel Frontier Darwin, this rooftop restaurant offers great views of the city and ocean. The à la carte menu offers modern Australian cuisine accompanied by a comprehensive wine list. It is open daily for breakfast and dinner. The hotel is moderately priced.

DARWIN Shenannigan's Irish Pub   ⓢⓢ
69 Mitchell Street, NT 0800 **Tel** *(08) 8981 2100*

Offering alfresco dining with full table service, this Irish pub has a plasma-screen TV that can be watched from the dining area. If you are not so interested in local sports, watch the passers-by on Mitchell Street. Entertainment is provided seven nights a week. The food is excellent – try the catch of the day or a rich Irish stew.

DARWIN Crustaceans on the Wharf ⓢⓢⓢ
Stoke Hill Wharf, NT 0800 **Tel** *(08) 8981 8658*

Situated in Darwin's wharf precinct, this restaurant offers a fabulous menu. The oysters are a must for starters. The barramundi fritters coated in spring onion, garlic and mild chilli egg wash, pan-fried and served with pappadum are a favourite. As for meat dishes, the double-boned lamb cutlets have plenty of flavour.

DARWIN Evoo ⓢⓢⓢ
Skycity, Gilruth Avenue, NT 0800 **Tel** *(08) 8943 8888*

Skycity Darwin is set in lush tropical gardens. Offering ocean views from an elegant private dining room, this casino restaurant has a fine wine list offering Australian and French wines. Try the pan-seared Evoo king prawns on lobster risotto with sautéd asparagus or maybe the chocolate lava pudding with strawberries for dessert.

FANNY BAY Pee Wee's ⓢⓢⓢ
Alec Fong Lim Drive, East Point Reserve, Fanny Bay, NT 0801 **Tel** *(08) 8981 6868*

This premier Darwin restaurant is situated in the East Point Nature Reserve only five minutes from Darwin's CBD. Pee Wee's offers spectacular views across the bay and has a reputation for fine dining. Try the fresh local saltwater barramundi, and for dessert the white chocolate and orange-oil mascarpone cheesecake.

JABIRU Jabiru Sports and Social Club ⓢ
Lakeside Drive, NT 0886 **Tel** *(08) 8979 2326*

Jabiru is a pocket of modern life in an ancient landscape. This community hub offers meals, welcoming visitors for a meal and a drink for lunch and dinner from Wednesday through to Saturday, lunch on Sunday, but no takeaway alcohol is permitted. The Jabiru Tourist Centre can be found at Jabiru Town Plaza. Payment is by cash only.

JABIRU Aurora Kakadu ⓢⓢ
Arnhem Highway, South Alligator, Kakadu National Park, NT 0886 **Tel** *(08) 8979 0166*

Dinner is served buffet style at this tropical restaurant situated in this wetlands lodge. The menu includes fish dishes, cold meats, chicken, stir-fries and roasts. There is a salad bar and a range of desserts. The price is inclusive of tea and coffee. Enjoy this convenient, sumptious buffet or have a snack at the bistro which offers burgers and sandwiches.

JABIRU Gagudju Crocodile Holiday Inn Escarpment Restaurant 📋 ♿ $$$

Flinders Street, NT 0886 ***Tel*** *(08) 8979 9000*

This unique hotel is shaped like a crocodile. It is located in the heart of the world heritage listed Kakadu National Park. The restaurant is open all day and offers a full breakfast, a snack lunch menu and both buffet and à la carte dinner menus. A cocktail bar adjoins the restaurant.

KATHERINE All Seasons Katherine 📋 ♿ ☂ $$

Stuart Highway, NT 0850 ***Tel*** *(08) 8972 1744*

This beautiful garden restaurant and bar is situated in the All Seasons Katherine, which is an Accor Hotel with a swimming pool and tropical environs. The restaurant offers alfresco dining for guests and visitors. It is conveniently located close to the Katherine Gorge, the Cuta Cuta Caves and the Mataranka thermal pool.

KATHERINE Katie's Bistro 🍸 📋 👶 ♿ $$

Cameron Street, NT 0850 ***Tel*** *(08) 8972 2511*

Located within Knott's Crossing Resort *(see p496)*, this casual bistro is named after local identity Katie Emma Knott. You can eat indoors in the air-conditioned restaurant or relax at a table on the patio which spills out into the resort's stunning tropical garden and overlooks the pool.

KATHERINE Kumbidgee Lodge Tea Rooms 🍸 ♿ ☂ $$

Gorge Road, NT 0850 ***Tel*** *(08) 8971 0699*

On the way to Nitmiluk, the traveller can stop here for breakfast or a Devonshire tea. The "bush breakfast" is a favourite with locals and travellers. It is generous and includes cereal, bacon and eggs, mushrooms, toast and tea or coffee. Try the barramundi for lunch or dinner. The pub menu offers steaks, lasagne, fish and chips and dessert.

TENNANT CREEK Margo Miles Steakhouse 📋 ♿ $$

146 Patterson Street, NT 0860 ***Tel*** *(08) 8962 2227*

This award-winning steakhouse offers great food, wine and atmosphere. Steaks include rump, rib, scotch fillet and T-bone, all done to the customer's preference and served with chips and salad. The menu also offers a range of seafood dishes, including grilled or battered barramundi. There is a comprehensive list of Australian wines.

THE RED CENTRE

ALICE SPRINGS Annie's Place 🥗 📋 ♿ ☂ $$

4 Traeger Avenue, NT 870 ***Tel*** *(08) 8952 1545*

One for the budget-conscious traveller who feels the need for a hearty feed. It's the sort of place you can take a load off, relax to some groovy tunes and chat with the friendly staff. The home-made pizzas for one are pretty popular while the pick of the menu is probably the spicy kangaroo curry. A cosy café atmosphere. Payment is by cash only.

ALICE SPRINGS Bar Doppio 🥗 🍸 📋 👶 ♿ ☂ $$

Shop 2, Fan Arcade, Todd Mall, NT 870 ***Tel*** *(08) 8952 6525*

One for the health-conscious snackers. Although not exclusively, Bar Doppio caters well for vegetarians and vegans, and has a variety of wholesome foccacias and soups available. It has funky fresh food and a friendly atmosphere. Patrons easily distracted by kitchen clatter might want to sit outside under the shade covers.

ALICE SPRINGS Casa Nostra Pizza and Spaghetti House 🥗 🍸 📋 $$

Shop 2, Undoolya Road, NT 870 ***Tel*** *(08) 8952 6749*

This is traditional Italian dining right down to the chequered tablecloths. Family owned and operated, it's affordable, hearty Italian cuisine. The pasta sizes are generous, as is the service. Garlic bread aficionados have something to write home about. Admirers of authentic Italian decor and relaxed family atmosphere will too. Payment is by cash only.

ALICE SPRINGS Oscar's Café and Restaurant 🍸 📋 👶 ♿ $$

Cinema Complex, Todd Mall, NT 870 ***Tel*** *(08) 8953 0930*

Winner of the 2004 Gold Plate award for Best Northern Territory Café. The menu is Mediterranean influenced, with seafood being a speciality. Try the baked barramundi fillet with lemon butter and herb/garlic glaze. The superb food is served by staff with a great attitude in a comfortable clean environment. Bookings are recommended.

ALICE SPRINGS Red Dog Australiana Café 🥗 🍸 📋 ♿ ☂ $$

64 Todd Mall, NT 870 ***Tel*** *(08) 8953 1353*

Good food and good value for money. A hearty bushman's breakfast or a lazy light lunch here won't set you back too much. Choose from the whole bacon and egg shebang or tuck into fresh sandwiches and coffee. It's a cosy café, with saddles and bridles and other horsey things all around. Payment is by cash only.

ALICE SPRINGS Samphire Restaurant 📋 ♿ $$

93 Barrett Drive, NT 870 ***Tel*** *(08) 8950 7777*

Named after an edible herb found in the salt marshes, this restaurant is well known for its quality contemporary Australian cuisine. Emu steak and tempura crocodile are just two of the delicious native delicacies on offer. Families are well catered for, poolside dining is an option and there is a special menu for children.

Key to Price Guide *see p524* **Key to Symbols** *see back cover flap*

ALICE SPRINGS Seasons Restaurant

$\$$

10 Gap Road, NT 870 Tel (08) 8952 1444

A truly international menu and a relaxed setting make this a place worth visiting. Choose from a wide variety of dishes, including European, Asian, Mediterranean and, of course, Australian. A children's menu is available, but you don't need to be young to enjoy the dessert speciality: a chocolate soufflé with locally made rum-and-raisin ice cream.

ALICE SPRINGS Ainslie's Restaurant

$\$\$\$$

46 Stephens Road, NT 870 Tel (08) 8952 6100

Local wonderchef Craig Lovewell takes care of all things food here. The à la carte menu is predominantly modern Australian cuisine with an international influence and an emphasis on quality produce. It's elegant yet affordable dining for the family in a relaxed atmosphere.

ALICE SPRINGS Barra on Todd Restaurant

$\$\$\$$

34 Stott Terrace, NT 870 Tel (08) 8952 3523

While the menu does try to cater for most tastes, the emphasis is definitely on seafood. Some of these dishes are simply mouthwatering. Try the char-grilled barramundi with lemon and dill risotto topped with a Moreton Bay bugtail and champagne caviar butter. It's a relaxed setting. You can dine by the pool or tuck yourself away in a quiet corner.

ALICE SPRINGS Bluegrass Restaurant

$\$\$\$$

Cnr Todd Street & Stott Terrace, NT 870 Tel (08) 8955 5188

Located in a heritage listed building with large leafy trees in the front courtyard, Bluegrass is Alice at its civilized best. The vast blackboard menu features Australasian Mediterranean cuisine, such as the seafood antipasti or the ginger chicken with stir-fried couscous. The bar is stocked with more than 100 wines.

ALICE SPRINGS Bojangles Saloon and Restaurant

$\$\$\$$

80 Todd Street, NT 870 Tel (08) 8952 2873

The food is quality and about as Outback as it gets, but with an international twist. Try a home-made camel and Guinness pie, or perhaps a Thai-style crocodile salad. At night there is a live radio show broadcast from the bar, which just adds to the already vibrant atmosphere.

ALICE SPRINGS The Lane

$\$\$\$$

58 Todd Mall, NT 870 Tel (08) 8952 5522

Offering French bistro cuisine, tasty tapas plates, wood-fired gourmet pizza and an extensive wine list, The Lane has worked hard to raise the bar on the Alice Springs dining scene. With tables that spill over onto the busy Todd Mall, The Lane is the perfect spot for a light lunch, a family meal or just a glass of wine and a nibble.

ALICE SPRINGS Oriental Gourmet Chinese Restaurant

$\$\$\$$

80 Hartley Street, NT 870 Tel (08) 8953 0888

For locals and tourists alike, this is the Asian restaurant of choice in town. Its affordable Cantonese cuisine is served in a buzzing friendly atmosphere. The signature dish is probably the honey prawns: battered prawns coated with honey and topped with sesame seeds. For a dessert with a difference, try the Galliano fried ice cream.

ALICE SPRINGS Sukra

$\$\$\$$

Lasseters Hotel Casino, 93 Barrett Drive, NT 870 Tel (08) 8950 7777

From India to Malaysia and Thailand to Singapore, this flashy fusion restaurant takes your tastebuds on a journey across Asia. The menu is a delight, offering laksas, noodles, salads and curries as well as meat and seafood dishes. Singaporean soft shell chilli crab is the superb house special and not to be missed.

WATARRKA Carmichael's

$\$$

Kings Canyon Resort, Luritja Road, Watarrka National Park, NT 872 Tel (08) 8956 7442

With outstanding views of Kings Canyon, this restaurant is a good one for families. Every paying adult allows an accompanying child under the age of 15 to eat for free. Choose from a huge buffet of seafoods, roast meats, salads and desserts. There's even some camel and buffalo for those with adventurous tastes. Bookings are essential.

YULARA Bough House Restaurant

$\$$

Outback Pioneer Hotel, Yulara Drive, NT 872 Tel (08) 8957 7605

This is a good place for families. Meals are free for children under the age of 15. There is an extensive buffet including a mouthwatering roast meat carvery, fresh seafoods, crispy salads and desserts. The rustic homestead-style decor only adds to the Outback experience, as does the restaurant's famous kangaroo pie.

PERTH AND THE SOUTHWEST

ALBANY Blue Jays Bistro

$\$$

42 Stirling Terrace, Albany, WA 6330 Tel (08) 9842 9696

This vibrant bistro serves modern Australian cuisine throughout the day, from big breakfasts to delicious lunches and hearty dinners. The menu offers consistently good food at affordable prices so Blue Jays is regularly fully booked on Saturdays.

AUGUSTA August Moon Chinese Restaurant

3 Matthew Flinders Shopping Centre, Allnutt Street, Augusta, WA 6290 **Tel** *(08) 9758 1322*

Authentic Chinese cuisine and a massive menu, this is the town's only Asian restaurant. The accommodating staff serve a large choice of Chinese dishes in a warm, inviting ambience. Popular and regular favourites include chow mein, chicken and cashew nuts and special fried rice. Ideally located in the centre of the township. BYO.

BRIDGETOWN Barking Cow Café

88A Hampton Street, Bridgetown, WA 6255 **Tel** *(08) 9761 4619*

Located in the centre of town, Barking Cow is a funky, café-style eatery with a deli. It serves light snacks and lunches consisting of fresh and healthy gourmet food. There's a good choice of vegetarian and gluten-free dishes. The Barking Cow serves great coffees too.

BUNBURY VAT 2

2 Jetty Road, Bunbury, WA 6230 **Tel** *(08) 9791 8833*

Bunbury dining at its best with vistas across the harbour and Jetty Baths. Modern Australian cuisine including the chef's grazing plate or the daily ocean catch. Other highlights are found on the tempting dessert menu (try warm chocolate pudding or freshly made honeycomb ice cream).

BUSSELTON Equinox Café

343 Queen Street, Busselton, WA 6280 **Tel** *(08) 9752 4641*

Prominently located beside Busselton's famous jetty *(see p314)*, the venue has three main dining areas and genuinely friendly service. The menu is contemporary and varied, with everything from tandoori chicken, chilli mussels, steak sandwiches and house-baked cakes. Popular with locals and tourists and open for three meals a day.

BUSSELTON Esplanade Hotel

Lot 2, Marine Terrace, Busselton, WA 6280 **Tel** *(08) 9752 1078*

Affectionately known by locals as the Nard, The Esplanade is touted as Busselton's most popular pub-restaurant, offering hearty meals at reasonable prices. They have a regular menu plus daily specials on the blackboard and a children's menu. Sit in the big open dining area or the beer garden and enjoy the amiable, informal atmosphere.

COWARAMUP Vasse Felix Winery and Restaurant

Caves Road (cnr Harmans Road South), Cowaramup, WA 6284 **Tel** *(08) 9756 5050*

Contemporary Australian cuisine combining fresh, regional ingredients with European and Asian influences. The winter and summer menus and excellent wines are well worth the steep prices. It has sweeping views of the vineyards. Open for lunch only. Later you can visit the permanent art collection.

DENMARK Mary Rose Restaurant

Base of Mount Shadforth Scenic Drive, 11 North Street, Denmark, WA 6333 **Tel** *(08) 9848 1260*

This easygoing establishment serves good, wholesome country food at exceptionally fair prices. Plates are varied and include old favourites with a modern twist. The restaurant has a seating area under a grand old veranda and is nestled beside the Old Butter Factory Gallery.

ESPERANCE Ollies Café

51 The Esplanade, Esperance, WA 6450 **Tel** *(08) 9071 5268*

Café-style eating surrounded by plain and simple decor, this is a well-liked local dining haunt. They offer hot and cold meals with a minimum of fuss. The retro eating booths are under-rated and the juicy steaks very well regarded. The café is part of Bonaparte Seafood Restaurant located above Ollie's. BYO and closed Mondays.

FREMANTLE Benny's Bar & Café

10 South Terrace, Fremantle, WA 6160 **Tel** *(08) 9433 1333*

Benny's menu is best described as contemporary Australian with a strong influence from Fremantle's traditional Italian flavours. The building was erected in 1897 but the interior has a sleek, modern design. Very popular for breakfast, lunch and dinner, the kitchen closes at 9pm but live music keeps the mixed crowd buzzing until midnight.

FREMANTLE Clancy's Fish Pub

51 Cantonment Street, Fremantle, WA 6160 **Tel** *(08) 9335 1351*

A top pub-style seafood eatery, Clancy's has become a household name in Fremantle and is hugely popular with both mainstream and alternative locals. A great family pub-like atmosphere and a varied menu, lacking only in good vegetarian options. Enjoy the youthful service, live music and a veranda out back.

FREMANTLE Maya Indian Restaurant

75 Market Street, Fremantle, WA 6160 **Tel** *(08) 9335 2796*

Renowned as one of Western Australia's best Indian restaurants and its prices have crept up slightly as a result. The scrumptious Indian cuisine on offer includes Goan fish curry. Both upstairs and downstairs get very busy from Friday to Sunday so book ahead. Located in the heart of Fremantle and open Tuesday to Sunday.

HYDEN Sandalwood Restaurant

2 Lynch Street, Hyden, WA 6359 **Tel** *(08) 9880 5052*

Buffet-style breakfasts and dinners in an informal setting at the Wave Rock Motel Homestead. It closes on some nights, when the homestead's sister, The Bush Bistro, serves grill-and-salad-style meals, otherwise it's seven days a week dining for breakfast, lunch and dinner.

Key to Price Guide *see p524* **Key to Symbols** *see back cover flap*

KALGOORLIE Saltimbocca $$

90 Egan Street, Kalgoorlie, WA 6430 **Tel** *(08) 9022 8028*

Centrally located and easily accessible, this eatery opened in 2003 and offers standard Italian meals and speedy service. Not surprisingly, the dish saltimbocca (a Roman speciality made with veal and prosciutto) is on the menu. Relaxed, casual atmosphere and a roaring tourist trade. Only open for dinner and closed on Sundays.

KALGOORLIE Top End Thai Restaurant $$

71 Hannan Street, Kalgoorlie, WA 6430 **Tel** *(08) 9021 4286*

Great Thai cooking set in an historic 1897 building, which is one of the oldest in town. It has three open dining areas in the garden and indoors. The menu's emphasis is on authentic Thai food and the wide selection of dishes include a vegetarian menu and a chef's speciality menu. BYO.

MANDURAH Jolly Frog Restaurant $$$

8 Rod Court, Mandurah, WA 6210 **Tel** *(08) 9534 4144*

Jolly Frog boasts an international menu with some highly original dishes, such as rack of lamb with crushed macadamia nuts or marinated kangaroo with redcurrants. Vegetarian choices are included in the menu and the seafood is guaranteed fresh. Superb views over the Dawesville Channel are another attraction.

MARGARET RIVER The Berry Farm and Tea Rooms $

Bessell Road, Margaret River, WA 6285 **Tel** *(08) 9757 5054*

A café-style eatery offering country hospitality located 15 km (9 miles) from the centre of Margaret River. This picturesque garden café has regular menu changes to reflect the seasons. A staple home-made favourite is beef and red wine pie. Wander around the farm to help burn off the delicious boysenberry pie.

MARGARET RIVER Arc of Iris $$

1/151 Bussell Highway, Margaret River, WA 6285 **Tel** *(08) 9757 3112*

Modern café cuisine in a somewhat eccentric, sometimes hippie and always fun atmosphere. An à la carte menu with a touch of France come thanks to the proud French proprietor. Popular with both locals and visitors, this funky eatery includes a room at the back with communal tables and armchairs.

MARGARET RIVER The 1885 at The Grange on Farrelly $$

Farrelly Street, Margaret River, WA 6285 **Tel** *(08) 9757 3177*

Located in a grand, 1885 building, this is a top-notch restaurant and hotel. The menu changes daily and boasts an exciting fusion of local and Asian ingredients and ideas. There is a good range of local wines and a warm, friendly ambience. They serve dinners daily except Sunday.

MARGARET RIVER Leeuwin Estate Winery Restaurant $$$

Stevens Road, Margaret River, WA 6825 **Tel** *(08) 9759 0000*

Classic European fare at the most prestigious restaurant in the Margaret River area. Honours include Prix d'Honneur, so not surprisingly this triple Gold Plate Award winner is formal and expensive. The menu reflects seasonal produce and intelligent wine selections. They only open for lunch plus Saturday for dinner (bookings are essential).

MARGARET RIVER Must Margaret River $$$$

107 Bussell Highway, Margaret River, WA 6285 **Tel** *(08) 9758 8877*

Located in the heart of Margaret River, this bar and bistro offers a comprehensive list of wines from the local region and around the world. A range of seasonal local produce drives the contemporary Australian menu but the bistro is best-known for its tender local beef. Patrons can see into the kitchen through the refrigerated, meat-aging cellar.

PEMBERTON Gloucester Ridge Café $$

Burma Road, Pemberton, WA 6260 **Tel** *(08) 9776 1035*

A relaxed, contemporary setting at the Gloucester Ridge Vineyard and the perfect stop on the way to the Gloucester Tree Top. There is a great decking area with tremendous views of the Karri Forest. The chef focuses on local products, such as grilled Pemberton marron. Open for lunch daily.

PERTH Jaws Kaiten Sushi $

Shop 1, 726 Hay Street, Perth WA 6000 **Tel** *(08) 9481 1445*

This popular revolving sushi bar is centrally located in the Hay Street Mall. A busy lunchtime trade among office workers and shoppers ensures high product turnover and optimum freshness. The pay-per-plate menu includes toned down options suitable for the western palate. An original taste of Japan in the heart of the main shopping area.

PERTH Dusit Thai Restaurant $$

249 James Street, Northbridge, Perth WA 6003 **Tel** *(08) 9328 7647*

Reputed as Western Australia's most award-winning Thai restaurant, they present creative Thai dishes in relaxed surroundings. Traditional meat dishes and many vegetarian choices are included on the menu. The chef's special is divine: marinated lamb with coriander, lemongrass, home-made chilli sauce and pickled vegetables. Closed Mon.

PERTH Romany $$

105 Aberdeen Street, Northbridge, Perth WA 6000 **Tel** *(08) 9328 8042*

An Italian food-lovers institution in Perth, Romany serves generous portions of classic Italian dishes at very reasonable prices. Although it is no longer run by the original family, it still holds its claim to fame as the oldest Italian restaurant in the city. It has a busy weekday lunch-time trade and fills quickly on Friday and Saturday nights.

PERTH C Restaurant

Level 33, 44 St Georges Terrace, Perth WA 6000 **Tel** *(08) 9220 8333*

Contemporary cuisine in a unique, revolving restaurant that allows for 360 degree city and river views. Popular with Perth socialites, it has the elegance to match its original menu. Examples include delights such as C Sashimi and Wagyu beef (listed on the menu as "the caviar of beef"). Late bar on Fridays and Saturdays.

PERTH Fraser's Restaurant

Fraser's Avenue, King's Park, West Perth, WA 6005 **Tel** *(08) 9481 7100*

One of Perth's finest restaurants in the privileged surrounds of King's Park. Modern European cuisine with subtle flavours from Asia, Fraser's emphasizes fresh, local ingredients and char-grilling. It has an extensive wine list and views of King's Park, the city skyline and the Swan River.

PERTH Funtastico

12 Rokeby Road, Subiaco, Perth WA 6008 **Tel** *(08) 9381 2688*

Mediterranean cuisine with an innovative flair, this trendy, popular and energetic restaurant specializes in modern Italian food. It has superb pasta, fish and vegetarian dishes, and the wood-fired oven pizzas are gaining fame as possibly the best on offer in the city.

PERTH Indiana Tea House

99 Marine Parade, Cottesloe, WA 6011 **Tel** *(08) 9385 5005*

Set right on Perth's famous Cottesloe Beach, the spectacular views of the Indian Ocean and the fine food justify the high-priced menu. The cuisine's theme is modern Australian creations. The Moreton Bay bug salad and other seafood delicacies are sure to please.

PERTH Simon's Seafood Restaurant

73 Francis Street, Perth WA 6003 **Tel** *(08) 9227 9005*

A multi-award winning seafood restaurant in the heart of Perth's nightlife and dining precinct. Simon's boasts fresh, local seafood served in pleasant surroundings and is fairly priced. Some pasta, poultry and red meat dishes are available as well as a children's menu. Crustacean fans should try the lobster mornay.

WILYABRUP Flutes Restaurant

Caves Road, Wilyabrup, WA 6284 **Tel** *(08) 9755 6250*

Flutes is part of Brookland Valley Winery and overlooks Willyabrup Brook and the estate gardens. The magical setting is matched by exquisite, contemporary European cuisine strongly influenced by the chef's French roots. There is also a fine dessert menu. Soak up the ambience and later browse the range of gourmet products on sale.

NORTH OF PERTH AND THE KIMBERLEY

BROOME Wing's Chinese Restaurant

Lot 18, Napier Terrace, Broome, WA 6725 **Tel** *(08) 9192 1072*

A very popular place with locals and visitors who fancy genuine Chinese cuisine. Located in the heart of Chinatown, diners can expect fresh meats and vegetables stir-fried with delicious Chinese sauces. Beef chop suey and vegetable spring rolls dipped in sweet chilli sauce are big favourites.

BROOME Black Pearl Restaurant

4/63 Robinson Street, Broome, WA 6725 **Tel** *(08) 9192 1779*

Offering stunning views across the mangroves to Roebuck Bay, the Black Pearl is the perfect place to watch the sunset while enjoying a great selection of good value, quality meals. The modern Australian menu emphasizes local produce, with fresh seafood, succulent meats and tropical flavours. Bookings are recommended.

BROOME Matso's

60 Hammersley Street, Broome, WA 6725 **Tel** *(08) 9193 5811*

A unique Australian-Asian themed restaurant situated in Matso's Brewery with views of Roebuck Bay. It serves delicious dishes, including a superb Indian curry, or for something different try crocodile shanks with spices, herbs and mango. Cold boutique beers are brewed on site.

BROOME Zanders at Cable Beach

Cable Beach Road, Broome, WA 6726 **Tel** *(08) 9193 5090*

Tourists come to watch the sunset over an outdoor dinner at this popular Cable Beach restaurant. A casual, contemporary Australian menu with global influences includes everything from fish, poultry, red meat, vegetarian, pasta, and bakery food. This relaxed and family-friendly restaurant is open for breakfast, lunch and dinner.

CARNARVON Water's Edge

121–125 Olivia Terrace, Carnarvon, WA 6701 **Tel** *(08) 9941 1181*

Standard pub meals served in the large indoor dining area or the small outdoor setting overlooking the sea. The food is excellent given the budget prices, with decent portions served in an informal and friendly atmosphere. The restaurant is part of the Carnarvon Hotel, which is popular with the town's residents.

Key to Price Guide *see p524* **Key to Symbols** *see back cover flap*

CERVANTES Sea Breeze Café
10 Cadiz Street, Cervantes, WA 6311 **Tel** *(08) 9652 7233*

A small, standard country café serving basic meals, fast-food takeaway and made-to-order sandwiches and rolls. They also serve tasty pizzas plus fizzy drinks and juices. The owner is very welcoming and used to visitors using the café as convenient pit stop for visits to the Pinnacles and Nambung National Park *(see p324).*

CORAL BAY Ningaloo Reef Café
Lot 1, Robinson Street, Coral Bay, WA 6701 **Tel** *(08) 9942 5882*

This place has something for everyone, including fish, steak, chicken and vegetarian dishes. It is also particularly famous for its made-to-order pizzas. Cheerful service and a happy to please attitude makes for a leisurely meal. The café has indoor and outdoor dining areas and also does takeaways.

DAMPIER Sirens Restaurant

Dampier Mermaid Hotel & Motel, The Esplanade, Dampier, WA 6713 **Tel** *(08) 9183 1222*

Dine alfresco in the Beer Garden or indoors at the bistro of the Mermaid Hotel & Motel. The menu is a tasty mix of modern Australian cuisine and great Australian hearty country dishes. Open for breakfast, lunch and dinner, and on Sunday evenings there's an all-you-can-eat BBQ in the Beer Garden.

DENHAM Old Pearler Restaurant
71 Knight Terrace, Denham, WA 6537 **Tel** *(08) 9948 1373*

Its claim to fame is that it is the only restaurant in the world made of coquina shell. It is also full of character and uses quality local seafood for many dishes. Apart from choice ingredients, the philosophy reflected in the menu is to emphasize healthy cooking (hence nothing is deep-fried). Bookings are recommended.

DERBY Point Restaurant & Café

1 Jetty Road, Derby, WA 6728 **Tel** *(08) 9191 1195*

Located right on the jetty, overlooking King Sound, the Point Restaurant & Café was completely refurbished in 2006 and now has an air-conditioned dining room, an outdoor area and a covered deck. Menu choices include fresh seafood, beef and chicken dishes, and a variety of other choices.

EXMOUTH Whalers Licensed Restaurant

5 Kennedy Street, Exmouth, WA 6707 **Tel** *(08) 9949 2416*

Whalers has the reputation of informal dining and quality food, with the speciality being Kailis prawns. It also presents other seafood dishes and tender steaks and are genuinely happy to accommodate vegetarian requests. It has an outdoor dining area and friendly country service. Open for breakfast, lunch and dinner.

GERALDTON Tanti's Restaurant
174 Marine Terrace, Geraldton, WA 6530 **Tel** *(08) 9964 2311*

The reputation of this Thai restaurant has spread, so much so that the Thai ambassador to Australia went out of his way to eat there in 2002. The decor may be simple but the food is exquisite. The main ingredients are mostly locally grown or caught, including fresh crustaceans and herbs. BYO.

HALLS CREEK Gabi's Restaurant

Roberta Avenue, Halls Creek, WA 6770 **Tel** *(08) 9168 6101*

Gabi's is part of the Kimberley Hotel and offers Mediterranean and international dishes. Open for breakfast, lunch and dinner, vegetarians will be pleased to know they are also catered for in the mainly carnivorous-orientated menu. There is a surprisingly good wine list and children's meals are available.

KALBARRI Finlays Fresh Fish BBQ
Magee Crescent, Kalbarri, WA 6536 **Tel** *(08) 9937 1260*

Situated on the old iceworks site, this seafood eatery is well frequented and recommended by most of the locals. Specializing in seafood barbecue-style cooking, it has outdoor seating and a great atmosphere. The barramundi and prawns with fresh damper and salad is excellent. Fish-free dishes are also on the menu. Closed Mondays. BYO.

KALBARRI Black Rock Café
80 Grey Street, Kalbarri, WA 6536 **Tel** *(08) 9937 1062*

This self-described "fine food restaurant and alfresco café" looks out onto the Murchison River. The international menu includes local ingredients with original results. Examples include kangaroo with half lobster mornay, local prawn and scallop mornay. Seafood platter for two is a popular choice. Closed Sunday nights and all day Mondays.

KARRATHA Etcetera Brasserie
Dampier Road (Cnr Hillview Road), Karratha, WA 6714 **Tel** *(08) 9187 3333*

This pavilion restaurant located at Karratha International Hotel offers fine dining with both classic and contemporary cuisine. Choose from the elegant interior tables or the poolside alfresco area surrounded by tropical gardens. There is also luxury lounge seating and a bar. A popular Pilbara mingling place for tourists and locals.

KUNUNURRA Kelly's Bar & Grill

47 Coolibah Drive, Kununurra, WA 6743 **Tel** *(08) 9168 1024*

Classic Australian food served with bush hospitality. Run by the Country Club hotel, it is open for breakfast, morning tea, lunch and dinner. Evening meals specialize in steaks and seafood. Dine inside in air-conditioned comfort or outdoors in the exotic garden. The bar is a quiet drinking place popular with locals.

NEW NORCIA New Norcia Hotel

Great Northern Highway, WA 6509 **Tel** *(08) 9654 8034*

Located on the top of a hill overlooking the monastic town of New Norcia, this imposing hotel was built in 1926 and exudes old-world charm. Its restaurant offers a comprehensive menu of modern Australian cuisine accompanied by locally brewed beers and wines.

SHARK BAY The Bough Shed

Monkey Mia Dolphin Resort, WA 6537 **Tel** *(08) 9948 1171*

This beachfront restaurant has the privilege of being a stone's throw away from where the Monkey Mia dolphins come in to greet tourists *(see p327)*. Meals are served throughout the day, including an excellent range of cooked breakfasts. Grilled Shark Bay pink snapper will please seafood lovers.

ADELAIDE AND THE SOUTHEAST

ADELAIDE Botanic Café

4 East Terrace, SA 5000 **Tel** *(08) 8232 0626*

Great for drinks and suppers, this ultra-hip restaurant is situated nicely on the fringe of Adelaide's bustling East End. The cuisine is modern Italian, with organic and fresh South Australian produce a speciality. There is a huge communal, marble table as the centrepiece of the striking interior design.

ADELAIDE Jerusalem Sheshkebab House

131B Hindley Street, SA 5000 **Tel** *(08) 8212 6185*

You'd be hard pressed to get a better meal in Adelaide at this price. This family owned and operated restaurant is one of the best kept secrets in the city's vibrant West End. The *kafta* with spicy yoghurt sauce is divine and the home-made hummus dip is to die for. It is BYO only and bills must be paid in cash but it's definitely worth the extra effort.

ADELAIDE Mandarin House

47A Gouger Street, SA 5000 **Tel** *(08) 8231 3833*

This family restaurant specializes in delicious Northern Chinese dishes. It's affordable and scrumptious fare. There is an almost overwhelming choice of dishes. The sizzling beef with snow peas has a nice bit of zing, and the vegetarian dumplings, either steamed or fried and served with a chilli sauce, must be tried.

ADELAIDE Thea Tea Shop

110 Gawler Place, SA 5000 **Tel** *(08) 8232 7988*

One of Adelaide's best-kept secrets, this tranquil traditional tea house exudes an atmosphere of peace. Its surprising menu is exclusively vegetarian and many options revolve around traditional Taiwanese-style dishes. Thea also specializes in hot and cold teas in a range of traditional and non-traditional flavours. Closed Saturday and Sunday.

ADELAIDE Ying Chow

114 Gouger Street, SA 5000 **Tel** *(08) 8221 7998*

Delicious affordable Chinese food is the order of the day at Ying Chow. It's a great place to grab a quick lunch or to share a few tasty dinner courses with friends. There is a huge range of dishes to choose from but you shouldn't miss the broad bean curd with Chinese chutney. The salt-and-pepper tofu is also very good.

ADELAIDE Goodlife Modern Organic Pizza

170 Hutt Street, SA 5000 **Tel** *(08) 8223 2618*

This is delicious, healthy pizza with a difference from the only fully certified organic restaurant in Adelaide. There are heaps to try but perhaps the pick of the bunch is the free-range roast duck pizza with shiitake mushrooms, spring onions and home-made ginger jam. It's tasty, affordable stuff in a relaxed environment with friendly, efficient staff.

ADELAIDE House of Chow

82 Hutt Street, SA 5000 **Tel** *(08) 8223 6181*

David and Roz Chow have gone to great lengths to create not only an aesthetically pleasing ambience but also the best in Asian gourmet cuisine. The restaurant prides itself on its consistency and has won numerous awards for excellence. An indoor aquarium with live coral makes a impressive restaurant centrepiece.

ADELAIDE Jasmin Restaurant

31 Hindmarsh Square, SA 5000 **Tel** *(08) 8223 7837*

It's the restaurant of choice for the South Australian Premier and with good cause. It's an exquisite dining environment with mahogany tables and chairs, flowers aplenty and art on the walls. The quality Northern Indian style food is heaven for the senses. The head chef has been there for nearly 26 years and deserves his outstanding reputation.

ADELAIDE Pranzo

46 Exchange Place, SA 5000 **Tel** *(08) 8231 0661*

Situated in the heart of Adelaide's business and judicial district, this slick city restaurant buzzes all day long with the sound of lawyers, politicians and stockbrokers tucking into some of the tastiest southern Italian food around. Try the poached baby chicken, ox tongue and cottechino sausage with salsa verde. Dress sharp and eat well.

Key to Price Guide *see p524* **Key to Symbols** *see back cover flap*

ADELAIDE Prince Albert Hotel
 $$

*254 Wright Street, SA 5000 **Tel** (08) 8212 7912*

This friendly relaxed inner-city pub has a great atmosphere and food to match. It's traditional pub fare and good value for money. Pride in preparation, presentation and service is a priority for the staff at the Prince Albert, and it shows. There's regular live acoustic shows to keep things ticking along and the interior is clean and warm.

ADELAIDE Stanley's Great Aussie Fish Café
 $$

*76 Gouger Street, SA 5000 **Tel** (08) 8410 0909*

This bustling restaurant specializes in fresh seafood, simply prepared. Friendly staff and good service make any visit well worth while. The grilled octopus and the Moreton Bay bugs are superb, while the chips are good enough to eat on their own. It's affordable enjoyable South Aussie seafood in a relaxed family setting.

ADELAIDE Worldsend Hotel
 $$

*208 Hindley Street, SA 5000 **Tel** (08) 8231 9137*

Excellent staff and an artistically hip interior make this a fine place to kickback for a beer and a decent meal. The restaurant prides itself on its quality pub food with an original twist. It has a constantly changing menu with Asian and Italian influences. Stick around after dinner and there's a good chance of hearing some live jazz or a DJ.

ADELAIDE Auge
 $$$

*22 Grote Street, SA 5000 **Tel** (08) 8410 9332*

Minimalistic decor and a stunning water feature provide a cool and modern setting in which Adelaide cultural movers and shakers come to enjoy this expertly prepared quality Italian cuisine. The friendly, smartly dressed staff are knowledgeable and highly efficient. The food is immensely satisfying. The experience is worth savouring.

ADELAIDE Crown & Sceptre
 $$$

*308 King William Street, SA 5000 **Tel** (08) 8212 4159*

Dining at the Crown & Sceptre can mean anything from an informal meal in the bar, beer garden or alfresco outdoor eating areas, through to an à la carte dining experience with all the trimmings. The staff are noticeably friendly and efficient, and the extensive and celebrated wine list has been recognized nationally.

ADELAIDE Jolleys Boathouse
 $$$

*Jolleys Lane, SA 5000 **Tel** (08) 8223 2891*

Situated on the bank of Adelaide's Torrens River, this is a lovely place to enjoy fine dining at its best. The menu is contemporary with a hint of Mediterranean and Asian influence. The wine list is extensive, the decor relaxed and the service second to none. It's ideal for a quiet business lunch or an evening with friends.

ADELAIDE Night Train Theatre Restaurant
 $$$

*9A Light Square, SA 5000 **Tel** (08) 8231 2252*

If you feel like something exciting and different, you should spend a Saturday night with the award-winning Night Train crew. The price of a meal includes three courses and a show. Fun and laughter are guaranteed as are quality large platters of delectable cuisine. Take a walk through the infamous Night Train tunnel and see where it leads you.

ADELAIDE Universal Wine Bar
 $$$

*285 Rundle Street, SA 5000 **Tel** (08) 8232 5000*

Situated in the heart of Adelaide's East End, the Universal Wine Bar sets a dining standard all of its own. The menu is modern Australian with a French twist. The warm duck salad tossed with shiitake mushrooms is a favourite, and with more than 300 different wines to choose from, you are guaranteed to find the perfect match to any meal.

ADELAIDE Alphutte
$$$$

*242 Pulteney Street, SA 5000 **Tel** (08) 8223 4717*

With an emphasis on quality Swiss-European style cuisine, this landmark Adelaide restaurant has won a swag of awards over the years. It's renowned for its authentic Swiss Roschti, a melt-in-the-mouth potato and onion cake that makes a delicious accompaniment to any of the tantalizing meals on offer.

ADELAIDE Gaucho's
 $$$$

*91 Gouger Street, SA 5000 **Tel** (08) 8231 2299*

Australia's first Argentinian restaurant has a heavy emphasis on char-grilled meat – the beef is even butchered and aged on the premises. Watch out for their spicy chimmichurri sauce, a combination of olive oil, lemon juice, garlic, herbs, spices and fennel. It's a taste sensation not to be forgotten. Gaucho's is always busy, so bookings are essential.

ANGASTON Vintners Bar & Grill
$$$

*Nurioopta Road, SA 5353 **Tel** (08) 8564 2488*

The beautiful vineyard setting and well balanced menu make Vintners one of the best places to eat in the Barossa. Head chef and co-owner Peter Clarke produces sophisticated country fare such as char-grilled kangaroo loin with lentil and barley toast, and lemon curd meringue tart with vanilla ice cream and mandarins.

BARMERA Bonneyview Winery Restaurant
$$$

*Sturt Highway, SA 5345 **Tel** (08) 8588 2279*

Like many restaurants attached to wineries, this is a family-owned establishment set in attractive surroundings. Summer is a great time to dine under the vines in the delightful Tuscan garden, while winter meals are best enjoyed inside by the open fires. Food is high quality traditional Australian cuisine with an emphasis on using local produce.

BRIDGEWATER Bridgewater Mill

$$$$

Mount Barker Road, SA 5155 **Tel** *(08) 8339 9200*

Set amongst a grove of colourful trees in the beautiful Adelaide Hills, the Bridgewater Mill provides the absolute finest of dining experiences. The exquisite food in this multi-award-winning restaurant is in the gloriously capable hands of one of the country's most respected chefs, Le Tu Thai. Food and service rarely come better than this.

CLARENDON Royal Oak Hotel Clarendon

$$$

47 Grants Gully Road, SA 5157 **Tel** *(08) 8383 6113*

Set in the picturesque Adelaide Hills, this old-style country pub restaurant is only a short but scenic drive from the city centre. The food is traditional modern Australian with an emphasis on quality seafood and steaks. It's a great place to sit out on a sunny veranda with a quiet beer and a hearty meal and watch the rest of the world go by.

COONAWARRA The Poplars at Chardonnay Lodge

$$$

Riddoch Highway, SA 5263 **Tel** *(08) 8736 3309*

This is a restaurant that has not closed for one day in the past 21 years. Business must be good, and it's not surprising when you consider they are serving mouthwatering dishes such as pan-fried kangaroo fillet with quandong relish and Spanish onion glaze served on wild rocket.

COONAWARRA Upstairs at Hollick

$$$

Ravenswood Lane, SA 5152 **Tel** *(08) 8737 2752*

Set amid the Coonawarra vineyards, this was the first winery restaurant in the area. The dining room features floor to ceiling windows that ensure uninterrupted views over the Hollick "Neilson's Block" vineyard and beyond to the broader Coonawarra region. The menu presents modern Australian cuisine using fresh quality local produce.

CRAFERS Jimmies on the Summit

$$

6 Main Street, SA 5152 **Tel** *(08) 8339 1534*

Half the menu changes on almost a weekly basis in this softly lit, wooden floored Adelaide Hills café. Best known for its delicious wood-oven pizzas and relaxed atmosphere, it's the sort of place you will drive a long way out of your way to visit. The food is an adventure to be enjoyed.

GLENELG Esca Restaurant and Espresso Bar

$$$

Shop 13–15, Marina Pier, Holdfast Shores, SA 5045 **Tel** *(08) 8376 6933*

This beachfront eatery and espresso bar has couches and fireplaces throughout. Relax, warm and toasty, with a perfect coffee. Or alternatively, move outside and enjoy ocean views while eating quality European cuisine such as the seafood *cataplana*: local seafood infused with a Portuguese broth of exotic spices, garlic, wine and tomato.

GOODWOOD Brown Dog Café

$$

143 Goodwood Road, SA 5034 **Tel** *(08) 8172 1752*

If you are looking for home-cooked comfort food with a gourmet twist, look no further. With a menu drawing on Asian, Indian and Cajun influences, Brown Dog is a comfortable café reminiscent of the Brunswick Street haunts in Melbourne. Hip and inviting, it's a great place to enjoy a tasty salt-and-pepper squid and a nice glass of wine.

HAZELWOOD PARK The Food Business

$$

4 Lenden Avenue, SA 5066 **Tel** *(08) 8379 8699*

Owners John Gabel and Cindy McFarlane have a passion for food and it shows. Their modern, clean restaurant is open daily for breakfast and lunch, and dinner on the last Friday of the month. Try the little oyster and leek pies: rich, petite delicacies in buttery coats topped with a sweet and sour shred of spinach with a hint of spice.

HINDMARSH The Governor Hindmarsh Hotel

$$

59 Port Road, SA 5007 **Tel** *(08) 8340 0744*

This landmark live music venue has a spacious yet cosy feel to the main eating area. The food is high quality pub food prepared with care. The prime grain-fed Scotch fillet is served on potato and parsnip mash and topped with roasted field mushrooms and a rich shiraz glaze.

HYDE PARK The Pot Food & Wine Restaurant

$$$

160 King William Road, SA 5062 **Tel** *(08) 8373 2044*

An extremely classy and yet comfortably cosy venue, this restaurant specializes in excellent modern European cuisine. The aptly named "4 P's" makes for an inviting entrée: pigeon, porcini, polenta and parmesan. Main courses are just as tastefully intriguing. Desserts have to be experienced to be believed.

KENT TOWN Tincat Café Restaurant and Gallery

$$$

107 Rundle Street, SA 5067 **Tel** *(08) 8362 4748*

Dine amongst an ever-changing display of local art. After dinner, enjoy some fine wine with a poetry reading. You never know quite what cultural treat is going to crop up at this marvellously bohemian retro hub of artistic activity. One thing is for sure, you are guaranteed fine food, excellent wine and superb service.

NORTH ADELAIDE The British Hotel

$$

58 Finniss Street, SA 5006 **Tel** *(08) 8267 2188*

There is always a buzz around lunchtime in the beer garden at The British Hotel. Choose from the range of quality modern Australian dishes, or if you prefer, you can select a prime cut of meat from the kitchen and cook it yourself on the communal barbecue. Whatever the case, the food is easy to enjoy and the atmosphere even easier.

Key to Price Guide *see p524* **Key to Symbols** *see back cover flap*

NORTH ADELAIDE Sparrow Kitchen and Bar

$$$

10 O'Connell Street, SA 5006 **Tel** *(08) 8267 2444*

Offering both indoor and outdoor dining, Sparrow Kitchen is open from early morning. The varied menu covers much ground, from full bacon and egg breakfasts to light lunches and big dinners. Fare is predominantly Italian with pizzas, pastas and other Italian mainstays. Small plates of tapas are also available in the evenings.

NORTH ADELAIDE The Wellington Tap & Grill

$$$

36 Wellington Square, SA 5006 **Tel** *(08) 8267 1322*

There is a range of quality dishes on offer but the speciality is Premium MSA grade steaks. It would be hard to find a better steak sandwich in all of North Adelaide. With 32 different beers on tap in the adjoining bar, a few hours at the Welly Tap & Grill can be every steak-and-beer lover's dream.

NORWOOD Martini Ristorante

$$$

59A The Parade, SA 5067 **Tel** *(08) 8362 7822*

This fine Italian restaurant is an integral part of Norwood's main culinary strip. It's chic: the walls are adorned with posters of 1950s film stars. The dishes are superb. Try the rabbit baked in a clay pot with potato, tarragon, wine and spices, or the taglierini with Port Lincoln blue swimmer crab meat, roma tomatoes, basil, chilli and mascarpone.

TANUNDA 1918 Bistro & Grill

$$$

94 Murray Street, SA 5352 **Tel** *(08) 8563 0405*

This restaurant gets its name from the foundation stone of the old villa in which it is housed. The interior has been tastefully modernized, the walls adorned with local art and pictures of vineyards. Open fires at each side of the main dining room provide a warm and cosy atmosphere in which to enjoy the excellent modern Australian cuisine on offer.

WEST BEACH Café Salsa

$$

5 West Beach Road, SA 5024 **Tel** *(08) 8235 1991*

This family run restaurant serves authentic mid-northern Italian cuisine. The interior is retro, with laminex-topped tables and chairs. There's a full range of tasty pastas available and some excellent vegetarian options, such as the eggplant parmigiana. The service is quite relaxed and the overall atmosphere is comfortable.

THE YORKE AND EYRE PENINSULAS

ARDROSSAN The Ardrossan Top Pub Restaurant

$$$

36 First Street, SA 5571 **Tel** *(08) 8837 3008*

If it's a good ice-cold beer and a decent meal that you seek, then this is the place to go. Family owned and operated, the restaurant caters for those wanting a simple pub meal as well as those who prefer à la carte. The chef has over 30 years' experience and there is an extensive dessert and coffee menu to work through.

AUBURN Rising Sun Hotel Restaurant

$$

Main North Road, SA 5451 **Tel** *(08) 8849 2015*

Traditional family fare and a friendly atmosphere are staples of this lively eatery. Choose from a variety of quality meat and fish dishes, or perhaps venture into the "stables steakhouse" and cook your own barbecue. Either way, it's all about relaxing and enjoying the quality food and wine.

AUBURN Tatehams

$$$

Main North Road, SA 5451 **Tel** *(08) 8849 2030*

A fine dining experience not to be missed and a contemporary European menu to be applauded. The highlight of this exquisitely delicious food would have to be the marinated beef served with taro and stuffed with blue cheese. Sit comfortably at the country-style long tables and indulge in excellent food and an extensive wine list.

BLINMAN Blinman Hotel Restaurant

$$

Main Street, SA 5730 **Tel** *(08) 8648 4867*

Relax on the veranda and enjoy quality modern Australian cuisine in picturesque surroundings. Try the baked pork fillet with honey or the native pepper leaf kangaroo. Sip some of South Australia's best wine by a Flinders Ranges sunset, then head back into the bar with its roaring open fire.

CLARE Artisan's Table

$$$

Main North Road, SA 5453 **Tel** *(08) 8842 1796*

Chef Roger Graham has created a diverse menu that takes your tastebuds around the Mediterranean, Spain and North Africa. Menu highlights include pan-seared duck livers with fettuccine and rich sage cream, and poached pork fillet served with *peperonata* and tomato and thyme sauce. Closed on Mondays and Tuesdays.

COOBER PEDY Umberto's

$$$

Desert Cave Hotel, 20 Hutchison Street, SA 5723 **Tel** *(08) 8672 5688*

It's the flagship restaurant of the world's only international underground hotel and there's something for everyone on the menu. Try the French onion soup with melted cheese and garlic croutons for starters. The Atlantic salmon fillet on roasted macadamia nuts, baked in paper bark and topped with Spanish onion salsa is also well worth a taste.

EDITHBURGH Sails Seafood and Steak Restaurant

Troubridge Hotel, Blanche Street, SA 5583 **Tel** *(08) 8852 6013*

As the name suggests, these guys like to keep the menu pretty simple. It's traditional pub fare with an emphasis on quality and local ingredients. Their signature dish is the Troubridge Rump, a nice thick piece of beef served with prawns on top and a wholegrain mustard sauce. Seafood and steak – not complicated, but delicious.

EDITHBURGH Faversham's

7 Edith Street, Edithburgh, SA 5583 **Tel** *(08) 8852 6373*

There's a comfortable Old World feel to this place, with its open fires and numerous antiques throughout. The owners won the 2004 SA Great Regional Award for best family business and it shows in the attitude of the service. It's affordable fine dining with a menu that stresses using local produce. Quality modern Australian cuisine.

MINTARO Mintaro Mews

Burra Street, SA 5415 **Tel** *(08) 8843 9001*

This restaurant caters beautifully for adults wanting a first-class meal in a warm, tranquil environment. The pot-belly stove and the flagstone floors help provide the perfect setting in which to enjoy a double-roasted duck or smoked rack of lamb. Up there with the best in modern Australian fine dining.

QUORN Old Willows Brewery Restaurant

Port Augusta Road, Pichi Richi Pass, SA 5433 **Tel** *(08) 8468 6391*

Built upon the remains of a burnt out brewery, this award-winning restaurant is notable for its friendly country feel and tasty Australian cuisine. You can feast on smoked kangaroo, barramundi and quandong pie, while the Pichi Richi steam train rumbles past just metres from the restaurant. Bookings are essential.

RAWNSLEY PARK Woolshed Restaurant

Rawnsley Park Station, Hawker-Wilpena Road, SA 5434 **Tel** *(08) 8648 2555*

The view of the sunset upon the Chace Range is stunning. The food here is high quality and distinctly Australian. Try the Drover's Mix of steak, sausages, lamb, bacon and egg. Good stuff for the stomach and soul. The Woolshed is often full of song, from casual patron sing-alongs to organized operatic events.

SEVENHILL Skillogalee Winery and Restaurant

Trevarrick Road, via Clare, SA 5453 **Tel** *(08) 8843 4311*

Open fires in winter and the veranda in spring make this an idyllic dining setting. It was the first full-time professional winery restaurant in the Clare Valley and the building itself is over 150 years old. The menu is seasonal and while internationally influenced, relies on the best local fresh produce. Simple yet superb.

WALLAROO The Boat Shed Restaurant

Jetty Road, SA 5556 **Tel** *(08) 8823 3455*

It's so close to the beach that a lot of the seafood on offer comes straight off the boats, and you can't get fresher than that. The menu is heavily seafood oriented, even the wood-fire oven pizzas have a predominant ocean twist. The sea views and the affordable tasty dishes make this coastal eatery a place well worth visiting.

WHYALLA Percy's on Playford

99 Playford Avenue, SA 5600 **Tel** *(08) 8645 9488*

This restaurant combines seafood caught along the Eyre Peninsula Coastline with the best locally farmed produce to create a menu that is consistently fresh and appetizing. Specialties are seafood, vegetarian fare and curries. For those who like a bit of family fun with their food, keep an eye out for the regular theme nights.

WILPENA Captain Starlight Bistro

Wilpena Pound Resort, Hawker-Wilpena Road, SA 5434 **Tel** *(08) 8648 0004*

This casual family orientated restaurant has a strong emphasis on food with an Australian twist. There's a kangaroo fillet served with roasted yam and native bush tomato salsa, and a Wilpena Pounder beefburger with home-made quandong and chilli sauce. Open wood fires in winter add a cosy touch.

WUDINNA Sturts Restaurant

72 Eyre Highway, SA 5652 **Tel** *(08) 8680 2090*

It's all about the fresh air in Wudinna and, of course, the Fresh Eyre Lamb Pot. This signature dish is a simmering pot of succulent lamb and bacon, braised in red wine and herbs and topped with a layer of golden pastry. It's country cooking at its best, and just the thing to tuck into after a long day's sightseeing.

MELBOURNE

CARLTON Brunetti

194 Faraday Street, VIC 3053 **Tel** *(03) 9347 2801*

This classy Italian venue with covered outdoor seating serves wonderful cakes, pastries, gelato, chocolates, nougat and biscuits, as well as club sandwiches, foccacia, calzone, bruschetta and coffee. The restaurant serves regional Italian cuisine. In 2005 they opened an outlet in the Melbourne City Square.

CARLTON Abla's

109 Elgin Street, VIC 3053 **Tel** *(03) 9347 0006*

Abla's has staked a claim with many Melburnians as the spark that ignited an abiding love affair with Middle-Eastern (particularly traditional Lebanese) cuisine. Its location in a Victorian terrace on a busy Carlton thoroughfare seems odd, but any misgivings soon dissipate as hearty classics and welcoming service take over.

CARLTON Shakahari

201-203 Faraday Street, VIC 3053 **Tel** *(03) 9347 3848*

This vegetarian stalwart has a reputation for good value, inventive menus with a mainly Asian feel. Gone are the days of stodgy lentil bakes served in an earnest but dreary setting. Here the food is fresh and light, served in simple surroundings highlighted by two magnificent 19th-century Indian cloth paintings.

CARLTON University Café

257 Lygon Street, VIC 3053 **Tel** *(03) 9347 2142*

This homely Lygon Street institution with on-street covered seating (a second home to generations of Melbourne University academics) has been serving up fine Italian pastas, seafood and foccacias since 1952. It's a great venue for people-watching, so be sure to secure an outside table early on sunny days.

CARLTON Esposito at Toofey's

162 Elgin Street, VIC 3053 **Tel** *(03) 9347 9838*

If you take your seafood seriously and fancy a step up from fish and chips, this licensed restaurant (with a worthwhile wine list) shouldn't be missed. Its casual but smart atmosphere wins praise, as does its menu which aims to do the simple things well, like crab and fennel soup, and beer-battered King George whiting.

CARLTON Hotel Lincoln

91 Cardigan Street, VIC 3053 **Tel** *(03) 9347 4666*

Map *1 C1*

The management of this once-neglected corner pub, one street back from Lygon Street's hectic Italian restaurant strip, is keen to ensure that a revitalized venue and menu does not put off the locals. It's inexpensive, quality gastropub cuisine that's not afraid to present unlikely sounding restaurant menu items, such as meatloaf.

CENTRAL MELBOURNE Pellegrini's Espresso Bar

66 Bourke Street, VIC 3000 **Tel** *(03) 9662 1885*

Map *2 D2*

Noisy, fast, Italian and retro before its time. For many Melbourne baby boomers, this institution is the site of their first encounter with "spag bol", lasagne and espresso. It's still the benchmark for standard Italian food, and it's always a pleasure to pull up a stool at the bar. Lively conversation is mandatory.

CENTRAL MELBOURNE Supper Inn

15 Celestial Avenue, VIC 3000 **Tel** *(03) 9663 4759*

Map *1 C2*

After ascending the flight of stairs leading from Chinatown's seedy Celestial Avenue, you may be disappointed at the lacklustre decor, but don't be deterred. The food here is as good and cheap as you're likely to find anywhere, with some oddities that are sure to challenge. A late-night haunt for Melbourne's hospitality workers.

CENTRAL MELBOURNE Yu-u

137 Flinders Lane, VIC 3000 **Tel** *(03) 9639 7073*

Map *2 D3*

Don't be mistaken in thinking you have been given the wrong address; this kooky little restaurant, entered from seedy Oliver Lane, serves good quality and reasonably priced Japanese classics. For anyone who has dined in Tokyo's Shibuya district, the smells here will take you back. Book ahead.

CENTRAL MELBOURNE Cafe Segovia

33 Block Place, VIC 3000 **Tel** *(03) 9650 2373*

Map *1 C3*

Cafe Segovia was quick to stake a claim when Melbourne's CBD alleys and arcades renaissance took off in the 1980s and 1990s. It was the first café in Block Place, and is still one of the best. Its great coffee, cramped indoor and outdoor seating, youthful vibe and Spanish inspired café menu ensure it's always hectic.

CENTRAL MELBOURNE Cookie

252 Swanston Street, VIC 3000 **Tel** *(03) 9663 7660*

Map *1 C2*

Boasting more than 85 imported beers, this festive beer hall is an odd setting for one of Melbourne's most affordable and popular Thai restaurants. Cookie attracts a large arty crowd with its retro 1950s interior, thumping music and late opening until 3am. If you're looking for atmosphere, this is where you'll find it.

CENTRAL MELBOURNE Cumulus Inc

45 Flinders Lane, VIC 3000 **Tel** *(03) 9650 1445*

Map *2 D3*

Cumulus Inc provides a grown-up alternative to the late-opening, later-closing booze houses dotting the city. If you want good design that isn't alienating, fine wine without stuffiness and great, unpretentious food, this is just the ticket. Serves breakfast, lunch and dinner Mon–Sat.

CENTRAL MELBOURNE Hanabishi

187 King Street, VIC 3000 **Tel** *(03) 9670 1167*

Map *1 B3*

Often voted Melbourne's best Japanese restaurant (with very good reason), this is the place for sashimi, steaming hotpots and melt-in-your-mouth tempura. The lunchtime menu and atmosphere is less formal than at night, and popular with the denizens of Melbourne's nearby legal and financial districts.

CENTRAL MELBOURNE Mask of China

115–117 Little Bourke Street, VIC 3000 **Tel** *(03) 9662 2116*   **Map** *2 D2*

An often-cited contender for Flower Drum's title as Melbourne's premier Chinese restaurant, and with good reason. As well as Cantonese dishes, this distinguished restaurant specializes in southern Chinese Chiu Chow cuisine. Its menu is as delicate as its table settings and the service is excellent.

CENTRAL MELBOURNE Becco

11–25 Crossley Street, VIC 3000 **Tel** *(03) 9663 3000*   **Map** *2 D2*

Cool, inspired and modern Italian with casual but professional service. After more than ten years of service, Becco has rightly staked a claim as one of Melbourne's finest. The restaurant serves up winners like roast duck with muscatel and grappa sauce, while the cheaper bar menu offers the likes of chilli flour-dusted calamari.

CENTRAL MELBOURNE Il Solito Posto

Basement, 113 Collins Street, VIC 3000 **Tel** *(03) 9654 4466*   **Map** *2 D3*

This restaurant is a popular lunchtime venue, although it also serves breakfasts and dinner. It is a welcoming, cosy and stylish basement trattoria, entered from George Parade, with slate floors, a bar and wooden tables. The menu is seasonal Italian, with an excellent wine list that offers local and Italian selections.

CENTRAL MELBOURNE Movida Bar de Tapas y Vino

1 Hosier Lane, VIC 3001 **Tel** *(03) 9663 3038*   **Map** *2 D3*

Book a table if you can, or take a chance on a seat at the bar in Australia's finest proponent of modern Spanish bar culture. Daily specials complement a solid list of tapas and small dishes to share. This restaurant is on Hosier Street, known worldwide for its graffiti and street art.

CENTRAL MELBOURNE The European

161 Spring Street, VIC 3000 **Tel** *(03) 9654 0811*   **Map** *2 D2*

One of Melbourne's best European wine lists is just the beginning at this top-end-of-town Parisian-styled bistro. It's smart and sophisticated and attracts the pre-theatre crowd. Politicians also duck in following question time at the state parliament across the road to enjoy the mainly French and Italian culinary repertoire.

CENTRAL MELBOURNE The Press Club

72 Flinders Street, VIC 3000 **Tel** *(03) 9677 9677*   **Map** *2 D3*

Chef George Calombaris has breathed new life into an old favourite, proving there is more substance to Greek food than merely grilled fish. Specialities include *kalamari makaronada*, and rabbit and *horta spanakopita* with poached egg. The extensive wine list includes some top Greek wines, as well as a selection of ouzos.

CENTRAL MELBOURNE Cecconi's Cantina

61 Flinders Lane, VIC 3000 **Tel** *(03) 9663 0222*   **Map** *2 D3*

Another award-winning favourite. Olimpia Bortolotto's restaurant, with views across the Yarra to the CBD, serves exquisite Modern Italian cuisine and classics, such as osso buco and risotto Milanese. For many well-heeled locals, this is quintessential Italian cooking. The wine list is heartily recommended.

CENTRAL MELBOURNE ezard

187 Flinders Lane, VIC 3000 **Tel** *(03) 9639 6811*   **Map** *2 D3*

Chef Teage Ezard explores the possibilities and complexities of Modern Australian cuisine's love affair with Asia in an ultra-modern (and often noisy) setting. The menu is flavour packed and the wine list and staff are excellent. You can dine à la carte or enjoy the eight-course degustation or express lunch menus.

CENTRAL MELBOURNE Flower Drum

17 Market Lane, VIC 3000 **Tel** *(03) 9662 3655*   **Map** *2 D2*

This Cantonese restaurant is often rated the best in Australia, let alone food-mad Melbourne. Although its regular clientele of media and sporting celebrities rubs shoulders with the Big End of Town, it's suprisingly relaxed and just as happy to accommodate a family celebration as a power lunch.

CENTRAL MELBOURNE Grossi Florentino

80 Bourke Street, VIC 3000 **Tel** *(03) 9662 1811*   **Map** *2 D2*

Definitely one for that special occasion: the rich modern Italian food served by attentive staff in the fin-de-siècle Mural Room is memorable. The Cellar Bar and Grill are cheaper and less subdued, but equally pleasing. The wine list is always a talking point, with several top French and Italian producers to choose from.

CENTRAL MELBOURNE Taxi

Level 1, Transport Hotel, Federation Square, Cnr Flinders & Swanston sts, VIC 3000 **Tel** *(03) 9654 8808*   **Map** *2 D4*

In 2005 Taxi won Melbourne's most prestigious Restaurant of the Year award. Modern Australian and Japanese cuisine combine with futuristic architecture and lighting and views over St Kilda Road, Southbank and Federation Square to deliver something truly special.

CENTRAL MELBOURNE Vue de Monde

430 Little Collins Street, VIC 3000 **Tel** *(03) 9691 3888*   **Map** *1 B3*

How does braised scallop with twice-cooked pork belly finished with spiced pumpkin purée sound? Melbourne's answer to Jamie Oliver, the youthful and European-trained chef-cum-author Shannon Bennett serves up exquisite modern French cuisine in his CBD premises in the historic Normanby Chambers.

Key to Price Guide *see p524* **Key to Symbols** *see back cover flap*

COLLINGWOOD Jim's Greek Tavern

32 Johnston Street, VIC 3066 Tel (03) 9419 3827

Melbourne has the largest Greek population of any city except Athens, and this is one of the best classic tavernas in the city. It has everything you could wish for in a Greek restaurant, including generous seafood platters, fried saganaki, metzes and charcoal-grilled lamb. And it's good value.

FITZROY Babka Bakery Café

358 Brunswick Street, VIC 3000 Tel (03) 9416 0091

This cramped but friendly café-cum-bakery made Brunswick Street sit up and beg when it opened. It serves light meals, many with a Russian flavour, although its meat pies and salad are a good value lunch option. Join the scene and grab an outdoor seat. The shoo-fly buns are also recommended.

FITZROY Café Provincial

299 Brunswick Street, VIC 3065 Tel (03) 9810 0042

A bustling, bohemian-type café which has undergone several changes of management but remains a Melbourne institution. They serve inexpensive French and Italian fare. It attracts a mixed crowd – backpackers to suits – and is a popular place with the locals at the end of a long night.

FITZROY Ladro

224 Gertrude Street, VIC 3065 Tel (03) 9415 7575

An award-winning restaurant located in cosmopolitan Fitzroy, the Ladro offers an intimate setting with daily specials, crispy wood-fired pizzas and reasonably priced wine list. There is even a roast of the day. It's breezy and hugely popular, so book ahead.

FITZROY Little Creatures Dining Hall

222 Brunswick Street, Fitzroy, VIC 3065 Tel (03) 9417 5500

The iconic Fremantle (WA) Brewery "Little Creatures" has set up shop in an old dressmaker's warehouse in Fitzroy. Close to the shops, it's the perfect place to wind down after a shopping spree. It's all about beer, and more beer, with decent pub food to match, including oysters, pizza, seafood and steaks.

FITZROY Mario's

303 Brunswick Street, VIC 3065 Tel (03) 9417 3343

Crisp white linen tablecloths, benchtop seats facing Brunswick Street and a couple on the street, classic café food (antipasto, pastas and specials) and slick waiting staff have made this bustling joint a favourite with the local art crowd. It's cramped and usually noisy inside, but well worth a visit. A Fitzroy favourite. Payment in cash only.

FITZROY St Jude's Cellars

389–391 Brunswick Street, VIC 3065 Tel (03) 9419 7411

This is a produce-driven restaurant and wine bar with a specialist wine retail shop front. Both the Modern Australian food and the wine at St Jude's are focused on quality local ingredients emphasizing sustainable farming and fishing, and organic, biodynamic and free-range produce.

NORTH MELBOURNE The Courthouse

86–90 Errol Street, VIC 3051 Tel (03) 9329 5394

In an area not known for its fine dining, this former corner pub now serves reasonably priced gastropub cuisine. It also offers a decent wine list and an intimate dining room with open fire. The menu is never extensive, but it knows how to impress with attention to detail and a careful choice of seasonal produce.

PRAHRAN Jacques Reymond Restaurant

78 Williams Road, VIC 3181 Tel (03) 9525 2178

Map 6 F3

Jacques Reymond's exacting standards, devotion to seasonal produce and determination to challenge modern Australian cuisine delivers a flamboyant yet accessible menu in a magnificent setting. The two-storey former Victorian residence is a mecca for those seeking the perfect setting for a big occasion.

RICHMOND Richmond Hill Café and Larder

48–50 Bridge Road, VIC 3121 Tel (03) 9421 2818

Map 4 D2

Stephanie Alexander, doyenne of Australian cuisine, opened this light and airy venue, which serves great coffee and light breakfasts, brunches and lunches. The treasures in its cheese room are to die for, and they even have a Cheese Club. Such is its popularity that evenings are reserved for private functions.

RICHMOND Pearl Restaurant & Bar

631–633 Church Street, VIC 3121 Tel (03) 9421 4599

Map 4 E3

A pleasing blend of Asian influences continues to draw the crowds, many of them seasoned regulars. The staff is professional, the decor sleek and inviting, and you can dine in the restaurant or the bar. Offerings range from salami and aubergine sandwiches to roast red duck curry and desiree potato gnocchi.

SOUTH MELBOURNE O'Connell's

407 Coventry Street, VIC 3205 Tel (03) 9699 9600

This convivial corner pub's menu delivers reasonably priced, modern Middle-Eastern cuisine with Lebanese, Turkish and North African influences. Enjoy a drink in the bar before your meal and choose a wine from their extensive selection.

SOUTH MELBOURNE The Isthmus of Kra $$$

50 Park Street, VIC 3205 **Tel** *(03) 9690 3688*   **Map** *3 A4*

A consistent and deserving award winner for its exotic decor, well-planned wine list and exquisitely presented Thai Nonya cuisine, including favourites such as red roast duck curry, king prawns in coconut crepe, and baked whole barramundi stuffed with lemongrass and chilli rempah and wrapped in bamboo leaves.

SOUTH YARRA Botanical $$$

169 Domain Road, VIC 3141 **Tel** *(03) 9820 7888*   **Map** *3 B4*

Named after the Botanic Gardens across the road, this restaurant is a favourite with South Yarra's well-heeled set. The decor is hard-edged contemporary and the atmosphere unsuited to a romantic tête-à-tête. Nonetheless, the Mod Oz cuisine and wine list consistently score praise from Melbourne's food critics.

SOUTH YARRA Caffè e Cucina $$$

581 Chapel Street, VIC 3141 **Tel** *(03) 9827 4139*   **Map** *4 E5*

This bustling Italian café and restaurant, with style and attitude aplenty, is a perennial favourite with Melbourne's younger celebrities and beautiful people. Inside it's dark and cramped. Outside, the Chapel Street tables and pocket-handkerchief balcony are perfect for people-watchers, and those keen to be seen.

SOUTH YARRA Caffé Sienna Ristorante $$$

Shop 2, 402 Chapel Street, VIC 3142 **Tel** *(03) 9827 1353*   **Map** *6 E1*

Located in trendy Chapel Street, Caffé Sienna is a popular spot and a celebrity favourite. The interior is modern, yet cosy and relaxed and punters come here to eat, drink coffee or sip cocktails. The menu is contemporary Italian and Australian and there is a great selection of cakes and desserts. Covered alfresco dining during the summer months.

SOUTH YARRA France-Soir $$$$

11 Toorak Road, VIC 3141 **Tel** *(03) 9866 8569*   **Map** *4 D5*

This energetic Traditional French bistro serves up "Plats de Résistance" such as filet de boeuf béarnaise, poissons du jour and boeuf bourguignon. Some claim it also serves Melbourne's best crème brûlée. The wine list and cellar are winners, and its French waiters play the part. Good fun and good value.

SOUTHBANK Walter's Wine Bar $$$

Upper Level, Southgate, Southbank, VIC 3006 **Tel** *(03) 9690 9211* **Map** *1 C4*

Offering views of the city, Flinders Street Station and the most lively stretch of the Yarra River, Walter's come up trumps for fine dining, and its wine list is up there with the very best. The setting is understated, the service impeccable, and the Mod Oz menu guaranteed to satisfy with offerings such as char-grilled kangaroo.

ST KILDA Cicciolina $$

130 Acland Street, VIC 3182 **Tel** *(03) 9525 3333*

Earthy, full-bodied comfort food with a Modern Italian sensibility is the order of the day at this cosy Acland Street favourite (the eye fillet is always a winner). They don't take bookings, but you can wait for a spare restaurant seat to materialize while sampling the wine list and a fine antipasto out in the back bar.

ST KILDA Il Fornaio $$

2 Acland Street, VIC 3182 **Tel** *(03) 9534 2922*   **Map** *5 B5*

One part industrial bakery, one part groovy café. Locals cruise through from breakfast till dark. It's a good place to enjoy a light lunch, or to find a healthy takeaway option in St Kilda. Try the filling ciabatta rolls with roasted vegetables. The coffee is always strong and the clientele makes it a place to be seen.

ST KILDA Donovans $$$

40 Jacka Boulevard, VIC 3182 **Tel** *(03) 9534 8221*

Views over the beach, the foreshore's cycle path, and Port Phillip Bay are just the beginning at Donovan's. Its beach-house inspired decor and self-assured Mediterranean menu can always be counted on to deliver finely rendered seafood dishes with ingredients such as Western Australian scampi and Balmain Bug.

ST KILDA Café di Stasio $$$$

31 Fitzroy Street, VIC 3182 **Tel** *(03) 9525 3999*   **Map** *5 B4*

Muted lighting, views onto Fitzroy Street, impeccable and friendly service in a small and cosy dining room, and a menu that takes homely Italian fare to another dimension sets this classy St Kilda establishment apart. The two-course set lunch menu, which includes a glass of wine, is recommended for diners on the run.

ST KILDA Circa, the Prince $$$$

2 Acland Street, VIC 3182 **Tel** *(03) 9536 1122*   **Map** *5 B5*

Subtle yet unexpected combinations define this modern European menu. The bill comes as a pleasant surprise after having enjoyed one of Melbourne's finest meals in a low-key but stylish setting. The wine list is befitting of Aladdin's Cave and the service is unobtrusive. Recommended treat for budget travellers.

ST KILDA The Stokehouse $$$$

30 Jacka Boulevard, VIC 3182 **Tel** *(03) 9525 5555*

Upstairs you'll find a casual restaurant with polished boards, floor-to-ceiling windows and fantastic bay views. Downstairs you'll find outside tables where the menu items are generally cheaper. Seafood is not the only draw, but it's hard to pass up offerings such as calamari salad with Asian herbs and a mint lime dressing.

Key to Price Guide *see p524* **Key to Symbols** *see back cover flap*

WESTERN VICTORIA

APOLLO BAY Bay Leaf Café

131 Great Ocean Road, VIC 3233 **Tel** *(03) 5237 6470*

A laidback and friendly licensed café and local favourite, with beach views and inexpensive excellent breakfasts, lunches and dinners. At dinnertime the menu and atmosphere is a little more formal, but in Apollo Bay that simply means leave your shorts and surfboard at home.

APOLLO BAY La Bimba

125 Great Ocean Road, VIC 3233 **Tel** *(03) 5237 7411*

This relaxed, innovative and very affordable restaurant has quickly become part of the Apollo Bay scene. The decor offers tiled Moroccan tables on the balcony and vivid wallhangings inside, while the menu combines the best of Middle Eastern and Asian influences with modern Australian cuisine, and includes plenty of choices for vegetarians.

APOLLO BAY Buff's Bistro

51–53 Great Ocean Road, VIC 3233 **Tel** *(03) 5237 6403*

Just down the road from the Great Ocean Hotel and across the road from the beach, this fully licensed and comfortable tavern-style bistro with open fireplace offers Mediterranean dishes with an emphasis on local seafood. There is also an inexpensive children's menu and a cake cabinet to tempt you.

APOLLO BAY Chris's Beacon Point Restaurant & Villas

280 Skenes Creek Road, Skenes Creek, VIC 3233 **Tel** *(03) 5237 6411*

Chef Chris Talihmanidis, who has owned this Greek restaurant since the 1970s, blends Mediterranean flavours with local produce, especially seafood. The restaurant was rebuilt and now has floor-to-ceiling windows to maximize the dramatic coastal views from this hilltop location. The wine list is excellent.

BALLARAT Europa Café

411 Sturt Street, VIC 3350 **Tel** *(03) 5338 7672*

Europa is a smart and inexpensive family friendly bistro, offering a traditional café menu spiced up with Middle-Eastern and Asian dishes. All-day breakfasts are popular and the wine list is one of the best in Ballarat. Lunches include burgers, pizzas, soups and pastas, while dinner options include tandoori chicken or lamb and prune tagine.

BALLARAT Oscar's Hotel and Café Bar

18 Doveton Street South, VIC 3350 **Tel** *(03) 5331 1451*

Housed in an Art Deco building in central Ballarat, Oscar's has a warm and friendly atmosphere and serves gourmet, pub-style food. The pub opens early for breakfast and is also popular for pre-theatre drinks – Her Majesty's Theatre and several cinemas are a short walk away. Excellent service; accommodation also available.

BALLARAT L'espresso

417 Sturt Street, VIC 3350 **Tel** *(03) 5333 1789*

This popular restaurant serves Mod Oz cuisine with an Italian influence. It's open for breakfast, lunch and dinner, and offers good quality coffee, cakes and gelati. For lunch there are the usual Italian menu items, such as pasta and risotto. Oven-baked Tasmanian salmon or char-grilled kangaroo fillet are often on the menu and worth trying.

BENDIGO The Puddler Restaurant

101 Williamson St, VIC 3550 **Tel** *(03) 5443 8898*

This elegant, award-winning restaurant is housed in a heritage-listed building in central Bendigo. Specialising in fresh seafood and grain-fed beef, it also has a good choice of vegetarian dishes with many gluten-free options. During the winter months, an open fire provides a cosy atmosphere and there is a secluded courtyard for alfresco dining in summer.

BENDIGO Whirrakee

17 View Point, VIC 3550 **Tel** *(03) 5441 5557*

At this warm and inviting restaurant in Bendigo's historic Royal Bank Building, the Mod Oz menu samples the world's great cuisines, including French, Indian, Indonesian, Mediterranean and Vietnamese. The wine list features several local wines, including the fine Blackjack Shiraz and Passing Clouds Sauvignon Blanc.

CASTLEMAINE Templeton Café and Accommodation

31 Templeton Street, VIC 3450 **Tel** *(03) 5472 5311*

This modest but smart café-restaurant in a small gold-rush era terrace enjoys a reputation with locals for quality dining in a relaxed atmosphere. The rear, north-facing courtyard is particularly popular on a sunny afternoon. Vegetarians are well catered for, as are those popping in for coffee and cake. Open Thu–Sun.

CASTLEMAINE Tog's Place

58 Lyttleton Street, VIC 3450 **Tel** *(03) 5470 5090*

A cosy Castlemaine favourite. The food is hearty Mod Oz with Mediterranean and Asian tendencies. There is outdoor seating under the broad verandah at the front, and upstairs on the rooftop deck. The owners also operate the excellent delicatessen next door, which supplies local gourmet produce, quiche, bread and cheese.

DAYLESFORD Cliffy's

$$
30 Raglan Street, VIC 3460 **Tel** *(03) 5348 3279*

Down the hill from the Botanic Gardens and a few minutes' walk from the lively Sunday Market, this light and airy old shop is now a relaxed and mega-friendly café and produce store. It's perfect for a hearty slow-paced breakfast or a quick lunch, especially if you've managed to get an outside table on a sunny day.

DAYLESFORD Koukla
$$$
82 Vincent Street, VIC 3460 **Tel** *(03) 5348 2363*

Frangos & Frangos' younger offshoot next door is a more humble affair, serving inexpensive Italian options such as pasta, risotto and pizza. It is open for breakfast, lunch and dinner, and its bi-fold doors, which open out onto Vincent Street, ensure that the atmosphere is relaxed and casual. Very pleasant on a sunny afternoon.

DAYLESFORD Frangos & Frangos

$$$
82 Vincent Street, VIC 3460 **Tel** *(03) 5348 2363*

This fine-dining option in a former pub on Daylesford's main street delivers Mediterranean (essentially Greek) cuisine in a romantic setting. It's popular with weekenders and Melbourne tourists who gravitate towards its sophisticated Melbourne ambience and quality wine list. Hence, it's quite a scene.

DAYLESFORD Lake House

$$$
King Street, VIC 3460 **Tel** *(03) 5348 3329*

Seasonal local produce works with a light and airy setting and service par excellence to deliver an award-winning Mod Oz dining experience. Dine beside the open fire or take a seat outside under a market umbrella and overlooking the picturesque lake. Regarded by critics as one of Australia's top restaurants.

DUNKELD Royal Mail Hotel Bistro

$$
Glenelg Highway, VIC 3294 **Tel** *(03) 5577 2241*

This 1850s pub on a lonely stretch of highway at the southern end of the Grampians mountain range was completely overhauled and modernized several years ago. It now offers fine Mod Oz cuisine in a sophisticated setting, complemented by an award-winning cellar and wine list, and great views of Mount Sturgeon.

ECHUCA Oscar W's Wharfside

$$$
101 Murray Esplanade, VIC 3564 **Tel** *(03) 5482 5133*

Overlooking the Murray River, Oscar W's takes the cake for perfect settings. Its Mod Oz menu sources local produce to create memorable dishes such as fettucine with yabbies, twice-cooked duck with cinnamon pearl couscous, and pavlova with dark chocolate sauce, passionfruit, fresh mint and double cream.

GEELONG Go Food

$
37 Bellarine Street, VIC 3220 **Tel** *(03) 5229 4752*

Great for all-day breakfasts, lunchtime burgers and foccacia, and inexpensive and casual dinners. A popular option with Geelong's smart young set, this licensed café serves great coffee and cakes. The sunny courtyard is popular and the retro interior decor and laidback service makes folks feel like settling in.

GEELONG Le Parisien
$$$$
15 Eastern Beach Road, VIC 3218 **Tel** *(03) 5229 3110*

For that Big Night Out in Geelong, most locals head to this classic French restaurant in a boatshed overlooking Corio Bay. The menu delivers classic Gallic favourites and standards such as French onion soup, bouillabaisse and soufflé au chocolat. For a French-Australian culinary detour, try the marinated kangaroo fillet.

LORNE Kosta's Taverna
$$$
48 Mountjoy Parade, VIC 3232 **Tel** *(03) 5289 1883*

Kosta's eponymous owner and his wife sold the business a few years ago, but this lively Greek seafood restaurant is still a great spot to tuck into calamari, grilled whiting or haloumi. The setting is light with white tablecloths and bentwood chairs right on Lorne's main strip and across from the beach. It's packed in summer.

MALMSBURY The Stables Pizzeria
$
75 Mollison Street, VIC 3446 **Tel** *(03) 5423 2369*

On Friday and Saturday nights only, locals round up their kids and head to the small township of Malmsbury on the Calder Highway for the best gourmet pizzas for miles. The bluestone courtyard behind the jointly owned bakery is a relaxed setting and the pizzas, which include dessert options, are excellent.

MILDURA Ziggy's Café

$
145 Eighth Street, VIC 3500 **Tel** *(03) 5023 2626*

A popular family owned and operated licensed café that serves up Mediterranean inspired breakfasts, brunches and lunch. The food is more upmarket than its prices would suggest, with daily specials such as king prawn and asparagus risotto. There is a children's menu and they do a brisk trade in coffee and cake.

MILDURA Stefano's Restaurant

$$$$
Langtree Avenue, VIC 3502 **Tel** *(03) 5023 0511*

Located in the Grand Hotel's cellar, Stefano di Pieri's eponymous Italian restaurant is classic award-winning quality. Well known as the host of a successful TV cooking series (*A Gondola on the Murray*), Stefano is a dynamic advocate of local produce. His signature restaurant is a testament to his passion. Bookings advised.

Key to Price Guide *see p524* **Key to Symbols** *see back cover flap*

MOONAMBEL Warrenmang Vineyard Resort

*188 Mountain Creek Road, VIC 3478 **Tel** (03) 5467 2233*

Lunches at this vineyard restaurant in Victoria's Pyrenees-style Ranges are a casual affair, while dinner is more formal. The Modern European cuisine offers light lunch specials such as warm potato and asparagus salad. For dinner you could expect wild hare and pork trotter with prunes, hickory nuts and truffle cream sauce.

PORT FAIRY Victoria Hotel

*42 Bank Street, VIC 3284 **Tel** (03) 5568 2891*

Chef Joshua Heard serves up a Mod Oz menu at this pleasantly renovated 1850s pub in the centre of historic Port Fairy. You can dine simply in the café/courtyard (a popular music venue) or splurge at night when the café is transformed into Port Fairy's fine dining Mecca.

QUEENSCLIFF Queenscliff Hotel

*16 Gellibrand Street, VIC 3225 **Tel** (03) 5258 1066*

If you've ducked down to Queenscliff for a romantic weekend, and your bank account is flush, don't leave town without dining in this grand 19th-century seaside hotel's award-winning formal dining room. Meals in the bistro are a cheaper option for the budget-conscious. The cuisine is Mod Oz and highly recommended.

QUEENSCLIFF Vue Grand Dining Room

*46 Hesse Street, VIC 3225 **Tel** (03) 5258 1544*

Another grand Queenscliff experience with a menu to match. The main courses swing from Asian dishes such as drunken chicken (marinated in sake) to European flavours like sebago potatoes served with caramelized chicory and almond and beetroot jus. The desserts are visually spectacular and the wine list impressive.

WARRNAMBOOL Pippies by the Bay

*93 Merri Street, VIC 3280 **Tel** (03) 5561 2188*

With views that take in the Southern Ocean, including Lady Bay and the Shipwreck Coast, it's easy to while away a few hours on Pippies' outdoor terrace. Proving it is more than just a great place to break a long drive, the menu devoted to modern Italian fare is superb.

WOODEND Holgate Brewhouse

*79 High Street, VIC 3442 **Tel** (03) 5427 2510*

This revamped 1902 pub's bar, lounge, restaurant and beer garden are the hospitable arm of the family owned Holgate micro-brewery enterprise. The menu is designed to complement the beers on offer, but wine lovers need not despair with local tipples on offer for lunch and dinner. Bookings are advisable at weekends.

WOODEND Campaspe Country House

*29 Goldies Lane, VIC 3442 **Tel** (03) 5427 2273*

Chef Brad Lobb (ex Frangos & Frangos and Warrenmang) creates exquisite modern European menus based on seasonal produce sourced from local suppliers, such as the Tuki Trout Farm and Harcourt apple orchards. The elegant restaurant is an easy day trip from Melbourne and overlooks the pool. Bookings advisable.

EASTERN VICTORIA

ALEXANDRA Stonelea Country Estate

*Connelly's Creek Road, VIC 3714 **Tel** (03) 5772 2222*

It would be just so easy to settle in here and never leave. A major restaurant guide awarded the restaurant its first chef's hat in 2006, and with good reason. You might start the meal with a duck, ginger and udon noodle broth and end with a trio of home-made sorbets with vanilla and hazelnut biscotti.

AVENEL Thyme and Place

*2 Queen Street, VIC 3664 **Tel** (03) 5796 2688*

Located in scenic countryside an hour outside Melbourne, Thyme and Place offers a relaxed, casual atmosphere in which to enjoy modern, bistro-style food. Fresh seafood is the speciality on Thursday nights and there is a selection of wines from local vineyards. Delicious home-made cakes and desserts and pretty verandahs for alfresco dining. Closed on Tuesdays.

BAIRNSDALE Comfort Inn Riversleigh

*1 Nicholson Street, VIC 3875 **Tel** (03) 5152 6966*

Enjoy modern European cuisine in the formal dining room, or sample a casual brunch or dinner in the conservatory bistro. If you've stayed overnight and the weather is fine, you'll find the courtyard a pleasant setting for a traditional buffet-style breakfast. The wine list highlights Gippsland wineries.

BEECHWORTH Gigi's of Beechworth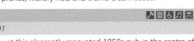

*69 Ford Street, VIC 3747 **Tel** (03) 5728 2575*

Open for breakfast, lunch and dinner, Gigi's regular clientele love the regional Italian cuisine, the extensive wine list (which features some of Italy's and northeast Victoria's best wines) and the imported Italian produce. The food is homely and filling, the coffee strong and inviting, and the service amiable. Closed Wednesdays.

BEECHWORTH Provenance Restaurant $$

86 Ford Street, VIC 3747 ***Tel*** *(03) 5728 2223*

A stately 1856 bank building with shady courtyard (and an adjoining guesthouse in converted stables and coach house if you need to linger), makes for an ideal culinary setting in this historic gold rush-era township. The food is Mod Oz and the cellar in the old gold vault is home to some fine Australian wine.

BRIGHT Sasha's on Bright $$

2d Anderson Street, VIC 3741 ***Tel*** *(03) 5750 1711*

The eponymous Sasha serves up Middle-European cuisine in this intimate, bistro-style restaurant. Roast duck with red cabbage and rösti is his signature dish (often preceded by a "duck call" from the kitchen). There are usually three children's specials on the menu. From November to May, book ahead. Open for dinner only.

BRIGHT Simone's Restaurant $$$

98 Gavan Street, VIC 3741 ***Tel*** *(03) 5755 2266*

Critics rave about the regional Italian cuisine served at Patrizia Simone's, where the emphasis is always on local seasonal produce. Signature dishes in this renovated heritage building on the main street include home-made pasta, pigeon, trout and goat, enhanced by local produce such as wild spinach.

DANDENONG RANGES Ripe $$

376 Mount Dandenong Tourist Road, Sassafras, VIC 3787 ***Tel*** *(03) 9755 2100*

This cosy weatherboard cottage is another eatery giving the Dandenongs an overdue culinary fillip. The menu shines with heartwarming favourites such as osso bucco, rabbit pie and lentil soup. On the lighter side there are baguettes and cakes. There's a deck out the back for summer dining and a corner fireplace in winter.

DANDENONG RANGES Wild Oak Café $$

Cnr Ridge Rd and Mt Dandenong Tourist Rd, Olinda, VIC 3788 ***Tel*** *(03) 9751 2033*

Wild Oak's award-winning formula is simple: deliver well-presented Mod Oz cuisine and fine wines in a relaxed contemporary setting. The menu features specials such as slow cooked confit duck leg and veal loin saltimbocca with fresh sage. There is live jazz on the last Friday of the month.

FALLS CREEK Astra Lodge Restaurant $$$

5 Sitzmark Street, VIC 3699 ***Tel*** *(03) 5758 3496*

Astra Lodge's restaurant starts the day with cooked and buffet breakfasts and ends with à la carte dining in the dining room. The menu is Mod Oz, specializing in local produce, for example, bush tomatoes and wild berries. There is an extensive wine list and the ambient Vodka Bar has almost 80 vodkas in stock.

LAKES ENTRANCE Nautilus Floating Dockside Restaurant $$$

Western Boat Harbour, The Esplanade, VIC 3909 ***Tel*** *(03) 5155 1400*

Unlike its Jules Verne's namesake, this floating restaurant keeps its head above water. It specializes in Gippsland wines, and given its position berthed alongside fishing craft, it couldn't help but offer Lakes Entrance scallops, Eden mussels and the catch of the day. Some say it's the best seafood in Gippsland.

MILAWA Milawa Factory Bakery & Restaurant $$

Factory Road, VIC 3678 ***Tel*** *(03) 5727 3589*

You can't blame the chef for insinuating Milawa cheeses into almost every menu item; it's one of Australia's best farmhouse cheesemakers. With relaxing views over the nearby ranges, the café menu has an Italian flavour, with inexpensive items such as polenta and grilled prosciutto with aged Milawa blue cheese sauce.

MILAWA The Epicurean Centre $$

Brown Brothers Winery, 239 Milawa–Bobinawarrah Road, VIC 3678 ***Tel*** *(03) 5720 5540*

The trick here is the attention paid to matching wine with local produce. Each dish is created to a balance with the flavours and textures of the wine. The menu is contemporary Asian and Mediterranean with locally sourced trout, nuts, mushrooms, beef, lamb, turkey, venison, berries and cheese.

MORNINGTON PENINSULA Coast 2827 $$

2827 Point Nepean Road, Blairgowrie, VIC 3942 ***Tel*** *(03) 5988 0700*

The staff here manage to keep everybody happy. Whether it's delivering a quick and satisfying brunch for the older customers, or keeping the little ones happy with a crayon and chips. At night the menu is likely to feature Asian-inspired seafood dishes. The decor is beach-shack chic and the atmosphere casual.

MORNINGTON PENINSULA Montalto Vineyard & Olive Grove $$$

33 Shoreham Road, Red Hill South, VIC 3937 ***Tel*** *(03) 5989 8412*

Combine contemporary architecture with French-inspired cuisine and views over the olive grove, vineyard and gardens and you have a winning formula. You can dine à la carte, or enjoy a casual meal at the café. They also cater for private picnics, which is an option worth considering in this picturesque area.

MOUNT BULLER Breathtaker Signature Restaurant $$$

Breathtaker All Suite Hotel, 8 Breathtaker Road, VIC 3723 ***Tel*** *(03) 5777 6377*

Open in winter, this smart restaurant offers views over Mount Buller Village and a contemporary menu with items such as barramundi with seasonal vegetables, oysters Kilpatrick and the popular dessert tasting menu – perfect on a winter's night. A café serves simpler fare all year round.

Key to Price Guide *see p524* **Key to Symbols** *see back cover flap*

MOUNT HOTHAM Zirky's $$$

Great Alpine Road, VIC 3741 **Tel** *(03) 5759 3518*

Zirky's offers à la carte dining in the restaurant, and breakfasts and lunches in the café and bar/bistro. The café serves cooked breakfasts, foccacias, hot chocolate and schnapps, while the Euro-centric menus in the restaurant and bistro/bar deliver hearty fillers such as lasagne and goulash. Open June to October.

NOOJEE The Outpost Retreat $$

38 Loch Valley Road, VIC 3833 **Tel** *(03) 5628 9669*

This rustic restaurant with wide verandahs is set beside the LaTrobe River en route to Mount Baw Baw. Chef John Snelling (ex Di Stasio) knows a thing or two about fine Italian food and his menu benefits from local produce, including Noojee trout. Open Friday nights and weekends only. The adjoining Toolshed Bistro offers cheaper fare.

OXLEY King River Café $$

Snow Road, VIC 3678 **Tel** *(03) 5727 3461*

If you're en route to Mount Buffalo, Falls Creek or Mount Hotham, the King River Café is a great halfway stop. The café occupies the town's charming 1860s post office and general store. The menu favours local King Valley wines and produce, and delivers fresh and ever-changing Mediterranean and Asian flavours.

PHILLIP ISLAND Harry's on the Esplanade $$

17 The Esplanade, Cowes, VIC 3922 **Tel** *(03) 5952 6226*

The cuisine is middle-European, with seafood delights such as crayfish thrown in for good measure. Close your eyes and tuck into veal with dumplings and you could be back in Budapest. Open them again and enjoy the ocean views from the balcony. The chef also prepares his own bread, pastries and ice cream.

PHILLIP ISLAND "Hotel" $$

11–13 The Esplanade, Cowes, VIC 3922 **Tel** *(03) 5952 2060*

With beach frontage and views to match, it's understandable that this old-timer's menu is heavy on the seafood, offering classics such as whole baby snapper and that 1970s throwback, the "surf and turf". Although char-grilled kangaroo with plum sauce might be more to your liking. The decor is rustic and homey.

YARRA VALLEY De Bortoli Winery and Restaurant $$$

Pinnacle Lane, Dixons Creek, VIC 3775 **Tel** *(03) 5965 2271*

The Wow Factor is big at this award-winning vineyard restaurant. The De Bortoli family are winemaking legends and the North Italian menu at their Yarra Valley restaurant sparkles with gems such as braised ox tongue with fennel, borlotti beans and salsa. Try the poached quince with star anise and honey for dessert.

YARRA VALLEY Eleonore's at Chateau Yering $$$

42 Melba Highway, Yering, VIC 3770 **Tel** *(03) 9237 3333*

It's best not to ponder the menu too long. Just dive in and drift from poached oysters to braised squab with chestnuts to prune and Armagnac soufflé. Chef Shane Delia will guarantee you won't be disappointed. The setting is elegant with garden views. The adjoining Sweetwater Cafe is marginally cheaper.

YARRA VALLEY Healesville Hotel $$$

256 Maroondah Highway, VIC 3777 **Tel** *(03) 5962 4002*

As if two Tucker Seabrook awards for their wine list weren't enough, this 1910 pub won *The Age*'s 2006 gong for Best Country Restaurant. The laidback bistro and stylish dining room menu rely on quality local produce, including Buxton salmon, Yarra Valley dairy cheeses and homegrown herbs, salad greens and venison.

TASMANIA

BATTERY POINT Da Angelo Ristorante $$

47 Hampden Road, Battery Point, TAS 7004 **Tel** *(03) 6223 7011*

This little piece of Italy located in historic Battery Point serves home-made pasta, pizza and ice cream. Much loved by locals for its excellent value for money and legendary pizzas, meals are presented with true Italian style and hospitality. A Hobart institution for many years, it is packed seven nights a week, so be sure to book ahead.

BATTERY POINT/HOBART Piccalilly $$$

Hampden Road, Battery Point, TAS 7004 **Tel** *(03) 6224 9900*

Piccalilly's imaginative menu groups its selections not by entrées, mains and desserts but instead by sweet or savoury flavours. Temptations include Sicilian white anchovies with chorizo and red onion purée, and carrot sponge with ginger sorbet and salted caramel. There's also a small selection of carefully picked wines.

CAMPBELL TOWN Zeps Café $$$

92–94 High Street, TAS 7210 **Tel** *(03) 6381 1344*

Definitely the best food stop on the Heritage Highway between Hobart and Launceston. This licensed cafe serves an all-day breakfast, great pizzas, toasted panini, pasta and more. There's a great range of sweets available, hot and cold drinks, plus excellent coffee to prepare you for the journey ahead.

COLES BAY The Bay Restaurant

Freycinet National Park, TAS 7215 **Tel** *(03) 6257 0102*

Set amidst the Freycinet National Park and the stunning Great Oyster Bay, this low-key but luxurious holiday lodge offers both formal and casual dining options. Richardson Bistro opens from 10am while the more formal Bay Restaurant serves breakfast and dinner, and offers a comprehensive wine list.

CRADLE MOUNTAIN Highland Restaurant

Cradle Mountain Lodge, TAS 7306 **Tel** *(03) 6492 1303*

Excellent Tasmanian wines (if a little high-priced) and modern Australian cuisine are the specialities of this sophisticated restaurant located on the edge of Tasmania's World Heritage wilderness area. The restaurant also offers an enormous buffet breakfast for guests wanting to make a solid start to a day of wilderness exploration.

CRADLE VALLEY Lemonthyme Lodge

Dolcoath Road, Moina, TAS 7306 **Tel** *(03) 6492 1112*

Award-winning restaurant offering fine food and wine. The dinner menu features Tasmanian produce, including game, local meat and seafood. The wine cellar has an extensive range of fine Australian and Tasmanian wines. After dinner warmth is provided around the huge open fire in the lounge.

HOBART Fish Frenzy

Elizabeth Street Pier, TAS 7000 **Tel** *(03) 6231 2134*

One of the best value eateries on the Hobart waterfront, serving big paper cones of excellent fish and chips in different incarnations, plus enormous seafood platters and other creations. Fish Frenzy caters for children and there are plenty of outside tables right on the water of Victoria Dock.

HOBART Marti Zucco's

364 Elizabeth Street, North Hobart, TAS 7000 **Tel** *(03) 6234 9611*

Marti Zuccos was one of the first restaurants in Hobart to serve "international" food. As popular as ever, Marti's is a eat-in or takeaway pizza and pasta restaurant, with a range of traditional Italian meat dishes and home-made gelato. Great prices, casual dining, BYO and fully licensed.

HOBART Siam Garden Restaurant

81a Bathurst Street, TAS 7000 **Tel** *(03) 6234 4327*

Tucked away upstairs off Bathurst Street in Hobart's CBD, Siam Garden could be easily missed as it is out of the main restaurant precincts. Serving really good Thai food that is excellent value for money in a relaxed and casual atmosphere. If you like your Thai extra-hot then ask the cheerful staff and the chef will gladly oblige.

HOBART Sirens

6 Victoria Street, Hobart, TAS 7000 **Tel** *(03) 6234 2634*

Sirens is a lusciously decorated, Persian harem-style restaurant in Hobart's CBD. Serving exquisite vegetarian dishes with vegan and gluten-free options, the menu at Sirens lends itself to the sharing of lots of small to medium-size dishes. Be sure to leave room for divine desserts, such as the decadent chocolate Cointreau tart.

HOBART The Point Revolving Restaurant

410 Sandy Bay Road, Sandy Bay, TAS 7005 **Tel** *1800 030 611*

Superb 360-degree views are a feature of this revolving restaurant in Australia's longest-running casino. The Point's international/modern Australian menu caters to a broad clientele. There is a lounge and cocktail bar for those just wanting to take in the ever-changing mountain, city and river vistas.

HOBART Prossers on the Beach

Beach Road, Sandy Bay, TAS 7005 **Tel** *(03) 6225 2276*

Set in the Sandy Bay Regatta Pavilion just metres from the popular Nutgrove Beach, Prossers has great views and a reputation for excellence. Its speciality is seafood and incorporating the finest Tasmanian produce into its quality dishes. Prossers has received Tasmania's best seafood restaurant award multiple times.

HOBART Drunken Admiral

17–19 Hunter Street, Old Wharf, TAS 7000 **Tel** *(03) 6234 1903*

Tasmania's most distinctive seafarer's restaurant serves fresh fish in both traditional and international styles. The Drunken Admiral offers a lot more than just seafood and there are a number of set menus to choose from, plus a children's menu. The nautical decor adds to the atmosphere.

LAUDERDALE Eating on the Edge

13 North Terrace, TAS 7021 **Tel** *(03) 6248 7707*

With a loyal following of regulars, both local and from across town, this beachside restaurant serves well-priced fine Italian food and seafood. Eating on the Edge boasts stunning views and a relaxed atmosphere. The servings are generous and the service friendly – excellent value for money.

LAUNCESTON Levee Food Co.

27 Seaport Blvd, Launceston, TAS 7250 **Tel** *(03) 6334 7011*

Enjoying a prime location on the Launceston waterfront, the Levee has a bright, airy dining room with lovely views of the ocean. The modern Australian and Mediterranean menu covers everything from pizzas and pastas to scotch fillet steaks and fresh Tasmanian seafood. The Levee burger is their signature dish.

Key to Price Guide *see p524* **Key to Symbols** *see back cover flap*

LAUNCESTON Jailhouse Grill
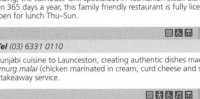
$$

32 Wellington Street, Launceston, TAS 7250 **Tel** *(03) 6331 0466*

Located in a heritage-listed, convict-built building, the Jailhouse Grill specializes in Tasmanian steak dishes, cooked how you like it with a myriad of sauces. Open 365 days a year, this family friendly restaurant is fully licensed, featuring a comprehensive wine list and is open for lunch Thu–Sun.

LAUNCESTON Pickled Evenings
$$

135 George Street, Launceston, TAS 7250 **Tel** *(03) 6331 0110*

This small restaurant brings modern Indian Punjabi cuisine to Launceston, creating authentic dishes made with aromatic spices. Specialities include *zaffrani murg malai* (chicken marinated in cream, curd cheese and saffron then cooked in the tandoor oven). There is also a takeaway service.

LAUNCESTON The Metz Café Bar
$$$

119 St John Street, Launceston, TAS 7250 **Tel** *(03) 6331 7277*

The Metz is a popular café/wine bar in central Launceston, offering casual dining in an often lively atmosphere. Their wood-fired pizza is very popular with locals and they also serve pasta, salads and traditional pub food plus an extensive wine list and beers on tap. The Metz has opened a sister café in the Hobart suburb of Sandy Bay.

LAUNCESTON Pierre's on George
$$$

88 George Street Launceston, TAS 7250 **Tel** *(03) 6331 6835*

Pierre's is a Launceston institution. The city's oldest café/restaurant was the birthplace of Launceston's café culture. Today, Pierre's stretches a block in the CBD, from street to rear courtyard. Offering quiet nooks for coffee contemplation plus plenty of people-watching opportunities.

LAUNCESTON Stillwater River Café

$$$$

Ritchies Mill, 2 Bridge Road, TAS 7250 **Tel** *(03) 6331 4153*

Offering a casual café atmosphere by day, it is Stillwater's evening dinner menu by chef Don Cameron that has won it acclaim. Situated in the old Ritchies Mill historic site, with views across the river, the Stillwater complex incorporates a providore and craft store upstairs and an amazing stone wine cellar below.

NORTH HOBART Annapurna

$$

Elizabeth Street, North Hobart **Tel** *(03) 6236 9500*

Located in Hobart's multicultural food district, Elizabeth Street, North Hobart, Annapurna serves great value Indian cuisine, using traditional recipes and cooking techniques. They offer great vegetarian options and a legendary Masala Dosa. This place is often packed to the rafters, so be sure to book. The banquets are exceptional value for money.

NORTH HOBART Raincheck Lounge

$$

392 Elizabeth Street, North Hobart **Tel** *(03) 6234 5975*

Groovy, retro-inspired decor and well-priced favourites have made the Raincheck Lounge a real hit. Café-style eatery by day, the establishment also boasts an impressive cocktail list making it ideal for those in for the long haul. Located on the cosmopolitan restaurant strip of Elizabeth Street, north of the CBD.

SALAMANCA Maldini Restaurant
$$

47 Salamanca Place, Hobart, TAS7004 **Tel** *(03) 6223 4460*

Crown Prince Frederick of Denmark dined here; so did swim star Ian Thorpe. Hobart's famous visitors are discovering what locals have known for years – Maldini serves fabulous Italian food. Located on historic Salamanca Place, this sleek café/restaurant also boasts great coffee and home-made cakes that keep it thriving all day long.

SHEFFIELD Weindorfers

$$

Wellington Street, Gowrie Park, TAS 7306 **Tel** *(03) 6491 1385*

In memory of Gustav Weindorfer (founder of Cradle Mountain National Park) and his wife, Kate, Weindorfer's serves generous portions of home-cooked country fare. Located in a rustic, shingled building beneath the mystical beauty of Mount Roland, Weindorfer's is a licensed restaurant seating up to 60 plus a private room for 100.

STRAHAN Franklin Manor
$$

The Esplanade, Strahan, TAS7468 **Tel** *(03) 6471 7311*

Strahan's most gracious mansion provides quality accommodation and a first-class dining experience. Admire the superb 19th-century garden from the dining room or the verandah. There is a strong emphasis on Tasmanian produce and there is a select selection of premium Tasmanian wines.

STRAHAN Risby Cove
$$$

The Esplanade, Strahan, TAS 7486 **Tel** *(03) 6471 7572*

This eco-tourism centre is situated right on the water's edge, overlooking Strahan's harbour. At Risby Cove the emphasis is on seasonal, fresh ingredients, complementary flavours and impeccable presentation. The knowledgeable staff and harbourside ambience create a wonderful dining experience.

WOODBRIDGE Peppermint Bay

$$

3435 Channel Highway, Woodbridge, TAS 7162 **Tel** *(03) 6267 4088*

Cruise from the Hobart docks or drive the scenic route to this world-class establishment incorporating a fine-dining restaurant, casual local bar serving quality pub food, and a craft and produce centre. Peppermint Bay supports local suppliers by sourcing produce from the surrounding region. The views are magnificent.

SHOPPING IN AUSTRALIA

Colourful craft shop sign in Margaret River

Australia has much to offer the visiting shopper beyond the standard tourist fare of koala bear purses and plastic boomerangs. The tourist shops can be worth exploring, some stock being of a high standard and including goods not available in other countries. In each state capital, especially Sydney *(see pp132–5)* and Melbourne *(see pp406–9)*, there are precincts and open-air markets with a range of shops, stalls and cafés to explore. Wine and gourmet food products are a major attraction, and a wide range of reasonably priced world-class goods is available. Australian contemporary design has a refreshing irreverence for convention – look out for homewares and fashion in the inner-city precincts. In country areas, unusual items made by local craftspeople make good buys. Australia has a goods and services tax (GST), adding 10 per cent to the cost of most manufactured items.

Browsers at a stall in Mindil Beach Sunset Markets, Darwin *(see p272)*

SHOPPING HOURS

Standard weekday opening times are 9am–5:30pm, Monday to Friday. Late night shopping is usually available on Thursdays or Fridays, when stores stay open until 9pm. Weekend hours vary greatly. Deregulation has meant that many stores, particularly in city locations, open on both Saturday and Sunday. In most country areas, however, stores will open only until 1pm on Saturday. A few supermarkets in city and suburban areas operate 24 hours. Bookshops and other specialist shops stay open late – until around 10pm – in downtown areas.

HOW TO PAY

Major credit cards are accepted by most stores, sometimes with a minimum purchase limit. Identification, such as a valid passport or driver's licence, is required when using traveller's cheques. Personal cheques are also accepted at the majority of larger stores, with identification, but a telephone check on your account may be made. Payment by cash is the preferred method for traders and can be used to negotiate a lower price for your goods in some instances.

RIGHTS AND REFUNDS

The laws on consumer rights in Australia vary slightly from state to state. If you have a complaint or query, look under "Consumer" in the government section at the front of the White Pages telephone directory. If the goods purchased are defective in any way, customers are entitled to a full refund. If you decide you don't like an item, try to get a refund, but you will probably have to settle for a credit note or exchange. As a general rule, the larger stores are more lenient – you can always ask to speak to a manager or customer relations officer if you are unhappy with the service you receive.

ESSENTIALLY AUSTRALIAN

Aboriginal art is available for purchase from community-owned or managed galleries in the Northern Territory and good specialist galleries in the cities. Take the time to discuss the work with the painter or gallery staff: spiritual and cultural meanings are inextricably linked with aesthetic properties, and the painting or artifact that you choose will be all the more valuable with a little knowledge. These

Shoppers in London Court, Perth's Tudor-style street *(see p304)*

A colourful arts and crafts stall in one of Australia's many markets

artworks are by their nature expensive, so do not be beguiled by cheaper imitations

Australia produces 95 per cent of the world's opals. Their quality varies greatly, so when considering a purchase a little research will go a long way. Opals are widely available at duty-free stores. Many other places will deduct the luxury excise tax from the price if you produce your passport.

Outback clothing is a specialist industry in Australia. Look for Akubra hats, boots by RM Williams and Driza-bone overcoats in camping and army stores. Surf clothing has become highly desirable among tourists, as it can be a lot cheaper to buy in Australia than abroad. Board shorts and bikinis are popular purchases.

Fresh fish on display at Wollongong Fish Market (see p186)

MARKETS

Most Australian cities have a large central produce market and a range of small community markets that operate at the weekend. The bustling city food markets are as sensational for their vibrant multicultural atmosphere as they are for the extraordinary range of fresh, cheap produce available. Look out for local

specialities such as cheeses, olives and unusual fruits. Melbourne's Queen Victoria Market (see p386) and the Adelaide Central Market (see p346) are particularly good and well worth visiting. Community markets, such as those in Paddington, Sydney (see p125), and Salamanca Place, Hobart (see p466), offer an interesting and eclectic range of locally designed clothing and crafts. In a class of their own, the Mindil Beach Sunset Markets in Darwin combine eating, shopping and entertainment in a spectacular tropical setting (see p272).

DEPARTMENT STORES

Department stores occupy the up-market end of the chain-store scale and sell quality merchandise. They include names such as Myer and David Jones (see p406) and some of the top stores are sumptuously decorated. Local and overseas designer fashions, top-brand cosmetics and all manner of household goods and furnishings can be purchased. These stores are competitive and will often match prices on identical items found at more down-market stores. Their shopper facilities and standards for customer service are excellent.

SHOPPING PRECINCTS

Because the city centres have been colonized by the retail giants in Australia, many small and interesting shops have moved out to the lively precincts that lie somewhere between the city centre and

suburbia. These precincts represent some of the best and most interesting shopping in the country. Young designer outlets, specialist book stores, craft studios and galleries sit next to food stores, cafés, restaurants and bars. Some of these precincts are decidedly up-market, while others relish their bohemian roots. There is nearly always a strong mix of cultural influences – Jewish, Italian, Lebanese, Vietnamese, for example – depending on the area and the city. Ask at tourist information centres for the best precincts in each city.

Herbal infusions on sale in Brisbane's Chinatown (see p218)

OUT OF TOWN

Shopping in Australian country areas can be a mixed experience. In some areas the range of standard items is limited and prices can be much higher than you would expect to pay in the city. However, there are always unexpected surprises such as dusty second-hand shops with rare knick-knacks at absurdly low prices and small craft outlets and galleries with unusual items that make great gifts.

The attractive tiled interior of a shopping arcade in Adelaide

SPECIALIST HOLIDAYS AND OUTDOOR ACTIVITIES

To make the most of a trip to a country as vast and geographically diverse as Australia, a specialist holiday is an excellent idea. Whether you're pursuing an interest, acquiring a new skill or learning about the environment, such holidays can be very rewarding experiences. There is a wide range of specialist operators to

Sign for glass-bottom boat tour in Western Australia

choose from. If travelling to Australia from abroad, the best starting points are the local Tourism Australia offices or your local travel agent. Once in the country, the state tourism associations *(see p575)* can offer expert advice, make bookings with reputable companies and contact local activity associations for information.

Bushwalking in Namadgi National Park in the ACT *(see p207)*

BUSHWALKING

National Parks are without doubt the best places for bushwalking in Australia. Not only do they preserve the best of the country's natural heritage, but they also offer expert advice and well-marked trails for bushwalkers. These parks are state-managed and each state has a central information service. Look under "National Parks" in the government listings at the front of the telephone directory.

Equipment, including backpacks, boots and tents, is available for hire from camping stores in city and country areas. Joining up with a tour is a good alternative for those planning long bushwalking trips, as tour members will benefit from a guide's expertise on local flora and fauna, and access to remote wilderness areas. Exceptional bushwalking regions in Australia include Cradle Mountain in Tasmania

(see p467), the MacDonnell Ranges in the Northern Territory *(see p284)* and the Blue Mountains in New South Wales *(see pp170–73)*.

CYCLING

With its vast stretches of near-empty roads, many of them without a hill in sight, it is no wonder that Australia is becoming increasingly popular as a long-distance cycling destination. Visitors can bring their own bicycles, but are advised to check first whether this is acceptable with the airlines. Trains and buses will usually carry bikes provided they are dismantled. To hire a bike in Australia, look under "Bicycles" in the Yellow Pages. Bike helmets are a legal

requirement throughout Australia and can be bought cheaply or hired.

Many cyclists spend several days on the road camping along the way, while others will arrange an itinerary that allows them to stop for the comfort of a bed and meal in a town. The wine-growing areas of South Australia *(see pp338–9)*, the Great Ocean Road in Victoria *(see pp428–9)* and almost anywhere in Tasmania *(see pp456–71)* are terrific cycling destinations.

Bicycling associations in Australia also arrange regular cycling tours that anyone can join. These include accommodation, food and vehicle backup; most of the organizations are non-profit-making, so the costs are generally low. Contact **Bicycle New South Wales** for a catalogue specializing in Australian cycling publications. They will also provide information on their sister associations in other states.

Cycling around Canberra's lake *(see pp194–5)*

ADVENTURE SPORTS

Appropriate training is a component of adventure sports in Australia, so novices are always welcome alongside more expert adventurers. Contact specialist tour operators or national associations *(see p569)* for information about anything from a one-day class to a two-week tour.

Abseiling, canyoning, rock climbing and caving are all popular in Australia, which has some fantastic natural landscapes ideally suited to these pursuits. The Blue Mountains are something of a mecca for enthusiasts of all the above. Naracoorte in South Australia *(see p355)* is a great location for caving, while the Grampians National Park in Victoria *(see p427)* attracts a large share of abseilers and climbers.

Climbing on Wilsons Promontory in Victoria *(see p444)*

GOLF

There are more than 1,500 golf courses in Australia and 1,580 golf clubs. Many clubs have affiliations with clubs overseas and offer reciprocal membership rights, so check with your own club. There are also public municipal golf courses in many towns.

Australian courses are of a high standard, and Melbourne is home to two of the top 30 courses in the world, the Royal Melbourne and Kingston Heath. A round of golf will cost anything from A$20–$250. The **Australian Golf Union** has a handbook that lists all of the golf courses in Australia.

Camel trekking along Cable Beach, Broome *(see p330)*

ABORIGINAL HERITAGE TOURS

Aboriginal heritage tours can range from a visit to an Aboriginal art gallery to days spent with an Aboriginal guide touring Arnhem Land or Kakadu National Park in the Northern Territory *(see pp276–7)*. With the highest percentage of Aboriginal land and people in the country, the Northern Territory has the greatest number of activities, but there are sights and operators all over Australia. The focus of activities varies and may encompass a number of themes, including traditional bush food, hunting, rock art and Aboriginal culture.

Perhaps the best aspect of many of these tours is the chance to see the remarkable Australian landscape from a different perspective; Aboriginal spirituality is closely linked with the land. In addition, some tours will journey to Australia's most remote areas and travel through Aboriginal lands that are usually closed to all but members of the local Aboriginal communities.

CAMEL TREKKING

Camels have been an invaluable form of transport in Australia's Outback since Afghan-run camel trains were used to carry goods across the Australian desert from the 1840s until the coming of the railway. Joining a camel trek today is still an adventure, and activities range from a one-hour jaunt to a two-week trek. Food and accommodation (usually camping) are provided by tour operators. Alice Springs *(see pp282–3)* is the most popular starting point, but tours are available country-wide.

AERIAL TOURS

Aerial Tours can provide an exhilarating overview of an area and are a good option for time-restricted travellers who want to see some of the more far-flung attractions. Aerial safaris, stopping at major sights, are popular in the Outback. For charter flights to Australia's furthest flung territory, Antarctica, contact **Croydon Travel**.

Seaplane moored at Rose Bay in Sydney, ready for a scenic flight

FISHING

Australia has around four million fishing enthusiasts and, given the country's natural advantages, it's not difficult to see why. Vast oceans, a 12,000-km (7,500-mile) shoreline and a large inland river system, all combined with a terrific climate, make Australia a haven for local and visiting anglers alike.

Fishing for barramundi in the remote inland waters of the Northern Territory and game fishing off Australia's tropical coastline for species such as black marlin and yellowfin tuna are among the world's best fishing experiences. You will need to join a charter as these activities require a great deal of local expertise. Most operators will provide equipment.

The inland waters of Tasmania are famed for their excellent trout fishing prospects. The estuaries and beaches in the southern states, such as the Fleurieu Peninsula in South Australia *(see pp350–51)*, are full of species such as bream, salmon and flathead. Small boats are readily available for hire and fishing tackle can be bought and occasionally hired at most popular fishing destinations. Each state has a government department with a special fisheries section. Staff provide excellent information on locations, restrictions, safety issues and obtaining fishing licences. Check the weather forecast and heed warnings about dangerous spots, particularly rock platforms.

Mural advertising water-based recreational activities

ECOTOURISM

This tourism concept has its roots in activities as old as bird watching and wildflower identification. It incorporates many of the activities mentioned in this section, but is generally distinguished by its emphasis on issues concerning the appreciation and conservation

Canoeing on the Roper River in the Northern Territory *(see pp268–9)*

of the natural heritage. Given Australia's enormous natural bounty, it is hardly surprising that the market is now flooded with operators offering an astonishing range of nature-based activities. These encompass wildlife watching (including whales, birds and dolphins), nature walks, and trekking and rafting expeditions to remote wilderness areas. Visitors can also stay at resorts which are operated along strictly "green" guidelines. These are eco-friendly and are usually located within some of the most environmentally valuable regions in the country. The **Ecotourism Association of Australia** can provide information on tour operators and publications.

WATER SPORTS

Australia is one of the world's great diving destinations, and the Great Barrier Reef is the centre of most of the diving activity *(see pp212–17)*. Visitors can combine a holiday on the reef with a few days of diving instruction from one of the many excellent schools in the area. There are opportunities for diving all around Australia, however, and other popular locations include Rottnest Island *(see pp308–9)* and Esperance *(see p319)* in

Western Australia and the beautiful World Heritage Area of Lord Howe Island off the coast of New South Wales.

Canoeing in Australia can mean a quiet paddle in a hireboat on a city lake, or an exciting adventure in a kayak on the high seas. It is a reasonably priced sport and is widely available throughout the country. Popular spots include the Murray River *(see p355)*, Sydney Harbour *(see pp144–5)* and the rivers of national parks nationwide.

Whitewater rafting is another favourite sport in this land of outdoor enthusiasts and there are many opportunities for people of all abilities to have a go. The inexperienced can try a day with an instructor on an easy run; the confident can tackle a two-week tour on the rafter's mecca, the Franklin-Gordon River system in Tasmania *(see p468)*.

Sailing in Gippsland Lakes Coastal Park, Eastern Victoria *(see p444)*

Long stretches of unspoilt coastline, remote bays and harbours, tropical reefs and uninhabited islands make Australia an excellent destination for sailing enthusiasts. Skippered cruises are the most usual kind of holiday, but some visitors will want to hire a vessel and set off for themselves – a practice known as bareboating. To do this you will need to prove to the operator that you are an experienced sailor. It is difficult to beat the tropical splendours of the Whitsunday Islands in Queensland *(see p216)* as a location. Other popular sailing areas include Pittwater in New South Wales and Queensland's Gold Coast *(see pp238–9)*.

Australia is also world-renowned for its abundance of outstanding surfing beaches. For more information about the country's best places to surf, see pages 38–9.

SKIING

The Ski season in Australia extends from June to September. Downhill skiing is restricted to the Victorian Alps *(see p446–9)*, the New South Wales mountains and two small resorts in Tasmania *(see p469)*. The ski villages have excellent facilities, but the fields can get crowded during school holidays and long weekends, and prices for ski-lifts and equipment hire can be high.

Upland areas around these resorts are superb for cross-country skiing. Traversing gentle slopes and rounded

Skiing Eagle Ridge on Mount Hotham in the Victoria Alps

peaks, skiers will be treated to glimpses of Australia's rare alpine flora and fauna, and spectacular sweeping scenery.

SPECTATOR SPORTS

Most sports enthusiasts will enjoy taking in a fixture during their trip, while a few visitors come to Australia especially for a sporting event, such as yacht races, cricket or tennis events. Early booking is advisable as competition for tickets can be fierce. Regular highlights include the Australian Tennis Open, Melbourne Cup and the Formula 1 Grand Prix, all Melbourne events, and international Test cricket and the Australian Open golf that moves each year *(see pp40–43)*. Rugby League and Australian Rules football are the most popular spectator sports. The finals are the main event, but excitement is high at almost any match.

AFL Australian Rules football grand final in Melbourne

DIRECTORY

CLUBS AND ASSOCIATIONS

Australian Golf Union
95 Coventry St,
South Melbourne, VIC 3205.
Tel (03) 9626 5050.
www.agu.org.au

Australian Parachute Federation
Unit 3, 2994 Logan Road,
Underwood, QLD 4119. *Tel (07) 3457 0100.* www.apf.asn.au

Australian Yachting Federation
22 Atchison St, St Leonards, NSW 2065. *Tel (02) 8424 7400.*
www.yachting.org.au

Bicycle New South Wales
1st Floor, Heritage Building A, 1 Herb Elliott Ave, Sydney Olympic Park, Homebush Bay, NSW 2127.
Tel (02) 9704 0800.
www.bicyclensw.org.au

Ecotourism Association of Australia
Tel (07) 3252 1530.
www.ecotourism.org.au

Gliding Federation of Australia
130 Wirraway Rd, Essendon Airport, VIC 3041.
Tel (03) 9303 7805.
www.gfa.org.au

New South Wales Snow Sports Association
PO Box 934, Jindabyne, NSW 2627. *Tel 0408 006 415.*
www.nswsnowsports.com.au

Skiing Australia
1 Cobden St, South Melbourne, VIC 3205. *Tel (03) 9696 2344.*
www.skiingaustralia.org.au

TOUR OPERATORS

Adventure Associates
Level 7, 12–14 O'Connell St, Sydney. *Tel (02) 8916 3000.*
www.adventureassociates.com

Croydon Travel
34 Main St, Croydon, VIC 3136.
Tel (03) 9725 8555.
www.croydontravel.com.au

STA Travel
Tel 134 782.
www.statravel.com.au

World Expeditions
Level 5, 71 York St, Sydney, NSW 2000. *Tel 1300 720 000.*
www.worldexpeditions.com.au

SURVIVAL GUIDE

PRACTICAL INFORMATION

International tourist information sign

Australia continues to surge ahead as a major tourist destination, and facilities for travellers have kept pace with this rapid development. Visitors should encounter few problems in this safe and friendly destination. Accommodation and restaurants *(see pp474–563)* are of international standard, public transport is readily available *(see pp584–91)* and tourist information

centres are everywhere. The following pages contain useful information for all visitors. Personal Security and Health *(see pp576–7)* details a number of recommended precautions, Banking and Local Currency *(see pp578–9)* answers all essential financial queries, and Communication and Media *(see pp580–81)* describes Australia's telephone, Internet and postal services.

Skiers enjoying the slopes at Falls Creek in Eastern Victoria *(see p449)*

WHEN TO GO

The northern half of the country lies in a tropical zone and is subject to "wet" and "dry" seasons *(see pp44–5)*. The dry season falls between May and October, and is regarded as the best time to visit this area. During the wet season, conditions are hot and humid, and many areas are inaccessible because of flooding. For those with an interest in wildlife, however, there are areas such as Kakadu National Park *(see pp276–7)* which are particularly spectacular at this time of year.

The southern half of the continent is temperate and the seasons are the exact opposite to those in Europe and North America. Victoria and Tasmania can be a little cloudy and wet in winter, but they are very colourful and quite balmy in autumn. The vast southern coastline is a popular touring destination during the summer months – the climate is warm, with a gentle breeze. Avoid the Outback areas during the

summer, however, as the temperatures can be extreme.

The popular ski season is between June and September and takes place in both the New South Wales Snowy Mountains *(see p187)* and the Victoria Alps *(see pp448–9)*. In the states of South Australia and Western Australia, there are spectacular wild flower displays between September and December.

ENTRY REQUIREMENTS

Visitors to Australia must have a passport valid for longer than the intended period of stay. All visitors, except New Zealand passport holders, must also have a visa issued before arrival. For stays of up to three months the easiest option for most is to get an Electronic Travel Authority (ETA), or an eVisitors, depending on the country of origin. Neither requires a stamp in your passport or has a visa application charge. They can be obtained from travel agents, airlines (usually when you book your flight) or can

be applied for online at the **Department of Immigration** website *(see p575)*.

For stays of three to six months, a tourist visa may be applied for in person at the Australian Embassy or by post. Visitors will be asked for proof of a return ticket and of sufficient funds for the duration of their stay. Some visitors, including British nationals, between the ages of 18 and 30 may apply for a 12-month working holiday visa.

TOURIST INFORMATION

Tourism Australia is the central tourism body, but each state and territory has its own tourism authority. Travel centres in the capital cities provide abundant information and these are often the best places to seek advice on specialist tours and to make bookings. Information booths can also be found at airports, tourist sites and in shopping centres.

Smaller towns often have tourist offices located in general stores, galleries or

Visitor information kiosk and booking centre

◁ **Caravan driving through The Olgas (Kata Tjuṯa) in the Northern Territory**

The platform and view of Sydney Harbour at Circular Quay station, accessible to disabled travellers

petrol stations – look for the blue and white information symbol. In remoter areas, national park visitors' centres will provide useful information on bushwalks and the local terrain.

OPENING HOURS AND ADMISSION PRICES

Most major tourist sites are open seven days a week, but it is always advisable to check first. However, many places are closed on

Aquarium sign in Queensland

Christmas Day and Good Friday. In smaller places, galleries and other sites are often closed during the early part of the week. Admission prices are generally moderate and, in some cases, admission is free. Exceptions are major touring exhibitions, zoos, theme parks and specialist attractions such as Sovereign Hill in Ballarat (see p433). Make the most of weekdays – locals will be competing for viewing space at weekends.

ETIQUETTE

While Australian society is generally laid-back, there are a few unwritten rules which visitors should follow.

Australians drive on the left and, generally, also walk on the left-hand side of a path, stairway or busy escalator, to allow others to pass. Eating and drinking is frowned upon while travelling on public transport, in taxis and also in many shops and galleries.

Dress codes are casual, particularly in summer when the weather can get very hot, but some bars and restaurants may require men to wear shirts and place a ban on jeans and sports shoes.

Topless bathing is accepted in designated areas on some beaches, but it is advisable to see what the locals are doing. While a tiny bikini may go unnoticed on the beach, it is considered polite to cover up when sitting in a café or restaurant.

Continental table manners apply in restaurants. Placing your knife and fork together on the plate indicates to wait staff that you have finished your meal. Tipping is optional; however, 10 to 15 per cent of the final bill for good service in a restaurant is customary, as is rounding up to the nearest dollar for taxi drivers, porters and bar tenders.

Smoking is prohibited in all public buildings, on public transport, in taxis, stores, sports grounds, cafés, and restaurants. Depending on the state, smoking is also banned to a lesser or greater extent in pubs and nightclubs, with many providing an outdoor smoking area. Ask about smoking policies when booking hotels.

To avoid causing offence, always ask before taking someone's photograph, especially if the person is an Aboriginal Australian. If taking photographs for commercial purposes, permission is required before photographing on private land.

DISABLED TRAVELLERS

Disabled travellers can generally expect the best in Australia in terms of facilities. Many hotels, restaurants, tourist sites, cinemas, theatres, airports and shopping centres have wheelchair facilities, and guide dogs for the blind are always welcomed.

Traditionally, public transport is a problem for wheelchair users, although most states are now making their systems more accessible to disabled travellers. Contact the transport authority state by state for more detailed information. Tourist information centres and council offices can provide maps that show sites with wheelchair access.

One of the most useful organizations for disabled travellers is the **National Information Communication Awareness Network (NICAN)** in Canberra. This nationwide database provides information on disabled facilities in different parts of the country and, if they don't have the appropriate information at hand, they will do their best to seek it out. They also have details of many publications written for disabled travellers in Australia.

One particularly good publication is *Easy Access Australia*, written specifically for people with mobility problems. The **Information on Disability and Education Awareness (IDEAS)** website has an extensive listing of disability-friendly accommodation in its travel section.

Mother and child feeding some of Australia's famous marsupials

TRAVELLING WITH CHILDREN

Australia is an ideal destination for children. Most hotels welcome children as guests and can usually provide cots, highchairs and, in some cases, babysitting. However, some of the smaller bed-and-breakfast places advertise themselves as child-free zones.

Restaurants are also generally welcoming to children and offer children's portions, although it is advisable to check first with the more up-market establishments. City department stores and most major tourist sites have feeding and nappy-changing rooms as standard features. Parents travelling with young children are also encouraged by a range of discounts on air, coach, train and boat travel *(see pp582–91)*.

National laws governing the restraint of children in cars were introduced in 2009. These stipulate that children under the age of seven must be restrained in an appropriate infant seat and must not travel in the front seat of a car. As many cars do not have these restraints as standard fixtures, it is essential that prior arrangements are made.

Car hire firms will generally supply car restraints for a small extra charge. **Gillespie's Hire and Sales Service** leases restraints, push-chairs, baby carriers and travel cots. It is also illegal to leave children unattended in a car.

Two informative websites filled with great destinations, attractions and other child-friendly information are **BYO Kids** and **Holidays with Kids**. Both offer useful tips even if you don't book through them.

STUDENT TRAVELLERS

The International Student Identity Card (ISIC) is available to all students worldwide in full-time study. The ISIC card should be purchased in the student's own country at a Student and Youth Travel office or online from the Student Travel Association (STA) website (www.statravel.com).

Card-holders are entitled to substantial discounts on overseas air travel *(see pp582–5)*, national train and bus services *(see pp586–7)*, as well as discounts on admission to theatres, galleries, museums and other establishments.

GAY AND LESBIAN TRAVELLERS

Within inner city areas, the gay and lesbian scene is accepted but you may still find homophobic attitudes across much of Australia. Legality and age of consent for homosexual sex varies according to state laws, ranging from 16 to 21 years in Western Australia. More information can be found on the **Gay and Lesbian Rights Lobby (GLR)** website.

The **Gay and Lesbian Tourism Association (GALTA)** is a not-for-profit organization promoting and listing tolerant businesses for travellers.

Free magazines designed for the gay and lesbian market are available in all major cities. Look out for the lesbian magazine *Cherrie* and the gay monthly, *AXN*.

BUDGET TRAVEL

Accommodation is more expensive in inner city and tourist areas than in outlying suburbs and country towns. Staying outside the cities and using public transport to get in is a good, cheap option

Petrol is more expensive in rural areas and varies from state to state; Queensland is always the cheapest. Eating out tends to be cheaper outside cities where good-value hearty meals are served at local cafés. Groceries, on the other hand, are more expensive in smaller towns.

AUSTRALIAN TIME ZONES

Australia is divided into three separate time zones: Western Standard Time, Central Standard Time and Eastern Standard Time. Eastern Australia is two hours ahead of Western Australia; Central Australia is one-and-a-half hours ahead. Daylight saving is observed in New South Wales, the ACT, Victoria and South Australia, from October to March, which adds an hour to the time differences.

City and State	Hours + GMT
Adelaide (SA)	+9.5
Brisbane (QLD)	+10
Canberra (ACT)	+10
Darwin (NT)	+9.5
Hobart (TAS)	+10
Melbourne (VIC)	+10
Perth (WA)	+8
Sydney (NSW)	+10

ELECTRICAL APPLIANCES

Australia's electrical current is 240–250 volts AC. Electrical plugs have either two or three pins. Most good hotels will provide 110-volt shaver sockets and hair dryers, but a flat, two- or three-pin adaptor will be necessary for other appliances. Buy these from electrical stores.

RESPONSIBLE TRAVEL

There is an annual nationwide environmental event known as "Clean Up Australia Day", when volunteers help to clear local areas of rubbish. Most councils across Australia also run recycling schemes, and encourage the separation of recyclable materials from general rubbish. However, discarded spring water bottles have become a huge environmental problem, and many councils now supply refilling stations, such as the one at Bondi Beach, to encourage people to reuse their bottles.

Collection point encouraging people to recycle cans

Drought is an ongoing issue, with government campaigns encouraging very careful use of water as well as mandatory water restrictions.

Australia has a wonderfully diverse ecosystem, which should be respected. When bushwalking keep to marked tracks or boardwalks. This is particularly important in coastal areas, where the regeneration of sand dunes is necessary to prevent beaches from being washed away.

Local farmers' markets are increasingly popular across the country and allow visitors to support the local economy and sample organic produce. Contact the **Australian Farmers'** Markets Association (AFMA) for details of local markets. Most shops offer plastic bags but shoppers tend to reject them in favour of reusable green fabric shopping bags.

Look for the **Green STAR** accreditation when booking accommodation – this indicates properties which are energy efficient, which minimize waste and take steps to prevent excessive water use.

CONVERSION CHART

Imperial to Metric
1 inch = 2.54 centimetres
1 foot = 30 centimetres
1 mile = 1.6 kilometres
1 ounce = 28 grams
1 pound = 454 grams
1 pint = 0.6 litres
1 gallon = 4.6 litres

Metric to Imperial
1 centimetre = 0.4 inches
1 metre = 3 feet, 3 inches
1 kilometre = 0.6 miles
1 gram = 0.04 ounces
1 kilogram = 2.2 pounds
1 litre = 1.8 pints

DIRECTORY

IMMIGRATION

Department of Immigration
3 Lonsdale St, Braddon, ACT 2612. *Tel* 131 881.
www.immi.gov.au

DISABLED TRAVELLERS

Easy Access Australia
www.easyaccessaustralia.com.au

IDEAS
Tel 1800 029 909.
www.ideas.org.au

NICAN
48 Brookes St, Mitchell, ACT 2911.
Tel 1800 806 769.
www.nican.com.au

TRAVELLING WITH CHILDREN

BYO Kids
www.byokids.com.au

Gillespie's Hire & Sales Service
13 Elizabeth St, Artarmon, NSW 2064.

Tel (02) 9411 2180.
www.ghss.com.au

Holidays with Kids
www.holidayswithkids.com.au

GAY AND LESBIAN TRAVELLERS

Gay and Lesbian Rights Lobby
www.glrl.org.au

Gay and Lesbian Tourism Association
www.galta.com.au

TOURISM AUSTRALIA OFFICES

Australia
Tel (02) 9360 1111.
www.australia.com

United Kingdom
Australia House, 6th Floor, The Strand, London WC2B 4LG.
Tel (020) 7438 4601.

USA and Canada
6100 Center Drive, Suite 1150, Los Angeles, CA 90045. *Tel* (310) 695 3200.

STATE TOURIST OFFICES

ACT
330 Northbourne Ave, Dickson, ACT 2602.
Tel (02) 6205 0044.
www.visitcanberra.com.au

New South Wales
Cnr Argyle & Playfair sts, The Rocks, NSW 2000.
Tel 1800 067 676
www.visitnsw.com.au.

Northern Territory
43 Mitchell St, Darwin, NT 0800. *Tel* (08) 136 768.
also at: 67 Stuart Hwy, Alice Springs, NT 0870.
Tel (08) 8951 8471.
www.ntholidays.com.au

Queensland
The Mall, Brisbane, QLD 4001. *Tel* (07) 3006 6290.
also at: Cairns Information Centre, 51 The Esplanade, Cairns, QLD 4870. *Tel* (07) 4051 3588. www.queenslandholidays.com.au

South Australia
18 King William St, Adelaide, SA 5000.

Tel 1300 655 276.
www.southaustralia.com

Tasmania
20 Davey St, Hobart, TAS 7000. *Tel* 1300 827 743.
www.discover tasmania.com.au

Tourism Australia
Tel (02) 9360 1111. **www**.tourism.australia.com

Victoria
Federation Square, cnr Swanston & Flinders sts, Melbourne, VIC 3000.
Tel 132 842.
www.visitvictoria.com

Western Australia
Albert Facey House, cnr Forrest Place & Wellington St, Perth, WA 6000.
Tel 1800 812 808.
www.westernaustralia.com

RESPONSIBLE TRAVEL

AFMA
Tel (02) 9360 9380. **www**.farmersmarkets.org.au

Green STAR
www.starratings.com.au

Personal Security and Health

National park sign

Australia has a low crime rate and is generally regarded as a safe tourist destination. There is a strong police presence in all the state capitals, and even small towns will have at least one officer. In terms of climate and environment, however, Australia is a tough country, and visitors must observe safety procedures whether travelling to remote areas or merely planning a day at the beach. If you get into trouble, contact one of the national emergency numbers or helplines in the directory opposite.

Police vehicle

Fire engine

Intensive care ambulance

LOOKING AFTER YOUR PROPERTY

Leave valuables and important documents in your hotel safe, and don't carry large sums of cash with you. Traveller's cheques are generally regarded as the safest way to carry large sums of money. It is also worth photocopying vital documents in case of loss or theft.

Be on guard against pickpockets in places where big crowds gather. Prime areas for petty theft are popular tourist attractions, shopping centres, beaches, markets, sporting venues and on peak-hour public transport.

Never carry your wallet in an outside pocket where it is an easy target for a thief. Wear shoulder bags and cameras with the strap across your body and with any clasps fastened. If you have a car, always try to park in well-lit, reasonably busy streets. Lock the vehicle

securely and don't leave any valuables or property visible that might attract a thief.

PERSONAL SAFETY

There are few, if any, off-limit areas in Australian cities. Red-light districts may be a little seedy, but the fact that they are often busy and well policed probably makes them safer than the average suburban street at night.

Avoid poorly lit areas and parks at night. Buses (and trams in Melbourne) are regarded as a safe means of travel at night. However, when travelling by train it is worth remembering that many stations are not staffed after hours, particularly in suburban areas. Travel in the train carriage nearest the driver or in those marked as being safe for night travel. Taxis are a safe and efficient way of getting around late at

night. Hitchhiking is not advisable, and is illegal in some states *(see p590)*.

Country towns can shut down fairly early in Australia, which is often a surprise to many visitors. It is advisable to reach a destination before nightfall and avoid wandering around looking for accommodation or a meal after dark. The majority of places are friendly to travellers but in remote areas visitors do stand out and as such are potential targets if a threat exists.

WOMEN TRAVELLERS

It is safe for women, generally speaking, to travel throughout Australia, although all the usual rules about personal safety apply. Drink "spiking" sometimes happens, so don't leave drinks unattended and only accept drinks from people you know. Sexual harassment of women can occur; if possible, ignoring it is the best course of action.

MEDICAL MATTERS

Australia's medical services are among the best in the world. Under reciprocal arrangements visitors from the UK, New Zealand, Malta, Italy, Finland, Sweden and Holland are entitled to free hospital and medical treatment provided by Australia's national insurance scheme, Medicare. Medicare does not, however, cover dental work, so dental insurance is worth considering. Visitors from countries other than those

Park ranger   **Policeman**   **Fire officer**

mentioned will face prohibitive medical bills if uninsured. Arrangements for adequate medical cover should be made before leaving home.

Dial 000 in any part of the country for ambulance assistance. Most public hospitals have a casualty department. For less urgent treatment, queues can be very long. There are 24-hour medical centres in the major cities, and doctors in or near most towns. Look in the local Yellow Pages under "Medical Practitioners".

There are dental hospitals in the state capitals providing emergency treatment. Call the **Australian Dental Association** for emergency advice and a list of dentists in your area.

PHARMACIES

Pharmacies (or chemist shops as they are known in Australia) are plentiful in cities and suburbs, but can be thin on the ground in remote areas. Unrestricted drugs such as painkillers and other goods such as cosmetics, toiletries, suncreams and baby products are standard stock items. Most pharmacies will provide free advice on minor ailments, but foreign prescriptions can only be met if endorsed by a local medical practitioner.

Hotel staff and hospitals will direct you to after-hours pharmacies in major cities.

ENVIRONMENTAL HAZARDS

Paid lifeguards dressed in blue and white, and/or volunteer lifesavers in red and yellow, patrol many beaches in populated areas. Safe swimming areas are indicated by red and yellow flags during spring and summer. However, there are vast stretches of unpatrolled beaches in Australia and many of these are subject to dangerous rips. Rips can often be identified as a darker and calmer stretch of water between the breaking waves. Do not falsely equate calmer water with safe swimming. Certain rips can be

Tasmania parks logo

so strong that even wading can pose a threat. Follow local advice and, if in any doubt, do not swim. You should never swim alone.

Even in well-trodden areas of the Australian bush, hikers can lose their way. Always inform someone of your route. Staff at national parks can offer expert advice along with maps, and will keep a note of your intended trip. Take a basic first-aid kit, food and water, and extra clothing. In many regions, temperatures plummet when the sun sets.

Australia shelters some of the most venomous creatures on earth. Basic precautions such as good boots and a wary eye are necessary. Snakebite victims should be kept calm while emergency help is sought. Try to identify the creature by size and colour so that the appropriate antivenom can be administered.

Crocodiles are fascinating but dangerous creatures. In the northern regions, heed the warning signs and make enquiries if you intend to swim in remote, unpatrolled areas. Box jellyfish patrol tropical waters between October and May and their sting is deadly. Again, observe the signs.

Bush fires are a fact of life in Australia. When planning a camping trip, ring the **NSW Rural Fire Service** to check on restrictions. Total fire bans are not uncommon during warm, dry seasons when use of electric and gas barbeques are restricted and many national parks are

closed to the public. Avoid high-risk areas and dial 000 if in immediate danger from fire.

PROTECTING YOUR SKIN

Australia has the highest rate of skin cancer in the world, caused by the harmful effects of ultraviolet radiation. The risk of skin damage is high, even on cloudy days. Always use a good SPF 30+ sunscreen and cover up by wearing sun protective clothing, a hat and sunglasses. Keep in the shade if possible, especially between 10am and 2pm. The **Cancer Council of Australia** website has more information, and check UV alerts in daily newspapers or at the Bureau of Meteorology (www.bom.gov.au).

Surf lifesaving sign indicating a dangerous undertow or "rip"

Banking and Local Currency

Branches of national, state and some foreign banks can be found in the central business districts of Australia's state capitals. Suburban shopping centres and country towns will often have at least one branch of a major Australian bank. If travelling to remote areas, find out what banking facilities are available in advance. Banks generally offer the best exchange rates; money can also be changed at bureaux de change, large department stores and hotels. There is no limit to the amount of personal funds that can be taken in or out of Australia, although cash amounts of A$10,000 or more must be declared to customs on arrival or prior to departure.

Using electronic transfer (EFTPOS) to pay for goods

High street bank logos

BANKING

Banks are generally open from 9:30am to 4pm Monday to Thursday and 9:30am to 5pm on Fridays. Outside banking hours, many transactions can be handled through automatic teller machines (ATMs). Current exchange rates are displayed either in the windows or foyers of most major banks.

Automatic cash dispenser

TRAVELLER'S CHEQUES

Australian dollar traveller's cheques issued by major names such as Thomas Cook and American Express are usually accepted (with a passport) in large shops. You may have problems, however, cashing these in smaller outlets. Banks are the best places to go to cash traveller's cheques, as their fees are lower. Foreign currency cheques can be cashed at all major banks, bureaux de change and established hotels in the main cities.

CREDIT CARDS

All well-known international credit cards are widely accepted in Australia. Major credit cards such as VISA, MasterCard, Diners Club and American Express can be used to book and pay for hotel rooms, airline tickets, car hire, tours and tickets. However, some companies, travel agencies for example, charge a fee of 1–3 per cent of the total purchase price for using them. Credit cards are accepted in most restaurants and shops. Check first, though, as many places don't accept American Express or Diners Club due to the large commissions they charge and smaller places may impose a minimum charge. You can also use credit cards in ATMs to withdraw cash.

You should carry some emergency cash, however, if travelling to remote areas, particularly the Outback. Credit cards may not be accepted at small stores and cafés, and alternatives, such as a 24-hour ATM, may not be available.

AUTOMATIC TELLER MACHINES AND ELECTRONIC TRANSFER

Automatic teller machines (ATMs) can be found in most banks, as well as in shopping and tourist areas. In most cases it is possible to access foreign accounts from ATMs by using a linked debit card. Ask your bank about making your card valid for this kind of use.

An appropriate debit card will also give you access to EFTPOS (Electronic Funds Transfer at Point Of Sale). Pay for goods using a card, and funds are automatically debited from your chosen bank account. In many stores customers will also be able to withdraw cash, providing a purchase has been made. This "cash-back" facility is useful if the town you are in doesn't have an appropriate ATM.

BUREAUX DE CHANGE

Australian cities and larger towns, particularly those popular with tourists, have many bureaux de change. These are usually open Monday to Saturday from 9am to 5:30pm. Some branches also operate on Sundays.

While the opening hours of bureaux de change make them a convenient alternative to a bank, their commissions and fees are generally higher. Post offices will also often change foreign money.

LOCAL CURRENCY

The Australian currency is the Australian dollar (A$), which breaks down into 100 cents (c). The decimal currency system now in place has been in operation since 1966.

Single cents may still be used for some prices, but as the Australian 1c and 2c coins are no longer in circulation, the total amount to be paid will be rounded up or down to the nearest five cents.

It can be difficult to change A$50 and A$100 notes, so avoid using them in smaller shops and cafés and, more particularly, when paying for taxi fares. If you do not have change, it is always wise to tell the taxi driver before you start your journey to avoid any misunderstandings. Otherwise, when you arrive at your destination, you may have to find change at the nearest shop or ATM.

To improve security, as well as increase their lifespan, all Australian bank notes have now been plasticized.

Bank Notes

Australian bank notes are produced in denominations of A$5, A$10, A$20, A$50 and A$100. All bank notes are made of plastic. Paper notes have been phased out and are no longer legal tender.

A$100 note

A$50 note

A$20 note

A$5 note

A$10 note

5 cents (5c)

10 cents (10c)

20 cents (20c)

50 cents (50c)

1 dollar (A$1)

2 dollars (A$2)

Coins

Coins currently in use in Australia are 5c, 10c, 20c, 50c, A$1 and A$2. There are several different 20c, 50c and A$1 coins in circulation; all are the same size and shape, but have different commemorative images on the face. The 10c and 20c coins are useful for local telephone calls (see pp580–81).

Communication and Media

Communications systems in Australia are fast, modern, efficient and of international standard. The majority of Australians have mobile phones and home Internet connections, and Internet cafés and Wi-Fi areas are also widely available in cities and large towns.

Postal services within Australia are often overnight and international mail can take less than a week. Online versions of Australian national newspapers are regularly updated with domestic and international news, while the standard of Australia's television and radio broadcasting is generally considered to be high.

Telstra Corporation logo

PUBLIC TELEPHONES

Payphones can be found on streets throughout Australia's cities and country towns. Most accept both coins and phone-cards, although some operate solely on phonecards and major credit cards. Phonecards can be bought from selected newsagents and news kiosks, and from other outlets with the blue and orange Telstra sign.

Although slightly varied in shape and colour, all public telephones have a hand-held receiver and a 12-button key pad, as well as clear instructions on their use (in English only), a list of useful phone numbers and copies of telephone directories.

Telstra payphones

PAYPHONE CHARGES

Local calls are untimed and cost 50 cents. Depending on where you are, "local" means the city and its suburbs, or outside the city, a defined country region. **Telstra** can provide information on exact costs. Dial freephone 1800 113 011 for an estimate of the cost of long-distance and international calls.

Credit card phones have a A$1.20 minimum fee. Long-distance calls are less expensive if you dial without the help of an operator. The cheapest method of calling long distance is by using a prepaid phonecard; they can reduce the rate of international calls to about 5 cents per minute. Check the different kinds available to find one that suits your needs. Prepaid phonecards can

be bought at newsagents, local shops, post offices and other retail outlets.

TELEPHONE DIRECTORIES

Each city and region in Australia has two telephone directories: the **White Pages** and the **Yellow Pages**. The White Pages lists private and business numbers in alphabetical order. It also has a guide to emergency services and government departments. The Yellow Pages lists businesses under relevant headings such as Dentists, Car Hire and so on. Both are available online.

MOBILE PHONES

Short-term mobile phone rentals are available for visitors, but if your phone is compatible it may be cheaper to bring it with you and buy a local Sim card once you have arrived. This way you can also avoid paying the high cost of international fees on incoming calls to your mobile.

Optus, **Telstra**, **Virgin** and **Vodafone** are the main mobile phone service providers. They differ significantly in the coverage and costs they offer, so it is worth looking into each one to find the best deal.

While international texting is relatively cheap, international calls are very expensive from mobile phones in Australia, so using a prepaid phonecard

---

REACHING THE RIGHT NUMBER

• To ring Australia from the UK dial **0061**, then the area code, then the local number.
• To ring Australia from the USA or Canada dial **011 61**, then the area code, then the local number.
• For long-distance direct-dial calls outside your local area code, but within Australia (STD calls), dial the appropriate area code, then the number.
• For international direct-dial calls (IDD calls) from a fixed phone line in Australia: dial **0011**, followed by the country code (USA and Canada: 1; UK: 44; Republic of Ireland: 353; New Zealand: 64, South Africa: 27), then the city or area code (omit initial 0) and then the local number.

• Directory information with automatic connection (incurs an additional charge) to local and national destinations: dial **12455**.
• Local and national directory enquiries: dial **1223**.
• Reverse charge or third party charge calls: dial **12550**.
• National and international operator assisted calls: dial **1234** or **12550.**
• National and international call-cost enquiries: dial **1800 113 011**.
• Numbers beginning with **1 800** are toll-free numbers.
• Numbers beginning with **13** are charged at the local call rate from anywhere in Australia.
• Numbers beginning with **04** are mobiles.
• See also Emergency Services, *p577*.

Standard and express postboxes

may be a better option if you need to make a lot of international calls. Making calls while driving is illegal and carries as stiff fine. Many places in remote Australia are not on the mobile network.

INTERNET

Internet cafés provide relatively cheap Internet and email access and are widely spread throughout tourist areas. Public libraries also provide Internet access, although terminals may need to be booked in advance.

Wireless local area network (Wi-Fi), which allows you to connect to the Internet using your own laptop in a "hotspot", is becoming increasingly common in Australia. Many hotels provide a Wi-Fi service but may charge a premium for it. Lists of free Wi-Fi hotspots are available at www.freewifi.com.au and www.wififreespot.com.

For a cheap alternative to long-distance phone calls download VoIP (Voice Over Internet Protocol) on to your laptop before travelling. The most popular one is Skype and many Internet cafés already have this installed on their machines.

POSTAL SERVICES

Post offices are open 9am–5pm weekdays and some are open on Saturday mornings. Most offer a wide range of services including poste restante and fax services. In country towns, the local general store often doubles as the post office. Most newsagents also sell stamps.

All standard domestic mail is first class. Post boxes for standard mail are red and can be found on most street corners. Express Post, for which you need to buy the special yellow and white envelopes sold in post offices, guarantees faster, often nextday, delivery within Australia. Postboxes for Express Post are yellow. Post offices also offer international courier services.

NEWSPAPERS, TELEVISION AND RADIO

Australia has two national newspapers, *The Australian*, a well-respected broadsheet with excellent national and overseas news coverage, and the *Australian Financial Review*, which largely reports on international business and monetary matters. *Time* magazine is Australia's leading weekly international news magazine, though many stories are taken from the American version of the magazine. All major foreign newspapers and magazines are readily available in cities and large towns. Each state capital also has its own broadsheet and tabloid newspaper.

The Australian Broadcasting Corporation (ABC) is a

Logo for the ABC network

nationwide television and radio broadcaster which provides excellent news and current affairs coverage, children's programmes and high-quality local and international drama. In addition, the corporation has its own local and national AM and FM radio stations which offer a wide range of services, including news, arts commentary, modern and classical music, women's programmes and an acclaimed nationwide channel for the under 30s called Triple J. SBS (Special Broadcasting Service) is Australia's other state-run television and radio network and caters to Australia's many cultures with foreign language programmes. There are also three commercial television networks, Channels 7, 9 and 10, all of which offer a range of soap operas, sports, game shows and other light entertainment.

In all state capitals there is an enormous variety of local FM and AM radio stations. Details of current programming are available in local newspapers. Of interest also are the community radio stations which cater to local cultural and social interests.

Illuminated sign at a local Internet café

TRAVEL INFORMATION

While some visitors to Australia may choose to arrive by sea, the vast majority arrive by air. Once here, flying between locations is also the most popular form of long-distance travel, but there are some other choices, all of which offer the chance to see something of the country along the way. The national rail network links all major

Airport Express bus into central Sydney

cities, while coach routes provide regular services to most provincial and country areas. If you have the time, driving in Australia is an excellent option. Boat travel is best if you want to visit Australia's islands, principally Tasmania, but regular services run to other island destinations such as Rottnest Island off the coast of Western Australia (see pp308–9).

GREEN TRAVEL

Given the location and sheer size of the country, and unless you have unlimited time, it is difficult to travel to and within Australia without using environmentally unfriendly, long-haul flights. A journey of four hours by plane can take three days by train and, in most cases, a flight is the cheaper option. However, if you can spare the time and money, there are some spectacular long-distance train routes through the country where, especially with the speciality "luxury" operators (see p586–7) the journey can become a worthy part of your holiday.

If you plan to hire a car, the Australian Department of Transport produces a **Green Vehicle Guide** which rates cars according to their carbon emissions and allows useful comparisons between vehicles. Within cities public transport is relatively cheap and efficient, and has the advantage of avoiding costly parking at each destination.

Arriving by Air

Australia is served by around 50 international airlines. The Australian airline **Qantas** has a worldwide network and offers the most flights in and out of Australia every week. Qantas is also one of the main domestic carriers in Australia (see p584). **Air New Zealand**, Qantas and **United Airlines** have regular flights from the US, with a range of stopovers. The large Asian and European carriers, **British Airways, Emirates, Singapore Airlines, Cathay Pacific** and **Japan Airlines**, also offer a variety of different routes and stopovers on the Europe–Asia–Australia run. Canadian travellers can fly direct using **Air Canada**.

INTERNATIONAL FLIGHTS

Flights between Australia and Europe take upwards of 22 hours, and with delays you may be in transit for more than 30 hours. A stopover in Asia is worth considering, especially if travelling with children, as is one in Hawaii or the Pacific islands for visitors from the US. Also, consider arranging flights so that they account for international time differences. Arriving in the afternoon, spending the rest of the day awake, then going to sleep in accordance with local time is

a recommended way to help to counteract jet lag.

Australia has several international air terminals so visitors can choose different arrival and departure points. Sydney and Melbourne have major airports servicing flights from all over the world. Sydney's Kingsford Smith Airport is the busiest and can be congested. Melbourne Tullamarine Airport is consistently voted one of the world's best airports by travellers. Hobart has flights from New Zealand in the summer months, while Adelaide has direct flights to Singapore and flights to Europe via Sydney or Melbourne. Visitors to the west coast can arrive in Perth from Africa, Asia and the UK. Darwin, Brisbane and Cairns mostly service Asia, but there are a few possibilities for connections from Europe.

AIR FARES

Flights to Australia can be expensive, especially during December, the peak season. January to April is slightly cheaper. During the off-peak

International Qantas flight arriving in Sydney

Singapore Airlines 747 taking off at Perth Airport

season, airlines offer Apex fares that are often 30–40 per cent below economy fares (*see p584*). Many stipulate arrival and departure times and carry cancellation penalties. Round-the-world fares are good value and increasingly popular.

Check with discount travel agents if you can fly at short notice, as they regularly receive unsold tickets from the airlines. In these cases, flexibility isn't usually a feature. Departure Tax is now included in the price of a ticket out of Australia.

ON ARRIVAL

Just before setting down in Australia you will be given customs documents to fill in. On arrival you will be asked to present your documents, including passport, at the Entry Control Point. You can then collect your baggage and, if you have nothing to declare, proceed straight into

the main area of the airport. Note that Australia has strict quarantine laws. Food, plants and wooden items must be declared at quarantine. Sniffer dogs are common and your bags may be X-rayed on arrival to check for banned goods. Most items will be allowed but there are stiff penalties for non-disclosure.

Larger airports such as Melbourne and Sydney have better services, but most have good shopping, postal and medical facilities. You can hire cars and change money at all airports. Taxis and buses are available for transport into city centres.

Arrangements for domestic flight connections are usually made when purchasing your original ticket. Airline staff will advise you how to proceed. In Melbourne's main airport, the domestic and international services are in the same terminal but in many places the terminals are separate and distances can be

DIRECTORY

AIRLINE CARRIERS

Air New Zealand
Tel 132 476.
www.airnewzealand.com.au

British Airways
Tel 1300 767 177. www.ba.com

Air Canada
Tel 1300 655 767.
www.aircanada.com

Cathay Pacific
Tel 131 747.
www.cathaypacific.com

Emirates
Tel 1300 303 777.
www.emirates.com

Japan Airlines
Tel 1300 525 287. www.au.jal.com

Qantas
Tel 13 13 13.
www.qantas.com.au

Singapore Airlines
Tel 131 011.
www.singaporeair.com

United Airlines
Tel 131 777.
www.unitedairlines.com

GREEN TRAVEL

Green Vehicle Guide
www.greenvehicleguide.gov.au

long – 10 km (6 miles) in the case of Perth. Free shuttle buses transfer passengers between terminals.

AIRPORT	 INFORMATION	DISTANCE FROM CITY	TAXI FARE TO CITY	BUS TRANSFER TO CITY
Sydney	*(02) 9667 9111* www.sydneyairport.com.au	9 km (6 miles)	A$30	30 mins
Melbourne	*(03) 9297 1600* www.melbourneairport.com.au	22 km (14 miles)	A$50	30-40 mins
Brisbane	*(07) 3406 3000* www.bne.com.au	15 km (9 miles)	A$35	30 mins
Cairns	*(07) 4080 6703* www.cairnsairport.com	6 km (4 miles)	A$20	10 mins
Perth	*(08) 9478 8888* www.perthairport.com	15 km (9 miles)	A$30	25 mins
Adelaide	*(08) 8308 9211* www.adelaideairport.com.au	6 km (4 miles)	A$20	20 mins
Darwin	*(08) 8920 1811* www.ntapl.com.au	6 km (4 miles)	A$25	15 mins
Hobart	*(03) 6216 1600* www.hobartairpt.com.au	22 km (14 miles)	A$32	20-30 mins

Domestic Air Travel

Air travel accounts for a large proportion of long-distance journeys in Australia and is by far the most practical way of taking in a country of this size, particularly for those with time constraints. The main domestic air carriers in Australia, **Qantas, Virgin Blue** and **Jetstar**, concentrate on the high-volume interstate routes, while a host of small operators handle air travel within states and to remote locations. Fares can be expensive, but with the range of discounts available in this deregulated and aggressively competitive industry it is unlikely that you will ever have to pay the full fare, providing you plan your air trips in advance. Spectacular speciality aerial tours of distant or hard-to-reach landmarks are also available *(see p567)*.

Cut-price domestic flight operated by Virgin Blue

Tiny domestic terminal in Birdsville, Queensland

AIR ROUTES AND AIRLINES

Australia's air network is vast, but reasonably streamlined, so arranging flights to even the most remote spots should never be a problem. It is possible to fly direct between most major destinations such as Sydney–Darwin or Melbourne–Perth. However, if you are travelling to smaller centres, you will invariably have to fly first to the capital city in the state before then taking another flight on to your final destination.

The small airlines that cover out-of-the-way routes are, in most cases, affiliated with Qantas, which means bookings can be made through Qantas' centralized booking services.

DISCOUNTS FOR OVERSEAS VISITORS

Discounted domestic air travel is often offered as part of an international package, so check with your travel agent about booking domestic trips before leaving home. Once you are in Australia, Qantas offers immediate discounts on domestic flights to overseas travellers, which range from 25–40 per cent; proof of overseas residence is required when booking these tickets.

Various air passes are available from Qantas which allow you to make a number of single flights for a set price. You can then move from leg to leg around the country rather than having to make return flights, which are normally expensive. When buying these passes before your trip, you are sometimes required to pay half the cost before leaving home and half when booking the flights. In these cases, avoid buying too many flights in case your plans change. The passes offer greater convenience than return flights and are usually fairly flexible, but restrictions do apply, so check when booking.

OTHER BUDGET FARES

The cheapest domestic flights are available from the budget, no-frills airline services of **Jetstar**, a subsidiary of Qantas, **Virgin Blue** and **Tiger**, who are associated with Singapore Airlines *(see p583)*. The best deals are found by booking direct with them online.

Watch out for "super" deals, when airlines flood the market with cheap seats, including "light fares", for which passengers are only allowed carry-on luggage. However, such deals offer little or no flexibility so make sure you understand the strict conditions and cancellations policies before booking.

Plane on the harbourside runway, Hamilton Island *(see p217)*

FLY-DRIVE DEALS

A great way to see Australia is to fly to a destination and then continue on by car. To make things more convenient, arrangements can be made for different pick-up and drop-off points for hire vehicles. For example, you could pick up a car in Sydney, drive to Brisbane and drop off the car, fly to Alice Springs and then pick up another car there.

Virgin Blue and Qantas both have deals with the major car hire companies, and they offer discounts to passengers who are travelling on those airlines *(see p588)*.

BAGGAGE RESTRICTIONS

Baggage restrictions vary considerably on domestic flights and depend on the type of ticket you have booked. Jetstar's Jetsaver Light fare does not allow for any

checked-in baggage at all; the Jetsaver fare allows for 20 kg (45 pounds) of baggage but at an additional fee of A$10 if booked online or A$40 if booked at the airport; and the Jetflex fare allows for 20 kg (45 pounds) at no additional cost. Virgin Blue's Go! and Blue Saver fares allow 23 kg (50 pounds) but at an additional charge of A$8 if booked online or A$20 if booked at the airport; and their Flexible fare allows 23 kg (50 pounds) with no fee. Regardless of the fare, Qantas domestic flights allow 20 kg (45 pounds) for checked-in baggage.

Additional baggage fees are charged for any excess baggage; bear in mind also that airlines do not guarantee that additional baggage beyond the normal allowance will be carried. Carry-on luggage weight allowances vary between 7 kg (15.5 pounds) and 10 kg (22 pounds), depending on the airline.

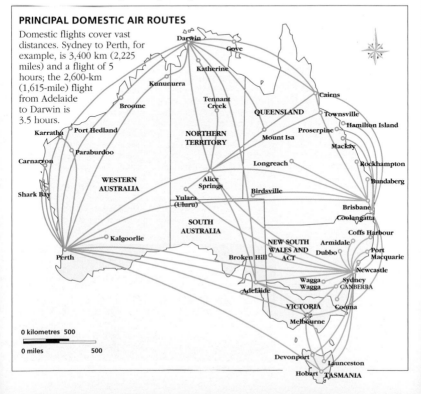

Qantas logo

CHECKING IN

Airlines request that you check in at least 30 minutes before your flight time, and many now offer online seat allocation up to two days before a flight. Check online to ensure that the flight is on time, and be sure to alight at the right terminal – some domestic and international terminals are at separate locations.

DIRECTORY

DOMESTIC AIRLINES

Jetstar
Tel 131 538.
www.jetstar.com.au

Qantas
Tel 131 313.
www.qantas.com.au

Virgin Blue
Tel 136 777 or
(61 7) 3295 2296.
www.virginblue.com.au

PRINCIPAL DOMESTIC AIR ROUTES

Domestic flights cover vast distances. Sydney to Perth, for example, is 3,400 km (2,225 miles) and a flight of 5 hours; the 2,600-km (1,615-mile) flight from Adelaide to Darwin is 3.5 hours.

Darwin
Gove
Katherine
Kununurra
Tennant Creek
Broome
QUEENSLAND
Cairns
Townsville
Hamilton Island
Karratha
Port Hedland
NORTHERN TERRITORY
Proserpine
Mackay
Mount Isa
Paraburdoo
Carnarvon
Longreach
Rockhampton
Bundaberg
WESTERN AUSTRALIA
Alice Springs
Shark Bay
Yulara (Uluru)
Birdsville
Brisbane
Coolangatta
SOUTH AUSTRALIA
Kalgoorlie
Coffs Harbour
Perth
NEW SOUTH WALES AND ACT
Armidale
Dubbo
Port Macquarie
Broken Hill
Newcastle
Wagga Wagga
Sydney
Adelaide
CANBERRA
VICTORIA
Cooma
Melbourne
0 kilometres 500
0 miles 500
Devonport
Launceston
Hobart TASMANIA

Travelling by Train and Coach

Rail Australia logo

Australia offers some of the most spectacular train journeys in the world. The vast and diverse continent offers rail travel across red deserts as well as through beautiful rainforests and spectacular coastal scenery; often the journey is as much about enjoying the view as arriving at a destination. However, the train network is not comprehensive – with its small population, Australia has never been able to support an extensive system of long-haul railways. Train journeys are useful for quick trips away from city centres, and regular services link the cities of the east coast. Coaches fill any gaps in overland travel, servicing major centres and remote outposts.

A railway journey across the Australian desert

THE AUSTRALIAN RAIL NETWORK

The Australian railway system is run by a complex group of several private and state-owned companies. The major tourist-orientated operators, including Countrylink, Great Southern Rail and Traveltrain, have formed an alliance called **Rail Australia**. You can get information and book tickets via the Rail Australia website.

Due to the advent of cheap flights, train travel is no longer cheaper than flying, and journey times are long. The Sydney–Brisbane trip takes 13.5 hours and Sydney–Melbourne takes 10.5 hours.

State governments accept responsibility for providing access to most areas. Queensland has increased its rail services of late, most of which are aimed at the tourist market. Increasingly, however, state-run coach services have replaced under-used railway journeys and, where there is no rail network, such

as in Tasmania, there will be an efficient, cheap coach network instead.

SPECIALITY TRIPS

The chance to take in some of the country's extraordinary landscapes is what makes rail journeys in Australia so special. Standards are high, often with a level of luxury reminiscent of the grand old days of rail travel.

The Indian Pacific route takes three days to cover the 4,352 km (2,700 miles) from Sydney to Perth. The 478-km (300-mile) crossing of the

Nullarbor Plain *(see p319)* is on the world's longest length of straight railway track. The fabled Ghan railway runs between Adelaide and Darwin. A museum in Alice Springs recounts its history *(see p283)*. The 2,979-km (1,852-mile) trip offers amazing scenery and takes two days.

Two different services run the 1,681 km (1,045 miles) between Brisbane and Cairns: the Sunlander and the Tilt Train. Another Queensland journey is aboard the Gulflander, a 152-km (95-mile) trip through some of Australia's most remote country.

The Overland (Melbourne–Adelaide) and the fast XPT (express passenger trains) services (Brisbane–Sydney–Melboune) have a rather more utilitarian approach to train travel.

TRAVEL CLASSES

There are three types of travel available on most interstate trains. Overnight services, such as Melbourne–Adelaide, offer first-class sleeper, first-class sit-up and economy sit-up. In addition, the Indian Pacific, the Ghan and various Queensland trains offer economy sleepers. All long-distance trains have dining facilities. First-class travel includes meals in the ticket price.

Motorail means you can travel with your car. The service is expensive, however, and you are better off hiring a car at your destination.

TICKETS AND BOOKINGS

Bookings for rail travel can be made with travel agents and at railway stations or via the

Mass Transit Railway Station in Perth

Greyhound coach station in Sydney

Rail Australia website. A choice of seven passes offer international travellers unlimited rail travel within either a three or six month period. The Backtracker Rail Pass allows between 14 days and six months of unlimited economy class trips between Melbourne, Sydney and Brisbane, while the Austrail Flexi-Pass offers either 15 or 22 days of travel over a six-month period.

Standard rail fares can be high, but there is a good range of discounts available for advance bookings.

COACH TRAVEL

Coach travel is cheap, efficient and generally safe. The two main operators are **Greyhound Australia** and **Premier Motor Service**. The latter only operates on the east coast.

There are a range of passes that reduce the cost of any extended travel. The Greyhound Oz Choice Travel Pass is available on 12 pre-set routes and allows you to jump on and off the bus as often as you like. The Oz-Flexi Travel Pass offers greater flexibility by allowing you to choose

either how many kilometres or for how many consecutive days you would like to travel. However, bear in mind that this kind of travel involves many days on the road, and nights spent sleeping upright.

There are a range of other companies operating locally – good for trips to particular sights or national parks. Tourist information bodies *(see p575)* in each state will give advice on which company services which route.

DIRECTORY

RAIL COMPANIES

Rail Australia
Tel 132 147.
www.railaustralia.com.au

COACH COMPANIES

Greyhound Australia
Tel 1300 473 946.
www.greyhound.com.au

Premier Motor Service
Tel 133 410.
www.premierms.com.au

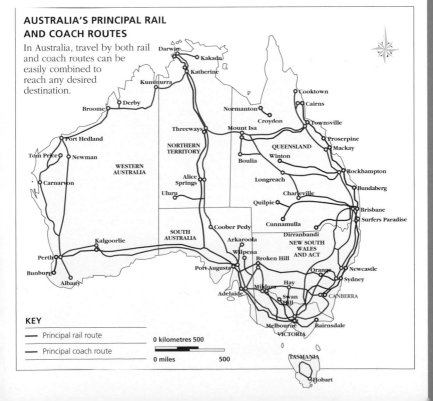

AUSTRALIA'S PRINCIPAL RAIL AND COACH ROUTES

In Australia, travel by both rail and coach routes can be easily combined to reach any desired destination.

Darwin
Kakadu
Katherine
Kununurra
Broome
Derby
Cooktown
Cairns
Normanton
Croydon
Townsville
Port Hedland
Threeways
Mount Isa
Proserpine
Tom Price
Newman
NORTHERN
TERRITORY
QUEENSLAND
Mackay
Boulia
Winton
Carnarvon
WESTERN
AUSTRALIA
Alice
Springs
Longreach
Rockhampton
Uluru
Charleville
Bundaberg
Quilpie
Brisbane
Cunnamulla
Surfers Paradise
Coober Pedy
Dirranbandi
Kalgoorlie
SOUTH
AUSTRALIA
Arkaroola
NEW SOUTH
WALES
AND ACT
Wilpena
Perth
Broken Hill
Orange
Newcastle
Bunbury
Port Augusta
Hay
Sydney
Albany
Mildura
CANBERRA
Adelaide
Swan
Hill
Melbourne
Bairnsdale
VICTORIA
KEY
— Principal rail route
— Principal coach route
TASMANIA
Hobart
0 kilometres 500
0 miles 500

Travelling by Car and Four-Wheel Drive

Great Ocean Road sign

It is well worth considering hiring a car when visiting Australia. Other modes of transport will get you around the cities and from one country town to another, but, once you arrive in a rural area or a small town, you may find it impossible to explore the area other than on foot or with a tour. Australia offers the motorist the chance to meander through areas such as the vineyard regions of South Australia *(see pp338–9)*, the Southern Highlands of New South Wales *(see pp186–7)* and the Great Ocean Road of Victoria *(see pp428–9)*, as well as the experience of Outback travel on near-empty roads.

Driving through the Pinnacles in Nambung National Park (see p324)

considering for inner-city driving, but not good value beyond the city limits where distances add up very quickly.

The smaller local operators offer very competitive rates, sometimes as low as A$25 a day, but read the small print carefully. Often, the quote does not include the extras that the larger companies consider standard. If travelling with children, make sure the car is equipped with restraints according to Australian laws *(see p574)*. A Global Positioning System (GPS) can also be hired for around A$11 per day or A$60 per week.

Credit cards are the preferred method of payment when hiring a car. If paying with cash you will usually be required to pay the full cost of the rental, plus a deposit.

INSURANCE

For peace of mind it is a good idea to have comprehensive insurance when hiring a car. "Third party fire and theft" insurance is standard and included in the cost of the hire, as is insurance against accidental damage to the hire car. However, you will have to pay extra to reduce the excess payment. From upwards of A$7 a day, you can bring the excess down from around A$2,000 to a more comfortable A$100. This option is usually only offered by the larger car hire companies.

Personal accident plans are also available, but they may not be necessary, depending on the cover offered with your own travel insurance. Four-wheel drive vehicles attract an excess rate of

DRIVING LICENCES

Providing your driving licence is in English and you have proof that you are a tourist, there is no need for an additional permit when driving in Australia. If the licence is not in English, you must carry a translation. It is a legal requirement that you have your licence with you at all times when driving.

CAR HIRE

Rental cars are available just about anywhere in Australia. They can be picked up at the airport on arrival, or arrangements can be made for delivery to your hotel. The big car rental firms **Avis**, **Budget, Hertz** and **Thrifty** have nationwide networks *(see p590)* – an advantage if you are considering making several different trips across the continent. Check with your travel agent before leaving home about discounts or special fly-drive offers.

Rates vary from around A$55 a day for a small car to A$100 a day for larger vehicles. It is invariably more expensive to hire a 4WD vehicle; rates average out at around A$120 and are more costly in remote areas where the demand is high. You can reduce daily rates by hiring over longer periods (usually three days and over), or if you accept a limited kilometre/mileage deal. These deals usually give you the first 100 km (60 miles) a day as part of the daily charge, and a per kilometre rate after that. This is worth

Car and van rental company in Sydney

around A\$4,000. For A\$20 a day this can be reduced to a A\$1,000, but never lower. Car hire companies will not offer insurance on any off-road driving, regardless of the vehicle type. Higher rates of insurance apply to drivers under the age of 25. Car hire in Australia is often not available to drivers under the age of 21.

Petrol station in Sydney

PETROL

Petrol is relatively cheap in urban areas compared to prices in Europe (though this may change), but in remote regions of the country prices rise considerably. Prices also vary according to the day of the week and it is usually cheapest to fill up on Tuesdays and Thursdays. Fuel is dispensed by the litre and can be purchased in regular unleaded, premium unleaded, diesel and LPG (liquid petroleum gas) grades. Most petrol stations are self-service and most accept major credit cards and have an EFTPOS facility *(see p578)*.

RULES OF THE ROAD

Australians drive on the left and give way to the right in all circumstances unless otherwise indicated. Drivers must also give way to emergency vehicles – if possible, pull over to the side of the road when you hear a siren. The speed limit is 40–60 km/h (25–37 mph) in cities, towns and suburban areas and 100–110 km/h (62–68 mph) on major highways. The wearing of seat belts is compulsory for drivers and passengers. Baby

capsules and child restraints must be used for all children up to the age of seven. It is illegal to drive a vehicle while using a hand-held mobile phone. This includes when the vehicle is stopped at traffic lights or in heavy traffic. Drink-driving laws are strictly enforced in Australia. The legal blood alcohol limit is 0.05 per cent. Should you be involved in an accident while over the alcohol limit, your vehicle insurance may be invalidated. Police in country areas are just as vigilant as their counterparts in the city, and it is not unusual to see a random breath-test taking place on an otherwise deserted road.

NEXT 5 km

Beware of kangaroos sign

Any accident involving injury in Australia must be reported to the police within 24 hours. In Western Australia all accidents must be reported and in other states it is advisable to do so if there is considerable property damage. Always get insurance details and a name, licence number and residential address from the other motorist.

The city of Melbourne has two road laws worth noting. First, motorists must stop behind a stationary tram to allow passengers to alight. Second, at certain city intersections motorists intending to turn right must pull over to the left *(see pp412–13)*. Called hook turns, they are designed to prevent traffic queuing across tram tracks.

Road rules are governed by the relevant state authority. Each has a website with traffic reports, highway conditions, road closures and webcams.

ROAD CONDITIONS

Stretches of multi-lane highways are found on most major routes, with the majority of other routes covered by two-lane highways. All are generally well sealed and signposted. Unsealed dirt roads exist in country regions, but are rarely the only means of getting to a destination.

Tollways are restricted to areas in the immediate vicinity of the large cities, such as the Western Motorway that covers part of the Sydney–Blue Mountains route. Melbourne has an intricate tollway system. Some tollways, tunnels and bridges, including Sydney Harbour Bridge, are now cashless and require payment by card or an electronic tag.

Service stations are plentiful along all the well-travelled routes, but are few and far between in the Outback. A particularly Australian and very dangerous road hazard is the prevalence of wildlife crossing country highways. At night danger increases when the nocturnal mammals, such as kangaroos and wallabies, are more active.

ROADSIDE ASSISTANCE

Car hire companies look after breakdowns of their rental cars and, if necessary, arrange for vehicle replacements. State-based motoring organizations provide roadside assistance for members around the country *(see p590)*. They also sell maps and guides in their central branches, and are a great source of information on road rules and conditions, and Outback driving. Members of motoring organizations in Great Britain, Canada and the US usually have reciprocal membership rights with Australian organizations.

Royal Automobile Association vehicle in Adelaide

South approach to the Harbour Bridge in Sydney

INNER CITY DRIVING

If you are planning to drive within any city, a good street directory will be essential. If possible, avoid peak-hour traffic (7:30–9:30am and 4:30–7:30pm). Traffic reports are broadcast on radio stations.

The larger the city, the more difficult it will be to park in the city centre. Parking restrictions are clearly signposted and usually specify an hour or two of metered parking. It's a good idea to carry coins for the meters, although most now take credit card payments. Many cities have clearway zones that apply in certain areas and parked vehicles will be towed away during the specified times; telephone the local traffic authority or the police to find out where your vehicle has been impounded. Car parks are also found in and around city centres.

OUTBACK DRIVING

For any Outback travel, it is important to first check your route to see if a 4WD is required. Although some Outback areas now have roads of a high enough standard to carry conventional cars, a 4WD is essential in some wild and remote areas. Motoring organizations and tourist information centres can provide information about this.

A number of basic safety points should be observed. Plan your route and carry up-to-date maps. If you are travelling between remote destinations, inform the local police of your departure and expected arrival times. Check road conditions before you start and carry plenty of food and water. Find out where you can get petrol and carry extra supplies if necessary. If you break down, remain with your vehicle – if you fail to arrive at the expected time, a search party will be sent out.

The **Royal Flying Doctor Service of Australia (RFDS)** offers safety advice. You can also hire radio sets with an emergency call button to the RFDS from **BTW Communications**.

Observe important guidelines to protect the land. Native flora and fauna should not be removed or damaged. Stick to vehicle tracks, carry a stove and fuel to avoid lighting fires, and don't leave rubbish. Be aware of Aboriginal boundaries and national parks, and leave gates as you find them: either open or shut.

HITCHHIKING

It is not considered safe to hitchhike in Australia. In Queensland and Victoria it is illegal; their laws do not allow obstructing traffic from the roadside. Elsewhere, pedestrians are not allowed on motorways or freeways but are permitted on highways and other roads where they can find rides.

DIRECTORY

CAR HIRE COMPANIES

Avis
Tel 136 333. www.avis.com.au

Budget
Tel 13 27 27.
www.budget.com.au

Hertz
Tel 133 039. www.hertz.com.au

Thrifty
Tel 1300 367 227.
www.thrifty.com.au

STATE ROAD DEPARTMENTS

Roads and Traffic Authority, NSW
Tel 132 213.
www.rta.nsw.gov.au

VicRoads, Victoria
Tel 131 171.
www.vicroads.vic.gov.au

MOTORING ORGANIZATIONS

National Roadside Assistance
Australia-wide breakdown service. *Tel* 131 111

New South Wales and ACT
National Road and Motorist's Association (NRMA). *Tel* 131 122. www.mynrma.com.au

Northern Territory
Automobile Association of NT Inc (AANT). *Tel* (08) 8925 5901. www.aant.com.au

Queensland
Royal Automobile Club of Queensland (RACQ). *Tel* 13 19 05. www.racq.com.au

South Australia
Royal Automobile Association of SA Inc (RAA). *Tel* (08) 8202 4600.

Tasmania
Royal Automobile Club of Tasmania (RACT). *Tel* 132 722. www.ract.com.au

Victoria
Royal Automobile Club of Victoria (RACV). *Tel* 13 11 11. www.racv.com.au

Western Australia
Royal Automobile Club of WA Inc (RACWA). *Tel* 13 17 03.

OUTBACK DRIVING

BTW Communications
Tel (02) 6884 5237.
www.btw.com.au

Royal Flying Doctor Service of Australia
Tel (02) 8259 8100 or (08) 8080 3777. www.flyingdoctor.net

Driving a 4WD along the Gibb River Road in the Kimberley

Travelling by Ferry and Cruise Boat

For an island continent, Australia has surprisingly few tourist cruises on offer. The most important route is that between Melbourne and Tasmania. Elsewhere ferries run between the mainland and island destinations such as Rottnest Island, Western Australia *(see pp308–9)*, and Fraser Island, off the Queensland coast *(see p242)*. There are, however, plenty of cruises of local waterways. Large cruise ships concentrate on the local Pacific area and in most cases sail in and out of Sydney.

Passenger ships berthed at Circular Quay, Sydney *(see pp75–85)*

ARRIVING BY BOAT

There is probably no better way of arriving in Australia than to sail into Sydney Harbour aboard a cruise ship. Cruising is expensive, however, and the services to Australia are very limited. To sail to Australia from the US or Europe, you may have to wait for the next world cruise on **P&O** or **Cunard Line** vessels. Another option is to fly to an Asian city such as Hong Kong and join up with **Princess Cruises**. Sydney is the main port of call for most cruise ships, and there are three passenger terminals, two in the heart of the city and a third at White Bay.

FERRIES TO TASMANIA

The *Spirit of Tasmania* takes just over 14 hours to cross the Bass Strait from Melbourne to the island state of Tasmania. It runs at 8pm, Monday to Saturday during winter and nightly during summer, departing from Port Melbourne and Devonport. The ship has every level of accommodation

ranging from reclining cruise seats and backpacker berths to fully equipped suites. There are restaurants, shops, and entertainment for children. The price is fair, considering the experience – a double cabin will cost around A$500 return for a couple in off-peak season, less if there is a special offer.

ISLAND CRUISES AND FERRIES

A **Sealink** ferry departs from Cape Jervis, south of Adelaide, for Kangaroo Island *(see p354)*. In Western Australia, **Rottnest Express** runs regular ferries to Rottnest Island from Perth. There are many services between the mainland and the Barrier Reef islands *(see p216)*. A boat also runs between Seisia, Cape York, and Thursday Island, *(see p252)*. Check the **Great Barrier Reef Marine Park Authority** website for a list of certified operators.

DIRECTORY

SHIPPING COMPANIES

Cunard Line
Sydney. **Tel** *132 441.*
www.cunard.com
Southampton, UK.
Tel *(0845) 071 0300.*

P & O
Sydney. **Tel** *132 469.*
www.pocruises.com.au
Southampton, UK.
Tel *(0845) 678 0014.*

Princess Cruises
Southampton, UK. **Tel** *(0845) 355 5800.* **www**.princess.com

Sealink
Kangaroo Island.
Tel *131 301, (08) 8202 8688.*
www.sealink.com.au

Spirit of Tasmania
Devonport. **Tel** *1800 634 906.*
www.spiritoftasmania.com.au

TOURIST INFORMATION

Great Barrier Reef Marine Park Authority
www.gbrmpa.gov.au

Rottnest Express
www.rottnestexpress.com.au

RIVERS AND HARBOURS

Hiring a houseboat is an excellent way of seeing some of Australia's spectacular river scenery. Popular spots include the Hawkesbury River, New South Wales, and the Murray River which runs through New South Wales, Victoria and South Australia. There are tours of Darwin and Sydney harbours, and cruises of the Swan River in Perth and the Yarra River in Melbourne. State tourist authorities can provide details *(see p575)*.

Taking the ferry to Rottnest Island *(see pp308–9)*

General Index

Acknowledgments

Dorling Kindersley would like to thank the following people whose contributions and assistance have made the preparation of this book possible.

Consultant
Helen Duffy is an editor and writer. Since 1992 she has managed and contributed to a range of tourist publications on Australia.

Main Contributors
Louise Bostock Lang has worked on a number of Dorling Kindersley Travel Guides.
Jan Bowen is a travel broadcaster and writer. Her travel books include *The Queensland Experience*.
Paul Kloeden lives in Adelaide. A freelance writer and historian, his work ranges from travel articles to government-sponsored heritage surveys.
Jacinta le Plaistrier is a Melbourne-based journalist, poet and librettist.
Sue Neales is a multi-award winning Australian journalist. Her travel articles have appeared in major Australian newspapers and magazines.
Ingrid Ohlsson is a Melbourne-based writer who has contributed to many travel publications.
Tamara Thiessen is a Tasmanian freelance travel writer and photographer.

Additional Contributors
Tony Baker, Libby Lester.

Additional Photography
Simon Blackall, DK Studio, Geoff Dunn, Jean-Paul Ferrero, Esther Labi, Jean-Marc La Roque, Michael Nicholson, Ian O'Leary, Rob Reichenfeld, Carol Wiley, Alan Williams.

Cartography
Lovell Johns Ltd, Oxford, UK; ERA-Maptec Ltd, Dublin, Ireland.

Additional Illustrations
Rockit Design.

Indexer
Hilary Bird.

Senior Revisions Editor
Esther Labi.

Design and Editorial
Duncan Baird Limited
PICTURE RESEARCH Victoria Peel
DTP DESIGNER Rhona Green
Dorling Kindersley Limited
SENIOR MANAGING EDITOR Vivien Crump
MANAGING EDITOR Helen Partington
PROJECT EDITOR Rosalyn Thiro
DEPUTY ART DIRECTOR Gillian Allan
ART EDITOR Stephen Bere
MAP CO-ORDINATORS Emily Green, David Pugh
PRODUCTION David Proffit
Ross Adams, Emma Anacootee, Rosemary Bailey, Lydia Baillie, Emily Bieber, Uma Bhattacharya, Hilary Bird, Hanna Bolus, Debbie Brand, Sue Callister, Wendy Canning, Sherry Collins, Laura Cook, Lucinda Cooke, Bronwen Davies, Stephanie Driver, Jonathan Elphick, Mariana Evmolpidou, Emer FitzGerald, Fay Franklin, Anna Freiberger, Camilla Gersh, Vinod Harish, Gail Jones, Christine Keilty, Esther Labi, Maite Lantaron, Stefan Laszczuk, Jude Ledger, Maria Leonardis, Nicola Malone, Nicolette Martin, Alison McGill, Ciaran McIntyre, Siobhan Mackay, Claudine Meissner, Sam Merrell, John Miles, Tania Monkton, Michael Palmer, Catherine Palmi, Manisha Patel, Sangita Patel, Alok Pathak, Marianne Petrou, Giles Pickard, Rachel Power, Rada Radojicic, Garry Ramler, Marisa Renzullo, Louise Roberts, Ellen Root, Lamya Sadi, Mark Sayers, Shailesh Sharma, Azeem Siddiqui, Kunal Singh, Deborah Soden, Naomi Stallard, Domenic Stanton, Adrian Tristram, Diana Tucker, Lynda Tyson, Dora Whitaker, Kim Wildman, Carol Wiley, Ros Walford, Steve Womersley, Ed Wright.

Special Assistance
Sue Bickers, Perth; Craig Ebbett, Perth; Peter Edge, Met. Office, London; Chrissie Goldrick, The Image Library, State Library of NSW; Cathy Goodwin, Queensland Art Gallery; Megan Howat, International Media & Trade Visits Coordinator, WA Tourist Commission; John Hunter and Fiona Marr, CALM, Perth; Vere Kenny, Auscape International; Selena MacLaren, SOCOG; Greg Miles, Kakadu National Park; Ian Miller, Auslig; Gary Newton, Perth; Murray Robbins, Perth; Ron Ryan, Coo-ee Historical Picture Library; Craig Sambell and Jill Jones, GBRMPA; Norma Scott, Australian Picture Library; Andrew Watts, QASCO; and all state tourist authorities and national park services.

Photography Permissions
Dorling Kindersley would like to thank the following for their kind assistance and permission to photograph at their establishments: Art Gallery of WA; Australian Museum; National Gallery of Australia; Australian War Memorial; Ayers House; Department of Conservation and Land Management (WA); Department of Environment and Natural Resources (Adelaide); Department of Environment (Queensland); Government House (Melbourne); Hermannsburg Historic Precinct; Jondaryan Woolshed Historical Museum; Museum and Art Gallery of NT; Museum of WA; National Gallery of Victoria; National Maritime Museum; National Museum of Australia; National Parks and Wildlife Services (all states); National Trust of Australia (all states); Parliament House (Melbourne); Port Arthur Historic Site; Powerhouse Museum; Rottnest Island Authority; Royal Flying Doctor Service of NT; Shrine of Remembrance Trustees (Victoria); South Australian Museum; *Spirit of Tasmania*; Supreme Court (Melbourne), Tandanya National Aboriginal Cultural Institute Inc; Victoria Arts Centre Trust; WA Maritime Museum; and all the other sights too numerous to thank individually.

Picture Credits

a - above; b - below/bottom; c - centre; f - far; r - right; t - top.

Works of art have been reproduced with the permission of the following copyright holders: Francois Gohier 455t; *Ngalyod and Ngalkunburriyaymi*, Namerredje Guymala, c.1975, Natural pigments on bark, The National Museum (Canberra) ©1978 Aboriginal Artists Agency Limited 13c,

The publisher would like to thank the following individuals, companies and picture libraries for their kind permission to reproduce their photographs: ALAMY IMAGES: Bill Bachman 12bc, 13tr, 388bl, 407tl; Cephas Picture Library / Mick Rock 10bl; Foodpix 520cl; Andrew Holt 89crb, 238bl; LEDPIX 57t; Chris McLennan 246tl; Ball Miwako 575tc; Matt Smith 231br; Doug Stely 521t, 521tl; David Wall 406cl; Rob Walls 521c; ALLSPORT: 539b, 42t; AQWA – THE AQUARIUM OF WESTERN AUSTRALIA: 306tr; ARDEA LONDON LTD: © D Parer & E Parer Cook 216tr; © Francois Gohier 455t; Jean-Marc La Roque 448cla; Peter Steyn 13ca; © Ron and Valerie Taylor 216cla; ART GALLERY OF NSW: © Ms Stephenson-Meere 1996, *Australian Beach Pattern* 1940, Charles Meere (1890–1961) oil on canvas, 91.5 x 122cm, 65tl; *Bridge Pattern*, Harold Cazneaux (1878–1953), gelatin silver photography, 29.6 x 21.4cm, gift of the Cazneaux family, 1975, 72bc(d); © Art Gallery of NSW *Sofala* 1947 Russell Drysdale (1912-81), oil on canvas on hardboard, 71.7 x 93.1cm 110cla; *Sunbaker* 1937, Max Dupain, gelatin silver photograph, 38.3 x 43.7cm 110ca; *Mars and the Vestal Virgin* 1638, Jacques Blanchard oil on canvas, 130 x 110cm 110cr; © Tiwi Design Executive 1996, *Pukumani Grave Posts, Melville Island* 1958, various artists, natural pigments on wood, 165.1 x 29.2cm, gift of Dr Stuart Scougall 1959, 111t; *Natives on the Ouse River, Van Diemen's Land* 1838, John Glover oil on canvas, 78 x 115cm 111crb; Art Gallery of NSW Foundation purchase 1990, *A Pair of Tomb Guardian Figures*, late 6th century AD Early, Unknown (China), sculpture earthenware with traces of red and orange pigment, 93 x 82cm, Art Gallery of NSW Foundation Purchase 1990 111cra; *The Golden Fleece – Shearing at Newstead* 1894, Tom Roberts, oil on canvas 104 x 158.7cm 111b; *Three Bathers* 1913, Ernst Ludwig Kirchner oil on canvas, 197.5 x 147.5cm 112tr; *Curve of the Bridge* 1928–1929, Grace Cossington Smith © Estate of Grace Cossington Smith oil on cardboard, 110.5 x 82.5cm 112cl; © Wendy Whitely 1996, *The Balcony 2* 1975, Brett Whitely (1939–92), oil on canvas, 203.5 x 364.5cm 112b; © ASSOCIATED PRESS, LONDON: 59t; AUSCAPE INTERNATIONAL: 39cr; © Kathie Atkinson 26clb; © Nicholas Birks 344bl; © Donna Browning 268br; © John Cancalosi 25clb, 245bl; © Kevin Deacon 25cr; © Jean-Paul Ferrero 2–3, 23b, 24t, 26cla, 159crb, 161trb, ba, 237, 242cl, 258–9, 260cb, 263t, 288cl, 455t, bra, 472–3; © Jeff & Sandra Foott 25br; © Brett Gregory 170b, 454bl; © Dennis Harding 27b, 452–3, 456; © Andrew Henley 40ra; © Matt Jones 277cra, b; © Mike Langford 27crb; © Wayne Lawler

161cr; © Geoffrey Lea 457b; © Darren Leal 24br, 243t, 244t, 245cr; © Reg Morrison 24bca, 242cr, 454tr, 455cl; © Jean-Marc La Roque 18t, 24cr, 27cr, 28-9c, 181t, 238cla, 239cb, 261br, 280l, 370-71, 376t, 377t, cb, 385cla, 426cr, 428t, cl, 430t, 572cl; © Jamie Plaza Van Roon 24bl, 25cl, 161t, cb, 234; © Becca Saunders 25cb; © Gary Steer 28tl; AUSTRALIAN BROADCASTING CORPORATION: 581c; AUSTRALIAN CAPITAL TERRITORY MUSEUMS AND GALLERIES: 206tl; AUSTRALIAN MUSEUM, SYDNEY: WWW.AUSTMUS.GOV.AU: 30cl, 94cla, 94clb, 95cra, 95crb; Nature Focus/John N Cornish; Stuart Humpries 65bl; AUSTRALIAN PICTURE LIBRARY: 18c, 158clb, 588cl, 587t; Adelaide Freelance 367b; Douglas Baglin 47ca; John Baker 20b, 21tr, 173t, 178ba, 249t, 415b, 431tr; JP & ES Baker 160b, 184, 471cra; John Carnemolla 15t, 29crb, 38l, 39cra, 40clb, 41t, l, 43cr, 142b, 158cl, 184t, 210cla, 262tr, 264cl, 334cb, 351t, 365t, 366bl, 372cl; Sean Davey 38–9c; R. Eastwood 470tr; Flying Photos 574tl; Evan Gillis 367t; Owen Hughes 253b; S & B Kendrick 335b, 354t; Ian Kenins 397t; Craig La Motte 211b; Michael Lees 427b; Gary Lewis 40t; Lightstorm 188b, 360b, 361c, 465cb; Johnathan Marks 185cr, 428crb; Aureo Martelli 171cra; Leo Meier 27t, 250cl, 252t, 263clb; PhotoIndex 257b; Fritz Prenzel 428b, 442b; Dereck Roff 40b; Stephen Sanders 352b; Peter Solness 38tr; Oliver Strewe 32cl, 33tr; Neale Winter 368b; Gerry Withom 171t; AUSTRALIAN REPTILE PARK: 168bl; AUSTRALIAN WAR MEMORIAL: 201c.

GREG BARRETT, THE AUSTRALIAN CHAMBER ORCHESTRA: 133b; BARTEL PHOTO LIBRARY: 175b; BILL BACHMAN: 26t, 28cl, 29c, 33tl, 43t, b, 165b, 167t, 210clb, 245br, 256b, 274t, 275c, b, 276bl, 287b, 296b, 327crb, 335bra, 438, 446tr; BERINGER BLASS WINE ESTATES: 338br; 357cr; BEST'S WINES: 378ca; © MERVYN BISHOP: 59cb; BOTANIC GARDENS TRUST, SYDNEY: 106cla; BRIDGECLIMB SYDNEY: 81tl; BRIDGEMAN ART LIBRARY LONDON/ NEW YORK: *Kangaroo Dreaming with Rainbow Serpent*, 1992 (acrylic) Michael Nelson Tjakamarra (b.c.1949), Corbally Stourton Contemporary Art, London © Aboriginal Artists Agency Ltd 8–9; *Bush Plum Dreaming* 1991 (acrylic) by Clifford Possum Tjapaltjarri (b.c.1932), Corbally Stourton Contemporary Art, London © Aboriginal Artists Agency Ltd 33cr; *Men's Dreaming* 1990 (acrylic) by Clifford Possum Tjapaltjarri (b.c.1932), Corbally Stourton Contemporary Art, London © Aboriginal Artists Agency Ltd 30c; *Kelly in Spring*, 1956 (ripolin on board) by Sidney Nolan (1917–92), Arts Council, London © Lady Mary Nolan 34bl; National Maritime Museum, London 49bla(d); British Museum 51cra; Mitchell Library, State Library of NSW 54tr, bl, 55tl; National Library of Australia 50tr(d), 53tl, cb, 54–5c; *Bush Tucker Dreaming*, 1991 (acrylic) by Gladys Napanangka (b.c.1920) Corbally Stourton Contemporary Art, London, © Aboriginal Artists Agency Ltd 253cr; *The Ashes*, 1883 (The Urn) Marylebone Cricket Club, London, 436b; PHOTO REPRODUCED COURTESY OF BRISBANE CITY COUNCIL: 233b; COURTESY OF BRISBANE MARKETING: 219bc; BRISTOCK-IFA/GOTTSCHALK: 260ca; GRANT BURGE WINES PTY LTD: 356b.

CANBERRA DEEP SPACE COMMUNICATION COMPLEX: D. Paterson 206bl; CANBERRA TOURISM: 191b, 566c; CENTREPOINT MANAGEMENT: 91br; CEPHAS PICTURE LIBRARY: Andy Christodolo 163t, 332-3, 338bla, 339c, 378cla; Chris Davis 334cl;

Mick Rock 19t, 36cl, 37cr; 162tl, cl, 163cr, 174tr, cla, 37br, 339c, 341b, 356cla, 357tr, 369t, ca; Courtesy of CITY SIGHTSEEING: 129br; PETER CLARKE: 402br; BRUCE COLEMAN LTD: John Cancalosi 69b; Alain Compost 337tl; Francisco Futil 68tr; Hans Reinhard 336bcl; Rod Williams 337bl; COLORIFIC: 31t; Bill Angove 263b, 293c; Bill Bachman 257t, 266, 359, 397b; Penny Tweedie 265t, 267b; Patrick Ward 235b; COO-EE HISTORICAL PICTURE LIBRARY: 9c, 32-3c, 33b, 34tl, 35cr, 49t, 50b, 51ba, 52bra, 56cr, 57clb, 157c, 209c, 259c, 291c, 333c, 433cr, 434b, 453c, 455bl, 469c, 473c, 571c; CORBIS: Free Agents Limited 449bc; Royalty Free 12tr; Kevin Schafer 11cl; Zefa/Stock Photos/R. Wallace 10c; SYLVIA CORDAIY PHOTO LIBRARY LTD: © John Farmer 334bl; Nick Rains 296c, 369t.

RUPERT DEAN: 36br, 356clb, bc, 357b, 379b, 522cla, 522crb; DINOSAUR DESIGNS: 406tc; Dixon Galleries, STATE LIBRARY OF NSW: 80tr; © DOMAINE CHANDON, AUSTRALIA: 443c; © KEN DONE: DRUNKEN ADMIRAL, HOBART: 460tl; © DW STOCK PICTURE LIBRARY: 188tr; P Brunotte 589b; M French 588b; ENVIRONMENTAL PROTECTION AGENCY, QUEENSLAND: 240c; EUREKA SKYDECK 88: Gollings Photography 382tr; MARY EVANS PICTURE LIBRARY: 61ca; FAIRFAX PHOTO LIBRARY: 58clb, bcb, 81bra, 146 cla, 169br(d), 272br; KEN JAMES: 133tr; McNeil 120b; FALLS CREEK ALPINE RESORT: 448tl, 449t; FOREST OF TRANQUILITY – AUSTRALIAN RAINFOREST SANCTUARY: 168cr.

GETTY IMAGES: AFP/Stringer 580br; David Woolley 578tr; RONALD GRANT ARCHIVE: Buena Vista 21b; Universal 35b; © GREAT BARRIER REEF MARINE PARK AUTHORITY: 215t, 217t, cr; Photo: S Browne 215bl; Photo: W Craik 212b; Photo: N Collins 212cla; Photo: L Zell 213b, 214ca; GREAT SOUTHERN RAIL: Steve Strike 586cl; ROBERT HARDING PICTURE LIBRARY: 290-91, 375t, 583t; © Rolf Richardson 298; © Nick Servian 340, 590t; C MOORE HARDY: 132br; HISTORIC HOUSES TRUST: 64cla; HOOD COLLECTION, STATE LIBRARY OF NSW: 81bl; HORIZON: © Andris Apse 279b; HUTCHISON LIBRARY: © R. Ian Lloyd 12, 570-71; © Sarah Murray 586c.

IMAGES COLOUR LIBRARY: 26b, 211ca, 287t, 289b; THE IMAGE LIBRARY, STATE LIBRARY OF NSW: 34tr, 36bl, 48tl, cb, 49c, 52bla, 55crb, 58t, 349br; ALI KAYN: 392cla; © DR RUTH KERR (Commissariat Stores, Brisbane): 222bl.

FRANK LANE PICTURE LIBRARY – IMAGES OF NATURE: 24clb, 215br, 336tl; © Tom & Pam Gardner 25bc, 337bcr; © David Hosking 25tr, 337tr, cb; © E & D Hosking 337crb, 455cra, cb; © M Hollings 336crb; © Gerard Lacz 161br; © Silvestris 216tl, 454tl; © Martin Withers 170cl, 336clb; LEISURE RAIL, RAIL AUSTRALIA: 586tl; LIBERTY WINES: 378br; LION NATHAN: 338ca; LOCHMAN TRANSPARENCIES: © Bill Belson 323r; © Wade Hughes 296t; © Jiri Lochman 307t, 307cl; © Marie Lochman 293tc, 309 t; © Len Stewart 303b; LONELY PLANET IMAGES: Glenn Beanland 388tl.

MAMBO: 134br; LINDSAY MAY PRS: 338cl; © GREG MILES (ENVIRONMENTAL MEDIA): 276br; © MIRROR AUSTRALIAN TELEGRAPH PUBLICATIONS: 58cr; MITCHELL LIBRARY, STATE LIBRARY OF NSW: 48blb; 50-51c, 52b, 68tl, 81cra, 108c, 109t; MOUNT BAW BAW ALPINE RESORT: James Lauritz

448clb; MUSEUM & ART GALLERY OF THE NORTHERN TERRITORY: 265ca; MULTIPLEX PROPERTY SERVICES: 98tr; MUSEUM OF CONTEMPORARY ART, SYDNEY: 64cl.

COLLECTION OF THE NATIONAL GALLERY OF AUSTRALIA, CANBERRA: Tom Roberts, *In a corner in a Macintyre* 1895, oil on canvas, 73.4 x 88.0cm, 202cl; Margaret Preston, *The Native Fuscia* 1925, woodblock print on paper, 44.8 x 28.2cm, 202cb; ADAGP, Paris and DACS, London 2011; Aristide Maillol, *The Mountain (La Montagne)* 1937, lead, 167,4 (h) x 193.0 (w) x 82.3 (d)cm 202b; Artist Unknown Kamakura period, Japan, *Prince Shotoku praying to the Buddha* c. 1300, wood, gesso and lacquer, height 48.2cm, 203tl; © ARS, NY and DACS, London 2011; Jackson Pollock, *Blue Poles* 1952, oil enamel and aluminium paint on canvas, 212.0 x 489.0cm, 203cra, © Bula'bula Arts, Ramininging Artists, Raminginging, Central Arnhem Land, NT, *The Aboriginal Memorial* 1998, natural pigments on wood: an installation of 200 hollow log coffins, height 40.0 to 327.0cm, purchased with the assistance of funds from gallery admission charges and commissioned in 1987, 203cr; NATIONAL GALLERY OF VICTORIA, MELBOURNE: 400cla; NATIONAL LIBRARY OF AUSTRALIA: 35t, 46, 49bra (original in possession of the WA Museum), 52ca, 53cra 55cra, 56tl, 197br; Rex nan Kivell Collection 49crb, b, 51crb; ES Theodore, Campaign Director, ALP State of NSW, Trades Hall 56clb; NATIONAL MARITIME MUSEUM, SYDNEY: 51tl, 97cra, 100tl, clb, 101cra, 101tl, bc; NATURE FOCUS: Carl Bento 64cla; H & J Bestel 454cl; Rob Blakers 454br; John Fields 68b; Dave Watts 454cr; Babs & Bert Wells 287cra, 336br; © Australian Museum 30tl, 32tr, NATIONAL MUSEUM OF AUSTRALIA: © Australia-China Friendship Society, *The Harvest of Endurance Scroll*. The scroll is of 18 segments, ink and colour on paper, mounted on silk and paper 205t, *Untitled* by Charlie Alyungurra, 1970 pigment on composite board 205c, *The Mermaid Coffin* by Gaynor Peaty, 205b; NATIONAL TRUST OF AUSTRALIA:© Christopher Groenhout 404cl, 405tl, b; NATURAL HISTORY PHOTOGRAPHIC AGENCY: © A. N.T 24cl, 161ca, 213t, 295bl, br, 454cra, cb, 458t; © Patrick Faggot 248; © Pavel German 286tl; © Martin Harvey 25ca; © Ralph & Daphne Keller 294bca; © Norbert Wu 214tl; PETER NEWARK'S HISTORICAL PICTURES: 29cr, 50clb, 371ca; TOURISM NSW: 178cl, cb; NORTHERN TERRITORY LIBRARY: 264-5c, 265crb; Percy Brown Collection 264br; N Gleeson Collection 264tr; NUCOLORVUE PRODUCTIONS PTY LTD: 53b.

PHOTOGRAPHY COURTESY OF THE OLYMPIC CO-ORDINATION AUTHORITY: 143 cla; Photo: Karl Carlstrom 143 clb; © OPEN SPACES PHOTOGRAPHY: Photo: Andrew Barnes 439b; Photo: Glen Tempest 358, 567cl, 569t; © OUTBACK PHOTOGRAPHICS, NT: Steve Strike 1994 288tr; Steve Strike 1995 289c; OXFORD SCIENTIFIC FILMS: © Mantis Wildlife Films 294cl; © Babs & Bert Wells 294clb; PARLIAMENT HOUSE: The Hon Max Willis, RFD, ED, LLB, MLC, President, Legislative Council, Parliament of NSW. The Hon J Murray, MP, Speaker, Legislative Assembly, Parliament of NSW. Artist's original sketch of the historical painting in oils by Algernon Talmage, RA, *The Founding of Australia*. Kindly loaned to the Parliament of NSW by Mr Arthur Chard of Adelaide, 82t; PHOTO INDEX: 59 b, 292clb, 293tr, b, 294t, bl, br, 294-5c, 302bla, 307b, 308tr, 310b, 313cr, 319t, c, b;

PHOTOLIBRARY: Rob Blakers 13bl; Perrine Doug 11tr; Geoff Higgins 448tr; Rob Jung 446clb; David Messent 591cl; PHOTOLIBRARY.COM: 160cl; © PHOTOTONE COLONIAL LIBRARY: 55b; PICTOR INTERNATIONAL: 218, 354lb; PLANET EARTH PICTURES: © Gary Bell 208–09, 212tl, 214tr, b, 215c; © Daryl Torkler 145b; © Norbert Wu 363b; © POLYGRAM/PICTORIAL PRESS: 29t; POWERHOUSE MUSEUM REPRODUCED COURTESY OF THE TRUSTEES OF THE MUSEUM OF APPLIED ARTS AND SCIENCES, SYDNEY: 50tl, 54tl, 57blb, 64tl, Marinco Kojdanovski 64br, 102clb; *Cricket Trophy*, Jean-Francis Lanzarone 102cla; William Kerr Sydney 1879 silver, + emu eggs, Gift of W.T. Kerr 1938 photographer 102tl; Sue Stafford 103tl; © SUSANNA PRICE 427tr.

QANTAS: 56brb, 585ca; COLLECTION OF THE QUEENSLAND ART GALLERY: R Godfrey Rivers, *Under the Jacaranda*, 1903, oil on canvas, 229t; Russell Drysdale, *Bushfire* 1944, oil and ink on canvas on composition board, 62 × 77cm, Gift of Capt Neil McEacharn through CL Harden 1954, 228c; © Succession Picasso/DACS London 2011, Pablo Picasso, *La Belle Hollandaise* 1905, gouache on cardboard mounted on wood, 77 × 66.3cm, purchased 1959 with funds donated by Major Harold de Vahl Rubin, 228clb; John Oxley Library, State Library of Queensland, *Bathers* 1906, oil on canvas, 229.2 x 250cm, purchased 1988, 228tr; © QUEENSLAND BALLET: 229clb; JOHN OXLEY LIBRARY, STATE LIBRARY OF QUEENSLAND: 242br; QUEENSLAND TRAVEL AND TOURIST CORPORATION: 210b.

RAVESI'S ON BONDI BEACH: 519cl; THE ROCKS DISCOVERY MUSEUM: 77tl; ROYAL FLYING DOCTOR SERVICE: 283TL; SAND HILLS VINEYARD: 162cra; SCIENCE CENTRE (BRISBANE): 222clb; © SKYSCANS/PHOTOGRAPHER: David Hancock 273crb, 265cr, b; SOUTHCORP WINES EUROPE: 36tl, 162tl, 523tr; SOUTHLIGHT PHOTO AGENCY: © Milton Wordley 335c, 338t, crb, 339br; SPECTRUM COLOUR LIBRARY: 28b, 30b, 41crb, 239cr, 262tl, 286-7c, 335tl, 369b, 584t; © TONY STONE IMAGES: 318; Doug Armand 278; Gary John Norman 39t; Fritz Prenzel 17b, 22–3c, 231t; Robin Smith 42b, 163b, 183b; Oliver Strewe 24crb; Penny Tweedie 31b; Ken Wilson 58 br; STORY BRIDGE ADVENTURE CLUB: Story Bridge Adventure Club 230tl; CHARLES STUART UNIVERSITY WINERY: 162b; SYDNEY FILM FESTIVAL: 134c; SYDNEY HARBOUR FORESHORE AUTHORITY: 73tl, 77ca, 96bc, 97cra, 97bl; SYDNEY JEWISH MUSEUM: 65br; SYDNEY OPERA HOUSE TRUST: 84tr, cla, clb, b, 85t, crb, bl; PHOTOGRAPHY COURTESY OF THE SYDNEY ORGANIZING COMMITTEE FOR THE OLYMPIC GAMES (SOCOG): 143t; Sydney Theatre: 136cl.

ST MARY'S CATHEDRAL APPEAL: 303cra; STATE LIBRARY OF TASMANIA: 51trb; TELSTRA: 580c; TENTERFIELD DISTRICT & VISITORS' INFORMATION: 159tl; TIME OFF PTY LTD: 232tc; COURTESY OF TOURISM NEW SOUTH WALES: Phase IX 160tr; TOURISM QUEENSLAND: 232cr; TOURISM VICTORIA: 143tr; TRIP & ARTDIRECTORS PHOTOGRAPHIC LIBRARY: Eric Smith 29bl, 206b, 447b; D Silvestris 350b; VIRGIN BLUE: 584tr; VISIONS OF VICTORIA: Peter Dunphy 385crb, 406br, 413br; Tim Webster 407c; COURTESY OF WATERMARK PRESS (SYDNEY): 57t; WELLCOM GROUP LIMITED: 578cla; © WILDLIGHT PHOTO AGENCY: Ellen Camm 158tr; Greg Hard 38tl; Carolyn Jones, 373cra; Tom Keating 297cr, crb; 321b; Mark Lang 156–7, 176t; Philip Quirk 19b, 21cl, 39b, 181b; 170tl; Sean Santos 180b; Grenville Turner 179cr, 297t, br; WORLD PICTURES: 22t, 23t, 60-61, 200c, 217b, 250b, 251t, 301r, 440l; YALUMBA WINE CO.: 522cra; ZEFA: 22cl, 477t.

Front Endpaper: All special photography except: AUSCAPE INTERNATIONAL: © Dennis Harding Rbc; © Jamie Plaza Van Roon Rtcr; AUSTRALIAN PICTURE LIBRARY: JP & ES Baker Rcrb; © BILL BACHMAN LBr; COLORIFIC/ Bill Bachman: Rtl; ROBERT HARDING PICTURE LIBRARY: © Rolf Richardson Ltl; © NICK SERVIAN Lclb; NHPA: © Patrick Faggot Rtcl; © OPEN SPACES PHOTOGRAPHY: Glen Tempest Lcl; © PICTOR INTERNATIONAL: Rtr; TONY STONE IMAGES: Doug Armand Ltr.

Jacket

Front - PHOTOLIBRARY: Fotosearch; Back - ALAMY IMAGES: Gerry Pearce cla, Pictures Colour Library clb, Travelscape Images bl, David Wall tl; Spine - PHOTOLIBRARY: Fotosearch t.

All other images © Dorling Kindersley.
For further information see: www.dkimages.com

SPECIAL EDITIONS OF DK TRAVEL GUIDES

DK Travel Guides can be purchased in bulk quantities at discounted prices for use in promotions or as premiums. We are also able to offer special editions and personalized jackets, corporate imprints, and excerpts from all of our books, tailored specifically to meet your own needs.

To find out more, please contact:
(in the United States) **SpecialSales@dk.com**
(in the UK) **TravelSpecialSales@uk.dk.com**
(in Canada) DK Special Sales at **general@tourmaline.ca**
(in Australia) **business.development@pearson.com.au**

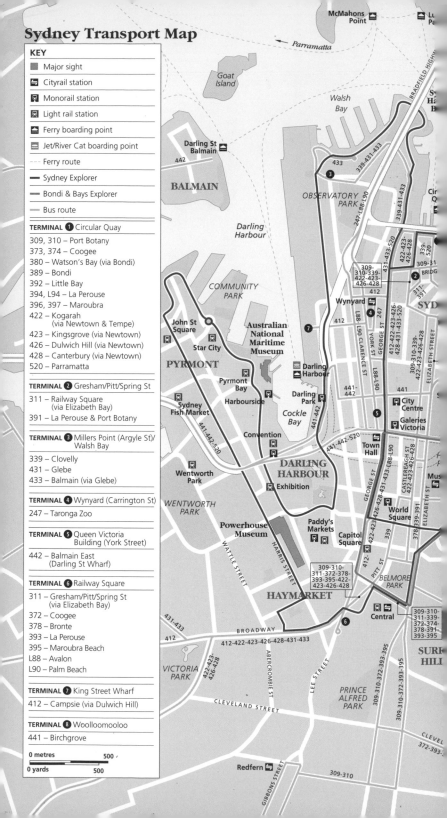

Sydney Transport Map

KEY

- ■ Major sight
- 🚇 Cityrail station
- 🚈 Monorail station
- 🚊 Light rail station
- ⛴ Ferry boarding point
- 🛥 Jet/River Cat boarding point
- --- Ferry route
- — Sydney Explorer
- — Bondi & Bays Explorer
- — Bus route

TERMINAL ❶ Circular Quay

309, 310 – Port Botany
373, 374 – Coogee
380 – Watson's Bay (via Bondi)
389 – Bondi
392 – Little Bay
394, L94 – La Perouse
396, 397 – Maroubra
422 – Kogarah
  (via Newtown & Tempe)
423 – Kingsgrove (via Newtown)
426 – Dulwich Hill (via Newtown)
428 – Canterbury (via Newtown)
520 – Parramatta

TERMINAL ❷ Gresham/Pitt/Spring St

311 – Railway Square
  (via Elizabeth Bay)
391 – La Perouse & Port Botany

TERMINAL ❸ Millers Point (Argyle St)/
Walsh Bay

339 – Clovelly
431 – Glebe
433 – Balmain (via Glebe)

TERMINAL ❹ Wynyard (Carrington St)

247 – Taronga Zoo

TERMINAL ❺ Queen Victoria
Building (York Street)

442 – Balmain East
  (Darling St Wharf)

TERMINAL ❻ Railway Square

311 – Gresham/Pitt/Spring St
  (via Elizabeth Bay)
372 – Coogee
378 – Bronte
393 – La Perouse
395 – Maroubra Beach
L88 – Avalon
L90 – Palm Beach

TERMINAL ❼ King Street Wharf

412 – Campsie (via Dulwich Hill)

TERMINAL ❽ Woolloomooloo

441 – Birchgrove

0 metres   500
0 yards   500